Make It!

Don't Buy It

Editor: John Warde

Designer: Barbara Field

Copy Editor: Felicia D. Knerr

Section Editors:
John Blackford
Marilyn Hodges
William H. Hylton

Contributing Writers:
Caroline Labonich
Elizabeth D. Miller
Melody Weisman

Contributing Illustrators:
John Carlance
Keith R. Heberling
Linda M. Heberling
John Hoover
Gene Mater
Frank Rohrbach

Photographer: Mitchell T. Mandel

Crafts Consultants:
Jim Eldon, Director of Design,
Rodale Design Group

Peggy Hobbs, weaver, spinner, fiber artist
Member: Philadelphia Guild of
Handweavers
Lehigh Valley Craft Association
Mid-Atlantic Fiber Association
Allentown Art Museum

Kathryn Price, fiber artist, weaver, fine
needleworker
Member: Philadelphia Guild of
Handweavers
Lehigh Valley Craft Association
Allentown Art Museum

Contributing Craftspeople:
Peggy Hobbs
Kathryn Price
Melody Weisman

Members of Rodale Design Group
Phil Gehret
Dennis Kline
John Kline
Fred Matlack
Alan Tenenbaum
Ed Wachter

Make It!

Don't Buy It

Home Furnishings and Accessories to Make with Wood, Metal, and Fiber

edited by John Warde

Rodale Press, Emmaus, Pennsylvania

Printed in the United States of America.

Library of Congress Cataloging in Publication Data
Main entry under title:

Make it! don't buy it.

    Includes index.
    1. Furniture making.   2. House furnishings.
3. Do-it-yourself work.   I. Warde, John.
TT194.M34 1983   684'.08   83-3336
ISBN 0-87857-450-6   hardcover

2 4 6 8 10 9 7 5 3   hardcover

Contents

List of Skills Boxes

Acknowledgments

Among the many people and organizations associated with this book who gave of their time and talents, the editors especially thank Mr. and Mrs. Fazil Erdogan, Bethlehem, Pennsylvania, for generously providing the location for the photographs of the Partition Screen with Handwoven Panels, which appear on pages 78 and 400; and the folks at Ritter Furniture, Emmaus, Pennsylvania, and Prints 'N Things, Lehigh Valley Mall, Whitehall, Pennsylvania, for loaning items used in the photograph of the Wall-Mounted Telephone Cabinet, on page 94. The design of the wooden hinges featured as part of the Partition Screen with Handwoven Panels is based on the screen-hinge design of woodcraftsman Tim Mackanness, Portland, Oregon, whose article detailing these hinges appears in *Fine Woodworking*, No. 10 (Taunton Press, Newton, CT 06470). Elements of the wedged-tenon design of the Double Bed on page 132 were suggested by woodcraftsman Sam Blagden, New Haven, Vermont.

Introduction

This is a book about making things. It contains plans, illustrations, photographs, and detailed instructions showing how to make literally dozens of useful items for your home. It also contains a wealth of information about three major crafts: woodworking, metalworking, and making textiles and textile products. With *Make It! Don't Buy It* as your guide, you can transform your home into a treasure trove of beautiful, one-of-a-kind furnishings of heirloom quality you can't buy in any store and which would cost a great deal of money to have custom-made by professional craftsmen.

But more than this is intended. Making things yourself is a satisfying and important activity. It is part of the basic human urge for self-expression, and this is an urge which is all too often thwarted by the elements of modern life. People need to make things. They need to have the sense of control over their lives that making things provides, and they need to perform acts that they and those around them can easily identify as constructive and complete, and beneficial to others as well as just themselves. There is a feeling of wholeness, unattainable any other way, that comes from working with your hands to give your inspirations useful, solid form. *Make It! Don't Buy It* aims to help you carry out this basic urge and to provide you with the opportunity for restoring to your life—or perhaps adding for the first time—this necessary and rewarding aspect.

In generations past, contact with handmade objects—and with the makers of those objects—was commonplace. Very little came from unknown sources. Much, in fact, was made right in the home. A child's father, like as not, made the bed in which the boy or girl slept as he or she grew up, and made as well the table and the chairs at which the family ate their meals each day. The mother made the coverlets and quilts, the rugs, the curtains, clothes, and table things. An uncle may have made the family's wagon; the man who shod the horses was, if not a relative, a neighbor known to all. Even in cities, objects that were not made at home were made by people one could visit, master craftsmen working in small shops with journeymen and apprentices. Clearly, things had makers, human makers, and links could be perceived, subliminally or otherwise, between people and objects. Humanity was much in evidence and obviously necessary. It must have been impossible to comprehend an object behind which there was no person as a driving or creative force.

Today all this is changed. Such contact is unknown. In fact it is impossible in many cases, because people seldom really make things anymore. Things are merely made, in factories, in other countries, by machinery, lately by computers. The old perceptions no longer form. Connections between humans and their works are clouded over. Unfortunately this shows, in many of society's greatest present ills. The value that we place on something now depends mostly on the sum of money we must spend to buy it, not on the effort another human being took to make it. And although the money we pay out may represent time spent by us at other labors (as money always has), the object we receive does not reflect the measure of human quality it would if we either had spent the time ourselves to make it—instead of working elsewhere—or knew that someone else had done so.

In spite of this—perhaps because of it—we cherish more than ever handmade objects and the crafts. It could be that we simply mourn the lack of need for them in ordinary life today, and revere them for their quaintness. But more than likely we are captivated by the qualities of humanness we see in handmade objects and their making and are drawn to them the more we recognize the emptiness of many of the things and occupations that surround us now. Truly, objects that are made by hand have value that is wholly different and undeniably greater than objects merely purchased, and this also is why you owe it to yourself to make things and owe it to others around you in the small sense and the large.

Useful handmade objects made by people close to those who will receive them are most valuable of all, and this is why the projects in *Make It! Don't Buy It* are designed to fill the home. Each project that you build or make not only serves a self-expressive purpose, it also performs a household function. It is something that

records and represents not just the time and care you spend to satisfy yourself, but also the generosity you feel toward your family and guests, and the esteem in which you hold them. Unlike money, things like time and care are irreplaceable: once they're spent, they're gone. Today, the time it takes to do handwork has become a premium commodity, and also, unlike in the past, there does exist the choice of whether to make a thing or buy it. Your choosing to make instead of buy the furnishings in your home is very much a statement of your feelings, even if the objects that you make seem small and unrelated to a larger issue. By choosing to invest your human worth in something that you make in turn for human use, you acknowledge both humanity and human purpose in a way that buying something never can.

Making things yourself is also self-reliant, and the objects prove your self-reliance. It's ennobling to see and know that you can build instead of buy, that you don't have to acquiesce to or rely on only what is made commercially to satisfy a public taste that may not be your own. Being able to hold in your hands what you yourself have conceived and made is a powerful symbol of security and independence and one which deeply strengthens inner feelings of self-worth.

And here a final note. Of all the links perceivable to those who know both objects and their makers, there is one which stands above the others: You get out of something just what you put in.

During medieval times craftsmen cloaked their work in secrecy. Even to this day the term *craft* carries with it secondary connotations of deceit or cunning. But there is no mystery or magic to making things by hand. There is only human effort: logic, patience, practiced skill, and faith. This is what the craftsmen hid. So simple were the underpinnings of their work, apparently they felt a need to make them seem like something more lest people lose appreciation for them or perceive that making things was not so special. Certainly the mastery of a craft takes work and dedication. But as an amateur, without the need to focus on the end result in order to survive, you have the opportunity to revel solely in the making of the objects that you choose, to pour yourself into the process only. Do this, for precisely in relation to your efforts will the end result be worthy of them and be as faithful a reflection of its human source as it will be a lasting record.

About This Book

Make It! Don't Buy It is really two books intertwined: a book of projects and a book of craft skills. At its heart are 34 attractive items you can make, each designed to serve a purpose in your home. The projects fall into three craft areas: woodworking, metalworking, and working with fiber and fabric.

Projects in the section Furnishings to Make with Wood are treated as a single unit, since woodworking as a craft is reasonably homogeneous. Projects in Furnishings to Make with Metal, though, are divided into groups according to the type of metalworking they require. Some projects involve sheet-metal techniques only; some are blacksmithing projects for which a forge is needed (plans for making an inexpensive forge are included), and the remainder are projects which require brazing or welding with small-scale conventional equipment. The projects in Furnishings to Make with Fiber also are separated into categories: those which center upon styles of handweaving and those for which no weaving is required.

Three of the items in *Make It! Don't Buy It* combine a project made in one craft area with one made in another. Each of the component projects, however, is designed to function as an item by itself. Instead of having to work in more than one craft area to complete an item consisting of combined projects, you can substitute a purchased part (or one acquired another way) for something you do not wish to make. For example, the large brass hinges featured as a metalworking project (see p. 222) are meant to be installed on the cedar-lined blanket chest that is a project in the woodworking section (p. 146). Naturally, the hinges may be made without the chest and mounted on any piece of furniture you wish—an antique cabinet, perhaps, or a drop-front desk. Likewise, the blanket chest need not carry the hinges. You may merely build it as a woodworking project and on it install commercially manufactured hinges that will do as well.

It's the aim of *Make It! Don't Buy It* to include as much material as possible on its pages and to present it in ways that are logical, concise, and clear. At the beginning of each main section is a brief introduction containing helpful general advice about the nature of the craft that follows. Then comes material dealing fully with the basic skills and background information necessary to begin the projects. For instance, in the woodworking section, you'll first learn how to obtain and prepare lumber, how to measure, cut, and true-up boards accurately to ready them for project-building, and how to build some elementary workshop equipment—benches and a sawhorse—so you'll have a place to work. In the metalworking section, you'll start out learning how to set up shop, finding out what tools you'll need and how to make decisions about the different kinds of metals. You'll also receive instructions on laying out a metalworking project: how to measure, how to cut. Later, in the introductory sections of chapters dealing with specific types of metalworking, you'll be filled in on the specialized information that relates exclusively to the area in which the projects in those chapters fall.

In the section Furnishings to Make with Fiber, two chapters are devoted to the craft's first category, handweaving. The first chapter contains the basics and the background—the kinds of fiber useful for making furnishings, the elements of good design, the ways of color, the different weaving styles—plus a group of projects based on the use of several kinds of looms. There's even a glossary of weaver's terms. After this chapter there's another one that deals solely with using a single type of loom, the multiharness. This chapter is set apart because the multiharness loom is more sophisticated than the other styles, and weaving on it actually can be considered a category all its own. The final chapter of the fiber section, of course, is the one that covers styles of textile work that don't require weaving.

Projects follow introductory material and

are arranged in order: simple to complex. Simple projects involve simple craft techniques; complex projects feature more sophisticated methods. Each project is presented in as uniform a format as possible. You see first a photograph of the finished item and underneath it an exploded view (project plan). On this same page is introductory advice outlining what's in store and advising you on special tips. At the top are also listed craft techniques featured in the project. On the facing page you'll find a list of materials required (under the heading What You Will Need) and also supplementary working diagrams and advice. Be sure to read the introduction before you start the project.

The project-making steps come next. These are numbered, step-by-step instructions written and arranged with care. You should follow them in order. Read through all of them first, though, thoroughly, so you'll be sure to understand the total picture and know what you'll be doing before you begin. Photographs are used to illustrate most steps. This is part of *Make It! Don't Buy It*'s strategy for clarity. Throughout the book, where you see a photograph, you're looking at a project being built. On the other hand, where you see an illustration—except a project plan or supplementary diagram—you're looking at information being given about a craft in general. (By the way, the photograph featured at the beginning of each project is of the actual item shown in stages of construction in the sequenced steps that follow. In most cases also, the very craftsperson commissioned to design and make the item is the person shown demonstrating the procedures.)

Interspersed throughout the project-building steps and also in the introductory material of each chapter you'll notice certain blocks of information—sometimes even entire pages—that are colored gray. These gray elements identify skills basic to the craft being presented in that section of the book, and are called skills boxes. Conceivably, all the skills boxes could be lifted out of *Make It! Don't Buy It* and bound together into separate smaller books. The result would be three concise, well-illustrated manuals of technique: one on woodworking, one on metalworking, and one on working with fibers and fabric. The skills boxes that accompany each project are selected to illustrate the techniques featured in its construction. As do the projects themselves, the skills boxes move from simple to complex throughout each section. Cross-referencing is heavy, so it's not necessary to build or make the projects in the order in which they're given. In most instances where instructions to a project call for a technique featured in a skills box somewhere in the book, directions—usually a page number for locating that box—are given immediately so you may quickly and easily look up the information you require.

Carefully arranged and researched, *Make It! Don't Buy It* is useful and accessible on several levels. For a beginner in any of the three crafts covered, it's a textbook leading to a thorough knowledge of these crafts, knowledge backed by sound experience as well. For the more accomplished craftsperson, it's a book of useful projects serving to challenge, refresh, and even enhance an already-gained facility with the tools and skills of handiwork. Finally, for sheer reading pleasure, or the satisfying of a curiosity or quest for information about a subject covered in the book, *Make It! Don't Buy It* functions as a fascinating and easily accessible reference encyclopedia: a lasting source of knowledge, entertainment, and—its editors sincerely hope—happiness.

Safety

Safety is an element of craftsmanship that must never be overlooked. In any craft there are tools, procedures, conditions, and even substances that are potentially harmful. Be aware of dangers, and if you can't avoid them, at least become alert to working in their presence. Safety is mostly a matter of paying attention to what you're doing and knowing enough to recognize potential hazards before they become real ones.

Your workshop should be well lighted and adequately ventilated. Good lighting not only makes for easier working conditions, but it cuts down on potential eye strain and headaches as well. A well-lighted area allows you to feel more relaxed and comfortable. If you're able without effort to see what you're doing, you'll do better at your craft, make fewer mistakes, feel less frustration, and in turn increase your ability to concentrate, by decreasing the overall level of distraction you must cope with. Ventilation, of course, is healthy and increases your ability to perform well. It's especially important where dust or toxic fumes — however slight — are by-products of your work. Woodworkers and metalworkers should give serious thought to installing special ventilation systems in their shops: local ventilation items such as dust collectors and vacuum devices which remove pollutants from their point of origin and general ventilation systems such as fans or air conditioners which dilute pollutants with fresh air. Naturally it's also recommended that you wear a respirator when working in conditions where breathing what is in the air around you may be harmful or even just uncomfortable. Be aware, too, of where the air from your workshop is vented. Shops in rooms attached to living areas of a house often transmit dust and fumes to these places as well; a definite hazard and cause of discomfort.

Neatness in the shop is also important, mostly because it makes for less distraction but also because it keeps in plain sight everything potentially harmful, or else keeps it safely out of harm's way. Don't let tools, materials, or trash pile up. The first can cut or otherwise injure you when you're not paying attention; the other two are fire hazards.

Don't smoke in your shop. This goes for textile craftspeople, too. Make sure all volatile fluids are kept tightly covered and in suitable, properly marked containers. Wipe up all spills right away, and keep the rags or paper towels you use for the job in a flameproof, closed container until you can safely dispose of them. Never eat or drink around your work area, either. You risk contaminating whatever you're consuming as much as you do spilling it on a project in progress.

When you have visitors while you're working — or even while you're not — make sure they're as alert about potential dangers as you are, and as protected. (Keep on hand extras of the safety items that you use: safety glasses, respirator, welding goggles.) If you're operating power tools or welding apparatus, be especially aware of who's there with you. If it means you'll be uncomfortably distracted to have them around while you're involved, it's better to have them come back later.

Don't work when you're not in the mood. Of course you shouldn't work when you've imbibed intoxicating substances (this is not a joke), but don't work either if you're tired or if your mind's on other things. The theory that working with your hands is a way to relax is only partly true. You've got to be mentally prepared for what you will be doing in order to avoid at least making embarrassing mistakes. Accidents resulting from your mind being elsewhere are often the most harmful.

It goes without saying that power tools and welding/brazing/soldering equipment are extremely dangerous. Most can permanently maim or even kill in less time than it takes to read this sentence. (Blacksmithing, with its open forge and constant proximity to hot metal, presents its own host of hazards; these are dealt with in the chapter on blacksmithing.) Learn to use your power tools safely. Read all literature that accompanies each item. Try to visualize beforehand how an operation might go wrong. Ground electric cords properly; make sure your shop is wired correctly and adequately; use adaptors for three-prong tools if your wall sockets will not accept them, or use double-insulated tools which have the conventional two-prong plugs. Make certain you're not standing in a wet spot when you switch on a tool or begin to use it. Keep tools disconnected as much as possible — especially when you're making adjustments to cutting blades, router bits, and such — but always, when you are around them, act as if they are plugged in.

When using power tools, wear appropriate protection (something which, on occasion, the craftsmen in the photographs in this book are not doing) — safety goggles or a face mask, perhaps at times a respirator — keep your sleeves rolled up, long hair out of the way, and jewelry removed. Leave in place the tool's safety guards and shields (something else the craftsmen pictured are not always doing) unless an operation can't be done without removing them, and then be extra careful. Use a notched stick of wood (called a push stick) to push wood past the blade of a table saw when your hand would otherwise come dangerously close, and always stand to one side of the blade in case of kickback. Be aware that noise is a distraction and can cause impaired reactions, not to mention long-term hearing damage. Wear ear protectors—the kind that muffle but do not eradicate the sound—and don't operate power tools for long periods without resting from the noise now and then. Keep a first-aid kit in the shop, and never work where a shout from you can't bring immediate assistance.

Hand tools also can be dangerous, especially those designed for cutting. Curiously, the sharper you keep your tools, the less likely you are to have accidents with them, because you need apply less force to make them work. A basic rule to follow is always to keep your body parts—and this includes your fingers, palms of hands, and crooks of elbows—behind the tool's blade, out of the way of possible deflected motions.

Less dramatic but also harmful are the poisons. Certain types of sawdust can irritate the nose and lungs and even the skin. Metal filings are not just dangerous in terms of the cuts and slivers they can give; some are also toxic when inhaled. Fluxes for soldering, brazing, and welding often are corrosive and will burn the skin and eyes, or cause damage if the fumes are inhaled. Solvents and finishes used in woodworking, and even some chemical dyes used in textile work, are dangerous as well. Extensively prolonged use of some of these has been linked to cancer.

When dealing with any of these, the best procedure is to know first what you are working with and what you are going to do. Work with proper ventilation, wear respiratory and eye protection, wear gloves and perhaps an apron of rubber or some other type of protective material, and keep your sleeves rolled down this time. In case of accidental contact with the skin—or what is very likely, a splash of something in the eye—work where you have instant access to running water and first aid. If children are around, keep them out of metal filings or sawdust that may be irritating. Make sure chemical items are completely out of reach, *and* marked, *and* sealed (you really shouldn't use these near children or even leave them open when they're in the room), and keep the number of a doctor or a poison control center within plain sight near the phone.

Furnishings to Make with Wood

Working with wood is a fascinating and richly rewarding activity. Each species of wood has its own qualities, each piece its own subtle personality. Throughout history, wood has been one of man's closest companions, instrumental in the development of his technology and vital to the expression of his creative urges.

Nowadays, wooden items are no longer as essential a part of daily life as they once were, and the skills of the woodworker are likewise less in demand. Yet wooden objects have not lost their appeal. If anything, we admire and cherish them even more today than before. Fine woodworking is becoming accepted as an art, and furniture made by hand often commands the same high prices as sculpture. Rightly so, for the skills of a master woodworker are not easily acquired.

Yet woodworking can be learned. The basic skills are not difficult, and even advanced techniques proceed methodically according to a logical pattern. Nothing is done at random or by magic. True, mastery of the craft may take a lifetime, but to a large extent the difference between a master woodworker and a skilled apprentice is only experience: the amount of time one crafts-

man has spent working with tools and wood compared to the other. The 11 projects that are presented on these pages contain the information and opportunity for experience necessary to make you a skilled apprentice, knowledgeable in wood characteristics, and adept at basic—and even not so basic—skills.

You do not have to build each project in order, since important techniques are cross-referenced, but the projects are arranged according to their complexity and do follow a systematic progression. In the early, simple projects, you will learn techniques that require practice to apply successfully to the more complex projects presented later on. Working through the projects in order affords this practice.

The key to successful, enjoyable woodworking lies in fostering an ability to work patiently, to concentrate fully, and to plan ahead. Develop an unhurried attitude and a love of precision. Take time willingly to sharpen tools, practice unfamiliar techniques on scrap wood, and test-fit pieces together before gluing. Relax, sink into your work, and enjoy the process of it without focusing too much on finishing up.

Working with Wood

If there is a golden rule in woodworking, it is probably to be found in the words of Thoreau: "Simplify, simplify." Basically, woodworking is simple, in concept and technique. It consists of shaping pieces of wood and fastening them together.

But nothing works without a plan. You should always have something in mind, something you're setting out to do, when you pick up tools and wood and commence to work. For one thing, shaping wood means taking some away, and once it is gone it can be very hard to replace. Patching up mistakes—even when it can be done—often takes more time and effort than making the entire project. The old-timers planned. What they didn't draw out first on paper they could see in their minds from years of past experience, including long apprenticeships. Their shops were full of patterns marked on scraps of lumber, and of templates hanging from the walls and rafters.

Drawing will help your planning. In fact, being able to visualize each piece in the way drawing demands is one of the most valuable woodworking skills you can learn.

Buy good tools. They needn't fall into the luxury class, but they should be of professional quality. Hardware stores often carry very good tools. Discount department stores generally do not. (However, if you know just what you're after, by all means shop for a bargain.) Acquire your tools gradually, as you need them for specific purposes. After you've put together a basic set, resist the urge to buy more until you're really sure you can't do the job without them. Many specialized tools—even old-fashioned ones—have evolved primarily because they save time for professional craftsmen who must work quickly to stay in business. An ordinary tool in combination with a homemade jig or guide often performs just as well, taking only a little more time, patience, and perhaps coordination.

Power tools are another matter. Many of them are impractical for amateurs, but some of them—saws, routers, drills, and perhaps sanders—are such enormous time-savers, and in practiced hands can perform such accurate work, that except for purely aesthetic reasons it seems incongruous in this day and age not to use them.

Obtaining and Preparing Lumber

The most obvious place to find lumber is at a lumberyard. If you are just getting started in woodworking, this is the place to go. At the yard you can get graded, seasoned, standard-size boards, or you can have them cut pieces to your specifications for a small fee. Most of the woodworking projects in this book can be built with lumber obtainable from any lumberyard. For the few projects which call for hardwood, you may have to find a lumberyard that carries wood specifically for cabinetmaking.

But there are also other ways to obtain lumber: buying from local sawmills, buying from other woodworkers or through informal woodworkers' exchanges, salvaging structures or furniture about to be scrapped, even making your own lumber from trees you cut and saw yourself (see p. 10). If you become truly interested in woodworking, chances are you'll develop a taste for lumber that comes from some of these sources as well. For one thing, it's often cheaper than buying from a lumberyard. For another, wood obtained from unusual sources is frequently unusual itself. It may be exotic in grain or species, or available in sizes not carried by yards.

When choosing lumber for a project, your first priority is deciding on a variety suitable for the job. Often many species will fill the bill structurally (p. 15); of these, you must narrow your choice down to which is easiest for you to obtain and work—some types of wood are very hard to cut; a softer wood may do as well—and is also easiest on your pocketbook.

After deciding on the species, then your task is to choose good-quality boards. To an experienced woodworker, even boards cut from the same tree have important and discernible differences. Defects, grain direction and texture, how the wood is sawn in relation to its growth rings and its center, and even how the lumber has been seasoned and stored since cutting are all factors to consider. Always try to match the quality and characteristics of wood you choose to the quality and intended use of the project.

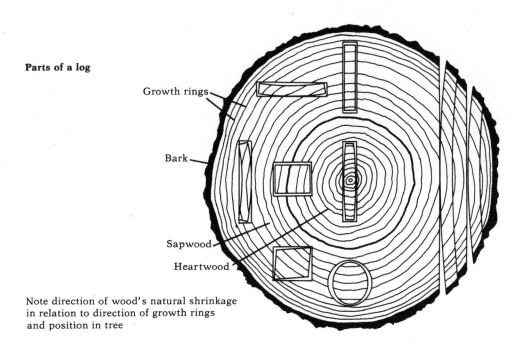

Parts of a log

Growth rings

Bark

Sapwood

Heartwood

Note direction of wood's natural shrinkage in relation to direction of growth rings and position in tree

Buying from a lumberyard

Most lumberyards cater to the home-building industry. They carry primarily the kinds of wood used for house construction, in sizes which are standardized to meet the requirements of ordinary building methods. However, provided that you know exactly what you're looking for and are able to select the boards yourself, lumberyards are a good source of stock for general woodworking and some cabinetmaking.

Learn the basics of commercial lumber grading and sizing so that you'll be able to ask correctly for what you need, and also so you'll be able to interpret the salesperson's replies. Take a tour of a lumberyard or two in your area if you've never done so, just to see what they've got and how their stock is arranged. Also do some comparative shopping. Prices between yards often vary.

When you are ready to place an order, be sure you have done your part to make the process go smoothly, by having your list of materials logically arranged. Group all the pieces you need according to their width. Then, together with the salesperson, you can calculate the number and sizes of actual boards you'll have to buy, based on the dimensions of stock the yard has on hand. Be prepared to do some figuring at the lumberyard, and buy a bit more wood than you'll actually use. About 10 percent more wood than your plans call for is good insurance against possible mistakes during construction. Bring along a tape measure and even, perhaps, a pocket calculator.

More and more, lumberyards are anxious to attract do-it-yourselfers and amateur woodworkers, so don't feel embarrassed or intimidated about describing in your own terms what you want, or asking questions when you don't understand a point of nomenclature or calculation. Different yards may use different terms to describe the same thing. More likely than not, unless you walk in on the middle of a deal for something like a wooden version of the Taj Mahal, you will find the sales staff friendly and helpful, willing to take the time to be of assistance.

Softwood—Lumber that comes from evergreen trees—pine, fir, spruce, and the like—is classed

Softwood Sizes	
Nominal	**Actual**
1 × 2	¾'' × 1½''
1 × 3	¾'' × 2½''
1 × 4	¾'' × 3½''
1 × 5	¾'' × 4½''
1 × 6	¾'' × 5½''
1 × 8	¾'' × 7¼''
1 × 10	¾'' × 9¼''
1 × 12	¾'' × 11¼''
2 × 2	1½'' × 1½''
2 × 4	1½'' × 3½''
2 × 6	1½'' × 5½''
2 × 8	1½'' × 7¼''
2 × 10	1½'' × 9¼''
2 × 12	1½'' × 11¼''
4 × 4	3½'' × 3½''
4 × 6	3½'' × 5½''
6 × 6	5½'' × 5½''
8 × 8	7½'' × 7½''

as softwood, even though some species may actually be harder than certain varieties classed as hardwood (and vice versa; see p. 15). Most lumberyards specialize in softwood, since it is the primary wood used in building construction, and stock it in standard dimensions and lengths and in graduated degrees of attractiveness and structural integrity. It's not always sold according to species, because for most construction purposes this doesn't matter, so ask if you want a particular kind. Usually softwood from a lumberyard is seasoned (dried) and planed smooth on all four surfaces, ready to use. (Even so, you should always store seasoned lumber from any source in your shop for at least two weeks—longer, if possible—before using it, to give it a chance to adjust to localized humidity. Wood shrinks when it's dry, swells when it's wet, and, no matter how well it's seasoned, will always seek to take on the same average moisture level as the surrounding air.) Occasionally some sizes may be stocked green—that is, unseasoned—and unplaned, but usually this type of lumber is available only at sawmills.

Nevertheless, for convenience in writing lumber orders and such, dried, surfaced, softwood lumber is always sold according to the size to which it was sawn at the mill. This is called the nominal size and it ignores the often relatively large amounts of wood lost during subsequent drying of the wood from its green state and the amount shaved off during the smoothing process, both of which, of course, contribute to the wood's actual size. You must be aware of nominal sizing when buying softwood at a lumberyard. If you ask for a 2 × 4, what you will get will measure 1½ inches by 3½ inches. The table on the page opposite gives a complete picture of what to expect.

Length, on the other hand, is no problem. Ask for a 10-foot board and you'll get a board that is 10 feet long. In fact, standardized softwood lumber is often priced by length (or, as sometimes termed, by the lineal, or running, foot). Standard lengths for softwood are in increments of 2 feet. The shortest boards you'll find at a yard are usually 8-footers (although most yards will gladly cut you a shorter length if you wish) and range upward to 16 and sometimes 20 feet.

Most of the softwood lumber you'll be looking for is also classed as yard lumber, and is categorized largely by its appearance, as either Select or Common. (Some lumber over 2 inches thick may be classed as Structural instead. This variety meets certain stress-test requirements not performed on yard lumber.) Select lumber is clear, virtually free of defects. Usually it is subdivided further by letter grades. Common lumber has visible knots. It is graded by numbers or names. The table on page 6 describes the softwood classes and grades.

For most woodworking, what you should ask for is either B and Better or clear (see table) if you want absolutely the clearest, most blemish-free softwood lumber available, or Number 1 or Number 2 Common, for projects that can stand a few knots here and there. Always look at lesser grades first, though, since softwood grading is based on the number and size of defects in an individual piece of wood, and often you can find boards with enough clear wood between defects to make them worthwhile for your purposes and a bargain as well.

Besides knots, which are merely where branches formed in the tree's trunk, lumber may have other defects, such as those shown in the illustration below: cracks of various kinds, pitch pockets, warps, etc. As long as you can avoid using those sections of the board which contain them, isolated defects such as these don't matter a whole lot to the overall quality of a board, be it softwood or hardwood. Tight knots are perfectly all right to include in most instances, except that they may prove hard to plane smooth.

Warped wood is a different matter. In the long

Defects in lumber

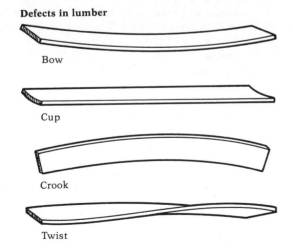

Bow

Cup

Crook

Twist

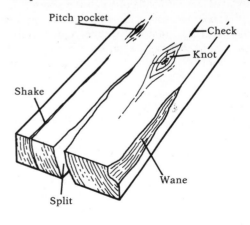

Pitch pocket

Check

Knot

Shake

Wane

Split

Classes, Grades, and Characteristics of Softwood

Class	Grade	Average Characteristics
Select	B and Better (or B & BTR; Clear)	Practically clear on both sides; no knots, virtually no blemishes.
	C	Slightly more blemishes than B & BTR. Occasionally very small knots. Sometimes one face of board qualified as B & BTR.
	D	One face of finish quality; recognizable defects on back.
Common	Number 1 (or Construction)	Evenly distributed small, tight knots no more than 2″ dia., surrounded by smooth grain. No knots near edges.
	Number 2 (or Standard)	Tight knots up to 3″ dia. in wide boards; otherwise similar to No. 1 Common.
	Number 3 (or Utility)	Some coarse or loose knots, or major blemishes, such as pitch pockets. Sometimes a single defect surrounded by otherwise usable wood.
	Number 4 (or Economy)	Numerous knots, knotholes, and defects. Some usable wood.
	Number 5 (or Economy)	Poor-quality wood, for use where neither appearance nor strength is required.

run it's best to avoid it. Boards that are cupped, if not too severely, can be planed flat (although obviously they won't be the same thickness they were when you bought them), but twisted, bowed, or crooked lumber is just plain unmanageable.

When judging any lumber, also consider the orientation of the growth rings (visible at each end of a board) to each other and to the board's sawn faces. This will tell you a lot about the overall quality of the wood, as well as how and to what degree it is likely to change shape further. Rings that appear evenly spaced and close together usually indicate better-quality wood than erratically spaced rings which seem far apart. Boards in which the growth rings are at or near right angles to the sawn faces will invariably have less tendency to warp—and especially cup—than boards whose rings appear as arcs running parallel to the faces. Sometimes—mostly in dealings with specialty lumber outlets, you may be lucky enough to find boards that have been intentionally sawn so their rings are perpendicular to their faces. This lumber is called quartersawn, because the log from which it was made was sawn first into quarters, then each quarter was repositioned and sliced into boards, as shown in the illustration to the left on the page opposite. Much lumber

was cut this way in former times, but the method is time-consuming and produces a lot of waste. Nowadays, nearly all lumber is plainsawn—merely sliced lengthwise through and through without regard to grain orientation—which is all most industries need, and as a result, is all most sawmills can afford to do.

Hardwood—All lumber from trees that lose their leaves each year is classed as hardwood. Except for oak, mahogany, and occasionally maple, it is difficult to find hardwood at ordinary lumberyards, because there isn't much demand for it from the building industry. Always ask, though; if nothing else, the yard may know of or be able to order from a supplier.

Hardwood is sold by an entirely different system than softwood. Since it is not needed as much in standardized lengths and widths, and since the aim of the sawmill cutting it is to maximize their profit from each log by selling as much of it as possible, hardwood is sold in whatever size it comes from the mill, usually in random widths and lengths. Specific thicknesses are available, however, and these are always stated in quarter-inch increments, usually beginning at 4/4—pronounced "four-quarter"—meaning 1 inch. A 5/4 board is 1¼ inches thick; a 6/4 board

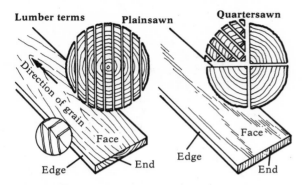

Lumber terms — Plainsawn — Quartersawn

Direction of grain — Face — Edge — End — Edge — Face — Edge — End

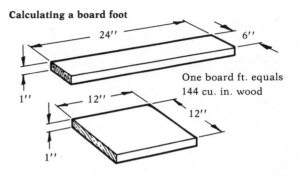

Calculating a board foot

24″ — 6″ — 1″

One board ft. equals
144 cu. in. wood

12″ — 12″ — 1″

is 1½ inches thick; an 8/4 board is 2 inches thick, and so on.

As with softwood, these are nominal sizes. In fact, lumberyards often stock hardwood in its rough state, just as it came from the sawmill, and it is customary for you to specify the degree of surfacing (planing)—if any—you wish to have done to it when you buy it. Abbreviations are used to designate this: S1S means to surface the wood on one side (face) only; S2S indicates surfacing on both sides; S1E means to smooth only one edge; S2E means smooth both edges. Although you can specify any combination (S1SE—surface one side and one edge; S1S2E—surface one side and both edges) usually you'll want to ask for S4S—surface all four sides—or S2S, which means the edges will be left rough. The surfacing operation does diminish the board's overall thickness, and unfortunately this is not by a standard amount as with softwood. A 4/4 board surfaced on one side will be 7/8 inch thick. Surfaced on both sides, the same board will measure ¹³/₁₆ inch. A 5/4 board, on the other hand, surfaced on both sides, will likely be only 1¹/₁₆ inches thick. It's always best to ask exactly what you'll be getting.

As for grading, hardwood classifications focus more on the number and sizes of clear pieces you can cut from a given board than on the nature of the actual defects the board contains. The grade of Firsts and Seconds (FAS) is given to the highest-quality hardwood boards. FAS lumber must have a minimum width of 6 inches and a minimum length of 8 feet and yield at least 81 percent clear cuttings, each of which must measure no less than 4 inches wide by 5 feet long,

or 3 inches wide by 7 feet long. Sound complicated? It is if you take it this far, which you probably won't if you can see the lumber and sort through the pile yourself. The other grades, in descending order, are Selects, Number 1 Common, Number 2 Common, Sound Wormy (you won't find much of this; it's as good as Number 1 Common but worm holes are allowed!), Number 3A Common, and Number 3B Common. The higher the grade, the more and larger defect-free pieces you can obtain.

Finally, since hardwood comes in such diverse sizes, it is sold by units of volume called board feet (see illustration above). One board foot equals 144 cubic inches. The board, however, may have any combination of measurements that, when multiplied together, yield this amount. The way to calculate board feet is first to multiply a board's nominal width in inches by its nominal thickness in inches, then multiply this by the board's actual length in feet, and then divide this product by 12. A board nominally 2 inches thick (8/4) by 6 inches wide, measuring 12 feet in length, contains 12 board feet. You won't be able to do this very easily on irregularly shaped boards; lumberyards and sawmills use formulas for this sort of thing. You also won't normally ask the yard for a certain number of board feet of lumber without also specifying the sizes of the boards you'll need. What you can do is use the board-foot measure to figure out from your materials list how much wood you will need for a given project, and then use that figure to shop for a bargain. What the lumber salesperson will do is figure up your order in terms of board feet—always based on nominal sizes—and charge you by it.

Manufactured wood products

Plywood and composition boards made of such wood by-products as sawdust, flakes, chips, particles, and fibers are all referred to as manufactured wood or wood products. They have gained more and more popularity among woodworkers, and will continue to do so, because they are easy to use, easy to buy, often far less expensive than equivalent amounts of solid wood, and perfectly strong and durable when used correctly. Manufactured wood products are available in any lumberyard, usually in a much broader range of types and grades than the same yard's stock of solid wood, and fall into more standardized (if no less complicated) categories than either softwood or hardwood lumber. For one thing, manufactured wood is practically always sold in 4 × 8-foot sheets (naturally the yard will cut it smaller if you ask), and in eighth-inch thicknesses, ranging from ⅛ inch to 1 inch.

One distinct advantage of manufactured wood over solid lumber is that it warps very little in any direction. Wide tabletops, for example, can be made of plywood or particle board (covered with a hardwood veneer or plastic laminate for attractiveness) merely by cutting them to size and fastening them in place. There is no need for the intricate construction techniques or special fastening procedures associated with making tabletops of solid wood, which must allow for large amounts of natural shrinking and swelling. Indeed, for many types of cabinetwork, hardwood-faced plywood or composition board has become the accepted construction material, which is partly why solid hardwood itself is so scarce!

There are drawbacks, though. The very hard and brittle glue—often urea formaldehyde—used in all types of manufactured wood products quickly dulls edge tools (power tools with carbide-tipped cutters are recommended for working with manufactured wood). Also, the standard-size sheets of the material are large and heavy, often unwieldy for one person to handle, and, finally, fastening pieces together sometimes requires special attention, since many of the common techniques of joining solid wood do not always work.

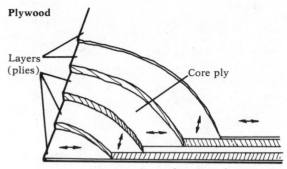

Plywood

Layers (plies)

Core ply

Arrows indicate direction of grain

Plywood—Basically, plywood is a sandwich of wood layers glued crisscross to each other on both sides of a central core. The core may be of wood or some other material. Plywood made of softwood is the most common variety—it has become the staple of the construction industry and is widely used in general woodworking as well. Grading softwood plywood is quite complex, since it can be put to so many uses. Being familiar with the grading criteria and knowing how to interpret the grading stamp that appears on each piece of plywood is helpful, but don't be afraid to ask a salesperson at the lumberyard for advice.

Plywood meant for use indoors is termed Interior. It is made with glues which are water-resistant but not fully waterproof. Plywood for use outdoors is termed Exterior. Its glues are waterproof. For woodworking, either type is acceptable, although you obviously won't want to use Interior plywood for an outdoor project.

Plywood is also rated according to the strength and stiffness of the woods used in its manufacture. These woods fall into five groups, and rather than specify which wood is used in each piece of plywood (in some cases they're mixed), the grading stamp indicates from which group the materials for the sheet have been drawn. Group 1 plywood is made from the strongest varieties of wood; Group 5, the weakest. Your choice for general use should be Group 1 or 2.

Finally, the appearance of each outer face of a plywood sheet is also graded. Clear-faced (virtually defect-free) plywood is graded N—the highest rating—for the face that fulfills this category. (N stands for natural finish. Plywood of this grade need not be painted.) Next in line follow grades A, B, C, and D. On the grading stamp, the first letter of the pair indicates the quality of the front (best) face, and the second letter indicates the quality of the back. Many, but not all, combinations of faces are manufactured. For instance, N-A, N-B, and N-D are made, but not N-C. What's more, certain combinations are made in Exterior that are not made in Interior, and vice versa. This is why you must ask for sales help at the lumberyard. More often than not, though, you should look for (and will probably find) plywood grades of A-C or better. Grades below B usually contain defects too pronounced to patch easily.

Hardwood plywood, since it is not rated for construction, is much easier to choose from. It is either Interior or Exterior and is categorized according to the type of wood from which its front face is made (since its inner layers and sometimes even its back may be of softwood). Ratings are given on the basis of the appearance of the front face: Premium (called Number 1), Good (also called Number 1), Sound (Number 2), Utility (Number 3), and Backing (Number 4). Normally, Good is acceptable even for cabinetwork.

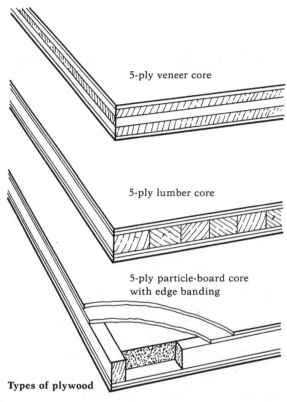

5-ply veneer core

5-ply lumber core

5-ply particle-board core with edge banding

Types of plywood

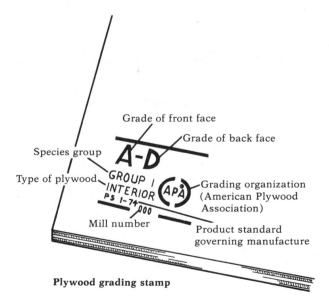

Grade of front face

Grade of back face

Species group

A-D

Type of plywood

GROUP I
INTERIOR (APA)
PS 1-74 000

Mill number

Grading organization (American Plywood Association)

Product standard governing manufacture

Plywood grading stamp

Composition boards—Construction materials made from wood by-products usually have trade names or are described as particle board, flake board, or chipboard, according to their ingredients. Usually they are not graded; their strength increases with their thickness and with the size of the particles used in their construction. They have no appearance qualities to speak of. Hardboard—Masonite—does come either standard or tempered (which is stronger), and either smoothed on one side or on both. These materials are strong when used on edge or when well supported if used flat. They are not resistant to moisture and should be sealed where exposed. Also, they do not hold fasteners well. Screws designed for joining sheet metal work best (drill the pilot holes undersize); small nails are a second choice. These should be cement-coated or specially made for composition board.

Making your own lumber

With the right equipment—logging tools and a portable chain-saw mill—felling trees and making your own lumber can reward you with varieties and sizes impossible to obtain any other way. The equipment is expensive, though, and the tasks are dangerous. Get some real experience by working with people who've done it themselves before trying it on your own.

Trees large enough to yield lumber must be at least 14 inches in diameter. Felling them is no small undertaking for a nonprofessional. Above all, be sure you understand what you are doing and what the hazards are before you start. That way you'll be programmed to work safely. The tools you'll need most are a chain saw with at least a 16-inch bar, a 3½-pound single bit axe, and a couple of felling wedges made of aluminum or plastic (available at chain-saw stores). Wear boots, a hard hat, goggles, gloves, ear protectors, and clothes that fit closely. Don't work alone. Have an assistant who is at least as knowledgeable as you are. Select trees both for their likeliness as good lumber producers and their ease of felling. Beginners should choose straight trees that clearly lean in a safe direction for falling and are not likely to fall against other trees nearby. Don't choose trees with excessive lean, though; these usually contain wood under stress, which will warp badly when made into boards. Before cutting anything, clear the path along the tree's direction of fall, and clear also two possible escape routes away from the felling area.

After the tree is down, cut off the limbs, then buck the trunk into lumber-size logs. These two operations can be quite dangerous. The limbs are usually under great tension, liable to snap if sawn carelessly, and as they are cut away the tree may roll or shift suddenly. Be especially careful of your footing and always stand so the trunk of the tree is between you and the limb you are sawing. When bucking, analyze how the log sections are supported and how they may roll when sliced through. If the saw blade gets pinched, shut off the engine and pry the sections apart with wedges or by levering.

Felling a Tree

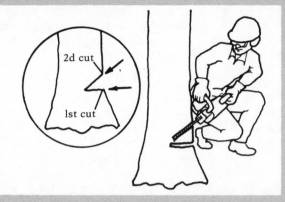

1. Felling a tree takes three cuts. Begin by making the first cut a short distance up from the ground. The cut should be horizontal and at a right angle to the intended direction of fall. Cut about one-third to one-half the distance through tree.

2. Start the second cut above the first at a height equal to, or somewhat more than, one-third the depth of the first cut. Angle the cut downward so it meets the deepest part of the first cut and forms a wedge-shaped piece. The two cuts should meet exactly on each side of the tree; if the second cut slants to one side, the tree will fall toward the narrower opening.

3. After checking escape routes and path of fall, start the final cut directly opposite and a few inches above the first cut. Do not cut clear through. The tree should begin to fall before the cut is finished, the uncut wood acting as a hinge. On trees that do not begin falling when the saw nears the center of the trunk, stop the saw and drive a wedge into the cut, directly in line with the path of fall. When the tree starts to fall, remove and shut off the saw, then retreat along your escape route. Before returning to the site, wait until broken branches from nearby trees have had a chance to fall also.

LIMBING

1. When the tree is down, saw off the limbs by working from the butt end of the tree toward the tip. Remove limbs from the top side of the tree first. Be very careful of side and bottom limbs. These may be under tension and will kick back at you or the saw when cut through.

2. To cut limbs under tension, first try to reposition the tree trunk to relieve stress. If this is not possible, cut the limb partway through at top of tension point, then sever the limb by cutting completely through from underneath. Trim limbed areas flush with the trunk to facilitate milling.

BUCKING

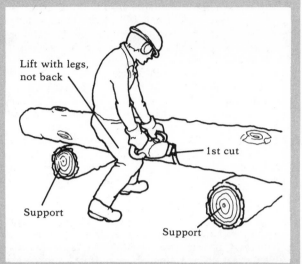

1. Measure the limbed trunk into usable lumber lengths, then mark intervals by notching the bark with an axe. Buck trunk into logs, using a chain saw. To avoid pinching the blade, first saw upward from beneath the log, to make a cut slightly more than halfway through. (Use your legs, not your back, to lift the saw.)

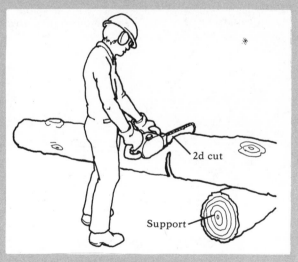

2. Complete the cut by sawing down to the first cut, keeping the blade just to one side of the kerf in case the log falls inward. The best technique is to work from one end of the tree to the other, removing support from beneath log sections before each cut, so the sections will fall away from the saw.

Using a Chain-Saw Mill

A chain-saw mill is simple: It's an adjustable frame—essentially a depth-of-cut guide—that attaches to the saw bar of a chain saw and allows you to rip logs lengthwise into boards of any given thickness. For serious do-it-yourself lumber makers, it's a dream come true.

With a chain-saw mill, you can custom-cut lumber in ways that would be prohibitively expensive to order from a commercial sawmill. You can also make lumber from unusual trees (such as exotic fencerow walnuts and maples) that commercial mills won't even touch for fear of encountering a stray piece of metal that can instantly ruin their saw blade (albeit at your expense). And, with a chain-saw mill, you can cut a log into boards right at the site. You don't have to worry about hauling large logs out of the woods; you bring out only finished lumber.

The problem with chain-saw mills, though, is that they're very hard on their most expensive component, chain saws. Lumber-making with a chain saw requires about three times as much power from the saw as using it for its normal function, which is crosscutting. Also, the saw must run for long periods of time at full power, not in short intermittent bursts. All of this means that for anything but the most incidental use you need a pretty hefty saw, and one with quite a bit of engine modification, a special saw bar, and a custom-sharpened chain as well. These items are available, but at a cost. Unless you are willing to invest the money, and/or are a skilled small engine mechanic with machine shop experience and can perform the almost constant high-level maintenance necessary to keep the equipment in running order, you're probably still better off buying lumber from local sawmills and wood dealers. Chain-saw mills are remarkable tools. The best advice, however, seems to be: Get some experience with one before you decide to buy.

Here's how they work. First determine the path the saw blade will take. The grain of quality wood runs parallel to the heart of the log. On extremely tapered logs, or where the heart is not located near the log's average center, prop the ends of the guide plank (see below) to compensate. If quality lumber is not needed, run the saw parallel to the log's average center; you'll get longer boards but they'll be of lesser grade. Large logs may be split with wedges, then quartersawn to produce superior lumber that resists warping.

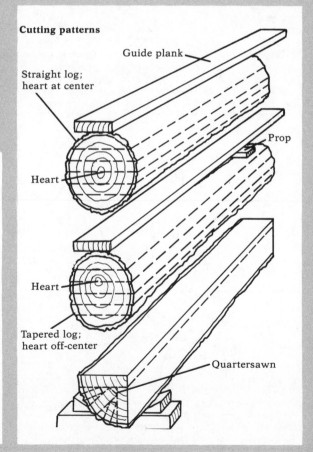

Cutting patterns

Guide plank

Straight log; heart at center

Prop

Heart

Heart

Tapered log; heart off-center

Quartersawn

Chain saw

Guard

Mill attachment

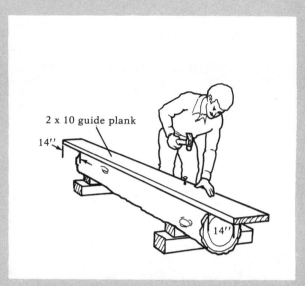

2 x 10 guide plank

14''

14''

1. For simple lumber-making on a log with minimal taper, first prop the log securely, and then nail a flat 2 × 10 board to the top of the log to act as a guide plank for the first cut. This board should overhang the ends of the log by about 14''. The nails must be short enough not to interfere with the saw blade passing beneath.

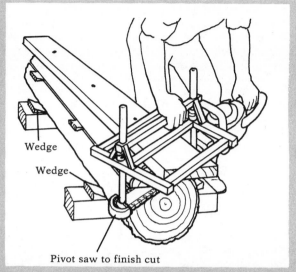

Wedge

Wedge

Pivot saw to finish cut

3. At intervals along the cut, insert wedges to prevent the top slab from pinching the blade. When the saw comes to the far end of the log, pivot the nose of the saw out first, then slide the rest of the saw out of the log and along the projecting end of the guide plank. Shut off the saw.

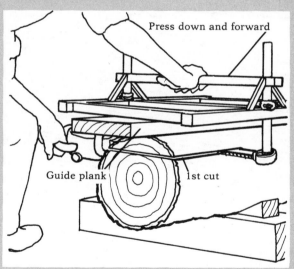

Press down and forward

Guide plank   1st cut

2. Determine the desired board thickness, then add the thickness of the guide plank. Set the chain-saw mill to this combined figure. Now start saw and slide it along the forward edge of the guide plank and into the log to begin cutting. Maintain firm downward pressure, while also moving the saw forward through the log.

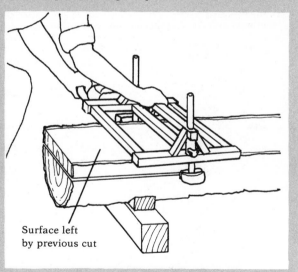

Surface left
by previous cut

4. Remove the top slab with the guide plank attached. For subsequent cuts, reset the mill to the desired board thickness only, and use the cut surface of the log as the bearing face for the mill. Pivot the saw carefully when starting and finishing the cuts (since there is no overhanging guide plank at this stage), both for accuracy and safety.

Drying Lumber

Freshly cut wood must be dried before it is used. Commercial lumber is usually kiln-dried in special ovens, but you may dry lumber you have cut yourself merely by leaving it in the open air, carefully stacked and protected. Air-drying in this manner takes time—wood 1 in. thick must usually be left to dry at least three months under ideal conditions, and six months or a year or more is not uncommon, especially with hardwoods—but many woodworkers feel wood dried this way is superior.

The keys to successful air-drying are plenty of air circulation, protection against rot, and some restraint against warpage. Under arid conditions you must not let wood dry too fast, either, or it will check (split).

As soon as possible after cutting, coat the ends of each piece with a sealer such as paraffin or urethane varnish. If the wood is very damp, apply a latex primer first. Then stack the wood so that air can circulate freely around each piece. Start the pile several inches off the ground, using poor-quality lumber for the bottom layers if the pile is outdoors, and place 1-in.-sq. spacers (called stickers) made of dry scrap lumber equal in length to the width of the pile between each succeeding layer. Locate the stickers at the ends of the boards—so there is no overhang—and at 16-in. intervals in between. Do not stagger them throughout the pile. At the top, again place poor-quality lumber, and on top of the last layer, a few bricks or other weights. Cover the top of outdoor piles with an overhanging layer of corrugated metal or plastic roofing, slanted to shed water. Mark each pile with the date it was stacked. Wood for furniture should be brought indoors and left to dry still further at least six weeks before using.

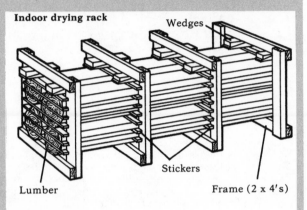

Indoor drying rack

Wedges

Stickers

Lumber

Frame (2 x 4's)

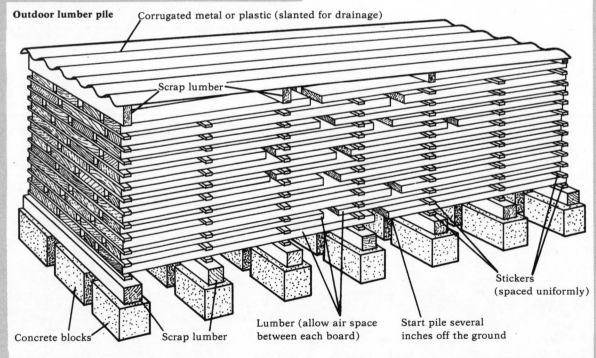

Outdoor lumber pile

Corrugated metal or plastic (slanted for drainage)

Scrap lumber

Stickers (spaced uniformly)

Concrete blocks

Scrap lumber

Lumber (allow air space between each board)

Start pile several inches off the ground

Common wood species

Beech—hardwood; a strong, heavy wood that works well and is resistant to impact. Beech takes a good finish. Though it shrinks a great deal, it has a fine, uniform texture, useful for flooring, furniture, wooden bowls, and utensils.

Cherry—hardwood; moderately heavy, but machines well. It is strong, stiff, and impact-resistant. The heartwood is reddish brown, is of uniform texture, and shrinks very little after seasoning. It is prized as furniture wood.

Cypress—softwood; light in weight, soft, and easy to work. Noted for its resistance to decay, it is often used for exterior siding and interior wall paneling as well as for furniture. Cypress is normally light brown and has a fairly coarse texture. Very old cypress trees often develop reddish heartwood, which is highly valued by cabinetmakers.

Douglas fir—softwood; strong and moderately resistant to decay, it is one of the world's most valuable structural woods. Douglas fir dries well and is easily worked. It is widely used to make plywood and lumber for housing, agriculture, and industry.

Eastern red cedar—softwood; not strong, but very resistant to decay; stable and cuts cleanly. Straight-grained, but with many knots, it is used for fence posts, chests, and closet lining. The heartwood, which accounts for most of the trunk, is dull red.

Eastern and western white pine—softwoods; stable, straight-grained woods of uniform texture that dry easily. They work well as furniture woods, take an excellent finish, and darken nicely with exposure to air.

Elm—hardwood; bends well, making it suitable for projects that require molded shapes. Slippery and American elm, both good for furniture and paneling, have nearly white sapwood and dark brown heartwood. The harder rock elm—light brown throughout—is often used for chair rockers.

Hickory—hardwood; exceptionally strong, tough, and resilient, making it valuable for tool handles, dowels, and furniture, but hard to work. Coarse-textured though fairly straight-grained, hickory is reddish brown in color.

Mahogany—hardwood; dimensionally stable and easy to work. An excellent furniture wood, it is reddish and takes an excellent polish. Mahogany does not grow in the United States.

Maple—hardwood; stiff, heavy, strong, and impact-resistant, with a fine, uniform texture. It is not difficult to work despite its density, and its durability makes it good for flooring, furniture, woodenware, and handles.

Red and white oak—hardwoods; heavy, tough, somewhat difficult to work but well suited for lumber and furniture. For fine woodworking, white oak is preferred over red, because it is stronger and can be steam-bent easily. White oak heartwood is impervious to moisture and resistant to decay.

Southern yellow pine—softwood; shrinks moderately but is stable when seasoned. It is used extensively for building—the dense wood for structural supports, the light wood for trim.

Walnut—hardwood; normally straight-grained, dimensionally stable, and easy to work. It's moderately heavy, strong, stiff, and impact-resistant, and ranges in color from deep brown heartwood to nearly white sapwood. Walnut is particularly attractive and regarded as America's most valuable furniture wood.

Yellow birch—hardwood; heavy, strong wood with good impact resistance and a fine, uniform texture. Despite its large shrinkage when seasoned, it is excellent for veneer, furniture, woodenware, and doors. Birch plywood is widely used for quality cabinetwork. Paper birch—used in birchbark canoes—is softer and weaker than yellow birch.

Yellow poplar—hardwood; medium in density and strength; generally straight-grained and uniform in texture. Second growth is often heavier and stronger than the old wood. The heartwood is yellowish brown with a greenish cast. Poplar is used for furniture, siding, interior trim, and core stock for plywood.

Yellow spruce—softwood; straight-grained, light, and strong, with a very uniform texture. It was once useful for building airplanes. It is still valuable for making violins and guitars, piano sounding boards, furniture, and boats.

Basic Procedures

Now that you've got your rough stock—wood obtained from a lumberyard or a sawmill or by your own hands—laid in, you need to know a few basic techniques for getting it ready to use in a project. This section will show you how to measure, cut, and prepare rough stock to the dimensions called for in the materials lists (What You Will Need) for each project that follows at the end of this chapter.

The measuring techniques and tool-handling methods described here are not just for preparing rough stock. You'll rely on them in every woodworking job you undertake.

Enlarging or Reducing Scale Drawings

Many scale drawings and patterns that you will find in this book and elsewhere require enlarging to make them full size. A common method for doing this is by the proportional grid technique shown here. The method also works for reducing large drawings to smaller size.

To begin, use a pencil and ruler to cover the original drawing with a grid pattern of evenly spaced vertical and horizontal lines. Draw lightly so you can erase; if marking directly on the original is not feasible, pencil a grid on tracing paper and fasten that to the drawing. On a blank piece of paper, make a copy of the grid, using the same number of horizontals and verticals as on the original, but spacing the lines closer or farther apart by some fixed or prescribed amount, determined by the desired size of the final pattern. The object is to reproduce the original grid so it has the same number of squares, only larger or smaller.

Now systematically fill in each square of the new grid with the portion of the drawing you see in the identical square on the original. As a guide, note primarily where the lines of the drawing contact the borders of individual squares. When reproducing complicated portions of a design, divide the squares of each grid still further—into quarters and even diagonally if necessary—to increase the number of reference points.

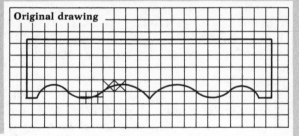

Original drawing

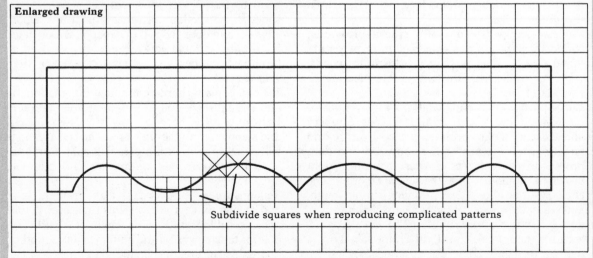

Enlarged drawing

Subdivide squares when reproducing complicated patterns

Tools for measuring

Accurate measuring tools are a must for your tool kit. To get started, you'll need at least a steel tape and a combination square. Buy a quality tape at least 8 ft. long. The ¾-in. width works best, because it is the most rigid. Don't worry if the tab on the front wobbles a little; it's supposed to. When buying a combination square, though, be sure that when tightened, there is no play at all in the blade. A combination square is likely to be your most-used measuring tool. It performs all the functions of a ruler, try square, miter gauge, depth gauge, marking and cutting gauge, and level. Most even have a built-in scribing tool.

Though pretty much outmoded by the combination square, a try square is still a good tool to buy. Use it for checking right angles. Some try squares have a 45° face also, which lets you check miters. Buy a well-made try square; for versatility, choose one with the blade shorter than that of your combination square.

A T-bevel is used for checking and laying out angles, in the same way as a try or combination square. Instead of the blade being fixed at a 90° angle, though, the T-bevel can be set at any angle.

With a compass you can lay out curved and radiused pieces, and divide long lengths equally. It is especially useful for scribing uneven surfaces against which mating pieces must be contour-fitted (see Compass, p. 18).

Marking, cutting, and mortise gauges are worthwhile if you do a lot of woodworking. They adjust to allow you to scribe lines a given distance from the edge or end of a board and are used for laying out saw cuts or the dimensions of joints.

Use a folding rule for carpentry. Because of its overlapping joints it's not as easy to read as a steel tape and so not always as accurate. It's more rigid, though, and can be extended outward, or into places you cannot reach, with greater success than a tape. A framing square is also a tool for carpenters. Primarily its use is as an on-the-job calculating device where angles are important, such as in laying out roof pieces or staircases. The two parts of the square—the tongue and the blade—represent two sides of a right triangle.

Measuring Techniques

STEEL TAPE

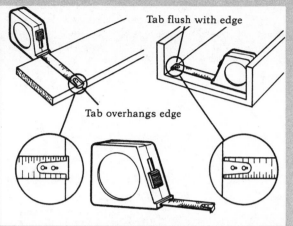

Tab flush with edge

Tab overhangs edge

Use the tab on the end of the hook when taking external measurements. Slots in the tab let it extend a distance equal to its own width, so the end of the tape is flush with the edge of the surface. When taking internal measurements, read the tape where it enters the case, then add 2 in., or as marked on case. The tab now retracts, so the end of the tape is flush against the edge of the surface.

COMBINATION SQUARE

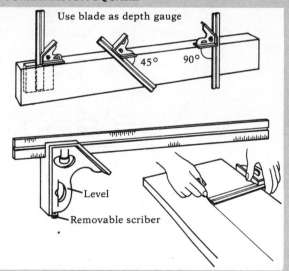

Use blade as depth gauge

45°   90°

Level

Removable scriber

Use a combination square to check 90° angles or 45° miters. Extend the blade into a mortise for use as a depth gauge. The level in the handle checks both

(Continued on next page)

Measuring Techniques—*Continued*

COMBINATION SQUARE—*Continued*
horizontal and vertical. To use as a marking or cutting gauge, set the blade so the end is the desired distance from the board edge. Press the square against the edge, and slide it forward while holding a scriber at the end of the blade.

TRY SQUARE

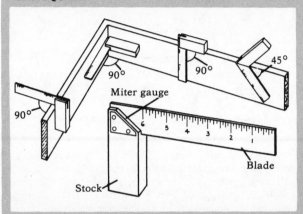

Hold the try square against the edge to check right angles or miters. Press both stock and blade into inside corners of the workpiece to check internal squareness. To test flatness, hold the blade against the board face at eye level; no light should show beneath the blade. Press the square against the board face and across the edge to check squareness of face to edge when truing up stock.

T-BEVEL

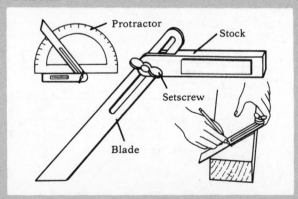

Set the T-bevel, using a protractor. Lock the blade by turning the lever or setscrew. To use, place the stock against the edge of the board and scribe along the blade.

COMPASS

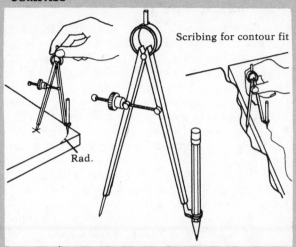

To radius a corner, set the compass to the desired radius, then place one end on a point equidistant from each side and equal to the radius dimension. Scribe the arc. To contour-fit uneven pieces, butt the pieces together, set the compass to the widest gap between them, then scribe the uncut piece by drawing the compass point along the edge of the irregular piece.

MARKING GAUGE

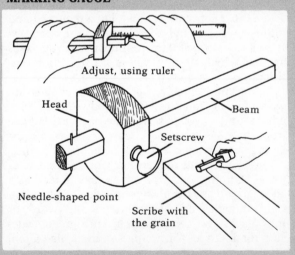

Use a marking gauge to scribe in the direction of the wood grain. The point of the gauge should be needle shaped. To use, adjust the distance between the head and the point, then press the gauge firmly against the side of the board and either push forward or draw toward you to scribe a line. Hold the gauge firmly, with your thumb extended toward the point. Rotate the gauge so the needle drags naturally when the gauge is slid forward or back.

CUTTING GAUGE

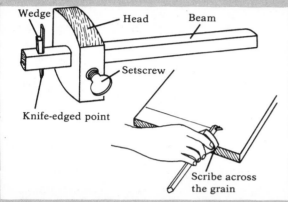

A cutting gauge is used across the grain of wood. The point should be knife-edged to cut wood fibers. To make a knife edge from the needle point of the marking gauge, first file the outside of the point flat, parallel to the surface of the gauge head, then bevel the side nearest the gauge head to form the knife edge.

MORTISE GAUGE

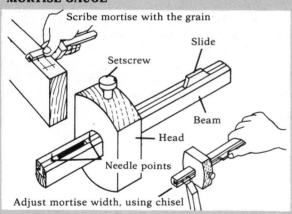

A mortise gauge is used exactly the same as a marking gauge, but separate needle points also adjust to scribe both sides of the mortise simultaneously. To use, first set the needles the desired distance apart (equal to the desired width of the mortise), then adjust the gauge head.

FOLDING RULE

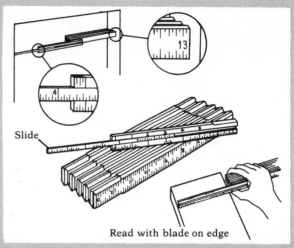

A folding rule is best read with the blade on edge, so the marks touch the wood directly. When measuring interior distances, open the rule as many sections as possible, then extend the slide. To read the measurement, add the distance shown on the slide to the distance shown at the end of the rule.

FRAMING SQUARE

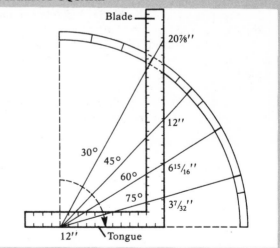

Commonly used angles can be found easily with a framing square by connecting markings on the tongue and blade. With skill, almost any problem involving right triangles (trigonometry) can be solved using the square.

Handsaws

Handsaws are the most basic tools for cutting wood. For making straight cuts, the ripsaw, crosscut saw, and backsaw are normally used. Coping and keyhole saws are used to cut curves.

Saws are sometimes distinguished by length, but most often by their number of teeth per inch. These are called points. The more points a saw has, the smoother the surface of the finished cut will be. However, more points also mean slower cutting. Saws designed for rough work—where smooth edges are not important—have fewer points so they will cut faster. Saws used for fine joinery—where speed is not much of a factor considering how small an amount of wood actually has to be sawn through—have many points, so that additional smoothing of the cut surface is not necessary.

Saw teeth are also set, that is, bent alternately to the left and right, so that they cut a path (called the kerf) that is wider than the saw blade's thickness. The kerf helps keep the saw from binding as it is pushed back and forth through the wood. Good handsaws (except backsaws) also have tapered backs—the blade thicker near the teeth than at the top—for the same reason.

A ripsaw is used for making cuts along the grain of a piece of wood. This process itself is called ripping. Most ripsaws are 26 inches long and have four or six points.

The crosscut saw, probably the most commonly owned saw, is used to cut across the grain.

Crosscut saws have smaller teeth than ripsaws, but most important, the teeth are filed differently and set at a greater angle. You can rip successfully (but slowly) with a crosscut saw, but you cannot make clean crosscuts with a ripsaw. Crosscut saws usually have 8 to 12 points, and are the same length as ripsaws.

Backsaws are smaller than the saws mentioned above, and have finer teeth, set and filed like those of a crosscut saw. Backsaws are used for precise work. A strip of steel or brass runs along the top of the blade to keep it from bending and to add weight to prevent bouncing. Most backsaws have 12 to 14 points and are made in various lengths. Small backsaws are called tenon or dovetail saws. Some of these may have up to 21 points.

Coping saws have a very thin, brittle blade strung between the ends of a U-shaped frame that keeps it under tension to avoid breakage. When sawing curves, the frame may be angled out of the way of the blade, and for extremely delicate work the blade may be installed with the teeth facing the handle, so that cutting takes place on the pull stroke for maximum control. Coping saws usually have 10 to 14 points and are 6 to 8 inches long.

A keyhole saw has no frame and is used to cut holes in wide panels beyond the reach of a coping saw. Keyhole saw blades are thicker than coping saw blades, and generally have 8 to 10 points. Keyhole saws come in a variety of lengths, up to 15 inches.

Types of handsaws

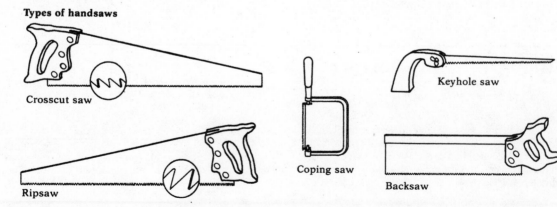

Crosscut saw

Ripsaw

Coping saw

Keyhole saw

Backsaw

Power saws

Power saws are time and effort savers, not substitutes for handsaws. Both take practice to use well, and the speed gained by using a power saw is often lost in the time required to set up the cut. For sawing tough woods like oak or manufactured products like plywood or particle board, however, you'll find a power saw a big help.

Most woodworkers begin with portable power saws: a circular saw for making straight cuts and a saber saw for cutting curves. If you do a lot of woodworking, sooner or later you'll want to get either a table saw or a radial arm saw to replace the circular saw and a band saw to supercede the saber saw.

Circular saws are capable of heavy-duty work. Saber saws are lighter, and their blades—which are unsupported—break more easily. Both saws are made in a variety of sizes and degrees of ruggedness. The circular saw you buy should be a quality brand and have a 6½- to 7¼-inch-diameter blade. A saber saw, likewise, should be of a quality make and as durably constructed as you can afford (blade size is not a factor). Specialized blades for ripping, crosscutting, cutting plywood—even for cutting masonry and metal—are available for both saws, and you should always use a blade appropriate to the task. Carbide-tipped blades, which stay sharp longer than regular steel blades, are available for circular saws. You might consider one for a table saw or radial arm saw, but they're quite expensive as saw blades go, and for very little money you can replace regular

circular saw blades that have become too worn to sharpen with brand-new ones. Also made for table saws or radial arm saws are pairs of blades with spacers to be sandwiched in between. These setups are called dado heads and are used for making very wide saw kerfs which serve as grooves (dadoes) or notches in boards being joined.

Types of power saws

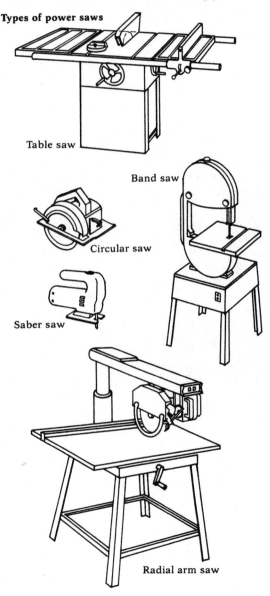

Table saw

Band saw

Circular saw

Saber saw

Radial arm saw

Making Crosscuts

HANDSAW METHOD

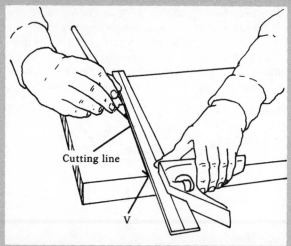

Cutting line

V

1. First, measure the board to length, using a steel tape or folding rule. Mark desired point with a V. Then square across the board, using a combination square or a try square. Align the blade of the square so its edge touches the point of the V, and scribe the cutting lines for the saw, using a sharp pencil held so only its point touches the square's blade.

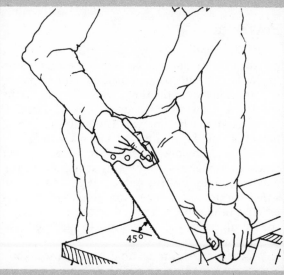

45°

3. Once the cut is started, increase the saw angle to about 45°. Withdraw your thumb, and use long, steady strokes to cut through the wood. Saw, using your shoulder muscles. Keep the blade in line with your forearm. You needn't grasp the saw tightly; it should cut smoothly almost under its own weight. If it binds, you are probably pushing it too hard.

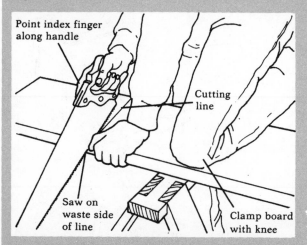

Point index finger along handle

Cutting line

Saw on waste side of line

Clamp board with knee

2. Place the board on the sawhorse so the cutting line and waste overhang the end or edge. Hold the board in place with your knee or a clamp. Grip the saw with your index finger pointed forward along the handle, and place the saw just to the waste side of the cutting line. Steady the blade against the thumb joint of your other hand, and start the cut by drawing the saw upward a few times at a shallow angle, until a kerf is formed.

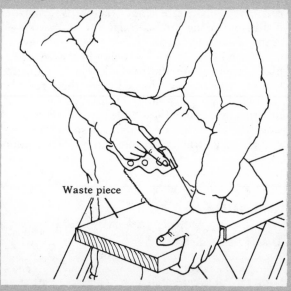

Waste piece

4. At the end of the cut, reach across the blade with your other hand, and support the waste piece so it does not splinter when cut off. Alternately, turn the board over and start a second cut to meet the first.

CIRCULAR SAW METHOD

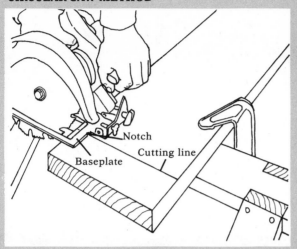

1. Mark the board (see Handsaw Method, on the page opposite), then clamp the board securely to the sawhorse. Set the saw's baseplate on the board, hold the saw level, and align the notch in the baseplate with the cutting line. (Experiment on scrap wood first.)

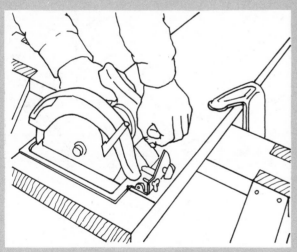

2. Start the saw with the blade at least 1'' from the board's edge, the guide plate resting on the board. Begin cutting by applying forward pressure, but do not press downward. Guide the saw along the cutting line, letting the saw do the work. If the saw binds or wanders, release the trigger, back the saw out of the kerf, and start over. At the end of the cut, slow the saw's forward motion slightly, then push the saw through quickly, right at the end, so the waste piece drops cleanly off without splintering.

HANDY SAW GUIDES

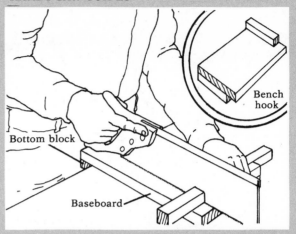

A bench hook protects the work surface and provides a stop for the work being sawn. The bottom block holds the hook against the work surface when in use. The blocks should be hardwood, perfectly squared, and attached at exact right angles to the baseboard with screws and glue. The baseboard may be softwood. Make several bench hooks, in various sizes.

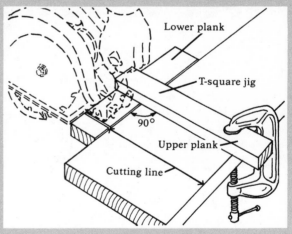

For a circular saw, make a T-square jig. Overlap squared planks at exact right angles, and fasten with screws and glue. Attach the jig to scrap board, align the saw's baseplate with the upper plank, then make a cut through the scrap board and lower plank. To use the jig, align the cut end of the lower plank with the cutting line, and clamp the jig to the board. Guide the saw along the upper plank to make the cut.

Ripping

HANDSAW TECHNIQUE

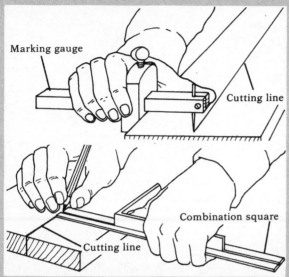

1. Lay out the cutting line by scribing along the board's face, using either a marking gauge or a pencil held against the end of a combination square. For each method to be accurate, be sure the edge of the board is flat and square to the face.

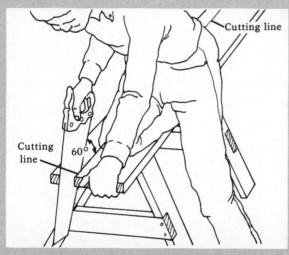

2. Place the board across a pair of sawhorses so that the end of the board projects about 8''. Hold the board in place with your knee or a clamp, and, with a ripsaw, start the cut as you would for a crosscut (see Making Crosscuts, p. 22). After the cut is started, raise the saw and continue while holding the saw at approximately a 60° angle.

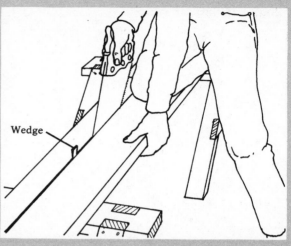

3. When the cut reaches the sawhorse, raise the board and saw, then reposition the sawhorse close to the board end already cut. Continue sawing between horses. At the end of the cut, reposition the second horse so the board end projects beyond it. If binding occurs during the cut, insert small wedges in the kerf near the blade.

RIPPING WITH POWER SAWS

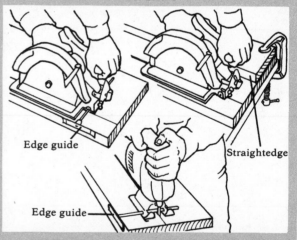

The setup for ripping with power saws is the same for handsaws, but be sure the board is clamped securely to the sawhorses. Saw freehand, using the edge guide that comes with the saw, or clamp a straightedge to the board face instead. With a circular saw, set the blade ¼ in. lower than the board's thickness. Stand to one side of the saw in case of kickback. When using any power saw, wear goggles when ripping, due to the large amount of sawdust.

Sawing Curves

USING A COPING SAW

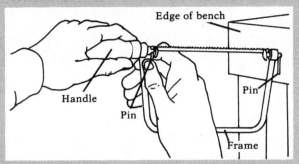

1. Install the blade with the teeth facing forward or back. First loosen the handle, then insert the blade in the pin at the forward end of the frame. Compress the frame against a hard surface until rear end of the blade will fit into the pin on the handle. Retighten the handle while holding the pins in line with the frame.

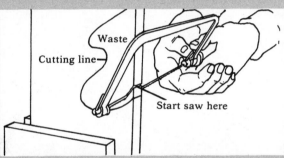

2. Start cut well on the waste side of the cutting line, using both hands to guide the saw. Gradually saw up to the line, and begin following the curve, staying always just inside of the line.

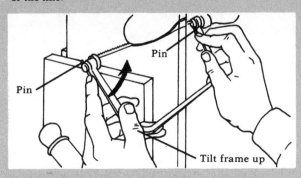

3. If the frame interferes with the cut, change the frame-to-blade angle by holding the pins at each end of the frame and pushing carefully against the frame with your thumbs. Don't twist the blade.

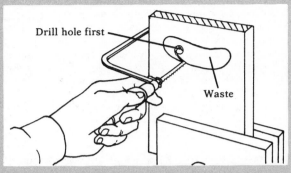

4. For interior cuts, first drill a hole in the waste, then disassemble the saw, pass the blade through the hole, and reassemble to begin cutting. Disassemble the saw to remove it when finished.

USING A KEYHOLE SAW

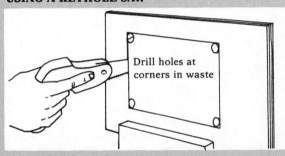

To saw out interior section, first drill a hole at each corner, then saw along the lines between the holes. Trim the corners square with a chisel when finished.

USING A SABER SAW

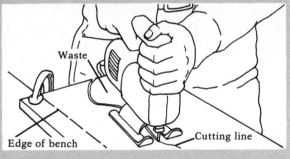

Clamp the work firmly to the edge of the bench top. Guide the saw along the waste side of the cutting line while holding the saw with both hands. Sight down on the line from directly above the saw. Check clearance between the saw blade and the edge of the bench frequently; reposition the work if necessary.

Sawing Large Panels

Plywood and manufactured wood products such as particle board and flake board have become popular and practical materials for woodworking because they are strong and considerably cheaper than solid lumber. Their major drawbacks, however, are that they come in large, unwieldy panels, and their composition (chiefly the glues used to bind either the laminations or wood fragments) causes rapid dulling of all but the hardest edge tools and saw blades.

Panels of plywood and composition boards are best cut with a power saw and help from an assistant. In fact, if your shop lacks adequate space or you lack adequate tools and equipment, you should consider having panels cut to size at the lumberyard. Most will make individual cuts for a very small fee, and, with their elaborate professional cutting jigs, lumberyards can perform work in minutes that might take you a couple of hours and cost you a saw blade as well.

If you do decide to do your own cutting—and on smaller pieces you undoubtedly will—you must have strong support equipment on which to work, straight-edge guides to make long cuts accurate, and sharp saw blades. Carbide-tipped blades are best for circular and related saws and stay sharp longest, but regular steel blades are sufficient for infrequent work. Whether for circular or saber saws, buy blades that are designed especially for the material you wish to cut. Plywood is especially troublesome, because the grain of each lamination lies at right angles to the one next to it and tearing of the grain somewhere is almost inevitable. Circular saw blades for plywood have small, equally sized teeth to minimize tearing. It also helps to score the cutting line with a knife before sawing. Be sure to cut plywood with the appropriate face up or down, as shown below.

WHICH SIDE UP?

LAYING OUT

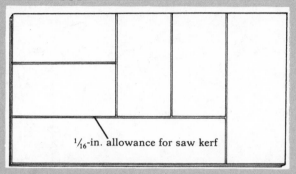

$\frac{1}{16}$-in. allowance for saw kerf

Efficient layout of pieces to be cut prevents excess waste. Mark panel on face that will be visible when sawing. Allow at least $\frac{1}{16}$ in. between pieces for kerf.

SUPPORTING PANELS

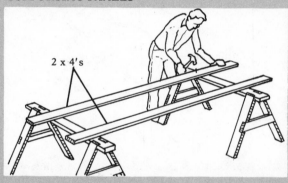

2 x 4's

Support large panels on sawhorses with 2 × 4's nailed between them. The distance between sawhorses is 2 ft. less than the length of the panel.

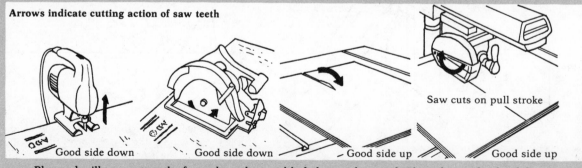

Arrows indicate cutting action of saw teeth

Good side down — Good side down — Good side up — Good side up

Plywood will tear out on the face where the saw blade leaves the wood. Place the good side of the plywood down when sawing with hand-held circular and saber saws. Keep the good side up when using a handsaw, radial arm saw, or table saw.

A JIG FOR CUTTING PANELS

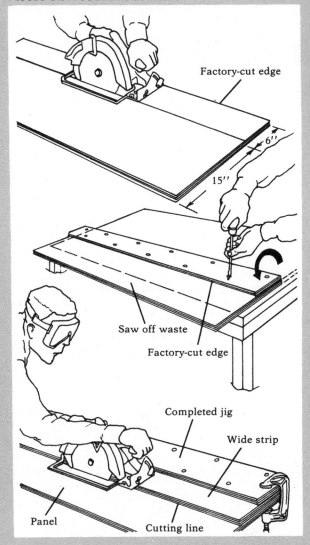

Factory-cut edge

6"

15"

Saw off waste

Factory-cut edge

Completed jig

Wide strip

Panel

Cutting line

This useful jig is easy to make and a great aid when cutting panels with a portable circular saw. Begin by cutting two strips of ½-in. or ¾-in. plywood, one 6 in. wide and the other 15 in. wide. The narrower strip should include the factory-cut edge of the panel. The strips should be as long as any of the cuts you'll be likely to make in panels later, but a good length to start with is 4 ft.—the width of an ordinary plywood sheet. Measure and cut the strips freehand; a perfectly straight cut isn't necessary. Next, glue and nail or screw the two strips together so that the factory-cut edge faces the middle of the wide strip. Clamp the assembly to a workbench or tabletop so that at least 6 in. of the wide strip projects beyond the edge, then, using the factory-cut edge as a saw guide, cut off the end of the wide strip to complete the jig. To use, merely align the edge of the wide strip with the cutting line on the panel, and clamp the jig in place. Rest the saw on the wide strip, and guide it along the factory-cut edge of the strip fastened above to make the cut.

RIPPING

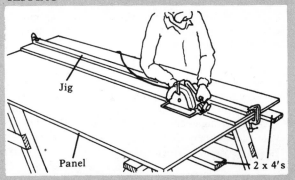

Jig

Panel

2 x 4's

A large jig for ripping panels can be fastened to the sawhorse setup shown on the page opposite. Be sure to adjust the depth of the saw blade carefully.

PANEL-CUTTING WITH A TABLE SAW

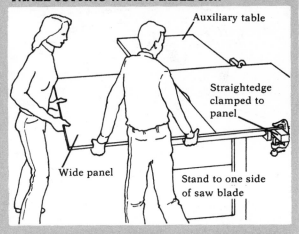

Auxiliary table

Straightedge clamped to panel

Wide panel

Stand to one side of saw blade

Cutting panels on a table saw is tricky and dangerous. Use auxiliary tables to support the panel, and have help from an assistant. If a rip fence cannot be used, clamp a straightedge to the underside of the panel as a guide. Beware of kickback.

Angled Cuts

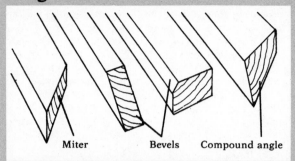

Miter   Bevels   Compound angle

Angled cuts fall into three categories: miters, bevels, and compound angles. Miter cuts cross the face of a board at some angle other than 90°, but are square to the board's edges. Bevel cuts are square to the board's face—if they are made across the grain—but angle across the edges. (Bevel cuts made with the grain are square to the board's ends instead. Normally these cuts are made using a plane when done by hand.) Compound angles cross both the face and the edge of a board at an angle other than 90°.

USING A MITER BOX

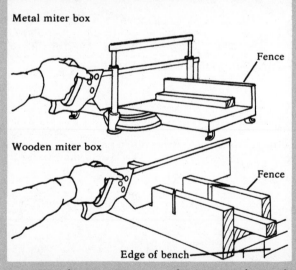

Metal miter box

Fence

Wooden miter box

Fence

Edge of bench

Miter boxes permit exact adjustment and control of the saw. Metal boxes are more versatile and accurate than the wooden ones used by carpenters. To use, set the saw to the desired cutting angle, then clamp or hold the marked board in place against the box fence, so that the saw cuts on the waste side of the line. Narrow boards can be sawn on edge to make bevels.

BEVELS WITH A HANDSAW

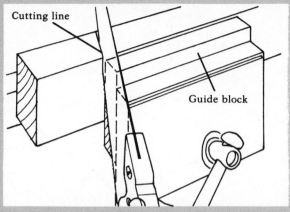

Cutting line

Guide block

Lay out the bevel cut on all four surfaces of the board. Clamp the board in a vise with a guide block. Hold the saw at a steep angle—handle downward—and begin cutting at the edge nearest you, following lines at both edge and face. When the saw reaches the far edge, reverse the board in the vise and make the second cut, allowing the saw to ride in the kerf from the first cut. Repeat steps until the cut is finished.

COMPOUND ANGLES WITH A CIRCULAR SAW

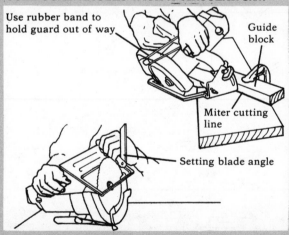

Use rubber band to hold guard out of way

Guide block

Miter cutting line

Setting blade angle

Compound angles can be cut in one operation with most power saws; with handsaws, two cuts must be made. To adjust a circular saw, first retract the blade guard and set the blade angle for the correct bevel, using the gauge on the saw or a T-bevel. Then align the saw with the miter cutting line. Make the cut, using a guide block for accuracy.

Sharpening Saws

Thorough saw sharpening should be done professionally. However, touching up your saw by the method shown below will keep it working well for a long time. Use a special saw file, available at hardware stores. Buy a file matched to your saw's number of points; it should fit perfectly in the gullets (spaces) between the teeth. Do not resharpen power saw blades. Ordinary ones are more easily replaced, and expensive ones should be sent to a sharpening service (check the Yellow Pages of your phone book).

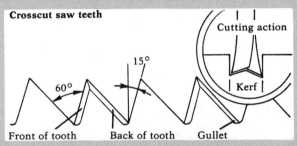

Crosscut saw teeth

Crosscut saw teeth are filed like tiny knives to sever wood across the grain.

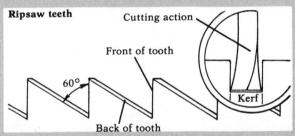

Ripsaw teeth

Ripsaw teeth are filed square across like chisels, to gouge wood in direction of grain.

STEPS FOR SHARPENING

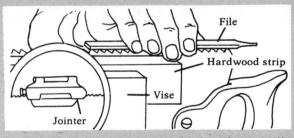

1. Clamp the saw in a vise between hardwood strips, 1/8″ below gullets. Slide a fine-cutting flat file or commercial saw jointer lightly along the tops of the teeth to flatten the point of each tooth very slightly. The flat spots act as sharpening guides.

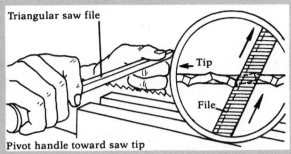

Pivot handle toward saw tip

2. Use a triangular saw file next. Starting at the tip of the saw, place the file in the gullet, in front of the first tooth set toward you. Rotate the file until it settles between the teeth, then, while holding the file level, pivot the handle toward the tip until the file matches the angle of the tooth's bevel. File gently with forward strokes until half of the flat spot is gone. Repeat process, repositioning file not in the next gullet but in the one after that. Continue filing in alternate gullets until the handle is reached.

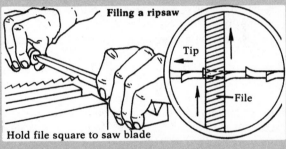

Filing a ripsaw

Hold file square to saw blade

3. Reverse the saw in the vise so the handle points in opposite direction. Repeat step 2, filing until remaining portions of flat spots disappear. (By following instructions exactly you will be filing the gullets you skipped.) To file a ripsaw, proceed just as in steps 1, 2, and 3, but hold the handle square to the saw; do not pivot the handle toward tip.

4. After several sharpenings, use a commercial saw set to return the teeth to their original flared angle if necessary. Adjust the tool, using the rearmost sawtooth (usually unworn, even on old saws) as a guide. Pressing the handles bends the teeth the correct amount.

Planes

Planes are for surfacing and smoothing wood. In use, they are pushed in, or at a slight angle to, the direction of the wood grain. Before the invention of power shapers such as routers, a woodworker usually owned dozens of planes, most of them handmade from wood, each designed to cut a certain shape. Nowadays, most planes are made of metal and not nearly so many varieties exist. As a beginner, you should buy a 14-inch jack plane for general smoothing and a 6-inch block plane for trimming end grain. Better, larger planes have a corrugated sole so they slide easily across the wood. Good block planes are fully adjustable and have the blade set at an angle of 12 to 20 degrees to the sole. Later, fill out your collection with a 10-inch smoothing plane for finish work and a 22-inch jointer plane for truing long edges.

Learn to adjust your planes properly, and keep them razor sharp. For most work, set the chip breaker (block planes don't have these) about $1/32$ of an inch from the edge of the blade, and align the edge of the frog with the upper edge of the sole's mouth opening. For rough work, increase the chip breaker's distance $1/16$ of an inch, and move the frog slightly to the rear. For finish work, or on wood with difficult grain, move the chip breaker as close as possible to the blade's edge, and adjust the frog forward. Store planes on their side with the blade retracted.

Types of planes

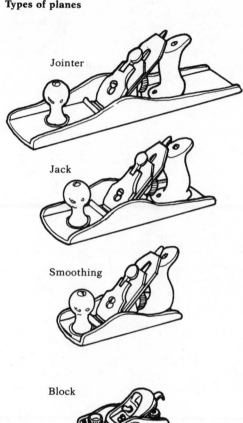

Jointer

Jack

Smoothing

Block

Corrugated sole

Parts of a plane

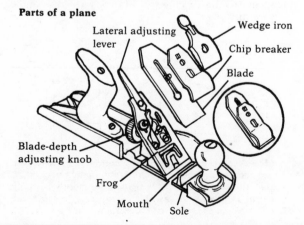

Lateral adjusting lever

Wedge iron

Chip breaker

Blade

Blade-depth adjusting knob

Frog

Mouth

Sole

Using Planes

ADJUSTING THE BLADE

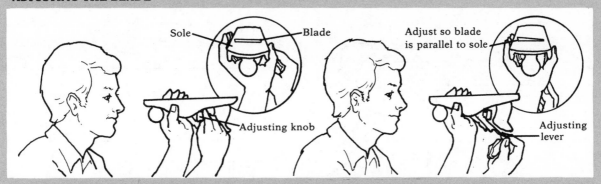

Hold the plane at eye level. For general work, turn the adjusting knob until the blade shows a hairline thickness above the sole. For fine work, the blade should only just be visible. Move the lateral adjusting lever to level the blade so the edge is parallel to the sole, otherwise the plane will leave scratch marks.

PLANING TECHNIQUE

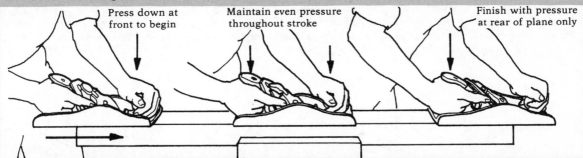

To plane correctly, press down at the forward end when beginning stroke, shift pressure to rear at end. Stand directly behind the work, with outer foot forward. Push plane by rocking the entire body forward.

PLANING EDGES

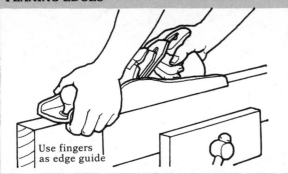

Use the fingers of the outer hand as a guide to keep the plane square to the board face. If the edge becomes unsquare, center the plane over the high edge.

PLANING END GRAIN

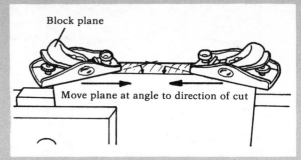

For best results, use a very sharp block plane set for a fine cut. Plane from both ends toward the middle to avoid splintering the wood at the corners. Hold the plane pivoted at a 15° angle to the direction of the cut.

(Continued on next page)

Using Planes—*Continued*

CHECKING FOR TWIST

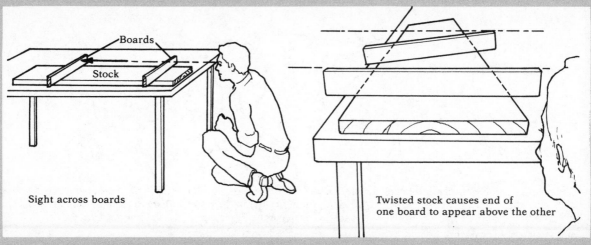

Sight across boards

Twisted stock causes end of
one board to appear above the other

Use two boards of equal dimensions and with perfectly squared corners to check for twist. Place the boards across the workpiece, then sight across their top edges. If a twist is present, a corner of one board will appear higher or lower than the others. To correct a twist, plane off high areas (usually at diagonal corners).

MAKING A SHOOTING BOARD

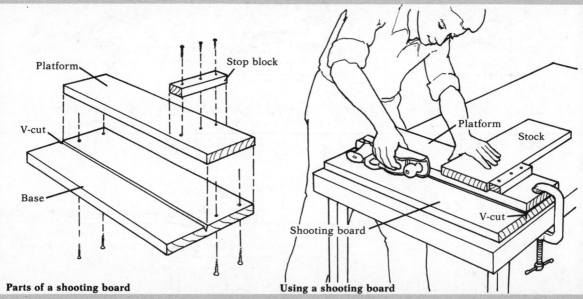

Parts of a shooting board

Using a shooting board

A shooting board is used for planing edges or ends. Make one or two in different sizes. Use hardwood or plywood for all parts. Pieces must be perfectly squared, as shown. Fasten with glue and nails or screws. Sink metal fasteners well below surface to protect the plane blade. To use, clamp or hold the workpiece against the stop block so the edge projects slightly beyond the raised platform. Slide the plane along the base to trim the edge square to face.

A SHOOTING BOARD FOR MITERS

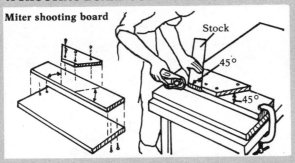

Miter shooting board

Stock

45°

45°

The base and platform of this shooting board are the same as shown on the page opposite. For the top piece, saw a square of wood or plywood in half diagonally, position the long edge flush with the outside of the base and platform, then mark and saw off the 90° corner before fastening. To use, press the work against one side of the top piece while sliding the plane along the base to trim the work flush with the inside edge of the shooting board. The angle of the finished piece will be 45°.

SHARPENING PLANES AND CHISELS

Until you become an expert, the most foolproof way to sharpen plane blades and chisels is by hand, using oilstones and a honing jig. Don't use an electric grinding wheel; you might ruin the blade's hardness.

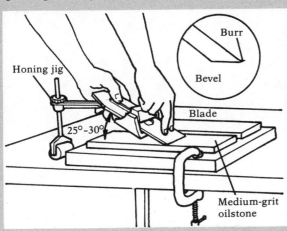

Honing jig

25°–30°

Burr

Bevel

Blade

Medium-grit oilstone

1. Clamp a medium-grit oilstone firmly to a level work surface. Install the blade, bevel down, in the honing jig, and adjust until the bevel fully contacts the stone (bevel should be 25° for planes, 30° for chisels). Work the blade forward and back over the stone—oiling often—until a burr forms.

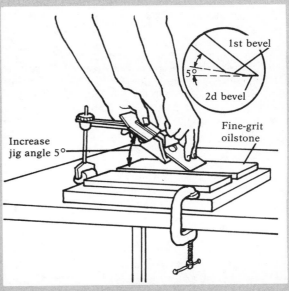

1st bevel

5°

2d bevel

Increase jig angle 5°

Fine-grit oilstone

2. Now increase the blade angle by about 5°. Work the blade over a fine-grit finishing stone until a second bevel appears evenly across the end of the blade and no shiny spots are visible when the blade is viewed end-on at eye level.

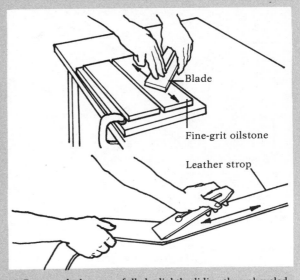

Blade

Fine-grit oilstone

Leather strop

3. Remove the burr carefully by lightly sliding the unbeveled side of the blade flat across the finishing stone. Strop the blade on smooth leather to achieve the final razor edge. Steps 2 and 3 can be repeated many times before step 1 is again required.

Truing-Up Stock

Most lumber you buy at a lumberyard does not require extensive preparation. However, rough-cut stock, or boards that are somewhat twisted or warped but still usable, need truing-up before use. Before using any piece of wood, even one that looks true, check its faces and edges for squareness, then complete the necessary steps (shown in these illustrations) to provide accurately sized pieces for your project before you begin. Truing-up stock by hand takes some practice at first but is a valuable skill and the quickest way to gain a really in-depth familiarity with wood.

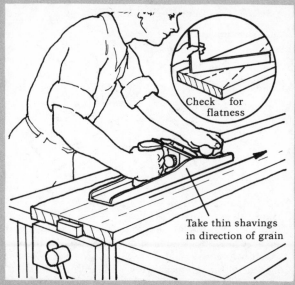

Check for flatness

Take thin shavings in direction of grain

2. Remove plane marks by planing with the grain. Use a jointer plane if possible, but a jack plane is also suitable. Take long, very thin shavings. Check entire board surface for flatness by holding a straightedge across the board at various angles. Light visible beneath the straightedge indicates that planing is still necessary.

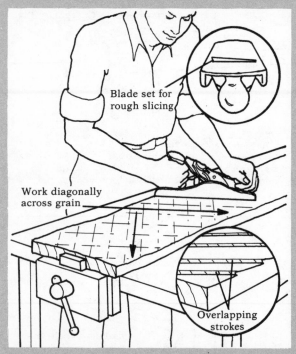

Blade set for rough slicing

Work diagonally across grain

Overlapping strokes

1. Begin by planing the best or convex face flat, using a jack plane. If the wood is dirty from storage, first brush it as clean as possible with a stiff bristle brush before beginning to plane it to size. Grit on rough-cut lumber will quickly dull any edge tool. Then plane diagonally across the grain in narrow, overlapping strokes, first from one direction, then the other. Plane obviously high areas first before planing across the entire width of the board.

To remove a great deal of waste wood quickly, adjust the plane so one corner of the blade protrudes farther below the sole plate than the other. This produces a slicing effect, allowing you to take coarser cuts with less effort. The plane will leave marks, however. Also set the mouth of the plane at a wider-than-normal opening so that the larger chips do not cause clogging.

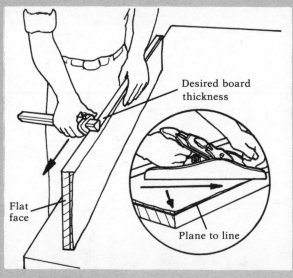

Desired board thickness

Flat face

Plane to line

3. When the face is flat, use it to guide the marking gauge for scribing the desired thickness of the board. Scribe around all four edges of the board, then plane the second face flat as in step 1, stopping at the scribed lines.

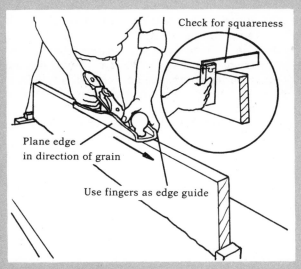

Check for squareness

Plane edge
in direction of grain

Use fingers as edge guide

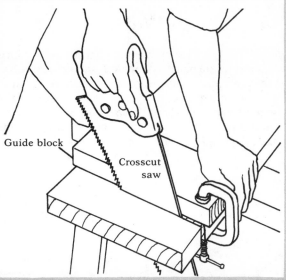

Guide block

Crosscut
saw

4. Now plane the best edge of the board, using a jack plane. Follow the grain of the wood; if planing leaves a rough surface, reverse the wood, or plane from opposite direction. Check the edge for squareness by holding a try square against the edge and face of the board. Sight from one end of the board while sliding the try square along the entire length. No light should show beneath the blade of the square.

6. Crosscut the board to the desired length. Use a guide block to assure that the cut is square to the board's face. To make the cut as close to the final dimension as possible without making the board too short, clamp a guide block to the "good" side of the line.

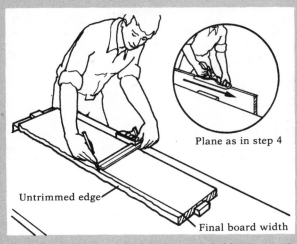

Plane as in step 4

Untrimmed edge

Final board width

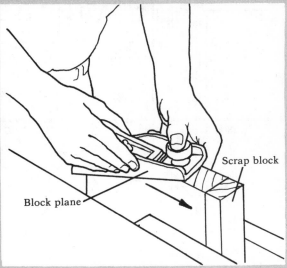

Scrap block

Block plane

5. Scribe the final width of the board by holding a pencil against the blade of the square and sliding the handle along the planed edge. Then plane the untrimmed edge square and to the line, checking frequently with a try square, as in step 4. Note: On hardwood boards where end-grain splintering is likely, you should perform steps 6 and 7 before this step.

7. Carefully plane the end grain of the board smooth, square, and to the board's final length, using a sharp block plane. To avoid splintering the grain at corners, keep the board pressed firmly against a scrap block, or plane from the corners toward the center. Check work with a try square, as in step 4.

A Place to Work

Your workshop should provide a comfortable and safe place to work and should contain all the tools and equipment you need, close at hand. Although few woodworker's needs are exactly the same, every shop should have a workbench, shelves, and a place to hang tools. Make sure to provide adequate lighting and ventilation, sufficient heavy-duty electrical outlets, and a fire extinguisher.

Individual needs and interests—as well as space and finances—will determine the type of workbench you choose. Build or buy a sturdy one, however, large enough to provide full support for your work and heavy enough to provide a solid base for hammering and planing. Mount a vise on the front (on the left-hand corner if you're right-handed), and another on an end, if possible. The top of the bench should be even with your hip.

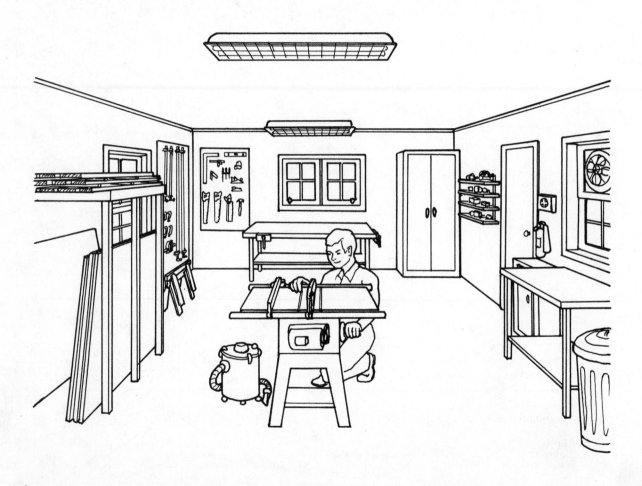

A Simple Workbench

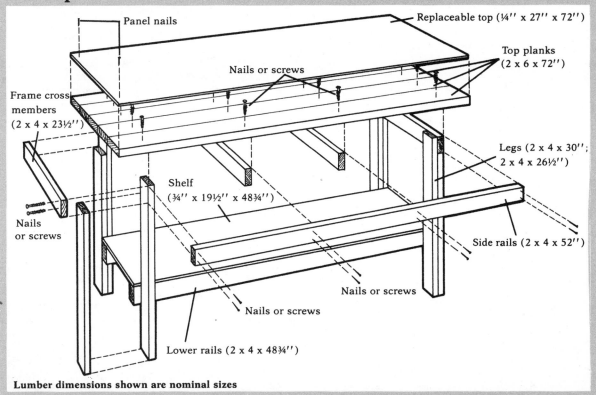

Panel nails

Replaceable top (¼'' x 27'' x 72'')

Top planks
(2 x 6 x 72'')

Nails or screws

Frame cross
members
(2 x 4 x 23½'')

Legs (2 x 4 x 30'';
2 x 4 x 26½'')

Shelf
(¾'' x 19½'' x 48¾'')

Nails
or screws

Side rails (2 x 4 x 52'')

Nails or screws

Nails or screws

Lower rails (2 x 4 x 48¾'')

Lumber dimensions shown are nominal sizes

This workbench is easy to build, using only hand tools and common-grade construction stock, available at any lumberyard. It is a good first bench to make if you are a beginner or only need a workbench for occasional use. Ideally, the bench should be set against a wall for stability, but it is sturdy enough to stand freely in the middle of your workshop for just about any operation except perhaps heavy hand-planing. With this, all but the most solid benches tend to slide around at least a little.

The legs shown here are made of doubled 2 × 4's, glued and nailed together. They're cheaper than 4 × 4's and not so prone to warping. Pairing long and short boards automatically forms the notches that support each outside corner of the top frame, saving you having to saw or chisel them out of solid lumber. The frame members are 2 × 4's also; however, the top is made of 2 × 6's laid next to each other, so their end grain patterns alternate up and down, as shown in the illustration. Nails are used to fasten all parts together. You may use screws if you wish, but they're more expensive. Carriage bolts may be used to fasten the completed top frame assembly and the bottom rails to the posts, which makes the workbench easy to disassemble. It is a good idea to install a replaceable bench top panel made of ¼-in.-thick plywood or Masonite over the 2 × 6's (just tack it in place with small paneling or finishing nails). Nail a piece of plywood across the bottom rails too, inside the legs, to make a shelf beneath the bench. This will add rigidity.

The length, width, and height of the bench shown are of dimensions most people will find comfortable. Naturally, you may alter them to suit yourself, but beware of making the bench any longer than it already is without adding extra bracing, or of extending the overhanging bench top more than 10 in. beyond the frame ends.

To construct the bench, cut and assemble the legs first, then cut the top frame and lower side rails. Assemble the top frame. Turn it upside down on the floor and attach the legs, then place the entire assembly right side up and attach the lower side rails. Cut out and fasten the 2 × 6's for the top next, and finally nail on the ¼-in. top panel and the lower shelf.

A Plywood Bench on Wheels

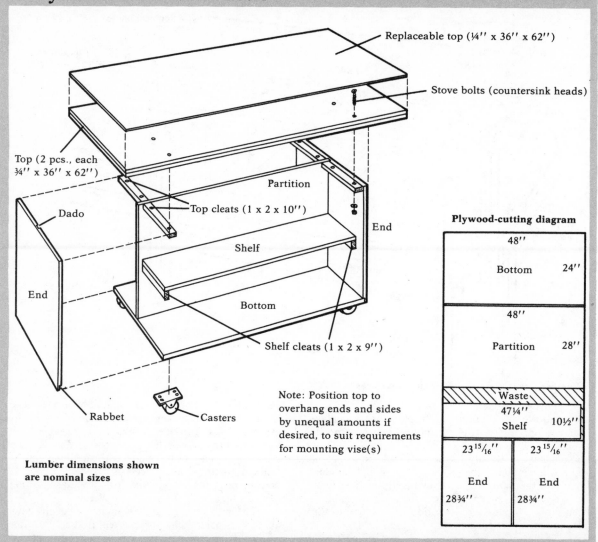

Replaceable top (¼'' x 36'' x 62'')

Stove bolts (countersink heads)

Top (2 pcs., each ¾'' x 36'' x 62'')

Dado

Partition

Top cleats (1 x 2 x 10'')

End

End

Shelf

Bottom

Shelf cleats (1 x 2 x 9'')

Rabbet

Casters

Note: Position top to overhang ends and sides by unequal amounts if desired, to suit requirements for mounting vise(s)

Lumber dimensions shown are nominal sizes

Plywood-cutting diagram

48''	
Bottom	24''

48''	
Partition	28''

Waste	
47¼'' Shelf	10½''

23¹⁵⁄₁₆''	23¹⁵⁄₁₆''
End 28¾''	End 28¾''

This workbench is more expensive to build than the one shown on p. 37, and it also requires the use of a power saw to cut out the major pieces and a router to rabbet and dado them for assembly. It's a very versatile bench, however, quite heavy and solid, yet with its casters (use at least one pair of the locking variety), readily movable as well. Additional shelves, and even swinging or sliding doors to enclose them, may be added. Notice that nonswiveling casters are used beneath the bench's vise end to provide stability when sawing or planing.

The entire bench base, including one shelf, can be cut from a single 4 × 8-ft. sheet of plywood. Use ¾-in.-thick A-C plywood. Remember to allow for the width (kerf) of the saw blade when cutting. The top is made of two ¾-in. thicknesses of plywood or particle board glued together, covered with a sheet of ¼-in.-thick plywood or Masonite tacked in place to provide a smooth, replaceable surface. Glue and nails are used to assemble the base; stove bolts, installed before tacking down the surface sheet, fasten the top in place, yet allow for removal if necessary.

A Sturdy Sawhorse

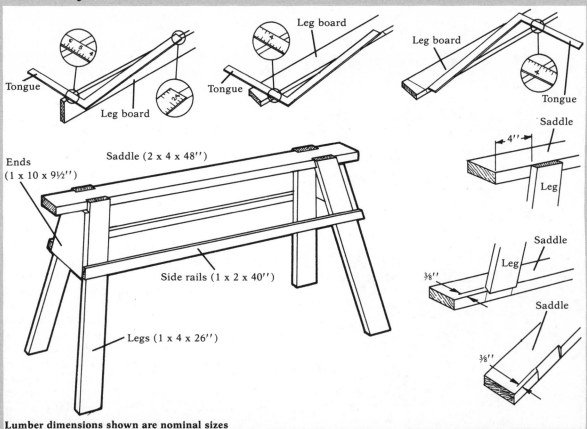

Tongue

Leg board

Leg board

Leg board

Leg board

Tongue

Tongue

Saddle

4''

Leg

Saddle

Leg

3/8''

Saddle

3/8''

Saddle (2 x 4 x 48'')

Ends
(1 x 10 x 9½'')

Side rails (1 x 2 x 40'')

Legs (1 x 4 x 26'')

Lumber dimensions shown are nominal sizes

Sawhorses are tricky to build because of their compound angles, but careful layout assures success. Use ordinary lumber. Assemble the pieces with nails and also glue if desired.

Begin by laying out the legs with a framing square. First, align the 5¼-in. mark on the square's tongue and the 24-in. mark on the blade along one edge of a board, as shown. Scribe along the tongue and across the end of the blade. Then lay the board flat, and align the square so the tongue's 4-in. mark contacts either end of one scribed line and the 24-in. mark on the blade touches the edge of the board on the same side. Scribe along the tongue only, then turn the square over, reverse it end for end, and realign it so the 4-in. mark on the tongue touches the end of the other scribed line, and on that same side the blade's 24-in. mark contacts the board's edge. (The blade should not lie on the line just scribed, but should be parallel to it and about ⅜ in. away.) Again scribe along the tongue. Continue the

lines around the other two surfaces if desired, and cut out the leg. Use it as a template to cut out the other three.

Now notch the saddle. Set it on edge and hold a leg against it, 4 in. from the end. Pivot the bottom of the leg away from the saddle's center until the tops of both pieces are flush. Scribe across the edge of the saddle on both sides of the leg. Repeat for all four legs. Next, lay the saddle face up, and scribe the depth of each notch, ⅜ in. from each edge. Then hold each leg in place above its notch lines and trace the shape of its base onto the saddle to mark the offset of the notch sides (these are not square with the saddle's edges). Saw along the lines on the edge and top of the saddle—cutting only into the saddle's top face—then chisel out the waste. Nail the legs in place with 8d common nails. Make the end braces from scraps of plywood or 1 × 10 lumber, and the side rails from 1 × 2 stock. Nail each in place.

Modular Boxes

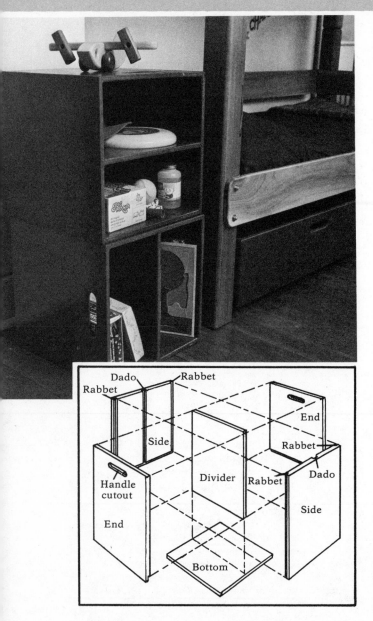

Dado · Rabbet · Rabbet · Side · Handle cutout · End · End · Rabbet · Divider · Rabbet · Dado · Side · Bottom

Routers
Clamps and clamping

These modular boxes are an excellent project for beginning woodworkers. Easy to build and inexpensive, these boxes are sturdy, attractive, and versatile enough to be used in any number of ways: for storage, shelving, even for seating or as supports for coffee tables. The construction processes involved provide an early and solid foothold on techniques which apply widely throughout the craft of woodworking. The dimensions of the boxes shown here are large enough to accommodate record albums; three complete boxes of this size can be cut from a single 4 × 8-foot sheet of plywood.

Plan before you build. Read all of the text carefully beforehand so that you understand the steps. If you decide to cut several pieces from a single plywood sheet, measure and draw *all* of the cutting lines first, before you saw. Remember to allow for the width of the saw blade when laying down the cutting lines, otherwise you may find the pieces turning out maddeningly short — by exactly the width of your saw blade! Labeling each piece as it is cut is also a good idea, since the pieces are hard to distinguish from one another, especially if many are being cut at once.

Any kind of saw — handsaw or power saw — may be used to cut out the box pieces. A table saw is probably the easiest to set up, as well as the most accurate, but a hand-powered cross-cut or portable electric circular saw generally is more available to beginning woodworkers and is actually easier to use when cutting up large sheets. The advantage is that you can more easily move the saw along the plywood than the other way around. To cut straight and square with a hand-held saw, simply clamp a straightedged 2 × 4 or something similar along the line you wish to cut. Lay the guide board against the inside of the line so that the saw cuts only on the waste side, and arrange the clamps so they do not obstruct the path of the saw.

Unless you do have a table saw, however, a router is nearly indispensable for this project, especially since plywood—which is tough to cut and hard on the honed edges of hand tools—is the material involved. A router is a high-speed, portable power tool, designed to remove or shape wood at a very fast rate, and it makes short, simple work of cutting precise grooves and notches into wood that would take even a skilled craftsman many hours with chisel and mallet. The use of a router is discussed in this section. Always remember to unplug the tool whenever you are changing or adjusting the bits, and make test cuts on scrap wood before you actually use the router on a project piece.

A final woodworker's trick to bear in mind when building this project, or any other that requires gluing, is to test the fit of the pieces by first assembling the project without glue. Any problems that arise at this stage are always more easy to remedy now than after the pieces are glued together. Only after all the pieces have been made to fit dry should you reassemble the project using glue. Apply whatever clamps you plan to use during the dry test as well. Clamping is often tedious, and the practice gained by trying the setup first will be a great help.

What you will need

1 sheet plywood, ½'' × 4' × 8' A-C
3d finishing nails
white or yellow glue
wood putty
interior high-gloss latex enamel
crosscut saw (or electric substitute)
keyhole or saber saw
router
drill and ½-in.-dia. spade bit
hand and measuring tools

Before you begin

To cut three boxes from a single 4 × 8-ft. sheet of plywood, first cut one 14-in.-wide strip lengthwise from the sheet, as indicated in the cutting diagram below. Cut the strip into six squares, each measuring 14 × 14 in. Label each square *side*. Then cut two more lengthwise strips, each 13½ in. wide. Cut one of these strips again at 14-in. intervals, and label these six pieces *end*. Cut the remaining strip at 13½-in. intervals. Label three of the 13½ × 13½-in. pieces *bottom* and the remaining three, *divider*. Discard the waste wood.

Cutting diagram for 4 × 8-ft. sheet of plywood

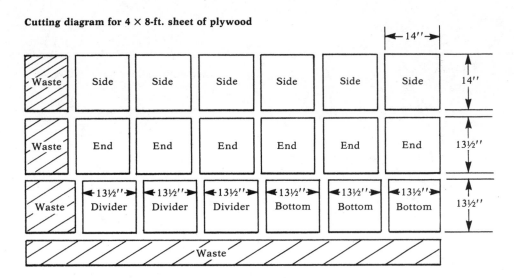

Routers

A router will greatly expand the range of wood-working tasks you can do. With a router, you can cut decorative edge moldings and make grooves, notches, dovetails, and even complex mortise-and-tenon joints. You can also trim thin wood panels and plastic laminates and cut the recessed openings necessary for door locks and hinges.

A single-horsepower router is a good size for a home shop. Models that have pistol-grip handles with a built-in on/off switch are best, since these allow you to start and stop the motor without taking your hands off the tool. To prepare a router for use, merely insert and tighten a cutter bit in the chuck, then raise or lower the baseplate to obtain the desired depth of cut.

Operating a router is simply a matter of turning it on and guiding it through the work, but there are some things of which you must be aware. One is the tendency of the router to twist whenever the motor speed increases, especially at starting. This is due to the extremely high speed at which the router operates, a speed which produces very smooth cuts but which also allows mistakes to happen fast. To counteract this gyroscopic motion, always have the router firmly braced with the bit away from the wood when starting, and always use some sort of fixed guide or fence to keep the tool in position when in use. Another thing to be aware of is the direction in which the router must be fed into the work. This must always be the *same direction* as the movement of the cutter bit's leading edge. Since the bit—when viewed from the top—revolves in a clockwise direction on most routers, this means feeding the router into the wood from left to right when routing along edges and moving in a counterclockwise direction when rounding corners. (To cope with splintering when shaping square corners, rout the end-grain portions of the wood first; any splinters will be removed when you then rout the long grain.) When making grooves—with wood on both sides of the cut—the direction of feed doesn't matter. If you mount the router upside-down beneath a router table such as the one shown in these pages, reverse the procedures; feed the *wood into the router*, moving from right to left.

Also important is the speed at which the cutter moves through the wood. You must vary this according to the density of wood you are routing, the depth of the cut, and the shape of the bit. Only practice will guide you. The motor should never labor; this indicates too high a rate of feed and will likely result in gouged or splintered work and perhaps an overheated—possibly ruined—motor. Neither should you feed too slowly; this will cause the cutter to enlarge or ripple the sides of the cut and may also overheat the cutter to the extent that it loses its hardness and is ruined. To avoid these problems, take shallow cuts—no more

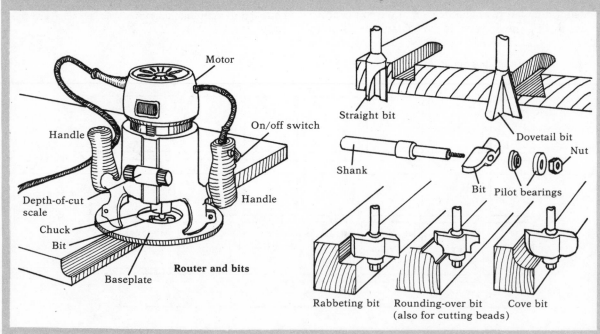

Motor
On/off switch
Handle
Handle
Depth-of-cut scale
Chuck
Bit
Baseplate
Router and bits

Straight bit
Dovetail bit
Nut
Shank
Bit
Pilot bearings

Rabbeting bit
Rounding-over bit (also for cutting beads)
Cove bit

than ½ in. deep at each pass—listen closely to the sound of the motor, and be aware of how the router behaves as it moves through the wood. The noise level should be consistent, and the router should cut smoothly with little pressure.

Besides the careful operation of the tool itself, the key to successful routing is taking time before each cut to set up a proper guide or fence to keep the router on course. And always make practice cuts in scrap wood before routing the actual workpiece. Even professional cabinetmakers do this. Most routers are furnished with edge guides, suitable for routing parallel to the edges of a workpiece, and this will suffice in place of a more elaborate setup in most cases. Of course, the edge of the piece against which the guide bears must be square and true. A simple, homemade guide for routing across the width of a board, or on any piece which is either not square or unsuited to the mounting of an edge guide, is merely a straightedged piece of wood clamped parallel to the cut to be made. Locate such a guide to one side of the cut line by measuring the distance between the outermost edge of the cutter bit and the outside edge of the router's baseplate on the same side. Guides and fences can be devised for virtually any type of cut. They are especially useful when a number of cuts requiring identical setups must be produced.

MAKING A ROUTER TABLE

To make a versatile router table for edging or cutting long grooves, construct a three-sided box as shown below that you can clamp or bolt to your workbench. For the top, begin with a piece of ¾-in.-thick plywood about 20 in. square. Remove the router's baseplate to use as a guide, center the plate near one edge of the plywood, and trace around it, then use a keyhole or saber saw to cut a circular hole into which the router will fit. Glue the plywood to the rough side of a 20-in.-square piece of ¼-in.-thick tempered Masonite. Now place the baseplate in the hole so it seats against the underside of the Masonite, and mark the locations of the baseplate mounting screws and center hole. Remove the baseplate, choose a drill bit the same diameter as the mounting screws which you removed in order to detach the baseplate from the router, then drill holes through the Masonite so you can attach the router underneath. Also drill out the area in the center for the router bit to protrude. Countersink the mounting-screw holes where they emerge through the top. Attach the router beneath the Masonite, without using the baseplate, by inserting the mounting screws through the Masonite and fastening them directly into the router. By having the tabletop overlap the sides by 2 in. or so, you can clamp a homemade fence to the top for use when making dadoes or tapered cuts.

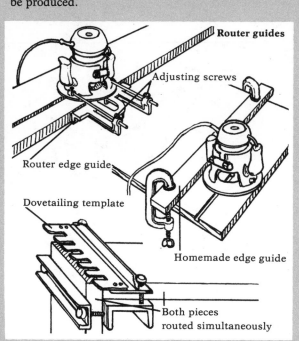

Router guides

Adjusting screws

Router edge guide

Dovetailing template

Homemade edge guide

Both pieces routed simultaneously

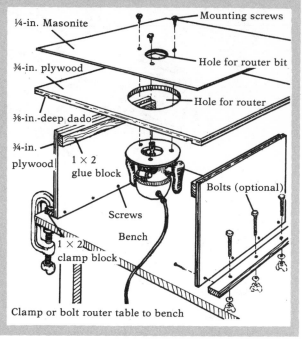

¼-in. Masonite

Mounting screws

¾-in. plywood

Hole for router bit

Hole for router

⅜-in.-deep dado

¾-in. plywood

1 × 2 glue block

Bolts (optional)

Screws

Bench

1 × 2 clamp block

Clamp or bolt router table to bench

Clamps and Clamping

Nearly every woodworking project requires clamps. They are versatile tools, capable of performing a wide variety of functions, and learning to use them skillfully will greatly enhance your own abilities as a woodcrafts-person. Aside from their most obvious use—holding glued parts together while they dry—clamps are also valuable for gripping work to the bench while sawing, routing, drilling, or chiseling and for holding pieces securely while measuring and marking out.

As versatile as they are, however, it is difficult to get along with only one or two. You should acquire as many as you can. The most frequently used varieties are C-clamps, bar (or pipe) clamps, and wooden-jawed cabinetmaker's screw clamps. Other types include spring clamps, miter clamps, and web clamps.

C-clamps are the least expensive and come in sizes with openings ranging up to 12 in. or so. Most useful are those with 6- to 8-in. capacities. Buy them in pairs. Since the depth of most C-clamps is relatively small, they are best suited for clamping narrow pieces of stock together and for clamping work near the edge of the bench. As with all metal-jawed clamps, thin pieces of scrap wood—or rubber clamp pads made expressly for the purpose—should be placed between the work and the jaws to avoid marring the wood when clamping up.

Bar clamps are used for clamping over very wide or long distances, such as when edge-gluing stock to make wide boards and especially when gluing-up furniture. They are invaluable. You should have at least two pairs that open to a minimum of 18 in. and additional pairs with capacities of 3 ft. or more. Several of the projects in this book require bar clamps that open at least 6 ft. Pipe clamps are substantially less expensive substitutes for bar clamps. You buy the fixtures and supply your own ¾-in.-dia. threaded pipe (available in scrap or from a plumbing supply house) in any lengths you prefer. Pipe clamps have a tendency to bow in very long lengths, but that is their only drawback.

Cabinetmakers' screw clamps are regarded by many professionals as the real workhorses of the craft. Their wooden jaws—with more depth than C-clamps—do not mar the work; their double-spindle adjustment allows them to grip nonparallel surfaces securely; and their shape permits them to be used in combination with other clamps as improvised bench vises or as integral parts of more elaborate homemade clamping setups. More than this, screw clamps can be made to direct a great deal of pressure over either a wide or a narrow area, depending upon how they are tightened. A pair whose jaws open to 6 in. is a good first purchase.

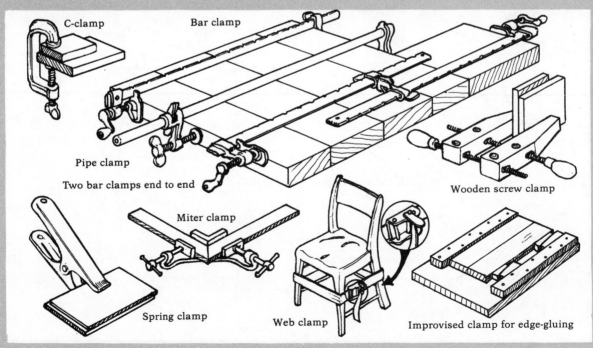

C-clamp   Bar clamp

Pipe clamp

Two bar clamps end to end

Wooden screw clamp

Miter clamp

Spring clamp   Web clamp   Improvised clamp for edge-gluing

SCREW CLAMPS

Cabinetmakers' screw clamps can be tricky to operate at first. To adjust them properly, hold them so your right hand grasps the rearmost handle, the one farthest from the jaws. Grip the inner handle with your left hand. Hold screw clamps this way whether you are right- or left-handed; it's easier in the long run. Now, to open the clamps, hold your left hand stationary and swing your right hand counterclockwise. The jaws should move toward your face, then down and away. To close the clamps, keep your left hand stationary and swing your right hand clockwise. When clamping a piece of work, adjust the jaws so they are parallel and spaced as nearly correct as possible, then slide them into place. Tighten the inner spindle first—it shouldn't require much turning—then give the outer spindle a strong twist.

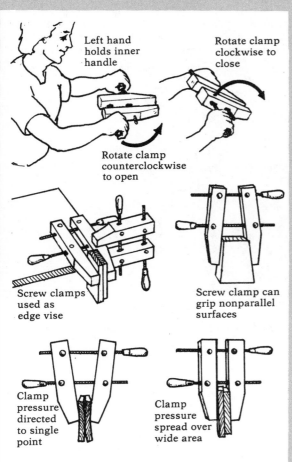

Left hand holds inner handle

Rotate clamp clockwise to close

Rotate clamp counterclockwise to open

Screw clamps used as edge vise

Screw clamp can grip nonparallel surfaces

Clamp pressure directed to single point

Clamp pressure spread over wide area

EDGE-GLUING

Edge-gluing is necessary to make wide boards. It is not difficult, but it does require care, planning, and an adequate supply of clamps, First, square the faces and edges of all the pieces to be joined. Next, arrange the boards side by side in the order you wish to glue them. Usually, it's best to alternate boards so they lie heartside-up/heartside-down next to each other to reduce total warpage. Number the boards when they are in position, then true the edges of each with a hand plane on a shooting board (see p. 32). To achieve invisible seams, plane one board with its numbered face up on the shooting board, and plane its mate with the numbered face down. Plane each edge slightly concave along its length; clamping mating boards tight will then place extra pressure on the ends. To glue up (after a trial dry run), spread white or yellow glue thinly and evenly along each edge, and place the boards side by side on sawhorses covered with wax paper to prevent sticking. Begin clamping at the center, and alternate clamps over and under the boards out to the ends. Hammer the boards flush with a mallet and scrap block before fully tightening the clamps. Add C-clamps at the ends if necessary, with wax paper between the clamps and the boards. Don't overtighten the clamps; stop when you see even beads of squeezed-out glue along each seam. When dry, replane.

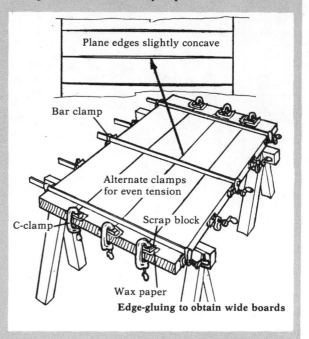

Plane edges slightly concave

Bar clamp

Alternate clamps for even tension

C-clamp

Scrap block

Wax paper

Edge-gluing to obtain wide boards

Step-by-step instructions

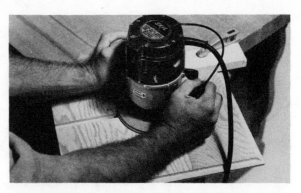

1. Begin by cutting out all the box pieces you will need. Cut each piece to size out of ½-in.-thick plywood according to the diagram on p. 41. Label each piece as it is cut. A table saw is accurate, but a hand-held electric circular saw is often easier to use, especially when cutting large sheets of material. Instructions for cutting plywood are given on p. 40.

3. Cut grooves (dadoes) down the centerlines of the two sidepieces to act as slots for the divider panel, which will be installed later. Use a router with a fence as in step 2, and make sure to press the router firmly against the fence as you cut. For a foolproof setup, clamp two fences parallel to each other (and to the centerline), one on either side of the router. Both the width and the depth of the dadoes should be ½ in.

2. Cut notches (rabbets) along three edges of each sidepiece and along one edge only of each end, using a router (see p. 42). Clamp (p. 44) a straightedged board across each piece to act as a fence. The width of the rabbets should be ½ in.; the depth should be ¼ in. Unless your router is a heavy-duty model equipped with a carbide-tipped bit, make each rabbet in two passes, cutting to a depth of ⅛ in. on each pass.

4. Drill starter holes for the handle cutouts in the pair of endpieces, using a ½-in.-dia. spade bit. Drill two holes in each piece, on centers located about 3 in. apart. Locate the holes 2 in. down from the top of each piece and about 5 in. from the sides. To prevent splintering, clamp a piece of scrap wood beneath the area you are drilling. Use a thick piece to avoid drilling through the scrap and into the bench top as well!

5. To complete the handle cutouts, use a ruler and pencil to square lines across the tops and bottoms of each pair of holes, then saw out the waste wood in between. Use a keyhole saw or hand-held electric saber saw. Round-over the edges of the cutouts, using a router fitted with a ⅛-in. rounding-over bit, or simply radius the edges by hand, using a wood rasp, file, or sandpaper.

7. Remove clamps when box is dry. Chip off excess glue with a chisel, fill gaps and nail holes with wood putty, then sand smooth. Finish with two coats of high-gloss latex enamel. See Wood Finishing, p. 162, for complete finishing instructions. Finish divider panel separately. Slide it into grooves in box when dry.

6. Assemble and clamp the sidepieces, endpieces, and bottom pieces together without glue to check the fit of each piece and to practice the clamping-up procedure. Then disassemble the box, and apply white or yellow glue in a thin layer to each piece being glued. Clamp the assembly back together, checking that all corners form precise 90° angles. Also measure between pairs of diagonal corners; each distance should be the same. Finishing nails can be used instead of clamps or to supplement an improvised setup.

Bunk Beds

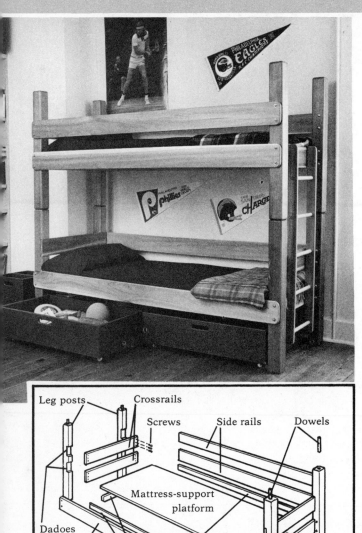

Leg posts
Crossrails
Screws
Side rails
Dowels
Mattress-support platform
Dadoes
Side rail
Mattress-support rails
Acorn nuts
Bolts
Leg posts

Circular-saw joinery
Bolts and other threaded fasteners

These childs' bunk beds are an uncomplicated project that a beginner can build in a relatively short time, say a weekend or two. No fancy joinery is required—parts simply bolt together—and all the materials can be easily obtained at ordinary lumberyards and hardware stores. The mattresses are standard bunk bed size: 30 × 75 inches.

The beds shown on these pages are made of cedar, a commonly available construction timber, chosen primarily for its attractiveness when treated with a clear finish. Pine would be as good a choice, as would any variety of lumber commonly used in building construction. Cedar's only drawbacks are its extra expense—it usually costs more than other types of construction stock—and its tendency to split when worked. If you choose to use cedar, be careful especially when drilling bolt holes; always use a scrap block to back up the wood through which you are drilling, or else drill partway through the workpiece from one side (until the bit just begins to emerge) and then complete the hole by drilling through from the other side. Likewise, go gently if you find you must use a hammer to install the bolts in their holes; if they emerge off-center they are likely to chip the surrounding surface wood.

The ladder has been designed to mount securely at either the sides or the ends of the beds. The storage drawers are optional—they make use of plywood left over after making the platforms which support each mattress—and are mounted on casters. The drawers roll in and out on the floor rather than slide from bed-mounted fixtures.

Care has been taken with this project to round-over all corners and projections that might cause injury. Though the instructions call for a router to accomplish this, you can achieve adequate results with a wood rasp and a file.

What you will need

handsaw, circular saw, or table saw
router
drill
white or yellow glue
brush-on lacquer
hand and measuring tools

To make the beds:
8 pcs. clear cedar, 3½'' × 3½'' × 3'
7 pcs. clear cedar, ¾'' × 5½'' × 31''
7 pcs. clear cedar, ¾'' × 5½'' × 82½''
4 pcs. #2 pine, ¾'' × 1½'' × 31''
4 pcs. #2 pine, ¾'' × 1½'' × 74½''
2 sheets plywood, ¾'' × 4' × 8' A-C
1 pc. hardwood dowel, 1'' × 2' (see step 24)
1 pc. hardwood dowel, ⅜'' × 3' (see step 17)
8 #10 flathead wood screws, 2½''
34 #10 flathead wood screws, 1½''
28 #10 flathead wood screws, 1''
28 carriage bolts with brass washers and acorn
    nuts, ⁵⁄₁₆'' × 4½''

To make the ladder:
2 pcs. clear cedar, ¾'' × 2½'' × 49''
1 pc. hardwood dowel, 1'' × 6' (see step 5)
1 pc. hardwood dowel, ³⁄₁₆'' × 2' (see step 6)
6 #6 flathead wood screws, 1¼''
2 #6 flathead wood screws, ¾''
4 steel corner brackets, ⅛'' × ¾'' × 3½'' × 3½''
self-adhesive felt

Ladder and drawers

The ladder designed for use with this bunk bed is strong yet light in weight. It is made of 1-in.-dia. hardwood dowels glued and pinned into side rails of cedar which match the rest of the beds. The ladder is hung by means of four ordinary metal corner brackets (angle irons) which are bent to hook over the bed rails. Self-adhesive felt covers the metal to protect the cedar bed rails. Because the ladder hangs securely on the brackets, it does not take up floor space, nor will it slide or fall down.

The two storage drawers which have been designed to fit between the leg posts beneath the lower bunk can be made from excess plywood remaining after you make the mattress-support platforms. The drawer components are rabbeted together and attached with glue and 4d finishing nails in exactly the same way as the modular boxes are constructed (see p. 40). No step-by-step instruction for the drawers is given. The drawers will probably look best painted. Mount them on 1¼-in.-dia. ball bearing casters for easy rolling.

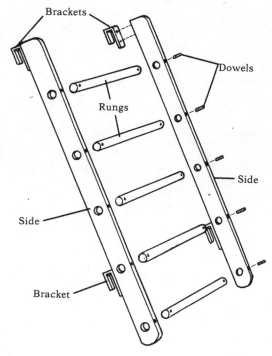

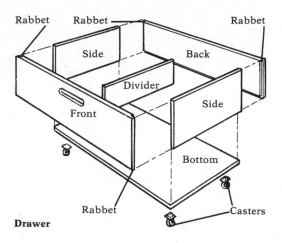

Drawer

Ladder

Circular-Saw Joinery

The circular saw can be an effective tool for cutting simple wood joints. In addition to basic square cuts, miters, and beveled cuts, the circular saw can also be used to cut rabbet joints, dadoes, and half-lap joints. The accuracy of the cuts depends upon the condition of the saw and the care with which you work. If your saw is old and the blade-height adjustment is unreliable, the joints may not fit well. For clean cuts, it's best to use a new or sharpened blade. Leave a small amount of waste wood, then trim by hand.

MAKING A RABBET CUT

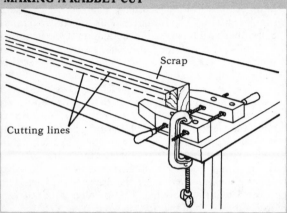

1. To lay out a rabbet cut, first determine the depth of both cuts. Next, mark the lines along the edge, face, and ends of the board. Then, turn the marked edge up. Clamp a scrap board adjacent to it at the same height to provide an even bearing surface along which the saw may slide smoothly.

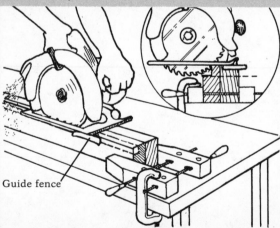

2. Adjust the height of the saw blade so that it corresponds with the depth of the rabbet. Set the blade and test it against the end; only the lowest tooth should touch the line. Position the guide fence to the desired width, so that the kerf runs just inside the rabbet's cut line. Now start the saw and make the first cut.

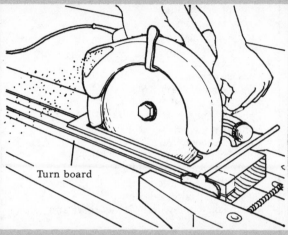

3. To make the second cut, remove the scrap board, and turn the wood so the marked line is up. Reset the blade height; the lowest tooth should not protrude below the kerf made in step 2. Also align the guide fence so the blade cuts just inside the line along which it will travel. Restart the saw and make the cut.

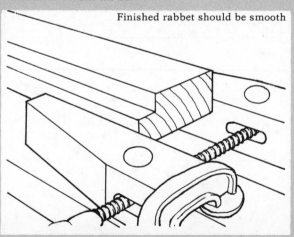

4. The waste wood should fall off easily to reveal a smooth rabbet cut. If the waste piece fails to drop out, you may have to lower the blade and carefully recut either or both lines until the rabbet is the desired size. Be careful not to overadjust the blade height. Clean up the edges with a sharp chisel or plane.

MAKING A DADO CUT

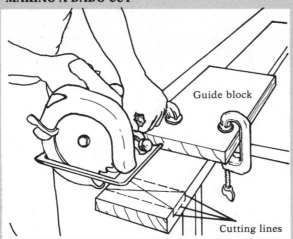

Guide block

Cutting lines

1. To make a dado cut on the face of a board, first mark out both lines across the face. Make sure the lines are parallel to each other and at right angles to the edge of the board. Measure and mark the depth of the joint on the board end. Set the saw's blade height to this depth, then, using a guide block, make a cut along the inside of one of the lines.

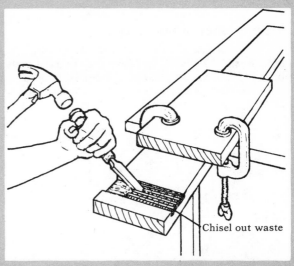

Chisel out waste

3. Make as many cuts as possible across the face of the board between the two outside lines to remove the maximum amount of wood with the saw blade. Clean out the remaining wood with a chisel, being careful not to gouge the wood. Keep the chisel flat and pare an even depth across the whole width of the joint.

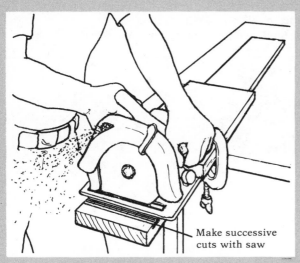

Make successive cuts with saw

2. Adjust the guide block, then make another cut along the inside of the second line. These two cuts mark the outside dimensions of the dado. To remove the waste wood from between these cuts, reposition the guide block out of the way if necessary, then make several successive passes between the lines with the saw, close together. The cuts need not be parallel.

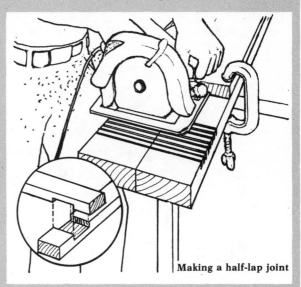

Making a half-lap joint

4. The finished dado should be square and clean. With this technique you can make dadoes as wide and as deep as you wish. To make a half-lap joint (see p. 71), follow the same procedure as for a dado, but to make sure the pieces will exactly match, clamp both pieces together edge to edge and cut both dadoes simultaneously.

Step-by-step instructions

1. Use a handsaw or a power saw to cut eight pieces, each 3½ in. × 3½ in. × 3 ft., for the leg posts of both beds. With a power saw, you will probably need to make at least two cuts to get through each piece. Label four posts *upper*, and four, *lower*.

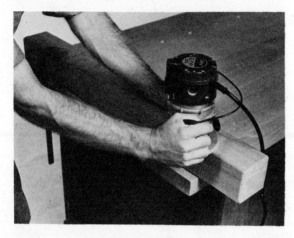

2. Radius (round-over) all edges and ends of the leg posts. Use a router (see p. 42) with a ½-in. rounding-over bit, or a rasp.

3. Lay out and cut two dadoes, each 5½ in. wide and ¾ in. deep, on the inside face of all lower leg posts and two of the upper leg posts. Begin the lower dadoes 12 in. up from the bottom of each post. Finish the upper dadoes 9 in. from the top. Cut lower dadoes only on the remaining two posts.

4. Drill a 1-in.-dia. × 2-in. hole in the center of the tops of the four lower leg posts and in the center of the bottoms of the upper four. Holes must be perfectly vertical.

5. Cut seven pieces of cedar, each ¾ × 5½ × 31 in., for the crossrails.

6. File or machine a ¼-in. radius on the edges of each crossrail. Stop 3½ in. in from each end.

7. Cut four pieces of #2 pine, each ¾ × 1½ × 31 in., for the mattress-support rails.

8. Glue and clamp (p. 44) the mattress-support rails flush against the bottom inside edges of four of the lower crossrails.

9. Drill two pilot holes (p. 73) in each rail assembly, 10 in. in from the ends. Counterbore ⅜-in.-dia. holes for plugs (see step 17). Install a 1-in. #10 screw in each hole.

10. Glue the crossrails into the dado cuts of the leg posts. Drill and counterbore three pilot holes in both ends of each rail. Install 2½-in. #10 screws into posts through support rail and crossrail. Install 1½-in. #10 screws where there is a crossrail only.
11. Work a ½-in. radius on the ends of each crossrail to match the radiused leg posts.
12. Cut seven pieces of cedar, each ¾ × 5½ × 82½ in., for the side rails.
13. Cut four pieces of #2 pine, each ¾ × 1½ × 74½ in., for the side mattress-support rails.
14. Position these support rails flush along the inside bottom edge of each of the four lower side rails. The rails should be 4 in. in from either end.

15. Glue and clamp the side mattress-support rails to the side rails, as in step 8. Drill and counterbore, then install five equally spaced 1-in. #10 screws.

16. With a router equipped with a ¼-in. rounding-over bit, or with a wood rasp and a file, work a ¼-in. radius on all edges of each side rail.

17. To fill all the screw holes, cut 70 plugs, each ¼ in. long, from ⅜-in.-dia. dowel. Glue plugs into place, then use a backsaw to cut off the excess wood. Protect the surface of the posts with a piece of thin scrap.

18. Drill ⁵⁄₁₆-in.-dia. holes into each leg post according to the diagram on p. 48. Locate the holes adjacent to each crossrail against which a side rail will be attached. To avoid making a mistake, dry-fit the side rails and note their position before drilling.

(Continued on page 56)

Bolts and Other Threaded Fasteners

Bolts

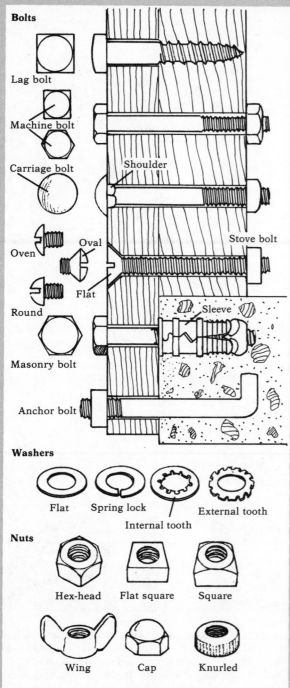

Lag bolt

Machine bolt

Carriage bolt

Shoulder

Oval

Oven

Flat

Round

Stove bolt

Sleeve

Masonry bolt

Anchor bolt

Washers

Flat   Spring lock

Internal tooth

External tooth

Nuts

Hex-head   Flat square   Square

Wing   Cap   Knurled

Bolts—except lag bolts (see illustration)—are threaded fasteners with flat ends. This distinguishes them from screws (see p. 73). Most bolts are designed for use with washers and nuts and are meant to be removable, again unlike screws, which are meant in most cases to be permanent fasteners. Bolts are sized by their diameter in inches, followed by their length, and sometimes by their number of threads per in. For example, a ½″ × 4½″ × 16 bolt would be ½ in. in diameter, 4½ in. long, and have 16 threads per in.

BOLTS

Lag bolts—actually large screws. They have square heads and pointed ends. They are used where extra strength is needed in a screwed joint, such as when fastening shelves to wall studs.

Machine bolts—used to secure a joint that is subject to frequent unbolting. They may have either square or hexagonal heads.

Carriage bolts—round-headed bolts with no slots. They have a square or hexagonal shoulder just under the head that bites into the wood as the nut is tightened and keeps the bolt from turning. Because the head is rounded, they are more attractive than stove or machine bolts.

Stove bolts—bolts with slotted heads which are flat, oval, round, or oven style. They are tightened with a screwdriver and a wrench.

Masonry bolts—special bolts used to fasten wood to concrete. They have a hexagonal head and a sleeve around the body of the bolt. As the bolt is tightened, the sleeve expands to grip the sides of the masonry.

Anchor bolts—used primarily to attach wooden house sills to concrete foundations. One end is threaded and the other is bent at an angle.

Washers—designed to distribute the force of a tightened nut over a greater surface area and to protect wood from being gouged by the nut. Washers may be used on either or both ends of a bolt. They can also act as spacers. Flat washers are simple disks of metal that distribute pressure and protect the surface. Lock washers, which come in various designs, force tension back against the nut to keep it from loosening.

Nuts—used to secure bolts by being tightened against the back of the joint. They come in various shapes for different purposes, but their thread sizes must match the bolts to which they are attached. Wing nuts and knurled nuts require no wrenches and can be tightened by hand. Cap, or acorn, nuts cover the end of a bolt, making it less jagged and more attractive.

OTHER THREADED FASTENERS

There is a variety of threaded fasteners that are

valuable in special situations and that can be used in some of the projects in this book.

Hanger bolts—headless screws and bolts, with threads for wood on one end and machine threads on the other. Use them in hard-to-reach spots where you need a tight joint. A hanger bolt and wood block, for instance, can replace a complicated corner brace in a table. Drive the wood-threaded end through the brace and into the corner post, then attach a square nut or wing nut to the protruding machine-threaded end and tighten the nut to draw the corner together.

Tee nuts—flanged metal washers with machine-threaded holes in their centers. To install a tee nut, countersink it on the exposed side of a joint, and cover it with a plug. Insert a bolt from the other side. As you tighten it, the tee nut, unable to rotate because of the flanges, will provide a stable anchor.

Wood inserts—similar to tee nuts in principle, but designed to be used in joints which are frequently dismantled. Install the insert by screwing it into a predrilled hole; the outside of the insert is threaded like a wood screw. A bolt can then be installed, the machine threads of which match those on the inside of the insert.

Toggle bolts—designed for installation in stud-framed hollow walls. The spring-loaded wings pass through a hole predrilled in the wallboard and then release, pressing against the back of the wallboard to hold the screw in place. To install a toggle bolt, first put the bolt through the object to be attached, then screw on the wings and insert the whole assembly in the wall. Tighten the bolt with a screwdriver until resistance is felt. Caution: The wings fall off if you withdraw the bolt!

Molly bolts—sophisticated versions of toggle bolts. Clips that bend permanently into place as the bolt is tightened hold the fastener in place. To install a molly bolt, first predrill a hole, then install the bolt and clip assembly. Set the clips by tightening the bolt until resistance is felt. Now remove the bolt, pass it through the object to be fastened to the wall, then reinsert the bolt into the clip fixture and tighten firmly.

Turnbuckles—used to draw a joint tight across a span. Often they are used in bed and chair repairs, where they remain out of sight. Half the sleeve has right-hand threads; the other half has left-hand threads. Tightening the sleeve draws the two screw eyes together.

Bed fasteners—used for attaching the side rails to the headboards and footboards of virtually any bed. They greatly simplify assembly and make dismantling easy also. They must be mounted firmly.

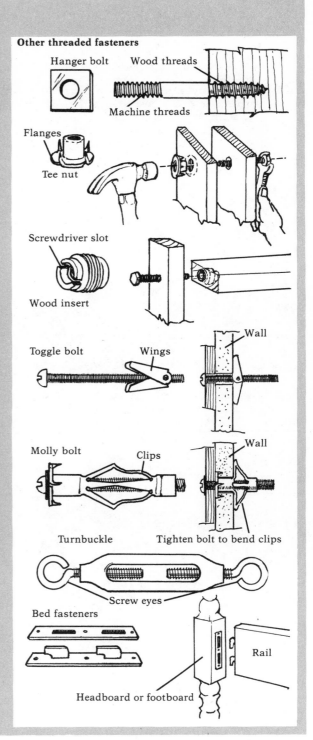

Other threaded fasteners

Hanger bolt   Wood threads

Machine threads

Flanges

Tee nut

Screwdriver slot

Wood insert

Toggle bolt   Wings   Wall

Molly bolt   Clips   Wall

Turnbuckle   Tighten bolt to bend clips

Screw eyes

Bed fasteners

Rail

Headboard or footboard

19. Drill 5/16-in.-dia. holes in the side rails according to the diagram on p. 48, aligning them with the holes drilled in the leg posts.

20. Make the two mattress-support platforms by cutting two pieces of 3/4-in. plywood, each 31 × 76 in. You will need a separate 4 × 8-ft. sheet for each.

21. Sand all of the components of each bed until they are smooth, then finish each piece, using two coats of brush-on lacquer. See Wood Finishing, p. 162, for complete finishing instructions.

22. Fasten the rails to the posts with 5/16 × 4 1/2-in. carriage bolts, brass washers, and acorn nuts. Insert the bolts from the inside of the leg posts.

23. Position one mattress-support platform on the support rails of each bed. It is not necessary to attach the plywood to the rails with fasteners.

24. To mount one bed on top of the other, begin by cutting four pieces of 1-in.-dia. dowel, each 4 in. in length. Chamfer (bevel) both ends of each piece for easy installation.

25. Insert one dowel into each of the four holes on the tops of the leg posts of what is to be the lower bunk. Gluing the dowels is unnecessary.

26. With help from an assistant, lift the upper bunk above the lower one, and carefully set it down so the dowels enter the holes in the bottoms of the leg posts.

Making the ladder

1. Cut two pieces of cedar, each 3/4 × 2 1/2 × 49 in., to make the sides of the ladder.

2. Use either a saber saw or a chisel, rasp, and file to form a 1-in. radius on the bottom ends (both sides) and top ends (outside only) of each side. Refer to the diagram on p. 49.

3. Drill five 1-in.-dia. holes through each side. Center the first hole 2 3/4 in. from the bottom end (both corners radiused); each successive hole is 9 1/2 in. higher.

4. Use a router or a rasp and file to form a ¼-in. radius on all edges of the ladder sides except where the brackets will be mounted.

5. For the ladder rungs, cut five pieces of 1-in.-dia. dowel, each 14 in. long. Glue them in place between the ladder sides, flush with the outside edges.

6. Drill ³⁄₁₆-in.-dia. × 2-in. holes through the sides and into each rung. Cut ten ³⁄₁₆-in.-dia. × 2-in. dowels, apply glue, then drive them into place.

7. Bend four ⅛ × ¾ × 3½ × 3½-in. steel corner brackets into U-shaped hangers over a scrap piece of ¾-in.-thick plywood. Hammer the metal to shape in gradual stages, holding one end firmly against the scrap block.

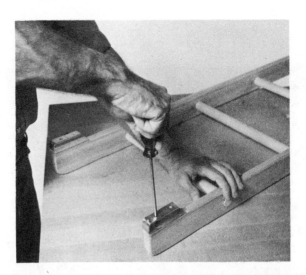

8. Drill ¼-in.-dia. holes through each bracket where necessary to accommodate the screwdriver and screws, then mount the brackets with #6 screws. Use the shorter screws in the upper holes of the lower brackets, even with the second rung from the bottom.

9. Cover the brackets with self-adhesive felt to protect the bed rails from scratches.

Laminated Hat Rack

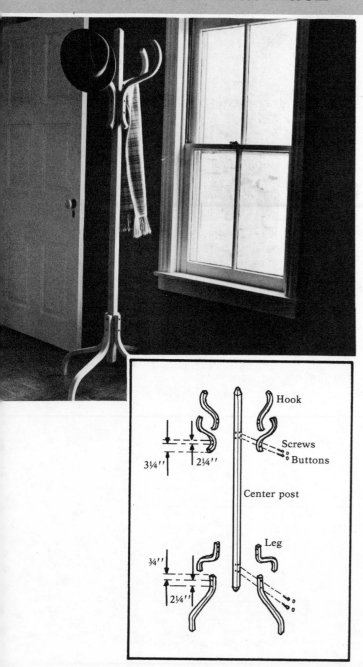

Laminating and bending wood
Glues and adhesives

This graceful hat rack will add a touch of elegance to your home. It is remarkably easy to build, and inexpensive as well. The one shown on these pages is made of clear pine, but nearly any blemish-free wood works just as well. You might even experiment with two different varieties—a dark wood such as mahogany, walnut, or cherry and a light wood such as pine, birch, or oak—and alternate the veneer strips that go together to make the hooks and legs to achieve a pleasing pattern of contrasts. Even the central post is made up of two pieces; you might wish to glue together one light-colored piece and one dark.

The lamination techniques this project demonstrates are not as difficult as they may appear. The wood for the bent pieces is cut very thin—each strip is only $\frac{1}{16}$ inch thick—and the pieces bend quite easily when moistened by the glue/water mixture that is used. It is important, though, that you select only absolutely clear stock for bending; even the slightest knot is liable to cause a strip to break instead.

When gluing, lay the strips—say, the amount you will use for one leg—flat on a table covered with freezer or wax paper. Thoroughly spread a thin film of glue mixed with lukewarm water (about 1 ounce glue to 1 teaspoon water) over the face-up surfaces of all the strips. Then combine the strips into pairs—matching glued face to glued face—and lay these pairs down flat again. Again spread glue on the face-up surface of each glued-together pair of strips, then combine the pairs into groups of four strips each. Continue this way until you have glued together the entire bundle. Remember to leave two outside faces free of glue; these will form the outer surfaces of the finished lamination. When the bundle of strips is glued up, place it between the plywood molds and clamp them tightly.

What you will need

1 pc. clear pine, 1¼'' × 8'' × 10' (see step 6)
2 pcs. clear pine, ¾'' × 1½'' × 66½''
1 pc. plywood, ¾'' × 4' × 4' A-C int.
16 hardwood buttons or 1 pc. hardwood dowel,
   ⅜'' × 6'' (see step 16)
16 #10 flathead wood screws, 1½''
white or yellow glue
clear varnish or polyurethane
paint roller or brush, 3'' wide
saber saw
table saw
router
drill
bar clamps
screw clamps or C-clamps
hand and measuring tools

Before you begin

You will need to construct forms, or molds (see p. 60), between which the glued-up veneer strips can be pressed to the proper shape. Since the curvature of the hooks is different from that of the legs you will have to make two molds, one for each part. Unless you have a band saw, it is best to make these molds by first cutting to shape several pieces of plywood, then stacking and gluing them together so that the completed molds are as thick as the strips are wide. If you wish, you can make as many as four of each mold to speed assembly time; however, since each laminated part generally needs to remain clamped no more than two hours, you will probably find this unnecessary. The layout for each mold is shown below. Notice that each consists of two halves. Attach a base piece to the bottom of one half of each mold. The base should be narrower than the total width of both mold halves plus the waste piece, so that the edge of the base won't prevent the clamps from tightening the mold completely.

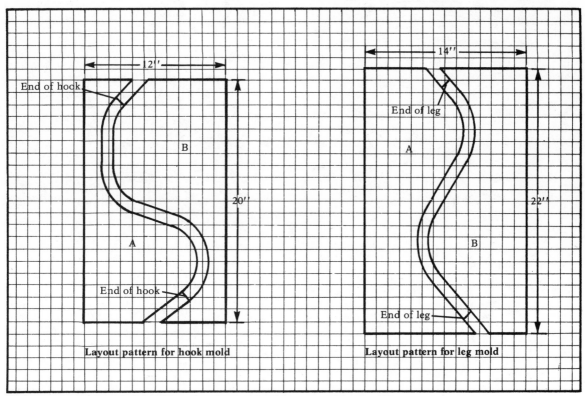

Layout pattern for hook mold

Layout pattern for leg mold

To draw patterns actual size, enlarge drawings, using 1-in. squares (see p. 16)

Laminating and Bending Wood

Laminating thin strips of wood together to form thicker pieces and bending wood to form curves are both simple processes in theory but can become quite complex in practice, due to the natural characteristics of wood. To minimize problems, always use absolutely defect-free stock, quartersawn (see p. 7) if possible, so that the grain runs as in the diagram below. Large pieces, or wood that must be bent to tight curves, must be soaked or steamed in water beforehand and then very quickly clamped into shape, a process requiring planning and assistance as well as good wood. Making curves by laminating thin strips is much easier; thin veneers bend easily with little moistening, and plainsawn (p. 7) stock can often be used if it is the correct thickness, since ripping it will yield veneers with proper grain orientation.

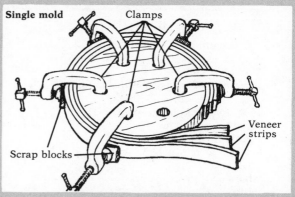

Single mold

Clamps

Veneer strips

Scrap blocks

Often a single mold is all that is needed for bending. Shape the mold as desired, using a saw, rasp, files, and perhaps sandpaper—then, if possible, cut holes on the interior for clamps to fit. Varnish and wax the mold. Place the wood to be bent—after soaking or steaming it in water until pliable—on the mold, and apply clamps every 3″, starting in the middle and working to the ends. Use a length of veneer or a series of scrap blocks to avoid marring the workpiece.

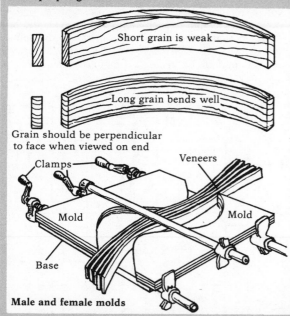

Short grain is weak

Long grain bends well

Grain should be perpendicular to face when viewed on end

Clamps

Veneers

Mold

Mold

Base

Male and female molds

To bend several layers of laminated veneers, construct male and female molds which can be clamped around the glued-up veneers to press them into shape as they dry. Use solid stock or built-up layers of plywood to make the molds, and wax or varnish them to prevent glue from sticking to them and possibly gluing the molds to the workpiece! Cut the veneers long enough to allow for the curves in the design of the finished piece, then glue them together in a bundle. Position the bundle between the molds, and begin by clamping across the middle. Work systematically out toward the ends, adding clamps on alternate sides to prevent buckling. Tighten all the clamps evenly to produce smooth curves.

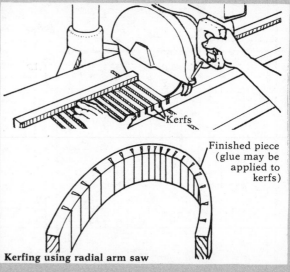

Kerfs

Finished piece (glue may be applied to kerfs)

Kerfing using radial arm saw

Cut kerfs across the face of solid stock to bend wood without moisture or lamination. Wood bent this way has little structural value but is adequate for use as face molding, say around a curving baseboard or counter top. Cut the kerfs across what will be the inside face of the wood, setting the saw's depth of cut to between $1/16$″ and $1/8$″ of the outside face. Determine the frequency of the kerfs by the sharpness of the curve to which the piece must be bent: the sharper the curve, the more kerfs per in.

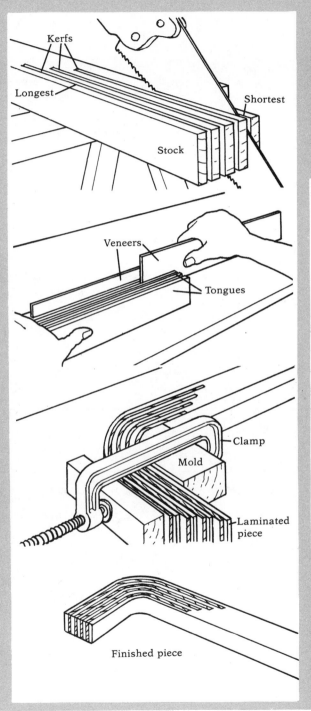

Kerfs

Longest

Shortest

Stock

Veneers

Tongues

Clamp

Mold

Laminated piece

Finished piece

An interesting way to bend the end of a piece of solid stock is to cut lengthwise kerfs into it and then to fit veneer inserts spread with glue into them. This maintains the original dimensions of the wood throughout the curve. Use a saw; each kerf must be longer than the one next to it. The shortest must be on the inside of the curve, and the longest — on the outside — should extend all the way around the bend. Also, the widths of the kerfs should equal the widths of the tongues of wood left between them. Make the veneers longer than necessary. Apply glue to both sides, then insert them and clamp the entire assembly between molds. When dry, saw off the waste veneer and sand smooth.

Rough laminations

Finished table

Stack lamination does not involve bending. It is a technique used to create a thick piece of wood which may then be carved or shaped as desired. The illustration above shows several layers of roughly shaped wood laminated to form a tall, hollow piece, the center post of a sculptured table. Stack lamination on this scale requires elaborate clamping techniques and facilities; however, much simpler pieces can be easily produced to make, say, carved furniture feet, or blocks from which wooden bowls may be turned on a lathe. By choosing woods carefully for stack lamination, the glued seams themselves can become part of the design, adding contrast and eye appeal.

Step-by-step instructions

1. Begin by making the molds for the hat rack's hooks and legs. All the pieces you will need can be cut from a single 4 × 4-ft. sheet of ¾-in. plywood. Refer to the diagram on p. 59, and cut a total of 10 pieces: two base pieces (one for each mold) plus two pieces each for the curved sections of the molds, which must be stack-laminated (see p. 60) to achieve the proper thickness. Label each piece as it is cut. Enlarge each diagram to full size by redrawing it on grid paper with 1-in. squares, then make templates of stiff paper or thin cardboard for each of the S-shaped waste strips. Trace the shape of each template onto the correct pairs of plywood pieces.

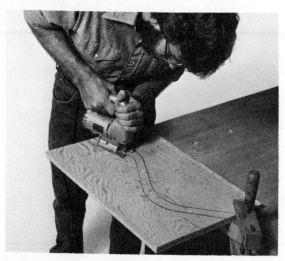

2. Carefully cut out the S-shapes from each of the mold pieces traced in step 1. Use a saber saw, and be certain to keep the blade within the traced lines. Try to follow each line exactly; the more accurate your saw cut, the less filing and sanding you will have to do to achieve a smoothly curved finished surface after each mold is completed. Position yourself so that you can sight straight down over the saw blade as you cut, and do not force the tool into the work too fast. Hold the saw firmly with both hands, but merely guide it as it cuts. To keep the work steady, clamp it securely (p. 44) — with two clamps if possible — to the side of the bench. Be careful, however, that the bench top does not lie in the path of the saw blade. If such is the case, make partial cuts, then reposition the board and the clamps and continue.

3. Stack the identically shaped pieces of each mold on top of one another, gluing and clamping each pair to form single stack-laminations, each 1½ in. thick. Keep the curved edges as flush with one another as possible, and be careful that they do not slide out of position while being clamped.

4. When the curved-mold portions are dry, scrape off any excess glue, then sand the surfaces smooth. Next, glue and clamp one section of each mold — for instance, each piece labeled *A* — to the correct base piece. Keep the squared edges of the curved pieces flush with the outside edges of each base.

5. Coat the surfaces of each mold (including the top surface of each base piece) with varnish or polyurethane, and allow to dry until hard. Then apply a layer of wax so that the mold pieces won't stick to the strips being laminated.

6. Now make the veneers for the four hooks and four legs. You will need 128 strips in all, each $\frac{1}{16} \times 1\frac{1}{8} \times 28$ in. These may all be cut from one $1\frac{1}{4}$ in. $\times$ 8 in. $\times$ 10-ft. board (five-quarter; see p. 6) which, when finish-sanded, will yield the $1\frac{1}{8}$-in. strips necessary, or several pieces of stock may be used, as long as they are at least 28 in. long and of the proper thickness. Absolutely clear material is a must. A table saw is best for making the veneers; it is such a simple task on this machine that you should have a professional shop do the job for you if you don't have the tool. The cost will be minimal. To make them yourself, first crosscut the stock into 28-in. lengths, then set the saw's guide fence $\frac{1}{16}$ in. from the side of the blade closest to the fence, and pass each of the boards through the saw, ripping $\frac{1}{16}$-in. strips until you have produced the required amount.

7. Each laminated part requires 16 strips. Lay out that many strips side by side for gluing. Prepare a mixture of white or yellow glue and water (1 oz. glue to 1 tsp. water), and apply it to the face-up surfaces of the strips, using a small paint roller or brush. Spread the glue thinly and evenly; the moisture will make the strips pliable.

8. Stack the glued-up veneers in pairs, glued face to glued face. Apply glue to the fresh sides, then stack again. Continue until a single bundle is formed. Do not apply glue to the outer faces of the bundle's topmost and bottommost strips.

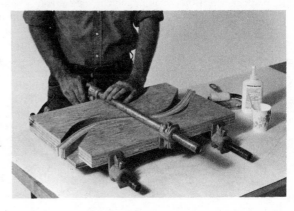

9. Position a mold so it rests evenly across two bar clamps. Open the clamps so that the space between the two mold sections is wide enough for the bundle of laminated strips to be placed between them easily. Then place the glued-up strips in the mold so that the 16 thin edges are up. Place a third bar clamp across the middle of the molds, and gradually draw the two halves of the mold together by tightening all three clamps in alternating succession. Allow at least two hours for drying.

(Continued on page 66)

Glues and Adhesives

Today's glues and adhesives are stronger and simpler to use than those of the past. Many are even stronger than the wood itself. Vinyl glues—both white and yellow—have become by far the most popular adhesives for home woodworkers, and are used by most professionals as well. Vinyl glue is inexpensive, easy to apply, quite strong, and dries in a relatively short time. In addition, the glue comes ready to use and has a long shelf life. Vinyl glue is not recommended for projects which will be exposed to moisture, but for most any other job it will do.

Use plastic resin or resorcinol for outdoor projects that must withstand water or extreme heat or cold. Plastic resin glue comes in powder form and must be

Common Glues

Type	Description	Uses	Application	Comments
Contact cement	Water-based acrylic latex, usually in bottle. Waterproof. Dries clear. Nonflammable. Nontoxic.	For porous and nonporous surfaces, indoors and out, where strength is not important. Bonding broad surfaces together: plastic laminates to counter tops, veneers, tabletops, other flat surfaces. Bonding dissimilar surfaces: leather, linoleum, thin-gauge metal. Jobs where clamping is not possible. Not for wood joints.	Sets instantly; no clamping necessary. Cures in 24–48 hours.	Expensive.
Cyanoacrylate resin	Cyanoacrylate ester. Also known as super glue or wonder glue. Water-resistant.	For mending nonporous surfaces (glass, china, metal, aluminum) that cannot be clamped together.	Sets instantly; no clamping necessary. Remove excess with acetone or nail polish remover. Cures in 48 hours.	Not as strong as epoxy.
Epoxy resin	Two-part polyamide resin and epoxy resin, in tubes or cans. Mix to form thick liquid. Very strong. Waterproof. Flammable. Toxic.	For porous and nonporous surfaces. Nonstructural wood repairs. Objects that get wet often: wooden boats, china, glass, fabrics, plastic, jewelry. Bonds dissimilar materials: metal to wood, glass to concrete. For patching up small gaps that can then be painted over.	Apply at temperatures between 70°–75°F. Sets instantly; no clamping necessary. Remove excess with acetone. Curing time varies from 5 minutes to over 8 hours, depending on brand.	Expensive. Best for small jobs.
Hide glue	Either liquid or flakes. Liquid is amber, ready to use. Flakes must be dissolved in warm water, then maintained at a warm temperature. Both have poor resistance to water and high humidity. Can be steamed apart.	For indoor furniture construction and repair. Slow setting time good for large work areas. Edge or face gluing, veneering, laminating, mortising, doweling. Hardboard, chipboard, leather, cloth, paper. For filling small gaps and rough spots in badly fitting joints.	Sets in 8 hours at 70°F. Clamp for 1 hour. Remove excess with warm water. Glue line dries to amber or light brown; may stain light-colored wood.	Liquid form much simpler to use than flake form.

mixed with water before use. It is highly water-resistant but not waterproof (fine for outdoor furniture, but don't use it to build boats). It is also comparatively inexpensive. Resorcinol, on the other hand, costs quite a bit but is absolutely impervious to the elements, including water.

There are many other glues, as the table below makes plain. Notice that old-fashioned hide glue—the glue of the past, made from horses' hooves, animal bones, and skins—is still available, precisely because of its weak adhesive qualities! Makers of musical instruments, especially, prefer hide glue to other types because of the ease with which it can be softened and removed for making repairs.

Common Glues—*Continued*

Type	Description	Uses	Application	Comments
Plastic resin	Urea formaldehyde. Powder, usually in a can. Creamy color when mixed with water. Very strong. Waterproof. Dries clear. Nonflammable. Nonstaining. Fumes toxic in large quantities.	For construction and repair of indoor furniture made of acid woods (oak, mahogany) but not oily wood. Gluing veneers. Do not use outdoors; high temperatures and humidity will weaken the bond.	Surfaces must fit tightly to set properly. Sets in 9–13 hours. Clamp for 12 hours at 70°F. or above. Clean excess with soap and warm water.	
Resorcinol	Two-part cherry-colored liquid resin and tan, powdered catalyst, in twin cans. Also known as waterproof glue. Mix to make a loose, brown paste. Pot life only 3 to 4 hours, once mixed. Dries brown. Very strong. Completely waterproof.	For making completely waterproof wood joints on boats, outdoor furniture, and other items immersed in water. Use on interior furniture too. Not for filling gaps.	Apply at temperatures above 70°F. Clamp for 16–24 hours. Remove excess with warm water while still wet. Not removable when hard.	Expensive.
White glue	Water-based, polyvinyl acetate (PVA), usually in squeeze bottle. Dries clear. Not strong. Not water-resistant. Nonflammable. Nontoxic. Odorless. Nonstaining.	For nonstructural wood projects where waterproofing is not required. Large veneer projects. Interior woodwork where nails or screws are also used. For porous surfaces: paper, fabrics, cardboard, leather. Corrodes metal. Not for use on objects subjected to excessive heat or moisture.	Sets in 30 minutes. Clamp for 1 hour. Remove excess with soap and warm water. Cures in 24 hours.	Inexpensive.
Yellow glue	Aliphatic, water-based resin, usually in squeeze bottle. Also known as carpenters' glue. Low water resistance. Dries clear. Nontoxic.	Specially made for nonstructural wood furniture building and repair tasks. Also good for bonding other porous surfaces, such as cloth, paper, leather. Not for filling gaps.	Apply at any temperature between 45°–110°F. in dry environment. Clamp for 30 minutes. Remove excess with warm water. Cures in 24 hours. Can be sanded.	Works like white glue, but forms a stronger bond and is more heat-resistant.

10. Before you remove the laminated piece from the mold, mark where each end is to be cut off to achieve the proper length (p. 59). When the piece is dry, loosen the clamps and remove it from the mold.

11. Prepare another group of 16 veneers to make the next piece, then repeat steps 7—10, using the appropriate set of molds. It is a good idea to rewax each mold section between setups. When all the hooks and legs necessary have been completed, saw off their ends where marked, scrape off any excess glue, then use either a router with a ¼-in. rounding-over bit (p. 42), or a wood rasp and file, to radius all four edges of each. Finally, sand each hook and leg until smooth.

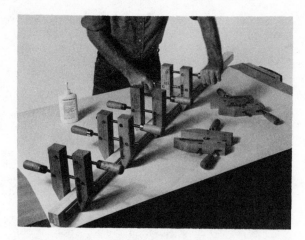

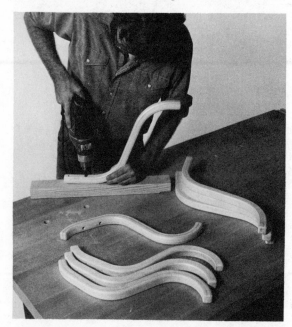

12. Drill pilot holes (p. 73) in each hook and leg to accept 1½-in. #10 screws. Using a ⅛-in.-dia. drill bit, make two holes in each piece. A power drill is easiest to use; it frees one hand to hold each laminated piece firmly against a backing block of scrap wood as you drill to prevent the holes from splitting out. To drill the hooks, locate the lower hole 3¼ in. from the bottom of each piece and the upper hole 2¼ in. above the first (p. 58). For the holes in each leg, locate the first hole ¾ in. from the top of each piece, and the second, 2¼ in. below it (p. 58). Counterbore all the holes ¼ in. deep, using a ⅜-in.-dia. bit, to allow plugging the holes later (see step 16).

13. Make the center post. First, cut two pieces of stock, each ¾ × 1½ × 66½ in. Carefully true-up and smooth two faces to be joined (for an absolutely invisible joint, the faces should be trued using a hand or power jointer plane—p. 30—however, in most cases, when using stock purchased to size, careful sanding is sufficient), then glue the two pieces together so that the dimensions total 1½ × 1½ × 66½ in. Use enough clamps— with scrap pieces of wood between the jaws and the workpiece—to distribute pressure evenly along the post's entire length.

14. After the post is dry, scrape off any excess glue. To point the ends, first scribe a line around all four faces of the post, ½ in. from each end, then place the post in a miter box (p. 28) and saw chamfers of 45° each, again on all four faces, cutting so as to just skim the scribed lines on each face with the saw. Use a block plane (p. 30) and sandpaper to smooth the cuts and to make them even if necessary.

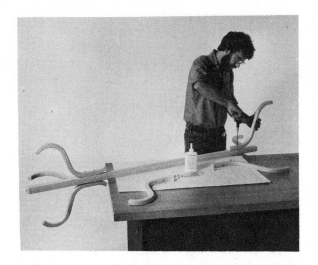

15. Using a ³⁄₃₂-in.-dia. bit, drill ¾-in.-deep pilot holes in the finished post for mounting the legs and hooks. Drill the lower holes for the legs on all four faces of the post 7¼ in. from the post's bottom end. Drill the upper holes 2¼ in. above the first. Drill the first series of holes for the hooks also on all four faces of the post, 14 in. from the post's top end, and the second holes 2¼ in. below them (p. 58). All holes should be drilled along the centerline of each face.

16. Align each hook and leg piece with the pilot holes drilled in the post, then attach each piece with two 1½-in. #10 screws. Cover the screws with ⅜-in.-dia. hardwood buttons or with pieces of dowel glued in place, then trimmed with a backsaw or chisel to fit flush with the post.

17. Apply clear varnish or polyurethane to finish the hat rack. See Wood Finishing, p. 162, for complete finishing instructions.

Mudroom Boot Bench

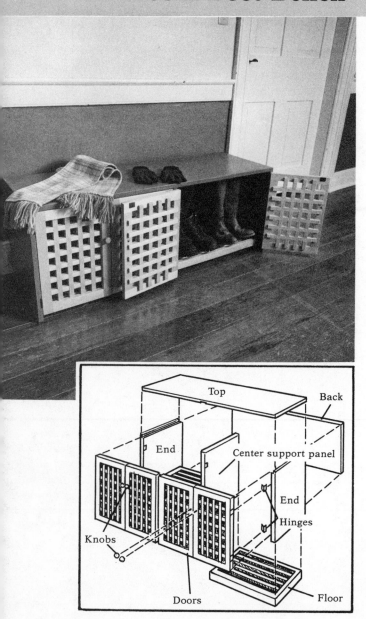

Top
Back
End
Center support panel
End
Hinges
Knobs
Doors
Floor

Half-lap joints
Choosing and using drills and screws
Nails and hammers
How to mount hinges

Here is an unusual and very practical item that makes a good intermediate woodworking project. Designed for storing wet boots and shoes out of sight but not out of circulation, this sturdy boot bench is just the sort of thing your mudroom probably needs to give it at least a semblance of neatness and order. The cabinet itself is made of ¾-inch plywood—strong enough to sit on while putting on or removing footwear—and the latticed doors and floorboards, designed especially to allow plenty of air circulation throughout the inside, are made of pine. The boot bench shown in this chapter is painted with two coats of tough latex interior semigloss enamel over a coat of latex primer, and the doors and floorboards are finished with polyurethane, for appearance as well as for durability. The floorboards are raised to allow ventilation underneath and also to make it easy to place a shallow pan or something absorbent like newspaper beneath the bench to catch water dripping off the articles inside. Both the floorboards and the doors are easy to remove when spring cleaning time arrives at last.

Although this project looks complex, really it is not. The plywood cabinet's construction is exactly the same in principle as the modular boxes (see p. 40) and the drawers that accompany the bolt-together bunk beds (p. 49): rabbeted and dadoed pieces held together with strong glue and nails. The technique of cutting half-lap joints (p. 71) is new and provides an easy introduction to the more complex world of woodwork joinery, challenging examples of which are to be found in later projects. Also covered are the facts you need to know about using drills and choosing screws, about selecting nails and how to hammer, and about the ways of mounting hinges.

What you will need

2 pcs. clear pine, ¾'' × 7½'' × 30''
2 pcs. #2 pine, ¾'' × 1½'' × 12'
2 pcs. #2 pine, ¾'' × 1½'' × 8'
1 pc. plywood, ¾'' × 4' × 6' A-C int.
6d finishing nails
4d finishing nails
16 #6 flathead wood screws, 1¼''
4 pr. loose-pin hinges, brass or steel, 1½'' × 1½''
4 magnetic cabinet catches
4 wooden knobs, 1-in. dia.
white or yellow glue
latex primer and interior semigloss enamel
polyurethane
table saw or circular saw
router
drill
C-clamps
hand and measuring tools

Before you begin

The most complex elements of the boot bench project are the half-lapped grid members that make up each cabinet door. The notches in these members must be cut quite accurately and uniformly if their appearance is to be neat. To achieve this, as well as to save a tremendous amount of time compared with chiseling out each notch individually, cut rabbets and dadoes across the width of wide boards according to the dimensions shown in the diagrams below, and then crosscut and rip the boards to the finished grid-member sizes. Use a table saw if possible, or a router—for this last you will need a hand ripsaw as well—to make the notches and perform the finish cuts. This way, since all the cutouts for each half-lap joint will have been made using a single blade or bit setting, all will be exactly the same size and should fit together perfectly. Be sure to test the accuracy of your saw or router setting on scrap stock before you attempt to cut into the actual piece of wood you intend to use.

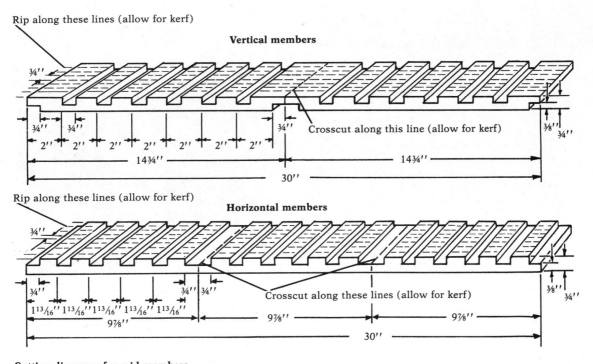

Cutting diagrams for grid members

Step-by-step instructions

1. Cut five pieces of ¾-in. plywood to make the top, ends, back, and center support panel of the bench. For the top, you will need one piece, ¾ × 16 × 47¼ in.; for the ends, two pieces, each ¾ × 16 × 18 in.; for the back, one piece, ¾ × 16¼ × 46½ in.; and for the center support, one piece, ¾ × 15¼ × 17⅜ in.

2. Along the inside top edge of each end panel, cut a notch (rabbet), ¾ in. wide and ⅜ in. deep, to seat the top panel of the bench. A router (see p. 42) or a table saw is best for cutting rabbets in plywood.

3. Rout or saw a groove (dado), ¾ in. wide and ⅜ in. deep, along the underside of the top panel to act as a slot for the center support. Cut the dado across the width of the panel, down the centerline.

7. Glue and nail the floor section pieces together, using white or yellow glue and 4d finishing nails. Clamps are not needed. Sand, fill, and finish each floor section with two coats of polyurethane before performing step 8.

4. Glue and nail the ends and the center support panel to the top, making sure that the front edges of each panel are flush with the front edge of the top. Then glue and nail the back panel in place. Use white or yellow glue and 6d finishing nails. Clamps are not required when using nails as well as glue.

5. To make finishing easier, sand, fill, and paint the plywood assembly now, then set it aside while you complete the remaining steps. The bench shown is finished with one coat of primer and two coats of semigloss latex enamel. See Wood Finishing, p. 162, for complete finishing instructions.

6. Cut 16 pieces of ¾ × 1½-in. #2 pine for the floor sections. This wood may be purchased as 1 × 2 stock at a lumberyard, or as wider material which you must then rip to the proper width. The lengths listed in What You Will Need, p. 69, are convenient and economical sizes. Specifically, you will need four pieces, each 12⅝ in. long, for end rails; four pieces, each 22⅞ in. long, for side rails; and eight pieces, each 21⅜ in. long, for the interior rails.

8. Drill pilot holes (p. 73) through each completed floor section into the ends and center panel of the plywood bench assembly. Attach the floor sections to the bench assembly, using 1¼-in. #6 screws. Install four screws per floor section.

9. Now cut 16 pieces of ¾ × 1½-in. #2 pine for the doorframes. Cut 8 pieces, each 16¼ in. long, for the vertical members; and 8 pieces, each 11⅜ in. long, for the horizontal members.

10. Cut half-lap joints on the ends of each horizontal and vertical doorframe member. Complete instructions for cutting half-lap joints are shown in the box to the right. An efficient method is to clamp (p. 44) each set of equal-length members together side by side, and make repeated passes across their ends with a router set to a depth of ⅜ in. Use a straightedged board as a guide fence for the router. Clamp the fence across the frame pieces, 1½ in. from each end.

11. Glue and clamp the jointed frame members together. The vertical members should overlap the horizontal members at both the top and bottom of each frame.

(Continued on page 75)

Half-Lap Joints

A half-lap joint is made by notching two pieces of wood. The notches are cut to precisely the same dimensions, then interlocked, usually at right angles, so they form a flush joint the total thickness of which is the same as the uncut thickness of each piece (or of the thicker piece if the two are different). Though each notch face should be flat, a neater fit is often possible if the faces are each pared to a slight V, with their centers a little lower than their sides.

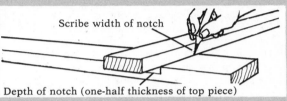

Scribe width of notch

Depth of notch (one-half thickness of top piece)

1. Place the pieces together as they will be when notched, then carefully scribe the width of each piece onto the piece it rests against. Also mark the depths each notch should be: one-half the thickness of each piece, or one-half the thickness of the thinner piece.

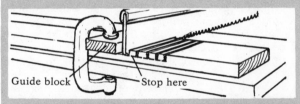

Guide block   Stop here

2. Saw across the grain of each piece to facilitate waste removal. Stop just above the depth-of-cut marks, and stay within the width-dimension lines.

Pare flat or undercut slightly

3. Carefully pare away the waste wood to the marked lines, using a sharp chisel. Work from the sides toward the center. Be sure to clean out corners thoroughly.

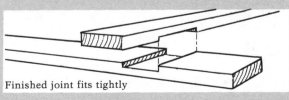

Finished joint fits tightly

4. The finished joint should press together for a tight fit.

Choosing and Using Drills and Screws

A good, portable, electric hand drill should be the first power tool you obtain. Buy one even before you invest in a twist drill or brace and bit; you may never need any other tool for boring. Power drills are simple to operate and inexpensive. In fact, a perfectly reliable model, adequate for just about any job, costs less than several well-known brands of hand braces, and the bits cost less, too. Power hand drills come in three chuck sizes: ¼ in., ⅜ in., and ½ in. The size refers to the shank diameter of the bits the drill will accept. Your best bet will most likely be a ⅜-in. size. Smaller drills have a very limited capacity, and larger ones are heavy and often awkward to use except in outdoor carpentry situations (and even there, many professionals use a ⅜-in. drill most of the time, even if they keep a ½-in. drill handy for special tasks). The size of the drill does not appreciably limit the diameter of the holes that can be drilled with it. Except in the case of a ¼-in. drill, many different varieties of bit—some of which, the spade bit in particular, have the capacity to drill very wide holes—come in both ⅜-in. and ½-in. shank sizes.

Operating a power drill is a cinch also. You just hold it steady and pull the trigger. The hardest part is making sure the drill is properly aligned with the wood so that it accurately bores the hole you intend it to. A number of commercial devices are available to assure proper alignment—perhaps the most useful is the Portalign tool shown on the page opposite—but homemade drilling guides are easy to make and work just as well in many cases. Most professionals simply develop an eye for drilling straight; it's not a difficult knack to acquire. Some drills also have a variable speed and a reversing feature. Both of these are handy; generally, you use a higher speed to drill small-diameter holes in thin stock, and a lower speed to drill wide holes, or holes through heavy stock. The reverse control lets you back the drill out of holes in which the bit has jammed. Make sure the drill you purchase either has a three-prong plug, which means it is electrically grounded, or is clearly marked double insulated if it is a two-prong model. Either of these features is crucial to your safety while operating the tool. Adapters that fit into three-prong plugs and allow them to be used in two-prong wall sockets do not diminish a grounded tool's safety if properly installed and cost practically nothing.

Next to a power drill, a small, hand-operated twist drill is probably most useful, but only as an auxiliary to the larger tool. With a twist drill you can bore tiny holes in awkward places, and they are perfect for making pilot holes for small screws such as those used on cabinet hinges and drawer pulls.

A brace and bit, on the other hand, while venerable and full of tradition, is nearly obsolete. It does have the capacity to accept large drill bits, which gives it the definite advantage of being cheaper to obtain for drilling large holes in heavy stock than a ½-in. electric drill. Also, a hand brace can be fitted with a screwdriver bit and the tool used very effectively for driving home a great many screws in a short time or for driving screws into extremely dense wood such as oak (it also helps to put soap or wax on the screw threads in such cases).

Most drilling procedures require that you bore completely through a piece of stock. When doing so, avoid splitting the wood on the underside as the bit emerges, either by clamping the workpiece to a scrap block (and drilling straight through into both pieces of wood) or by removing the bit from the hole as soon as it begins to come through, and then finishing up by drilling into the hole from the other side. To drill a hole to a predetermined depth, first measure the distance the depth should be along the length of the drill bit itself, then wrap a piece of masking tape around the bit to act as a gauge. Stop drilling when the tape touches the wood.

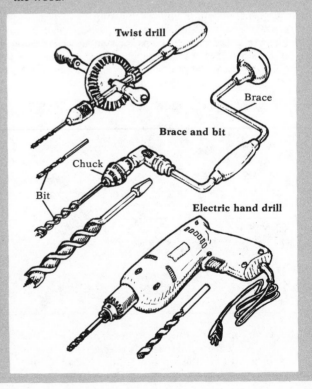

Twist drill

Brace

Brace and bit

Chuck

Bit

Electric hand drill

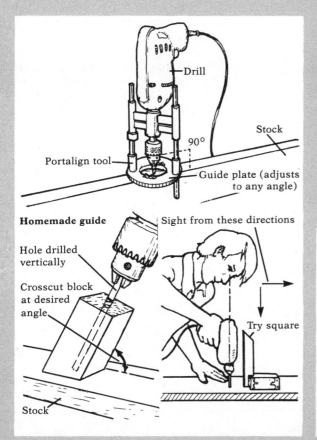

Drill

90°

Stock

Portalign tool

Guide plate (adjusts to any angle)

Homemade guide

Sight from these directions

Hole drilled vertically

Crosscut block at desired angle

Try square

Stock

the clearance hole, is bored for the screw shank. Finally, the top of the hole is drilled with a countersink bit so the screw head will lie flush, or with a bit large enough to recess the head if the screw is to be concealed. A screwsink bit, available in many sizes, performs all these tasks at once.

CHOOSING THE RIGHT SCREW

Flathead screws are the most common for woodworking. They can be set either flush with the top surface of the wood, or countersunk and concealed. Screws with oval heads are easier to remove without marring the work. When countersunk, their top surfaces are slightly higher than the surrounding wood. Use roundhead screws when there is no need for countersinking.

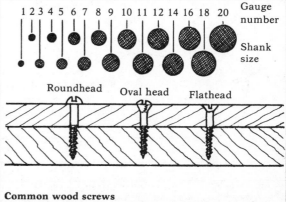

Common wood screws

DRILLING PILOT HOLES

Screws require predrilled holes to prevent them from splitting the wood as they are driven in and so their threads will hold tightly. Usually these are made in three stages: First the pilot hole is drilled for the threaded portion, then a larger-diameter hole, called

Choose screws large enough in diameter to hold the work but not so large as to split it. Their correct length is, three times the thickness of the top piece of wood; that is two-thirds, of the screw—usually the entire threaded portion—should extend into the lower of the two pieces being joined.

Chart of Pilot Hole Sizes for Screws

Screw gauge number	1	2	3	4	5	6	8	10	12	14	16	18	20
Drill bit size for clearance hole	$5/64$	$3/32$	$7/64$	$1/8$	$9/64$	$5/32$	$11/64$	$3/16$	$7/32$	$1/4$	$9/32$	$5/16$	$11/32$
Drill bit size for pilot hole in softwood	$1/32$	$1/32$	$3/64$	$3/64$	$1/16$	$1/16$	$1/16$	$3/32$	$7/64$	$7/64$	$7/64$	$9/64$	$11/64$
Drill bit size for pilot hole in hardwood	$1/32$	$1/16$	$1/16$	$5/64$	$5/64$	$5/64$	$3/32$	$1/8$	$1/8$	$5/32$	$3/16$	$3/16$	$7/32$

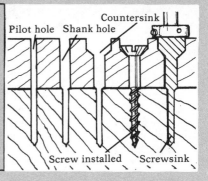

Countersink

Pilot hole   Shank hole

Screw installed   Screwsink

Nails and Hammers

Nails fasten wood together by the friction that results from the wood pressing against the metal shank. They grip even better when driven into the wood at a slight angle. In the past, many different types of nails were common, each with a different use. There were clench—or clout—nails, made to be driven clear through two pieces of wood and then bent over, or clenched, and there were nails that were square or rectangular in cross section, with sides that tapered toward each other, called cut nails. These latter still survive, so-named because they are actually cut from a flat sheet of metal, and are used primarily to fasten wood flooring. If driven properly, they hold floorboards so tightly that squeaking almost never develops. The secret is to drive cut nails into the wood so the long sides slice through the grain at right angles. That

long as the thickness of the top piece of wood into which it will be driven.

Hammer size should be considered, too. For rough work and common nails, a 16-oz. hammer is probably about right. For making furniture and driving finishing nails, a 7-13 oz. hammer will provide more control. When driving finishing nails, avoid denting the wood with hammer marks. This takes practice, but your plan should be to drive the nail only to about 1/8 in. from the wood surface, then sink the nail completely, using a nail set. In hardwood, such as oak, drill a pilot hole before hammering in the nail (this avoids splitting the wood and/or bending the nail), and use a nail set after you have driven the nail just to where the head touches the wood.

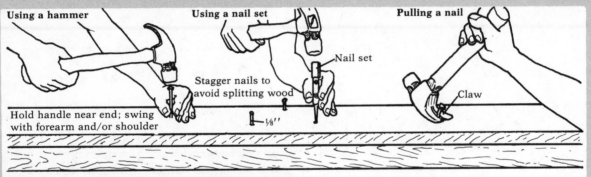

Using a hammer

Hold handle near end; swing with forearm and/or shoulder

Using a nail set

Stagger nails to avoid splitting wood

1/8''

Nail set

Pulling a nail

Claw

way there is no chance of splitting the wood—since the grain is in no way distorted—and at the same time the friction of the wood against the nail is maximized.

By far the most frequently used nail today is the wire nail. These are straight-sided and round in cross section since they are actually cut from wire; in fact, their diameters even correspond to conventional wire-gauge dimensions. There are two basic varieties: common nails, which have large, flat heads and are used mostly for rough work, and finishing nails, which have virtually no head at all and are meant to be completely recessed into the wood and concealed with wood putty.

All nails are sized according to the penny system, designated by the antiquated English currency notation *d*. This now refers to the length of the nail, but it originally meant the price per 100 nails. In sizes up to 10d, the length of a nail can be figured out by dividing the penny size by four, then adding 1/2 in. An 8d nail, for example, is 2 1/2 in. long (see table to the right). A correctly sized nail is one which is about three times as

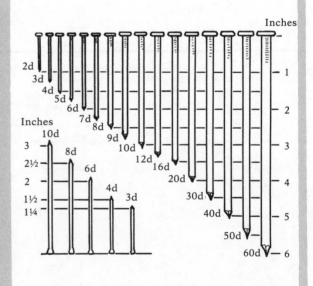

12. To make the grid sections of the doors, cut rabbets and dadoes across wide boards, then crosscut the boards to length and rip them to width (p. 69). Use 2 pieces of ¾ × 7½ × 30-in. clear pine. Mark each board according to the dimensions on the grid-member diagram on p. 69. Allow for saw kerfs as indicated. You will need to cut 16 vertical pieces, each ¾ × ¾ × 14¾ in.; and 24 horizontals, each ¾ × ¾ × 9¹³⁄₁₆ in. Notice that the wide dadoes cut across each board are to be split exactly down their centers when the pieces are crosscut to length, so that each side becomes a rabbet on the ends of the finish-cut members.

14. Glue and clamp the finished grid sections to the finished doorframes. The rabbeted ends of the grid pieces should be glued to the undersides of the doorframes (the sides where the horizontal frame members overlap the verticals and extend across the entire width of the frame). Sand and finish each of the four completed doors with polyurethane, as directed in step 7. Also apply polyurethane to each of the four wooden knobs to be attached later, in step 16.

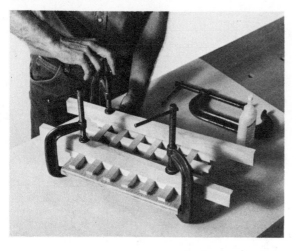

13. Assemble each of the four grid sections by joining together four vertical grid members and six horizontals. Glue the pieces, using white or yellow glue. Clamp if necessary, sandwiching the grid pieces between scrap blocks of lumber and a backing piece of plywood.

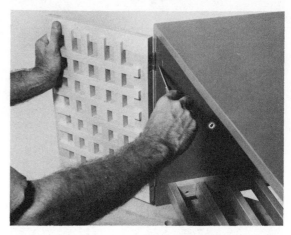

15. Attach two 1½ × 1½-in. loose-pin hinges to each door, following the instructions given in How to Mount Hinges (p. 76). Mortises (gains) for hinges should be located on the vertical doorframe members. The outer edge of each mortise should be even with the seam of the half-lap joint.

16. After the doors are hung, drill a single hole in each of the doorframes, and attach 1-in.-dia. wooden knobs. Use care in measuring and drilling so that all the knobs are in line with each other and also so that they form a horizontal line parallel to the top edge of the bench.

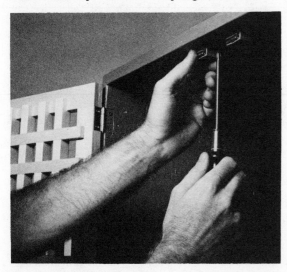

17. To complete the bench, install magnetic cabinet catches on the underside of the bench top. First attach the small metal plates to the doors, then install the magnets loosely, and adjust them for a perfect fit.

How to Mount Hinges

Hinges come in a wide variety of styles. By far the most common are butt hinges. Usually these are mounted with one leaf fastened on the side of a door and the other on the inside face of the adjacent doorframe. When the door is closed, only the hinge pin enclosure is visible. Surface-mounted hinges are generally more decorative than butt types and are fastened so that both leaves are visible on the outside of the cabinet. Concealed and semiconcealed hinges—a third category—are designed to be as inconspicuous as possible. These are usually reserved for designer-built custom cabinetry. The rule of thumb for placing all types of hinges is to locate them away from the top and bottom edges of the swinging piece they are to be mounted on, either the same distance or a little more than the length of one of the hinges themselves.

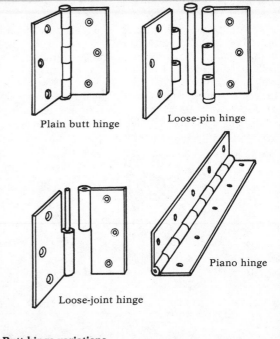

Plain butt hinge

Loose-pin hinge

Loose-joint hinge

Piano hinge

Butt hinge variations

Plain butt hinges do not come apart. They are reversible, however: either end is up. Loose-pin hinges disassemble by removing the hinge pin. Loose-joint hinges incorporate the hinge pin into the leaf that is fastened to the door frame. To disassemble, simply open and lift up on the door, freeing the other leaf. Piano hinges are actually continuous butt hinges. Often they are used on heavy chest tops and drop-front desks which must support a great deal of weight.

Surface-mounted hinges

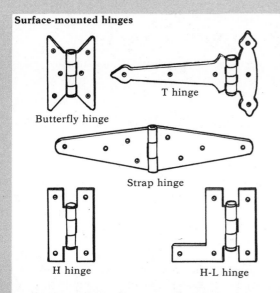

Butterfly hinge

T hinge

Strap hinge

H hinge

H-L hinge

Surface-mounted hinges are available in a wide range of styles and metals. Many kinds you can make yourself.

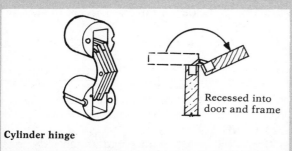

Recessed into door and frame

Cylinder hinge

Cylinder hinges are concealed, invisible when the door is closed. They cannot be used on stock less than 1 in. thick.

Pivot hinge

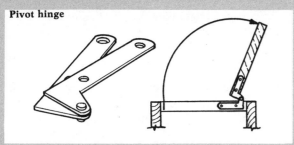

Pivot hinges are semiconcealed. They mount at top and bottom of doors. When closed, only tiny hinge pins are visible.

MORTISING A HINGE LEAF

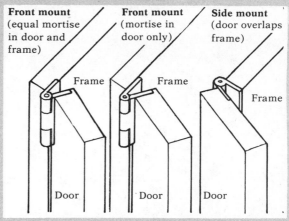

Front mount (equal mortise in door and frame)

Front mount (mortise in door only)

Side mount (door overlaps frame)

Frame

Frame

Frame

Door

Door

Door

Butt hinges may be attached in several different ways.

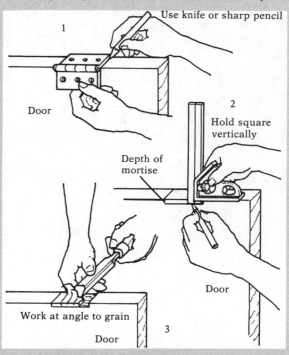

1

Use knife or sharp pencil

Door

2

Hold square vertically

Depth of mortise

Door

Work at angle to grain

Door

3

Door

1. To mortise hinge, begin with door-side leaf. Mark length of mortise by tracing hinge onto edge of door.
2. Square lines from step 1, then set try square to thickness of leaf and hold vertically to scribe depth mortise must be cut.
3. Mark outline of mortise using sharp chisel, then carefully pare away waste, holding chisel flat.

Partition Screen with Handwoven Panels

Doweling

This partition screen, made of woven fabric framed with wood, offers a decorative way to divide a room or provide an area of privacy. The self-supporting screen consists of three separate frames joined with homemade wooden hinges. Panels of fabric are stretched inside each frame and held in place with staples and molding. Directions for weaving panels similar to the ones shown here can be found on page 400.

The wood used in this particular screen is ¾-inch clear mahogany. The vertical and horizontal members of each panel are joined with hidden dowels. The lower members all are wider than the upper ones so the panels do not appear top-heavy. Each frame is rabbeted at the back, around the inside perimeter, to accept the woven panel and molding.

The wooden hinges that join the frames are a special feature of this project. The body of each hinge is made of mahogany, to match the frames. For maximum strength, the hinge bodies are designed with the wood grain running horizontally. The hinge pins are short lengths of ordinary hardwood dowel. The pins are positioned in pockets cut into the screen frames and are entirely concealed, both for strength and appearance, with mahogany inlays sanded flush with the edges of the frames. The design of these hinges allows the screen frames to fold back upon themselves. This makes possible a variety of positionings, as well as easy storage. When completely folded up, the entire screen takes up only slightly more room than one frame.

Though the panels in this screen are made of handwoven fabric, it is, of course, possible to use other materials, both homemade and purchased. When choosing materials for panels, however, consider the type and texture of wood you are using in the frames so the panels and the wood complement each other.

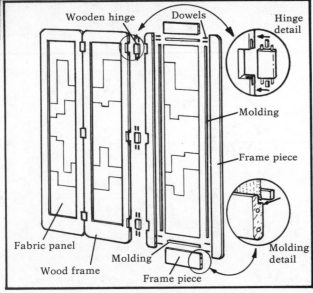

Wooden hinge — Dowels — Hinge detail — Molding — Frame piece — Molding detail — Fabric panel — Wood frame — Molding — Frame piece

What you will need

3 pcs. clear mahogany, ¾'' × 5½'' × 13''
3 pcs. clear mahogany, ¾'' × 3½'' × 13''
3 pcs. clear mahogany, ¾'' × 3'' × 1⅞'' (see
  step 18)
6 pcs. clear mahogany, ¾'' × 2½'' × 6'
6 pcs. clear mahogany, ¼'' × ⅜'' × 63¾''
6 pcs. clear mahogany, ¼'' × ⅜'' × 13¾''
24 pcs. clear mahogany, ¼'' × ¼'' × 1¼''
1 pc. hardwood dowel, ⅜'' × 4' (see step 11)
1 pc. hardwood dowel, ¼'' × 3' (see step 21)
16-ga. wire nails, ⅝''
staples, ¼''
white or yellow glue
wood putty
brush-on lacquer or polyurethane
table saw, saber saw, or hand saws
router, drill, doweling jig, heavy-duty staple gun
bar clamps
hand and measuring tools

Before you begin

The diagram below shows the construction of the wooden hinges, and the mortises within which each hinge is housed. The mortises are cut into the edges of the vertical frame members. Use a backsaw and saber or coping saw to cut the mortises and a router (see p. 42) for the pockets. A special router guide is shown and described in steps 6–8.

Step-by-step instructions

1. Cut six pieces of clear mahogany, each ¾ in. × 2½ in. × 6 ft., for the vertical members of the frames.
2. Cut three pieces of clear mahogany, each ¾ × 3½ × 13 in., for the top horizontal members of the frames.
3. Cut three pieces of clear mahogany, each ¾ × 5½ × 13 in., for the bottom horizontal members of the frames.

4. Use a backsaw to start the hinge mortises on the four interior vertical frame members. The lowest cuts are on a line with the upper edge of each bottom horizontal frame member, 5½ in. from the bottom of the frame. The lower of each pair of middle cuts is 35½ in. from the bottom of the frame; the highest cuts are on a line with the lower edge of each top horizontal, 3½ in. from the top of the frame. Each pair of cuts should be made 3½ in. apart.
5. Use a saber saw or coping saw to finish the hinge mortises, then, using a file, carefully clean the waste from the corners.

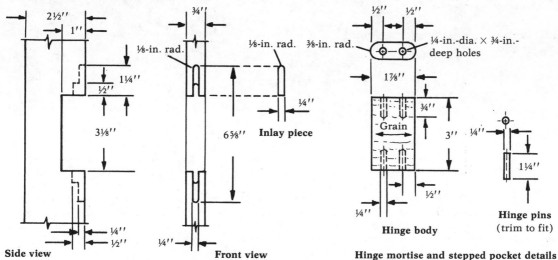

Side view   **Front view**   **Inlay piece**   **Hinge body**   **Hinge pins** (trim to fit)

Hinge mortise and stepped pocket details

6. To cut the stepped pockets in each hinge mortise, construct a router guide. The width of the guide's open area must be made exactly equal to the width of the desired groove (¼ in.), plus twice the distance between one edge of the router plate and the outside of the cutter bit nearest that edge. Figure the length of the guide the same way: the length of the desired groove (5⅝ in.), plus twice the distance between one edge of the router plate and the nearest surface of the bit. Butt-join and glue the pieces of the guide together. Also make inserts to fit against the inside of each end of the guide to limit the router's travel by ¾ in. at each end. These are for making the deep steps.

7. Screw a lengthwise fence along the underside of the guide. The fence should be ⅜ in. to one side of the guide's centerline (or half the thickness of the frame piece being grooved). Position the guide with its fence against the outside of a mortised frame piece, then clamp another fence against the piece to secure the guide and provide a wide surface for the router to travel along.

8. With the guide—inserts removed—in place on a mortised frame member, rout a ¼ × ¼-in. groove on each side of the mortise, using a ¼-in.-dia. straight router bit. Each groove should be 1¼ in. long.

9. Position the inserts at each end of the guide, then rout ¼-in.-wide grooves, ½ in. deep, measured from the surface of the wood, in effect deepening ½-in.-long sections of the grooves made in step 8. Perform steps 8 and 9 on both mortises of each inner frame piece.

10. Drill ⅜-in.-dia. holes 1 in. deep for the dowel joints in the corners of the vertical and horizontal frame members, as shown in the diagram (see p. 78). Use a doweling jig (p. 83) for accuracy, and locate the center of each hole by measuring from the same side of each frame member to avoid misalignment. The holes in the lower frame members should have their centers at 1½ in. and 4 in. from the bottom, and the holes in the upper members should have centers ¾ in. and 2¼ in. from the top.

11. Cut 24 pieces of ⅜-in.-dia. hardwood dowel, each 1⅞ in. long, for the dowel joints in each frame. Chamfer (bevel) both ends of each dowel (p. 82).

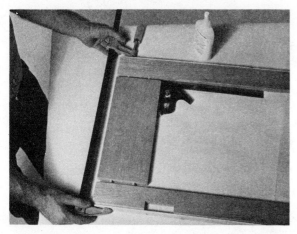

12. Join the members of each frame. First, apply glue to one end of each dowel, then tap the dowels into the holes in the horizontal members. Apply glue to the frame pieces, insert the dowels into the holes in the vertical members, and clamp the frame together, using bar clamps (p. 44). Use scrap blocks to avoid marring the wood.
13. With a saber or coping saw, cut a 2-in. radius at the corners of the frames, then, with a router and ⅜-in. rounding-over bit, machine a radius along the exterior edges of each completed frame.

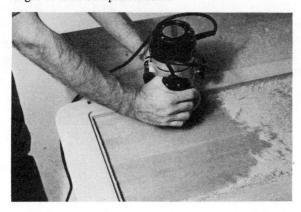

14. Use a router also to machine a ⅜ × ⅜-in. rabbet around the inside perimeter at the back of each frame, to accept the panel material and molding strips.

15. Cut six pieces of clear mahogany, each ¼ × ⅜ × 63¾ in., for side molding strips to fit the rabbeted frames.
16. Cut six pieces of clear mahogany, each ¼ × ⅜ × 13¾ in., for top and bottom molding strips.
17. Saw off each end of the molding strips at 45° so they will meet in a miter joint in the corners of the frames. Round the corners of each strip to match the radius in the corners of the rabbet cut.
18. Cut six pieces of clear mahogany, each ¾ × 3 × 1⅞ in., for the hinges. Note that the width is greater than the length.

19. Using a router, work a ⅜-in. radius on the end-grain edges of all the hinges.

20. Center and drill two ¼-in.-dia. holes, each ¾ in. deep, in both ends of each hinge for the hinge pins. Position the holes ⅞ in. apart, ½ in. from either end.
21. Cut 24 pieces of ¼-in.-dia. hardwood dowel, each 1¼ in. long, for the hinge pins. Chamfer the ends.
(Continued on page 84)

Doweling

Typical dowel joints

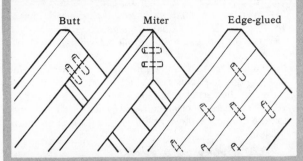

Butt   Miter   Edge-glued

Dowel joints are relatively simple to make and don't require fancy or expensive equipment. Properly installed, they add enormous strength to such weaker joint varieties as butts and miters and are often an effective substitute for more elaborate joints such as dovetails and mortise-and-tenon joints.

The technique of making good dowel joints begins with selecting the dowels themselves. Their diameter should be about one-third the thickness of the wood they are to join. The holes for installing dowels should be drilled at least one-third of the way through each board; the correct length for dowels is about ⅛ in. less than the total length of both holes.

When freshly glued, dowels tend to swell in diameter. Therefore, it is necessary to chamfer (bevel) their ends—use a file or sandpaper—prior to applying glue, so that they tap easily into place with a hammer, but are not so tight that they split the surrounding wood. Do not drill holes oversize. Loose-fitting dowels are ineffective. Cutting some type of groove along the length of dowels is also a good idea; this allows trapped air or glue, which would otherwise prevent the dowel from seating fully, to pass from the hole.

Always use dowel centers or a doweling jig when laying out and drilling dowel holes. Hardware stores carry a variety of styles, all designed to produce holes that will align exactly in mating boards. Doweling jigs are more expensive than centers; however, jigs also help ensure that the holes you drill will be perfectly perpendicular, thus assuring alignment in two directions instead of only one. Regardless of whether you use centers or a jig, when marking initial layout lines to locate dowels, remember that boards joined together will have adjacent outer, as well as inner, faces. Before layout, mark the outer or inner faces on the boards to be joined, then when setting up, make measurements only from the marked side of each board. This will assure that at least one surface will join flush.

PREPARING DOWELS FOR USE

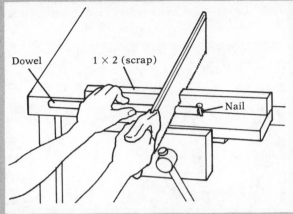

To cut a quantity of dowels to the same length, make a jig of scrap wood. Carefully located nail acts as a stop.

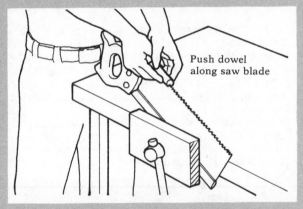

Saw a kerf in the dowel to release trapped air and excess glue from the dowel hole during installation.

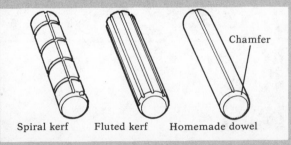

Spiral kerf   Fluted kerf   Homemade dowel

Commercially made dowels have elaborate kerfing. Homemade dowel appears at right. All dowels should have their ends chamfered (beveled) for easy installation.

USING DOWEL CENTERS

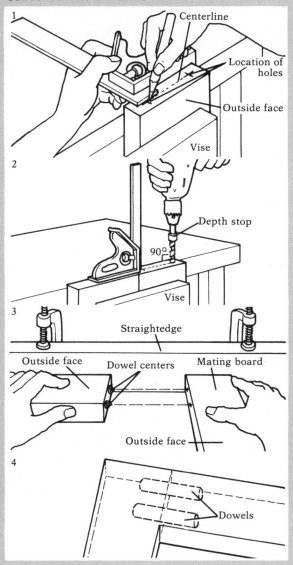

USING A DOWELING JIG

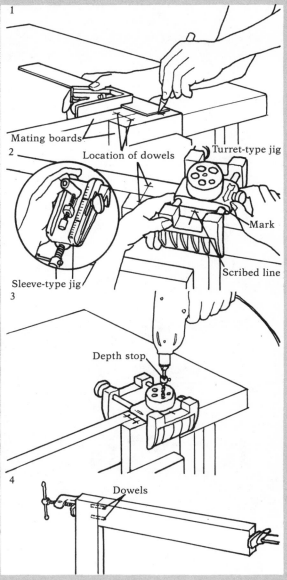

1. Measure and mark desired center points of dowel holes in one board.

2. Drill dowel holes to correct depth, exactly perpendicular to surface of board.

3. Insert dowel centers in holes, then mark mating board by sliding both boards together, using straightedge as guide.

4. Separate boards, remove centers, then drill holes in mating board. Apply glue and insert dowels. Clamp and glue boards together until dry.

1. Clamp mating boards face to face, then square lines across edges of both to show dowel locations.

2. Adjust and position jig according to manufacturer's instructions, usually by aligning mark on jig with lines from step 1.

3. Drill holes to correct depth in each board.

4. Apply glue, insert dowels, then glue and clamp boards together until dry.

22. Apply glue to one end of each hinge pin, then tap the pins into the holes in the hinge bodies.

23. Test-fit the assembled hinges in the mortised frame members and stepped pockets. Trim pins if necessary.

25. Use a backsaw to cut across the grain of each piece to make the ¼-in.-wide segments (the inlays) each 1¼-in. long. Only one end of each inlay should have a radius; the other end should be square.

26. Apply two coats of brush-on lacquer or polyurethane to the frames, hinges, and molding strips. Do not apply finish to the inlays at this time.

27. Reinsert the hinges into the mortised frames. Be sure the pins fit into the ½-in.-deep stepped pockets.

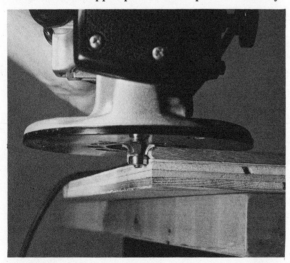

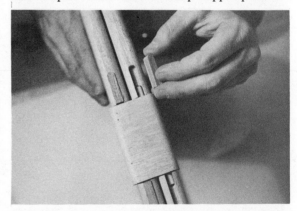

24. For the inlays which cover the hinge pins, you will need 24 pieces of clear mahogany, each ¼ × ¼ × 1¼ in. To make them quickly, begin by routing a ⅛-in. radius across the ends of several wide pieces of ¼-in.-thick stock, then saw 1¼-in.-long kerfs, ¼ in. apart, along the grain of each piece. Use a thin-bladed saw, such as a saber saw, which will make straight cuts.

28. Glue the inlays in place with the radiused end of each inlay fitted into the radiused end of each pocket. Keep glue from getting on the hinges or pins.

29. Sand the inlays so they are flush with the surface of each frame. Now apply finish to inlays and sanded areas. See Wood Finishing, p. 162, for complete finishing instructions.

30. To attach the panel material to each of the three frames, first position each panel in the rabbets on the back of each frame. Be sure the front side of the fabric faces the front of the frames, and lay out all three panels before attaching any of them to see that all will line up according to the diagram and photo on p. 78. Using a heavy-duty stapler, attach the fabric to the frames with ¼-in.-long staples, spaced evenly around each frame.

33. Use a razor knife to trim any excess fabric from the ends of each panel so that no loose strands protrude between the upper and lower frames and the molding.

31. Apply a line of fray-preventing fluid (available at weaving stores) across the top and bottom of each panel to keep the ends of the woven material from unraveling.

32. Predrill pilot holes in each molding strip, then nail the top and bottom molding strips in place on each frame. Use ⅝-in.-long wire nails, and set them about ¹/₁₆ in. below the surface.

34. Attach the side molding strips in place, also with ⅝-in.-long wire nails. Space the brads evenly to secure the molding, and set them as in step 32.

35. Fill all the brad holes with wood putty, stained to match the color of the molding strips.

Clothes-Drying Rack

Wedged-tenon joinery
Laminated mortises

This folding rack for drying clothes is designed so that articles may hang from each of the outer racks without those on the upper rungs touching those below. When not in use, the outer racks, which pivot, fold against the center rack, which is firmly pegged in place. Coated with durable, waterproof, clear polyurethane, this functional yet decorative home accessory can withstand existence out of doors — on the back porch, say — as easily as it can inside, next to the wood stove, or in the kitchen, laundry, or utility room. Wet clothes or other items won't hurt the finish, either, and since the chains that link each pivoting rack are made of brass, even they won't suffer from excessive dampness. Unobtrusive nylon furniture glides are fastened to the bottom of the clothes rack's bases and provide a steady four-point surface on which the rack can rest without wobbling.

As a project for developing your skills in woodworking, the clothes-drying rack can be classed as intermediate. It draws on basic skills as well as those that were the featured techniques of previous projects and prepares the way for projects yet to come. The stack-laminated, mortised bases you'll be building here, and the simple wedged-tenon joints that are also featured, introduce techniques for making complicated versions of these joints which you'll find later on, should you choose to build the dining table (see p. 108) or the double bed (p. 132). And working here in pine — a softwood — will build your confidence and expertise for working later on in the hardwoods that the more advanced projects require.

Of course, you can build this rack of any wood. Maple, birch, cherry, hickory, ash, or even oak would do as well. Regardless of the wood you choose, however, you'll find that the special design features of this project make it an elegant expression of your craftsmanship.

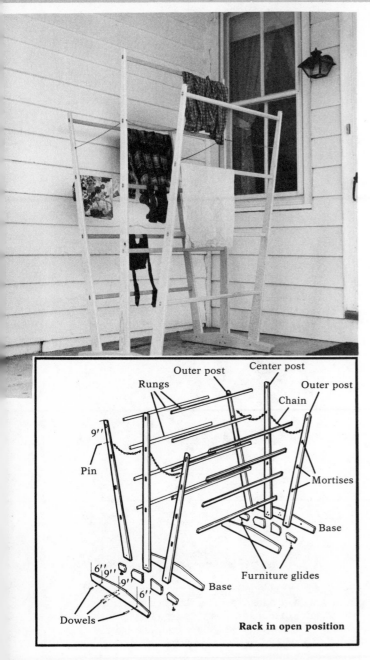

Rack in open position

Labels: Outer post, Center post, Rungs, Outer post, Chain, 9'', Pin, Mortises, Base, 6'', 9'', 9', 6', Furniture glides, Base, Dowels

What you will need

6 pcs. #2 pine, ¾'' × 3¼'' × 30''
2 pcs. #2 pine, ¾'' × 3'' × 68½''
4 pcs. #2 pine, ¾'' × 3'' × 58''
12 pcs. #2 pine, ½'' × 1'' × 3'
1 pc. walnut, ½'' × 1'' × 10'' (see step 20)
1 pc. hardwood dowel, ⅜'' × 3' (see step 12)
6d finishing nails
brass sash chain, 6'
4 nylon furniture glides
white or yellow glue
wood putty
polyurethane
saber saw
table saw
router
drill
long-nosed pliers
C-clamps
hand and measuring tools

Before you begin

One of the most important construction features of the clothes-drying rack is the assembly of the base pieces. Although each of the two bases appear to be shaped from a single, thick block of solid wood, actually they are made up of three thicknesses of thinner stock, glued together according to the process of stack lamination described on p. 60 and also on p. 91. To form the mortises—the holes running through each base into which are fitted the vertical posts of the rack—sections are merely cut out of the middle member of each set of base pieces to be laminated, before they are glued together. The spaces formed by the missing sections yield the mortises.

This technique makes it easy to produce with precision mortises whose inside faces must be cut to certain angles, such as is the case with the drying rack, whose outer vertical posts must be able to pivot both toward and away from the center. Trying to carve these angled faces accurately from a solid block, using a drill and chisels, would be a real test of cabinetmaking skill, and a time-consuming one at that. With the laminated method, the entire process involves only the accurate use of a try square and a crosscut saw. Cut each piece to shape according to the diagram at right, then mark the positions of the middle inserts before gluing-up. Glue the inserts to one of the outer pieces first; when dry, glue on the other outer piece.

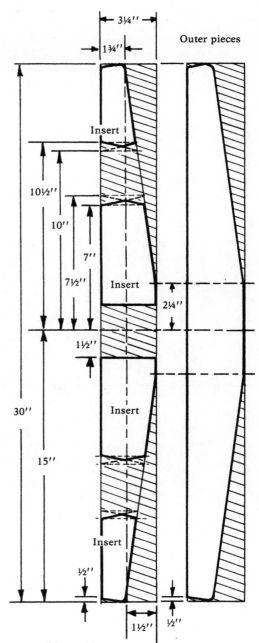

Layout of base pieces

Step-by-step instructions

1. Cut six pieces of #2 pine, each ¾ × 3¼ × 30 in., for the stack-laminated bases (see p. 87). Each base is made up of three thicknesses of wood. Choose the four clearest pieces of stock and mark them to be the outside faces of each base, then mark the remaining two pieces for use as middles, to be inserted between the outer faces.

2. On each of the pieces selected as an insert, use a tape measure and try square to locate and mark a perpendicular centerline across the face of each board. The centerline should be 15 in. from each end. Also on both boards, mark additional perpendiculars across the face of each, 1½ in. to each side of the centerline, so that you lay out the 3-in.-wide section to be cut from the center of each insert to form the mortises for the rack's center posts.

3. Measure from the centerline of each board 7 in. along the bottom in both directions, and mark the points with a sharp pencil. Also mark points 7½ in, 10 in., and 10½ in. from each centerline. Do the same along each board's top edge. Now refer to the diagram on p. 87 once again, and carefully scribe straight lines connecting diagonal pairs of points as shown, so that your marks resemble two Xs, as in the photo above.

4. Use a backsaw and scrap block to cut vertically through the boards along each scribed line. Label the pieces to be used *insert*; discard waste sections.

5. Position each group of insert sections on the inside face of one of each pair of boards between which they will be glued, then trace around their outlines for reference. Glue and clamp the inserts to the boards. When dry, glue on the remaining boards to complete the stack-lamination of each base.

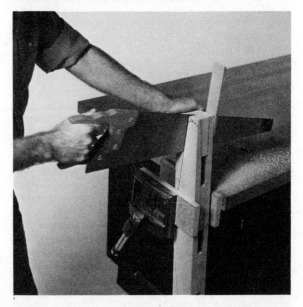

6. Lay out and cut the tapered top and end surfaces of each laminated base. To mark the top surface of each base, measure out from the centerline 2¼ in. in both directions, then measure down 1½ in. from the top along each end. Connect the two points on each side of the board's centerline with a straight line, which should slope downward, as shown in the photo above. On the bottom of each base, measure from the ends toward the center a distance of ½ in., and also up along each end a distance of 1¾ in. Connect these points to mark the taper at the ends. When the lines are laid out, use a crosscut saw and a straightedge guide to cut each taper. Then, with a router and a ¼-in. rounding-over bit, radius all the edges of each base. Smooth the ends to a gentle curve with a file.

7. Cut four pieces of #2 pine, each ¾ × 3 × 58 in., for the rack's outer pairs of vertical posts.

8. Cut two pieces of #2 pine, each ¾ × 3 × 68½ in., for the center pair of vertical posts.

9. Lay out and cut the taper on each of the six posts. First, measure in from each edge toward the post's lengthwise centerline a distance of ¾ in. The two points you mark should be 1½ in. apart. Now connect each point with a long, straight line to the outer edge nearest it on the opposite end of the board, so that when cut, the posts will be 3 in. wide at one end, and 1½ in. wide at the other. Saw along the outside of each line to remove the waste. (If you use a portable saw, such as the saber saw shown in the photo above, you will have to interrupt each cut several times to reposition the clamps.) Then radius the edges of each post with a router and a ¼-in. rounding-over bit, as in step 6.

10. Mark the positions of the mortises to be made in the vertical posts (p. 86). Measure 2 in. from the top (narrow) end of each post to mark the center of the first mortise, then mark the centers of three more mortises, each 14 in. apart. Each mortise is made by drilling several holes a small distance apart, then removing the waste between. Drill out the mortises, using a ⅜-in.-dia. bit.

11. Each mortise should measure 1 in. long and ½ in. wide. Use a saber saw to cut away the excess wood between the drilled holes, then smooth out the inside surfaces, using a file. Be careful not to mar or accidentally round-over the mortise edges.

12. Cut ten pieces of ⅜-in.-dia. hardwood dowel, each 2⅜ in. long.

13. Place the vertical posts in the mortises in each of the base pieces. The bottom surface of each center post should be flush with the bottom surface of each base; the outer posts, however, should be fitted into place as if the rack were in its open position (p. 86), and only the outside corners of the posts should be flush with the bottom of the base.

14. Drill ⅜-in.-dia. holes through the base and positioned posts according to the locations shown in the diagram on p. 86. Glue and insert dowels into the center holes of each base to secure the middle posts, then insert—but do *not* glue—a dowel into each of the outer post holes.

15. After the glue has dried on the center dowels, trim all of the dowels flush with the surface of the base using a backsaw or chisel and sandpaper. Be careful

not to split the dowels. The best method for trimming them is to work your way around their entire circumference with whatever tool you are using, and then snap the excess off in the center, rather than cutting straight through from one side to the other. Do not attempt to trim dowels with more than ⅛ in. excess using a chisel. When using a backsaw, tape a piece of cardboard or scrap veneer to the area surrounding the dowel to protect the surface of the base piece from scratches.

16. Cut 12 pieces of #2 pine, each ½ × 1 × 3 in., for the rungs of the rack.

17. Use a router and a ¼-in.-dia. rounding-over bit to machine a ¼-in. radius, as in step 6, on all long edges of each rung. Do not radius the end grain portions of the rungs, since these must remain square in order to fit flush against the outside faces of the posts when the rack is assembled and the joints are wedged tight.

18. Sand each rung smooth.

19. Saw pairs of slots (kerfs) in the ends of each rung to accept the wedges. To make the slots, use a sharp backsaw, dovetail saw, or other fine-toothed saw. Each kerf should be slightly more than 1/16 in. wide and ⅝ in. deep, and should divide the rung-end into three approximately equal parts. Be careful not to cut the slots too deeply into the rungs or they will show on the inside—where the rungs emerge from the posts—after the piece is assembled.

Wedged-Tenon Joinery

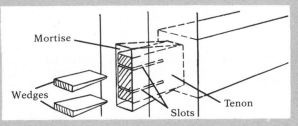

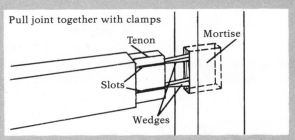

Pull joint together with clamps

Mortise-and-tenon joints always require precise layout and cutting to make them strong as well as neat in appearance. For beginners, however, reinforcing mortise-and-tenon joints with wedges often is a way of remedying loose-fitting joints caused by inexperience. Loose joints can be made strong, and strong joints even stronger, by installing wedges either in the manner shown above—where slots are cut into the tenon to receive them—or as shown below.

Fox wedges are not really a beginner's technique, since it is hard to estimate the correct length and thickness to make the wedges. They are used when the tenon does not protrude all the way through the mortised piece. Properly made, the joint can't be pulled apart, even if the glue fails.

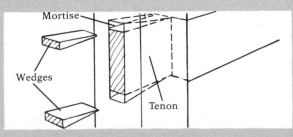

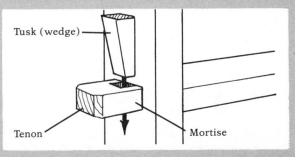

Wedges inserted above and below the tenon mean you don't have to slot the tenon beforehand. They greatly strengthen any mortise-and-tenon joint but are a particularly good solution to ill-fitting joints that have already been glued together.

Tusk-wedged (usually called tusk-tenoned) joints are excellent for use on items which require frequent disassembly or are subject to great stress, such as trestle tables and beds. Since the wedging action of the tusk is very powerful, ample wood should surround the mortise to prevent splitting.

Laminated Mortises

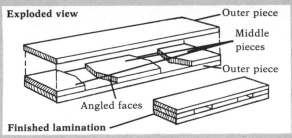

Stack-laminating complicated mortises in thick—or even relatively thin—stock is not only an excellent method for beginners lacking experience with hand tools, but is also a less time-consuming and often more

precise way of obtaining accurate results even for expert professional woodworkers. Usually, three thicknesses of stock are used, sandwiched and glued together to form the finished piece. The two outer thicknesses are left whole to form the sides of the piece; the inner thickness is cut into sections, some of which are discarded, so that the spaces they leave behind form the mortises. The two parallel-sided mortise faces are automatically formed by the two outer thicknesses of stock. To cut the other two faces, simply lay out the angle you desire across the face of the middle piece, and then cut straight down along the lines you mark, using a crosscut saw. When glued-up with the other pieces, these edges will form the angled sides.

20. Cut 48 pieces of walnut, each ⅛ × ½ × ⅝ in., for wedges to be inserted into the slots cut in the rungs. To produce a number of wedges quickly, first rip ⅛-in.-wide strips from the ½-in.-thick stock. Mark off ⅝-in. lengths along each strip, then cut each wedge by placing a sharp chisel on the mark and striking firmly with a mallet. Protect the surface of the workbench with a piece of scrap wood.

21. Apply white or yellow glue to the rungs, then insert them in place so their ends are flush with the outside faces of each upright post. No clamping is needed.

22. Insert a walnut wedge—with a small amount of glue applied—into each slot sawn in the ends of the rungs, then tap each wedge into place with a hammer. Strike squarely to avoid splitting or breaking the wedges or marring the posts. Drive each wedge into its slot until strong resistance is felt or the wedge is driven flush with the end of the rung.

23. Carefully saw, chisel, or file the ends off of any wedges that protrude, then sand the rung-ends smooth and flush with the outside faces of the posts.

24. Before righting the rack, drill ⅜-in.-dia. holes in each post to accept the chains. Locate the holes according to the diagram on p. 86. The holes on each outside post are centered 9 in. down from the top of the post, and those on the center posts are located 16 in. from the top, even with the center of the second rung. Drill each hole to a depth of ½ in.

25. For the pins (trimmed 6d finishing nails; see step 28) which fasten the chains in place, drill tiny ³/₃₂-in.-dia. holes on the *inside* face of each post to intersect at right angles the larger holes drilled in step 24. Drill only through the inside of each post, and stop when the bit breaks through into the larger hole.

26. Apply two coats of polyurethane to the drying rack. Sand the finish smooth when completely dry. See Wood Finishing, p. 162, for complete finishing instructions.

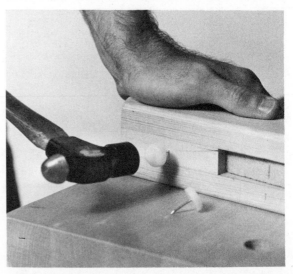

27. Install two nylon furniture glides on the bottom of each base to prevent the rack from wobbling. Center the glides across the thickness of each base, and tap them into place 1½ in. from each end.

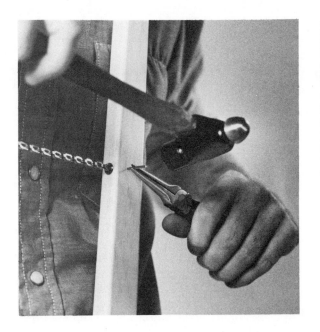

28. Cut four pieces of brass sash chain, each 16½ in. long. Also cut the heads off eight 6d finishing nails. Use the nails as pins to fasten the chains to the posts.
29. Stand the rack upright on its bases. Insert an end of one of the chain lengths into one of the ⅜-in.-dia. holes drilled in step 24, then insert one of the headless nails into the $3/32$-in.-dia. hole on the inside face of the post, and thread the pin through a link of chain. Hold the pin in place with long-nosed pliers, and tap it into the outside face of the post with a hammer. Repeat this procedure for all the lengths of chain connecting all the posts.
30. Snip or file off the protruding end of each pin, then drive the pins below the surface, using a nail set (p. 74). Fill the areas above the pins with wood putty.

Wall-Mounted Telephone Cabinet

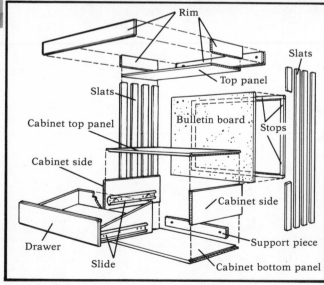

Drawer construction
Drawer hanging

Here is a hanging telephone cabinet that looks attractive in the living room, not just in the kitchen. Its special design incorporates a variety of features, yet its unobtrusive good looks keep it from being just another gadget. Mounting is simple; four long screws through the back of the cabinet hold it securely to the wall studs.

The shelf on which the telephone rests is large enough to hold a message pad as well. The back of the cabinet is cork bulletin board, which provides a handy place to pin messages, and a tidy one as well. The sides of the cabinet, slatted to give a lightweight appearance, keep anything pinned to the bulletin board all but out of sight. The flat panel that forms the top of the cabinet serves as a small shelf for miscellaneous items—there is a rim around its perimeter which makes it a perfect catchall for odds and ends—or as a surface on which to set a small vase or other decorative object. The drawer beneath the phone shelf is designed especially to hold an open phone book and is the cabinet's most special feature. The slanted drawer bottom props the book up at an angle for easy reading.

This project involves skills which are of intermediate complexity—no new techniques are featured—but the precision involved in measuring and working to close tolerances is advanced. You will probably find the drawer most challenging. It must be made to fit within the cabinet, not so wide that it binds, yet also not so narrow that the slides, which are in two halves—one part attached to the drawer side and the other to the inside of the cabinet—won't fit properly. It is best, in fact, to purchase the drawer slides before you begin to work on the drawer itself. That way, the exact thickness of the slides, as well as their particular mechanism, can be taken into account. Ideally, the drawer front should be about ⅛ inch narrower than the cabinet opening. The lips at each side of the drawer front will cover the gaps and hide the drawer slides.

The telephone cabinet shown on these pages is made of solid mahogany. Surprisingly, its cost is very often comparable to furniture-grade pine, and is almost always easier to obtain in clear stock. To give the finished piece a uniform hue, a wax- or oil-base stain works well as a finish, covered simply with paste wax, or with lacquer or polyurethane for extra stain resistance.

Drawer — front detail

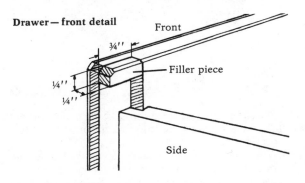

Drawer — exploded view

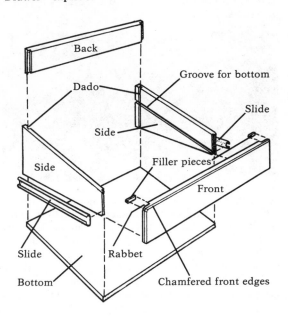

What you will need

8 pcs. clear mahogany, ½'' × 5½'' × 24'' (see steps 1 and 5)
2 pcs. clear mahogany, ½'' × 5⅛'' × 15''
2 pcs. clear mahogany, ½'' × 4¼'' × 14¼''
1 pc. clear mahogany, ¼'' × 3¾'' × 20⅞''
2 pcs. clear mahogany, ½'' × 2'' × 22''
1 pc. clear mahogany, ½'' × 2'' × 19⅜''
2 pcs. clear mahogany, ½'' × 2'' × 10''
1 pc. mahogany, ½'' × 1¾'' × 18'' (clear not necessary)
8 pcs. clear mahogany, ½'' × 1½'' × 2'
2 pcs. mahogany, ½'' × ½'' × 22'' (clear not necessary)
2 pcs. mahogany, ½'' × ½'' × 15⅜'' (clear not necessary)
2 pcs. clear mahogany, ¼'' × ¼'' × ¾''
1 pc. hardboard (Masonite) ¼'' × 14¼'' × 19⅜'' (see step 33)
1 pc. rigid cork board, ⅝'' × 16⅜'' × 22''
4 #10 flathead wood screws, 2''
1 pair full-extension drawer slides, 14''
white or yellow glue
wax- or oil-base stain (optional; see step 40)
brush-on lacquer
table saw
router (router table, optional)
drill
hand and measuring tools

Drawer — side view

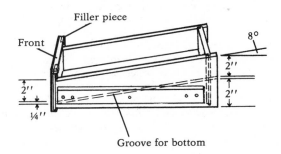

Step-by-step instructions

1. Begin by making the top and bottom panels of the drawer cabinet. For each panel you will need a piece of clear mahogany, $\frac{1}{2} \times 15 \times 22$ in., which you must ordinarily make by edge-gluing several pieces of narrower stock (see p. 45), say, three pieces, each $\frac{1}{2} \times 5\frac{1}{2} \times 24$ in. The additional width and length allow for exact jointing of the edges prior to gluing and for exact trimming to length afterward. Use white or yellow glue to join the edges, then plane and sand the panels flat.

2. Cut two pieces of clear mahogany, each $\frac{1}{2} \times 5\frac{1}{8} \times 15$ in., for the sides of the drawer cabinet.

3. Use a router (p. 42) or table saw to make rabbets, $\frac{1}{4}$ in. deep and $\frac{1}{2}$ in. wide, on the ends of each top and bottom panel. When assembled, the sidepieces fit into the rabbets, between the top and bottom panels.

4. Glue the pieces of the drawer cabinet together and clamp them securely (p. 44). Scrap wood next to the clamps prevents damage to the workpiece.

5. Make the flat panel that is the upper part of the telephone cabinet by edge-gluing two pieces of $\frac{1}{2} \times 5\frac{1}{2} \times 24$-in. clear mahogany as in step 1, and trim to obtain one piece, $\frac{1}{2} \times 10 \times 21\frac{1}{2}$ in.

6. For the pieces which form the rim around the panel, cut two pieces of clear mahogany, each $\frac{1}{2} \times 2 \times 10$ in., for the sides; and two pieces of clear mahogany, each $\frac{1}{2} \times 2 \times 22$ in., for the front and back.

7. Use a router or table saw as in step 3 to make rabbets, $\frac{1}{4}$ in. deep and $\frac{1}{2}$ in. wide, on the ends of front and back rim pieces. Also cut rabbets with similar dimensions along the bottom inside edges of all four

rim pieces, so that when assembled, the panel made in step 5 will be recessed flush with the lower edges of the completed rim.

8. Assemble the rim pieces around the panel without glue. Use a square to be sure that the outside corners form right angles.

9. Turn the assembly upside down, then glue and clamp the pieces in place. Protect the mahogany surfaces with strips of scrap wood. Be sure clamping pressure is even on all sides so that the panel does not develop a twist during gluing. When glue is dry, chip off excess.

10. Using a hand-held router or one mounted beneath a router table (see Making a Router Table, p. 43), and a chamfering bit with a pilot bearing, machine a $\frac{1}{8} \times \frac{1}{8}$-in. chamfer (bevel) on all exposed edges of the drawer cabinet. To chamfer the inside edges of the cabinet using a hand-held router, either clamp the cabinet in a vise, with the cabinet opening facing up, or clamp the cabinet on one of its wide panels so the opening is flush with the side of the bench and facing away from the bench top. (In this second position, hold the router on its side and move it counterclockwise.) On a router table, turn the cabinet so its opening is face down on the table surface. Even though the bit will be hidden as you move the cabinet in a clockwise direction around it, the pilot bearing will ensure accuracy.

11. As in the previous step, machine a ⅛ × ⅛-in. chamfer on all exposed edges of the upper panel and rim assembly. First cut the chamfers on the four inside edges of the rim pieces, then cut their outside vertical edges. Finish by cutting chamfers along the top and bottom outside edges of all rim pieces, which should remedy any chipping-out of the end grain which may have occurred.

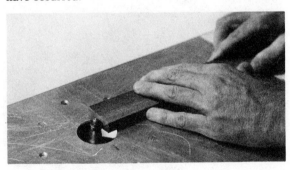

12. Cut eight pieces of clear mahogany, each ½ in. × 1½ in. × 2 ft., to make the slats for the sides. These will connect the drawer cabinet to the upper panel and rim.

13. Use a hand-held or table-mounted router to cut ⅛ × ⅛-in. chamfers around the edges of each *end* of the eight side slats. If you are using a table-mounted router, begin by cutting the chamfers on the ½-in.-thick edges before machining across the 1½-in. widths. Due to the narrowness of the stock, if the width is chamfered first, there will be no bearing surface for the

router when it comes time to chamfer the thickness. To chamfer the thickness-edge of each slat, place the slat on edge against the table surface. To chamfer the width, lay the slat on its wide sides.

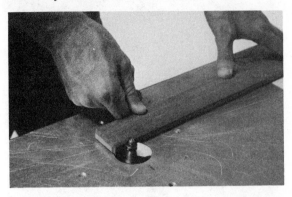

14. Now use the router to machine ⅛ × ⅛-in. chamfers on the four long edges of each side slat. If you are using a router table, pass the pieces from right to left across the bit. If the router is hand-held, move it from left to right along the work.

15. Glue the side slats to the drawer cabinet and upper panel assembly. Position the rear slats flush with the backs of both the cabinet and the rimmed panel. Position the foremost slats flush with the front of the panel's rim and 4½ in. from the front edge of the drawer cabinet. Space the remaining slats 1½ in. apart between those already in place.

16. Cut two pieces of mahogany, each ½ × ½ × 22 in., for the horizontal bulletin board stops.

17. Cut two pieces mahogany, each ½ × ½ × 15⅜ in., for the vertical bulletin board stops.

18. Glue and clamp the horizontal stops across the top and bottom of the rear opening between the drawer cabinet and top panel, flush with the back edge.

19. Glue and clamp the vertical stops flush with the back edge of the two rear side slats.

clearance holes through both the support piece and the rear rim piece (in the top panel) that will align the cabinet with wall studs in which to anchor the 2 in. #10 screws used for mounting. To do this, first locate the wall studs (usually positioned so their centers occur at 16-in. intervals when measured from a corner), then hold the support piece level, against the spot on the wall you wish the cabinet to occupy. Mark lines across the top edge of the piece to show where it crosses the center of each hidden stud. Using a try square, transfer these marks to the flat sides of the piece, and then drill a single 3/16-in.-dia. hole centered on each line to accept the screws. You may then use the support piece as a template for drilling holes in the rim piece. Do this by centering the support piece over the rim piece so that each end is an equal distance from the outside of the cabinet. Insert a nail into the holes in the support piece, and prick marks on the rim piece. When finished, glue and clamp the support piece into place, flush against the back edge of the bottom panel of the drawer cabinet, and centered exactly as it was when used for marking the rim piece. Double-check the alignment of the holes in the two pieces, then drill a 3/16-in.-dia. hole at each mark in the rim piece.

20. Cut one piece of mahogany, ½ × 1¾ × 18 in., for the support piece. At this time you may also wish to determine the location of the finished cabinet and drill

21. Cut one piece of cork, ⅝ × 16⅜ × 22 in., for the bulletin board. Place it against the bulletin board stops, then glue and clamp in place. To apply pressure without damaging the side slats, use wood blocks which extend higher than the slats. Note: If you plan to stain the cabinet, perform this step after finishing is completed (see step 40).

(Continued on page 104)

Drawer Construction

Being able to make neat, well-fitting drawers is one of the marks of an accomplished cabinetmaker. Well-constructed drawers slide in and out of their cabinets smoothly and without any tendency to move to one side or the other. The joinery at the corners is flawless, whatever the type of joints used, and the sides, front, and back always meet at precise right angles. These are the basic requirements! In addition, close-fitting drawers often need to have allowances designed into their construction for seasonal shrinkage and expansion, and some cabinetmakers even taper drawers very slightly so they are narrower at the back than at the front to insure perfect fits.

One of the most important considerations in making drawers is keeping the construction style of the drawer consistent with the style and quality of construction used to build the larger piece of furniture that surrounds it. Basically, there are three levels of drawer construction; they might be termed simple, contemporary, and classic.

A simple drawer is usually constructed of butt-joined pieces and is fastened together primarily with nails and glue. A simple drawer's appearance, however, need not be crude.

Contemporary drawers may be singled out as those which are built more solidly and with greater effort than simple drawers, but whose joinery techniques generally are based more on the ease and speed with which they can be cut by ordinary or factory power tools than on their ultimate strength and beauty. Most often drawers of this style are perfectly adequate for their intended purpose. They are almost always strong (modern glues have done away with most of the traditional problems of drawer-joinery) and economical to build; they look nice, and they do not require an inordinate amount of time to construct.

Classic drawers, on the other hand, generally do, even if you have the necessary equipment (usually a dovetail-template assembly for use with a router; see p. 42) to perform the task with power tools. Invariably, classic drawers have dovetailed corners for the last word in strength, durability, and design appeal.

Of course, all three styles of drawers may have either a lipped front, where the ends of the drawer front project beyond the thickness of the sides, and sometimes even to the outside edges of the cabinet itself, or be flush-fronted, resembling an ordinary box or tray whose sides meet edge-to-end at right angles. Drawer fronts may also be dropped, that is, project below the level of the bottom panel, usually in order to hide parts of a cabinet-mounted sliding mechanism underneath the drawer.

SIMPLE DRAWER

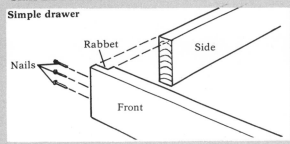

Simple drawer

Simple drawer construction relies on nails and glue for strength. Rabbet the drawer front for a neat appearance, and attach the sides with nails entering the end grain of the drawer front. The corner joints will remain fairly strong since the most frequent stress, occurring when the drawer is pushed or pulled, is always at right angles to the nails.

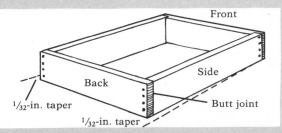

The rear of the drawer is usually butt-joined with flush corners. Nails may be installed in either direction, since the drawer back receives little stress. When making drawers which must fit closely against cabinet sides, cut the drawer back 1/16'' less than the length between the rabbets of the drawer's front, to produce slight narrowing of the drawer toward the rear.

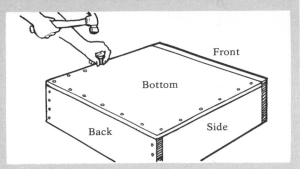

Cut drawer bottom to fit flush with all four sides, or to butt against dropped lower edge of drawer front, as shown. Attach bottom to lower edges of sides, back, and front (if applicable) with common or finishing nails. Be sure to place and drive nails accurately.

(Continued on next page)

Drawer Construction—*Continued*

Contemporary drawer

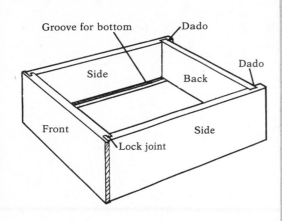

Mitered lock joint

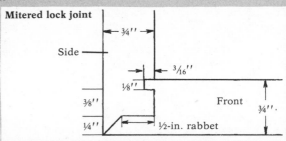

A mitered lock joint is best cut on a table saw. First cut a dado in the sidepiece, to a depth of one-quarter of the board's thickness. Then cut a groove in the end of the drawer front, as deep as the full thickness of the side-piece. Rabbet the end of the sidepiece. Measure (you won't be able to fully assemble the joint), then pare away the inner tongue to fit the dado in the sidepiece. Make the 45° miter cuts last. Trim the inner tongue for a perfect fit.

CONTEMPORARY DRAWER

Contemporary drawers are of a higher quality of construction than simple drawers. Often they show very fine craftsmanship and should not be thought of as mediocre. The interlocking joints used in making drawers of this type range from simple to quite complex, but all are based on the ability of power tools to make the cuts required. As a rule, contemporary draw-ers are glued together; nails are almost never used. Drawer bottoms are fitted into grooves located in the drawer's sides and front and are permitted to "float" without fasteners, which prevents splitting or warping due to seasonal changes in moisture content.

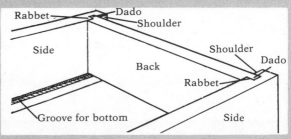

To fasten the back to the sides, use a combination rabbet and dado. Make rabbet cuts across the ends of the back piece (on the inside face), and dadoes—cut very slightly deeper than the tongues of the rabbets—along the inside faces of the sides. Leave ample wood at the ends of each side to form sturdy shoulders behind the back pieces.

Lock joint

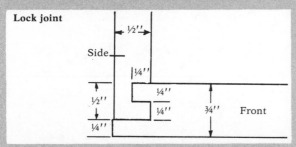

A lock joint is strong and easy to make with either a router or a power saw. Begin by cutting a dado in the sidepiece. Next, cut a groove in the drawer front twice the depth of the sidepiece dado. Carefully pare away the inner tongue until a perfect fit is achieved. On a drawer made with a front of ¾-in. stock, dimensions for cuts are as shown.

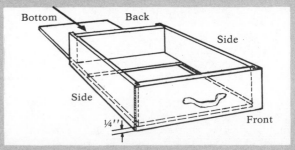

Fit the drawer's bottom panel into grooves cut in the sides and front, about ¼'' up from the bottom edge of each piece. On a contemporary drawer, the back piece nor-mally extends down only to the level of the bottom panel and so is not grooved. The bottom is installed after the other pieces are assembled and is usually left unfastened.

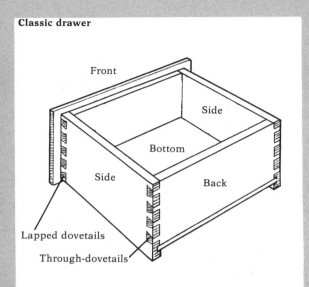

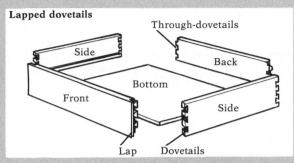

On lipped-front drawers, dovetails are the lap variety so end grain of tails is hidden from view. When laying out pins and tails of joints, tails should occur at top and bottom. Grooves for bottom panel should be cut after ends of each piece are notched.

CLASSIC DRAWER

Classic drawers have dovetailed corners (see p. 150). In the front, the dovetails are most commonly lapped; that is, made so they are visible only from the side. Occasionally—on flush-front drawers only, of course—through-dovetails, which are visible from the front as well as the side, are used, as much for appearance as for strength. At the back of the drawer, through-dovetails are always the rule. The bottom panel of a classic drawer is held by grooves on three sides as on a contemporary drawer. Since dovetails are not well suited to plywood, classic drawers are most often made of solid wood.

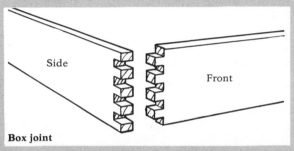

Box joint

Box joints (also called finger joints) are excellent substitutes for through-dovetails. They are easy and quick to make, using either a router or table saw. Large surface area for gluing gives them as much strength as dovetails. If you wish, use wood for the sides that is lighter or darker than for the drawer front, to obtain a contrasting checkerboard effect at corners.

Through-dovetails

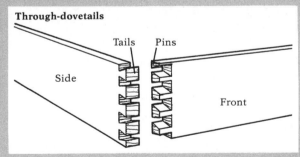

Through-dovetails are easiest to make. Cut on drawer fronts, they look particularly well if their pins taper almost to points. To resist stress most effectively, the tails, which appear rectangular when viewed from the end, should be made on the ends of the drawer's sidepieces.

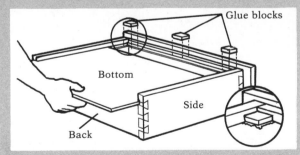

The drawer's bottom panel slides into grooves after other pieces are assembled and glued. To prevent the panel from moving or developing a rattle due to extreme seasonal dryness, use glue blocks to fasten it in place along the front edge only. Any shrinkage that occurs will thus be at the rear of the drawer.

Drawer Hanging

There are three main ways to hang drawers: with simple corner guides, with a center guide, and with side rails. To a certain extent, the system you choose should be based on the design and function of the piece of furniture you are building. However, the way you plan to hang the drawers should be an integral part of your design-thinking right from the start and should be one of the earliest decisions you make about how to proceed. If you choose to hang drawers using commercially made fixtures, you will do well to have these in hand even before you start building. Since it is impossible to trim these to fit, you must actually plan your work around their fixed dimensions.

Other features to include when planning drawer installation are kickers which keep the drawers from tilting forward and possibly spilling their contents when fully extended and stops which prevent drawers from being pushed too far back into the cabinet. On flush-front drawers without stops, this usually means only an unsightly appearance where the drawer front meets the edges of the cabinet opening. On lipped-front drawers, however, repeated hard contact between the sides of the cabinet opening and the inside faces of the drawer overhangs can weaken the drawer's front corner joints.

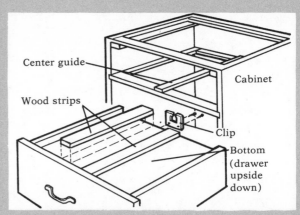

Center guides can be used on drawers with dropped fronts in cabinets whose interior framing acts as side supports for the drawers as well. The guide is a strip of wood attached between the front and back of the cabinet. Two additional strips of wood are fastened across the bottom of the drawer, evenly spaced on either side of the drawer's centerline, so that the guide strip fits closely—but not tightly—between them when the drawer is in place. Plastic clips that extend below the bottom surface of the drawer and fit over the guide strip may be purchased. These keep the drawer from tilting forward when fully open. Commercially made guide assemblies are available at hardware and cabinetmaking supply stores.

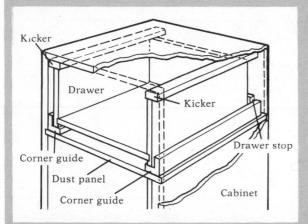

Simple wooden corner guides run between the front and back pieces of the cabinet and provide support for drawers as well as a bearing surface upon which they may slide. Usually corner guides rest on the upper surfaces of the cabinet's interior framing or dust panels, but on light work such as small tables, the corner guides may act as framing as well. Small wooden blocks at the rear of the guides act as stops. Strips of wood above the drawer are kickers. Wax or silicone on the surfaces of the guides allows the drawers to slide easily.

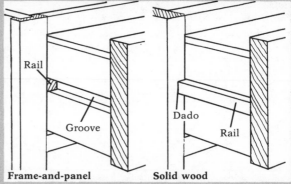

Frame-and-panel   **Solid wood**

Side rails are a means of hanging drawers in cabinets which offer no interior framing for support. On cabinets whose construction is frame-and-panel, attach the rails to the cabinet sides, and cut grooves in the sides of the drawers for the rails to fit. On solid wood cabinets, attach rails to the drawers instead, and cut dadoes in the cabinet sides. Side rail systems such as these will work for small drawers. On large drawers, however, and those which become heavy when filled, increased friction makes side rails a poor choice. Commercially made slides with rollers are more effective.

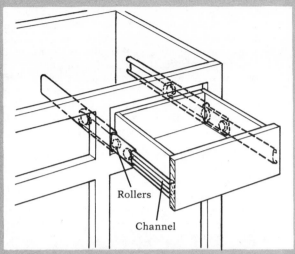

Rollers

Channel

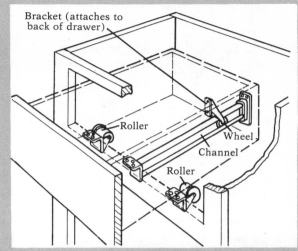

Bracket (attaches to back of drawer)

Roller

Wheel

Channel

Roller

Metal drawer slides are excellent for moderately heavy drawers, as well as items such as sliding trays and pull-out shelves for stereo turntables. Varieties which allow the drawer to be pulled completely out of the cabinet without falling are called full-extension drawer slides. Most metal slides have nylon or plastic rollers which attach to the drawer and ride in channels attached to the cabinet sides. One of their best features is their super-smooth operation. When installing slides, the fixtures on both sides must be correctly aligned, otherwise the drawers will stick. Slides must be used with lipped drawers to hide the ends of the fixtures.

Center slides with auxiliary rollers are suitable for very heavy drawers such as those in filing cabinets. The single central slide is mounted between the front and back of the cabinet, usually below the drawer but occasionally above it. A bracket with a wheel attached is fastened to the rear of the drawer and rolls back and forth along a channel in

the slide. Additional rollers mounted to the front of the cabinet frame support the drawer as it is extended forward. On very wide drawers, two slides may be used, parallel to each other and spaced evenly some distance apart on each side of the drawer's centerline.

HOW TO MAKE SELF-CLOSING FILE DRAWERS

By tapering the bottoms of the drawer sides, large file cabinet drawers fitted with central slides and auxiliary rollers can be made to close by themselves. Plan the cabinet opening to be at least ½'' taller than the height of the drawer sides, and design the drawer fronts to extend above the sides to cover the opening when the drawer is closed. Cut a gentle taper beginning 5'' from the front edge of the drawer, narrowing the width of the sidepieces by ⅜'' where the sides meet the front. Install the center slide, but fasten it ¼'' lower in the back than in the front. The drawer will close by itself when pushed to within 5'' of the opening.

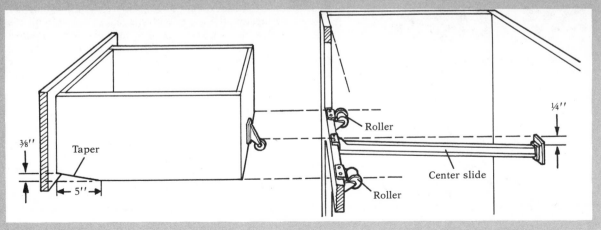

⅜''

Taper

5''

Roller

Center slide

Roller

¼''

22. Begin making the drawer by cutting one piece of clear mahogany, ½ × 3¼ × 20⅞ in., for the drawer front. (By designing the drawer front to be less than the height of the cabinet opening, a finger-space is provided instead of a drawer-pull for opening the drawer. See the diagrams on p. 95.)

23. Using a hand-held or table-mounted router and a chamfering bit with a pilot bearing, first refer to the diagrams on p. 95, then machine a ⅛ × ⅛-in. chamfer on all four outside edges of the drawer front. Follow the procedures outlined in steps 10-14. To remedy end-grain chipping, chamfer the edges of the board first, then chamfer the long edges so that any chips resulting from the initial cross-grain cuts will be removed. Do not chamfer the edges of the drawer front which come into contact with the sides of the cabinet; these must remain square to fit neatly without gaps.

24. Use a router or table saw to cut a rabbet, ¼ in. deep and ¾ in. wide, along the inside edge of the drawer front at each end. The outside edges of these rabbets become the lips at each side of the drawer, which cover the ends of the drawer slides.

25. Now rout or saw a groove, ¼ in. deep and ⁵⁄₁₆ in. wide (or a little wider; up to ⅜ in.), along the full length of the drawer front, to house one edge of the drawer's ¼-in.-thick bottom panel. You must make the groove slightly wider than the panel's thickness so that enough clearance is available to accommodate the rise of the panel as well, since it seats at an upward-sloping

angle to the drawer front, rather that at a right angle to it. Make the groove parallel to the long edges of the drawer front, ¼ in. from the bottom inside edge. Unless you are using a ⁵⁄₁₆- or ⅜-in.-dia. router bit, you will have to make at least two passes with the router (as you will also with a saw; most power saw blades produce a kerf about ⅛ in. wide). Be careful not to make successive passes that extend the groove *below* its specified distance (¼ in.) from the drawer front's lower edge, otherwise the bottom panel won't fit properly.

26. To make the drawer sides, cut two pieces of clear mahogany, each ½ × 4¼ × 14¼ in. Lay out a taper on the upper surface of each piece by making a mark on the front edge of the piece, 2¼ in. from the bottom, and connecting that point with the rear top edge (which is 4¼ in. in height). Use a ripsaw and straightedged guide board to cut along this line, staying to the waste side of the line at all times. To make the pieces exactly the same, clamp them together after they are cut, and with light strokes of a hand plane, gently true both tapered edges at the same time as if jointing a single piece of stock.

27. Use a router or saw to cut a ¼ × ¼-in. rabbet across the inside face of the 2¼-in. end of each sidepiece. See the diagrams on p. 95 and the photo at top left on the page opposite. Be sure you make one right-hand piece and one left-hand piece.

28. Rout or saw a ¼ × ¼-in. dado across the inside face of both sidepieces, ⅜ in. from the rear edge of each.

29. To house the sides of the bottom panel, rout or saw a ¼ × ¼-in. groove parallel to the tapered edge of each sidepiece. Refer to the diagrams on p. 95. The bottom edge of each groove (the surface on which the panel will rest) should begin ¼ in. above the bottom edge at the front of the sidepiece (the end which measures 2¼ in. high) and end at a height of 2¼ in. where it passes through the rear (4¼-in. end) of the board. Measured from the groove's bottom surface, a constant distance of 2 in. from the tapered edge should be maintained throughout.

30. Cut one piece of clear mahogany, ½ × 2 × 19⅜ in., for the drawer back.

31. Using a protractor, lay out 8° angles across the top and bottom edges of each end of the drawer back. The lines you mark should each slant in the same direction. Then, using a hand plane, bevel the top and bottom

edges of the drawer back to match the slanted lines marked across each end. By holding the finished drawer back at right angles to each of the two side-pieces, you should find that the beveled top edge of the back matches the tapered top surfaces of the sides, and the beveled bottom edge of the back matches the rise of the groove running the length of each side. The beveled bottom edge of the drawer back will rest on top of the drawer's bottom panel when assembled.

32. To ensure that the drawer sides will be parallel once the drawer is put together, measure the distance between the two rabbets cut across the inside face of the drawer front, then lay out ¼-in.-deep rabbets at each end of the drawer back which are exactly the same distance apart as the rabbets in the drawer front. If the plans have been followed precisely, these rabbets should each measure ¼ in. wide. Cut the rabbets with a router or saw.

33. To make the bottom of the drawer, cut one piece of hardboard, ¼ × 14¼ × 19⅜ in. Due to the accumulation of small errors while making the other drawer pieces, you may have to alter these dimensions slightly.

34. Make a trial assembly of the drawer pieces without glue to test the fit of each piece. Use clamps to hold the components in place. The sidepieces seat with their rabbeted ends against the drawer front. The ends of the drawer front should extend ½ in. beyond the thickness of each sidepiece, or enough to hide the ends of the drawer slides (to be installed later; see step 41). The top edges of the sidepieces should slant upward toward the rear. The grooves in the sidepieces and drawer front should all have a common bottom surface and appear to form one continuous groove around all three sides of the drawer. Slide the bottom panel into the grooves until it seats in the drawer front, then fit the beveled drawer back into position by placing it on top of the bottom panel; its rabbeted ends fit into the dadoes cut in the sidepieces.

35. All the pieces should fit without gaps and without having to be forced into place. If they don't, first determine which pieces are incorrectly cut, then carefully trim them for a better fit. Extra care and patience is the key to accurate drawer construction. When you are ready, take the drawer apart and reassemble it with glue. To clamp it, cut two pieces of scrap wood, each slightly longer than the width of the drawer, and position these along the drawer front and the drawer back. Apply pressure with bar clamps running the length of the drawer sides. Clamp the sidepieces to the drawer's front and back by positioning bar clamps across the width of the drawer, one at the front and one at the back. Use small scraps of wood between the clamps and the drawer sides to protect the mahogany. As you apply pressure to the clamps, check the corner joints frequently with a try square to make sure they remain at 90°. Also measure between diagonal corners; the distances should be equal.

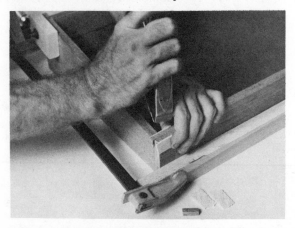

36. To fill in the rabbeted portions extending above the drawer sides at each end of the drawer front, cut two small pieces of clear mahogany, each approximately ¼ × ¼ × ¾ in. Glue these in place, even with or slightly above the top inside edge of the drawer front. Spring clamps — with thin scraps of wood placed between the jaws and the filler pieces — work well for this job. You may, if you wish, make the filler pieces larger (say, ¼ × 1 × ¾ in.), so they cover the entire rabbeted portions of the drawer front above the sides, but since the drawer is enclosed completely within the cabinet, the gaps left by the smaller filler pieces are not noticeable since they are never viewed from the side.

37. Using a hand plane, cut "by eye" a ⅛ × ⅛ in. chamfer on the top inside edge of the drawer front — trimming the tops of the filler pieces flush in the process — to approximate the appearance of the chamfer on the drawer front's outside edge. Take long, light strokes with the plane, shaving off only a little bit of wood each time.

38. Use a file to chamfer the end of each filler piece. Work from the top edge down to avoid splitting them.

39. Lightly sand the entire cabinet and drawer; be careful not to round-over the crisp edges of the chamfers.

40. Apply stain if desired, then finish with brush-on lacquer on all parts. See Wood Finishing, p. 162, for complete finishing instructions.

41. Turn the cabinet on its side to install the drawer slides. Position a slide along the bottom edge of one side of the cabinet, with the end of the slide flush against the cabinet's back edge. The front end of the slide's fixed portion should not extend beyond the front edge of the cabinet opening. Drill pilot holes (p. 73) for the mounting screws, which should come with the slides. Install the slide, then turn the cabinet over and install the remaining slide.

42. Position the drawer-mounted portions of the drawer slides even with the bottom edges of the drawer's sidepieces. One end of each slide should butt against the rabbeted portion of the drawer front. Drill pilot holes for the mounting screws, then attach the slides to the drawers. Finally, install the drawer in the cabinet by joining together the halves of each slide mechanism according to the manufacturer's instructions.

Dining Table

Installing plastic laminate
Tabletop edging
Fasteners for tabletops

This handsome dining table is practical and affordable, as well as good-looking. It's an advanced project, but with care and patience it is really not too difficult to build. A table saw is required. You will find it indispensable not only because of the amount of precise cutting involved, but also because of the extreme hardness of the wood—oak—used in the table's construction. The table shown on these pages is made of white oak and matches the chairs (designed as companion pieces) whose construction is shown beginning on page 120. Red oak might also be used, or, of course, any clear hardwood. Pine or other softwoods would probably be disappointing.

Two features of this table bring it within most woodworkers' budgets: the plastic-laminate-covered top, whose inner core is a ¾-inch sheet of inexpensive manufactured flake board available at ordinary lumberyards, and the table legs and frame, which are stack-laminated to thickness (see p. 60) from ¾-inch stock. Hardwood lumber in small thicknesses such as this is far less expensive than even short lengths of thicker stock; also, very thick pieces, such as those required for the table legs, are prone to cracking (checking) with seasonal changes in temperature and humidity.

The plastic tabletop is heat, moisture, and alcohol resistant, and the flake board core—properly sealed with lacquer as specified in the project instructions—is unlikely ever to shrink, swell, or warp. Traditional tabletops, on the other hand, made by edge-gluing boards together (p. 45), require a great deal of ingenuity and careful joinery to accommodate the inevitable movement of such a wide expanse of solid wood.

This dining table is also easy to take apart for storage or moving. Unscrewing a single bolt in each leg is all that's necessary to remove them.

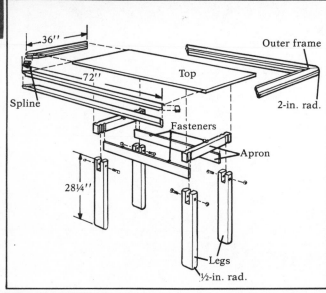

36''

72''

Spline

Outer frame

Top

2-in. rad.

Fasteners

Apron

28¼''

Legs

½-in. rad.

What you will need

2 pcs. clear oak, ¾'' × 4⅝'' × 6'
2 pcs. clear oak, ¾'' × 4⅝'' × 3'
12 pcs. clear oak, ¾'' × 4'' × 28¼''
2 pcs. clear oak, ¾'' × 3'' × 43''
4 pcs. clear oak, ¾'' × 3'' × 29¹⁵⁄₁₆''
4 pcs. clear oak, ⅛'' × 1'' × 1½''
4 pcs. #2 pine, 1⅛'' × 1⅛'' × 3'' (see step 32)
1 pc. hardwood dowel, ⅞'' × 2'' (see step 47)
1 pc. hardwood dowel, ⅜'' × 15'' (see step 22)
1 sheet flake board, ¾'' × 4' × 8' (see step 2)
1 sheet plastic laminate (choose color as desired),
   ¹⁄₁₆'' × 3' × 6'
1 sheet plastic backing laminate, ¹⁄₃₂'' × 3' × 6'
12 pcs. corrugated cardboard, 4'' × 40''
   (approx.; see step 4)
24 #8 flathead wood screws, 1''
12 #8 flathead wood screws, ¾''
4 machine bolts with washers, ⁵⁄₁₆'' × 3''
6 figure-8 mounting clips and screws
4 tee nuts, ⁵⁄₁₆-in. dia.
1 qt. liquid contact cement
white or yellow glue
brush-on lacquer
table saw or circular saw
router
drill
drywall or masonry trowel
socket wrench
bar and cabinetmakers' clamps
hand and measuring tools

Before you begin

As shown in the diagram at the top of the column to the right, the natural rabbet formed by gluing together the narrow and wide pieces of the table's outer frame must be made deeper in order for the tabletop to seat flush with the frame's top surface. After measuring the extra depth needed (see step 19), deepening the rabbet is easily done on the table saw, using the rip fence. First, set the saw's blade height to 1½ in. (the width of the rabbet), then position the frame piece with the 3-in. face against the rip fence and the double-thick edge of the frame facing up. Now slide the rip fence, together with the frame piece, toward the saw blade until you can see that the desired amount to be cut away is in the path of the blade. Lock the fence in place and make the cut. Check and cut each frame piece individually.

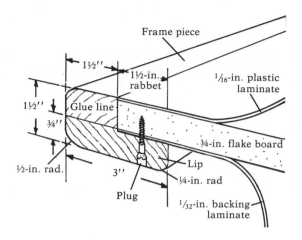

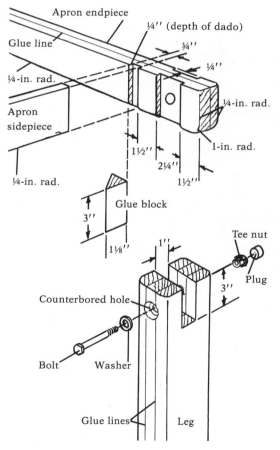

Step-by-step instructions

1. Spread liquid contact cement thinly and evenly onto the underside of a piece of backing laminate, $\frac{1}{32}$ in. $\times$ 3 ft. $\times$ 6 ft. Use a drywall or masonry trowel for a spreader, or use a piece of thin plywood. Allow the layer of contact cement to dry (it behaves somewhat like rubber cement), then remove the backing laminate to a safe location where it can be stored flat, glued side up, of course, while you prepare the flake board. Be careful not to chip the laminate while moving it.
2. Cut one piece of flake board, $\frac{3}{4} \times 33 \times 69$ in., for the tabletop. Use a table saw or circular saw with a sharp blade.
3. Spread contact cement onto one surface of the flake board, exactly as you did in step 1.
4. Cut approximately 12 strips of corrugated cardboard, each about 4 in. wide and 40 in. long. When the cement on the flake board has dried, gently lay the strips down on its surface (they will not stick), spacing them evenly along the board's entire length.

5. Now carefully lay the backing laminate—glued side down—on top of the row of cardboard strips. It is important that the laminate not come into direct con-

tact with the flake board at this time. Should the two glued surfaces touch, they will bond instantly and be impossible to separate. Carefully position the laminate so that it extends beyond all edges of the flake board, then remove the strips one by one by sliding them out from between the laminate and the flake board. Begin at one end and work toward the other. As you remove a strip, press the laminate down against the flake board and rub the entire area with the heel of your hand so that complete bonding is achieved.

6. Using a router (see p. 42) equipped with a flush-cutting laminate trimming bit and a pilot bearing, or a carbide-tipped bit and the homemade trimming guide shown on p. 112, trim the edges of the laminate flush with the edges of the flake board. Be sure to use a sharp, undamaged bit to avoid chipping the brittle laminate.
7. With help from an assistant (to lessen the risk of chipping the corners of the laminate), turn the flake board over. Then repeat steps 1, 3, 5, and 6 on this side, using a sheet of plastic laminate, $\frac{1}{16}$ in. $\times$ 3 ft. $\times$ 6 ft., in your choice of color. (Laminate also comes in a variety of textures and patterns. You should choose a surface that is easy to wipe clean, and one with a color that either harmonizes or contrasts with the solid wood portions of the table. The laminate shown on these pages is beige.) This laminate will be visible as the top surface of the table.

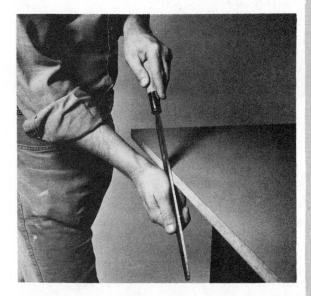

8. Trim any unevenness in the flake board edges square with the top and bottom laminates, using a wood file. Hold the file as shown in the photo above, and apply pressure only on the downward stroke, to avoid chipping the edges of the laminate.

9. When you are finished, brush the edges of the completed tabletop free of sawdust, then apply a coat of brush-on lacquer to the edges to seal the flake board. Set the tabletop aside in a safe place, so it won't be damaged while you perform the steps which follow. Be careful not to chip the edges or corners of the top as you move it.

10. Rip two pieces of clear oak, each ¾ in. × 4⅝ in. × 6 ft., into two pairs of strips for the sides of the tabletop's outer frame. Each pair of strips should be made from a single board. The dimensions of one strip of each pair should be ¾ in. × 1½ in. × 6 ft.; their mates should each be ¾ in. × 3 in. × 6 ft.

11. Glue and clamp (p. 44) the members of each pair of strips together to form the completed sidepieces of the tabletop's frame.

12. Cut two pieces of clear oak, each ¾ in. × 4⅝ in. × 3 ft., then repeat steps 10 and 11 to make the two endpieces of the tabletop's frame.

13. Using an accurate table saw with a sharp blade, cut 45° miters on the ends of each of the four pieces of the tabletop's frame.

14. Use a router equipped with a ½ in. rounding-over bit to radius the outside edges (top and bottom) of each frame piece. If desired, use a ¼-in. rounding-over

Installing Plastic Laminate

Plastic laminates, such as Formica, are easy to apply and economical. Laminates are brittle, though, and when in place must not overhang the surface which supports them. Use a power saw with a carbide-tipped blade to cut laminate. Cut the piece slightly larger than the finished dimensions, then trim it flush later with a file or router (see Tabletop Edging, p. 112). Prepare the support surface by sanding it smooth and filling any holes. Apply liquid contact cement to both the laminate and the support surface, and allow each to dry before pressing them together, as shown below.

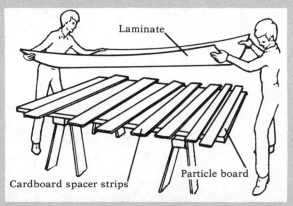

Cement-coated surfaces bond instantly on contact with each other and cannot be adjusted once they meet. To assure accurate positioning, first distribute strips of wood or cardboard across the support surface to act as spacers. The strips will not stick. Lay laminate on top of strips.

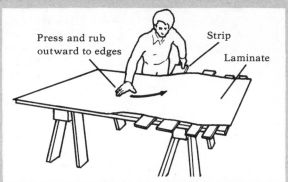

Adjust laminate until it is correctly positioned. Then, while holding it in place, remove the strips one at a time, working from one end toward the other. As you remove each strip, press down on the laminate with the heel of your hand. Rub entire area to bond surfaces fully.

bit to radius the bottom inside edge of each piece as well. Do not radius the rabbeted edges that will come into contact with the tabletop.

15. On the underside (the 3-in.-wide face) of each frame piece, ½ in. from the inside edge, drill evenly spaced ¹¹⁄₆₄-in. clearance holes (p. 73) for the screws which fasten the frame pieces to the tabletop. Counterbore the holes to a depth of ³⁄₁₆ in., using a ⅜-in.-dia. bit. Drill four holes in each endpiece and eight holes in each sidepiece.

16. Using a table saw with the blade height set at ½ in., cut slots for the splines along the mitered ends of each frame piece. To do this, set the saw's rip fence ¾ in. from the blade, and pass each frame piece over the saw, always with the 3-in.-wide face of the frame piece in contact with the fence.

17. Cut four pieces of clear oak, each ⅛ × 1 × 1½ in., for the splines used at each corner of the tabletop's frame. First though, measure the width of the saw kerf cut in each frame side to be sure the kerfs measure ⅛ in. wide. If they don't, use whatever width the kerfs do measure as the thickness dimension for your splines. Be particularly careful to cut each spline so the grain of the wood runs across the width of the spline, at right angles to the spline's length.

18. Set the tabletop upside down, with the backing laminate face up, on a work bench. The sides of the tabletop should extend beyond the bench if possible.

Tabletop Edging

Traditional tabletops, made from solid wood, require edge treatment only to cover exposed end grain. This is done partly for appearance but mostly because end grain has a tendency to take on or give up moisture at a greater rate than the rest of a piece of wood. By covering the end grain this tendency is lessened, and the rate at which the wood responds to moisture is equalized over its entire surface. With manufactured boards, edging is required more for appearance than for warpage control. Normally, however, it is applied around all four sides.

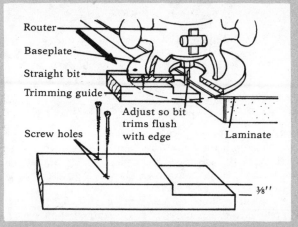

Edging for laminate-covered tops should be cemented on prior to installing the top itself, so that the top can overlap the edging to form a seamless surface. Apply edging with contact cement, then trim it with a router and special laminate-trimming bit, or use a carbide-tipped straight bit and a homemade wooden trimming guide, as shown above.

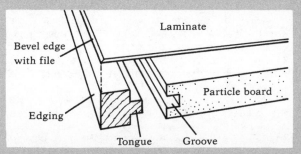

Tongued edging which fits into a sawn or routed groove in the sides of the tabletop also works well. Manufactured edging, both wooden and synthetic, can even be purchased in this form. As mentioned above, if the tabletop is to be covered by laminate, install the edging first.

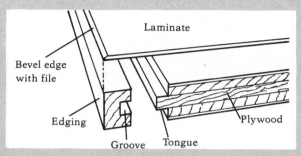

Sometimes you may find it easier to cut a groove in the edging and a matching tongue in the manufactured board. This is an acceptable method when working with plywood, but the result tends to be weak when done in particle board or flake board, since neither has a grain structure to give it strength.

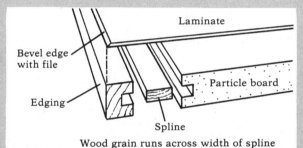

Wood grain runs across width of spline

Splines make strong joints on particle board or flake board. To install splined edging, saw or rout matching grooves in both the edging and the board, then cut the spline to fit the grooves and allow for glue. Where splines meet at corners of the table, miter each end for a perfect fit.

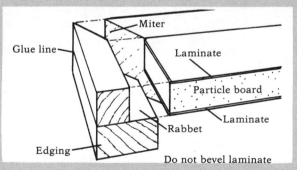

Do not bevel laminate

When you want the edging to show on the surface of the tabletop, rabbet a thick piece, or glue a narrow piece on top of a wider one. Form the rabbet so the top of the table is flush with the top of the edging, and miter the ends of each piece so they meet attractively at the corners.

BREADBOARD ENDS

Breadboard ends are a traditional way of covering the end grain of tabletops made from edge-glued solid wood (see p. 45). Not only is the end grain covered, but warping caused by structural differences between each of the edge-glued pieces is minimized also. By using the combination of round and elongated-oval holes as shown below, and by fastening the ends with dowels or screws instead of nails or glue, the ends can be made to fit tightly to the tabletop, yet allow for sideways expansion and contraction of the edge-glued pieces.

To make breadboard ends, cut wide tongues at each end of the table, and correspondingly deep grooves in the endpieces. Fit the ends onto the table and clamp them so they are drawn tightly toward the center of the table. Drill holes for the dowels or screws. Holes for dowels should go straight through, but for screws mounted from the top (holes for these should be counterbored for plugs) you should drill only partway into the lower half of the breadboard end. Screws may be mounted from underneath instead and thus be invisible from the top. In this case, drill only partway into the upper half of the endpieces. After the holes are drilled, remove the endpieces. Elongate all but the *center* hole in each tongue, by drilling a single, similar-size hole on both sides of the ones already drilled. Now replace the endpieces, and fasten them through the holes in the tongues. Use glue for dowels, but apply it only to their upper portions.

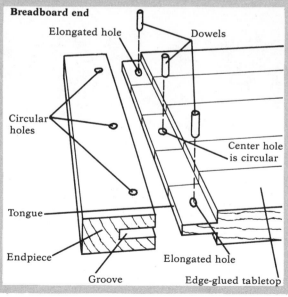

Breadboard end

19. Now fit the pieces of the frame around the tabletop. Begin by placing each piece in position right side up against the edges of the tabletop (it doesn't matter that the top is upside down). Check whether the surface of the top is higher than the upper surface (the 1½-in.-wide face) of the frame. If it is, measure the difference in heights, and remove this amount of wood from the bottom surface of the frame piece's rabbet (p. 109). Then, turn the endpieces upside down and fit them against the edges of the tabletop exactly as they should go. Clamp them in place, and drill $^3/_{32}$-in.-dia. pilot holes, ¾ in. deep, into the tabletop, using the existing clearance holes as guides. Remove the clamps and fasten the endpieces to the tabletop, using 1-in. #8 screws.

20. Fit each sidepiece of the frame into position, trimming the miters with a very sharp block plane until a precision fit is achieved. Apply glue to the

mitered edges and to the splines, insert the splines in the slots in each endpiece, then clamp the sides in place.
21. Drill pilot holes as in step 19, and fasten the sides to the tabletop, using 1-in. #8 screws.
22. Cut 24 pieces of ⅜-in.-dia. hardwood dowel, each $^3/_{16}$-in. long, for plugs to cover the screws. If desired, stain the plugs to match the surrounding wood.
23. Glue the plugs into the counterbored screw holes. When dry, sand the plugs flush with the frame's surface.
24. If desired, use a saber saw to round the corners of the table to a 2-in. radius. If you choose to leave the corners square, carefully trim the splines flush, using a fine-tooth backsaw or saber saw or a chisel.
25. If, due to adjustments during fitting, the rounded-over edges of the frame pieces do not mate precisely, or if you have radiused the corners in the previous step and so cut off the rounded edges, perform step 14 over again, taking the router around the entire perimeter of the frame in one continuous motion. Turn the tabletop over (right side up) to round-over the frame's outside edge.
26. Cut four pieces of clear oak, each ¾ × 3 × 29$^{15}/_{16}$-in., then glue and clamp pairs of pieces together face to face to form the two endpieces of the table's apron. Each glued-up apron end should measure 1½ in. thick.
27. Cut two pieces of clear oak, each ¾ × 3 × 43 in., for the apron sides.

28. Using a router equipped with a straight bit, cut ¼-in.-deep dadoes into the ends of each apron endpiece, according to the measurements shown in the

Fasteners for Tabletops

Tabletops are seldom fastened directly to the legs or other underparts of a table. Usually some form of fastener is used which allows the top to shift slightly from one position to another to accommodate the natural movement of the wood during seasonal changes of temperature and humidity and to minimize any possibility of the tabletop splitting due to the individualized warping of perhaps only one or two boards. Mounting tabletops made of manufactured boards does not require the use of fasteners as safety devices, since tabletops of plywood, particle board, and flake board — when properly sealed — are virtually unaffected by moisture. However, it is often much easier to use fasteners than it is to drill deep mounting-screw holes in wide table aprons, say, or legs. Fasteners also make assembly and disassembly of a table's components much easier.

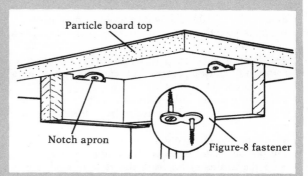

Figure-8 mounting clips work well with manufactured boards. Cut a notch in the upper edge of the apron so each clip is flush with the edge when attached, then use screws to secure one half of the mounting clip to the tabletop and the other to the apron.

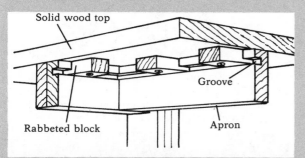

One way of attaching a tabletop to the apron is to use rabbeted wood blocks. Cut a groove around the inside of the apron to accept the tongued portion of the blocks, but make the groove slightly wider than the width of the tongue to allow for movement. Attach the blocks to the table with screws.

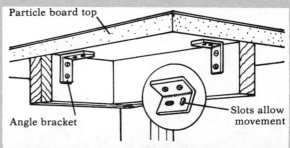

Angle brackets need no notching of the apron's upper edge as do figure-8 clips. Some types are even slotted and work as well on solid as on manufactured boards. When mounting angle brackets, make sure the tabletop rests fully on the apron and does not shift upward during installation of screws.

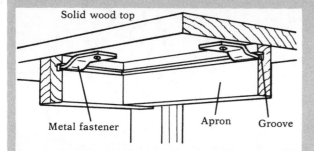

Metal fasteners can also be used. The ones shown work just like the rabbeted wood blocks shown above and fit into a groove cut around the inside of the apron. The groove in the apron is normally narrow enough so that it may be cut with a single pass on a table or radial arm saw.

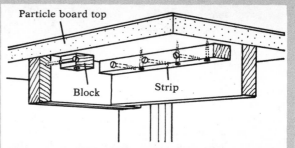

Wood blocks or strips can be used to secure manufactured board tabletops directly to the apron. Although the sturdiest method is to have a strip of wood run all the way around the table, it is sufficient to use blocks of wood placed at intervals. Pilot holes must be drilled carefully.

diagram on p. 109. The wide dadoes form joints with the table legs; the narrow dadoes house the sidepieces of the apron.

29. Using a wood rasp and file—or a saber saw—round the bottom corners of each endpiece to a 1-in. radius.

30. Using a router and a ¼-in. rounding-over bit, work a ¼-in. radius along the ends and bottom edges of each end piece.

31. Using the same router setup as in step 30, radius the bottom edges of each of the apron's sidepieces. Stop the radius ¼ in. from the ends of each piece, though, so they will fit snugly in the endpiece dadoes.

32. Cut four knot-free pieces of #2 pine (or other scrap wood) into triangular pieces, each 1⅛ × 1⅛ × 3 in., for corner blocks.

34. Mark positions for six figure-8 tabletop fasteners around the top (unradiused) surface of the apron after it is dry. Space the fasteners evenly—one centered on each end and two placed on each side.

33. Assemble the apron by gluing and clamping the sidepieces into the narrow dadoes cut in each endpiece, so that the unit forms a rectangle, but with the ends extending beyond the sides. Lay the pieces into position first—all the radiused edges should be in contact with the bench surface—then use bar clamps when gluing-up. Check the corners with a framing square to make certain each angle measures 90°. Also, measure between diagonal corners; the dimensions should be equal. While the apron is still in clamps, install the corner blocks with glue and finishing nails. (In the photo above, the clamps have been removed from the apron for clarity.)

35. At each location, chisel a shallow mortise as wide as the fastener and just deep enough so that the fastener will lie flush with the surface of the apron when installed.

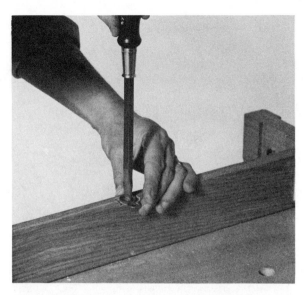

36. Drill ³/₁₆-in.-dia. pilot holes, ¾ in. deep, in each of the mortises. Hold a fastener in place as a guide as you drill. Then install the fasteners into the mortises, using ¾-in. #8 screws. The small-diameter portion of each fastener should face the inside of the apron.

37. Now lay the tabletop upside down on the workbench. First make sure the bench top is free of grit that might scratch the dining table's laminate. (You may

even wish to spread an old blanket over the bench top as further protection.) Center the apron carefully on the underside of the bench, then, using the figure-8 fasteners as guides, drill ³/₁₆-in. pilot holes, each ¾ in. deep, into the underside of the tabletop. Be careful not to make the holes too deep. Finally, fasten the apron to the tabletop with ¾-in. #8 screws installed in the figure-8s.

38. Cut 12 pieces of clear oak, each ¾ × 4 × 28¼ in., for the table legs.

39. Glue and clamp groups of three boards each together face to face, to make four individual legs, each measuring 2¼ × 4 × 28¼ in.

40. Lay out a notch 1 in. wide and 3 in. long across one end of each glued-up leg section for attaching the legs to the apron's dadoed endpieces. Carefully saw down the sides of the notch, using a backsaw. Straightedged scrap blocks aligned with the layout lines of the notch and clamped to each side of the leg act as guides. Be sure to saw only on the waste side of each line and be especially careful not to let the saw cut too deeply into the leg and travel below the notch's bottom line. Make saw cuts in all the leg sections before proceeding to the next step.

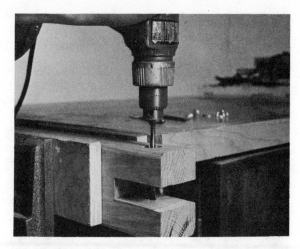

43. Drill ⅞-in.-dia. counterbores ½ in. deep into the edges of each leg on opposite sides of the notches. Then drill a ⁵⁄₁₆-in.-dia. hole through each leg, centered at the bottom of each counterbore.

44. Finally, on one edge of each leg only—the edge you designate to face outward from the table when it is assembled—counterbore the ⁵⁄₁₆-in. hole further, using a ⅜-in.-dia. bit. Drill this counterbore ⅝ in. deep to accept the barrel of a tee nut (see step 46) whose outer flanges will seat at the bottom of the ⅞-in. counterbore around it.

41. Clamp a leg firmly to the bench top, then carefully chisel out the waste wood between the sawn lines to form the completed notch. To chisel the notch correctly, first hold the chisel vertically—with its bevel facing toward the notch—on top of the notch's bottom layout line, the one uncut by the saw. With a mallet, strike the chisel a few times to make a stop-cut across the grain of the wood. Be careful not to let the chisel stray from the mark as you strike it; try to make the stop-cut as square and clean as possible. Then hold the chisel as in the photo above, and split out a layer of waste wood as thick as the stop-cut is deep. Repeat this two-step procedure until you are a little more than halfway through the notch, then turn the leg over and chisel from the other side. Continue until all the legs have been evenly notched.

42. Using a router equipped with a ½-in. rounding-over bit, machine a ½-in. radius on all edges on each leg except at the top, where the legs contact the underside of the table.

45. Assemble each leg in position by slipping it over the dadoed portion at each end of the apron pieces. The fit should be very snug but not so tight that sharp malleting is needed (too tight a fit can cause the legs to split). With the legs seated against the underside of the table, insert the 5/16-in. drill into the prebored hole in each leg and drill through the apron piece.

46. Remove each leg and tap a tee nut into place in each, seating the barrels of the tee nuts in the 5/8-in. counterbore drilled in step 44.
47. Cut four pieces of 7/8-in.-dia. hardwood dowel, each 3/8 in. long, for use as plugs to cover the tee nuts. Stain the dowels to match the color of the table legs, if desired. (If you have access to a wood lathe, these plugs may be cut from oak and made invisible when fitted into the legs.)

48. Glue the plugs in place over the tee nuts, then sand the plugs flush with the outside surfaces of the legs.
49. Before final assembly of the table, sand all wooden surfaces, then apply three coats of brush-on lacquer. See Wood Finishing, p. 162, for complete finishing instructions.

50. To assemble the finished table, fit the legs into position with the plugged holes toward the outside of the table, then install 5/16 × 3-in. machine bolts with washers in the open holes of each leg, and tighten them firmly into the tee nuts, using a socket wrench. With help from an assistant, turn the table right side up.

Dining Chairs

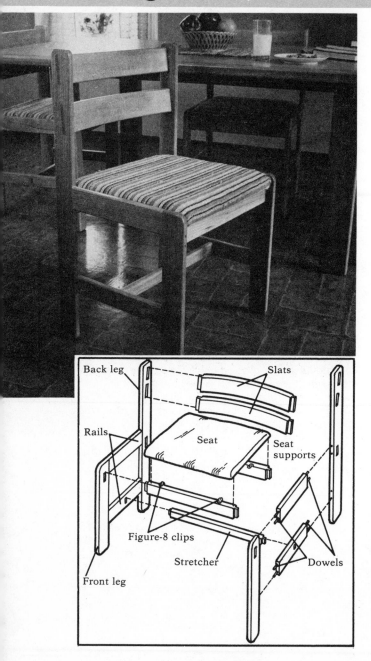

Back leg

Slats

Rails

Seat

Seat supports

Figure-8 clips

Stretcher

Dowels

Front leg

Seat upholstery

Elegant chairmaking is an art, and chairmakers themselves occupy a special niche in the world of woodworking. You will find these chairs challenging—they are an advanced project—but not technically very difficult, provided you have on hand good tools for the job and are willing to take pains to work accurately and with patience. For details on how to cut the mortise-and-tenon joints which are an important feature of the design, see page 138. You should practice the technique as well, if it is new to you, before attempting to perform it on the project pieces. Oak is the wood specified (although, as with all the hardwood projects in this book, any other hardwood may be substituted) and, due to its extreme toughness, power tools, at least for sawing and rough sanding, are virtually a must. Carbide-tipped router bits are also worthwhile items to have on hand.

Reflected in these chairs are basic elements of sound structural design, sturdy construction, and pleasing lines, all of which go into the making of a fine chair. Each part is functional; all the parts together unite into a harmonious whole. The chairs are also designed to complement the oak dining table described in the previous project (see p. 108) and to be upholstered with the handwoven fabric detailed on page 396. (Of course, upholstery fabric purchased from a store may also be used.)

The construction of the seat is quite simple: Fabric is merely stretched over a base of cushioned plywood and stapled underneath. The entire seat is removable for cleaning if desired (it is held in place by mounting clips similar to those used in fastening the dining table top), and the fabric itself can be easily replaced to meet redecorating needs or should some damage to the seats occur.

The list of materials you will need details what is required to build just one chair.

What you will need

To make one chair:

4 pcs. clear oak, ¾'' × 3'' × 19¾''
2 pcs. clear oak, ¾'' × 2½'' × 32''
2 pcs. clear oak, ¾'' × 2½'' × 18''
2 pcs. clear oak, ¾'' × 2½'' × 1'
2 pcs. clear oak, ¾'' × 2'' × 19¾''
2 pcs. clear oak, ¾'' × 2'' × 1'
1 pc. clear oak, ¾'' × 1½'' × 19¾''
1 pc. plywood, ¾'' × 16¼'' × 17¾'' A-C int.
1 pc. hardwood dowel, ⅜'' × 3' (see step 11)
1 pc. hardwood dowel, ¼'' × 3' (see step 26)
1 pc. hardwood dowel, ³⁄₁₆'' × 3½'' (see step 28)
4 figure-8 mounting clips and screws
staples, ⁵⁄₁₆''
1 pc. urethane foam, 1½'' × 16¾'' × 18¼''
1 pc. upholstery fabric, 2' × 2'
1 pc. stiff paper, 3'' × 20''
white or yellow glue
wood putty
paste wood filler
brush-on lacquer
band saw
saber saw
router
drill
belt sander
doweling jig
heavy-duty staple gun
bar or pipe clamps
hand and measuring tools

Before you begin

Success in building this chair depends largely on accurate measurements and precise joinery. Use the template pattern shown in the column to the left to lay out the curved back slats. Enlarge the pattern to actual size, by following the instructions for enlarging grid diagrams shown on p. 16. Notice that the tenon-ends of the slats do not follow the curve of the piece but are positioned so they pass through the mortises in the chair's side frames at right angles. Also note that the distances between the tenon shoulders at opposite ends of each slat, seat support, and stretcher (there is only one of these), must be equal—18 in. is specified—in order for the chair to be of uniform width throughout and for all the mortise-and-tenon joints to fit snugly without gaps. The doweled joints in the side frames must be made carefully as well, and the frame pieces must be made to fit together at exact 90° angles. Study the diagram on the following page to be sure of all the chair's dimensions before beginning.

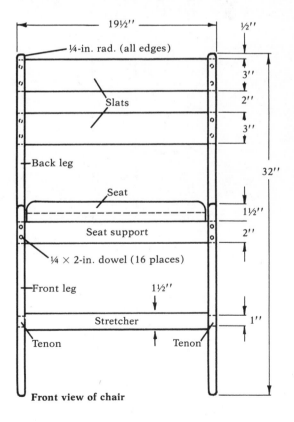

Front view of chair

Back slat

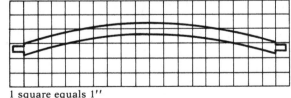

1 square equals 1''

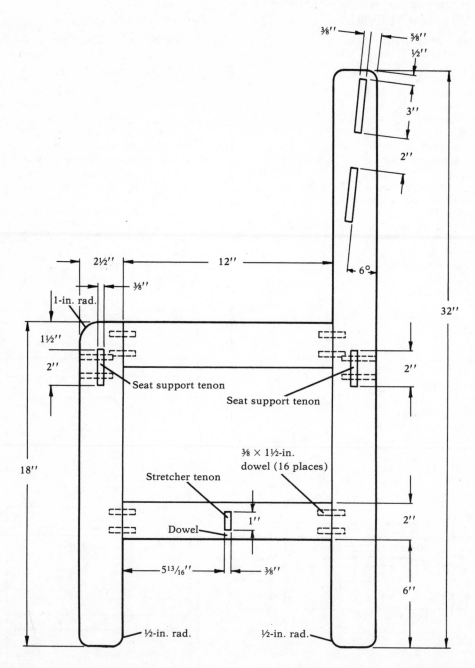

Side view of chair

Step-by-step instructions

1. Cut four pieces of clear oak, each ¾ × 3 × 19¾ in., to make the block from which to saw out the chair's back slats.

2. Glue and clamp these four boards together face to face to form a single block whose dimensions are 3 × 3 × 19¾ in.

3. Enlarge the back slat diagram shown on p. 121, transferring the full-size design onto stiff paper to make a template for cutting the back slats out of the block.

4. Place the template on one of the block's face sides. Do not place it on an edge-grain side, where the glue lines are visible. Position the template so the top of the arc is as close to the edge of the block as possible, in order to leave enough room for a second slat to be laid out as well. With a fine-pointed felt tip pen or sharp pencil, carefully trace around the template to transfer its shape onto the wood. When you are finished, reposition the template and trace a second slat onto the block.

5. Use a band saw to cut out the back slats. Be sure to keep the saw blade on the waste side of each line. When you have finished, sand each slat smooth, using a belt sander.

6. Cut two pieces of clear oak, each ¾ × 2½ × 32 in., for the chair's back legs.

7. Cut two pieces of clear oak, each ¾ × 2½ × 18 in., for the chair's front legs.

8. Cut two pieces of clear oak, each ¾ in. × 2½ in. × 1 ft., for the top rails of the chair.

9. Cut two pieces of clear oak, each ¾ in. × 2 in. × 1 ft., for the chair's bottom rails.

10. Use a doweling jig (see p. 83) to drill two holes in the end of each rail to accept the dowels used to join the chair together. Use the jig to drill matching holes in the chair legs as well, where the rails are to be attached. For the location of each of the 16 holes required, see the diagrams on pp. 121 and 122.

11. Cut 16 pieces of ⅜-in.-dia. hardwood dowel, each 1¾ in. long, to use for attaching the rails to the legs.

12. Assemble the rails and legs to make the two side frames. Before gluing up, make a trial assembly to see that the legs are parallel to each other and that the rails are level with the floor. Glue and insert the dowels into the rails, then join the rails to the legs. Clamp the joints, using bar or pipe clamps. Allow glue to dry.

13. Cut two pieces of clear oak, each ¾ × 2 × 19¾ in., for the seat supports.

14. Cut one piece of clear oak, ¾ × 1½ × 19¾ in., for the stretcher, which attaches between the chair's two lower rails.

15. Lay out two mortises on each back leg to accept the two back slats. Their positions are indicated in the diagram on p. 122. Begin by marking a point on each leg ½ in. down from the top and ⅝ in. from the back edge. From there, use a ruler and protractor to draw parallel lines downward and toward each leg's front edge, 6° from perpendicular. Follow the diagram to complete the layouts. Each mortise is 3 in. long; there is a 2-in. gap between them.

16. To cut the mortises, first select a drill bit slightly smaller in diameter than the thickness of the tenon-ends of the slats cut in step 5. (Although the diagram on p. 122 shows this thickness as ⅜ in., in actuality it may vary, so measure the mortise widths from the tenons themselves.) Using the bit, drill out the bulk of the waste wood from the mortise, then pare the sides smooth, using a very sharp chisel (p. 139). Use a doweling jig for accuracy, or mark a line down the center of the mortise and use it to locate the top of the drill bit. Clamp a block of scrap wood to the back of the chair leg each time you drill, to avoid splitting it where the drill emerges. When you finish each mortise, test-fit its mating tenon, then mark the pieces for accurate reinstallation later.

17. Lay out and cut mortises on each front and back leg for the seat supports. Follow the procedures described in the previous step, but use a ⅜-in.-dia. drill bit to remove the mortise waste (since the tenons have not yet been cut, all the mortises may be made a uniform width). Each mortise should measure ⅜ × 2 in. Their locations are shown in the diagram on p. 122.

18. In each lower rail, lay out and cut a mortise to accept the stretcher (see p. 121 for front view; p. 122 for side view). The long sides of these mortises run across the grain and measure ⅜ × 1 in.

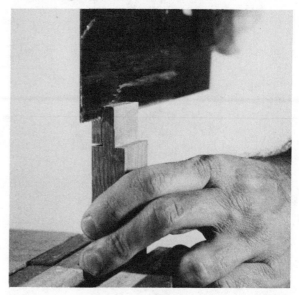

19. Lay out and cut a ⅜-in.-thick tenon, ⅞ in. long, on each end of the two seat supports to fit into the mortises cut into the legs in step 17. Make sure that the distance between the tenon shoulders at both ends of each support piece is exactly 18 in., since this length determines the distance between the chair's side frames. The tenons themselves may be a bit longer or shorter than ⅞ in. (since they project through the mortises and will be sanded flush after assembly), but the 18-in. distance between them must be constant. Cut the tenons with a backsaw, and use a guide block; the shoulders must be square (p. 138).

20. Now lay out and cut a ⅜ × 1 × ⅞-in. tenon in each end of the stretcher to fit into the mortises cut in the lower rails. Follow the same procedures as in the previous step, and again use a guide block to cut the tenon shoulders square. The distance between the shoulders of the tenons at each end of the stretcher must measure exactly 18 in.

(Continued on page 128)

Seat Upholstery

Upholstering simply designed chairs is not difficult. Even covering complicated furniture such as sofas, overstuffed armchairs, and the like is more a matter of practice than skill. Reupholstery is often even simpler: The old fabric, carefully removed, serves as the pattern for cutting the new. Full-scale upholstery, however, does require a great variety of materials and special tools, and does involve quite a number of specialized techniques. The sequences shown on this and the following pages should enable you to cover ordinary dining chairs, such as the ones found in this book, as well as common straight-back chairs, footstools, and benches.

UPHOLSTERING A REMOVABLE SEAT

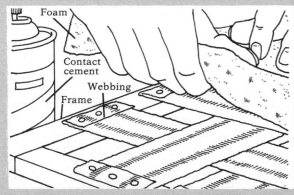

1. Removable seats may be a flat piece of plywood or a frame with webbing as a base. Cover each with a 1½-in.-thick pad of foam, cut to shape. Glue the foam to the base with contact cement.

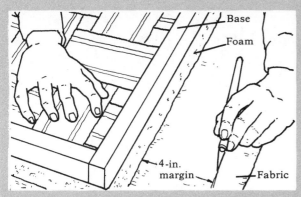

2. Place the upholstery fabric wrong side up on a flat surface. Position the padded seat base upside down on the fabric and trace around the base, allowing a 4-in. margin on all sides. Then cut away the waste fabric.

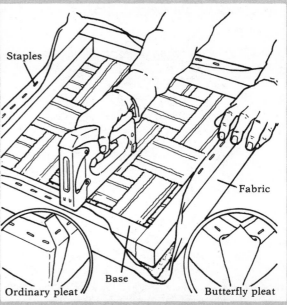

3. As if wrapping a package, draw the fabric snug from opposite sides and staple it to the underside of the seat base. Start in the center of each side and move to the corners. Form pleats at corners, trim excess, then staple in place so no wrinkles show.

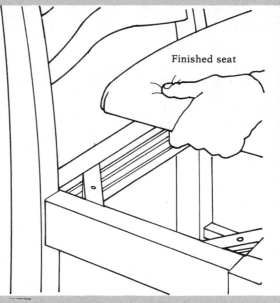

4. Reinstall finished seat.

(Continued on next page)

Seat Upholstery—*Continued*

RE-COVERING A SIMPLE CHAIR

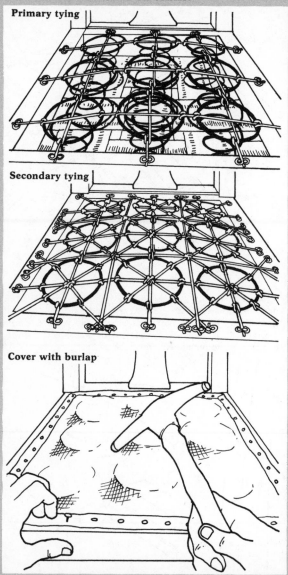

Primary tying

Secondary tying

Cover with burlap

1. Begin by replacing broken springs or worn webbing, then retie springs with twine. Primary tying joins rows of springs together back to front and side to side. Begin with center row. Tie twine to top coils of springs for rounded seat. Center springs should be no more than 2″ above chair rim when tied. Secondary tying joins twine between rows and diagonally. When finished, tack or staple burlap cover over springs.

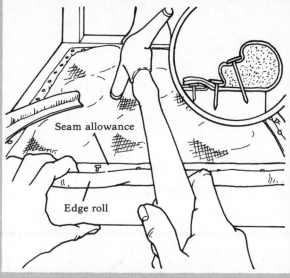

Seam allowance

Edge roll

2. Tack or staple edge roll, made of filler material wrapped in burlap, around the perimeter of the chair to contain the padding and keep the fabric from wearing against the chair's edges. Install fasteners along seam allowance of roll so they are hidden when roll is in place.

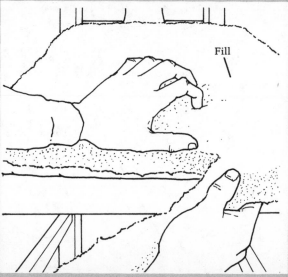

Fill

3. Install cotton, synthetic fill, or foam padding in even layer, 4″-6″ thick, or enough so that the springs cannot be felt when pressed. Never cut cotton or synthetic fill, since this will create a hard edge. Instead, tear it gently to shape while holding it in place on the chair.

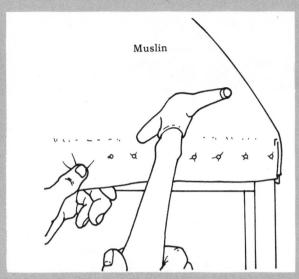

Muslin

4. Cover padding with muslin cut 2″ oversize on all sides. To install, tack muslin temporarily to one side of chair, pull taut, then tack or staple to other side. Now unfasten first side, pull taut to recenter padding, then refasten. Repeat on front and back sides. Form pleats at corners (see p. 125).

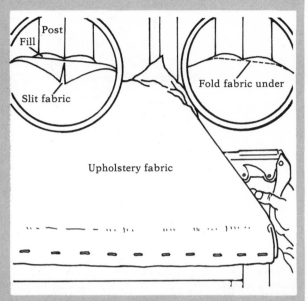

Post

Fill

Slit fabric

Fold fabric under

Upholstery fabric

6. Install upholstery fabric over stitched-down muslin. Begin by tacking or stapling fabric once in the center of each side as you pull it snug, then work outward to corners. Form and fasten pleats. Carefully slit fabric, fold under, and trim to fit around rear posts and tops of front legs.

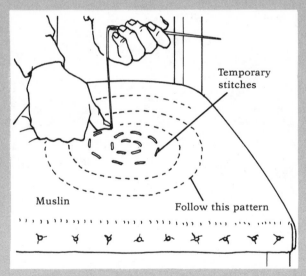

Temporary stitches

Muslin

Follow this pattern

5. Temporarily compress seat by tying one end of a length of twine to the chair bottom and then stitching up through the entire seat and down again at 2″-3″ intervals, following contour of seat. Compress springs and padding firmly as you pull twine taut. Tie twine off underneath chair when finished.

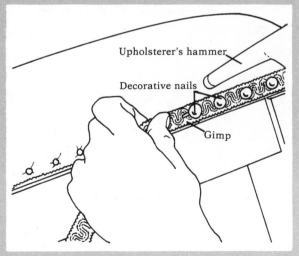

Upholsterer's hammer

Decorative nails

Gimp

7. Hide fasteners by gluing or decoratively tacking finishing tape called gimp over them, after trimming fabric's raw edges with razor knife. When covering is finished, cut and remove compression stitching by working from underneath chair.

21. Use a band saw (or substitute a saber saw) to cut a 1-in. radius on the top outside corner of the front legs, and a ½-in. radius on both bottom corners, as well as on the top and bottom corners of the back legs (p. 122). Lay out each radius carefully, keep the saw blade on the waste side of each line, and finish each cut by smoothing with a file and sandpaper.

22. Use a router equipped with a ¼-in. rounding-over bit to machine a radius on all edges of each side frame. Also radius the long edges of the stretcher and the lower edges (long ones only) of the seat supports.

23. Make a trial assembly of the chair, using no glue. Enlist the aid of a helper if possible, and plan on the job taking a bit of time and patience. Begin by

placing one of the side frames flat on the work surface (which should be clean and perhaps padded to prevent marring the wood) and tapping all the tenoned pieces in place. Use a rubber mallet for seating parts, or hold a scrap of softwood (such as pine) over the joint area and knock the pieces together with a hammer. After the tenoned pieces are in place, have your helper position the other side frame, while you proceed from tenon to tenon around the piece, tapping each one gradually into place by stages. Trimming some of the tenons may be necessary. Do so carefully with a rasp or file. Do not at this time trim tenons which are too long and protrude beyond the surface of a mortise. Tap thin shims or small wedges of wood into loose-fitting joints.

Once all the parts are seated, check the joints with a try square to make sure each corner forms a 90° angle. Place bar or pipe clamps in position during the trial assembly, on alternate sides of the legs to equalize their drawing pressure and prevent twisting of the joints. The clamps may be used to make fine adjustments in squaring up the joints, but do not rely on them to force a tenon into place which obviously needs trimming instead.

24. After performing the trial assembly, take the chair apart, then reassemble it again, using glue. While clamping up, check each piece for squareness. Allow the glue to dry thoroughly.

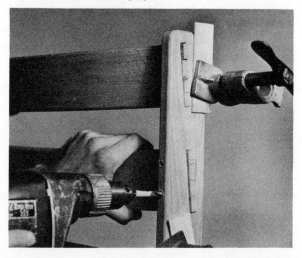

25. Before removing the clamps from the chair, lay out and drill ¼-in.-dia. holes, each 2 in. long, through the mortise-and-tenon joints in the back slats and seat supports. Drill the holes through the slats and rear support from the back of the chair. Drill the holes

through the remaining support from the front. Space each pair of holes evenly across the width of the tenon.
26. Cut 16 pieces of ¼-in.-dia. dowel, each 2 in. long, to insert into the holes drilled in the previous step.

27. Drill a single ³/₁₆-in.-dia. hole, 1½ in. long, into the mortise-and-tenon joint at each end of the stretcher. Drill the holes from the underside of the chair, locating them so they pass through the centers of the tenons.
28. Cut two pieces of ³/₁₆-in.-dia. dowel, each 1½ in. long, to insert into the holes drilled through the stretcher tenons.

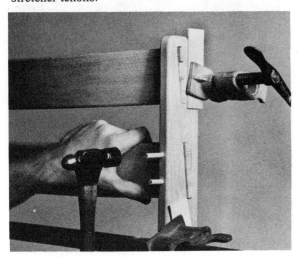

29. Apply glue and insert all 18 dowels, tapping each one home as you install it. Use glue sparingly, applying it to the front portion of the dowel only.

30. Remove the clamps from the chair. Sand the dowels flush with the wood surface. If necessary, carefully trim the dowel ends with a sharp chisel before sanding, but be careful not to chip their edges. The best technique is to work all the way around each dowel, tapping the chisel lightly with a mallet, then snap or shave the excess off so that the high point is in the center of the dowel. If any dowels are too short to come up flush with the surface, plug the holes with wood putty, then sand smooth.

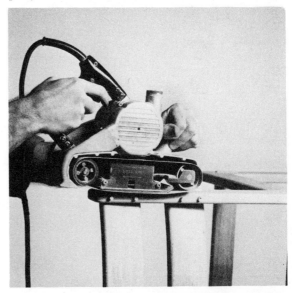

31. Use a belt sander to sand the projecting tenon ends of the various chair parts flush with the frames. Practice with the sander before you apply it to the chair itself, so you get a feel for how fast it removes wood. If no sander is available, trim the tenons as flush as possible, using a sharp chisel, then sand by hand. When chiseling, be careful to avoid chipping the corners of the tenons.
32. When the dowels and tenons have been smoothed flush with the surface of the side frames, sand the entire chair by hand in preparation for finishing.
33. Apply paste wood filler to the chair, to fill the oak's open grain.
34. Apply two coats of brush-on lacquer after the filler has dried. See Wood Finishing, p. 162, for complete finishing instructions.

Making the seat
1. Cut one piece of ¾-in. plywood, 16¼ × 17¾ in., for the seat base.

4. Cut one piece of urethane foam, $1\frac{1}{2} \times 16\frac{3}{4} \times 18\frac{1}{4}$ in., for the seat padding.

5. Attach the foam to the upper face of the plywood base by gluing the foam to the wood at each corner.

2. At each corner of the plywood base, lay out and cut a $\frac{1}{2}$-in. radius. Use a saber saw to make the cuts, then smooth them with a wood rasp or file.

6. Cover the seat with a piece of upholstery fabric. Place the fabric face down on a flat work surface, then place the seat (padded side down) on the fabric, centered so there is a generous overlap of material on all sides. Draw the fabric up from opposite sides. Using a heavy-duty staple gun, staple the fabric to the underside of the seat base. First secure the fabric by installing one staple on each side, then add staples to opposite sides as you pull the fabric evenly snug. Avoid distorting the pattern or compressing the foam. Fold fabric corners over and staple them to the underside of the seat so no tucks are visible on the upper side.

3. Use a router equipped with a $\frac{1}{4}$-in.-dia. rounding-over bit to radius the bottom edges of the seat base. Do not radius the top edges.

Attaching the seat

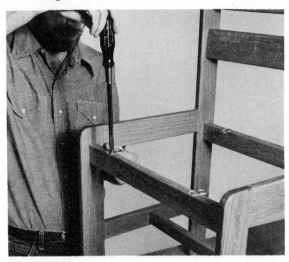

1. Mount two figure-8 mounting clips on the upper edge of each seat support, using a chisel to notch the top edge of the supports so each clip is flush with the wood surface. Position the clips 3½ in. from the ends of the supports. Drill pilot holes for the screws, then secure the clips in place.

2. Position the seat on the seat supports, and turn the chair upside down. Drill pilot holes through the seat base from the bottom, using the figure-8 clips as guides. Attach the seat to the clips with screws, making sure the screws do not completely penetrate the plywood base.

Double Bed

Mortise-and-tenon joinery
Frame-and-panel construction
Drawboring

Here is a bed of heirloom quality that combines simplicity of construction with graceful design and traditional good looks. Together with its companion piece, the dovetailed blanket chest featured on page 146, this bed is worthy of your finest work. The building techniques involved are not difficult or even, for the most part, newly presented; even so, you might consider holding off on this project until you have developed the habitual skills of craftsmanship a piece such as this deserves. Your abilities as a woodworker will be reflected in this bed for many years to come. Building the clothes-drying rack (see p. 86) is good preliminary practice, since many of the techniques used for the bed are presented in that project under much less exacting circumstances, involving less-expensive, more easily obtained materials.

Metal fasteners to hold the frame together are not used in this bed. Instead, the side rails are notched to form half-dovetail tenons, and these are inserted into corresponding mortises in each leg and then locked into place with wooden wedges. Pegs of wood instead of screws are used as well, with or without glue, to anchor the crossrails, headboard, and footboard to the legs. This reduces the chances of wide headboard or footboard stock splitting due to impaired movement while shrinking or swelling during seasonal humidity shifts. The wedged construction makes assembly and disassembly of the bed an easy matter.

The bed shown here is made of mahogany—of course, any hardwood such as oak, maple, cherry, or walnut will do quite well—and is designed to accommodate a double or full-size mattress/box spring combination, the standard dimensions of which are 54 × 75 inches. Modifications of the design to suit different-size mattresses and box springs are easily made.

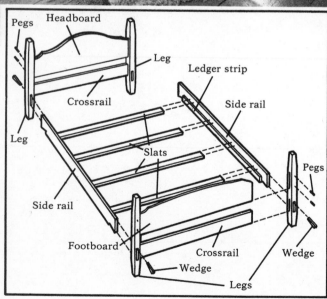

What you will need

2 pcs. clear mahogany, ¾'' × 5½'' × 80''
6 pcs. clear mahogany, ¾'' × 5½'' × 54½''
1 pc. clear mahogany, ¾'' × 5½'' × 53¾''
4 pcs. clear mahogany, ¾'' × 2¼'' × 54''
6 pcs. clear mahogany, ¾'' × 2¼'' × 41½''
6 pcs. clear mahogany, ¾'' × 2¼'' × 31½''
2 pcs. clear mahogany, ¾'' × 2'' × 74''
4 pcs. clear maple, ¾'' × ¾'' × 6½''
1 pc. hardwood dowel, ¼'' × 3' (see step 23)
10 #8 flathead wood screws, 1''
2 pcs. stiff paper, 16'' × 30'' (approx.; see steps 10 and 12)
white or yellow glue
stain
brush-on lacquer
table saw
saber saw
router
drill
bar or pipe clamps (must have 60-in. reach)
hand and measuring tools

Before you begin

The diagrams below and on the following page will help you to understand how the components of the bed fit together.

Also from the diagrams you will be able to determine how to alter the size of the bed to fit mattress/box spring combinations of different sizes. To modify the interior dimensions of the bed you must alter the lengths of the crossrails, headboard and footboard, side rails, ledger strips, and slats. The legs and wedges may be left alone, as may be the dimensions of the joints themselves. Their size is adequate even for the construction of a queen-size (60 × 80 in.) or king-size (76 × 80 in.) bed from the ¾-in. stock listed. Hardwood should be used, however; if you wish to substitute softwood such as pine, consider using thicker stock for the legs and the side rails.

Many possibilities exist for creating your own headboard and footboard designs. Since these pieces contribute very little to the strength of the bed (the legs and the side rails are the load-bearing components), as long as their ends fit and are pinned into the leg mortises, any style is acceptable.

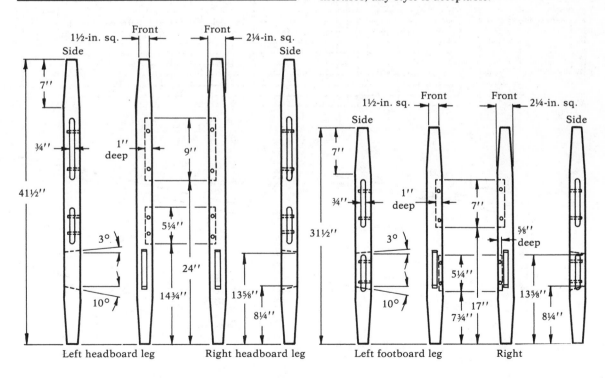

Left headboard leg   Right headboard leg

Left footboard leg   Right

Headboard pattern

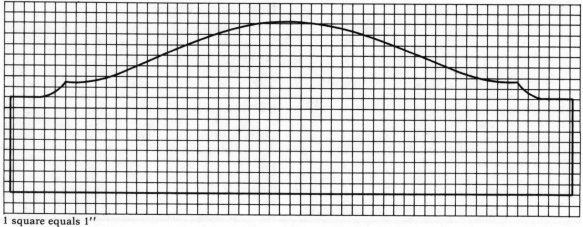

1 square equals 1''

Footboard pattern

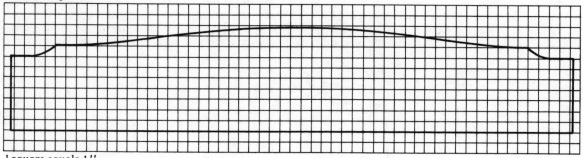

1 square equals 1''

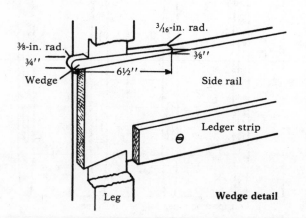

³⁄₈-in. rad.
³⁄₁₆-in. rad.
³⁄₄''
³⁄₈''
Wedge
6½''
Side rail
Ledger strip
Leg
Wedge detail

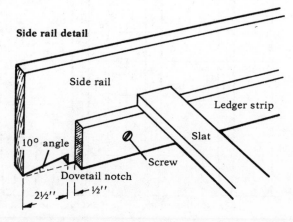

Side rail detail

Side rail
Ledger strip
10° angle
Slat
Screw
Dovetail notch
2½''
½''

Step-by-step instructions

1. Cut six pieces of clear mahogany, each ¾ × 2¼ × 41½ in., for the headboard legs.
2. Cut six pieces of clear mahogany, each ¾ × 2¼ × 31½ in., for the footboard legs.

3. Each leg is made by stack-laminating (see p. 60) a group of three ¾-in.-thick boards together to form a single piece 2¼ in. square in crosssection. Laminated mortises (p. 91) are incorporated into each leg to accommodate the side rails and locking wedges. Begin by labeling each piece as either *inside, outside,* or *middle,* and indicate which end of each piece will be at the top of the leg or at the bottom. Then square two lines across the lower end of each middle piece, marking one line 8¼ in. from the bottom and the other 13⅝ in. from the bottom (p. 133). Now hold a protractor along the lower line, against one edge of the board, and lay out a slope of 10°, beginning at the edge and running toward the bottom. Mark the slope, using a straightedge and sharp pencil. Hold the protractor also along the upper line on each board—against the same edge—and mark out a sloping line of 3°, running from the edge toward the top.
4. The sloping lines indicate the shape of the waste portion which must be removed from each piece to form the mortises for the side rails. Mark the wood between the sloping lines *waste,* then, using a backsaw and guide block, carefully cut each board in two along the 3° sloping line.

5. The long sections of the boards will form the upper middle portion of each laminated leg. Cut the short sections in two, following the 10° slope, and retain the unmarked sections. These will form each leg's lower middle portion. Discard the wood marked *waste.*

6. Assemble each leg. Begin by laying each inside piece flat on the work surface. Next, position the two sections of each middle piece, as shown in the photo above, to create the mortise. Be sure the mortise sides flare rather than form parallel lines. Finally, place the outside piece of each leg in position on top of the pairs of middle pieces. After this trial assembly, take the legs apart and reassemble them, using glue and clamps (p. 44). Be careful not to get glue in the mortise areas, and do not allow the pieces of each leg to slide out of position during clamping.

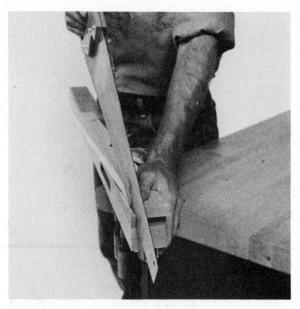

7. Use a router equipped with a straight bit (p. 42) to cut the mortises in each leg to accept the crossrails and either the headboard or footboard ends. The mortises are centered on the inside face of each leg, at right angles to the laminated mortises, and care must be taken to create both right and left legs by making sure that when the bed is assembled the larger openings in the laminated mortises face away from each other. Make a router guide such as the one shown above (a similar guide is also shown on p. 80) to help you cut the mortises precisely. The guide shown above is clamped together, but you may also use screws and glue. The inner dimensions of the guide must form a rectangle whose length equals the length of the mortise you wish to cut, plus twice the distance measured from the edge of the router's baseplate to the nearest edge of the router bit, and whose width equals the width of the desired mortise plus the same measurement of twice the distance from baseplate to bit. On the footboard legs, the crossrail mortises are each ¾ × 5¼ in., and ⅝ in. deep. The bottom of each mortise is located 7¾ in. from the base of each leg. The mortises for the footboard itself are each ¾ × 7 in., and 1 in. deep. Their bottoms are located 17 in. from the leg bases. The mortises for the headboard crossrails are each ¾ × 5¼ in., and 1 in. deep. Their bottoms are 14¾ in. from the base of each leg. The headboard mortises each measure ¾ × 9 in., are 1 in. deep, and are located with their bottoms 24 in. from the leg bases.

8. Lay out and cut tapers on the top and bottom of each leg. Begin each taper 7 in. from the end, and, using a guide block, saw wood off all four sides so the end of the leg is 1½ in. square. Smooth the faces of the legs with a rasp and sandpaper.

9. Edge-glue (p. 45) two pieces of clear mahogany, each ¾ × 5½ × 54½ in., to make the footboard. Trim the piece to 10 in. in width.

10. Lay out the shape of the footboard on stiff paper by enlarging (p. 16) the grid diagram on p. 134. Then trace the pattern onto the footboard. Only half the pattern need to be laid out on paper; flopping it will produce the complete shape.

11. Edge-glue three pieces of clear mahogany, each ¾ × 5½ × 54½ in., to make the headboard. The finished piece should measure ¾ × 16½ × 54½ in.

12. Lay out and trace the headboard pattern (p. 134) onto the headboard by repeating step 10.

13. With both the headboard and footboard laid out, secure each to the workbench and cut to shape, using a saber saw. Work carefully, making sure to keep the saw kerf in the waste portion of the wood.

14. Using a router equipped with a ¼-in. rounding-over bit, machine a ¼-in. radius along the upper and lower edges of the headboard and footboard. Radius both the inner and outer edges of each. If necessary, round the ends of both boards further, using sandpaper, so they will fit in the mortises cut in each leg.

15. Cut one piece of clear mahogany, ¾ × 5½ × 54½ in., for the headboard crossrail. Cut a similar piece 53¾ in. long for the footboard crossrail. Trim both to 5¼ in. in width.

16. Using the router and a ¼-in. rounding-over bit, radius the upper and lower edges of each crossrail, as in step 14, and trim further with sandpaper if necessary.

17. Cut two pieces of clear mahogany, each ¾ × 5½ × 80 in., for the side rails. Trim to 5¼ in. in width.

18. Lay out the dovetailed notch at bóth ends of each side rail (p. 134), along the rail's lower edge. The notches are cut to the same 10° slope as the lower portion of each laminated mortise. Use a protractor to lay out the notches. Each notch is 2½ in. long (measured along the edge of the rail) and ½ in. deep at its deepest point. Between notches, each rail should measure 75 in. in length. Carefully, using a backsaw and guide block, cut out each notch. Trim away any waste wood, especially in the corners, with a sharp chisel. Be careful not to cut the notches too deep, otherwise compensation will have to be made—not only in the sizes of the locking wedges, but in the positioning of the ledger strips as well. Leave the top edge of each rail square.

19. Use a router equipped with a ¼-in. rounding-over bit to radius all upper and lower edges of each side rail. Do not radius the edges of the notches.

(Continued on page 144)

Mortise-and-Tenon Joinery

Mortise-and-tenon joints are among the strongest in woodworking. They are primarily used to fasten pieces together at right angles. Since it is possible to modify the shapes of both mortises and tenons, innumerable variations of the joint have evolved, suited to all types of cabinetmaking and carpentry. Making a basic form of a cabinet-style mortise-and-tenon joint is shown on these pages.

A few overall tips: Although shoulders are not necessary to the function of the joint (in some cases they do add extra strength), they are often cut into all four sides of a tenon to hide the rough edges of the mortise. The thickness of a shouldered tenon should never be less than one-third the thickness of the wood from which it was made. When cutting mortises and tenons, do not attempt to smooth the cut surfaces; their roughness provides a better gluing surface between the mating parts. When cutting a blind mortise (as illustrated below), let its depth be about ⅛ in. greater than the length of the tenon, to allow for glue which may collect at the end.

Types of mortise-and-tenon joints

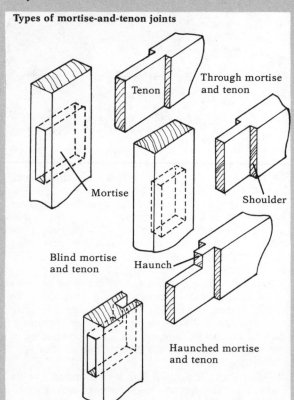

Tenon

Through mortise and tenon

Mortise

Shoulder

Blind mortise and tenon

Haunch

Haunched mortise and tenon

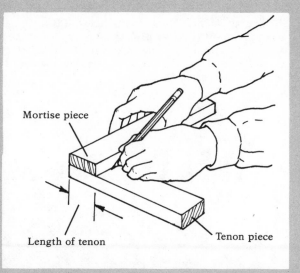

Mortise piece

Length of tenon

Tenon piece

1. Start by marking the length of the tenon. Use a ruler to measure the correct distance in from the end of the tenon piece, or use the mortise piece as a guide, laying it over the top of the tenon piece, as shown. After marking the length on one face, use a try square to extend the line around all four sides of the piece.

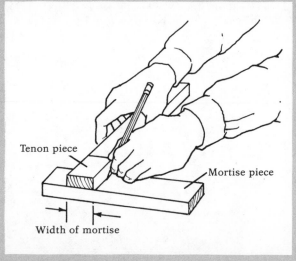

Tenon piece

Mortise piece

Width of mortise

2. Now mark the width of the mortise on the mortise piece, either by using the tenon piece as a guide (if the top and bottom of the tenon are to be shoulderless) or by using a ruler (to lay out the tenon width minus the top and bottom shoulder dimensions). As in step 1, extend the lines around all four sides of the mortise piece, using a try square.

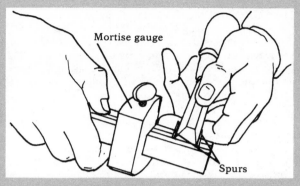

Mortise gauge

Spurs

3. Use a mortise gauge to mark the mortise thickness. (If you don't have a gauge, skip this step.) First select a chisel to cut the mortise (the mortise thickness should be approximately one-third the thickness of the mortise piece), then set the gauge's spurs to match the chisel's blade width.

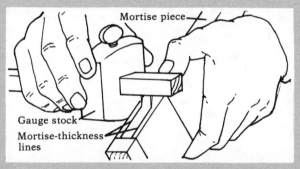

Mortise piece

Gauge stock
Mortise-thickness lines

4. Set the gauge stock so the spurs are centered equally from the sides of the mortise piece, then scribe the mortise-thickness lines by pushing the gauge between the two mortise-width lines scribed in step 2. If you don't have a gauge, lay out these lines with a ruler, and scribe with a pencil.

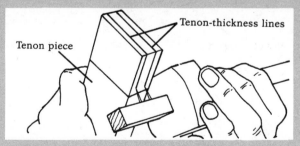

Tenon-thickness lines

Tenon piece

5. Without altering the setting of the gauge spurs, scribe around the end of the tenon piece, as shown above, to lay out the tenon. Adjust the gauge stock only if the tenon piece differs in thickness from the mortise piece. If you have no gauge, lay out the tenon using a ruler and pencil.

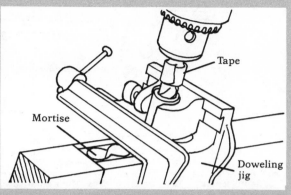

Tape

Mortise

Doweling jig

6. Drill out bulk of waste from mortise, using drill bit that is slightly smaller in diameter than mortise thickness. Tape on bit acts as depth gauge. Use a doweling jig for perfectly vertical holes. Drill end holes first.

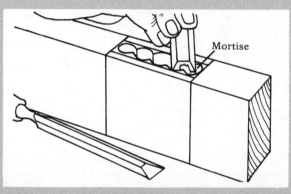

Mortise

7. Carefully pare remaining waste wood from the sides of the mortise, using very sharp chisels whose dimensions are as close as possible to those of the mortise. Mortise walls should be perfectly vertical; corners should be square.

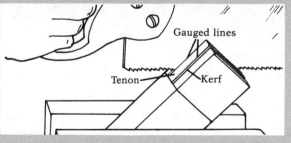

Gauged lines

Tenon   Kerf

8. Clamp tenon piece at angle in vise. Saw down waste side of gauged edge and end lines as shown above, then turn piece around, reclamp at angle as before, and saw down remaining edge. Stop saw just short of scribed tenon-length lines.

(Continued on next page)

Mortise-and-Tenon Joinery — *Continued*

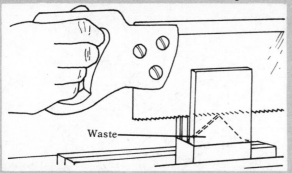

9. Clamp tenon piece vertically in vise. Make final saw cuts straight down to tenon-length lines, removing remaining V-shaped waste between cuts from previous step.

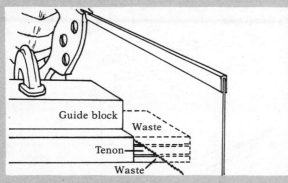

10. Place tenon piece flat on bench, then cut shoulders along tenon-length lines to free waste pieces from cheeks. Shoulder cuts must be exactly square; use a guide block to ensure accuracy. Be sure saw cuts only on waste side of lines.

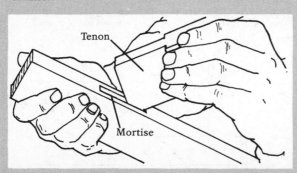

11. Check the fit of the tenon in the mortise by trying each corner. To assemble fully, apply glue sparingly to rim of mortise and lower edges of tenon. Seat pieces, using bar clamps rather than mallet, to avoid splitting mortise piece. (Joints may also be drawbored; see p. 143.)

FRAME-AND-PANEL CONSTRUCTION

Frame-and-panel construction is a particular style of woodworking in which thick stock is mortised and tenoned together to create a rigid framework within which is attached a thin, non-load-bearing panel to cover the open area. The most familiar examples of frame-and-panel construction these days are probably doors, although cabinets, chests, and bureaus were commonly made this way in the days before plywood. The technique combines strength, lightness, and economy, and also provides the chance to use finely figured or carved wood, or even glass, as panels, without concern for its structural qualities. Panels may be fitted permanently into grooves cut into the frame pieces or made removable (the best method if using glass) by being held in place with strips of molding tacked to the inside of the frame. Panels should never be glued or fastened directly. Unless they are free to shrink or expand during seasonal humidity changes, they may split.

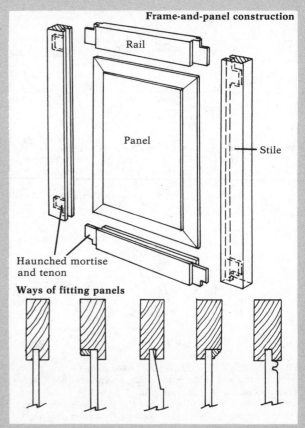

Frame-and-panel construction

Rail

Panel

Stile

Haunched mortise and tenon

Ways of fitting panels

Making a frame

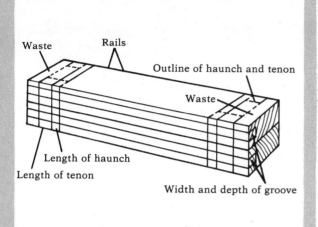

Waste · Rails · Outline of haunch and tenon · Waste · Length of haunch · Length of tenon · Width and depth of groove

1. Establish length and width of finished frame, then lay out rails as a pair, marking them along their edge, ends, and outside faces. Then separate them, and square the lines around each piece. Mark the groove location (width and depth; chosen to suit panel), tenon length, and haunch length (equal to groove depth). Haunch width may be selected arbitrarily.

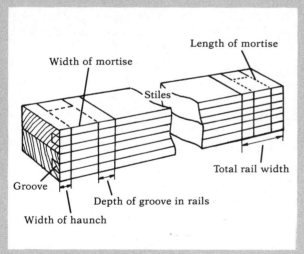

Width of mortise · Length of mortise · Stiles · Total rail width · Groove · Depth of groove in rails · Width of haunch

2. Lay out stiles, also as a pair. First mark total rail width at stile ends. Then, to obtain mortise dimensions, subtract tenon's haunch width from stile ends, and groove depth from scribed rail-width lines. Lay out groove dimensions identical to rails. Mark mortise depths slightly greater than tenon lengths.

Groove · Homemade jig

3. Use a router equipped with a straight bit to cut the grooves marked out on the inner edge of each piece. Cut grooves along entire length of pieces. Use a jig for accuracy. Deep grooves will require more than one pass with the router.

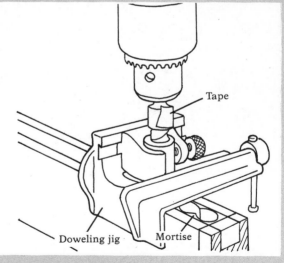

Tape · Doweling jig · Mortise

4. Drill out bulk of mortise waste, using drill bit of slightly smaller diameter than mortise thickness (which equals groove width). Use a doweling jig for accuracy. Tap on bit acts as depth gauge. When finished, pare remaining waste from mortise walls, using very sharp chisels.

(Continued on next page)

Mortise-and-Tenon Joinery—*Continued*

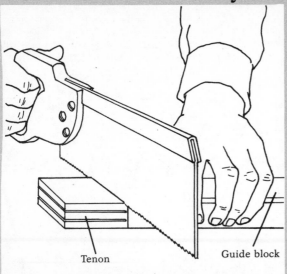

Tenon   Guide block

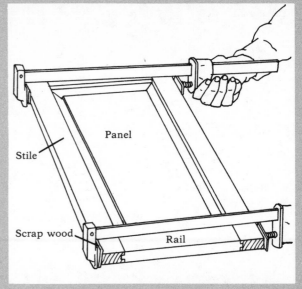

Stile   Panel

Scrap wood   Rail

5. Cut the tenons on each end of the rail pieces by following the tenon-cutting instructions illustrated on pp. 139 and 140. At this stage, each tenon should be wider than its mortise by an amount equal to the tenon's haunch width.

7. Frame pieces may now be assembled (use glue or drawboring method; see page opposite), together with finished panel. Draw frame tight, using bar clamps. Assembled frame should have continuous inner groove around all four sides; tenon haunches should fill portions of grooves at ends of stiles.

Making a panel—Panels may be of uniform thickness or may be raised, that is, made of thick wood decoratively beveled on four sides to fit the grooves in the frame. Wooden panels fitted permanently into frames should have finish applied before installation.

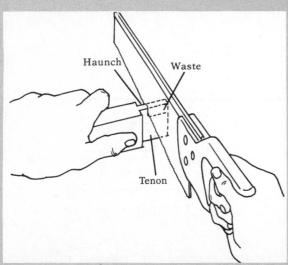

Haunch   Waste

Tenon

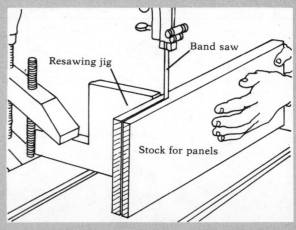

Resawing jig   Band saw

Stock for panels

6. Use already-cut mortises as guides for scribing haunch-widths precisely, by laying tenons at right angles against mortises so grooved lower edges of pieces are even. Carefully cut away upper portions of tenons, allowing for haunch length (equal to groove depth), then cut straight down along haunch-length lines to remove waste.

Thick boards may be sliced in half (resawn) and edge-glued to form panels with unusual grain patterns.

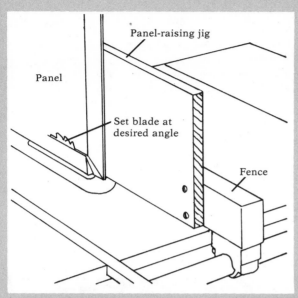

Panel-raising jig

Panel

Set blade at desired angle

Fence

The most common method of raising a panel is to use a table saw. Set the blade to the desired angle and depth of cut, then pass the piece through the saw. Make the end-grain crosscuts first.

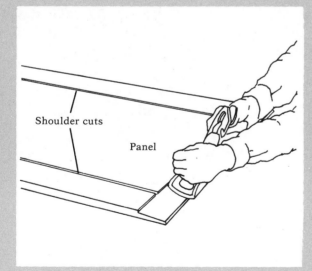

Shoulder cuts

Panel

Traditional raising method is to use a plane. Saw shoulders of bevels first, using backsaw and guide block. Then, after scribing thickness lines on edges of panels, plane off waste, working end-grain areas first. Smooth surfaces with file or sandpaper.

DRAWBORING

Drawboring is a traditional way to fasten mortise-and-tenon joints. A wooden peg driven through slightly misaligned holes bored in each piece pins the joint tightly together. No glue is needed.

Stop drill when bit contacts tenon

1. With the tenon seated fully in the mortise, drill through one side until the bit just touches the tenon. Remove the tenon and continue drilling through the other half of the mortise, using a scrap block in place of the tenon to keep the bit from wandering. The two mortise holes should be in alignment with each other.

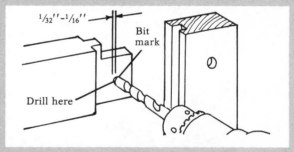

$1/32''$–$1/16''$

Bit mark

Drill here

2. With the tenon removed, locate the drill bit mark. Drill a hole through the tenon with the same bit, $1/32''$–$1/16''$ closer to the shoulder than the bit mark.

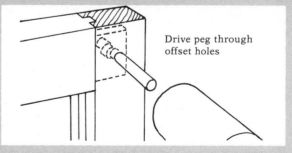

Drive peg through offset holes

3. Replace the tenon in the mortise, and drive a long, tapered wooden peg through the hole to secure the joint. Saw the peg off flush with the mortise sides.

tive crossrail and headboard or footboard end. Be sure the large openings of each laminated mortise are oriented in the proper direction. Disassemble the parts. If you wish to drawbore the assemblies together, follow the explanation of this technique on p. 143. Otherwise, reassemble the pieces, using glue, then pull each assembly together firmly, using at least two bar or pipe clamps.

22. When the glue is dry, but before removing the clamps, drill (p. 72) four ¼-in.-dia. holes, each 1¾ in. deep, into the back of each leg (the side where the laminated-mortise opening is larger) to accept pegs which will lock the components of each assembly together. Locate each hole according to the diagram on p. 133.

23. Cut 16 pieces of ¼-in.-dia. hardwood dowel, each 1¾ in. long, for pegs. Apply glue to the pegs and insert them into the holes. Carefully trim or sand the pegs flush with the legs, then remove the clamps.

20. Cut four pieces of clear maple or other hardwood, each ¾ × ¾ × 6½ in., to make the locking wedges. Shape each wedge with a plane, rasp, or file, so it tapers from ¾ in. thick at one end to ⅜ in. at the other. With a rasp, radius each end to a smooth curve, then sand the wedges smooth. Leave the edges of each wedge square.

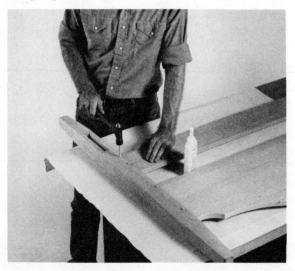

21. Now join all the pieces except the side rails and wedges to form the headboard and footboard assemblies. First, make trial fits of each leg onto its respec-

24. Cut two pieces of clear mahogany, each ¾ × 2 × 74 in., for the ledger strips.

25. Position a ledger strip flush along the lower edge of each side rail, centered so each end of the strip is ½ in. from the notch at each end of the rail, then glue and clamp the strips to the rails.

26. When the glue is dry, remove the clamps and drill five pilot holes (p. 73), evenly spaced along the length of each ledger strip, to accept the 1-in. #8 wood screws. Install the screws.

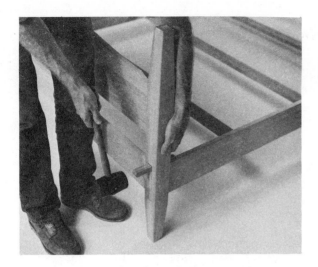

27. Cut four pieces of clear mahogany, each ¾ × 2¼ × 54 in., for the slats. These are not fastened; their ends merely rest on the ledger strips after the bed is assembled.

28. Sand all parts of the bed, stain if desired, then apply two coats of brush-on lacquer as finish. See Wood Finishing, p. 162, for complete finishing instructions.

29. To assemble the bed, position the headboard and footboard assemblies opposite each other, with the larger openings of the laminated mortises in each leg facing away from each other. Insert the notched ends of each side rail into the small openings of the laminated mortises, then push down on the rails to seat them. Install the locking wedges from the outside ends of the bed. Use a mallet to drive the wedges firmly into place.

30. Install your choice of mattress and box spring after placing the slats in position.

Cedar-Lined Blanket Chest

Dovetail joints
Box joints
Inletting a mortise lock

This classic cedar-lined blanket chest should be built as a labor of love. Not only will it store and protect your finest blankets, linens, and other family treasures, but as an heirloom it will also preserve a record of your own abilities as a craftsman, for many, many generations. A woodworker with intermediate abilities can build this chest, using great care and patience, but really it is an advanced project best left until you are confident of your skills and have acquired a diligence and strength of concentration that is second nature. The chest's main feature is its exacting dovetailed construction, for which there are no shortcuts or any way of making up for mistakes. In addition, the chest's extreme simplicity of design—basically it is only a six-sided box—places enormous emphasis on maintaining a high level of accurate workmanship throughout.

The chest is designed to stand at the foot of the double bed whose construction is shown on the preceding pages. Matching wood may even be used. The hinges shown are those described on page 278. When installing them, drill two pilot holes side by side (to form a single, oval-shaped hole) in the lid for each mounting screw, but only one hole per screw in the lid brace underneath. This will allow the hinges to be fastened securely to the chest but will still allow the lid to expand or contract across its width due to humidity changes.

The sliding tray reflects in miniature the design of the chest. The spacing and dimensions of the dovetails are the same. When making it, be sure that its height does not bring it into contact with the lid braces.

The entire chest is lined with aromatic red cedar, a natural moth-deterrent. Never apply a finish to the cedar; just sand it lightly every five years or so to renew its effectiveness.

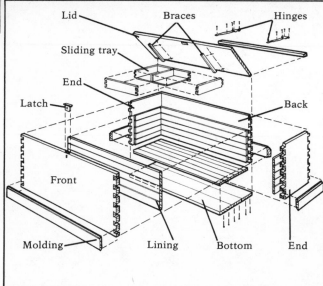

Lid · Braces · Hinges · Sliding tray · End · Latch · Back · Front · Molding · Lining · Bottom · End

What you will need

4 pcs. clear mahogany, ¾'' × 9½'' × 46½''
4 pcs. clear mahogany, ¾'' × 9½'' × 18½''
3 pcs. clear mahogany, ¾'' × 7½'' × 4'
3 pcs. clear mahogany, ¾'' × 7½'' × 46½''
2 pcs. clear mahogany, ¾'' × 2½'' × 4'
2 pcs. clear mahogany, ¾'' × 2½'' × 20''
4 pcs. clear mahogany, ¾'' × 2½'' × 16¾''
1 pc. clear mahogany, ¾'' × 1⅞'' × 16''
1 pc. clear mahogany, ¾'' × 1¾'' × 4'
2 pcs. clear mahogany, ¾'' × 1'' × 15'' (optional; see step 47)
2 pcs. plywood scrap, ⅛'' × 1'' × 43½''
2 pcs. plywood scrap, ⅛'' × 1'' × 15½''
⅜'' aromatic red cedar closet lining, 20 sq. ft. (approx.; see step 26; usually sold in tongue-and-groove random widths)
6d common nails
6d finishing nails
18-ga. wire nails, ⅞''
miscellaneous screws (see step 42)
2 brass strap hinges (see step 47)
1 cabinet latch (mortise type) and striking plate
1 escutcheon
2 brass corner stays
white or yellow glue
stain
brush-on lacquer
table saw
router and router table
bar or pipe clamps
hand and measuring tools

Before you begin

Dovetails are difficult, because they are hard to visualize. Carefully study the layouts of the chest and sliding tray corners shown below, and practice cutting a few dovetail joints on scrap wood before actually cutting the joints for this project.

Sliding tray

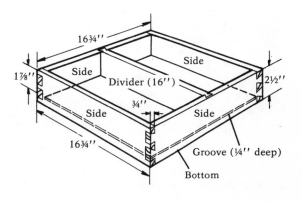

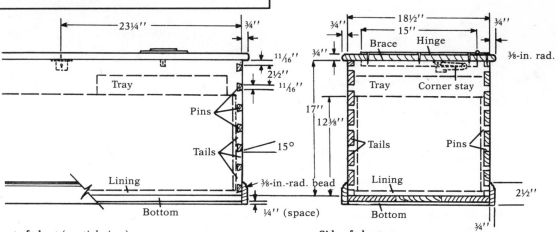

Front of chest (partial view)   **Side of chest**

Step-by-step instructions

1. Cut four pieces of clear mahogany, each ¾ × 9½ × 46½ in., to be edge-glued (see p. 45) to form the chest's front and back panels.

2. Cut four pieces of clear mahogany, each ¾ × 9½ × 18½ in., to be edge-glued to form the chest's end panels.

3. Each panel is made up of two boards, joined with hidden splines. Select which edges are to be joined, then, with the table saw, cut a single groove, ⅛ in. wide and ½ in. deep, along each of those edges to accept the splines. Stop each groove 1½ in. from the ends of each board.

4. From scrap plywood, cut two pieces, each ⅛ × 1 × 43½ in., for the front and back panel splines, and cut two pieces, each ⅛ × 1 × 15½ in., for the end panel splines.

5. Apply glue in the grooves and on the edges of two boards to be joined. Insert a spline in one groove, and position the pair of boards for clamping.

6. Clamp the pieces evenly, using bar or pipe clamps (p. 44). Repeat for the other three panels.

7. Using the table saw, rip each panel to 17 in. wide by removing equal amounts from each side.

8. On the outside face of each end panel, lay out the pins for the dovetail joints (p. 150). Refer to the diagram on p. 147. Scribe seven pins at each end of each board. The upper edge of the first pin starts ¹¹⁄₁₆ in. below what will be the top edge of the panel. Scribe the upper edges of each succeeding pin at 2½-in. intervals, then scribe the lower edges of the pins, each ¹¹⁄₁₆ in. below the first marks. Use a pencil, try square, and straightedge to square the marks along the face of each board and to scribe the baseline indicating the depth of cut, which should be about ¹⁄₃₂ in. greater than the width of the front and back panels.

9. Mark areas of waste wood. Carefully adjust the saw's blade height to cut just to the baseline scribed in the previous step, then set the saw's miter gauge so wood will pass over the blade at a 75° angle (to give each pin a 15° slope). Use the oversize miter gauge extension shown on p. 151 for safety and accuracy. Now make cuts along *every other* scribed line, and make parallel cuts to remove waste wood halfway along each notch.

11. Lay out each set of tails on the front and back panels by using the set of pins marked for each specific corner as a template. Position the pins upright on the inside face of the panel on which you will cut the corresponding tails. Indent the pin board slightly (about ¹/₃₂ in.) from the end of the tail board, but keep the top and bottom edges of each exactly flush. Clamp the pin board in place with a bar clamp. Using a sharp knife, trace around each pin to mark out the tails.

10. Readjust the miter gauge to cut at 75° on the other side of perpendicular. Set each partially notched panel against the extension exactly as before—with the same side of each panel facing the blade—and saw out the remaining portions of each notch to leave only the pins. Lightly letter or number the corners of each panel in pencil, and identify their tops or bottoms as well.

12. Remove the pin board. Use a straightedge and the knife to scribe the baseline, by connecting the already-scribed bottoms of the tails, then square the baseline around the top and bottom edges of each panel, using a try square. Turn the panel over, and scribe a new baseline across the panel's outside face, by connecting the visible points of each end line, using the straightedge.

(Continued on page 154)

Dovetail Joints

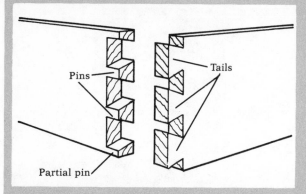

Pins

Tails

Partial pin

The two parts of a dovetail joint are the pins and the tails. When looking at the face of the wood, the pins appear square or rectangular. On the end grain their top and bottom edges flare at angles to each other. Tails are just the opposite. Their top and bottom edges flare when seen from the face; on the end grain their corners are square-cut. The sloping angles resist pulling apart. Made properly, dovetail joints fit so tightly that glue is often not required.

PINS BY MACHINE

An accurate table saw can add extra precision to dovetail joints, since the saw will make repeated identical cuts once it is set up. It is best to cut only the pins with the saw, then use them to scribe the tails. The tails should be fitted individually by hand.

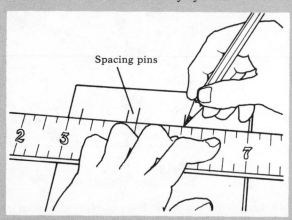

Spacing pins

1. Make sure the boards to be joined are finish-cut, with all edges square.
2. Decide width of pins arbitrarily (usually they are all of equal size, smaller than tails), then mark their positions on the board's outside face, using an accurate ruler or tape.

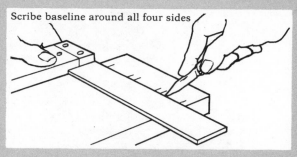

Scribe baseline around all four sides

3. Use a knife and try square to scribe a baseline indicating the depth to which the pins must be cut. This should be about $1/32''$ greater than the thickness of the mating board, to allow for final sanding.
4. With a try square, continue the baseline around the edges of the board and across the inside face so that all four surfaces are marked with a knife-scribed line.

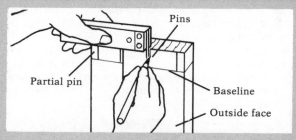

Pins

Partial pin

Baseline

Outside face

5. Use a try square to connect marks from step 2 from the baseline to the edge. With practice you may now skip directly to step 9.
6. Clamp board so end grain is up. Decide arbitrarily on angle that sides of pins should slope (15° is common), then set sliding T-bevel to this angle, using a protractor if needed.

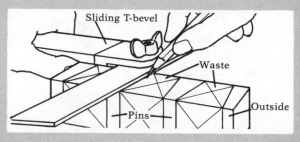

Sliding T-bevel

Waste

Pins

Outside

7. Scribe angled lines across end grain to indicate top and bottom edges of pins. Make sure outward flare of pins is toward inside face of board.
8. Place the board on its outside face, then, using a try square, connect the visible points of the end-grain lines with the scribed baseline. Now each pin is fully outlined. Plainly mark the waste wood to be removed.

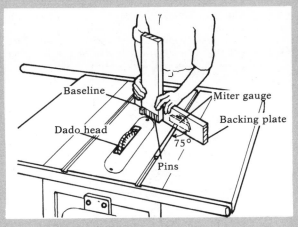

Baseline
Miter gauge
Backing plate
Dado head
75°
Pins

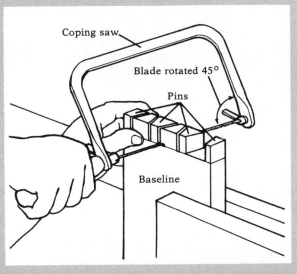

Coping saw
Blade rotated 45°
Pins
Baseline

9. Set saw so blade barely contacts baseline. Adjust crosscut miter gauge to angle of slope. Attach oversize extension (scrap wood) as backing plate for safety and accuracy.

10. Cut all sides of pins which coincide with angle of miter gauge. Position board carefully so blade barely touches pin-width lines and always is on waste side. Use saw's dado head, or make repeated passes to clean out waste halfway across notch.

11. Reset miter gauge to same slope angle, but on other side of perpendicular. Then cut remaining sides of pins by repeating procedures from step 10. Pins are now complete.

PINS BY HAND

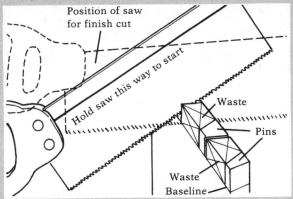

Position of saw for finish cut
Hold saw this way to start
Waste
Pins
Waste
Baseline

1. Lay out pins by following steps 1–8 in Pins by Machine (see page opposite). Then clamp board so end grain is up and use a dovetail saw or fine-tooth backsaw to make the vertical cuts for each pin. Saw as close as you can to the lines, but stay always on the waste sides. Begin by sawing on an angle to follow both visible lines as shown. Hold the saw horizontal to finish the cut. Stop often to check your progress.

2. Using coping saw, cut along the baseline to remove waste. Rotate saw blade about 45° so bar does not strike wood. Begin with saw in kerf, then curve cut to follow baseline. For best results, follow one line at a time, saw across one face, then pivot saw and cut across the other.

3. Carefully clean out baseline cuts with a sharp chisel. Indent the centers of each notch slightly so edges form the highest surface. This will ensure neat-appearing joints.

TAILS

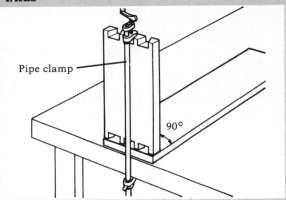

Pipe clamp
90°

1. Regardless of whether you cut pins first (preferred method) or tails, always cut the mating pieces of the joints by hand for accuracy. To do this, first scribe the already-cut pieces onto the mating board. To scribe tails from pins, as shown, clamp pins against inside face of piece from which tails will be cut. Indent pins 1/32'' so tails will be slightly oversize to allow final sanding, but keep inner and outer edges of both boards flush.

(Continued on next page)

Dovetail Joints—*Continued*

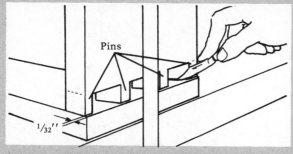

2. Using a sharp knife blade, scribe carefully around each pin to trace the exact outline onto the wood.
3. Remove the pin board.
4. Using a straightedge, scribe a baseline across the inside face of the board by connecting the bottom portions of the tails scribed in step 2. Then use a try square to continue the line across both edges of the board and across the outside face so all four surfaces are marked.

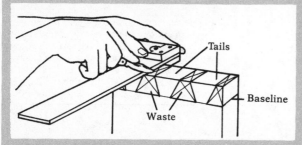

5. Square across the end grain to outline the top and bottom of each tail. Beginners should also measure the locations of the points where the sloping lines of each tail intersect the baseline of the inner face and transfer the points to the baseline of the outside face. By connecting the transferred points with the end-grain lines, each tail can be outlined fully. Mark the waste wood in between on all sides.

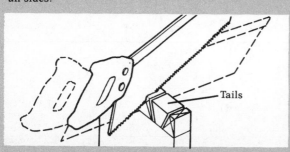

6. Using a dovetail saw or a fine-tooth backsaw, carefully cut down along the slanting lines of each tail while also following the scribed end-grain lines. Place the saw so one

row of teeth is actually on the lines; the other row should be on the waste side. A helpful technique is to hold the wood at an angle in the vise and saw vertically. Begin at a corner with the blade tilted up. Saw to the baseline, then pivot the saw to horizontal and finish the cut.

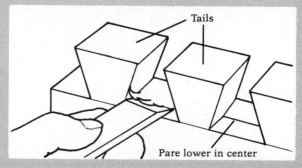

7. Cut along the baseline with a coping saw to remove the waste wood, then clean out each notch with a paring chisel. Follow the procedures given in steps 2 and 3 in Pins by Hand (see p. 151). Be careful not to trim away too much wood.

ASSEMBLY

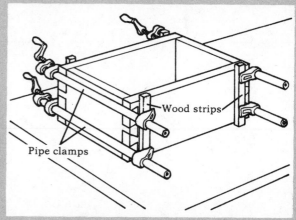

1. Dovetail joints fit tightly only once, since properly made, each piece slightly compresses another. Assemble the pieces only partway to test them; take them apart and trim them very carefully with a chisel if necessary. When it is clear the pieces will fit, reassemble them (partially) and apply small amounts of glue on the upper edges of the pins. Pull the pieces completely together with bar clamps, by tightening them in even stages. Use strips of scrap wood to protect the surfaces of the finished joint.
2. When dry, sand the projecting surfaces of the joints flush, using a belt sander or sandpaper wrapped around a sanding block. Be careful not to chip end-grain pieces.

SLIDING DOVETAILS

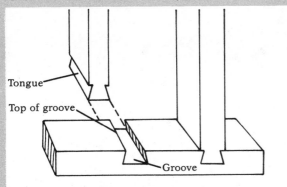

Sliding dovetail joint

Sliding dovetails are useful, particularly for joining shelves to uprights. Cutting them by hand requires special tools, but they can be easily made using a router and router table (see p. 42). You must design your work around bit sizes commercially available; for shelves made of ¾-in. stock, a dovetail bit that cuts a groove ⁹/₁₆ in. wide at the bottom (a standard size) is recommended and shown here. For thicker stock, wider grooves (but not deeper ones) can be cut, using multiple passes with the router. The success of this joint depends on careful setup of router and table. This is most precisely done by trial and error using scrap wood. Sliding dovetails are tricky to get right, but work patiently and you will be very pleased with the end result.

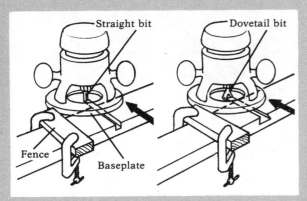

1. Lay out the groove first, then remove most of the waste wood by routing along the center of the groove, using a ¼-in.-dia. straight bit, set slightly less than the finished groove's depth of cut. Then install the ⁹/₁₆-in.-dia. dovetail bit without moving the router's fence. Set the bit to the full depth of cut, and then rout the finished groove. If you are making shelves, or some object which requires a number of similar grooves, rout them all at this time.

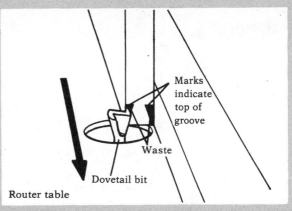

2. Cut the dovetail tongue, using the router table. First measure the width of the groove across the top, and mark on both sides of the mating piece the waste to be removed in order to cut the tongue to fit. Using scrap wood the same thickness as the mating piece, adjust the fence and cut one side of the tongue, removing the marked amount of waste. Do not move the dovetail bit from its setting in step 1.

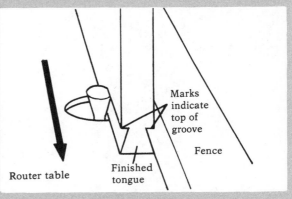

3. Cut the second side of the tongue without moving the fence, then check the fit of the practice tongue in the groove. The fit should be tight, yet require no more than light mallet blows to fit, otherwise the wood may split. (Applying paste wax to the tongue helps.) Adjust the fence until a perfect setting is achieved. Remember that, for the tongue to remain centered on the end of the board, waste must be cut equally from both sides, so once the fence is approximately correct only slight adjustments are necessary. Above all, do not cut away too much wood from the tongue; loose fits are useless.

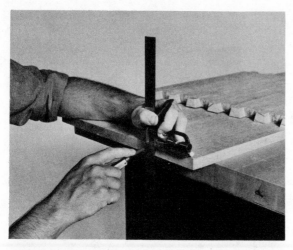

13. Locate the points where the sloping faces of each tail will make contact with the new baseline by measuring and transferring those same points from the reverse side of each board. Square around the end grain as shown above, then, with a knife and straight-edge, connect the visible end points with the points on the baseline to complete the outlining of the tails.

15. Using a coping saw, cut along the baseline between pairs of previous cuts to remove waste wood. Adjust the saw blade to about 45° for easier cutting. Follow the baseline as closely as possible.

14. Label each set of tails to correspond with the pins from which they were laid out. Also indicate each panel's top or bottom and inside or outside face. Now clamp a panel in the vise, and, using a dovetail saw or fine-tooth backsaw, slice down along the end grain, carefully (*very* carefully) following the scribed lines, keeping the saw kerf on the waste side. Stop at the baseline.

16. Clean out the cuts with a sharp chisel. Take very small cuts, on the diagonal, to pare the area between the tails down exactly to the scribed lines. Clean out the angles where the coping saw rounded the corners. Do not cut beyond any scribed lines. Angle the cuts downward toward the middle just a fraction so the edges, becoming the highest surface, will fit tightly.

17. Assemble the sides and ends of the chest by partially fitting the joints together. Determine that they will fit—make very careful adjustments if necessary—then apply glue to the exposed top portions of the pins and seat the joints completely, using bar clamps as shown. Strips of scrap wood protect the mahogany; place them just beyond the baselines of the front and back panels.

18. Trim three pieces of clear mahogany, each ¾ × 7½ × 46½ in., so that the width of each piece is 6⅛ in.

19. After removing the clamps, turn the chest upside down and nail the three boards in place as the bottom, using 6d common nails.

20. Cut two pieces of clear mahogany, each ¾ in. × 2½ in. × 4 ft., for the side molding and two additional pieces of clear mahogany, each ¾ × 2½ × 20 in., for the end molding.

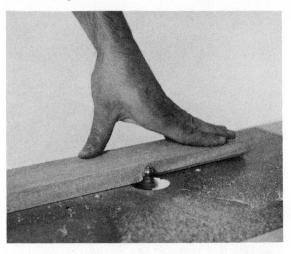

21. Using a router equipped with a ⅜ in. rounding-over bit, machine a bead on the upper edge of each piece of molding. To form the bead, set the rounding-over bit high enough so that it cuts a step in the wood in addition to a simple radius.

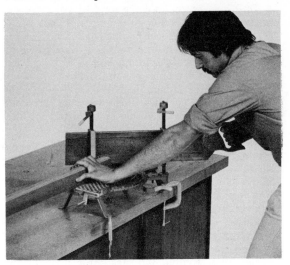

22. Miter the molding to fit around the base of the chest. Begin by cutting both ends of one piece, then cut and test-fit each successive piece individually.

23. To attach the molding, first set the chest upright on ¼-in.-thick blocks of scrap plywood. (Be sure the work surface is uniform.) This raises the bottom of the chest slightly so that only the molding rests on the floor and reduces the likelihood of the chest wobbling if it is placed on an uneven surface.

24. Drill holes in the molding for 6d finishing nails, spacing them evenly along the length of each piece. Measure up ⅝ in. from the bottom edge of the molding to locate the holes, so the nails will then enter the center of the edges of the bottom boards. Use a drill bit slightly smaller in diameter than the nails.

25. Now start the nails in the holes, apply glue to the inside face of the molding, position it, and drive the nails. Hammer only to within ⅛ in. of the molding surface, then use a nail set to bury the heads.

26. Now you are ready to line the chest. Cover the bottom first. Cut strips of ⅜-in.-thick cedar closet lining to fit the inner dimensions of the chest (approximately 17 × 45 in.). Using the 18-ga. nails, tack the strips in place, making sure they also overlap the joints in the mahogany bottom boards. Drive the nails into the tongue of each strip so that they will be hidden by the grooved portion covering it. Bury the heads, using a nail set.

27. Next, line the front and back of the chest. Follow the procedures of the previous step. Position the strips with their tongues up on one side, however, and down on the other.

28. The height of the lining, measured from the surface of the bottom lining, should be 12 in. For the top strips, rip a single piece of cedar and attach each strip with its smooth edge up. A scrap piece of paneling is useful for seating the tongue-and-groove strips together without damage.

29. To line the ends of the chest, cut ⅜-in.-thick cedar as for the bottom, back, and front, and nail it in place, using the techniques described in steps 26–28.

30. Cut one piece of clear mahogany, ¾ in. × 1¾ in. × 4 ft., for the hinge board.

31. Use a router and a ⅜-in. rounding-over bit to machine a ⅜-in. radius (not a bead) on both ends and one long edge of the hinge board. Radius both the top and bottom edges.

Box Joints

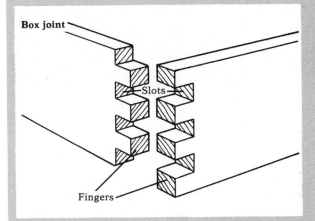

Box joint

Slots

Fingers

1. Box joints are variations of dovetail joints and can be made completely using only a table saw equipped with a dado head. Box joints must be glued, but due to their large surface area, they are virtually as strong as dovetails. Lay out the joints by dividing the width of one board into identical sections designating the fingers and slots. The layout must create full-dimension fingers at both the top and bottom edge.

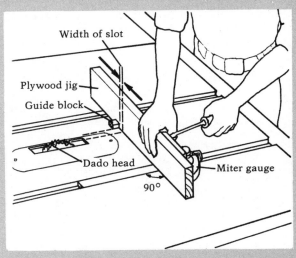

Width of slot

Plywood jig

Guide block

Dado head

Miter gauge

90°

2. To prepare the saw, first assemble the dado head so it equals the desired width of a slot, and install it so its height equals the desired depth of cut (1/32'' greater than the thickness of the wood to be slotted). Using this setup, slot a piece of ¾'' plywood for use as a jig, and install in the slot a guide block the same thickness as the slot but a few inches longer. Clamp the jig to the saw's miter gauge (set to 90°) so the block is exactly one slot-thickness away from the blade. Test the jig by performing steps 3 and 4

(below) on scrap wood and joining the pieces. If the fit is too tight, move the plywood so the block is closer to the blade; if the fit is too loose, shift the jig farther away. When the fit is correct, screw the jig to the miter gauge.

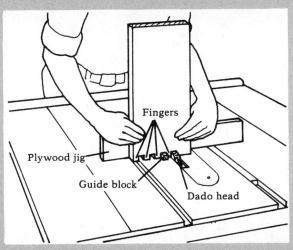

Fingers

Plywood jig

Guide block

Dado head

3. To make the fingered piece, hold the board against the guide block, and pass it through the saw to make the first finger. Make the second finger by placing the just-cut slot over the guide block and passing the board once more through the saw. Repeat the process to make all the fingers.

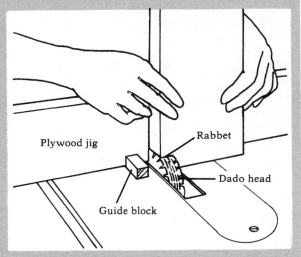

Plywood jig

Rabbet

Dado head

Guide block

4. To make the slotted piece, repeat step 3, but begin by holding the board so that a rabbet is cut at the edge, exactly the thickness of the dado head. The last cut should also form a rabbet, identical to the first in size.

32. Glue and nail the hinge board onto the upper edge of the chest's back panel, using 6d finishing nails. Position the board to overhang the back of the panel ¾ in. and to extend ¾ in. beyond both ends as well. Set the nails.

33. Cut three pieces of clear mahogany, each ¾ in. × 7½ in. × 4 ft., to make the panel for the chest lid. As in step 3, cut grooves in the edges, stopped 1½ in. from each end, to accept ⅛ × 1 in. splines. Glue and insert the splines and clamp the boards together, following the procedures in steps 3–6. Trim the finished lid to 18¼ in. wide, as in step 7.

35. Install the cabinet latch. First, center the keyhole along the front panel (23¼ in. from each end). Place the latch body on its side as shown above, and, with a knife, scribe its width onto the top edge of the panel. Then hold the latch upright so its bottom edge rests on the panel, centered between the width lines, and scribe the latch's thickness. Be sure the upright latch is also centered between the panel's inner and outer edges.

34. Use a router and a ⅜-in. rounding-over bit to work a ⅜-in. radius on three sides of the lid, on both the top and bottom edges. Using a hand-held router is often easier than working on the router table (as shown above).

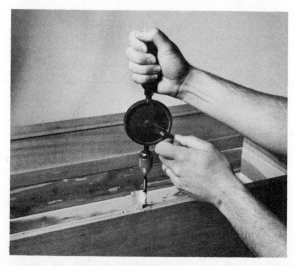

36. Measure the height of the latch, both the body and the flange, then drill out the bulk of the mortise. Use a hand or power drill (p. 72). Wrap masking tape around the drill bit as a depth gauge.

37. Clean out the remaining wood with a chisel, using gentle blows with a mallet. Pare the sides of the mortise so they are straight and square. Trim carefully as needed until the latch body fits. For more on cutting mortises, see p. 138.

38. Insert the latch body in the mortise, then use a knife to scribe around the mounting flange. Hold the knife perpendicular to the flange for accuracy.

Inletting a Mortise Lock

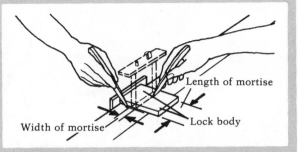

Length of mortise

Width of mortise

Lock body

1. First determine the desired position of the lock, then scribe the length and thickness of the lock body onto the wood by holding the lock against the edge where it is to go. Using a drill the same diameter as the lock's thickness, (taped to indicate the depth the mortise should be), carefully bore a series of vertical holes to remove the waste. Pare the sides of the mortise smooth with a sharp chisel.

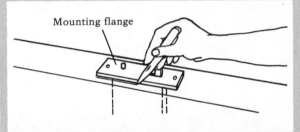

Mounting flange

2. Insert the lock body into the mortise, and scribe around the mounting flange. Use a chisel to inlet this area just enough so the flange will be flush with the wood's surface.

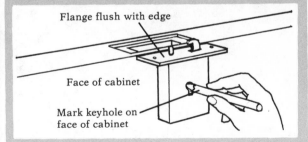

Flange flush with edge

Face of cabinet

Mark keyhole on face of cabinet

3. While holding the lock against the face of the board, with the top surface of the mounting flange flush with the top surface of the board, insert the point of a pencil through the keyhole to mark its position. Or, if the keyhole does not go through, make a paper template of the lock and hold it in position against the face of the board directly in front of the mortise. Drill a hole through the front face. File the hole to fit the key, then cover the area with an escutcheon to hide the hole's edges.

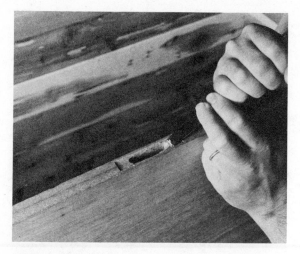

39. Use a chisel to cut away enough wood within the scribed lines so the top of the mounting flange will rest flush with the top edge of the panel. Cut small shavings at a time, using only hand pressure.

40. Fit the latch in place, mark the locations of the mounting screws, then remove the latch and drill pilot holes (p. 73) for the screws.

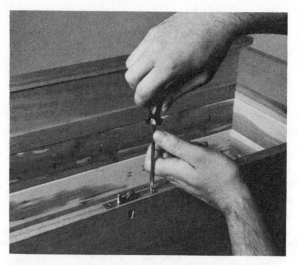

42. Replace the latch in the mortise and secure it temporarily with short, narrow-diameter screws. Check that the keyhole lines up with the hole in the latch.

41. Now position the latch on the front face of the panel so the flange is flush with the top edge. With a pencil, mark the location and size of the keyhole to be drilled through the front of the panel into the mortise. Remove the latch. To rough out the keyhole, drill a large hole above a smaller one. Finish by removing the wood between the holes with a file.

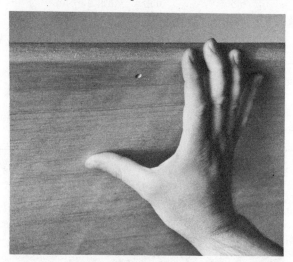

43. Place the lid in position on top of the chest. To determine where to drill the lid to accept the latch's alignment pin, hit the lid firmly with your hand to make a dimple on the underside of the lid. Turn the lid over. Measure the pin and drill the hole.

44. Place the striking plate on the underside of the lid, surrounding the hole. Scribe around the opening for the catch. To realign the plate later, also mark the locations for the screw holes.

45. Chisel out a mortise to accept the catch.

46. Replace the striking plate, and scribe around its perimeter with a knife. As in step 39, chisel away wood so the plate rests flush with the lid.

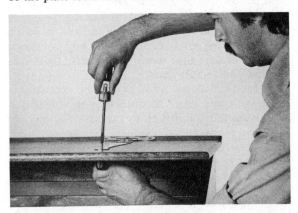

47. With lid in place, center brass hinges 10 in. from the ends of the hinge board, and drill pilot holes for mounting screws. If using the hinges shown, screw them into ¾ × 1 × 15-in. clear mahogany braces beneath the lid. Do not glue the braces to the lid.

48. Remove all the cabinet hardware, then sand all parts of the chest. Apply stain and two coats of brush-on lacquer as finish to all wood *except* the lining. See Wood Finishing, p. 162, for complete instructions.

49. When finish is dry, install the hinges, latch, and striking plate permanently. Mount the escutcheon so it surrounds the keyhole, using the fasteners provided.

50. Fasten sturdy brass corner stays inside the chest at both ends to prevent the open lid from slamming shut.

Making the sliding tray

1. Cut four pieces of clear mahogany, each ¾ × 2½ × ¾ in., for the sides of the tray. Trim length if necessary so tray will fit into chest and rest on top edges of lining.

2. Lay out dovetail pins on both ends of two sides. Space pins the same as on chest (see p. 147). Note, though, that at top and bottom only partial pins are cut.

3. Cut the pins as in chest steps 8-10.

4. Using the pins as templates, lay out tails on the remaining sidepieces as in chest steps 11-13. Cut and label tails as in chest steps 14-16.

5. Using a router with a ⅜-in.-dia. straight bit, cut a ¼-in.-deep groove the full length of each sidepiece on which *tails* were cut, to house the tray bottom. Locate the groove's lower edge ¼ in. from the bottom of each sidepiece (p. 147).

6. Cut a similar groove in each of the pieces on which *pins* were formed, but stop the ends of the groove ¼ in. past the baseline of each set of pins. Do not run the groove the full length of the pieces.

7. Cut one piece of clear mahogany, ¾ × 1⅞ × 16 in., for the tray's divider.

8. Cut a sliding dovetail (p. 153) on each end of the divider, using the hand method.

9. Cut a groove for the dovetail on the inside face of each of the sides which have tails at each end.

10. Cut and assemble with glue, ⅜-in.-thick strips of cedar closet lining to make the tray bottom, approximately 16 × 16 in., or of a size to fit into all four grooved sides when the tray is assembled.

11. Assemble the sides of the tray—locking the bottom in the grooves as you do so—using glue and clamps as in chest step 17. Do not glue the tray bottom.

12. Press the divider into place; glue is optional.

13. Sand the tray; finish same as chest.

Wood Finishing

Wood finishing is the final stage of the long progression from tree to finished object. It is the crucial work that turns bare wood into a warm and glowing piece of furniture, protected from grime and enhanced in grain.

Raw, unfinished wood, though beautiful, is highly vulnerable. The cellular structure of bare wood behaves very much like blotting paper, absorbing dirt not just from direct contact, but from the environment as well. Unfinished wood also responds much more than finished wood to changes in humidity, by contracting when it is dry and expanding when it is damp. Finally, wood needs protection from spills, burns, stains, scratches, and nicks.

Time was when workaday domestic furniture got its shine and protection from nothing more than the repeated application of salt pork, or cedar oil, or oil and tallow accidentally spilled and rubbed into the wood. Fine furniture, on the other hand, was solely the province of finishers who spent years developing a sensitivity of touch and a working knowledge of the many processes and formulas that were necessary to create finishes and apply them.

Modern chemistry has turned this once esoteric craft into an accessible, though still tricky, do-it-yourself activity. Now it is possible to apply to wood ready-mixed products that approximate the hand-rubbed finishes of the past and protect even better than they did, yet achieve these ends in hours of work rather than days.

Finishing is still a multistep process, however, and it still requires patience and energy. There are many different methods to finish any given piece of furniture and many products to accommodate each method. Think of finishing as a creative rather than as a mechanical process, but don't improvise haphazardly. A well-made piece of furniture can be ruined by insufficient preparation of the surface or an incompatible choice of finishing materials.

A good finishing job always depends on the best choices from several alternatives, as well as careful planning and meticulous execution. Work one step at a time, and remember the goals: protecting and beautifying the wood.

Steps to a fine finish

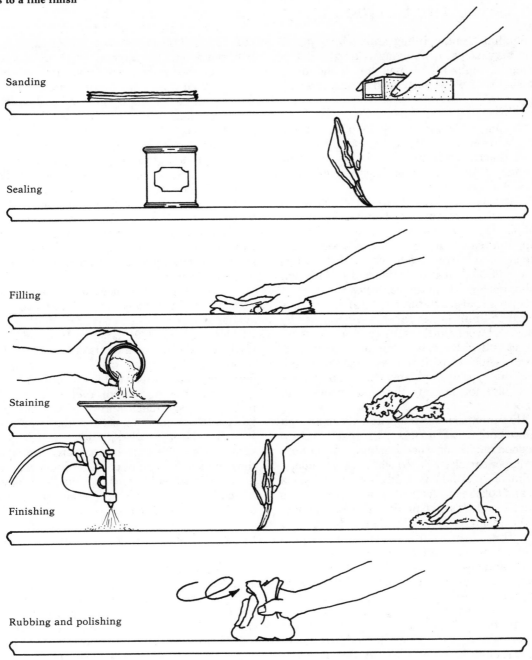

Sanding

Sealing

Filling

Staining

Finishing

Rubbing and polishing

Preparing the Surface

Sanding, sealing, filling, and staining are all preliminary steps to applying a finish. Before sanding, though, fill all nail holes and other blemishes with wood putty such as plastic wood.

Sanding

Sanding is the process of smoothing wood. Your goal is to eliminate all the scratches and imperfections that would otherwise show up under the finished surface, using progressively finer grades of abrasive paper.

There are four kinds of sandpaper in general use, but all are comprised of mineral particles glued to paper. Flint-coated paper is natural, cheap, and readily available in hardware stores. It's too dull to use on wood, but it's useful when you need to sand an already finished surface that is going to clog the sandpaper quickly.

Garnet is also a natural mineral, but it lasts longer than flint. Garnet paper is widely used by professional wood finishers. As the abrasive granules break off with use, new granules are exposed, a process which considerably extends the usefulness of this type of sandpaper. Garnet paper is a good choice for sanding the wood projects in this book.

Aluminum oxide is tough and sharp enough to use on both wood and metal. Like garnet paper, it's a good choice for wood finishing. Aluminum oxide paper can also be used with power sanders.

Silicone carbide is made by fusing silica sand and coke in an electric furnace. The process is a lot like nature's own production of diamonds, and the result is similarly diamond-hard and sharp. Use silicone carbide paper on lacquer, plastic, metal, and composition materials.

All abrasive papers come in a variety of grades from very coarse to superfine. Flint-coated papers are labeled with a descriptive word, but the other types are usually designated by a number. There are two different numbering systems: the first ranges from 60 to 400; the second from 1/0 to 12/0. One or both numbers usually appear on the paper you purchase. In both systems, the higher the number, the greater the number of particles and, therefore, the finer the grit.

Abrasive paper is either open-coat or closed-coat. The grit particles on open-coat papers cover between 50 and 70 percent of the surface, while on closed-coat papers they cover the whole surface. Closed-coat paper cuts faster, but clogs faster, too, when used on softwood or paint. Open-coat paper clogs less, because there is more space between particles.

There are many backing materials for abrasive particles, but for home use, paper and cloth are best. Like grit, paper comes in grades. Paper labeled A is lightweight, has abrasive particles of fine grit, and is called finishing paper. Papers labeled C and D are medium weight, have abrasive particles of medium fineness, and are called cabinet papers. Grade E paper (known as roll stock) is heavyweight and is not generally used in home projects.

You will probably need to use only a small percentage of the many kinds of abrasive papers available. Garnet, open-coat paper with a paper backing in 80-grit (1/0), 120-grit (3/0), and 180-grit (5/0) will suffice for most tasks. Use 80-grit for rough sanding; switch to 120-grit to remove surface imperfections, then to 180-grit for fine sanding.

Using a sequence of ever-finer abrasives removes the scratches left by the previous grade. Start with coarser grits, because they work faster. Switch to the next higher grit when you can see no scratches on the surface that are deeper than those which the sandpaper has produced. Examine the scratches in cross-light to check. Always remember to sand with the grain of the wood, even when using the finest grit.

When sandpaper becomes dull, discard it. But if it is only clogged, you can restore it by brushing out the dust.

As a final step, when the surface feels smooth as glass to the touch, run a damp sponge evenly over the surface. The dampness will slightly raise the wood fibers that have been pressed down by sanding. Brush off the sanding dust, wipe the wood with a tack cloth (see p. 171) and let dry overnight. Sand once again the next day, using the finest grade of sandpaper you finished up with.

How to Use Sandpaper

SANDING A FLAT SURFACE

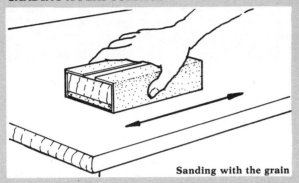

Sanding with the grain

To maintain even pressure, use a sanding block. Start in one corner and rub in a straight line along the grain. Sanding with the grain creates scratches that are easier to remove than cross-grain scratches. Use a light touch, and let the sandpaper do the work. Clean the paper frequently.

Making a sanding block—Store-bought sanding blocks waste paper and tend to weigh more than home-made ones. It's easy enough to make your own out of cork, which is firm and light, or wood. Make it about $1\frac{1}{2} \times 3 \times 4\frac{1}{2}$ in.—a size that will fit the hand. If you use wood, glue a $\frac{1}{4}$-in.-thick layer of foam rubber or felt to the working surface of the block. It will reduce heat buildup and lessen the possibility that debris caught between the wood block and the sandpaper will gouge the wood surface.

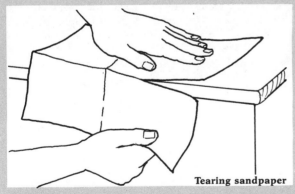

Tearing sandpaper

Fold a piece of sandpaper in quarters, unfold, and tear the creases along the sharp edge of a piece of wood. You may damage your scissors or knife if you use them to cut sandpaper. Wrap the paper around the cork or foam rubber, and shift it to a fresh section as it dulls.

SANDING CHAIR LEGS AND SPINDLES

Sanding a spindle

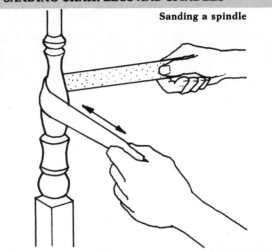

Tear sandpaper into thin strips along a sharp edge, and run masking tape along the back of each strip to prevent it from tearing. Sand back and forth, using a shoeshine motion, working up and down and all around. Use only a fine sandpaper, such as 180 (5/0). Rougher grits can flatten or distort rounded areas.

SANDING CARVED AREAS AND CREVICES

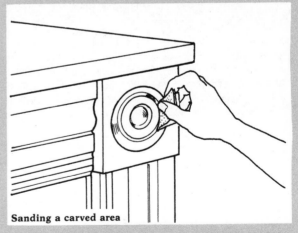

Sanding a carved area

Use a fine sandpaper, such 180 (5/0). Sand lightly and slowly along the grain. Push the paper into crevices with your fingers, and fold it to conform to indentations. To smooth a concave curve, wrap sandpaper around a dowel that has the same diameter as the curve. Push it carefully back and forth along the curve.

Alternatives to Hand Sanding

SCRAPERS

There's more than one way to smooth a board. Before there were abrasive papers, there were scrapers, and they are still widely used in cabinet-making. Scrapers come in two forms: hand scrapers, which are simply rectangular pieces of steel all of whose edges can be sharpened; and cabinet scrapers, which have a blade that is similar but is mounted in a cast-iron frame. There is also a variety of smaller, curved scrapers that work very efficiently on moldings and curved pieces.

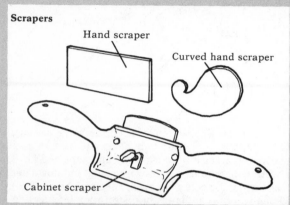

Scrapers

Hand scraper

Curved hand scraper

Cabinet scraper

The cutting edge on both hand and cabinet scrapers is about 3/100 in. thick and cuts the fibers of the wood into paper-thin shavings. It does not produce grain-clogging dust the way sandpaper does.

Use either a pulling or a pushing action, moving along the grain but at a slight angle to it. After each pass, shift the angle from slightly to the left to slightly to the right. Pulling allows more control and produces a cut as wide as the blade. Pushing is best for rough jobs like removing dried glue or an old finish.

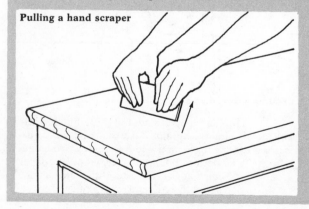

Pulling a hand scraper

To pull: Use the four fingers of each hand to support the scraper, while your thumbs in front control the degree of curve at the cutting edge. Tilt the top of the scraper toward you so that the cutting edge bites into the wood at an angle of about 80°.

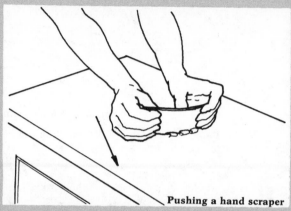

Pushing a hand scraper

To push: Bow the center of the scraper blade slightly outward by applying pressure with your thumbs. Curl your other fingers over the ends of the blade. Push the scraper away from you so that the cutting edge bites into the wood at an angle of about 80°.

A cabinet scraper is easier to use, but more expensive than a hand scraper. It eliminates the need to exercise perfect control with the hands and fingers and to maintain an exact angle. A setscrew controls the blade's curve. Hold the scraper firmly by the handles, then simply push it along the grain of the wood.

How to sharpen a scraper—When a scraper produces dust instead of fine shavings, it is time to sharpen it. The technique requires some getting used to. The goal is to produce a burr, which is the hooklike surface that runs along the cutting edge.

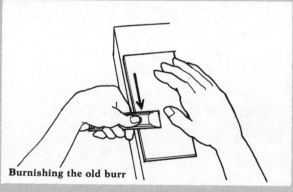

Burnishing the old burr

First, burnish the old burr down. Begin by lightly oiling both sides of the scraper blade and the back of a chisel. Place the scraper flat on a bench. Holding the chisel between your thumb and index finger, run the back of it along the whole length of the blade. The back of the chisel should be flat against the scraper and tilted slightly in the direction you're going. Make several passes, increasing the pressure slightly each time.

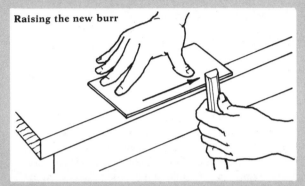

Raising the new burr

To raise the new burr, upend the scraper on the bench. With the chisel at an angle of 85° to the face of the scraper, run it lightly toward you for the full length of the blade. Only one edge of the back of the chisel should be making contact with the end of the scraper blade. After several passes, you should barely feel the burr when you run your finger along the face of the scraper. The cutting edge is ready at that point. Repeat the procedure on each of the three remaining sides.

STEEL WOOL

Steel wood does not leave tiny scratches on the wood surface like sandpaper does. It is, therefore, very useful for the final smoothing of surfaces that you have finished sanding, particularly end grains, turnings, and carved areas. Use 3/0 steel wood for smoothing. To smooth the surface between coats of finish, use 4/0. To rub the top coat, use either of the extra-fine grades, 5/0 or 6/0.

Use steel wool with a light touch to avoid cutting into the surface. Clean off remaining particles with a damp cloth or tack cloth.

POWER SANDING

Using a power sander requires a bit of practice, because it can quickly do a great deal of damage. A belt sander, for example, is so tough and fast that it can cut right through thin veneer almost on contact. It is, however, the best bet among sanders for heavy-duty finishing work. Orbital and disk sanders—though less expensive—operate in a circular pattern and leave

cross-grain scratches on the wood. Some orbital sanders have an optional back-and-forth motion, which makes them worthwhile for fine finishing after the rough work is done.

To use a belt sander, hold it in both hands, switch it on, then make contact with the surface. Keeping it flat on the surface, move it from one end of the work to the other. Changing direction midway can make scratches. Switch it off only after you have lifted it from the work.

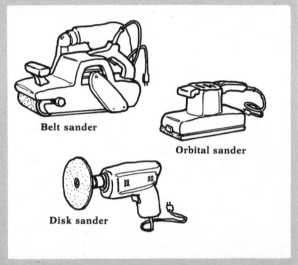

Belt sander

Orbital sander

Disk sander

Sand in a 45° angle in one direction, then 45° in another, and finally sand back and forth with the grain to remove marks left by the angled passes. Work with increasingly finer grits, and end with hand sanding. Use 60-, 80-, and 120-grit paper, or whatever grits you would normally use for hand sanding. Do not skip more than two grit numbers when progressing from coarse to fine papers.

An orbital sander, also called a finish sander, is much lighter than a belt sander. Use its back-and-forth mode for medium and light work, and its orbital mode for polishing or smoothing wood between layers of finish.

A disk sander is good for odd-shaped sanding work. It holds a round disk of sandpaper fixed to a flexible rubber disk backing. In two-speed models, use the fast speed only for removing an old finish, and the slow speed (with a lamb's wool bonnet fitted over the rubber disk) for polishing. Do not use it for finishing. It can't produce an even surface and it won't go into corners.

Sealing

A sealer provides a tough and transparent division between layers of finish. There are several points in the finishing process when you should apply a sealer. After staining, brush a sealer over the stain to prevent it from bleeding through to the subsequent finish above. Sealer will also stiffen the minute wood whiskers raised on the surface by water stain (see p. 169), making them easy to sand off. If you intend to use filler (below), again seal the wood first. This will make it easier to wipe excess filler off the surface. Even if you are not going to stain or fill the wood, you may wish to use a sealer over particularly porous raw wood to prevent surface coatings from soaking deeply into the wood. Sealer used this way is known as a wash coat.

Shellac is a good sealer. Buy the 4-pound base (p. 177), and mix 1 pint of it with 8 pints of denatured alcohol. This combination produces a very thin shellac. Keep in a glass jar with a tightly fitting lid.

You can also buy commercial sealers that have a longer shelf life. You'll probably have to thin them with lacquer thinner. Sanding sealer is also a popular commercial sealing product. It is formulated to be very easy to sand and doesn't become gummy.

To apply sealer, just brush it on with a soft brush. It will dry rapidly and should be problem-free. Sand the surface lightly with a fine-grit sandpaper, and wipe up the dust with a tack cloth. Repeat a second time.

Filler

Sanding may make wood very smooth, but it cannot do the job perfectly if the wood has obvious pores. Filler is used to fill those pores so that they will be inconspicuous. You can apply filler either before or after you stain the wood, if you stain it at all. Filler used before staining should be in a natural wood tone. When filling after staining, buy a filler that matches the stained wood.

Not all woods need filler. It's a step you can skip if you're working with close-grained wood or open-grained wood that you are intending to

finish with a penetrating sealer. But if you're working with an open-grained wood and you intend to finish it with a surface coating like varnish, lacquer, or shellac, then fill the pores to ensure a smooth, glassy surface effect. If you do not, the finish coat you apply may look rippled on the surface.

Filler comes in both liquid and paste form. The paste is best for open-grained wood. Before you start spreading it on, you must thin it with whatever the manufacturer suggests on the label. Aim for a consistency approximating thick cream. If in doubt, it's better to make it too thin than too thick. It should run when you pour it on the surface.

Apply filler with a very stiff brush. A stencil brush with a 1½-inch diameter is a good choice. Otherwise, use an old paintbrush (or a cheap new one) with the bristles cut back to 2 to 3 inches long.

Load the brush with filler, and brush it on thickly in the direction of the grain. Then brush across the grain to work the filler into the pores. This is messy work, more like scrubbing than brushing.

The filler will take on a dull cast as it starts to dry. Depending on the kind you use, this will

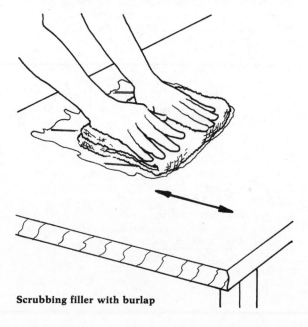

Scrubbing filler with burlap

happen in from 5 minutes to an hour. At this point, take a rough rag or a piece of burlap and rub it across the grain. Timing is important here; if you start scrubbing too soon the filler will lift out of the pores; wait too long after it has turned dull and it will be tacky and resist removal.

Rubbing packs the filler into the pores and removes it from the surface of the wood. Working cross-grain, continue to wipe the filler off the surface. If you leave any, it will make the wood less smooth, which is the opposite of what you are trying to accomplish, and there will be a cloudy appearance under the finish you apply.

Let the filler dry for 24 hours, then sand the surface with a very fine sandpaper.

Staining

If your wood is uninteresting, or variable in tone, a stain will make the grain more pronounced, deepen the color, and unify the wood tones. Light woods such as beech, birch, poplar, ash, gum, and new pine will brighten up considerably if stained. If your wood is new and you want it to look old, that's another good reason to stain it.

But if your wood is darker and already heavily grained, it may have sufficient natural beauty to make staining unnecessary. Cherry, maple, rosewood, and mahogany, unless they are uneven in tone, do not need staining.

Some wood finishers contend that no wood should be stained; variations in tone are natural, as are variations from one piece of furniture to another in the same room. Mass-produced furniture is frequently stained to create uniformity among all the pieces in a set, but this practice obliterates the individual character of each piece. Remember that changing the color of wood does not always enhance it. It may obscure the grain.

Try a simple test before you decide to use stain. Wet your finger and run it over the newly sanded wood. This will approximate its finished look. Better yet, if you have your chosen finish already at hand, brush a bit of it on some inconspicuous spot. You may find that the finish alone will enhance the wood sufficiently to make staining unnecessary.

Stain is different from paint. It is relatively

Making Your Own Stain

Powdered aniline dyes and water make the most brilliant and transparent of all stains and are also the least expensive. You can add standard colors available in powdered form to water to create your own stain, and you can pick from among at least 36 colors pre-blended to cover the spectrum of wood tones. Aniline dye stains penetrate deeply and do not fade. Use a water stain only on new wood. Do not try to use a water stain on any surface that has been finished before, however. Even wood that has been stripped of its finish will not be able to absorb a water stain.

Powdered aniline dyes made especially for use by furniture finishers carry both a color and a wood name. The common ones are yellow (oak), orange (maple), red (mahogany), and brown (walnut). You can experiment with blending these colors and with adding dark blue and black to make any number of wood shades.

To prepare a water stain, boil 1 qt. water (preferably distilled water), pour it into a metal container, and slowly stir in 1 oz. of the powder. When the mixture cools to room temperature, the stain is ready. Make sure that you buy water-soluble powder when you are shopping for stain colors. Some stain powders are meant to be dissolved in liquids such as shellac, varnish, and penetrating sealer, and these will not work in water.

After using a water stain, seal it and apply a surface finish like shellac, lacquer, or varnish that will protect it. Do not use an oil finish over a water stain.

Store aniline powders in an airtight container. Do not keep liquid stain for later use, because it may lose some of its color in storage. Whether you mix your own powders or use only one, keep a record of the stain you created.

transparent, in order to let the grain show through, but it actually dyes the wood. A good stain should go on easily, dry quickly, and penetrate well. Applying a stain is less of a challenge than is choosing the right shade of stain for your wood. There are several categories of stains, each with its own color range.

Penetrating oil stains—Though simple to apply, penetrating oil stains present a much more limited choice of colors than water stains you mix yourself. They are a mixture of aniline dyes and turpentine. Use them on pine and softwoods, but not on hardwoods, because they do not penetrate evenly.

To apply a penetrating oil stain, either wipe on with a cloth or sponge, or use a wide, flat-bristle brush. Seal any end grain first with shellac or linseed oil, because it is much more porous. Stain the sides, front, back, and top, brushing in the direction of the grain. Because it is oil based, penetrating stain will take 24 hours to dry. If it isn't dark enough, restain. Before going on to a filler or surface coat, first apply a wash coat of sealer, otherwise the stain will bleed through the finish. (This effect will be rich and transparent, but will fade with time.)

Water stains — Inexpensive and fast to apply, water stains are nothing more than aniline dye powder mixed with hot water. The powders come in many rich colors, and the more powder you use, the darker the stain (see Making Your Own Stain, p. 169).

To use a water stain, moisten the wood with warm water, let it dry, and sand it. Otherwise the grain will raise when you apply the stain. Apply the stain with a brush or spray, then wipe. Since the stain does not blend in from stroke to stroke, brush on carefully in long strokes that do not overlap. Complete one whole surface before going on to another. To lighten the color, wait 2 or 3 minutes, then wipe the surface. The stain dries in 12 to 24 hours.

Pigmented oil stains — Nonfading and nonbleeding, pigmented oil stains are composed of the same kind of pigment used in paint, mixed with linseed oil, turpentine, or mineral spirits. They have excellent clarity and do not raise the grain.

To use pigmented oil stains, apply liberally to softwoods only, using a brush or rag. Let set for 5 to 10 minutes, then wipe with a soft cloth along the grain.

Wiping stains — Pigmented oil stains in concentrated form are called wiping stains. They are applied and wiped off in order to create highlights and shading.

Non-grain-raising stains (NGR) — These stains do not fade or bleed, and they penetrate evenly. They are a combination of aniline dyes and denatured alcohol or methanol. Though they dry much more quickly than penetrating oil stains, they cost more, and are more difficult to apply.

Color selection is more limited than among water stains.

To use NGR stains, apply to hardwoods only, with a brush or cloth. Start with light coats and recoat, rather than use a heavy coat.

Choosing a Finish

There are several factors to consider before you can choose the best finish for the job. The most important are the purpose your furniture project will serve and the kind of wood from which it is made. If your project will be used for food preparation or serving, it will require a nontoxic finish, resistant to moisture and stains. Varnish or polyurethane would be appropriate. But if aesthetic considerations are uppermost, an oil finish that you are willing to renew periodically may be preferable.

Consider, too, the natural color of the wood. The finish you choose should complement the other pieces of furniture in the room. The degree of gloss you prefer will also influence your choice of finish. Do you prefer the matte effect of a penetrating resin or the antique, glossy look of a shellac finish?

Decide on the degree of difficulty you can take on. Spray lacquering and French polishing are time-consuming undertakings, requiring skill and special equipment. Oils are simple and fast to apply.

Clear finishes fall into two categories: penetrating and nonpenetrating. Penetrating finishes soak into the wood, while nonpenetrating finishes coat the surface. The kind of wood you are working with will help determine which kind of finish you should use.

Generally, open-grained wood with its obvious pores soaks up a penetrating finish well. Open-grained woods with beautiful texture — new mahogany, new walnut, old oak, teak, rosewood, and ebony — gain clarity and intensity with a penetrating resin finish. Fine-grained woods such as old mahogany, old walnut, and new oak have pores that are not visible and require surface coating. Maple, birch, pine, cherry, gum, basswood, and beech also should have a surface finish.

Some woods, such as oak, mahogany, chestnut, pecan, walnut, and ash can be treated with either an in-the-wood or an on-the-wood finish.

There are, of course, exceptions to these rules. You can use a nonpenetrating finish on an open-grained wood by first sealing its pores with a penetrating finish. And you can use a penetrating finish on a close-grained wood, but, because the finish will not penetrate as far, it will be less effective. You can also buy or mix a finish that combines the qualities of both penetrating and nonpenetrating finishes.

In-the-wood finishes include boiled linseed oil, tung oil, and penetrating resins. Generally, they are easier to apply than surface finishes. Since the liquid soaks in, it eliminates the two nemeses of nonpenetrating finishes: telltale brush strokes and traces of surface dust. To apply an oil finish, just pour it on, work it in with rag, hand, or brush, and let it soak in, then wipe off the excess. Periodic reapplication is necessary, but easy. As it hardens between the fibers, the finish will actually strengthen the wood.

The surface will retain its tactile wood qualities and look natural in a way that is appropriate to modern furniture. The uncoated surface will, however, be more vulnerable to stains and abrasions.

Nonpenetrating finishes include all the traditional methods of covering wood: shellac, lacquer, and the many kinds of varnishes. These finishes, built up one coat at a time, shield the wood very effectively from dirt and damage. Except for spraying lacquer, surface finishes are applied with a brush and are subject to lap marks. Their generally slow drying time makes them vulnerable to dust settling on the surface.

Unfortunately, there is no one clear finish, either built up or rubbed in, that is a perfect blend of ease of application, durability, and beauty. The trick is to find the combination of wood and finish that comes closest to being perfect.

One characteristic that all clear finishes have in common, though, is being flammable. Get rid of the rags and newspapers you use at the work site immediately. Find a dust-free, nonhumid, well-ventilated place to work in.

Dealing with Dust

A TACK CLOTH

A tack cloth is simply a sticky cloth. It is used to lift dust from the pores of wood you have finished sanding after you have wiped off all the dust you can readily see or feel. You can also use the tack cloth as a final wiping-up step before you add a new coat of finish. Use a brush or vacuum for initial clean-up stages, and save the tack cloth for the final wipe.

To make a good tack cloth, use a diaper, handkerchief, or any lint-free cloth that has been washed often enough to be very soft and free of sizing. Soak the cloth first in water, wring it out, then immediately soak it in turpentine, and wring it out again. Smooth out the cloth and sprinkle it with enough varnish to dot the surface liberally. Work the cloth together until it is uniformly yellow and just barely damp and sticky. Now it is ready for use.

Store a tack cloth in a screw-top jar so it will not dry out. If you renew the cloth occasionally by sprinkling it with water and turpentine, it will actually improve with age.

A PICKING STICK

When hair, dust, or the odd brush bristle drops onto your newly finished surface, a small device can accomplish what your fingernails can never quite manage. A picking stick, merely a sliver of wood with a sticky tip, can touch down on the offending particle and lift it straight off your otherwise perfect surface.

To make a supply of picking sticks, first collect some bamboo cocktail skewers. Buy crushed or powdered rosin in a music store or sporting goods store. In the top of a double boiler, with boiling water beneath, gradually stir 8 parts rosin into 1 part varnish. When the two form a small, sticky ball, the mixture is cooked. Dip each stick in the ball, and extract a small amount, then, with wet fingers, form a little ball on the tip of the stick. Roll it in your palm until it is firm. Store the picking sticks in a tall jar with a screw-top lid.

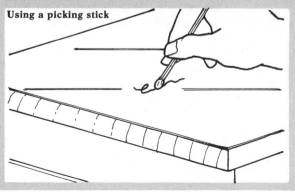

Using a picking stick

Natural and synthetic varnishes

Natural varnish has been used for hundreds of years. It coats furniture with a handsome, rather formal surface layer that is impervious to heat, water, alcohol, and the rigors of daily use. This very hard surface has warmth and depth, darkening the wood only slightly and giving it a golden tone.

The ingredients in traditional varnish are natural resins, tung or linseed oil, turpentine, and a chemical drying agent. This is a difficult combination to work with. The varnish is applied with a brush in several thin coats. Each coat requires skillful brushing to eliminate lap marks and bubbles on the surface. Varnish dries very slowly by oxidation. Unless the work is done in a dust-free location, airborne particles have ample time to settle and stick on the surface.

Modern synthetic varnishes dry just as hard and protect just as well as natural varnish, but sidestep its shortcomings. There are now varnish formulations designed for every possible wood surface, presenting a confusing range of choices. Though there are hundreds of products, those for indoor furniture fit into only two categories: polyurethane and alkyd varnish.

Polyurethane, sometimes called plastic varnish, is formulated to provide a rock-hard layer of protection. The price of this protection is a surface that looks and feels like plastic. It's not for fine woods but is useful for everyday pieces that get a workout around the house. Brush strokes are self-leveling; drying time between coats is 3 or 4 hours, rather than 24. It comes in high gloss, satin, or flat finishes. Polyurethane is so hard that it requires a power sander if you decide to remove it. Paint stripper can't always do it.

Most varnishes on the market are alkyd varnishes. They produce an attractive finish that is tough, but not quite as tough as polyurethane. Alkyd varnishes containing tung oil have greater resistance to moisture than those containing linseed oil.

Phenolic resin or spar varnish is meant for outdoor furniture and boats. It yellows too much to use on indoor furniture.

How to Apply Varnish

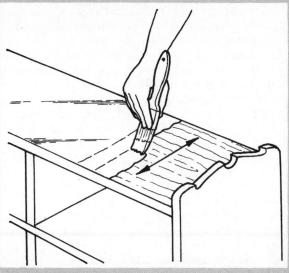

1. Work in a dust-free room with the temperature between 65° and 85°F. Clean the sanded surface with a tack cloth. Use a new brush, first shaking off any dust. Fill the brush with varnish, and brush across the grain with long strokes. Refill the brush, then, starting 2″ beyond where you stopped, work back to it, then away from it.

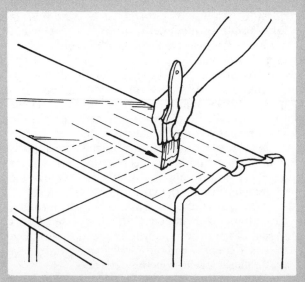

2. When the area is coated, dry the brush along the rim of the varnish can. Use the dry brush to brush along the grain. The goal is to make the varnish as even and level as possible. As you work, continue to dry the brush against the can.

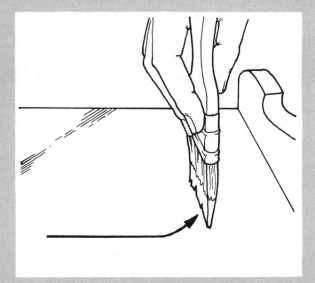

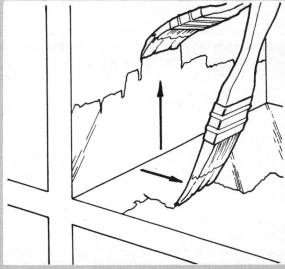

3. Still working with the dry brush, smooth the varnish further and remove brush marks by stroking with just the tip of the brush. This is called tipping off. Hold the brush almost vertical, and work in the direction of the grain. Work in rows. Coat each section of the piece by following this 3-step sequence.

5. At an inside corner, coat the horizontal surface first, working out from the corner. Next, coat the vertical surface, working up from the corner. This method will prevent varnish from building up in the corner. Thick spots of varnish take longer to dry and may crack as the varnish gets older.

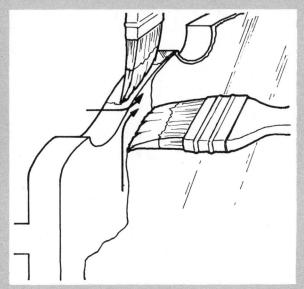

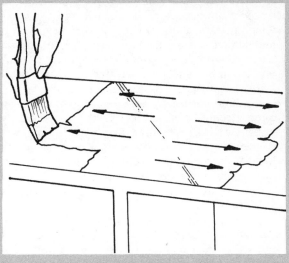

4. Work in a horizontal plane whenever possible to prevent the varnish from running or sagging. At an outside corner, brush the varnish toward the corner, lifting the brush just before it gets to the edge.

6. On large surfaces, start in the center, and work with the grain toward one end; then go back to the center and work toward the other end. Do not work from end to end. On turned areas, work lengthwise.

Between the first and second coats, sand with 7/0 sandpaper, and clean with a tack cloth.

Lacquer

Because lacquer dries faster than any other finish, it is the most commonly used coating for mass-produced furniture. But lacquer fumes are both volatile and toxic, necessitating elaborate safety measures that are difficult to organize in a home workshop. Using a spray gun, you apply the finish in many thin coats, while working within the confines of a booth constructed of sheet metal or fire-resistant wallboard. The booth must be open at one end and equipped with an exhaust fan at the other end that can vent fumes outside the house and catch spray in a filter.

Given these requirements for lacquering full-size pieces, it is more practical to use lacquer at home only for projects small enough to complete with an aerosol spray or portable spray outfit. In aerosol spray form, lacquer comes in high gloss, satin, and matte finishes, as well as in many vivid colors. Aerosol spray lacquer won't work well on large pieces of furniture, because the spray pattern is not reliable enough. For small pieces of modern furniture or special objects make of fine-grained wood, however, lacquer is a good choice, and better than varnish. There is a form of lacquer which dries just slowly enough to be brushed on and which can be used on larger pieces, as an alternative to the aerosol variety, provided your workshop has adequate ventilation. This type of lacquer is available in clear form.

While varnish is easier to apply than lacquer, it cannot be rubbed to the same highly polished finish. With lacquer, a mirror-smooth, rubbed finish is possible, with a mellow, satiny look. Any wood will accept a lacquer finish, but mahogany and rosewood contain oils that will bleed through unless a thin coat of shellac is applied first as a sealer.

Lacquer has nearly the protective strength of varnish, and certainly more than shellac. It is moisture-proof enough to use on bar tops and heat-proof enough to use on kitchen tables and coffee tables. The surface will last indefinitely. Of all the finishes, it is the most transparent, intensifying the grain and color of the wood without changing it.

How to Apply Lacquer

SPRAY LACQUER

1. When applying lacquer with a portable spray outfit or a spray can, work in a well-ventilated room, wearing a mask over your mouth and nose and goggles to protect your eyes. Mix lacquer thinner and lacquer for the spray outfit, as recommended by the manufacturer. Hold the spray gun or can 6''–10'' away from the wood. Experiment to find the best distance, and use it throughout the job. If the spray gun or can is too close, the lacquer will sag on the surface; if it is too far away, the lacquer will reach the wood as it is drying and will look dull.

Right method

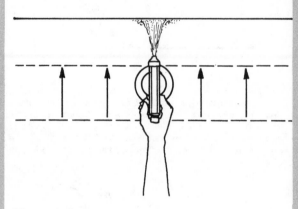

Wrong method

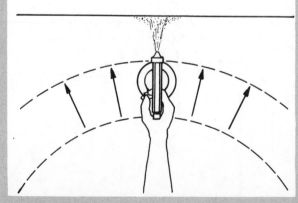

2. Maintain the spray gun or can perpendicular to the surface of the work, and move your arm along as you spray in horizontal bands. Do not wave the spray gun or can back and forth. Keep it the same distance from the surface at all times.

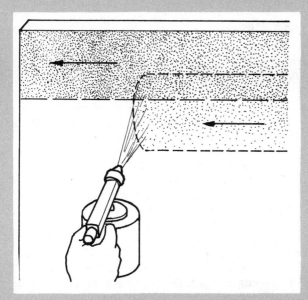

3. Overlap a third of each new band with the band above it. The spraying pattern, which should be oval or fan-shaped, will then even out from one row to the next.

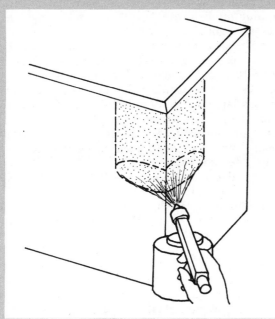

4. At corners, hold the spray gun or can so that it covers both surfaces at once. If the corner extends for some length, spray down it in short rows.

BRUSH-ON LACQUER

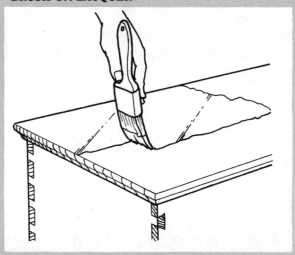

1. Work with the surface well lighted and horizontal. Use a soft brush 2″—3″ wide. Load one-third of the length of the brush with lacquer. Tap off the excess on the inner side of the can as you withdraw the brush. Hold the brush at a 45° angle, and flow the lacquer, which is very thin and watery, onto the surface. It is self-leveling and does not require brushing back and forth as varnish does. Working quickly, spread the lacquer with bold strokes along the grain of the wood.

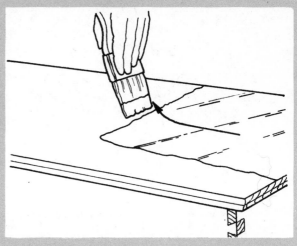

2. Work from an uncoated area toward the last area you coated. Avoid overlapping where one brushful meets the next by lifting the brush. When your fingernail won't dent the surface, sand with fine steel wood, clean with a tack cloth, and recoat.

How to Apply Shellac

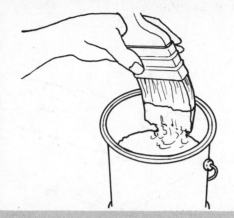

1. Dilute the shellac with denatured alcohol to the proper cut, or concentration, according to label directions. For use as a sealer, a ½-lb. cut is best. For use as a finish, a 1-lb. cut is best. Load a wide brush with shellac and pat it against the inside wall of the can as you draw it out. Quickly shift the full brush to the work surface, holding the brush upright as you move it to prevent dripping.
2. With the brush fully laden, brush gently with the grain in long, even strokes. With each new brushful, work toward the previous stroke, starting 2″ from it, then brush away from it along the grain. Lap marks will be softened and smoothed out by successive coats.

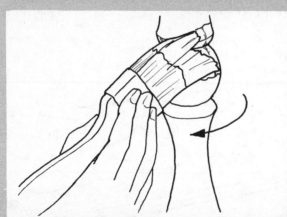

3. To shellac curved areas, brush around the leg or spindle section by section. Do not work up and down. Dry the brush and go over the section while it is still wet in order to pick up the excess shellac.
4. Shellac dries within minutes, but wait at least 3 hours between coats. Sand lightly between coats with very fine sandpaper, then clean with a tack cloth. After three coats of shellac, apply paste wax.

Shellac

The lac bug, native of India and Ceylon, secretes a gum, which when cleaned, refined, and dissolved in denatured alcohol, produces shellac. Shellac, in turn, produces an excellent, mellow surface on furniture, and like varnish and lacquer, it goes on in several thin coats that build on the surface. It dries fast and goes on easily, leveling off to conceal faulty brushwork. It's so flexible and crack-proof that it's used on floors in bowling alleys. Museum-quality furniture with its soft shine often has a shellac finish. Under the right conditions, it lasts a long time.

It's also fragile. Moisture on the surface will turn it white; heat will soften it and mark the surface. Extreme heat will crack the finish. Scratches leave white streaks. Alcohol will act as a solvent and remove the finish. Shellac is only really useful on furniture with fine veneers, or on walnut or mahogany pieces that do not get handled. It also makes a hard, transparent undercoat over raw or stained wood. An excellent sealer, nothing applied over it will penetrate under it, and what goes over it will adhere well.

Shellac comes in two colors: orange, which is its natural color, and white, which is a bleached form. Use white shellac when you definitely do not want to alter the color of the wood. It's appropriate for light and dark woods. Orange is best for darker woods such as walnut, mahogany, teak, and mission oak, giving them an amber tone. It will also give a pleasant yellow tone to light pine and maple.

Shellac also comes in different concentrations, called cuts, requiring that it be thinned with denatured alcohol before being used as a sealer or finish coat (see How to Thin Shellac, on the page opposite).

The most exalted use of shellac is in French polishing, an old, arduous, and complicated process of hand rubbing and polishing, which produces the most beautiful wood finish possible. It takes time and talent to master, but there is a product called Qualasole, which provides a shortcut to a finish that comes close to the look of French polishing.

French Polishing

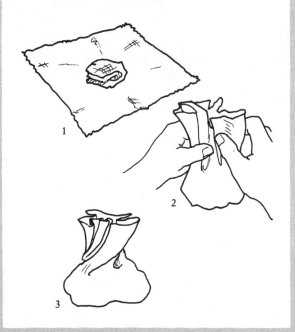

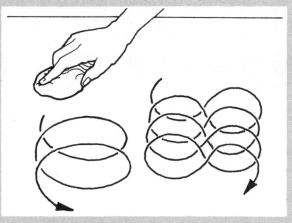

1. Mix 2 tbs. boiled linseed oil into 1 pt. orange shellac diluted to a 1-lb. cut. Place a wad of cheesecloth about 2'' in diameter in the center of a square of linen about 6'' square. Pick up the four corners of the square, and twist them together. Hold the pad in your fingers, and make a fist so the palm of your hand applies pressure on the pad when you hold it on the wood surface. Make sure the rubbing surface is free of wrinkles.

2. Dip the pad lightly into the shellac/oil mixture, moistening it but not soaking it. Sprinkle a light dusting of pumice (see p. 181) on the surface. Gently rub the surface in a figure-8 or circular motion, keeping it moving at all times. Put light pressure on the pad, working in circles between 4'' and 8'' in diameter. Do not repeat the same motion in the same spot twice in a row, or it will soften the finish. After about 45 minutes to an hour of rubbing the surface, rub in the direction of the grain in order to eliminate circular marks. When the surface is even and glossy, let it dry for 24 hours. Repeat the procedure a second time, and then a third time in two to three days. In a week to ten days, apply paste wax.

Qualasole, the modern alternative to the arduous work of French polishing, is a premixed liquid you apply with a rubbing pad. The procedure involves only one operation and gives results that compare favorably with traditional French polishing techniques.

How to Thin Shellac

Desired Cut (in lb.)	3-Pound Base		4-Pound Base		5-Pound Base	
	Shellac (in parts)	Denatured Alcohol (in parts)	Shellac (in parts)	Denatured Alcohol (in parts)	Shellac (in parts)	Denatured Alcohol (in parts)
½	1	4	1	5	1	7
1	3	4	1	2	1	2
2	5	2	4	3	1	1
2½	5	1	2	1	3	2
3	...	...	4	1	2	1

Finishing Products That Work Together

Finish	Sealer	Filler	Stain
Natural varnish	Shellac; thinned varnish	Any kind	Any kind
Synthetic varnish	Thinned varnish; sanding sealer	Check label	Any kind
Lacquer	Thined lacquer; thinned shellac; sanding sealer with a lacquer base	Lacquer base is best; let any other kind dry 48 hours	Water; non-grain-raising; lacquer base
Shellac	Thinned shellac	Any kind	Any kind except alcohol base
Wax	Sealing bare wood optional; if staining, use wash coat of sealer before and after applying stain	Any kind	Any kind
Oil	Do not seal	Any kind	Any kind except water base
Penetrating resin	Do not seal	Any kind	Oil base is best; do not use varnish base or vinyl base
Enamel	Thinned shellac	Any kind	Do not stain

How to Apply a Wax Finish

PASTE WAX

1. Apply sealer if desired. Rub wood with 4/0 steel wool, and clean with a tack cloth.
2. Apply a thin layer of wax with a ball of cheesecloth. Allow it to dry thoroughly.
3. To buff, first use a soft fiber shoe brush, followed by a lamb's wood buffer for the final polishing. To do the buffing and polishing mechanically, use a power brush that attaches to the chuck of an electric drill or power tool.
4. Apply several thin layers, buffing and polishing each layer completely.

SEALER STAIN

1. Apply stain evenly along the grain with a cloth or brush. Leave it on for 10-15 minutes, then wipe off the excess with a cloth. Apply the second coat in 24 hours.
2. Apply paste wax 24 hours after the second coat of sealer.

Wax

The chief virtue of a wax finish is the mellow beauty it gives to close-grained wood. This asset can override its chief deficiency: Wax does almost nothing to protect the wood surface. It offers no resistance against abrasion, scratches, alcohol, or water. It is, however, easy to repair with the application of a bit more wax and a bit more buffing.

Wax is best used over a protective layer of sealer. If you intend to stain the wood before waxing it, you must apply a wash coat of sealer both before and after applying the stain, or apply a sealing stain. You may also use a colored paste wax over a clear sealer.

Minwax produces sealing stains, which are a combination of pentrating oil stains, wax, and a drying agent. This all-in-one approach simplifies the finishing process considerably and produces a soft wax finish that is, in fact, tougher than using paste wax alone.

Oils and penetrating resins

Oiling furniture is as old as the idea of wooden furniture itself. Oil and wood have a natural affinity for each other. The traditional penetrating oil finish is boiled linseed oil, usually mixed with up to 50 percent turpentine. (In its raw state, linseed oil does not dry. When it is labeled boiled, Japan dryers have been added. It has not literally been boiled.) The final result is a rich and beautiful varnishlike finish, but it takes weeks to achieve and is not durable.

The task of applying a long succession of sticky coats of linseed oil has been eliminated by a second generation of penetrating resin-oil finishes, and by tung oil. Tung oil is an oil extracted from the nut of the Chinese tung tree. It is easy to apply, penetrates the surface quickly, and retains the beauty of traditional oil finishes.

Linseed oil and tung oil are often mixed with other finishes to enhance their capacities. Tung oil varnish, for instance, both penetrates and coats the surface. Tung oil mixed with polyure-

How to Apply a Penetrating Finish

OIL

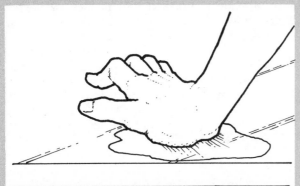

Make a pad out of a piece of cheesecloth. Pour oil onto the surface of the wood and work it in with a circular or figure-8 motion. When an even layer of oil coats the surface and the wood can absorb no more, rub the surface along the grain with the heel of your hand. The warmth your hand generates will increase the oil's ability to penetrate the surface. Wipe off all excess oil with a clean cloth. The number of coats and the extent of hand rubbing will vary from one type of oil to another. Follow manufacturer's instructions.

MIXING PENETRATING AND SURFACE FINISHES

Mix tung oil, boiled linseed oil, raw linseed oil, or Watco with an equal portion of 3-lb.-cut shellac or any varnish. Apply to the surface with a rag. Keep stirring the mixture. Watch the surface until it gets tacky (make sure it doesn't dry). Remove all the mixture from the surface with 3/0 steel wool. Clean the surface with a cloth.

PENETRATING RESIN

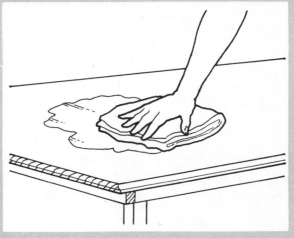

Apply penetrating resin with a brush, cloth, or 4/0 steel wool. Spread it thickly and evenly over the surface. Keep applying it until the wood stops absorbing it. Watch the surface for about an hour, adding more resin to dry spots as they appear. The surface should stay wet and shiny. After an hour, wipe off any excess finish with clean rags. No wet or shiny spots should remain. Let the surface dry for 24 hours. Wipe off any wet spots that appear. Before adding a second coat, smooth the surface gently with 4/0 steel wool and wipe with a tack cloth.

thane is the basis of Danish oil, or teak oil, which can be used on any wood to preserve its natural look and feel.

Penetrating resins, also called penetrating sealers, are now widely used to give wood the look of an oil finish without the hand rubbing that oil finishes require. This finish sinks in and hardens between the wood fibers, actually strengthening it while it does wonders to enhance the grain. The more open-grained the wood—that is, the larger its pores—the more resin will seep in, and the more lustrous and protective the finish will be.

The grain and natural markings of oak, walnut, rosewood, and teak are particularly receptive to penetrating resin. The effect is not so dramatic in close-grained woods like maple, birch, and cherry.

The darker the natural color of the wood, the greater will be the darkening effect of the resin. Light maple will not darken much, which is desirable, while the brown in rosewood will become nearly black, which is also desirable. Applied to any surface, this finish, though it will lack depth, will look natural, uncoated, and exceptionally handsome.

Use it on floors, paneling, any large expanses, or any intricately carved surfaces. It is the easiest of all finishes to apply. Pour it on, work it in with rag, hand, or brush, and wipe it off. Recoat when the product label specifies, but never more than a day later. No other filling or sealing is necessary beforehand, nor is waxing necessary afterward.

Next to varnish, this is the strongest finish around. It resists the usual range of mishaps furniture is heir to—heat, water, alcohol, and scratches. The simplicity of its application also eliminates the two nemeses of the wood finisher: the surface dust that clings to slow-drying varnish and the lap marks left by varnish and lacquer.

A penetrating resin is different from a penetrating oil. The former, because of its hardening qualities, offers much more protection, though both oils and resins are applied in similar fashion. Watco, clear Minwax, Dupont's Wood Finish, and Clear Rez are all penetrating resins.

Enamel

Enamel is a varnish with pigment added for color and opacity. It is different from paint in composition, dries harder, and is a much more protective finish for furniture. Finish furniture with enamel for the pleasure of color, to hide flaws in the wood, or to cover a wood that does not have sufficient natural beauty for a clear finish. Enamel is available in the whole spectrum of colors and glosses. The glossier the shine, the more durable the finish.

How to Apply Enamel

1. Sand the wood, filling and sealing if necessary. Clean the wood with a tack cloth. Paint on an undercoat of primer in order to produce a good working surface for the enamel to adhere to. Thinned enamel is a good undercoat. Use 4 parts enamel to 1 part of the solvent recommended on the enamel label. Otherwise use white undercoat.

Turn chairs and tables upside down and paint legs and undersides first; do chair seats and tabletops last. On horizontal areas, apply the undercoat across the grain, then brush along the grain, working in 10-in.-square areas. On vertical areas, keep the brush nearly dry, and work from dry areas to wet.

2. Sand the wood with 7/0 sandpaper. Clean with a tack cloth. Apply the enamel in long, smooth strokes along the grain, then stroke across the grain. Finally, with the brush nearly dry, tip off the enamel by again brushing along the grain. Try for a thin, even coat. Thick coats dry very slowly. Work from an unpainted area toward a painted area when you reload the brush. Work with the brush filled only one-third of its bristle length. Check for runs and sags as you work and while the enamel is drying; tip them off as you spot them.

3. When the first coat has hardened, sand it with an extrafine-grit sandpaper, then clean with a tack cloth. For a very glossy finish, apply three or four coats.

4. If you want the strength of a gloss finish, but not the high shine, there are several ways to diminish the gloss. To knock the gloss down just a little, rub the final coat with rubbing oil. For a satin finish, rub down the final coat with pumice and water. For a matte finish, wet the final coat with a sponge, then sand it lightly.

Rubbing and Polishing

Rubbing the wood with an abrasive between coats of finish levels out the surface and gives it a "tooth" to grip the next layer. Polishing then adds lustre and smoothness.

Rubbing and polishing are steps to use on surface finishes. Penetrating finishes are rubbed and polished as they are applied, and nothing more need be done to the surface, except perhaps waxing. There are several routes to a smooth and shiny surface finish. See Steel Wool and Power Sanding on page 167 for some suggestions. Below are other possibilities.

Pumice and rottenstone—This is the traditional combination for rubbing and polishing the top coat. Pumice (actually volcanic ash) is an abrasive that comes in different grades. Grade F is for coarse rubbing. Grades 2/F and 3/F are for fine rubbing. To use pumice, put it in a flour sifter and sprinkle some out on the surface. Add enough water to the surface so that when you start rubbing, the water and pumice will form a paste. Rub with a 3 × 5-inch pad of felt about 1 inch thick. A blackboard eraser or part of an old felt hat will do. Rub with the grain and keep adding water, but not more abrasive, which would introduce fresh scratches to the work.

Check the work often by moving the paste aside with the side of your hand. The smoothing process goes quickly, and you will have to take care not to rub through the finish. When it is smooth, wash the surface with a damp cloth.

You can also use pumice with mineral oil, either stirring the two together to the consistency of cream, or working with the oil and pumice in

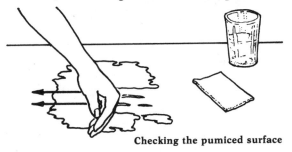

Checking the pumiced surface

separate containers, dipping the pad first in one and then in the other. (On a shellac finish, which is not waterproof, you must always use mineral oil as the lubricant.) Water, while faster and cleaner, is not as easy to judge as mineral oil. Apply mineral oil and pumice just like water and pumice, but clean up with a cloth dampened with mineral spirits.

Rottenstone is a gray powder abrasive derived from slate. It feels like talc and has no cutting action. Use it to shine the dull, smooth surface left by pumice. To use rottenstone, soak a felt pad in mineral oil and rottenstone, and rub the surface, checking often to see if the surface is shiny enough for your taste.

Rubbing compound—Available in liquid or paste form, rubbing compound comes already mixed and is available in several grades of fineness, to smooth the final coat.

Furniture polish—A common commodity, furniture polish is used to add shine to a finish. It requires frequent reapplication. Apply with an old piece of velvet, a clean powder puff, or an old pair of socks worn over your hands like gloves.

To make your own polish, mix 2 tablespoons olive oil, 1 tablespoon white vinegar, and 1 quart warm water. Apply from a spray bottle, then rub dry with a clean cloth. For furniture that does not have a surface coating, mix 1 tablespoon lemon oil into 1 quart mineral oil. Apply from a spray bottle, then rub dry with a clean cloth.

Wax polish—Use paste wax as a buffer to shield the finish it covers, as well as to enhance its beauty. Carnauba wax, made from the leaves of a palm tree native to Brazil, is the most common ingredient in most paste waxes. It is too hard to use on its own, but in combination with other ingredients, it protects well and polishes to a high gloss.

To make your own paste wax, put 1 tablespoon carnauba wax and 1 pint mineral oil in the top of a double boiler. Heat and stir until the wax is completely melted. Stir in 3 or 4 drops lemon oil if you like. Cool the mixture, and store it in a metal or glass container. Apply with a soft cloth, then buff with a second cloth. Always work in one limited area at a time, allowing the wax to set before you buff it.

Repairing the Finish

Furniture is subject to all the shocks of daily life. To repair the inevitable stains, scratches, dents, and other injuries that may befall it, start with the gentlest solutions, then work up to more heavy-duty remedies if these fail. Remove only as much of the finish as you have to, and always work in the direction of the grain.

Chips—A sharp blow to the surface can chip the finish. First carefully scrape away any loose finish from around the chip with the flat, sharp edge of a craft knife. Then use 4/0 steel wool very lightly to smooth the edges of the chip. Go over the area with a cloth moistened with mineral spirits. Let it dry, then apply the new finish with a delicate brush. Let dry, then lightly sand with 4/0 steel wool, and wax the whole surface.

Cigarette burns—Sand the burn mark with a 4/0 steel wool pad moistened with mineral spirits until the mark disappears. Wipe the area with a clean cloth, and wax the whole surface.

Cracks—Cracks need filling. Fill tiny cracks by wiping them with a putty stick in the appropriate shade, then smoothing with your finger. Wood putty also works on cracks but can be noticeable on the surface. Shellac sticks, which are usually undetectable on the surface, are the most professional approach and come in many shades.

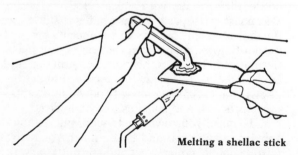

Melting a shellac stick

Use a shellac stick on shellac and varnish. Use a lacquer stick on lacquer. For a heat source that will heat the putty knife that in turn heats the shellac stick, use an alcohol lamp or propane torch. Hold the shellac stick over the putty knife and the putty knife over the flame so the stick melts slowly. Do not let the knife get red-hot.

When the stick is soft as putty, quickly press it into the crack and smooth with the knife. Fill the crack very slightly, then heat the tip of the knife, and press the blade over the crack to flatten the excess shellac. Let it set for an hour or two, then sand with 5/0 garnet paper. Apply shellac, then sand with 4/0 steel wool.

If the crack is quite deep, you can fill it almost to the top with wood putty first, then fill the top with the shellac stick.

Raising a dent

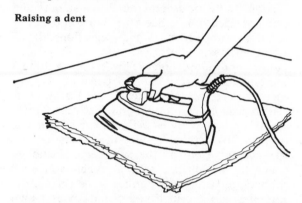

Dents—Soft woods like pine dent easily. To get to the dent, remove the finish immediately around it with fine sandpaper. If the dent is shallow, a couple of drops of water sprinkled on the dent, then left to penetrate the wood for a day or two, will raise it. Be sure to wet only the dent. If that doesn't work, try heat: Place a damp cloth folded into quarters over the dent, and press it with a

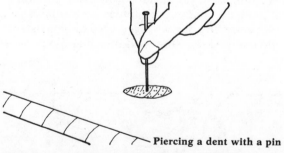

Piercing a dent with a pin

warm iron. Don't let the iron come in direct contact with the wood. If the dent still remains, buy a commercial wood-swelling liquid.

If the dent is deeper than shallow and the above methods don't apply, push a pin or needle into the wood several times to a depth of about ¼ inch. Pull the pin out with a pliers each time. Add drops of water and allow the tiny pinholes to help the water penetrate the wood and swell the dent. The pinholes themselves will become invisible.

When the dent is gone, by whatever means, let the wood dry for a week, and then refinish as you would for a chip (see the page opposite).

Ink stains—If they have not gone through the finish to the wood, ink stains will disappear if you buff them with a cloth moistened with mineral spirits, then rinse with a damp cloth. Dry, wax, and polish the surface. If the ink remains, rub the surface with 4/0 steel wool moistened with mineral spirits. Then rinse the wood with a damp cloth, dry, wax, and buff.

Paint, crayon, lipstick, grease, and tar—These marks usually stay on the surface. Lift whatever dry matter you can from the surface with a putty knife, proceeding very carefully to avoid scratching the finish. Moisten 4/0 steel wool with mineral spirits, buff the surface, wax, and polish. If the mark is paint and you can catch it while it is still wet, wipe it off with mineral spirits if it is oil-based or with water if is latex.

Paper—Saturate stuck-on paper with olive oil. Let it soak in, then rub it off. Sand with 4/0 steel wool.

Scratches—For shallow scratches, rub a broken piece of walnut, pecan, or Brazil nut over the raw marks, and the oil in the nutmeat will darken them. Rubbing on paste wax with 4/0 steel wool, then buffing with a soft cloth, also works on shallow scratches.

Try new iodine to cover scratches on red mahogany. Old, dark brown iodine works on

Applying paste shoe polish

brown or cherry mahogany, and iodine diluted to half-strength with denatured alcohol works on maple.

Shoe polish can also effectively cover scratches. Try brown paste shoe polish on walnut, cordovan on mahogany, and tan on light finishes. Dab the polish on with a cotton swab, then buff dry. The polish will shine, so do not apply it to a dull finish.

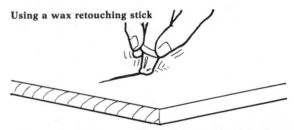
Using a wax retouching stick

For deeper scratches, buy a wax retouching stick in a color that matches your finish. Fill the scratch with wax. Rub it in with your finger, and remove the excess with a soft cloth. When the wax is dry, buff it.

A process called reamalgamation works on lacquer and shellac surfaces that have extensive scratches (or the kind of cracking and crazing that sunlight or temperature variations can create on older pieces). The idea is to soften the surface and then let it heal and harden to a smooth finish.

First clean the area with turpentine or mineral spirits. Using denatured alcohol on shellac and lacquer thinner on lacquer, apply with a natural bristle brush in long strokes over an area no more than 2 feet square. Work fast, and don't let the brush get dry. Apply second and third coats only if scratches remain. When the surface has turned dull, buff it with 4/0 steel wool, then wipe with a tack cloth. Apply a fresh coat of lacquer or shellac if the amalgamated surface seems very thin. When it dries, sand lightly with 4/0 steel wool, wax with a paste wax, and buff.

Water, alcohol, and perfume stains—Remove these stains from varnish with a medium-thick paste of 3/F pumice and linseed oil. Apply with a soft cloth in a circular motion. Check frequently to see if the mark is gone by pushing aside the paste with the side of your hand.

Furnishings to Make with Metal

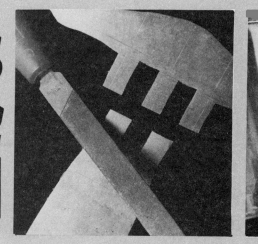

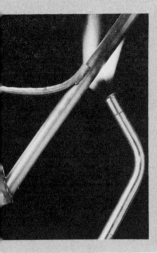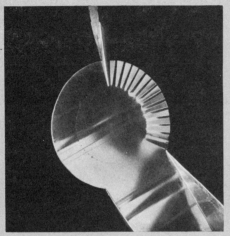

If you've never tried your hand at metal-working, you've been missing something. Probably you'll find it far easier than you imagine. In fact, in many ways metal is a lot less difficult to work than wood. For one thing, metal is a ductile material like clay; it flows. Often all that is required to make an object is to bend it or to beat it to shape with hammers.

Heating metal causes it to flow more freely, the same as adding water does to clay. Blacksmiths use heat and hammers to bring steel within the range of human strength to fashion. The tools and techniques used by smiths today are essentially the same as those used centuries ago.

Welding, on the other hand, at least the type done nowadays with gas torches or electric arcs, is new and really still evolving. Basically, though, it's nothing more than joining pieces of metal by heating their edges simultaneously until they melt and flow together by themselves.

Naturally there's skill involved, and metal working can become enormously complex, but not in this book. Begin by crafting some sheet metal if you've never done so—use scrap 1-gallon cans and such, or buy some copper flashing from a building supply company—and see if you don't get bitten by the bug. The projects in the sheet-metal portion of this section begin with very simple items. You may be able to make the first (see Candle Sconce, p. 208) in only an hour or two. Very few tools are needed, and no large-scale heating of metal is required.

Blacksmithing, brazing, and welding do require pretty substantial investment and commitment, and you'll need a special place to work. Before you take the plunge in earnest it may be worth your while to gain some initial experience to see what's really involved and how you might fare. Visit a historical museum or recreated village and watch a master smith at work. Sign up for a night-school class in welding. (Many adult education programs offer these; a few even offer blacksmithing.)

Above all, don't let making things with metal sound intimidating. Much of it can be self-taught through reading, practice, and trial and error.

Working with Metal

Making metal objects has a strong conceptual kinship with making wooden or textile objects. You must start with a plan for the object that breaks it down into its component parts. You must collect the tools and materials you need. Then you must make the pieces. And, finally, you must assemble them.

But metalworking can be intimidating. The raw materials are not as readily available as cloth or lumber. Once acquired, the materials seem to resist the manipulations that quickly transform cloth or lumber.

The key is using the right tools and techniques. Don't be put off. Making things of metal is fun and practical, too. Whether you choose to try your hand at blacksmithing, tinsmithing, or brazing and welding, you start with a plan, you make the pieces, and you put them together.

Materials

Start with the material itself. There are dozens of metals, and most come in dozens of forms and shapes. Knowing a little about the characteristics of the most common metals and about available shapes and sizes can help you plan your projects most effectively.

A few definitions to start. Pure metals are those that have but a single constituent: iron, copper, gold, silver. As a practical matter, the only pure metal you are likely to use is copper. Ferrous metals are all the iron-based metals: iron in its various forms, the carbon steels, and the alloy steels. The ferrous metals will be the basis of most of your metalworking. Nonferrous metals, obviously, are all the metals that have no iron in them. Alloys are metals made up of two or more constituent metals. There are a great many steel alloys: nickel steel, chromium steel, and the like. Brass and bronze are alloys.

Metallurgists have defined a series of properties of metals to help in the selection of metals for particular uses. Ductility is the capacity of the metal for being drawn out into thin shapes, such as wires, without breaking. The opposite of this is brittleness, which is the quality of being breakable. A brittle metal is not ductile and will fracture or shatter if you try to hammer it. Elasticity is the capacity of the metal to return to its original form after being bent or twisted. Malleability is the capacity of the metal to be hammered, rolled, or bent. A brittle metal is not malleable. Hardness is the capacity of a metal to resist being dented or penetrated. A hard metal will be brittle unless it also has toughness. Toughness is the capacity of a metal to resist bending, breaking, cracking, or stretching.

Metals

You will find that only a limited number of metals will be of genuine use to you in your home metalworking projects. These include the carbon steels for blacksmithing and general metalworking, aluminum for general metalworking, and several coated sheet steels, aluminum, copper, and perhaps brass for sheet-metal work.

Carbon steel—Smelting iron ore yields what is known as pig iron, an impure iron. To make steel, the pig iron is resmelted in a way that burns out the contaminants and reduces the carbon content to 1.50 percent or less. The resulting product is carbon steel.

Carbon steels are classified according to the amount of carbon they contain. A steel with 0.10 to 0.30 percent carbon is a low-carbon steel, frequently called a mild steel. One with 0.30 to 0.60 percent carbon is a medium carbon steel, sometimes called machine steel, and one with 0.60 to 1.50 percent carbon is a high carbon steel, often called tool steel. The more carbon the steel contains, the harder it is. Thus, tool steel, being the highest in carbon, is the hardest and is used to make drills, punches, and chisels that are used to cut mild steel and other metals.

For all the projects in this book and for all other general-purpose metalworking, mild steel is the best steel to use. It is available in all shapes and is the basis for all the coated steel sheets that are used in sheet-metal work.

Aluminum—This familiar silver gray metal is easily as widely used and as versatile as steel. It's most outstanding characteristics are its light weight, its corrosion resistance, and its malleability and ductility. It is quite easy to cut, bend, shape, and drill, though it is definitely not the stuff of the blacksmith. Although aluminum is not particularly strong in its pure state, when alloyed and heat-treated, its strength can be increased into the range of structural steel. And almost all aluminum *is* alloyed.

Aluminum is available in as many shapes and sizes as steel. You can use it in all sorts of sheet-metal and general metalworking projects.

Coated sheet steels—Plain steel makes a very workable sheet, but it quickly rusts and corrodes. Primarily to inhibit this, steelmakers apply coatings of other metals.

Galvanized steel has been dipped in molten zinc. It has a characteristic mottled, semishiny appearance. You'll find it most useful for more utilitarian projects. The single caveat to its use is that if the zinc is heated enough to burn off, it will burn off in a toxic cloud.

Tin-plated steel, often simply called tin plate, is usually made by electroplating steel sheets with tin. It is very corrosion-resistant and is nontoxic, hence its wide use for packaging. Tin cans are an excellent source of tin plate for small projects.

Tin plate is hard, so it takes sharply defined bends very well, but it is also malleable, so it is fairly easily shaped with more gentle curves. It is easily pierced and soldered. Perhaps best of all, it takes and holds a very high polish, making it a good sheet to use where appearance is important.

Copper—The oldest metal known to man, copper is also one of the most useful metals. It is extremely malleable and ductile, so it can be rolled into very thin sheets and drawn into very thin wires. It conducts both heat and electricity well and is corrosion-resistant. It is the basis for all the brass and bronze alloys.

If copper has drawbacks, they are its expense and its patina, a poisonous green oxide called verdigris that forms on it. The expense cannot be avoided. The patina *must* be prevented wherever the copper will be used in cooking or eating utensils by coating it with a film of pure tin in a process called tinning. In other uses, the patina is often regarded as a visual plus, and it is the patina that in fact seals out deep corrosion.

Shapes and Sizes of Steel Stock

Name	Shape	How Measured	Typical Size Range*
Strip†‡	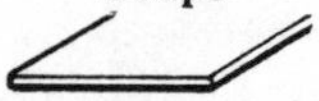	Thickness × width	16-ga. × ½″ to ³/₁₆″ × 12″; 16′ to 20′ lengths
Flat†‡	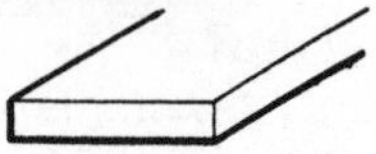	Thickness × width	¼″ × ⅜″ to 5″ × 8″; 10′ to 12′ lengths
Sheet†	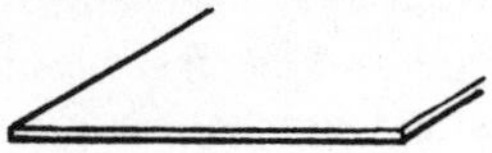	Thickness × width × length	30-ga. × 24″ × 96″ to ³/₁₆″ × 72″ × 240″
Plate†		Thickness × width	¼″ × 9″ to 14″ × 120″; lengths to 40′
Round‡ (rod)		Diameter	⅛″ to 12″; 10′, 12′, 20′ lengths
Square‡		Width	⅛″ to 6″; 9′, 10′, 12′, 20′ lengths
Hexagon‡		Distance from flat to opposing flat	¼″ to 4″; 9′, 10′, 12′ lengths
Round tubing		Outside diameter × wall thickness	⅛″ × 24-ga. to 14″ × 2″; lengths to 24′
Square tubing	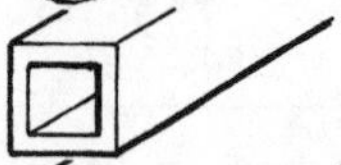	Outside width × wall thickness	½″ × 20-ga. to 10″ × ⅝″; 20′, 24′, 40′ lengths
Rectangular tubing		Outside width × outside height × wall thickness	1½″ × ½″ × 16-ga. to 12″ × 8″ × ⅜″; 20′, 24′ lengths
Pipe		Nominal size	⅛″ to 12″; 10′ to 20′ lengths
Angle		Leg width × leg width × leg thickness	½″ × ½″ × ⅛″ to 9″ × 4″ × ½″; 20′, 40′ lengths
Channel		Depth × flange width × web thickness	¾″ × ⅜″ × ⅛″ to 2½″ × ⅝″ × ³/₁₆″; 20′ lengths
Tee		Flange width × stem depth × stem thickness	1½″ × 1½″ × ³/₁₆″ to 2½″ × 2½″ × ⅜″; 20′ lengths

* The listings here are typical in the sense that they reflect the range of sizes listed in the catalogs of several national distributors of metals.

† The distinction between strips and flats and between sheets and plates is the thickness. Generally, strips and sheets run up to ³/₁₆ inch thick, while flats and plates begin at a ¼-inch thickness. There *are* thicker strips and sheets and thinner flats and plates.

The distinction between strips and sheets and between flats and plates is the width. Generally, strips run up to 12 inches wide, while sheet widths start at 24 inches. Flats run up to 8 inches wide, and plate widths start at 9 inches.

‡ Strips, flats, rounds, squares, and hexagons are often referred to collectively as bar stocks.

Copper is easily worked, though it will become increasing hard and brittle if it is hammered a great deal. These qualities can be diminished by annealing, a process in which the metal is heated red-hot, then allowed to cool very slowly. It is easily joined by soldering and brazing. The reddish brown metal takes a polish very well, though it will slowly darken and eventually develop its patina.

Copper is available in a wide variety of shapes and sizes, usually in soft, half-hard, and hard forms; you will find the soft to be the most workable.

Brass — This copper-zinc alloy is in many ways similar to copper. It is harder than copper, which makes it somewhat more difficult to work, but like copper it is responsive to both work-hardening and annealing. It solders and brazes well. Brass is somewhat more resistant to dampness than copper, but it will develop the same poisonous patina that copper will. Its color ranges from a reddish to a yellowish brown, depending upon the amount of zinc it contains. It takes a high polish.

Other metals — There are a number of other metals used in the various metalworking trades, but they are far less likely to find their way into the home shop.

Bronze, available in shapes and sizes similar to brass, is a copper-tin alloy. It is harder than brass and costs more, but in most respects it is like brass. Modern pewter, sometimes called Britannia metal, is a tin-antimony-copper alloy (no lead). The softest of the alloys, it works easily, doesn't work-harden, and solders well. Gar-alloy is a zinc-copper-silver alloy that is sometimes used as a substitute for pewter. It works and polishes well.

Shapes and sizes

Metal is formed in a myriad of shapes in a myriad of sizes, as demonstrated by the table Shapes and Sizes of Steel Stock, on the page opposite. There *are* more shapes than are shown, but those shown are the ones you may find some use for in a home shop.

Not all metals are available in all shapes. Aluminum is available in all the shapes shown and others besides. Copper, brass, and bronze are available in sheets and bar stocks. Copper tubing, of course, is also available.

The variety of sizes available isn't fully appreciated unless you get an opportunity to page through a catalog from a steel manufacturer or a large metals distributor. While the table indicates the range of sizes for each shape, it does not list the number of sizes available within the range. Rounds, for example, are made in as many as 110 different sizes within the ⅛-inch to 12-inch range.

The gauge system used to measure very thin stocks is not consistent from metal to metal, though this should not present a problem to you as a practical matter. There are several systems in use, including the U.S. Standard system applied to steels and the Brown & Sharp and the American Standard systems applied to copper, brass, and some other metals. A 16-gauge copper sheet is not quite the same thickness as a 16-gauge steel sheet. But in every case, the higher the gauge number, the thinner the sheet.

Sources

Acquiring metal stock for your home projects can be an adventure or a headache. Every sizable community has a home building center, stocked with a reasonable selection of lumber and putting up with, if not actively catering to, home craftsmen such as you. But there are no such metals centers. You must shop around.

Start with a fingertip tour of the Yellow Pages. Look for listings under the particular metals you want. Look for listings for welding shops, machine shops, blacksmiths, even scrapyards. Make some exploratory telephone calls.

Give some thought to what you *really* need. Most blacksmithing projects a beginner will tackle require only short scraps of stock. Small sheet-metal objects can be fashioned from flattened cans. It's only when you get to welding up a trailer or the like that you really do need long pieces of new material.

Check with local metal fabricators or welding shops or scrapyards to see if they'll allow you to pick through their discards for materials you might use. A pickup load can frequently be had for a modest sum.

Even if you need full lengths of new stocks, you may be able to strike a deal with a fabricator or a welder. Or look for a local distributor willing to sell small quantities to private customers.

Setting Up Shop

To do your metalworking and to house all of your tools, equipment, and materials, you will need a shop. If all you plan to do is small-scale sheet-metal projects, the shop can be a corner of a family or utility room. But it's more satisfactory, in fact imperative, if you plan to set up a smithy or to get into welding, that a separate room or outbuilding be devoted to your work.

The point here is not to explain how to organize a shop but to establish the value of having a special place to work. Most metalworking will generate a fair amount of dirt and a considerable amount of noise. Some of it involves open flames, showers of sparks, and coal dust. It really isn't compatible with the domestic scene.

Here are a few guidelines to help in picking your spot.

• It should have as much space as you can get. You need room to set up a workbench; room for shop tools, a welding rig, a forge and anvil (if you have any or all of them); room to assemble the largest project you figure you'll tackle; room to store all your tools and materials properly.

• It should be sufficiently isolated from the living area that the noise and dirt won't be troublesome.

• It should have adequate access. Lugging metal stock up and down steps or finagling completed projects through narrow doorways gets old in a hurry.

• It should be adequately wired, so you can have good lighting, both background and task, and enough power to start and run your power tools. If you have an arc welder, it should have its own 230-volt circuit.

• A smithy or welding shop should have a dirt or concrete floor and, if at all possible, masonry walls.

Whatever setup you do establish, make sure you have a good, solid workbench and storage for tools and materials. Even if you only arrange your tools and materials on shelves, you've taken a substantial step toward establishing a well-organized, safe, and pleasant workplace.

Tools and Equipment

Certain tools and equipment are basic to all metalworking. If you choose to focus your efforts on a particular aspect of metalworking, like blacksmithing, you will need to acquire specialized tools. But to start, build a basic tool kit.

The first item of equipment you need is a workbench. Whatever else it is, it should be sturdy and well braced. It can be wooden, framed of 2 × 4's or 4 × 4's, and topped with a thick, heavy working surface. You should cover all or a good part of the top with fairly heavy sheet metal, which can be replaced if it gets excessively dented or scuffed up.

A good-quality machinist's vise should be bolted to the left front corner of the bench. The ideal machinist's vise is a 5-inch swivel-base model. The 5-inch designation means the jaws are 5 inches wide; on such a vise, the jaws will usually open

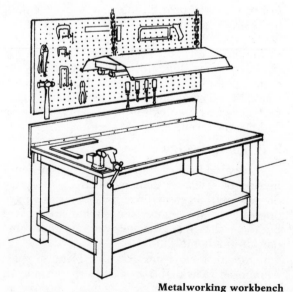

Metalworking workbench

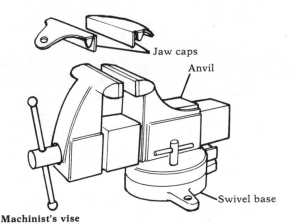

Machinist's vise

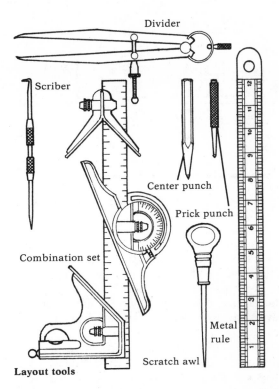

Layout tools

about 6 inches. A good option is to have removable jaw inserts, with the basic inserts being knurled tool steel and the alternates being either soft metal or hard rubber. On a top-quality vise, curved pipe jaws are an integral part of the jaw casting and are located below the main jaws. The swivel base allows the vise to be turned without being unbolted from the workbench. Such a vise will have a smallish anvil face, and sometimes an anvil horn, integral with the vise body. It will weigh 35 to 40 pounds. Smaller vises with fewer options are, of course, available.

Depending upon the work you'll be doing, you may want to supplement your workbench with one or more metal worktables. Plans for a welder's worktable appear on page 287.

Layout tools

The success of any metalworking projects begins with proper layout of the pieces. Only a few tools are needed for most layout tasks.

The primary measuring tool is the rule. You can use a tape measure or folding rule, but you should depend on a good-quality metal ruler for measuring and as a straightedge.

A multipurpose measuring and layout tool is the combination set. Its foot-long rule has etched graduations of 8ths, 16ths, 32nds, and 64ths. It has three heads that can be adjusted to any spot along the rule or removed completely. One is a square/miter head that has a spirit level and a small scriber. The protractor head is indexed

180 degrees and usually has a spirit level too. The center-gauge head allows quick and accurate marking of diameters and center points.

For marking metal, you should have tools with hardened, pointed tips: a scratch awl or machinist's scriber, a prick punch, and dividers.

Cutting tools

No one tool is ideally suited for cutting all metal stock. If you will be doing general metalworking, you should have several tools.

Saws—The hacksaw is probably *the* basic metal-cutting tool. The typical hacksaw has a frame that adjusts to accept 8-, 10-, and 12-inch-long blades. An 18-tooth-per-inch blade is a good general-purpose blade. A carbide chip blade, which is actually a ¼-inch rod, cuts in any direction and can be used to make curved cuts, including quite tightly radiused curves. It does cut a wide kerf, however.

To cut curves and have only a thin kerf, use a

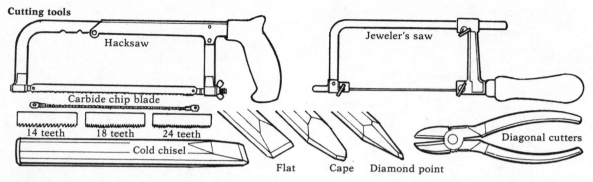

Cutting tools

Hacksaw

Jeweler's saw

Carbide chip blade

14 teeth   18 teeth   24 teeth

Cold chisel

Diagonal cutters

Flat   Cape   Diamond point

jeweler's saw, which looks a lot like a woodworker's coping saw. This saw, however, has an adjustable frame. It is used primarily for very fine work.

Metal-cutting blades are available for saber saws, circular saws, and band saws.

Chisels—Cold chisels are also used to cut metal. Blacksmiths usually collect enormous numbers of chisels, but every metalworker as well should have a chisel or two. The flat chisel has a wedge-shaped tip and is used for rough shaping, splitting, and shearing the heads off bolts and rivets. A cape chisel, which has a much narrower wedge to its tip, cuts grooves, while a diamond-point chisel, with a sharply pointed tip, cuts fine lines and squares off inside corners.

Snips and cutters—Sheet metal up to about 18-gauge can be cut with snips. You can buy common snips, compound-action aviation snips, and a variety of other, more specialized snips.

For cutting wire, use diagonal cutting pliers, not snips. Compound-action bolt cutters are available that will allow you to clip bolts and bar stocks up to ⅜ inch thick.

Files—Files come in a surprising array of shapes, sizes, and cuts. Choose flat, half-round, round, square, and triangular shapes in accordance with your needs. The same with sizes. The cuts range from rough (the coarsest) through coarse, bastard, second cut, and smooth cut. There are single cut, double cut, and curved-tooth cutting edges. Curved-tooth files are used with soft metals.

Whenever you buy a file, also buy a handle for it. And when you buy your first file, buy a file card, which is a short-bristled wire brush specially designed for cleaning the file teeth.

Grinders—Bench grinders and portable sander-grinders are also used to shape metal. Even if you get no other power tools, think seriously about

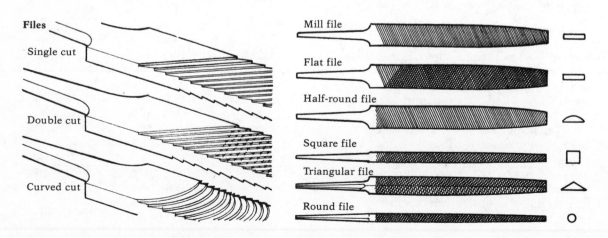

Files

Single cut

Double cut

Curved cut

Mill file

Flat file

Half-round file

Square file

Triangular file

Round file

getting a bench grinder. Hand-cranked models are available relatively inexpensively.

Drilling tools

The metal worker doesn't have the woodworker's wide variety of bits to choose from for making holes. He has only twist drill bits, but they are made in a hundred or more sizes, graduated in wire gauges, millimeters, fractions of the inch, and letters A to Z. The best drills are made of high-speed steel, although bits made of other steels are available.

The bits can be driven by a hand drill or a portable electric drill. The hand drill is more than adequate for boring sheet metal, but with heavier stocks a power drill is better. Electric drills are made in ¼-, ⅜-, and ½-inch sizes, the size being a measure of the chuck capacity (a ¼-inch drill will take a bit with a shank diameter of ¼ inch). The larger a drill, the more powerful its motor and the slower it turns.

Hand-guided drills are okay for most general-purpose work, but where holes must be bored with special precision, the drill press is a must. The drill press always drills holes in precise alignment, an important consideration. Both floor and bench-mounted versions are made.

If you get a drill press, get a drill press vise, too. The vise is clamped or bolted to the drill press table, and the stock being drilled is secured in its jaws. V-blocks can be used to secure round stocks for drilling.

Large holes—1 inch up to 2½ inches—can be "drilled" using hole saws. Hole saws will cut through steel plate up to ½ inch thick.

Assembly tools

Assembly is often a matter of fastening the pieces together with screws, bolts, or rivets. For these tasks you need wrenches and pliers, screwdrivers, and riveting tools.

At the least, you should have several adjustable wrenches. If your budget will allow, get a set of open-end, box, or combination wrenches, or even a socket set, as these tools fit bolt heads most securely.

Pliers are made for many special purposes. You should have general-purpose slip-joint pliers and a pair of groove-joint pliers whose jaws open as much as 2 inches. Locking-grip pliers are also very useful, serving as clamps as often as they serve as pliers. They are made in a variety of sizes and with several kinds of specialized jaws (for welding, sheet-metal work, and the like).

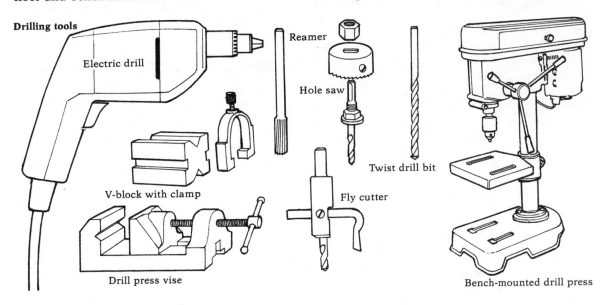

Drilling tools

Electric drill

Reamer

Hole saw

V-block with clamp

Twist drill bit

Fly cutter

Drill press vise

Bench-mounted drill press

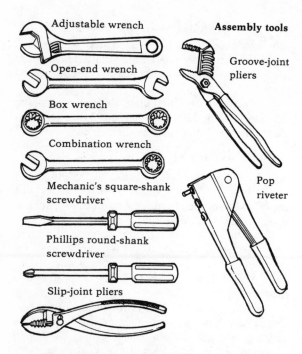

Adjustable wrench

Open-end wrench

Box wrench

Combination wrench

Mechanic's square-shank screwdriver

Phillips round-shank screwdriver

Slip-joint pliers

Assembly tools

Groove-joint pliers

Pop riveter

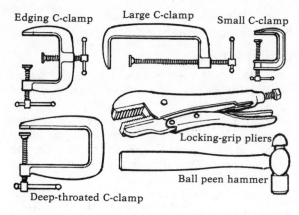

Edging C-clamp   Large C-clamp   Small C-clamp

Locking-grip pliers

Ball peen hammer

Deep-throated C-clamp

In assembly work, there's no substitute for the right screwdriver. Screwdrivers are so commonplace that we tend to take them for granted. Don't do *that*. Get good-quality screwdrivers, with both slot-head and Phillips-head tips.

Hammers and clamps

Two indispensable tools figure in more than one metalworking operation: hammers and clamps.

The basic metalworking hammer is the ball peen. It is used in every phase of metalworking, from sheet-metal work to blacksmithing to machine work. Get two or three, in different sizes: a 12-ounce for light work, a 32-ounce for routine work, and a 2-pound for serious persuading.

As you begin to specialize in one area or another, you may find a need for more specialized hammers. Blacksmiths generally accumulate the grandest array of hammers: ball peens, straight peens, cross peens, and forging and sledge hammers. Sheet-metal workers collect various soft-face mallets and at least one tinner's setting hammer. A welder needs a chipping hammer.

The basic clamp is the C-clamp. It comes in

lots of sizes, ranging from 1 inch up to 8 inches and more. Deep throated versions are available, as are edging clamps, with an adjusting screw in the center of the throat.

Safety equipment

Don't fail to get appropriate safety gear. For general metalworking, you need eye protection and a pair of sturdy work gloves. The eye protection, which could be goggles, safety glasses, or a face shield, should be worn when drilling, sawing, chiseling, and grinding. Leather work gloves should be worn when you'll be dealing with rough edges or hot metal. To protect your midriff, you may want to get a leather apron.

Basic Procedures

Basic metalworking procedures aren't markedly different in concept from those of woodworking. You begin with a plan. You lay out the pieces, then cut them out and shape them. Finally, you assemble them. But the material is notably different. So in execution the procedures are unique to metalworking.

Each metalworking discipline—blacksmithing, sheet-metal work, brazing and welding, and others—has a number of processes and procedures seemingly unique to it. But there's a fundamental unity to the work, those basic procedures that you have to know, regardless of your area of special interest.

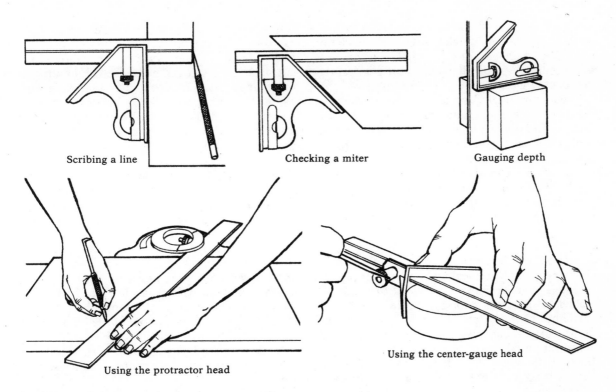

Scribing a line   Checking a miter   Gauging depth

Using the protractor head

Using the center-gauge head

Using a combination set

Layout

The layout of any and every project has to be right. If you do everything correctly but the layout, the project will not be a total success. You may be able to make little adjustments and compensations as you work, but the project will be flawed.

A pencil, you'll find, is seldom the best marking device in metalworking. Its mark is broad, indistinct, and too easily smudged or rubbed off. You may get by with a felt tip marker for some work, and where the metal is to be heated, a soapstone pencil's mark will not burn off. A scriber of some sort that scratches the metal surface is best, *except* where a scratch will cut through a surface coating, such as galvanizing, and expose the base metal.

Wherever appropriate, use a square or a combination set to guide your scriber and ensure that lines are made at the correct angles. The

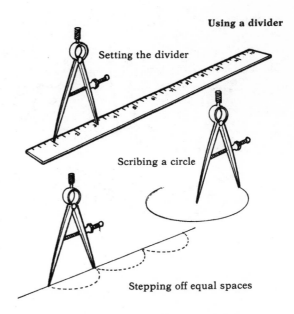

Using a divider

Setting the divider

Scribing a circle

Stepping off equal spaces

combination set will enable you to lay out accurate squares and rectangles, square off stock for cutting, mark angles of any degree, and quickly and accurately mark diameters and find center points of circles.

For marking circles and curves, use a divider. Locate the center point and mark it with a prick punch. Then adjust the divider to the desired radius, set one leg on the center mark, and pivot the tool to mark the curve.

A divider can also be used to step off and mark uniform intervals and to scribe lines parallel to an edge (the combination set can also be used for this task).

Cutting

Metal can be cut in a variety of ways. The sheet-metal worker, dealing with sheets up to 18-gauge, can use snips for most cutting jobs. A welder with access to a gas cutting torch can easily burn through metal of considerable thickness. But you can also saw through metal, or chisel through it.

Using a hacksaw—The first step in hacksaw cutting is selection of the proper blade. You want to get two or more teeth on the section at all times, so if you are cutting angles, channels, light bar stock, or tubing, you should select a fine blade, one with 24 teeth per inch or more. When cutting thicker stock of mild steel, aluminum, or other relatively soft metal, choose a blade with 14 or 16 teeth per inch. Very light stock can sometimes be bulked up with scrap wood: clamp sheet metal between two pieces of wood, or slip a dowel inside thin-wall tubing.

The hacksaw cuts on the push stroke. Make sure the blade is so installed.

Position the stock in the vise or clamp it to the workbench so you'll be cutting through the broadest section. Use a file to score the cutting line, so the blade has a slight groove to contain it. Grasp the saw by the handle and the front of the frame, and set it on the work at a very shallow angle. Bear down on the forward strokes and let up on the return strokes. Saw in a steady rhythm; working too fast can generate enough heat in the metal to draw the temper out of the blade.

For cutting curves, use a carbide chip blade, actually a thin rod. Since the entire surface of the rod is abrasive, you can cut up and sideways, as well as down.

Using a chisel—A chisel can be used to cut stock

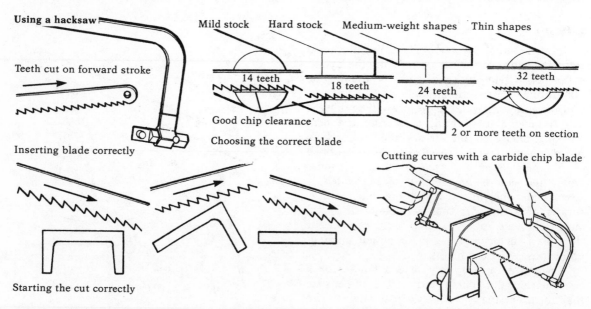

Using a hacksaw

Teeth cut on forward stroke

Mild stock   Hard stock   Medium-weight shapes   Thin shapes

14 teeth   18 teeth   24 teeth   32 teeth

Good chip clearance

Choosing the correct blade

2 or more teeth on section

Inserting blade correctly

Cutting curves with a carbide chip blade

Starting the cut correctly

in either of two ways. In the first method, you clamp the stock in a vise with the cut line just above the jaws. Set the chisel at about a 30-degree angle to the face of the stock, with the bevel resting on the jaws and the cutting edge against the cut line. Strike the chisel with a ball peen hammer, shearing the metal.

In the other method, you lay the stock on the workbench and set the chisel on the cut line. Strike it with a hammer. Move the chisel along the line and strike again. When the work is completely scored, move the chisel back to the beginning and repeat the process. With each pass you'll score progressively deeper and eventually cut all the way through.

Using a file—Some of the most simple shaping can be done with a file. It completes rough shapes created by cutting or finishes off edges. For example, a concave or convex curve can be roughly cut in a metal plate using a hacksaw, then be filed to the final smooth, even curve.

Most filing is what's known as cross-filing. The file is held in both hands, with the thumbs atop the tool and parallel to it. Bear down on the forward stroke, and lift the file slightly on the return, working diagonally across the metal. The

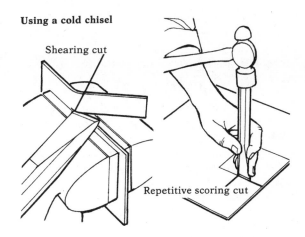

Using a cold chisel

Shearing cut

Repetitive scoring cut

more pressure you use, the faster the file will cut. To produce a square surface, you should try to avoid rocking the file as you work.

For a particularly smooth finish, you should draw-file. To do this, hold a mill file in an overhand grip. Stroke the file perpendicularly over the work, filing on the forward strokes. Work the entire surface with each stroke.

With any file operation, a slight burr will be created along the edges of the surface. Your fin-

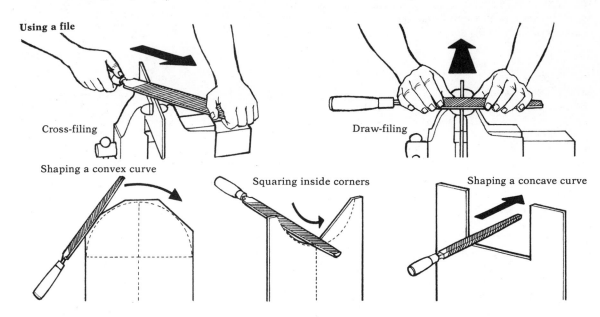

Using a file

Cross-filing

Draw-filing

Shaping a convex curve

Squaring inside corners

Shaping a concave curve

ishing touch should be to file the edge slightly to remove this burr.

Clean the file with a file card after each use. This will greatly extend the life of the tool.

Bending and shaping

For so strong a material, metal can be remarkably plastic. It can be bent, folded, twisted, stretched, compressed, formed, and molded.

Some of the most important procedures of sheet-metal work involve folding sheets to create basic shapes, to make hems (see p. 212) and to form seams (p. 222). Sheets are shaped to form curves (p. 233).

The blacksmith and the welder generally work with heavier stocks. The smith will work with forge, hammer, and anvil, and a variety of other tools, to create enormous changes in the forms the metal takes. The basic procedures for him include drawing, bending, upsetting, shouldering, flaring, and twisting. The metalworker with a gas welding rig can use it to heat metal to perform simple forging and bending operations.

Not all bending operations require the metal to be heated, however. Lightweight bar stocks can be clamped in a vise and bent by hand or with the help of hammer blows. A variety of homemade forms and jigs can be made to help shape metals (pp. 302, 308).

Drilling

To create the typical bolt, screw, or rivet hole, twist drill bits are used. The motive force for the bits can be provided by a hand-cranked drill, a portable electric drill, or a drill press.

You should provide a starting point for the bit with a center punch. Mark the center point first with a prick punch, then enlarge it with the center punch. If you don't, the bit may wander and create the hole a little off the mark.

The work should always be clamped for drilling, especially when using a drill press. If you don't clamp the work, the drill could easily wrench it out of your grasp and injure you.

The speed at which you bore is important. To bore a small hole in soft metal, you need high revolutions per minute (RPM). To bore a large

hole in hard metal, you need very low RPM. If you have a drill press, follow the manufacturer's recommendations as to the speeds to use for different metals. Judging the speed of a hand-held electric drill is more difficult. A ½-inch drill will generally peak at 750 RPM, while a ¼-inch drill will peak at about 2,500 RPM.

Drilling can generate a lot of heat. To help dissipate the heat, use cutting oil. Squirt a bit on the center point as you start to drill, then feed more into the hole as it is bored. If smoke begins to drift out of the hole, ease up a bit and feed more oil into the hole.

To drill a hole ⅜ inch or larger, bore a pilot hole first, then bore it out to the desired diameter.

In instances where a hole will be tapped (see p. 310), the hole should be reamed to ensure it is exactly the right diameter. You can use either machine-driven reamers or hand reamers.

Very large holes—1 inch to 2½ inches—can be drilled using hole saws or fly cutters. These tools are usually used only with light stock.

Drilling holes

Marking the centerpoint

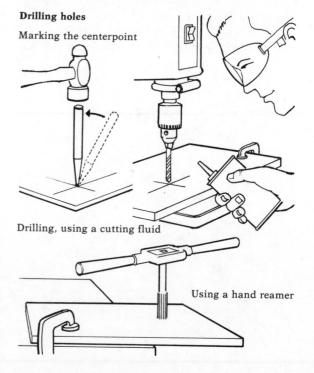

Drilling, using a cutting fluid

Using a hand reamer

Assembly

Assembly in general metalworking is frequently a matter of fastening parts together with screws, bolts, or rivets. There is an almost bewildering array of fasteners available: machine and sheet-metal screws with flat, pan, oval, round, and fillister heads; machine, carriage, stove, and tap bolts using flat, lock, and star washers; and hexagonal, jam, square, cap, and wing nuts. In certain situations, you may use a castle nut that can be locked in position with a cotter pin or a hitch-pin clip fit through a hole drilled in the bolt. Setscrews or thumb screws might be required in a project. Even rivets aren't simply rivets: there are flathead, countersunk head, buttonhead, panhead, and truss head rivets.

Bolts and screws are generally used where

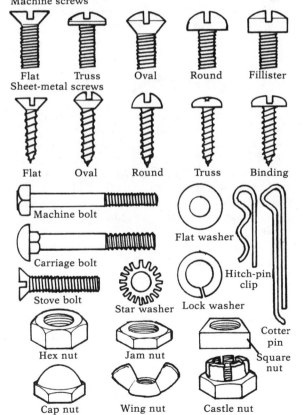

Machine screws

Flat Truss Oval Round Fillister

Sheet-metal screws

Flat Oval Round Truss Binding

Machine bolt

Carriage bolt

Stove bolt

Star washer Lock washer

Flat washer

Hitch-pin clip

Hex nut Jam nut Square nut

Cotter pin

Cap nut Wing nut Castle nut

eventual disassembly of the project is a possibility. In all cases, it is best to clamp together the parts to be joined and drill the necessary holes. With self-tapping screws, a pilot hole of appropriate size is drilled, then the hole in the top piece is enlarged so the screw will pass through it without binding. When the screws are driven, they cut their own threads in the bottom piece. Machine screws are used when the bottom piece has enough mass to allow threads to be cut in it with a tap (see p. 310).

When driving screws or stove bolts, be sure the tip of the screwdriver really fits the slot. If it is too big or too small, the slot can easily be butchered.

Tighten nuts and bolts with wrenches, not pliers. And select a wrench that fits precisely.

Setting rivets with a commercial rivet set is easy. Put the set over the rivet so the shank extends up the hole in it. Strike the set with a hammer, driving the pieces together. Remove the set and roughly form the head with a hammer. Then fit the set over the head and strike it with the hammer, finishing the head.

Not all assembly work involves the use of fasteners. Often in sheet-metal work, the edges of the pieces being joined are folded, then fitted together and forcefully locked together with a hand groover and hammer, making a seam (p. 222). Sometimes the parts are soldered together (p. 214). Welding is the most strong and durable method of joining metal parts together (p. 284).

Safety

In none of these basic procedures can safety be overlooked. In every metalworking project, the potential exists for cuts, impact injuries, eye injuries, burns, and the like. If you use power tools, the potential is increased by the accelerated speed at which things happen.

Exercise appropriate caution. Dress the part. Wear gloves when cutting sheet metal or working hot metal. Wear eye protection. Keep the shop cleaned up, using a brush or broom to sweep up shards of metal, drill turnings, and filings. Make sure your tools are sharp and in good repair.

Metalworking is fun and productive. Don't let a foolish, preventable injury spoil the experience.

Sheet Metal

Sheet-metal work may be the best area of metalworking for the complete novice to tackle. It requires relatively few tools, the materials often can be scavenged, and only a modest work area is needed. Yet remarkably attractive and useful projects can be successfully completed in a short time.

While a sheet is a piece of metal wider than 6 inches but no thicker than 3/16 inch, most home sheet-metal work involves pieces ranging from 28 to 16 gauge and no more than a couple of feet square. Sheets are made of steel, aluminum, copper, brass, and some other metals.

The work itself usually progresses quickly with modest noise and little dirt. Most projects can be built in tight quarters. The required tools are few, though you can assemble quite a collection if you really get into it. The items you can make range from the purely utilitarian to the exclusively decorative, with stops at spots at once useful and attractive. The four projects that follow this chapter should give you ideas for others you can make.

Setting Up Shop

No elaborate shop facilities are required for most home sheet-metal work. Small items, such as the candle sconce on page 208, can be crafted at a kitchen table, as long as you cover the table with a 3- or 4-foot-square panel of plywood to protect it. Keep your tools neatly organized in a tool chest. You won't need much room to store tools, your portable work surface, and a small supply of sheets.

If you can establish yourself in a fixed location—the back of the garage, a corner of the basement, even an uncarpeted spot in the family room—so much the better. You should still have a place for everything, and you should keep everything in its place, but at least you don't have to pick *everything* up just so the family can eat dinner.

In this situation, you should have a good workbench, measuring about 2½ feet by 4 or 5 feet, and of a comfortable working height. A vise should be bolted to the left front corner of the workbench. For sheet-metal work, you can use either a machinist's vise or a woodworking vise. If you have one or the other, stick with it; if you own neither, let your ultimate plans—will you branch out into other metalworking areas? or will you take up woodworking?—guide your choice.

Tools can be hung from pegs on the wall, laid out on shelves above the workbench, or stored in drawers beneath the work surface. Don't just heap them up on the workbench, though. The size and amount of material you keep in stock will dictate the space and facilities you need to store it. Smallish sheets can be put on a shelf under the workbench. Larger sheets can be slid between the workbench and the wall. Or you may devise a storage rack that will allow you to separate sheets of different composition and thickness.

Proper lighting can make the work easier. You should have a decent level of background lighting, such as that provided by an overhead fluorescent fixture. But you should also have directional task lighting, from a movable light source, so you always have light falling correctly for layout work. Scribed lines can be difficult to see on shiny tin plate or copper. Sometimes it's best to turn off the background light and just use task lighting.

Tools and Equipment

You don't need a whole lot of exotic tools to do simple sheet-metal projects, such as the four projects that follow. But there are quite a few specialized sheet-metal tools made, and if you choose to make sheet-metal work an important pastime, you will surely collect more than the few tools you need to get started.

Layout tools

Typical metalworking layout tools—combination set, steel rule, divider, scriber or scratch awl, prick punch, and center punch—are all the layout tools you need. Although not a necessity, a framing square, usually used by carpenters, is a very useful layout tool for sheet-metal work. It is a square, so it can be used to mark right angles. It's long enough to serve as a rule and has enough heft to be a good layout straightedge. And it is graduated in a variety of ways.

Cutting tools

Sheet metal can be cut with anything from a utility knife to a power shear. Holes can be cut in it with punches, drills, and other tools. Even files are useful for particular cutting jobs.

Snips—The primary cutting tool for sheet metal is snips. There are several varieties, and you may eventually collect all of them, but to start, you really only need one pair: straight-cutting snips.

Common snips, which look like clumsy scissors, are the tinsmith's traditional tool. The largest versions, a foot long or more, will cut through 18- to 16-gauge sheets without too much difficulty. For cutting curves, snips with curved blades are available. Hawk-billed snips, which have more graceful and slender blades, are used to cut internal openings.

Aviation snips are now quite widely used in the sheet-metal trades. These have compound action to increase and boost cutting power (though they'll still only cut up to 18-gauge sheets). Their plastic grips are color-coded: yellow for straight cuts, red for left cuts, green for right cuts. Offset snips, which place your hand above the cut, rather than in the cut, are also available in straight-and curve-cutting versions.

Other cutters—A common utility knife can be used to cut light sheets. The metal is scored with the knife guided by a straightedge, then carefully

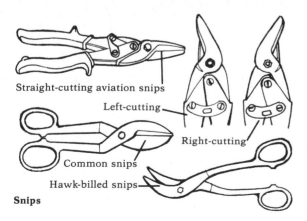

Straight-cutting aviation snips

Left-cutting

Right-cutting

Common snips

Hawk-billed snips

Snips

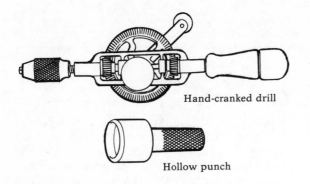

Hand-cranked drill

Hollow punch

bent along the line and flexed one or two times to tear or break it.

A saber saw can be used to cut sheets when fitted with a metal-cutting blade. Its use is generally limited to cutting sheets thicker than 16 gauge. It can be used to cut curves, of course, and internal openings.

While chisels do cut sheets, their use also would generally be limited to quite heavy sheets. They are frequently used, however, for decorative piercing.

Drills — Twist drill bits are used to bore holes in sheet metal. Brad-point bits, which resemble twist drills but which have a sharp center spike and cutting flanges similar to a woodworker's auger bits, will cut more precise holes.

A hand-cranked drill is the best motive tool

to use with either kind of bit. It is very easily controlled, and it doesn't require much effort to penetrate sheets. If you have an electric drill, of course, use it.

Large-diameter holes — up to 2½ inches — can be cut with holes saws or an adjustable fly cutter.
Punches — Common punches are used in sheet-metal work. Hollow-cored hole punches cut fairly large-diameter holes. Some versions are struck with a hammer, while others are fitted in a plierslike tool. The latter punches are used primarily to punch mounting holes in flanges, and they are limited by the throat-depth of the pliers.
Files — Every cutting tool leaves a burr, and the file is used to remove it. Therefore, first- and second-cut files will be used most frequently in sheet-metal work.

Shaping tools

Much of the work of the tinsmith involves the shaping of sheets, either in broad or tight curves or in hard creases called folds.
Stakes — Cast-iron or forged steel stakes, roughly T-shaped, are used by the tinsmith as forms for shaping sheets. The stakes are fitted in mortises in a bench plate, and you either form the sheets over the stake by hand or with a mallet. A hatchet stake, which has a sharply beveled edge, is used to form folds. A conductor stake, which has two round extensions of different diameters, is used

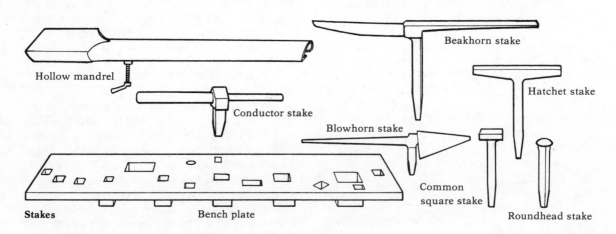

Hollow mandrel

Conductor stake

Beakhorn stake

Hatchet stake

Blowhorn stake

Common square stake

Roundhead stake

Stakes   Bench plate

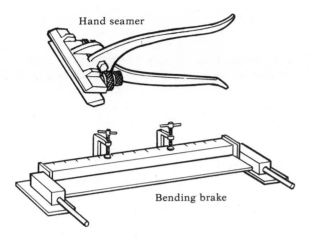

Hand seamer

Bending brake

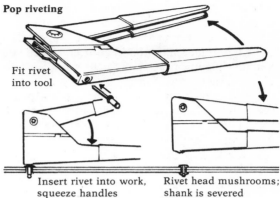

Pop riveting

Fit rivet into tool

Insert rivet into work, squeeze handles

Rivet head mushrooms; shank is severed

to form tight, even bends. A hollow mandrel, with a broader curved surface, forms broader bends. Blowhorn and beakhorn stakes, which have extensions similar to the horn of an anvil, can be used to form conical shapes. Spikelike square and roundhead stakes can be used to stretch areas of sheets into bowllike depressions.

You can clamp strips of bar stock or pipe in a machinist's vise to create your own stakes. These will work just as well and will cost far less.

The mallet you should use when hammer-forming sheets is either a plastic-faced mallet or a mallet with a head of tightly rolled rawhide. These will bend metal without denting or marring it.

Bending brake—Folds are most commonly made using a device called a bending brake. The sheet is slid horizontally between a hinged anvil and a clamping bar with the fold line aligned with the edge of the bar, which is then tightened down. A lever is lifted, pivoting the hinged portion of the anvil and folding the sheet against the clamping bar. The capacity of all brakes is limited by their width, but many can create a fold anywhere along the length of the sheet.

You can make a more limited brake to be clamped in a vise, or you can use the edge of the workbench, a strip of hardwood or bar stock, some C-clamps, and a mallet to create a bending break (see p. 212).

Hand seamer—To make folds for hems or seams,

which are invariably located within a ½ inch or so of the sheet's edge, you can use a plierslike device called a hand seamer. The seamer works best where the hem or seam is only a few inches long, but by working progressively along a fold, you can use it to make quite long folds. A locking-grip pliers with sheet-metal jaws will do much the same work.

Crimpers—Plierslike crimpers are used to press small, regular folds into the edges of sheets, as in the candle sconce's reflector (p. 208). A needle-nose pliers can do the same work, however.

Assembly tools

Sheet-metal objects are assembled using

Hammers

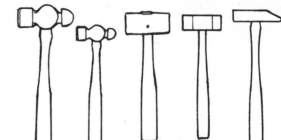

32-oz. ball peen hammer

16-oz. ball peen hammer

Rawhide mallet

Plastic-faced mallet

Tinner's setting hammer

mechanical or soldered (or occasionally brazed) seams or with rivets or sheet-metal screws.

For greatest strength, seams should be locked using a hammer and a hand groover, which you can make yourself (see p. 222).

The tools you need for soldering include a propane torch with friction lighter and a brush for applying flux. You can use a soldering iron for small joints, but it is difficult to heat joints more than an inch long with a soldering iron. Soldering guns are strictly electronics tools.

Sheet-metal screws, of course, are driven with a screwdriver.

For riveting you can use a rivet set and ball peen hammer, or a pop riveter. The pop riveter is a plierslike device that, when squeezed, simultaneously mushrooms the head of the special pop rivet and severs its shank.

Basic Procedures

Before you embark on any sheet-metal project, you must have an understanding of the basic procedures, how the sheets are cut and formed, and how the pieces are fitted together. Some simple projects can be formed of a single piece; it is simply folded into shape and soldered. But most projects, including those that follow, involve the fabrication of pieces and subassemblies that come together to form the finished project.

In sheet-metal work, perhaps more than in any other form of metalwork, the planning is critical. The finished projects are often geometric shapes: cubes, boxes, pyramids, cones, even frustums. To provide stiffness and safe edges, the metal must be hemmed. Interlocking seams are formed on edges. Every little tab and flange must be accounted for in the initial pattern, or the project won't come together properly.

In many circumstances, it is best to work up a full-scale pattern, called a stretchout, on heavy paper. The stretchout can then be folded into shape to ensure that it will indeed work. However, for simple pieces, such as the candle socket for the candle sconce or the various strips used in the chandelier, the outlines can be scribed directly on the sheet metal.

Planning

Begin the planning process with a pad of paper and a pencil. Sketch what you want to make as best you can. The drawing doesn't have to be pretty; the lines don't have to be straight; the shape doesn't need to be in true proportion.

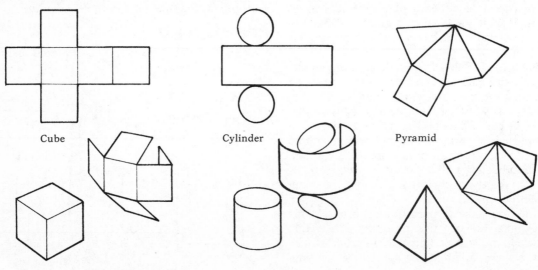

Cube   Cylinder   Pyramid

Stretchouts for solid geometric shapes

Next, try to visualize how you could make the item from a sheet—whether paper or metal. Remember that you can fold and bend the sheet, so each new plane doesn't necessarily require a new sheet. If you think about it, you'll see that any three-dimensional geometric shape—a cube, a cylinder, a pyramid—can be opened up and stretched out in one plane.

The problem for you, as a sheet-metal worker, is not only to develop a stretchout for your geometric shape, but to include the necessary seams and hems. And to work out the dimensions correctly. And to work out the order in which you will fold and form your two-dimensional sheet into the third dimension.

When you feel you have the concept in hand, begin developing the actual stretchout in full scale. Lay out the bottom, then the sides, and, if appropriate, the top. Then account for any hems that must be made, for lap seam tabs and lock seam folds. Study the stretchout and mentally

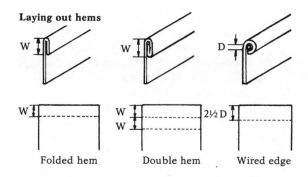

Laying out hems

Folded hem   Double hem   Wired edge

assemble the piece. Pick out the lines that indicate places you'd fold, rather than cut. Mark them by putting a couple of little Xs on the line. Look now for places where seams or hems will overlap. Here you should clip the corners to prevent the overlaps. The corners of tabs for lap seams are usually clipped too.

When you feel you have the stretchout completed, cut it out. Don't cut along any of the fold

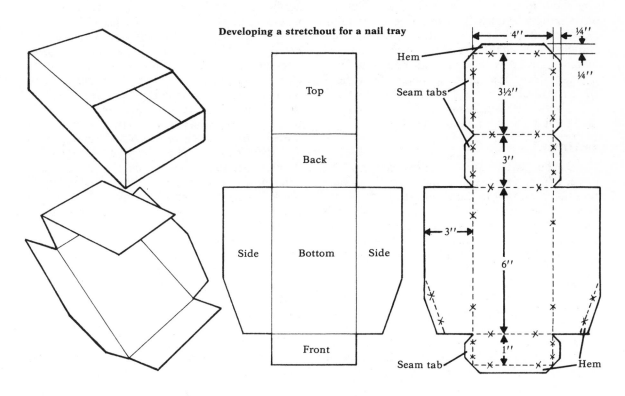

Developing a stretchout for a nail tray

Top

Back

Side   Bottom   Side

Front

Hem

Seam tabs

4″   ¼″

¼″

3½″

3″

3″

6″

1″

Seam tab   Hem

lines, but do clip corners and tab ends as indicated. Then fold along every line indicated as a fold line. Bring the sides and top up from the bottom and into position. See if the thing really works. If it does, you are all but ready to transfer the stretchout to the metal sheet.

But if it doesn't work, you have revisions to make. Figure out why it doesn't work. A mismeasurement? A miscalculation of how the planes relate to one another? Keep working, preparing the new full-scale stretchouts until the pattern works.

Of course, not all projects involve single-piece stretchouts. All the projects that follow have at least two. The process involved in developing multipiece stretchouts is the same. You can't easily fit the separate paper stretchouts together, but you can assure yourself by cutting out and folding the separate pieces that they work individually and that they should fit together.

The last thing to do before you transfer the stretchout to the metal sheet is to work out the order in which you will make the cuts and folds and lock or solder the seams. The hems are usually folded and flattened first, then seams are folded, followed by the folds and bends that form the item itself. You can make notes about these concerns directly on the stretchout.

And when that planning is done, you are ready to lay the piece out on metal.

Layout

Layout is a matter of either scribing the pattern directly on the sheet metal, or of transferring the stretchout to the sheet metal.

Direct layout—Creating the layout directly on the metal is not markedly different from creating the stretchout. But a mistake here will cost you a piece of metal, not a sheet of paper. You'll be scribing the metal, not sketching pencil lines. The marks can't be erased if you mismeasure or allow the scriber to wander.

The generally accepted procedure is to start in the lower left-hand corner of the sheet. Using a square, make sure the edges of the sheet are straight and square. If they are, use them as your reference lines throughout the process. If not,

Layout tips

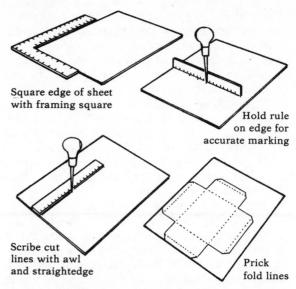

Square edge of sheet with framing square

Hold rule on edge for accurate marking

Scribe cut lines with awl and straightedge

Prick fold lines

scribe along both inside edges of the square and use these lines as the reference lines.

When laying out measurements, set the rule on edge, so the graduations are against the sheet. Use the scriber or a prick punch to mark the extremities of each line, then lay the rule flat and use it to guide the scriber as you connect the marks with a single, unbroken stroke. Fold lines can be distinguished from cut lines by marking them with a series of pricks, rather than scribing them.

Circles and curves should be laid out with a divider. Always mark the center point with a prick punch, and set one leg of the divider on the mark. Sweeping curves that involve more than one divider setting or position probably should be worked out on a stretchout.

In scribing and pricking the metal, it isn't necessary to score the metal deeply. If the sheet is thin, it's possible to weaken it seriously by scoring too deeply. You simply want to make a line that you can follow as you cut, or pricks that you can see to line up in a bending brake. You don't want to mar the appearance of the finished product with scriber scars.

Tracing a stretchout—Transferring a stretchout to the metal is largely a matter of tracing with a scriber. Here, as in direct layout, begin in the lower left-hand corner of the sheet. Spread the stretchout on the sheet and tape it down.

Using a scriber, trace around the edges of the stretchout. You should make only one stroke for each line. Fold lines can be pricked directly through the stretchout.

If the stretchout has been created from very thin paper, you can use a prick punch to mark reference points—the extremities of each line— then join the marks with a straightedge and scriber after you remove the stretchout from the metal.

Cutting

With the layout completed, the piece can be cut from the sheet. The usual technique is to use snips of one kind or another, but if the sheet is heavier than 18 gauge, a saw of some kind must be used. Holes are then drilled or punched. Each cut edge and each hole must be lightly filed to eliminate the burr. Decorative piercing, crimping, chasing, or embossing is usually completed at this point also.

Forming

The item must next be folded and shaped. Keep in mind the order in which the various forming operations must be performed, so that the existence of one fold doesn't interfere with the creation of another. This should all have been worked out as you created your stretchout.

Folds made close to an edge, such as those for hems or seams, can be formed with a hand seamer or a bending brake. Others must be formed over a hatchet stake or the edge of the workbench. The forming of uncreased bends is done over stakes or mandrels. When the metal is too thick to be formed by hand easily, you must use a hammer or mallet to hammer-bend it.

Assembly

Assembly is usually a simple matter of riveting or soldering lap seams and hooking and locking mechanical seams. Lock seams need to be soldered only when they must be waterproof.

The idea of soldering may seem intimidating,

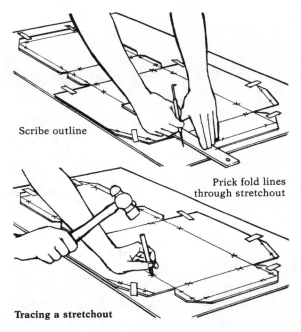

Scribe outline

Prick fold lines through stretchout

Tracing a stretchout

and even after you read how to do it, you may be suspicious of its seeming simplicity. But it is in fact quite easily done. Don't rivet a project just because you figure that method to be more simple than soldering.

Finally, keep in mind that assembly is seldom an isolated procedure. Most projects have subassemblies. And working out the proper and most efficient sequence in which to make any item is a vital bit of planning.

Safety

The closing note on sheet-metal work, before you begin the projects, is on safety. There are dozens of ways you can hurt yourself in any workshop environment. The real dangers generally are inattention and carelessness. The same is true in the sheet-metal shop.

Be careful. You can have fun and do productive work in a shop without cutting yourself, burning yourself, or getting other injuries. Just as you plan each move in laying out, cutting, forming, and assembling your projects, so should you plan for your own physical well-being. Use your head. Do the work the safe way.

Candle Sconce

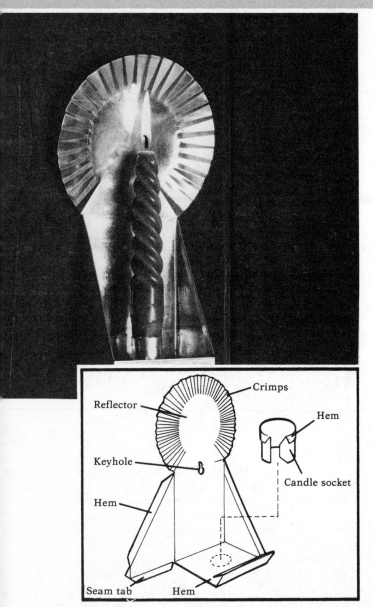

Reflector
Crimps
Keyhole
Hem
Seam tab
Hem
Hem
Candle socket

Cutting sheet metal
Folding and hemming
Soldering
Crimping

The candle sconce is an excellent first project. It introduces most of the fundamental sheet-metal skills; it requires only a few basic tools; it's made from a common tin can; and the product is not at all mundane, as many first-try projects are.

The initial challenge is the pattern, shown scaled down on the page opposite. It has straight and curved lines to cut out, hems to be folded, holes to be drilled, and crimps to be made. All have to be laid out on the sheet quite precisely if the project is to succeed. Although the project directions depict the layout being done directly on the sheet, you are well advised to make a paper stretchout in actual size to ensure you get it right.

Cutting out the sconce shouldn't be too difficult, even for the beginner. There are no long cuts to be made, but there are intricate inside corners and tabs that must be cut properly, and, of course, there is the curved reflector cut to deal with.

You get valuable practice at folding, for there are many short hems and folds in the project. All can be easily made using the bending brake described on page 212. The brake is easily and inexpensively made, and it will be a much-used device in all your sheet-metal work.

The soldering required is not difficult, but appearance is important here. Poorly mated joints and sloppy soldering should be avoided. Although a soldering iron could be used for some of the joints, the propane torch is a better all-around device to use. Use 50/50 solid wire solder and flux, applied with an acid brush.

The sconce is a duplicate of an Early American design and will add warmth and charm to most any room of the house. Because they are so easily made, you find yourself making extras to give to relatives and friends.

What you will need

1 empty 1-gal. paint thinner can
knife
straight-cutting snips
circular-cutting snips
drill
vise
file
ignition file
mallet
bending brake (see p. 212)
needle-nose pliers
locking-grip pliers with sheet-metal jaws
awl
layout tools
flux
50/50 solid wire solder
propane torch

Step-by-step instructions

1. Begin construction of the candle sconce by cutting the top and bottom from a clean 1-gal. paint thinner can. Use a can opener or sturdy knife, cutting close to the seams so that the edges of the tin-plate sheet are

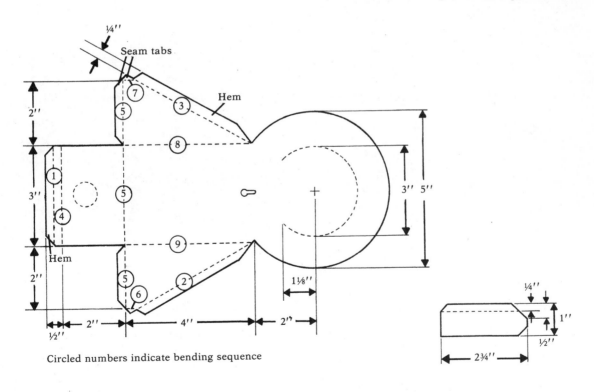

Circled numbers indicate bending sequence

Cutting Sheet Metal

While there is more than one way to cut sheet metal, the most common method is with snips. Snips are very much like heavy-duty scissors, and when you use them, you are essentially using paper-cutting skills.

You may satisfactorily complete a few simple projects with only one pair of snips, but eventually your stable of snips should include straight, circular-cutting, and hawk-billed snips. The straight- and circular-cutting snips do what their names imply. The hawk-billed snips are used to cut interior circles. If you go for aviation snips, you should have left-, right-, and straight-cutting models (see p. 201).

The most accurate way to cut sheet metal is to do it in two stages: rough cut and finish cut. Cut about ⅛ in. shy of the cut line while rough cutting. With only a thin waste strip to bend out of your way while finish cutting, you can concentrate more on the cutting. This method can actually be faster than attempting to cut on the line the first time around.

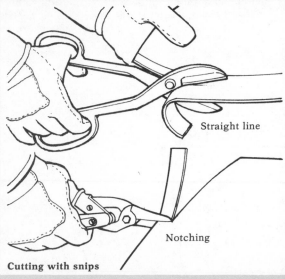

Straight line

Notching

Cutting with snips

Think of the sheet as a piece of heavy paper you are about to cut with scissors. Hold it in one gloved hand, with the snips in the other. As you cut, open the snips completely, making each cut nearly as long as the blades, increasing the efficiency of your work and producing a cleaner edge. Avoid closing the blades completely, since this creates a little nick along the cut edge. As you work, bend the waste metal up or down so that, as much as is possible, it is out of your way.

Cutting broad outside curves involves the same process. But you must use snips designed to cut curves. Cutting a scrolled edge with aviation snips may involve switching from one pair to another as the cut progresses.

When cutting inside corners or notching adjoining hems, be careful not to cut too far. This is the only situation in which you should cut with the blade tips. Align the blades precisely so the tips will close *at* the corner, not shy of it or beyond it.

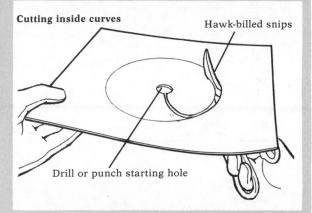

Cutting inside curves

Hawk-billed snips

Drill or punch starting hole

To cut an inside circle, you must first create a hole through which you can insert the snips' blade. The hole can be cut with a fly cutter or hole saw or with a hollow punch. In a pinch, you can use a chisel to slash an entryway for the snips. Work the blade into the hole from beneath the sheet, then rough cut the larger hole. Then make your finish cut.

If you make the rough cut too close to the actual cut line, you may have trouble during the finish cut with the snips bending the waste, rather than shearing it off. You could have the same trouble if the snips are dull. Keep your snips sharp, and always leave yourself enough waste to make a good finish cut. If, despite your best efforts, you do run into this trouble, try reversing the direction of the cut. This usually works a different blade and changes the angle of the cut. If that doesn't help, cut as much as you can, then file the edge.

Regardless of how careful you are, you will often have an edge that's crimped, nicked, or bent. Flatten this edge with a mallet. Hold the piece on a clean, flat work surface, and tap the edge lightly.

Every edge will have a slight burr. Use a file to remove it. Fine sandpaper *can* be used, but there's a danger that a rough edge or sliver will cut through the paper and into your fingers. Better to use the file.

straight when you are finished. After removing and discarding the top and bottom, cut along the vertical seam with snips to open the can into a sheet. Be careful of the sharp edges.

2. Flatten the sheet by bending the corners over the edge of the workbench. Flatten the edges and remove any kinks or dents with a mallet. Be careful not to stretch the metal out of shape.

3. Lay out the pattern on the sheet's shiny side. Use a metal rule, a scriber, and a divider to mark the cut and fold lines. A light line is sufficient for the fold lines, but use a heavy line to mark the cuts.

4. Cut the sheet using snips. Use circular-cutting snips to cut the edge of the reflector. Cut the 1 × 2¾-in. strip

for the candle socket from the remainder of the sheet, then discard all scraps to keep the work area clean. File the burr from all edges with a smooth-cut file.

5. Lay out and drill the keyhole for hanging the sconce. Center-punch and drill the ¼-in.-dia. bottom hole first, then center-punch and drill the ⅛-in.-dia. top hole. Clean the edges of the resulting keyhole with a small ignition file.

6. Fold the hems using the hardwood bending brake (see p. 212). Position the brake in the vise and fit the cutout in it to the depth of the fold lines, then tighten the vise. Start the hems by hand-bending the metal over the beveled edge of the brake until the fold is uniform and flat. Be sure to start each fold in the right direction: The hems should double over onto the shiny side of the sheet.

(Continued on page 215)

Folding and Hemming

A fold is a sharply creased bend. In sheet-metal work, folding is one of the fundamental techniques that must be mastered. While it is important in the creation of angular shapes, it is even more important in creating hems and seams. Hems stiffen the edges of sheet-metal objects and make them safe. Seams are interlocking folds that join one or more sheets into a shape. The details of making seams are on p. 222.

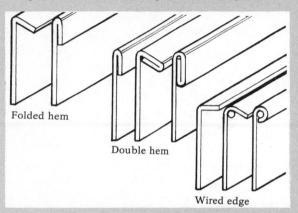

Folded hem

Double hem

Wired edge

There are three ways to finish an edge: the folded hem, the double hem, and the wired edge. The most commonly used is the simple folded hem. The edge of the sheet is folded completely over and hammered flat against the sheet. The double hem takes off from a folded hem: the hem is folded over completely and hammered flat, adding another thickness of metal to the hem and making it still more stiff. The strongest hem is the wired edge, which is created by folding and setting the metal edge over a strand of galvanized steel or copper wire.

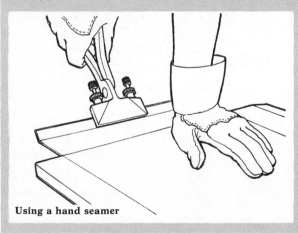

Using a hand seamer

Hems can be folded using a hand seamer, a special pliers with very wide, flat jaws. Some have adjusters that govern the depth to which the metal can slide into the jaws, so you don't have to align the jaw edge with the fold line each time you move the seamer.

Folding a short hem—one no longer than the width of the seamer jaws—is relatively easy. Lay the sheet flat on the workbench and hold it down. Align the seamer jaws with the fold line, and grip the metal's edge tightly. Make the bend with a rocking motion: as you lift the handles, simultaneously press the lower jaw against the workbench, so the fold is made at the jaws' edge. Bend the sheet about 130°–140°. You can then flatten the hem with a mallet.

Folding a long hem takes more care, since it is all too easy to get the hem slightly skewed: proper alignment of the seamer with the fold line at each bending point is critical. Start in the middle of the hem and work toward the ends. Work in stages, bending the middle slightly, then bending the ends into alignment, then bending the middle further, then the ends, and so forth.

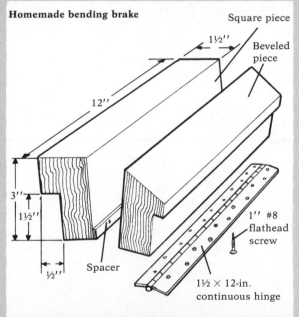

Homemade bending brake

Square piece

Beveled piece

1½''

12''

3''

1½''

½''

Spacer

1'' #8 flathead screw

1½ × 12-in. continuous hinge

Hems can also be made in a handy, homemade bending brake, used in conjunction with a vise. Cut two 1½ × 3 × 12-in. pieces of hardwood. Plow a ½ × 1½-in. rabbet along one face of each, as shown. Bevel the top edge of one piece to 45°. Glue a ½-in.-wide spacer strip, no thicker than ⅛ in., to the other, as shown. Join the two pieces with a 1½ × 12-in. continuous hinge.

To use the brake, drop it in a vise, with the rabbets resting on the tops of the jaws. Fit the sheet metal in the brake and align the fold line with the edge of the brake. With the sheet tightly clamped in the brake, hammer-bend it over the beveled edge with a mallet. Slip the piece out of the brake and lay it on the workbench to close the hem with the mallet.

Forming a wired edge

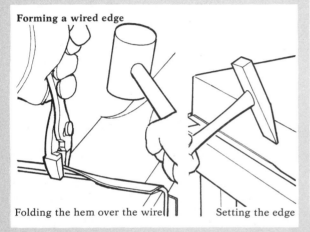

Folding the hem over the wire | Setting the edge

A wired edge is a bit more difficult to form. The wire enclosed by the hem not only stiffens the edge, it also ties adjoining edges together. Hence, until the edges actually adjoin, the wire can't be installed (though the folds should be formed as an initial step).

Layout is particularly critical. For a proper fit, the width of the fold must be 2½ times the diameter of the wire plus twice the thickness of the sheet. In practical terms, then, forming a 24-ga. steel sheet around a 12-ga. steel wire would require a fold ⁵⁄₁₆ in. wide (the sheet is 0.0239 in. thick, the wire 0.1055 in. dia.).

The fold is formed as for any hem. Then the wire is fitted into the fold and held in place with a pliers while you flatten the hem with a mallet. To prevent the jaws of the pliers from marring the metal, wrap them with tape. To complete the edge, use the tapered peen of a tinner's setting hammer to drive the edge of the sheet fully against the wire.

Since the wired edge usually forms the perimeter of a shape, it has to be bent to the proper shape and size prior to installation. The ends should meet at least 1½ in. from any corner.

Folds that help shape the finished object are made

Folding

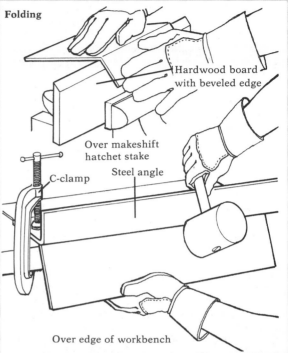

Hardwood board with beveled edge

Over makeshift hatchet stake

C-clamp

Steel angle

Over edge of workbench

after hems are completed. Because they usually don't occur close to the edges of the sheet, they seldom can be made with a seamer or a bending brake.

Many folds can be made over a hatchet stake or some makeshift variety of it. A hatchet stake can be made by cutting or grinding a 45°-60° bevel on the edge of a hardwood board or a steel bar or plate. Clamp the piece in a vise and use it as you would a stake.

To form a fold over the stake, align the fold line of the sheet along the edge of the stake. If the sheet is light enough, you can fold it by hand, using the stake's edge as the fulcrum. Otherwise, use a mallet to hammer the sheet over the stake's edge.

Another technique is to use the edge of a workbench as the fulcrum. Position the sheet with the fold line aligned over the edge of the work surface. Clamp it in place with a length of bar stock or wood and C-clamps. Then bend the sheet by hand or by using a mallet.

A critical factor in making these latter kinds of folds is the order in which you make them. You must be able to make each without previous folds getting in the way. Use the stretchout, rather than the metal sheet, to plan the sequence.

Soldering

Soldering is a technique of joining metals that's frequently used in sheet-metal work. It is one of the basic skills that must be mastered. In brief, the metal pieces being joined are heated. Then the solder, which is the glue that will hold the joint together, is applied to the joint. There it melts and, upon cooling, bonds the pieces together.

Solder itself is a tin-lead alloy that melts at about 400°F. The most common solders, often called soft solders, are 40/60, 50/50, and 60/40. The first number indicates the amount of tin in the alloy, the second the amount of lead. You will need only 50/50 solder for the projects in this section. It is sold in wire form, which is what you will use, and in bars, powders, and other forms.

Where greater strength than that provided by soft solder is needed, the so-called hard or silver solders are used. These contain silver and melt at a higher temperature than soft solders. Aluminum must be soldered with a special solder composed of zinc and either tin, aluminum, copper, or lead.

For proper bonding to occur, the pieces being joined must be scrupulously burnished with steel wool to clean them, and flux must be applied. All metals will develop a film of oxide or tarnish, which interferes with the bonding of the solder to the metal. It is this film that must be removed by burnishing. The use of flux does three things. It helps lift the oxides from the metal, it prevents the further formation of oxides, and it lowers the surface tension of the molten solder and helps it spread through and over the joint.

Fluxes are either corrosive or noncorrosive. The corrosive fluxes are acid-based. You must clean any residue of such fluxes from the joint after it is soldered. This can be done with steel wool or with a baking soda-and-water solution. If you don't do this, the flux will promote long-term corrosion and consequent weakening of the joint. Acid flux can be used on any metal.

Noncorrosive flux—rosin is the common one—is used in electronics work, where the residue can't be cleaned of the finished joint. It will work on clean copper and tin plate, so you can use it when soldering those metals.

Buy a paste flux and a brush to apply it. And keep the brush clean.

The necessary heat can be applied either by an electric soldering iron or by a propane torch. Soldering guns and tiny soldering pencils are used in electronics work and won't deliver enough heat for soldering sheet metal.

Soldering irons are made in various sizes, usually

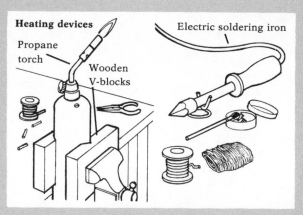

Heating devices — Propane torch — Wooden V-blocks — Electric soldering iron

ranging from 100 to 350 watts. A 100-watt model may be adequate for small jobs, but for long seams and large sheets, you need the heat produced by the larger models. It isn't enough to be able to melt solder, you have to be able to heat the metals sufficiently that they can melt the solder. Be sure, if and when you buy a soldering iron, that you get a holder, which supports the tip of the iron when you set it down.

For a soldering iron to work properly, transferring heat quickly into the metal being joined and sliding smoothly along the joint, its tip must be tinned with solder. To do this, file the faces of the copper tip until they are smooth and shiny. Plug in the iron and let it heat up. Then lightly touch solder to each of the faces, spreading a thin film of solder over them. The iron will have to be retinned periodically.

Perhaps the best all-around heating device is the common propane torch. All the soldering on the projects in this section was done with such a torch. Follow the manufacturer's directions in setting up and using the torch. It should always be lighted with a friction lighter rather than a match.

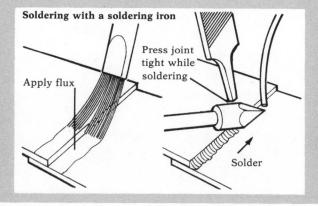

Soldering with a soldering iron — Apply flux — Press joint tight while soldering — Solder

The usual technique in using the torch is to secure it in some way, so your hands are free to hold the workpiece and/or the solder. Stands for such torches are commercially available and are commonly used by jewelrymakers. If you choose to clamp the torch in a vise, make a pair of V-blocks from scrap lumber so the vise will have a better purchase on the propane bottle. Whatever you do, don't just stand the torch on the workbench; it can be too easily knocked over.

Soldering any joint begins with the preparation of the joint itself. It must be smooth, tight, and, of course, clean. Flux the joint.

If you are using a soldering iron, touch its heated tip to one end of the seam, heating the metals. Periodically touch the seam with the solder. When it melts, begin moving the iron very slowly along the seam. It will pull a film of molten solder along the seam with it. To maintain a supply of the solder, occasionally touch the solder to the seam near the iron's tip. Don't touch the iron with the solder, however. Let the solder cool and harden before you move the workpiece.

When using the propane torch, the procedure is a

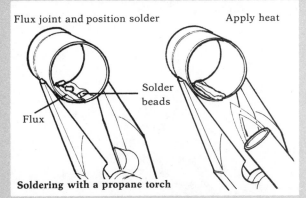

Flux joint and position solder — Apply heat

Flux — Solder beads

Soldering with a propane torch

bit different. Nip little beads of solder from the roll and place them in the flux along the seam. You don't need to use a lot of it. Grip the seam tightly with a pair of pliers, and pass the workpiece through the flame of the torch, heating it until the solder melts. It will flow along the seam; if necessary, you can rock the piece a bit to encourage the flow.

Where you want as little solder as possible to show, you can tin the mating surfaces—much as you tin the tip of the soldering iron—before assembling the joint. After clamping it together, reheat the seam to remelt the solder. When the seam cools, the pieces will have been bonded.

7. As each hem is folded, flatten it with a mallet on a flat, clean surface. The finished hems must be straight and uniformly smoothed. The hems are not soldered, but the edges are flattened so that they are strong and will not cut or scratch. Fold and flatten the hem for the front edge first. Then return the piece to the brake and fold the right side hem. Complete it, then fold and flatten the left side hem.

8. Complete the 90° folds in the sequence indicated on the pattern (p. 209). The sconce bottom must be kept square and the overall shape symmetrical. Fold the sconce to shape so that it will hold together while the seams are soldered. Bend the sides until they stay in alignment with the bottom edges.

Crimping

Crimping is a way of decorating flat sheet metal that also adds strength to the piece. It's a series of organized bends along the edge of a sheet, each crimp a separate flute. Although crimping is really easy, considerable planning and some practice is necessary so that the crimps stay uniform and work out symmetrically.

Begin by carefully measuring the space to be crimped. Plan the size of the flutes so that each will be of a uniform size, or so that they will diminish in size in a symmetrical fashion. The flutes can range uniformly from corner to corner, or symmetrically from the corners to a center point, or, if tapered, around a curved edge, as in the candle sconce project.

Cut the edge to shape, then file it to remove metal slivers and sharp edges. The edge must be smooth and clean before you crimp; it is very tedious to finish the edge after it is crimped.

Use a prick punch or awl to mark the location of each flute. You will use needle-nose pliers to make the crimps. By lining up the tips of the plier jaws with the punch mark, you'll be easily able to control the length and location of each flute. Grasp the metal in the pliers and twist the pliers. Practice on a scrap of metal to determine how much to twist to produce the kind of flute you want.

With practice you'll be able to execute truly creative crimping. The finished product is limited only by your imagination and experience.

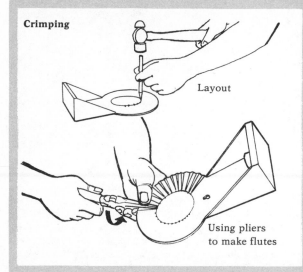

Crimping

Layout

Using pliers to make flutes

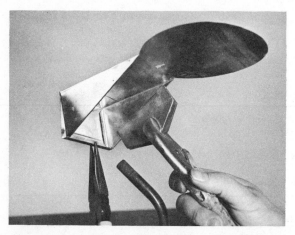

9. Clean the areas to be soldered and apply flux. Cut ⅛-in.-long beads of 50/50 solid wire solder, and wedge a piece in each of the bottom seams. Heat the seams from the bottom with a propane torch. Hold the seams together with two pliers, as shown. When all the solder has melted and the seams are tight, remove the piece from the heat, allow it to cool, then wipe off any flux residue.

10. Fold and flatten the hem along the top edge of the candle socket strip. Scribe a line on the tab to mark the position of the overlapping straight edge. Shape the strip around a ¾-in.-dia. dowel with the hem on the outside.

11. Solder the joint. Clean and flux the ends of the strip. Grip the socket with needle-nose pliers, lay a bead of solder inside by the seam, and hold the piece over the torch to solder it. The bottom of the ring must be level to fit the sconce body properly.

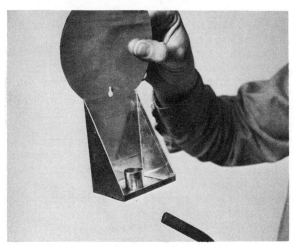

12. Center the candle socket on the sconce body, and lightly mark the position. Clean the entire bottom of the sconce body and flux it. Place the socket, hem up, in the flux, which will help to hold it in position. Cut a ⅛-in. bead of solder and lay it inside the socket. Heat the sconce from the underside until the solder melts, keeping the socket centered as you do so. If it moves, reheat the piece and reposition the socket when the solder melts.

13. Lay out the sconce reflector for crimping. Lightly scribe a 3-in.-dia. arc on the reflector, paralleling its edge. Punch decorative holes on this line to mark the length and positions of the crimps. Lay the sconce on a piece of scrap wood, and, using a small awl, punch the holes. Space them uniformly around the arc. Try to punch with the same impact at each spot, so that, as much as possible, the holes are all the same size.

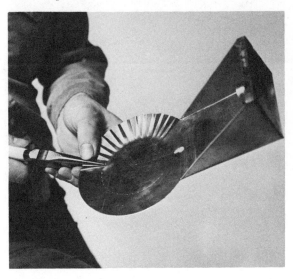

14. Crimp the reflector with needle-nose pliers and a twisting motion. Start at one side of the reflector and work around the edge. Align the tips of the pliers with the holes, and try to keep the flutes uniform.

Chandelier

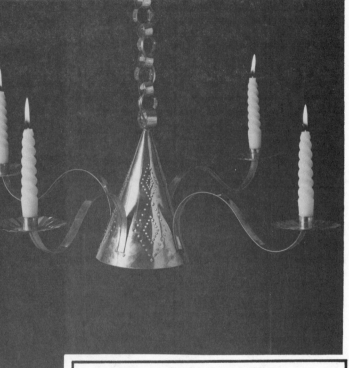

This chandelier, formed of tin-plated steel, is both an attractive and a functional project. It's a good second project, for it calls upon all the skills acquired in making the candle sconce and adds a couple new ones, including a vital skill, seaming.

The chandelier combines traditional candle-power with electric power. The four graceful arms support candle holders, and the pierced conical body hides—except when it's turned on—a light bulb. The whole unit is suspended by a chain formed of sheet-metal loops.

The materials should cost next to nothing. You must buy only the electric socket, wire, plug and switch, and a few brass fittings. The chandelier itself is fabricated from the metal recycled from two 1-gallon paint thinner cans. If you can't find them in your own trash barrel, look through someone else's. By all means, however, look for cans with paper labels glued to them; those with the label painted or printed directly on the metal won't do.

When you do go shopping for the electrical supplies, be sure you get electric cord with clear insulation, rather than the usual white or brown. The cord is woven through the loops of the chain, and cord with clear insulation is probably the least obtrusive variety to use in this situation.

Once you have the raw materials, the next major step in the project is layout. Here, as in the previous project, you can lay out the various parts directly on the metal, as did the Rodale craftsman who made the one shown. But if you are a relative novice, it is a good idea to prepare a stretchout. Then transfer the stretchout to the metal.

There are quite a number of small pieces to cut out for the chandelier, including four drip pans and candle-socket strips and, depending upon the length of the chain you make, quite a few chain-loop strips. Play around with the

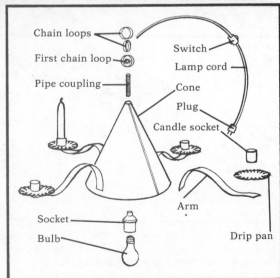

arrangement of the pieces on the metal you get from the cans before scribing any lines. Don't waste your metal by cutting out the initial pieces thoughtlessly. Even if you work frugally, you will probably have to use the tops and bottoms.

The new skills introduced in this project are piercing and seaming. Piercing is primarily a decorative technique. Seaming is a fundamental skill, one that you'll draw upon again and again as you do sheet-metal work.

Completing the chandelier is a matter of working slowly and carefully through the steps. Just take every step in order, and you shouldn't have any difficulty making a unique and attractive home furnishing.

Step-by-step instructions

1. Begin the project by cutting two clean 1-gal. paint thinner cans open and flattening the metal. Use a sturdy old knife to slice the tops and bottoms from the cans, then use snips to cut the cans along the seam. Save the tops and bottoms. Flatten the metal by bending the corners over the edge of the workbench and hammering the metal edges and any kinks or dents with a mallet.

What you will need

2 empty 1-gal. paint thinner cans
1 switchless short electrical socket
1 pipe nipple, 1½'' × ⅛''
1 brass pipe coupling, ⅛''
1 brass pipe thread nut, ⅛''
18-ga. clear lamp cord, 15'
1 quick-connect switch
1 quick-connect plug
knife
straight-cutting snips
circular-cutting snips
drill
vise
8-oz. ball peen hammer
mallet
bending brake (see p. 212)
needle-nose pliers
awl
hand groover
layout tools
flux
50/50 solid wire solder
propane torch

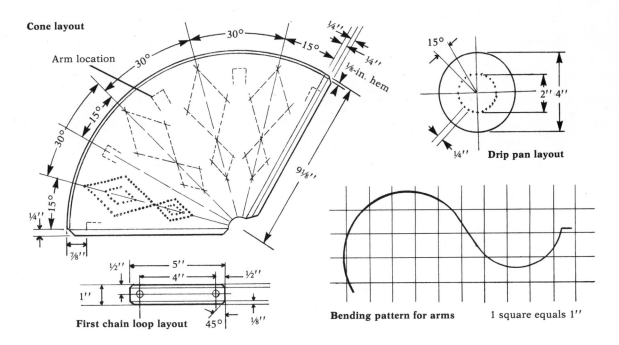

Cone layout

Arm location

30°   30°   15°

¼''

¼''

⅛-in. hem

15°

30°   15°

30°

15°

9⅛''

¼''

⅛''

7⁄8''

15°

2''   4''

¼''

Drip pan layout

½''   5''   ½''

4''

1''

⅛''

First chain loop layout   45°

Bending pattern for arms   1 square equals 1''

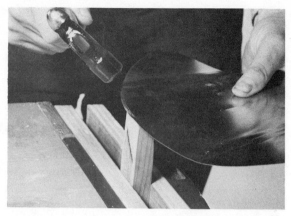

2. Lay out the pieces for the chandelier. It is best to prepare a paper stretchout first, then transfer it to the metal. Enlarge the pattern on p. 219 in preparing the stretchouts for the cone, the drip pans, and the first chain loop. The dimensions of the other pieces are given in subsequent steps. Lay out the pieces as close together as possible, to conserve the tin plate. Scribe the cut lines deeply, the fold lines lightly.

4. Hem the cone and fold the edges for the lock seam. Hem the long curved edge first, using a hammer and a hardwood stake. Make three or more passes to bend the edge, then flatten the hem with a mallet. The seam folds can be made using the homemade bending brake (see p. 212). Flatten these folds over a shim, so they aren't completely closed, which would prevent you from hooking them. Be sure to fold one edge over what will be the outside of the piece, the other over the inside.

3. Cut out the first piece, the cone, using snips. Use circular-cutting snips for the curved edges, straight-cutting snips for the straight edges. Rough cut, then finish cut the piece. The other pieces, though laid out, don't have to be cut from the sheet until you are ready to work them.

5. On paper, lay out the pattern for the piercing, using the dimensions for one 30° section of the cone. The pattern will be repeated four times. Tape the paper pattern in place, lay the metal on a scrap board, and pierce the metal, using a hammer and awl. Punch the holes into the shiny side of the metal, so the rough edges will be on the inside of the finished cone. When one section is finished, lift the pattern and move it to the next for piercing.

Piercing

Piercing is a time-honored way of decorating sheet metal, altering it to allow light and air to penetrate. The idea is simply to punch an attractive pattern of holes in the sheet using a punch or chisel.

Begin this process as you do many others, with a blank sheet of paper. Sketch the lines of the pattern, then work out the spacing and locations of the holes. The paper pattern is taped to the sheet, and the punch is driven through paper and metal.

Any number of tools can be used. Experiment on scraps of the sheet you are using to see what sorts of holes the different tools make. A nail will make a ragged, irregular hole. Awls and punches will produce round holes, but will also stretch and flare the metal surrounding the hole. To produce a clean, undistorted hole, use a hollow punch. A chisel can be manipulated to produce a teardrop-shaped hole, while a screwdriver should yield an oblong slot.

Regardless of the tool you use, lay the sheet on a scrap board while you punch. The board will provide support so the metal doesn't dent with each piercing blow.

Traditional pierced tinware always has the design punched from the back of the sheet, so the rough edge is seen, rather than hidden. You don't have to be a traditionalist, but you *should* decide beforehand which side of the finished piece will have the rough edge, and work accordingly.

Follow your predetermined design as you work. Arriving at a symmetrical pattern is not difficult. Lay out only half the pattern on paper, tape it in position on the sheet, punch it, then turn the paper over as if turning the page in a book. Tape it down once again and punch the second half of the overall pattern. As long as you position the layout paper carefully, the result should always be symmetrical. A repeated pattern is also created by laying out the basic pattern once, then repositioning it wherever you want to repeat it.

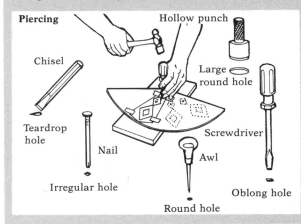

Piercing — Hollow punch, Chisel, Large round hole, Teardrop hole, Screwdriver, Nail, Awl, Irregular hole, Oblong hole, Round hole

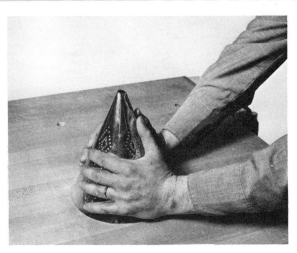

6. Form the flat sheet into a cone and hook the folds. Be careful in forming the cone so you don't get kinks or creases in it. The metal is light enough to form easily by hand.

7. Lock the seam. Make a mandrel by cutting a 12-in.-long board in half on a diagonal. Clamp it in a vise with the pointed end projecting from the side. Slide the cone over the mandrel with the seam up. Fit a hand groover over one end of the seam, and strike it with a hammer to lock it. Work along the seam to lock its entire length.

(Continued on page 224)

Seaming

Seams are sheet-metal joints. The edges can simply be overlapped and riveted or soldered together, or the edges can be folded, hooked, and either hammered together firmly or folded further. The best seams are smooth and accurately folded, and they hold the edges of the metal together through years of normal use. Only a few commercial tools and a couple of home-made tools are needed.

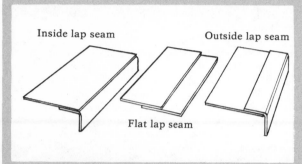

Inside lap seam   Outside lap seam

Flat lap seam

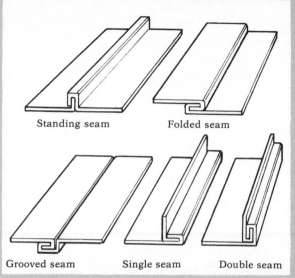

Standing seam   Folded seam

Grooved seam   Single seam   Double seam

Lap seams are the most simple. One edge overlaps the other by ¼-½ in. The seam is secured with sheet-metal screws, rivets, soldering, or even brazing. Despite their simplicity, lap seams can be both strong and waterproof.

Lock seams are more complicated. They are formed by interlocking folds made on the metal edges and can yield strong joints without further bonding, although they are frequently soldered.

The folds for seams are formed as for hems. But instead of flattening them completely, as in hemming, you flatten them loosely over a shim the thickness of the metal sheet that's to interlock. The shim is removed and the folds are hooked together, then locked by hammering them flat. Slide the hooked seam over a mandrel, real or makeshift, to provide support as the

seam is hammered. Use a rawhide or plastic mallet to lock the seam without marring the metal. This process will produce a folded seam.

A grooved seam is produced in similar fashion, but a hand groover or a grooving rail is used to create an additional crimp that provides extra strength. Hand groovers are commercially available, but you can make your own from a scrap of hardwood. Cut the wood into the shape of a truncated triangle. Plow a ¼-in.-wide by ⅛-in.-deep groove the length of the base edge. In similar fashion, a grooving rail can be made by plowing a ¼-in.-wide by ⅛-in.-deep groove along the edge of a length of hardwood.

The outside seam is made by supporting the hooked seam with a mandrel and locking it with the hand groover. Fit the groover over one end of the seam,

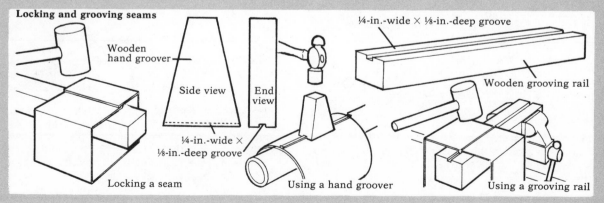

Locking and grooving seams

Wooden hand groover

Side view

End view

¼-in.-wide × ⅛-in.-deep groove

¼-in.-wide × ⅛-in.-deep groove

Wooden grooving rail

Locking a seam

Using a hand groover

Using a grooving rail

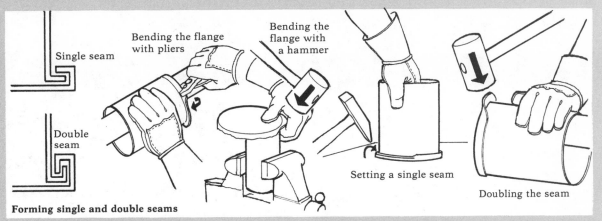

Forming single and double seams

aligning the groove over the hooked folds. Rap the groover smartly with a hammer. Move to the other end of the seam and do the same. Then lock the entire length of the seam in the same manner.

The inside seam is made by using the grooving rail as a mandrel. The hooked seam must be aligned over the groove. Use a mallet, rather than a hammer, to smite the seam and lock it.

Single and double seams are used to attach bottoms to containers. A flange is formed around the base of the container body. The bottom is fitted in place and its edges folded over the flange and set. This is a single seam. It can be folded against the sides of the container, forming a double seam.

Folding the flange on an angular shape is easily done with a hand seamer or a bending brake. The flange should be $1/8$-$3/16$ in. wide for a single seam, $1/4$ in. wide or more for a double seam.

Folding the flange on a cylindrical shape is somewhat more difficult. Use slip-joint pliers, with the jaws wrapped with tape to protect the sheet metal. Support the cylinder on a mandrel. Be sure to work to a fold line, so the flange is of a uniform width. Make a shallow bend at first, working around the entire edge of the piece. Then bend more on a second pass and complete the bend on a third or even a fourth pass. Trying to complete the 90° bend in one pass can distort the metal and yield an unsatisfactory flange.

The bottom piece must also be flanged before it can be fitted to the body and the seam set. With an angular shape, again, folding the flange is a simple folding operation. With a disk, the flange is less easily produced. You can use pliers, forming the flange in several passes as with the cylindrical body. Or you can hammer-bend the flange over a flat stake. Hold the disk

over the stake and hammer the edge, bending it slightly and forming a crease at the fold line. Work around the circumference of the disk, moving it so the fold line is always aligned with the edge of the stake.

When both flanges are formed, fit the pieces together. If you laid out the pieces correctly and formed the flanges precisely, the fit should be snug. Use a mallet to bend the bottom's flange over the body's flange, then switch to a tinner's setting hammer to set the seam.

Doubling the seam is a matter of sliding the nearly completed container over a mandrel and using a mallet to hammer-bend the seam yet again, setting it against the container side. With an angular container, the corners of the single seam must be notched before this step can be undertaken.

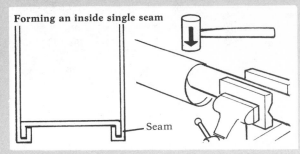

Forming an inside single seam

A variation on the single seam, used on the watering can (see p. 230), could be called an inside single seam. Here a seam fold is formed on the bottom of the body cutout before it is shaped and joined. The bottom is flanged, then dropped down through the assembled body piece and fitted into the seam fold. The seam is set with a mallet over the edge of a mandrel.

8. Solder the brass pipe coupling into the cone. Burnish the coupling and the edges of the small opening in the cone. Flux both and force the coupling into the opening until only ⅛ in. of it projects. Drop a small bead of solder into the up-ended cone, so it lodges between the coupling and the cone. Heat the area evenly until the solder melts.

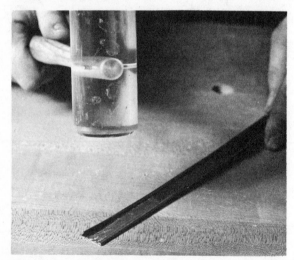

9. Cut the four chandelier arms and triple-hem them. Each arm is formed from a strip 1½ in. wide and 14 in. long. After cutting out the strips, fold and flatten a ⅛-in.-wide hem along each long edge. Fold and flatten each hem again, and then a third time. The triple hems are necessary to provide enough stiffness for the arms to support the weight of the drip pans, candle sockets, and candles.

10. Shape the arms. Enlarge the pattern on p. 219 to full size and shape each arm to the pattern's contour. Clamp a mallet in a vise and use the head as a mandrel to form the curves. The hems should be on the inside of the larger curve.

11. Cut out and crimp the drip pans. Each pan is 4 in. in diameter. Lightly scribe a 2-in.-dia. circle on the center of each disk, then use a prick punch to make a mark every 15° around the circle. Use needle-nose pliers to crimp the pieces.

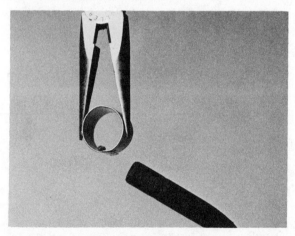

12. Make the four candle sockets next. Form each from a strip 1 in. wide and 2¾ in. long. Prick fold lines for a ¼-in.-wide hem along one long edge and a ¼-in.-wide assembly tab across one short edge. Nip the corners off the hem and tab, then fold and flatten the hem. Form the socket with the hem on the outside. Flux the tab, lay a bead of solder next to the seam, and hold the socket in the torch flame as shown to solder it.

13. Solder the candle sockets to the drip pans and the drip pans to the chandelier arms. Center the fluxed socket on the pan, place a bead of solder inside against the seam, and, using pliers, hold the pan in the torch flame. Turn the pan upside down on a scrap of wood, flux the pan and arm, and position the arm as shown, with a bead of solder at the arm's edge. Heat the assembly with a torch.

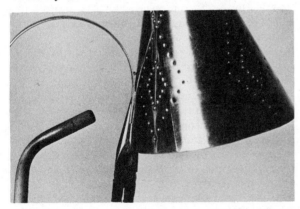

14. Join the arms to the cone. One arm is soldered directly atop the seam, ⅞ in. above the bottom edge. The other three are evenly spaced around the cone. After fluxing the parts, clamp them together with needle-nose pliers, and wedge a bead of solder where the arm curves down to join the cone. Heat as shown. The melting solder will be drawn into the joint.

15. Make the chain from which the chandelier hangs next. The first loop is formed from a strip 1 in. wide and 5 in. long. Drill a ⅜-in.-dia. hole at each end of the strip, centered on the midline, ½ in. from the end. Nip the corners, then fold and flatten a ⅛-in.-wide hem

along each long edge. Form the strip into a loop, hem in, with the holes aligned, and solder the loop closed. The other loops are formed from strips ¾ in. wide and 4 in. long. Hem both long edges of each, form them into loops, hems in, link the loops into a chain, and solder them closed. A foot-long chain has about 14 loops.

16. Wire the chandelier. Turn a 1½-in.-long, ⅛-in. nipple into the base of a switchless light socket, and tighten the set screw. Feed the electric cord through the nipple, wire the socket, and snap it into the base. Feed the other end of the cord through the coupling in the cone and turn the nipple-socket assembly into the coupling.

17. Install the chain. Fit the hole in the first loop over the end of the nipple, and secure the chain with a brass nut of the correct size. Install a quick-connect switch at an appropriate spot along the cord and a plug on the end, and the chandelier is ready to hang. All you need to add is a bulb.

Brass Hinges

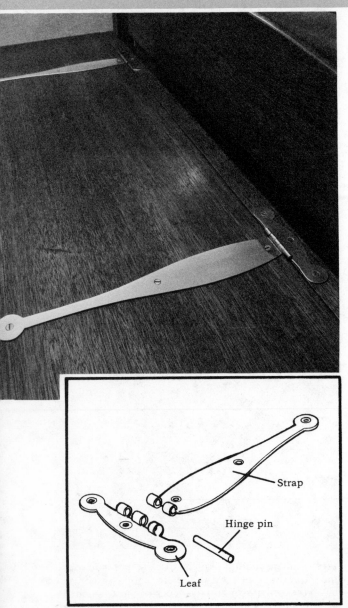

Strap

Hinge pin

Leaf

Polishing

Fine hardware adds just the right finishing touch to any cabinet work. Imagine your next woodworking project showcasing a set of custom-designed, handmade hinges. It can. And you can make the hinges yourself from sheet metal. Chances are that after making your first hinges, you'll never again compromise your work with mundane factory-made hinges.

The hinges shown here were made for the lid of a handcrafted, cedar-lined mahogany blanket chest (see p. 146). They are a good example of simple yet elegant hardware, made from highly polished yellow brass. You don't, of course, have to use them on the blanket chest, nor do you have to stick to the strap-hinge design. You could scale them down for use on cabinet doors, or you could use symmetrical leaves.

However you choose to make the hinges, do draw and cut out a pattern of heavy paper before you actually cut the metal. This allows for proper sizing and fitting. Trace the outline from the paper pattern to the metal. Lay out a leaf and a strap for each hinge set.

The metal can be cut with a jeweler's saw or a saber saw equipped with a metal-cutting blade. Exercise some discretion in choosing the tool you'll use. Cutting with a jeweler's saw may be tedious, but a moment's hesitation on the trigger of the saber saw can ruin a leaf.

The hinge knuckles are formed by cold-forging the metal with a lightweight hammer over a wooden anvil. A metal anvil, such as that on a machinist's vise, could be used, but soft metal like brass tends to stretch when worked over unyielding metal.

The hinges look best when polished to a high luster. Be sure to follow the suggestion to mount the hinges on a scrap board to buff them, for without backing, they can easily be twisted or bent during this operation.

Hinge pattern

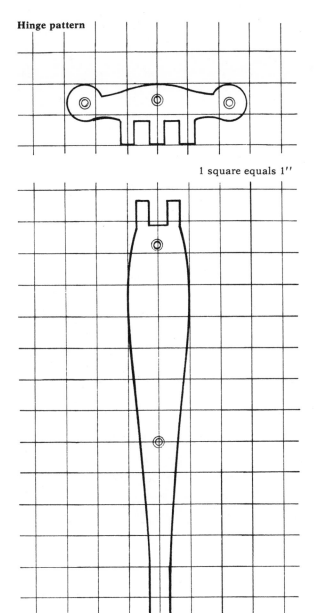

1 square equals 1''

What you will need

1 pc. 14-ga. yellow brass, 16'' × 10''
3 10d nails
12 #8 brass flathead wood screws, ¾''
jeweler's saw
8-oz. ball peen hammer
C-clamps
file
drill
countersink
screwdriver
bench grinder with buffing wheel
1 spray can clear lacquer
layout tools

Step-by-step instructions

1. Enlarge the pattern for the hinges (to the left) to full size on a sheet of heavy paper, taking care that the fingers of the strap and the leaf fit precisely. Trace the paper pattern on a piece of 14-ga. yellow brass, using a felt tip marker or a scriber. Lay out two straps and two leaves.

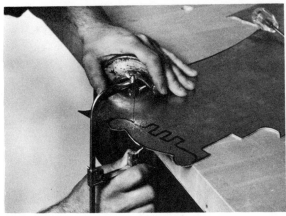

2. Cut out the pieces. Clamp the sheet to the work-bench with the area to be cut projecting over the edge. Cut with a jeweler's saw, keeping to the waste side of the cut line and allowing a modest amount of metal to be removed when filing the finished edge. Pair the straps and leaves, marking them so you'll know which strap goes with which leaf. File the edges to the cut line, finishing with a 45° bevel. Be sure the fingers of each hinge pair interlock precisely.

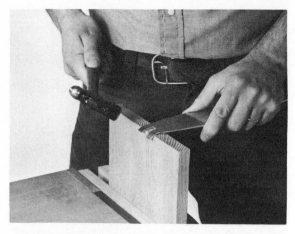

3. Begin to form the knuckles of the hinges by bending the fingers. The best anvil to use in this situation is a scrap of hardwood, clamped end-grain-up in a vise. Hold the workpiece with the fingers extending over the edge of the board, and bend the tips down with a light ball peen hammer. When the fingers are equally bent, turn the piece over and continue hammer-bending them into the appropriate shape to house the hinge pin.

4. To close the knuckles, lay the hinge piece on a scrap of hardwood on the bench top, and fit a 10d nail into the developing hinge-pin sockets. Close the fingers loosely around the nail with the hammer.
5. Lay out and drill three $3/16$-in.-dia. holes in each piece. Center-punch each hole location so the bit doesn't wander off the mark before it bites into the metal.

6. Assemble the hinge pairs and fit the hinge pins. Use 10d nails for the pins. The head and point of the nails can be cut off before or after installing, though it is easier to do it beforehand. Fit the pin in place and hammer the knuckles more tightly closed. Peen the ends of the pin slightly so that it doesn't fall or work out of the knuckles.

7. Countersink the mounting holes. Clamp the hinge to a scrap of wood on the bench top, and use a hand-cranked drill. Trial-fit a #8 flathead screw in each hole as you work to gauge your progress.
8. Finish the completed hinges by polishing and buffing them to a high luster, then coating them with clear lacquer to protect the luster. To buff the hinges safely, mount them on a scrap board. This prevents the screw holes from becoming distorted, prevents the hinge from inadvertently swinging and digging into the spinning wheel, and gives you something to hold that won't become unbearably hot.

Polishing

Polishing is the final step in many sheet-metal projects. The metal is worked with increasingly fine grades of sandpaper, abrasive cloth, or steel wool, removing any roughness, nicks, or scratches. If a high luster is desired, the piece can be buffed with a buffing wheel mounted on a bench grinder. The luster can be preserved with a thin coat of lacquer.

All finishing work, of course, is made easier if you work carefully while cutting and assembling the item. In all probability, any marks that must be polished away will have been put in the metal by you. Keep that in mind from the start.

Work first with the finest grit of abrasive material that will do the job. If the piece is in good condition, polishing with a fine abrasive may be all that's necessary. If there are deep scratches to be removed, however, you should start with a coarse-to-medium abrasive, then change to a medium abrasive, and finish with the fine. Putting a few drops of oil on the metal as you work can speed the polishing. Some craftsmen use a well-worn piece of fine abrasive cloth for the final polish, or even the back of the abrasive cloth.

Buffing applies the final luster to the metal. Buffing wheels of one sort or another are available for electric drills and portable sander-grinders, but the best tool to use is the bench grinder. When installing the cloth wheel, remove the housings that surround much of the wheel, if possible. For buffing large objects, these housings, vital safety devices when grinding wheels are being used, may get in the way.

The wheel must be loaded with a small amount of a polishing compound. Four are used: pumice or tripoli for preliminary buffing, rouge or whiting for final buffing. All are available in sticks, which you hold against the wheel as it spins. Don't use more than one compound in any wheel; use one wheel for preliminary work, another for final buffing.

Hold the workpiece firmly, and apply it to the lower part of the buffing wheel. You don't want it to be wrenched from your grasp. Since the buffing action will generate a lot of heat in the metal, you probably should wear gloves. In some situations, as with the brass hinges, you may find it helpful to mount the workpiece on a board. Wear eye protection: goggles or a face mask.

As you work, polishing compound will build up on the workpiece. This is especially true if you apply too much to the buffing wheel. The buildup can be washed off with alcohol or mild soap and water.

After the piece has been buffed, then washed, it can be coated with clear lacquer. You can apply the lacquer with a brush, but for best results, spray it on. Spray the lacquer sparingly. Apply two or more thin coats to avoid runs. If you misjudge and do get a run, clean the piece with lacquer thinner and try again.

Polishing

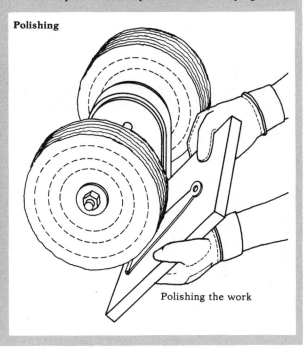

Polishing the work

Watering Can

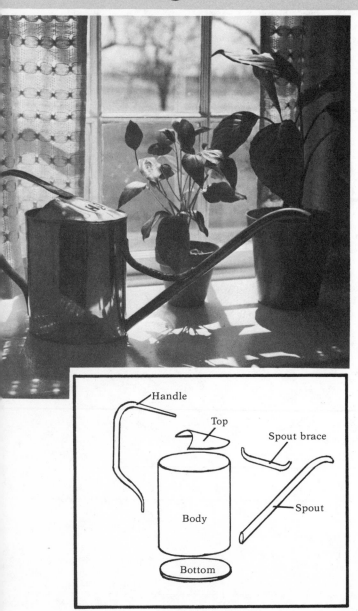

Handle

Top

Spout brace

Body

Spout

Bottom

Shaping sheet metal
Annealing
Chasing and embossing

Every house-plant lover will value this unique and attractive copper watering can. The can holds enough water to sate a dozen thirsty plants, and the long spout enables you to water the most bushy plants with ease. And when the watering chore is done, you won't feel compelled to hide the watering can in a closet or under the sink.

The project is the logical culmination of your introduction to sheet-metal work. While it is no snap for the beginner to make, it does present a reasonable challenge for anyone who has successfully completed the candle sconce and chandelier. It introduces some new techniques and a new material—copper.

The techniques include the hammer-shaping of the spout brace and handle and the chasing or embossing of decorations into the metal.

The procedures for shaping sheet metal grow out of those introduced in the creation of the arms for the chandelier. Sheets can be formed by hand or over a stake or mandrel, still by hand. But as the metal worked increases in thickness, so must the force used to shape it increase. The blows of a hammer provide that force here. The fulcrum in the work here is different too. Rather than a standard stake or mandrel, you use a forming board that helps you produce just the shape you need.

Because of the amount of hammering you have to do to shape the brace and handle, the copper used will become work-hardened, making it necessary to anneal it.

In chasing and embossing, the metal is stretched out of the plane of the sheet to create decorative form and texture. In either case, the process is the same: blunt punches or chisels are used to dent the metal but not puncture it. Chasing is done on the face of the metal to recess it; embossing is done on the back to relieve the metal. When chasing and embossing are combined, the process is called *repoussé*.

The watering can project will also challenge your skills at folding and hemming and at soldering.

Although the watering can could be made of any sheet metal, the one shown was made of copper. The copper materials used—copper flashing and copper tubing—are available at most home building centers.

Step-by-step instructions

Making the forming board

Cut a 4 × 12-in. piece of ¾-in. plywood. In the center of one long edge, file a semicircular notch. The notch should have a diameter of ½-in., meaning it should be ½ in. wide and ¼ in. deep. The square edge of the plywood will be used as a mandrel over which to hammer-bend the handle and spout brace for the watering can. The notch will serve as a form in which to dish the same two pieces.

Making the watering can

1. Start the watering can project by collecting the necessary tools and materials. Then prepare a full-size stretchout for the three sheet-metal pieces that form the body, top, and bottom of the can. Follow the pattern below. After using the stretchout to ensure that all the measurements are in order, transfer the layout from the stretchout to the copper flashing.

What you will need

1 pc. ¾-in. plywood, 4″ × 12″
1 pc. copper flashing, 7¼″ × 17″
1 pc. copper flashing, 6¼″ × 4½″
1 pc. copper flashing, 5¼″ × 5″
1 pc. copper flashing, ⅜″ × 16½″ (see step 3)
1 pc. ½-in. copper tubing, M temper, 14″
1 pc. ½-in. copper tubing, M temper, 11″
1 pc. ½-in. copper tubing, M temper, 5¼″
straight-cutting snips
circular-cutting snips
needle-nose pliers
vise
round, flathead stake
8-oz. ball peen hammer
20-oz. ball peen hammer
bending brake (see p. 212)
hand groover
hacksaw (to cut tubing)
1 16d common nail with rounded point
2 or 3 large screw clamps
bench grinder with buffing wheel
1 spray can clear lacquer
layout tools
flux
50/50 solid wire solder
propane torch

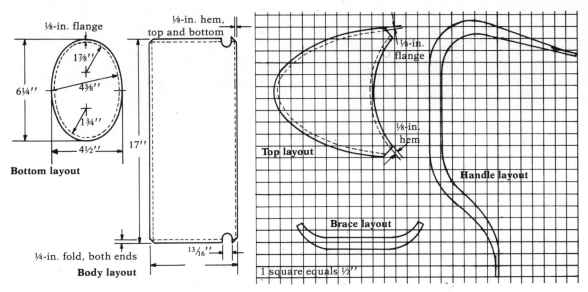

⅛-in. flange

1⅞″

4⅜″

6¼″

1¾″

4½″

Bottom layout

⅛-in. hem, top and bottom

17″

¼-in. fold, both ends

Body layout

13⁄16″

⅛-in. flange

⅛-in. hem

Top layout

Handle layout

Brace layout

1 square equals ½″

2. Cut out the piece that will form the can body using tin snips. Nip off the corners as indicated on the pattern, then cut out the semicircular notches that will eventually form the hole for the spout. Don't cut the notches too big. File the burr from the cut edges.

4. Fold, seam, and lock the watering can body. Make matching ¼-in.-wide folds along the ends of the body piece. Be sure to fold them over opposite faces of the sheet. Form the sheet into a cylinder freehand, and hook the seam folds. Slide the workpiece over a mandrel with the seam up, and lock it with a hand groover and hammer (p. 222). The can may be formed to a roughly elliptical shape by hand, and the shape will be refined as the bottom is installed.

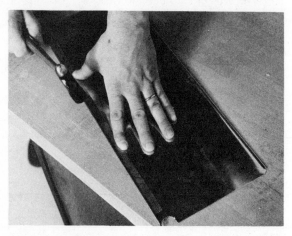

3. Using a bending brake (see p. 212), make folds along the top and bottom edges. The fold at the top is a hem and can be flattened completely. The fold along the bottom is for a seam and should not be closed completely. Instead, fit a narrow strip of flashing into the fold and lightly flatten the seam over it. The strip acts as a shim to ensure that enough of a gap will exist to permit the bottom to fit into the seam fold. Leave the shim in place until after the body is formed and seamed.

5. The shim, which kept the bottom seal fold from kinking closed at any point, may now be removed. With a pair of needle-nose pliers, grasp the shim and work it out of the fold, being careful not to pull the seam fold open as you do so.

Shaping Sheet Metal

Shaping is the process of forming uncreased bends in metal sheets. Rather than introducing sharply the angled folds necessary for hems, seams, or boxlike shapes, here you are creating curves of varying radii, forming graceful scrolls or cylindrical or conical shapes.

While shaping is seldom confined to a specific stage of the overall construction process, it almost invariably is done *after* all folds are made and *after* any piercing or embossing is done.

Since the results of freehand bending can be quite unpredictable, it is always best to shape the sheets over a form of some sort. And where the sheets are of too heavy a gauge to be easily shaped by hand, even over a form, a mallet is used.

While any metalworking task is completed most easily and efficiently using tools designed for it, in shaping sheets, as in other jobs, you can use makeshift tools. A sheet-metal tradesman, for example, will use a variety of stakes for shaping operations—the conductor stake, the blowhorn stake, the mandrel, and others. You can use less costly substitutes. A length of 1- or 2-in.-dia. round stock can be used instead of a conductor stake. A length of 4–6-in.-dia. pipe or round tubing of heavy gauge can be used instead of a mandrel or blowhorn stake.

When using these forms, clamp them very firmly in a vise, with the working surface extending beyond the edge of the workbench. A good machinist's vise will have semicircular pipe jaws below the familiar straight jaws, with serrations to grip large-diameter rounds or pipes. If your vise doesn't have these jaws, or if you are working with a woodworker's vise, cut a pair of wooden V-blocks to use with round stocks. You don't want your makeshift stakes to slip out of the vise as you work.

Because sheet metal is elastic, that is, springy, you must usually work with a form that has a tighter curve than the one you want to introduce into the metal. While some experimentation is in order, a good rule of thumb to follow is to use a form with a radius at least 25% shorter than the radius of the curve you want in the finished piece.

Cylindrical shapes are formed by simply bending the sheet metal, by hand or with a rawhide or plastic mallet, over a stake or form of the proper size. If the form is very close in size to the desired curve, hold one end of the metal tightly against its side and push the free end down and around it. If you use a mallet, strike glancing blows to bend the sheet.

If you are using a relatively small form to produce a broad curve, lay one end of the sheet atop the form and support the other end with your gloved hand. With the other hand, also gloved, or with a mallet, begin bending the sheet, gradually feeding it across the form as you bend. The trick is to create an even shape, rather than an irregular series of bends. It's better to work the sheet over the form several times, gradually tightening the curve with each pass, than to overdo it on the first pass.

A conical shape is most easily created over a blowhorn stake, but it can also be produced by feeding the sheet over a length of pipe. Start the operation as you would in shaping a cylinder. But as you feed the sheet across the form, move it in a curved line (rather than a straight line), so the long edge of the sheet moves across the form faster then the short edge.

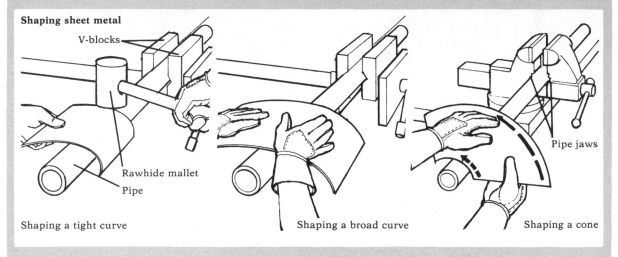

Shaping sheet metal

V-blocks

Rawhide mallet

Pipe

Shaping a tight curve

Shaping a broad curve

Pipe jaws

Shaping a cone

6. Make the bottom next. Cut the piece that's been laid out on the copper flashing and file the edge. Form a ⅛-in.-wide flange around the edge. To do this, clamp a 1- to 2-in.-dia. round upright in a vise as a flathead stake. Hammer-bend the flange using a medium-weight ball peen hammer. Don't try to complete the bend on the first pass. Rather, form it progressively, in several passes.

7. Fit the bottom into the can body. First, burnish the bottom's flange and the body's seam fold. Flux both, then fit the bottom piece into the body from the top, forcing the body into the final shape. Carefully work the bottom down through the body and seat it in the seam fold.

8. To waterproof the can and to secure the bottom in its seam, solder both the vertical lock seam and the single seam around the bottom. Hold the can horizontally, place several beads of solder along the seam inside the

can, and heat the outside with a propane torch. As the solder melts, capillary attraction will draw it into the seam. Next, lay beads of solder around the bottom seam, inside the can. Hold the can in the torch flame, heating the perimeter of the bottom until the solder melts and is drawn into the seam. Though the solder in the vertical seam may melt during the second heating, it won't run out of the seam.

9. Cut the piece of copper tubing for the spout and, using the form board and a medium-weight ball peen hammer, bend one end of it. Rest the tubing in the notch in the board, as shown. Strike lightly, so you don't dent or kink the tubing. Complete the task by flattening the opening to an oblong shape.

10. Forming the spout brace is a three-step process. Begin by cutting a piece of tubing for the brace. Use the same stake employed in step 6 as an anvil on which to flatten the tubing. Hammer it completely flat with the medium-weight ball peen hammer.

11. Form bends on both ends of the flattened tubing. Clamp the form board in the vise, and use the square edge as a mandrel. Apply the necessary force to bend the piece with the ball peen hammer. It is likely that during this work the piece will become less and less malleable and more difficult to work. This is a sign it is work-hardening. Stop work and anneal it (p. 235). If you don't, it may crack.

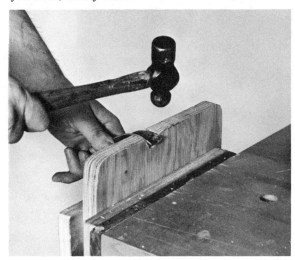

12. Finally, shape the brace in the form board's notch using the ball peen of the hammer. Dish the stem of the brace as much as desired, but fit the appropriate ends to the spout and body so you achieve a tight fit. Again, annealing will probably be necessary during this step.

Annealing

A number of metals, particularly copper and brass, are prone to work-hardening. That is, the more you hammer them, the harder and more brittle they become, to the point that they may crack or break. To compensate for this characteristic of the metal, you must occasionally anneal it by heating it, then allowing it to cool slowly.

To anneal a piece of copper or brass, simply heat it with a propane torch until it glows dull red. Cut the flame, and let the air cool the piece. When it is cool enough to handle, the annealing process is completed, and you can resume working the piece.

When heating the metal, work in subdued light so you can better judge the metal's color. You don't want to overheat the piece. Lay the piece on a firebrick to heat it. You don't want to lay it on a wooden surface for obvious reasons, nor do you want to lay it on a metal surface, which would draw heat away from the workpiece and slow the heating process. Leave the piece where it is until it cools, since the cooling really shouldn't take all that long.

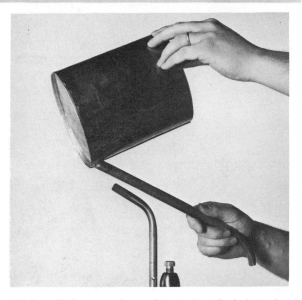

13. Install the spout by pushing it into the hole in the can and soldering it in place. The hole should be a bit too small for the spout, so file it until a snug fit is achieved. Burnish and flux the pieces and fit them together. Lay a bead or two of solder on the joint inside the can, and hold the can in the torch flame to complete the soldering job.

Chasing and Embossing

Chasing and embossing are decorative techniques. The idea is to introduce a pattern of shallow dents. In chasing, the dents are made in the face of the metal, so the pattern forms a recess. In embossing, the dents are made in the back of the sheet, so the pattern is raised. When the techniques are combined, creating a pattern of recesses and reliefs, the process is called *repoussé*.

The tools used are blunt punches and chisels.

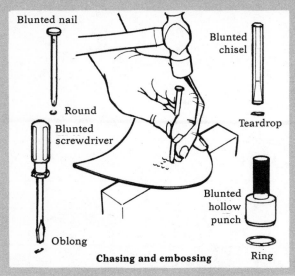

Chasing and embossing

Simple tools can be made by grinding the sharp points off nails, old chisels or punches, even old screwdrivers.

The sheet being worked must be supported by a relatively soft backing. A scrap pine board, a lead plate, or a piece of heavy leather all provide firm support for the work, yet give under the impact of the chasing and embossing tools.

After transferring the design to the metal, position the workpiece on the backing. If necessary, drive brads or small nails around its edge to keep it in position. You do want to be able to turn the entire setup from time to time during the course of the work.

Hold the chosen tool vertical. Use a lightweight hammer, holding it with index finger extended along the handle. Tap the blunt punch or chisel lightly, delivering the blows from the wrist. Keep your eyes on the surface being worked.

Outline the pattern first, then go back over it, refining and, if necessary, deepening the dents. Remember to work with some reserve, since you can always expand or deepen the dents, but you can't easily remove them.

Depending upon the metal being worked and the scale of the design, chasing and embossing can cause the sheet to become work-hardened. This effect will become evident as the metal resists deformation. Rather than risk cracking the metal, stop and anneal the piece (see p. 235).

14. Install the brace next. Burnish and flux the joint areas and position the brace. Carefully squeeze the brace to the can with needle-nose pliers, as shown. Lay a bead of solder against the end of the brace on the spout, and heat the joint area with the torch. Repeat the process to solder the brace to the can.

15. Cut out the top next, and hem the edge that will be exposed. Work over the flathead stake using a lightweight ball peen hammer to form the initial fold. Make several passes along the edge to fold it, so the metal doesn't overstretch. Turn the piece over and flatten the hem against the stake with the hammer.

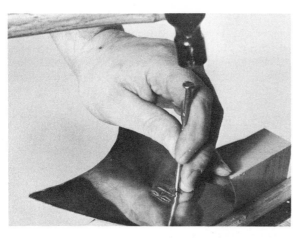

16. Emboss or chase the monogram "H$_2$O" in the top. As shown, the monogram is being chased in the top, using a rounded-off 16d common nail as a chasing tool and the end grain of a scrap board as a backing surface. To emboss the monogram, work from the back of the piece.

18. Make the handle from a length of copper tubing, following the procedures used to make the spout brace (see steps 10–12). Flatten the tubing over the flathead stake, then form the bends over the edge of the forming board. Dish the handle as much as desired in the form board's notch. You will have to anneal the workpiece before the handle is done.

17. Form the top and join it to the can. Begin this task by folding a flange around the perimeter of the top. Work over the flathead stake with the lightweight hammer, forming the fold in several passes. Shape the bulge in the top freehand, trial-fitting it to the can as you work. Burnish and flux the pieces, fit the top on the can, and clamp the two pieces together using several screw clamps joined end to end, as shown. Lay beads of solder on the seam inside, and heat the seam from the outside to solder the top in place.

19. Solder the handle to the can. Burnish and flux the joint surfaces, then hold or clamp the pieces together. Lay a bead of solder at the edge of one seam and heat the metal, and the heat of the metal will melt the solder and draw it into the joint. Repeat the process to solder the second joint.

20. Complete the watering can by polishing and buffing it to a high luster (see Polishing, p. 229). To maintain the luster without periodic polishing, coat the outside with two or three light coats of clear lacquer.

Blacksmithing

The blacksmith used to be what the local car mechanic is today—the one who kept the wheels turning. He could repair a broken cart axle so you didn't have to wait weeks or months for a replacement, mend your plow blade, or forge harness fittings for the team.

Mass production and machined parts put an end to most of that work, and today blacksmithing as a commercial venture is largely the province of high-priced artisans or those who demonstrate the craft at local fairs or in historical villages.

But the truth is that blacksmithing remains an immensely practical, if underutilized, skill. With a modest forging setup, you can repair or replace some hand tools and some parts for household appliances and equipment. You can also forge attractive, durable articles for use around the home—hinges and door latches, decorative stovepipe supports, towel racks, even iron patio furniture.

How difficult is it to practice this venerable craft? Not hard at all. In fact, farmers and tradesmen used to maintain a forge to do the little jobs that didn't require the talents of the local journeyman blacksmith. Now as then, you can respect the abilities of the full-time smith without hesitating to try your own hand at the forge.

And the forge is where smithing is best learned. Heating steel or iron and working it will teach you more than endless reading about the subject, though there *are* things to learn before you begin. The ideal situation is to work with, or at least learn from, a practicing smith. But even if you don't know a blacksmith, you can start with the projects in this section and learn the basics step by step.

The work involves selecting the correct type of steel for the job, heating it to the right temperature, and hammering it properly.

The projects in this section are arranged so that you begin with simple skills, which you should master before tackling the more demanding projects later on. Thus making simple forged hooks and chain indoctrinate you in keeping a fire and judging temperatures correctly.

When that comes easily, you begin the simple

bending and drawing operations that form the basis of much of the later work. These tasks are done by hammering hot metal on the anvil. The hammering—working the steel—can take many forms according to how the hammer is wielded and where the workpiece is placed on the anvil. Accessories that fit into the anvil and tools such as punches or chisels broaden the range of procedures you can perform. And the more articles you make, the greater facility you'll develop in the various techniques.

If you want to try your hand at smithing before you arrange an entire forge, see if you can use another smith's shop—perhaps by doing some work free. If you do set up a forge, you may be able to do all of your metalworking there. Everything that's required for a forge is compatible with other metal craft.

Setting Up Shop

A basic smithy requires adequate space to move around in and to store supplies in, good ventilation, a fireproof floor, decent lighting, tools, coal storage—and a forge, anvil, and workbench arranged convenient to one other.

The forge can put out a lot of smoke and must be vented outside, just like a wood or coal stove. This will require a masonry or insulated-metal flue installed according to standard fire

A well-equipped smithy

Materials storage rack

Forge

Leg vise

Workbench

Anvil on stump

Tool rack

Homemade Forges

One of the biggest stumbling blocks for the beginning smith, or more specifically, the person who'd *like* to be a beginning smith, is the forge. You need a safe yet accessible spot for a tight, hot fire. You need to be able to fan the fire with a blower at some times, and not at others.

The professional blacksmith or the well-heeled aficionado will have a factory-made cast-iron forge, complete with tuyere and electric blower, set in masonry. The farrier, who these days must carry his forge and anvil to the horse, will have a factory-made portable forge, complete with hand-cranked blower. Either represents a substantial outlay of cash.

What are the alternatives, you ask?

There are a few. The most rudimentary forge, but one that's perfectly satisfactory, is made of a barbecue grille. Choose the sort with a shallow pan for the charcoal supported on three tubular legs. Discard the

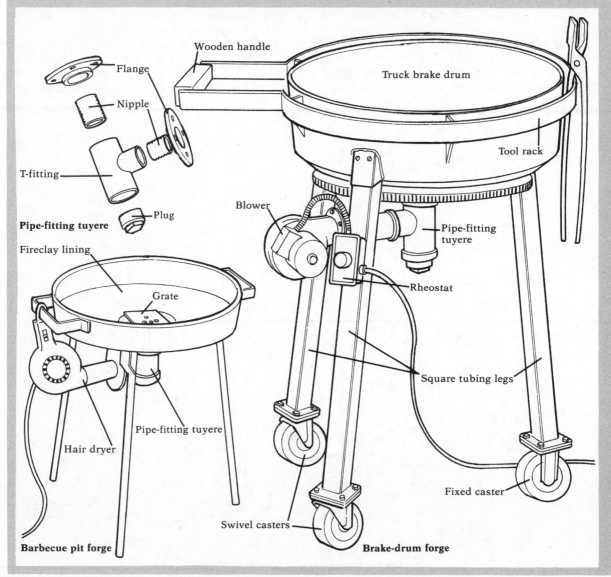

Flange

Nipple

T-fitting

Pipe-fitting tuyere

Plug

Fireclay lining

Grate

Hair dryer

Pipe-fitting tuyere

Barbecue pit forge

Wooden handle

Truck brake drum

Tool rack

Blower

Pipe-fitting tuyere

Rheostat

Square tubing legs

Fixed caster

Swivel casters

Brake-drum forge

grille itself. Cut a 2½–3½-in.-dia. hole in the center of the pan for a homemade tuyere.

Assemble the tuyere from standard 2-in. steel plumbing fittings. You need a T-fitting, a plug, two threaded nipples, and two flanges. Turn a nipple into the branch opening of the T-fitting and another into one of the main-line openings. The third opening gets the plug. From beneath the forge pan, fit the main-line nipple through the hole you cut, then turn one of the flanges onto the nipple. The tuyere will simply hang in place.

You need a grate to prevent the fire from falling into the tuyere, so make one from a scrap of ¼-in. plate—3-4-in. square will do—by drilling a half-dozen ¼-in. holes in it and laying it over the tuyere opening.

If you are *really* scrounging, use a hair dryer for a blower. Hang it from the barbecue pan's handle with the nozzle stuck in the tuyere. An alternative here is to acquire a squirrel-cage fan, mount it on the remaining flange, and turn the flange onto the nipple.

To extend the life of the pan, line it with fireclay.

This is the kind of forge you'd use in an outdoor smithy. If breezes become a problem, cooling the fire and blowing the smoke in your eyes, rivet a sheet-metal windbreak around a portion of the pan. If you find you like blacksmithing enough to make it a year-round hobby, and you set up an indoor smithy, set this forge under a hood.

A more durable, albeit somewhat smaller, forge can be made using a brake drum. This project may require some welding and machining skills on your part, and certainly more than a little ingenuity. The basic idea is to weld or otherwise attach three legs of angle iron or steel pipe to a large brake drum. A pipe-fitting tuyere is attached over the hub hole in the drum. How you actually make such a forge depends upon the materials you assemble, the skills you have, and the services you are willing to pay for. You may be able to bolt one together using steel pipe and flanges. If you can weld, it may be easier for you to weld the unit together. Or you may just hire someone to assemble the parts you collect.

The craftsmen in Rodale's Design Center built a brake-drum forge (see illustration) that incorporates a number of interesting and quite useful features. A length of steel strap was fastened to brackets welded around the outside of the drum, creating a tool rack and handle. The unit is mounted on large, rubber-wheeled casters, so it can easily be moved about. All of the projects that follow were made using this forge, so you need not feel you'd be limited by a homemade forge.

and building codes—and you may have to have it inspected.

You may also want some ventilation near the ceiling, not for smoke but for the heat that collects there. In summer, drawing this heat away can make a lot of difference—forging is hot, heavy work as it is. A simple convection-operated vent or even a fan mounted in the top of a window will do. You'll also need an air intake near the floor to replace the vented air.

Fire protection is a must. A floor of concrete, brick, or dirt will minimize the danger of fire, although concrete can crack when heated (water trapped inside turns to steam). Avoid that problem by using dirt or bricks on the floor, and never leave rags or combustible trash around. If you use an oil quench, make sure it is tightly covered and out of the way when not in use. Get a large fire extinguisher and perhaps a smoke alarm, too.

The key to a safe operation is an uncluttered work area, especially the floor. It's partly a matter of cleaning up periodically and partly the result of a workable floor plan with adequate storage space. The effort you give to planning up front will result in a much smoother, safer operation later on.

Kitchen planners have found that a triangular arrangement between the main areas is most efficient, and in the smithy, too, the work triangle has its place. The forge and anvil should be close to each other, on the short leg of the triangle. The workbench, perhaps with a vise at one end, should be at the apex. Position the anvil so the smith need make only a quarter turn to move from the forge to the anvil.

The forge

A good forge is the heart of a blacksmith's shop. In it he heats steel until it's soft and malleable. He controls the heat by varying the position of the workpiece in the bed of coals and by changing the air blast.

The forge consists of a firebox—usually, though not always, lined with firebrick or fireclay—and a duct for forced air, called a tuyere. The blower—either hand powered or electric—forces air through the tuyere at the base of the fire

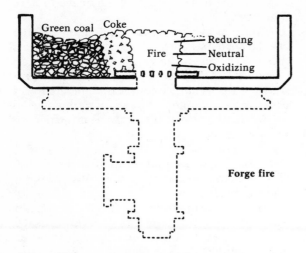

Green coal Coke

Reducing
Fire — Neutral
Oxidizing

Forge fire

to keep it burning hot. Smoke must be contained by a hood and vented through a flue, unless the forge is outdoors.

It is important to be able to control the flow of the air forced into the forge, by means of either a rheostat on the blower motor or a valve on the air pipe leading to the forge. The variable blower switch is simpler.

By reducing the airflow, you can avoid overheating small pieces in the forge; by increasing the flow, you can raise the temperature of the fire quickly. Shut off the blower completely, and let the workpiece soak up heat if you want to be sure the piece is heated evenly throughout. Turn off the blower when there is no steel in the fire, to avoid wasting fuel.

The flue above the forge should be attached to a small hood that collects the smoke, preventing any from escaping into the workshop. Proper sizing and elevation of the hood are important, both to contain the smoke properly and to assure that it won't be in the way while you work.

The hood should be just about the size of the forge and positioned with the bottom of the hood below eye level. The hood often extends down to the firebox at the back and sides. Make sure that the hood doesn't obstruct your vision into the center of the fire and that you can reach easily into all parts of the forge.

The fire

The secret of a good forge fire is to establish a good bed of coke—that's what remains after the impurities burn off the coal. Coke burns hot with practically no smoke. Since the impurities are gone, they can't combine with and weaken the heated steel. Make sure you have built up a good bed of coke around the grate before you begin to heat steel in the forge.

Forming this bed of coke is part of the process of lighting the fire. First place new coal (called green coal) around the perimeter of the forge, and stack wadded newspaper and sticks on top of the grate, shielding the tuyere. Light the paper, then turn on the blower when the kindling begins to burn well. Drop a few pieces of coal at a time onto the blaze, taking care not to smother the fire.

As the coal begins to burn, start raking in coal from the perimeter. Gradually pile the burning coal around the grate, leaving the space above the grate open. Slope the sides of the pile down to the grate and pack the coal down, using a small shovel. As you do this, sprinkle water on the sides of the burning coal. The packing and sprinkling process causes coke to form—it's a tough, sticky mass. Prod it with a poker to see if it has fused together. When it has and is glowing clear orange, you can start forging.

As the fire continues to burn, dark masses will appear in the coke; these are clinker, an unburnable substance that cools to a hard, glassy lump. Clinker causes cool spots in the fire and has a tendency to clog the grate. So pick it out with tongs and discard it in an ash bucket. If you have a shaker attachment, rattle it periodically to remove ash and clinker from the grate. Otherwise, reach down with a poker and pry the clinker away. Then use the tongs to discard it.

Gradually rake in new coal to replace the coke as it burns off, sprinkling water on the new coal to make coke. You can continue this process for hours, adding fresh coal to the perimeter of the forge and working it in.

Near the grate, there is, because of the air blast, more oxygen than the fire can consume.

This is the oxidizing part of the fire. If you put your steel there, a heavy coat of scale will form (scale is oxidized steel), and you may burn the outer surface of the stock.

Above the oxidizing region is a neutral area, and at the top of the coke a reducing fire, where there is actually less oxygen than the fire needs. A thin coat of scale forms in the neutral area, practically none in the reducing zone. The reducing fire also keeps any remaining impurities in the coke from combining with the steel. Thus, the reducing zone is usually the ideal place for heating steel. Place the workpiece in the coke; rake some of the coke on top to keep the air above the forge from oxidizing the top surface of the piece.

When you are ready to shut down the forge, turn off the forge blower, and rake the coke away from the center. The fire will soon go out. Reuse this coke the next time you light the forge. Kindling will light it easily with very little smoke, speeding up the whole procedure.

Fuel—To get a clean-burning fire that forms coke easily, you need good coal. This is low-sulfur coal that has a low percentage of impurities. Unfortunately, there isn't a great deal of demand for it, so it can be hard to come by.

Try asking local blacksmiths where they get theirs. It may happen that a local smith has cornered such a small-scale source that he won't want to tell you, or you might not live near any smiths. In that case, try small quantities of coal from different suppliers until you find what you need.

Ideally, the coal should be pebble size, with about 20 to 30 percent coal dust, or fines, mixed in. The fines are important in forming coke. Break a couple of pieces of coal and examine the interior. White specks or brownish spots are impurities. The less of these, the less clinker you'll get.

Next, try some in the forge. It should form a uniform bed of coke that burns with a bright orange color. Good coal burns longer and without hot spots that can make forging more difficult.

Most blacksmiths use the best quality bituminous coal they can find. Bituminous is soft and can be broken apart in your hand. You *can* use anthracite (hard coal), which by nature tends to have less sulfur and impurities, but check it in your forge to be sure.

The trouble with anthracite is that it is hard to light and burns hot. If you use some soft coal to get it started, it will burn with a clean, hot flame. Set your blower down to avoid overheating your work.

Steel and iron

Most forging work is done with what is called mild steel, meaning it has a very low carbon content. Iron has quite a bit of carbon in it. Many blacksmiths loosely refer to mild steel as iron. Part of the reason is that there just isn't much iron around to work anymore.

Pig iron is low-grade cast iron. Early foundaries worked some of this into wrought iron, the true material of the blacksmith. Wrought iron has excellent qualities for forging, but foundries no longer make it.

Mild steel is easy to work, and it has the advantage of being widely available—often at nominal cost in the form of scrap steel sold by the pound. High-carbon steel is harder and can be heat-treated to make tools and cutting edges. Old truck springs from junk yards are a good source of such tool steel.

The anvil

Anvils have changed slowly over the years as smiths have tried out new ideas, hoping for small improvements in efficiency and ease of use. The anvil design that finally evolved, called the London pattern, is a marvelously economical one.

Most prominent is the long, pointed end that sticks out from one end. This is the horn, whose surfaces allow stock to be hammered into curves of many different sizes and shapes. Since the horn tapers, though, you don't bend bar stock tight against the horn unless you want the bar's inner surface to taper like the horn's. Instead, use the curve of the horn as a fulcrum for your hammering, repositioning the stock as you hammer to form the curve.

The point of the horn can be used as a large punch, and circular objects can be spread by hammering them over the point.

Anvil and hardies

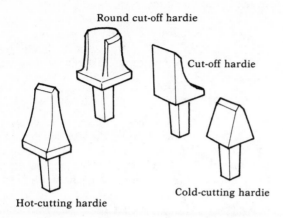

Round cut-off hardie

Cut-off hardie

Cold-cutting hardie

Hot-cutting hardie

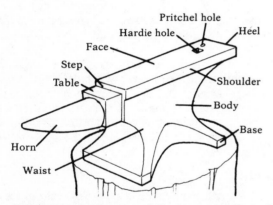

Pritchel hole

Hardie hole

Heel

Face

Step

Shoulder

Table

Body

Base

Horn

Waist

The anvil face forms the main working area. Keep this surface as smooth and unmarred as possible and, since it is hardened, avoid striking it with the hammer or other tools.

The edges of the face, especially toward the middle of the anvil, are used for starting bends and forming right-angle bends. (Lay the workpiece on the face with the end extending past the edge, and hammer down on the end.) To avoid chipping these edges, grind them to a rounded shape (if they haven't been already) rather than leave a sharp right angle. The edge nearest where you stand is the inner edge and should be ground to a ¼-inch radius, while the outer edge should form a ⅜-inch radius.

Near the end of the anvil known as the heel, there are two holes. The square hardie hole holds attachments such as hardies, fullers, and swages. The round pritchel hole is used with punches and drifts.

A good anvil rings when it's struck and actually bounces the hammer. If you are shopping for a second-hand anvil (and new ones are quite expensive), it is extremely important to test this by tapping the anvil lightly with the hammer. A dead anvil is tiring to use, adding unnecessary difficulty to the work. Before you buy, also check the horn for deep gouges or dents that can't be ground off. The face should be smooth and the edges free of chips.

Mount the anvil on a hardwood stump, fastening it securely with heavy spikes and perhaps a chain wrapped around the feet and anchored by spikes. To make it really stable, sink the bottom of the stump about a foot into the ground.

Anvil accessories

Cutting and shaping tools of all sorts fit into the hardie hole, making it a versatile part of the forge's capabilities. And you can easily forge other special tools to fit the hardie hole. They all have a short, square extension that fits snugly—not tight enough to stick—into the square hole.

Most important are the hardies. A hardie is a cutting tool against which the workpiece is held while being hammered. Generally, the piece is turned between blows, so it is cut on all sides but

Between the horn and the main surface of the anvil is a small, flat surface called the table. Neither the horn nor the table is hardened, so chisels or other tools that happen to strike them won't be damaged.

If there's a chance you might hit the anvil surface with a punch or chisel, use the table rather than the harder anvil face, which might ruin your tool or become marred. A block of soft steel on the bench is better yet, but sometimes in the heat of the action, it's hard to resist using the anvil.

The step between the table and the main surface (the face) forms an inside right angle that can be useful in forming metal—you brace stock being forged in the corner, which keeps its end from spreading.

is never completely severed on the hardie. When the piece is nearly severed, it can be broken by hand, with tongs or pliers, or with a hammer. This procedure keeps the surface of the cut smooth, but more important, it assures that the hammer won't strike and dull the cutting edge of the hardie.

Hardies designed to cut hot metal have a fairly thin taper—the edge actually cuts into the soft steel like a knife. Hardies for hot cutting don't have to be hardened to the same degree as those for cutting cold steel. But they do have *some* temper, and a heavy piece of steel can heat up the hardie enough to ruin that temper if you cut straight through. Pause in midlift each time you turn the piece to allow the hardie to cool; the heat will pass into the anvil, which acts as a heat sink.

Hardies for cold cutting have a much broader taper—they are wedges, really, that push their way into the workpiece as you hammer. The steel you are cutting with the hardie must, of course, be softer than the hardie, so you are limited to mild or medium carbon steel. Any time you strike steel against steel, there's a chance that a chip will fly off—and it will fly fast. Always wear safety glasses when you're working with the hardie, especially the one for cold cutting.

Chisels are often used with hardies, but the operation takes two people. One holds a wooden-handled chisel—which looks a lot like a cross peen hammer—on the workpiece, with its cutting edge directly over the hardie. The other person strikes the chisel with a hammer.

Other tools for the hardie hole are fullers, swages, and mandrels. A fuller is a tool used to spread iron in such a way as to reduce its cross section. It looks a little like a cold-cutting hardie with the edge rounded off. Usually it's used in conjunction with a fuller fitted with a handle, just as hardies and chisels are used together. A spreading fuller is similar to a cold-cutting hardie, except that the two sloped faces are at right angles to each other. It is used to spread metal apart when the work is hammered onto it. In addition to spreading operations, this version will form a right angle in any fairly thin strap steel that's hammered over it.

Swages are used to form iron, usually to

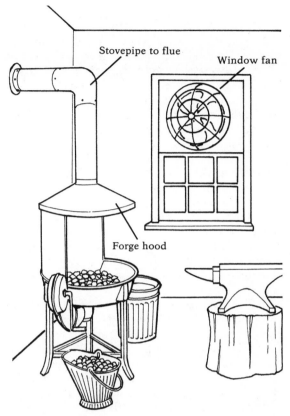

Stovepipe to flue

Window fan

Forge hood

Elements of good ventilation

create a new cross-sectional shape. They are always used in pairs.

Mandrils are cone-shaped tools used in making circular shapes and rings. They come in many different sizes, some floor-mounted, some hardie-mounted.

The pritchel hole doesn't have as many uses as the hardie hole, but it's important whenever you drive a punch through metal. The punch is centered over the pritchel hole, whose small diameter keeps the punched piece from sagging under the force of the hammer blows. Heading tools are also used over the pritchel hole—with the header hole over the pritchel hole, you hammer the nail or rivet you are heading into the pritchel hole, allowing the entire header to rest on the anvil so you can strike it evenly and hard.

Ventilation and lighting

Before you invest in a full-scale smithy, you can work outside in the open air or in a screened shed, letting the breezes eliminate waste heat and smoke. With your tools locked in a weathertight cabinet and a portable forge stored indoors, you can be flexible about where you work. You can set up the anvil beneath an overhang next to a shed where you store tools and supplies.

Eventually, you'll want to set up shop inside, so you can work in any weather. When you do, you will want a work area with the proper ventilation and light.

Ventilation—A properly sized flue of sufficient height will have enough draft, when warmed up, to exhaust the smoke from your forge easily. Of course, if the flue isn't right, not only will you have an excessively smoky smithy, you may have a fire hazard as well.

The very best flue is one constructed of brick or masonry block, flue liners, and mortar. Prefab metal flues are less costly and more easily erected, and they will work perfectly well. In practice, ordinary stovepipe extends from the forge hood to the wall of ceiling, where it links to the flue proper. The single-wall pipe should never be within 18 inches of combustible material such as wooden walls, and the top of the chimney (protected by a cap) should rise 3 feet above the surrounding roof and 2 feet above anything within 10 feet—other chimneys, trees, or the roof peak.

If you have a portable forge, the hood can be free-standing, rather than attached to the forge. When you want to work indoors, wheel the forge under the hood and light the fire. Portability is also useful when you are using the forge area for other projects—you can wheel the forge out of the way and even detach the hood from the flue.

As noted earlier, you'll probably want a window fan or roof vent to draw out the heat that builds up when you operate the forge indoors.

Lighting—Contrary to what's best for nearly every other craft and trade, a blacksmith's shop requires dim lighting—enough light to see what you're doing, but not so much so that you are unable to judge the color of glowing steel accurately. For this reason, if you do work outside, a shed roof overhang will not only keep off rain, it will reduce the light level as well.

Try not to depend exclusively on daylight as a light source, because it changes widely and unpredictably. Outdoors, you must compensate mentally for the changing level of light. Indoors, arrange a few light fixtures to provide an even, but fairly low level of background light. Supplement this with fixtures over the workbench and anvil that you can turn on to examine something closely.

A floor plan

The main work of the blacksmithing is heating and hammering, moving back and forth between forge and anvil as you go. Work out a comfortable

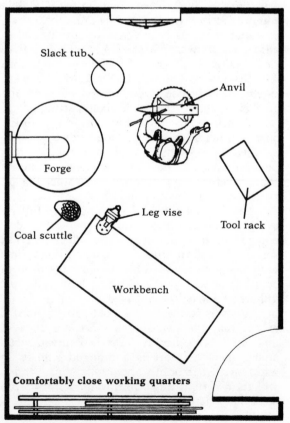

Slack tub

Anvil

Forge

Leg vise

Coal scuttle

Tool rack

Workbench

Comfortably close working quarters

arrangement between these two, and set up the rest of the shop in relation to them.

Usually the anvil is placed a quarter turn (90 degrees) from the forge, so that you can lay the heated stock on the anvil with a turn and maybe a step or two. Place the anvil to the right or left of the forge, whichever feels best. The anvil is usually placed so the horn is to your left, the heel to your right. Your knuckles should rest comfortably on the anvil face.

The slack tub (a container of water used to cool forge-heated metal) is often between the anvil and forge, set back so it isn't underfoot. You can store your coal almost anywhere you have room for it, but keep a scuttleful next to the forge on the side opposite the anvil. Hang pokers, ash rakes, and tongs nearby— next to the forge, on the coal bin, or on a wall rack.

Hand tools, such as hammers, chisels, and punches, should also be hung on a rack of their own—to the far side of either the coal bin or the anvil. This keeps them within reach but not cluttering up the operation. A bench or table behind the anvil gives you a convenient place to set tools while you are working.

At your back as you face the forge, place a workbench, perhaps with a heavy vise at one end. The bench can be covered with a metal slab if you need additional space for working hot metal, or simply surfaced with wide planks or particle board. Mount a grinding wheel, if you have one, on the bench.

You'll also need space for hardies, fullers, and anvil accessories. Keep a large trash bin well away from the forge. Also useful are storage racks for metal stock and an out-of-the-way metal shelf where you can set forge work to cool undisturbed. In fact, good storage counts high in the actual efficiency of the workshop.

Storage

Good storage, whatever else it is, is a state of mind. You've got to have places for everything— tools, projects in progress, materials, scrap—to be sure. But you've also got to have the discipline to keep everything in its place when it isn't being actively used. If you can't find the tool you *do*

need because all the ones you *don't* need are in the way, storage is the problem.

Good storage is really a process that begins with realistic planning and is modified according to demand. If your storage space is adequate and located conveniently, there's no need to start piling things up in every open space, particularly floor space. Steel rods, half-finished projects, and who knows what will end up there if you aren't careful, creating an awkward, risky situation.

Use the walls, not the floor, for storage. Build some brackets to hold long pieces of stock. Provide as much shelf and cabinet space as possible, and store seldom-used items in drawers or cabinets where they won't get dusty.

Tools and Equipment

A forge without hand tools is worth no more than one without a blacksmith, because smithing remains strictly a trade of human dimensions— where the tools and the person who uses them form a whole.

Welding machines are common in industry, and sheet metal is formed and folded to a thousand fantastic shapes by machine, but you'll never see forged work without a blacksmith wielding the age-old tools of his trade.

Forging hammer

In the days when most blacksmiths had apprentices, the smith would strike a blow with his hammer, and his assistant, called the striker, would match it with a heavier sledge of anywhere from 5 to 20 pounds. But for the individual blacksmith working alone, a 2- to 3-pound hammer (that's the weight of the head only)—or at most a 5-pound hand sledge—is all the hammer you need.

The forging hammer is by far the most important, often-used tool in the blacksmith's shop. Nearly every operation, from bending to punching to cutting, involves the hammer. The anvil and its accessories (in conjunction with punches, chisels, and drifts) provide the surfaces to shape hot steel, but the hammer provides the force.

When you look at a new forging hammer,

you'll see that the perimeter of the striking face is beveled. If you use it like that, you'll mar whatever you strike, leaving small dents. Before you put the hammer to regular use, dress these beveled edges round on a grinding wheel.

Some forging hammers have a striking face at each end of the head, while others combine a striking face with a cross peen. Either hammer is fine, though you get two tools for a single price with the combination.

If your hammer comes with a varnished handle, strip off the varnish; it makes the handle too slippery. Refinish the handle with tung oil or linseed oil.

Ball peen hammer

The ball peen hammer is the primary striking tool of the metalworker. In the smithy, a ball peen with a 20-ounce head makes a good, light forging hammer.

The ball end spreads metal evenly in all directions, useful for flaring metal (for example, to make a mounting surface for screws or a broad surface that can be bent into a finger loop for a door latch). A cross peen, by contrast, spreads metal in two directions only, so it's best for thinning a section without widening it.

A ball peen has a long handle to allow plenty of leverage for striking, and, next to the forging hammer, it's the most important hand tool for blacksmithing.

Cross peen hammer

A cross peen hammer has a head with one end shaped like a wedge with a dulled edge. As noted, it spreads metal in two directions only, permitting you to thin a section without widening it. Fullers do similar work but are more rounded, giving a smoother finished surface.

Medium-weight forging hammers often have a cross peen opposite the striking face, a good arrangement because the cross peen is often used for heavier work than the ball peen.

Hammers

32-oz. ball peen hammer

3-lb. straight peen hammer

32-oz. cross peen hammer

3-lb. hand sledge

3-lb. forging hammer

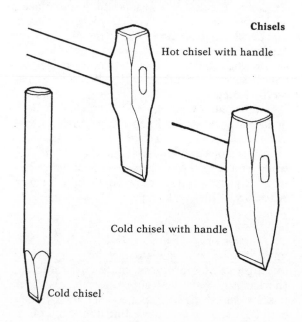

Chisels

Hot chisel with handle

Cold chisel with handle

Cold chisel

A Cold Chisel

Metal objects can be used over and over by reheating and forging them into a new form. High-carbon steel of the type used in files is particularly useful for making cutting tools such as this cold chisel. Any large rat-tail file whose teeth have dulled beyond usefulness will do fine.

Before shaping the file, you must soften it in a process called annealing. If you don't, it could shatter when you try to forge it. To anneal, heat the file cherry red, cut the forge's blower, and let the file soak up the heat for a few minutes. Turn it occasionally to prevent any spots from overheating. Bury the file in dry ashes for a few hours to cool it slowly, and the hardness will be gone. If you can cut the annealed piece with another file, it is soft enough to work.

Cut off the file's tang by heating the tang end to bright orange and setting it on the cutting edge of a hardie. Hammer and turn the file until you've cut almost through. Then tap off the tang with the forging hammer.

Taper the end you've just cut: Hold the file on the anvil face at a slight angle and strike with the forging hammer. Repeat on the other side of the file so the two tapered surfaces slope together to form a cutting edge.

Cut the piece to length by heating the area about 6½ in. back from the tapered edge. Bright orange is the best heat. Place the heated section over a hardie, and strike with a forging hammer. If the file is too hot to hold, use tongs. After every few blows, turn the file 90°, continuing until you have nearly cut through. (Be sure not to strike the edge of the hardie.) Knock off the piece with a few blows of the hammer.

To harden (p. 256) the cutting end of the piece (which is now beginning to look like a chisel), heat it to cherry red, cut the blower, and again let the piece soak up heat for a few minutes to assure that it is heated all the

Chisel made from rat-tail file

way through. Move it around to avoid any overheating.

Quench only the tapered section in water, moving it up and down in the water an inch or so to prevent stress cracks from too drastic a temperature difference.

Quickly polish the quenched end bright with emery cloth, sandpaper, or a piece of brick, and watch the polished part as the temper colors run down from the handle end. There will probably be enough heat left in the handle to temper the chisel, but if not, heat the handle briefly in the forge.

Quench the tip just before the blue band reaches the cutting edge. Place the chisel in water about 1½ in. deep to maintain it at the proper temper, and let the chisel cool for several hours.

Grind a 60° cutting edge, using a grinding wheel or a file, and smooth up the edge with a whetstone. Chamfer the opposite end of the chisel to remove any burrs.

With only two hammers — a ball peen and a cross peen forging hammer — you get four different striking surfaces, each with a distinct use. When you are just getting started, a medium-weight hammer with a cross peen face and a light ball peen will cover your basic requirements.

Chisels

Chisels are cutting tools. Some are simply short lengths of steel with a flat surface at the end that's struck and a cutting edge at the opposite end. Others have a hammerlike handle.

These set chisels have a head that looks somewhat like a forging hammer, but with a cross peen parallel to the handle, rather than perpendicular to it. What looks like the cross peen is a cutting edge. Never strike anything with a set chisel. Instead, hold it on stock to be cut — usually with a hardie underneath — and strike the flat surface with a hammer.

Cold chisels, like cold-cutting hardies, are tempered very hard and taper gradually to the cutting edge. Hot chisels aren't as hard and have a sharp taper to the edge.

A Hot Punch from an Old Hammer

You'll need a good, hot punch to make holes for screws or nails in such things as towel bars or hinges—anything mounted to a wall or door. A punch with a wooden handle is easier to use than one that must be held with tongs, and you can use an old ball peen hammer to make one.

The striking face of such a hammer contains enough metal to be drawn to an excellent punch. Place the hammerhead in the forge, and let the handle burn out of the eye. When the hammerhead is cherry red, use tongs to hold the hammer's striking surface on the anvil face, then strike the ball end with a forging hammer, flattening the peen a little to make a good, flat surface (for the forging hammer to strike when the punch is finished).

Now heat only the striking surface of the hammerhead, and hold it on the anvil face with tongs. Begin hammering and turning to form the striking surface into a four-sided section.

Continue forging the piece until you've drawn it out (see p. 260) to a square taper, about 6 in. from the peen end to the tip. This may require several heatings. Heat once more and carefully round the corners of the taper, working it from the square cross section into a round one. You may want to switch to a lighter hammer for this rounding operation, for better control.

Heat only the tip of the taper, stand it on the anvil face, and tap the peen end lightly with a forging hammer to flatten the tip. At this point, you can add a handle and use the punch as is, or harden it by heat treating.

If you heat treat, bring both the flattened peen and the punch end to moderate hardness—the punch will be striking hot steel, which doesn't require great hardness, and the peen end needs only to be hard enough to maintain its shape.

Heat the entire punch to the critical temperature (between dark cherry red and cherry red for hammer steel). Quench the peen end first, and rub it with emery cloth, sandpaper, or a piece of brick until it is bright. Then let the temper colors run to a dark straw color as they pick up heat from the rest of the hammerhead. Set the peen end in water to keep it from getting hotter, and let the head cool to room temperature. Next heat the tapered end to dark cherry red and repeat the same quenching, tempering, and cooling steps. Both ends are now medium hard.

To install the handle, select one whose end closely matches the eye of the punch. Insert it in the eye and tap it snug. Cut off the protruding part ⅛ in. above the eye, then hammer a hardwood wedge into the slot of the end of the handle. Cut off the remaining ⅛ in., so the handle end is flush with the eye. Finish off by driving a metal wedge into the end so that it crosses the wooden wedge. The punch is secure and ready to use.

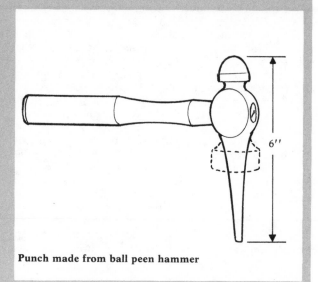

Punch made from ball peen hammer

Punches and drifts

Like chisels, some punches and drifts have wooden handles, while others are straightforward metal tools that, in use, are held in the hand or with tongs and struck with a hammer.

Punches have a flat, rather than a pointed, end, so they knock out a round plug of a particular size. With the workpiece set over the pritchel hole, the punch is hammered partway through.

Then the piece is flipped over and the punch pounded the rest of the way through, producing a clean hole. Some punches are hollow in the middle, allowing them to cut out a larger plug. The oval punch that cuts out the eye in axe and hammerheads is an example.

Drifts enlarge holes already made by a punch. Some are oval in cross section, some round, and others square. In making a hammer, an oval punch is used first to knock out a plug about half

Blacksmith's Tongs

Tongs are invaluable for holding lengths of steel while you hammer—especially short lengths that soon get too hot to handle. A pair with flat jaws will serve many purposes and is easy to forge.

You'll start by forming a jaw at each end of a length of steel. The space between the jaws must be drawn out to a rod shape, and the rod cut in two, yielding the two tong halves. Doing it this way rather than cutting the bar first gives more length to work with, so the part you're holding won't get too hot.

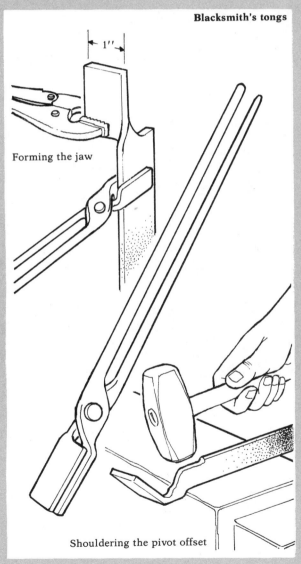

Blacksmith's tongs

Forming the jaw

Shouldering the pivot offset

Form the first jaw by setting a ¼ × 1 × 24-in. bar (its end heated to orange) on edge on a hardie. Make a ⅜-in.-deep cut 1½ in. from the end of the bar by hammering the bar onto the hardie.

Twist the jaw (the 1½-in. section) to a right angle to the bar by heating the end of the bar to cherry red, gripping above and below the cut with tongs or pliers, then twisting the tongs 90°. Repeat the process at the bar's other end to make the second jaw.

To form the pivot offset behind each jaw, first heat the area and set the handle on edge on the anvil face, with the cut directly above the anvil's outer edge and the jaw extending past the anvil. Tap the jaw with a forging hammer, bending it down 45°. Turn the bar over, so the other edge is now on the anvil face with the cut facing up. Position the bar so the cut is 1 in. past the anvil's outer edge, and create a shoulder (see p. 275) by hammering the edge that sticks out beyond the anvil edge.

Angle the hammer blows back toward the edge of the anvil, driving the work against it. The shouldering operation will also force the jaw down. Stop when the jaw is parallel to the rest of the bar. Repeat the process at the other end of the bar.

Heat and punch a ¼-in. hole in the center of each offset section.

Draw out and taper (p. 260) the section of the bar between the two offsets, making the middle the thinnest part. Cut the middle, producing the two tong halves. You can either cut the two halves to slightly different lengths and scroll one end to provide a decorative hook (p. 263), or cut them the same length.

Draw a ⁵⁄₁₆-in. mild steel rod until the end is ¼-in. in diameter and 1 in. long. Cut most of the way through the ⁵⁄₁₆-in. part on the hardie, ¼ in. above the drawn portion (1¼ in. from the end), then break the piece off. The thicker part will form one rivet head. Heat and form the head on a heading tool that has a ¼-in. round hole. Insert the rivet through one arm of the tongs, and heat both. Quickly place the tong half on the anvil face, rivet head down, and set the other tong half over the rivet. Hammer the exposed rivet end with a ball peen hammer to form a rough head. See p. 272 for a more elaborate method.

Eventually, you'll make additional tongs, for the longer you work at blacksmithing, the more pairs of tongs you'll need. And you can make them all. The directions given here can be followed—with adjustments of measurements and the stock used—to make huge tongs for heavy stock and small ones for relatively delicate work. Too, you'll find yourself making a special pair of tongs for each different stock you work.

the size of the hammer eye. Then a larger drift of the same shape is used to enlarge the eye to finish the job.

Since both punches and drifts taper to a narrow dimension, they are liable quickly to draw heat out of the piece being worked. Quench them frequently to avoid drawing out the temper and softening the end. The corollary danger is that if one does heat up to cherry red, and you then quench it, the tool will become brittle. Anneal and reharden it before you use it again (see Heat Treating, p. 256).

Tongs

Tongs hold things you can't grip by hand—hot steel, punches or drifts without wooden handles, even clinker that needs to be taken out of the fire.

Tongs aren't hard to make, and little by little you may create quite a set of them. The most basic type has flat, unmarked gripping jaws. You can branch out to tongs having jaws with serrated teeth, grooved jaws designed to grasp a single type of stock, or rounded jaws—and on to short- and long-handled tongs. But to start, a couple of pairs are enough.

Additional equipment

You can do a lot of forge work with a couple of hammers, an anvil, a few hardies, and such home-forged tools as tongs, chisels, and punches. But once you get started, there's always some other tools you can use, and here are a few.

Leg vise—You may already be using a machinist's vise to hold things being forged, and that's fine for light work. But a leg vise is made of sterner stuff—a typical one is heavier and has jaws that open wider than a machinist's vise.

The jaws of the leg vise pivot open and are joined directly to the leg, which extends to the floor where it's anchored to a block. The force of your hammer blows travels right to the floor, putting no pressure on the threads that open the vise jaws. (On a machinist's vise, strong blows can damage the threads.) The leg vise is a valuable tool for heavier work.

Bench grinder—This important accessory consists of an abrasive wheel powered by hand or motor. You can use it to grind domes on steel rod ends for making rivet headers; it's also great for

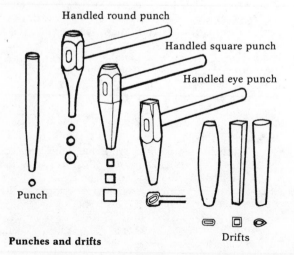

Handled round punch

Handled square punch

Handled eye punch

Punch

Punches and drifts

Drifts

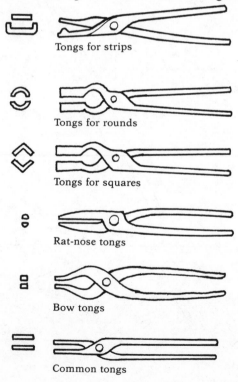

Tongs for strips

Tongs for rounds

Tongs for squares

Rat-nose tongs

Bow tongs

Common tongs

Tongs

removing large burrs or bulges, for dressing (smoothing) tools, and for a host of other forming and finishing jobs.

Drill press and band saw — These are standard tools in a machine shop, and good ones are quite expensive. They aren't required for basic smithing, but if you have them, so much the better.

Hand tools — Files in several varieties are essential for knocking off burrs and testing the hardness of stock. As they wear out, use them as an excellent source of high-carbon steel.

Hacksaws, like files, are invaluable for any kind of metalwork. You need only one handle, but get several replaceable blades with various tooth spacings. The blades wear out fairly quickly.

You'll probably want some locking-grip pliers (great for clamping parts together while you forge) and perhaps a pair of regular slip-joint pliers. A wire brush is essential for removing scale and rust. Get metal measuring tools, which won't be damaged by heat. Nail and rivet headers are worth having, and you can learn how to make them beginning on page 268.

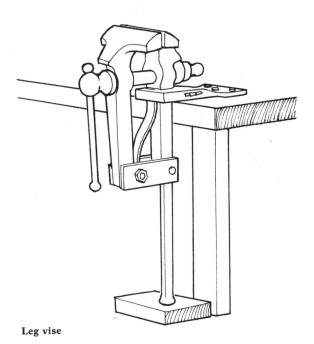

Leg vise

Basic Procedures

The basic operation of blacksmithing is hammering. The hot metal is caught between a hammer and a hard place, and both contribute to the shaping of the metal. Punches and headers and all the other blacksmithing tools play a part, but the motive force is the pounding of the hammer, repeated over and over.

Smithing involves another important factor that's independent of the shaping of the metal — the qualities of the steel itself. The more carbon contained by the steel, the harder the steel tends to be. The smith takes advantage of this by choosing steel most suitable for his purposes, and by heat-treating high-carbon steel to further adjust the hardness and toughness for such tools as punches and chisels.

When a piece of stock has been worked into shape — and heat-treated if that's required — it must be finished to protect it from the scourge of steel and iron — rust. With a layer of oil, the piece takes its place as a useful product, one you make yourself, that could prove its worth for a long time to come.

Working steel

The hotter steel and iron become, the softer and more workable they are. To make what he needs, the smith heats a piece in the forge until it begins to glow, then places it on the anvil and begins to hammer it to shape. As it cools, the metal becomes duller in color and harder to work, so he must not delay. Soon a rhythm develops of heating and forging, heating and forging. With practice the smith is able to accomplish in a single heating what once required two or three.

A good exercise for a beginner is simply to heat a piece of steel, then hammer on it a bit. Observe the range of colors evident as the steel heats up, and think about the correlation between the color of the steel and the effect of the hammer's blows.

Steel can be forged at temperatures ranging from 1000°F. to about 2600°F. The blacksmith may not know temperatures, but he must know the colors steel takes on as its temperature rises, and he must know how the steel responds to his hammer at different colors (temperatures). Roughly speaking, the forging colors range from dark red (about 1050°F.) to cherry red (1420°F.) to orange (1800°F.) through increasingly lighter yellows to white (about 2550°F.), the top forging color for wrought iron. At dazzling white, or 2800°F., wrought iron burns.

Individual interpretations of color enter in, of course, and light levels change color perception. But knowing that steel becomes nonmagnetic at cherry red allows you to use a magnet to establish what cherry red looks like. You can work from there.

Working metal, the main task of blacksmithing, includes the basic procedures of bending, cutting, drawing or tapering, flaring, punching, shouldering, splitting, twisting and scrolling, and upsetting. More detailed how-to explanations of each are included with the project where the procedure is first required.

Bending

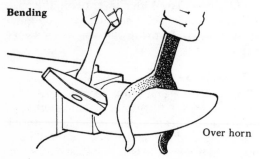

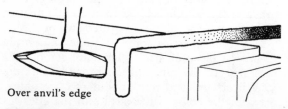

Over anvil's edge

Bending—One of the key operations in smithing, bending is done by hammering heated steel held against the anvil horn or—to make right angles—over the edge of the anvil.

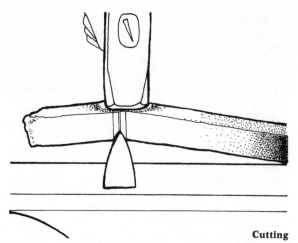

Cutting

Cutting—Iron is cut by heating it orange and hammering it over a hardie. The trick is to cut the piece in two without actually striking (and thus dulling) the cutting edge of the hardie.

Nearly every project involves cutting the workpiece to size from a larger section of stock. Although the materials lists call for pieces precut to size, you'll often find in practice that it's easier to do some initial shaping before you size the piece—because you have more to hold on to.

Drawing

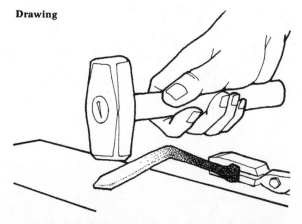

Drawing or tapering—This operation is accomplished by hammering and turning a heated piece held on the anvil face. The metal thins and lengthens at the same time. Hooks, fireplace pokers, nails, and hinges all require drawing.

Flaring

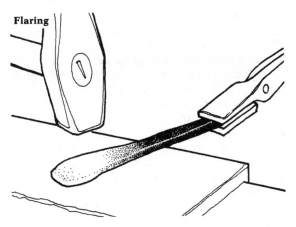

Flaring—The metal is thinned, as in drawing, but broadened rather than lengthened. Flaring is useful in forming a flattened area to support screws—as in the towel bar and stovepipe support—and to serve as a stop in a simple mechanism such as the door latch.

Punching

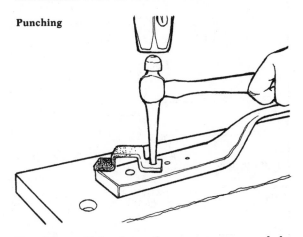

Punching—Holes for nails or screws are made by hammering a tapered metal rod (a punch) through a heated workpiece that's placed over the anvil's hardie or pritchel hole, or on a heading tool.

Shouldering—This useful technique involves forming a step in a workpiece by laying it over the edge of the anvil and hammering on it. Since the part on the anvil face will be flattened, shouldering is usually done as part of a drawing or flaring operation.

Splitting

Splitting—This is similar to cutting, except that the cut is usually along the length of the stock but only along *part* of the length. Hinge leaves are split and tapered, both as a decorative effect and to separate the screws for better holding power.

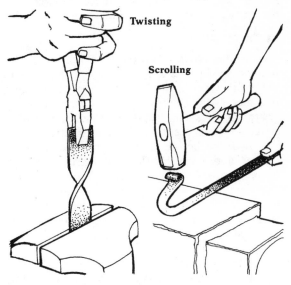

Twisting and scrolling—These are simple decorative techniques. A twist can be added to a piece of stock by clamping one end of it in a vise and rotating the free end with tongs. When done in moderation, twists make a plain object more attractive than its utilitarian counterpart. Scrolling, likewise, adds a decorative curl or two to tapered ends of projects such as the stovepipe support.

Upsetting

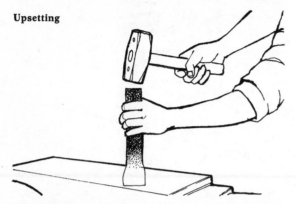

Upsetting—The opposite of drawing, in upsetting, heated metal is shortened and thickened instead of thinned and lengthened—by standing it straight up on the anvil face and hammering on the end. This requires very hard blows and lots of heat in the metal. Use caution, because a glancing blow could strike your hand or tongs.

Heat-treating

Steel is a tough, durable metal that's ideal for items as diverse as knives to cut butter, nails to penetrate wood, and high-speed drills to bore into metal. It has many uses, because its internal characteristics change dramatically according to its carbon content and its heat-treatment.

As its carbon content goes up, steel becomes harder and more brittle. High-carbon steel is used for razors, stone drills, and precision cutters that *must* hold an edge. A tougher steel with a little less carbon makes better tools for rough treatment—twisting and pounding. In this category are some tools you may need to make at the forge—chisels and punches.

Objects that don't have to hold an edge and aren't subjected to sharp twisting or pounding can be made of low-carbon mild steel. All the items in the projects section of this book can be made of mild steel.

Hardening—To harden steel, heat the piece evenly to a dark cherry red, then shut off the blower and let the metal soak up heat for a few minutes. Turn the blower back on and bring the piece up to a bright cherry red, turning frequently.

Remove the steel from the forge to check the color, examining it quickly in dim light. As soon as it has reached the proper color, quench it in water, moving the piece up and down in the quenching bath to avoid cracks resulting from too sharp a temperature difference along the metal.

Most tools are hardened selectively, with the cutting edge being harder than the rest of it. For a punch, the end to be struck is partially hardened so it won't crack when hit, yet will retain its shape. Heat the entire tool, but quench only the portions to be hardened or partially hardened.

When the quenched part no longer glows, set the tools in the quench medium to cool, leaving the unhardened part out. The liquid prevents the hardened part from heating back up by absorbing

Color, Temperature, and Forging Operation

Color	Degrees Fahrenheit	Operation
Dazzling white	2800	
	2700	Welding
White	2600	
	2500	
	2400	
Light yellow	2300	
	2200	
Yellow	2100	
	2000	
	1900	Cutting
Orange	1800	
	1700	
Light cherry	1600	
	1500	
Cherry red (critical temperature)		General working
	1400	
Dark cherry	1300	
Blood red	1200	
	1100	
Dark red	1000	

residual heat from the unquenched section.

Tempering—Hardened steel is too brittle as is to be useful for most tools; it must be tempered. As higher temperature is applied to hardened steel, it gets tougher and less hard.

How do you know how much heat to apply in tempering? Polish a section of the metal surface using an abrasive—emery cloth, sandpaper, or even a chunk of brick. This bright section will go through a series of color changes from a light straw color to brown to purple to dull gray.

Heat the metal slowly. The temper colors should appear in bands a couple of inches wide. Remove the tool from the fire before the proper temper color reaches the edge, because the object will retain some heat—less for a small one such as a punch, more for a large part such as an axe head. Lay the piece on the anvil or dip it for a moment in the quenching bucket to slow the tempering, if necessary.

Finishing

Iron and steel must be protected from rust, which attacks any ferrous metal that's in contact with air and moisture. Once started, rust will continue to form, even under a sealant.

Remove rust and scale, down to bare metal. Power sanders are helpful on even surfaces, but you'll need a wire brush to get into crevices. You can take off scale by quenching the workpiece in a 10 percent brine solution or by hammer-refining the still-glowing piece.

Rub motor oil or heated wax onto the bare metal, or dip the project in a container of oil. For cooking utensils, use vegetable oil. Place the piece in the forge for a moment, to singe the oil, then apply another coat. Oil or wax will wear off with time, but can be easily replaced.

If your project will be used outdoors, finish with primer and exterior paint rather than oil.

Before you begin

Since the projects that follow are scaled in complexity, with the simpler ones first, the skills required tend to build on one another, with those learned for earlier projects used again and again. To get the most from this arrangement, it's best to do them in order. If you skip one, practice the skills needed for it before moving on.

For these projects, it's essential to have a serviceable forge, an anvil, and a pair of tongs. A slack tub, which is simply a metal tub or bucket filled with water, should be handy to forge and anvil for wetting the fire or quenching hot steel. You *should* wear safety glasses whenever you are working at the forge, but wearing gloves is another matter. Some smiths always wear gloves. Others feel more confident of a bare-handed grip on the hammer, but will occasionally don one glove if the workpiece is uncomfortably hot to handle. If you choose to use gloves, select leather ones that will ensure you a secure grip.

Most of the step-by-step instructions describe actions to be performed on heated steel. At first, you may have to heat the steel several times to complete a single operation. With experience will come confidence and greater efficiency. You'll do each step in fewer heats. Unless the directions state otherwise, forge heating is required whenever hammer work or cutting is called for. And unless the directions state otherwise, cherry red is the color best for most work.

Dimensions are given for most projects, but you'll find that blacksmithing is not as exacting as working sheet metal or wood. It's difficult to work to fractional tolerances when the workpiece is glowing light cherry. You *can* use a metal rule and a file to nick the workpiece in laying out a project, but most smiths exercise their senses of proportion instead. Part of the pleasure of hand-forged work, after all, is the uniqueness of each piece. In doing the projects that follow, then, view the dimensions more as approximations than as specifics.

It's natural to want the projects to proceed smoothly, but mistakes are part of the process, and so is learning how to deal with them. If the metal you're working starts to fissure, scrap it. If repairing a mistake looks as hard as the project itself, you may be better off starting over.

But if you do the projects in order, there won't be many mistakes. Experience with new skills on scrap so when you start a project, you'll be ready to do it for keeps.

Hooks and Chain

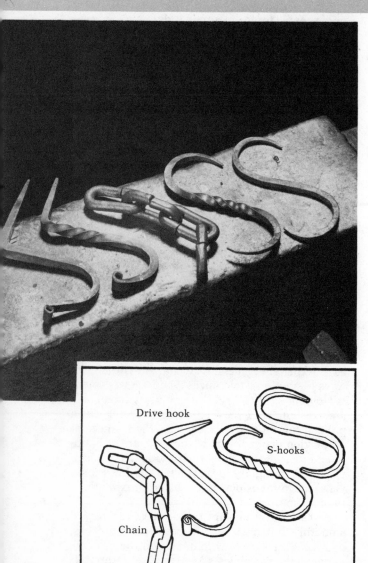

Drive hook

S-hooks

Chain

Drawing a taper
Bending on an anvil
Scrolling

Blacksmithing, for the most part, consists of simple techniques combined in novel ways. Repetitive hammering to change the shape and dimension of iron, bending hot iron over a form; these are elementary processes by themselves. But in combination, they can yield not only attractive but also useful objects.

A very good way to start in blacksmithing, then, is to learn these fundamental processes by making useful products—in this instance, hooks and chain.

Hooks and chain are fairly easy to make and don't require precise measurements—you can vary the size or relative dimensions without compromising the usefulness of the finished product. It's possible to relax and develop some skills while still having something worthwhile to show for your efforts at the forge.

The required skills are two of the most basic in blacksmithing: drawing (or tapering) and bending. Drawing a piece of iron elongates and thins or tapers it. It's done by laying the heated stock on the far edge of the anvil with the piece at a very shallow angle to the face, then hammering on it, just where it touches the anvil. Curves are made by hammer-bending the stock over the horn or some other form.

Curls can be made simply by varying the edge or surface used as the form. Scrolls are double curls. They are trickier to forge, but they add a particularly special touch to a hook.

Forged hooks make attractive additions to a country-style kitchen. You can hang cast-iron skillets and utensils of all kinds from hooks mounted on walls or driven into exposed beams. Hats and coats can be hung on hooks mounted by the door. A plant can be hung from a hook with a length of hand-forged chain.

Step-by-step instructions
S-hook

1. Draw out each end of a ¼ × ¼ × 6-in. piece of stock, working at an orange heat. Work the final 1½ in. of each end evenly, completing one point before starting the other. Rotate the piece as you work to keep the taper even.

2. (Optional.) Put a twist in the middle of the length of steel by heating that area to a light cherry red, quickly clamping one end in a vise, and, in one continuous motion, twisting the other end with a pair of pliers or an adjustable wrench (see p. 267).

(see p. 267)

What you will need

1 pc. mild steel bar, ¼″ × ¼″ × 6″ (for S-hook)
1 pc. mild steel bar, ¼″ × ⅜″ (for drive hook)
1 pc. mild steel bar, ⁵⁄₁₆″ × 1¼″ (6″–8″, for
   forming block)
¼-in.-dia. mild steel rod (3¾″ for each link)
medium-weight forging hammer
light cross peen hammer
cut-off hardie
cold-cutting hardie
pliers
locking-grip pliers
vise
basic blacksmithing equipment

3. Form the piece into an S-shape on the horn of the anvil. This requires forging the length of metal into two opposite curves, each with the same radius. Heat to light cherry; be careful to avoid burning the tips. Start at the part of the horn with the desired curve, and slowly shape the workpiece. Continue hammering until the piece is bent completely against the horn. If necessary, work on the anvil face to keep the curve from curling to the side.

Drive hook

1. Bring the end of a length of ¼ × ⅜-in. stock to an orange heat, then draw and flatten the end. Don't draw it into a pointed taper; rather thin and taper the stock while slightly increasing its width. Concentrate the blows on top and bottom to do this.

2. Curl the tip. The roll or curl is a decoration made by heating to light cherry — don't burn the tip — and laying the piece on the anvil face with ½ in. extending over the edge. Strike down on the tip, then in toward the anvil side. Lay the piece on the anvil face with the tip up, and close the curl with a cross peen hammer.

3. Shape the metal into a curved hook with a bend made on the anvil face. Heat the piece to light cherry. Hold it on the anvil face with the curled end extending past the edge. Hammer straight down, then in, bending the bar 90°. Turn it over (with the curl up) and refine the curve. Using a light hammer, strike at the curl with blows directed toward, rather than away from, yourself.

4. Until now, you've worked the end of a fairly long piece of the initial stock, obviating the need to use tongs. Now, however, the nascent hook must be cut from the larger piece. Bring the iron to an orange heat, hold it over the cut-off hardie, and strike. When the iron is well notched on both sides, strike a shearing blow beyond the hardie and break off the hook. The hook's proportions should suggest where to cut.

Drawing a Taper

Bring the end of the workpiece to an orange heat, and lay it over the face of the anvil, with the heated end tilted slightly downward and extending past the outer edge. Strike with medium strokes using a medium-weight hammer, its striking surface contacting the workpiece squarely. The hammer face should fall at the anvil edge. This will produce small dimples on the underside. Pull the piece toward you until the entire end has been worked.

Turn the piece 180° and repeat the process. Do the same on each of the two remaining sides, then reheat the metal. Continue drawing the taper, working more toward the end. Smooth out dimples by forging with the piece flat on the anvil face. If desired, you can round the edges by working them at an orange heat before the finish step.

To finish, heat once more, and scrape off any scale. Let the work cool to a dark red. Use light hammer blows to finish and draw the final point.

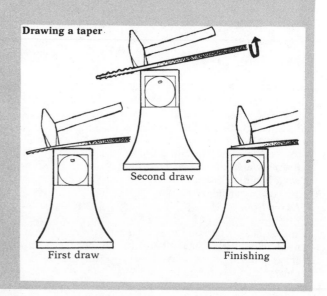

Drawing a taper

First draw

Second draw

Finishing

Bending on an Anvil

Using the horn of the anvil and a hammer, you can bend rods and lengths of bar stock into curves of almost any radius. In brief, you lay the heated stock across the horn where its curve matches the radius of the curve you want to make, then hammer on the piece until it takes the shape of the horn.

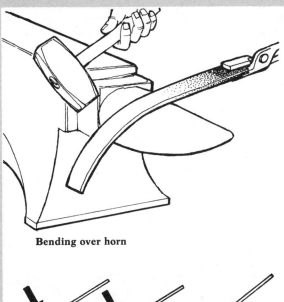

Bending over horn

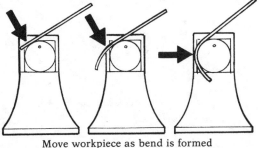

Move workpiece as bend is formed

To start, heat the piece to a light cherry, then position it so it overhangs the horn by several in. Strike the end to start the curve, then gradually push the piece away from you and continue forging to drive the work against the horn. You will be reaching over the anvil, swinging back toward where you are standing. As the piece begins to take the shape of the horn, hold the hammer with its face in a more vertical position, and hammer against the piece. As you work, you may need to reposition the piece slightly to end up with a curve of the desired radius. The procedure may require several heatings.

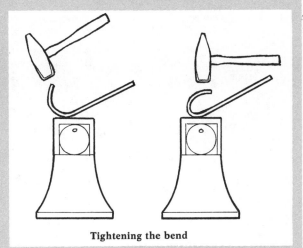

Tightening the bend

If the curve must be tighter than the one produced at the horn, place the piece on the face of the anvil, with the open part of the curve facing up. Hammer down on the end until the desired curve is reached. Use the same procedure to curve a tapered tip, but be careful not to overheat the tip, which can be easily burned. A tapered piece will require more frequent heatings, since it will cool quickly. When first starting a tapered piece, strike back from the tip a little to avoid mashing it.

Curling the tip

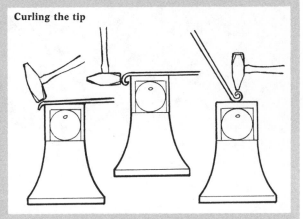

If you put a decorative curl in the tip, do it before you make the larger curve. Heat the tip to a light cherry, avoiding overheating, and lay the work on the anvil face with less than an in. over the edge. Strike down, then in toward the anvil with a light hammer. Lay the piece on the face and close the curl with a cross peen hammer.

5. The newly cut end must now be drawn to a taper. Bring the end to an orange heat, and, with tongs, hold it over the anvil's edge at a very shallow angle to the face. Drawing the taper requires that you forge all faces of the hook's end. As you rain blows on the hot iron, slowly pull it toward you over the anvil's edge. Rotate the piece 180° and repeat the forging. Then work the remaining edges, bringing the end to a nice point.

6. The shaft of the hook can be decorated with a twist, if desired. Before heating the piece for the operation, set the vise so you can quickly secure the hook, using only a partial turn of the vise's screw. Heat the midsection of the piece to light cherry, moving the piece around in the fire as necessary to concentrate the heat at the right spot. Quickly clamp the tapered end in the vise, grasp the curved end with pliers, and twist.

If the hook is a large one and you have a helper, you can make a reverse twist. Clamp the heated piece in the vise and hold the tapered end firmly with locking-grip pliers. The helper grips the center of the shaft with pliers and rotates it, creating the reverse twist.

7. The final step is to bend the pointed end at right angles to the shaft of the hook. Heat to light cherry. Hold the piece on the anvil with an in. or more of the point extending beyond the edge. Strike down, then in. Strike to either side of the bend, but not directly on the bend itself, which would weaken it. Since you'll be driving the hook into a wooden post or beam, you want that point to be as strong as possible.

Chain links

1. Chain has been forged in a variety of ways, but here it is made by bending each link around a scrap of bar stock clamped in a vise. The forming block is $5/16 \times 1\frac{1}{4}$ in.; a piece 6–8 in. long will do. Clamp it tightly in a machinists' vise or, better, a leg vise, so that about 3 in. of it projects from one side of the jaws.

2. Each link is forged from a 3¾-in. length of ¼-in.-dia. rod (although smaller rod could be used to make a lighter chain). Cut the link sections you need cold on the hardie. With a file, lightly chamfer the ends of each piece to remove burrs or protrusions.

3. The individual links are formed next. In brief, the process requires you to heat the link piece, withdraw it from the fire with tongs, clamp it to the forming block with locking-grip pliers, then hammer it into shape with a medium-weight forging hammer. The piece will lose heat quickly, so you must have your tools carefully arranged and your moves practiced.

Bring a link piece to a cherry red heat. Clamp it to the forming block with about an equal amount extending above and below the block. Hammer one end over, down, and firmly against the forming block. Hammer the lower end over and up, but don't completely close all the links. At least half of them should be left partly open so that the links can be joined to form the chain.

4. Assembling the chain, like forming the links, should be practiced cold so you can arrange your tools and parts and plan your moves. You must heat an open link to a cherry heat, extract it from the fire with tongs, slip at least one closed link onto it, hold it on the anvil face with the open end up, then take up a medium-weight forging hammer and pound the link closed. All the while, the link will be losing heat, so you dare not fumble too long.

The chain can be assembled a link at a time, in which case all of your links should be left open except one. Or, you can speed the work by adding two links at a time to the chain, as shown. Hook the open link onto the chain, then add a closed link too.

5. (Optional.) Braze or weld each link where the ends meet. An experienced blacksmith would forge-weld the links, a process that requires a very hot fire, flux, and considerable skill.

Scrolling

A scroll is a decorative, S-shaped double curl at the tip of a forged piece. A lightweight piece can be scrolled easily with a pair of needle-nose pliers, but a heavy piece must be scrolled by hammer-forging.

In either case, heat the taper to a light cherry. The tip is easy to burn, so be sure not to overheat the piece. Using pliers, simply grasp the taper just shy of the tip and bend a curl into the piece. Reposition the pliers and bend the curl back, creating the S-shape.

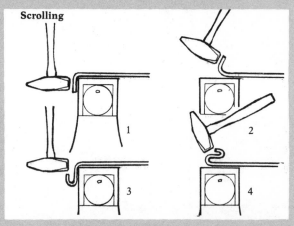

Scrolling

Using a light hammer, hold the tip of the piece over the anvil's outer edge and strike down, then in. Twist the piece 180° and pull it back onto the anvil face. Using the cross peen of the hammer, tap the curl closed.

To form the second part of the scroll, reheat the end, then quench just the curl, so it isn't deformed by your hammer blows. Hold the piece over the anvils' outer edge, curl up, and strike down, then in. Pull the piece back and twist it, then tap the reverse curl closed.

Towel Bar

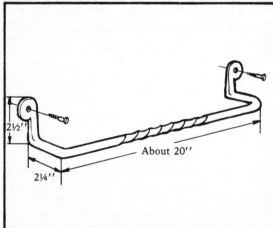

2½"

About 20"

2¼"

Punching a clean hole
Twisting

A towel bar is a good project to sharpen the skills you developed while forging blacksmithing tools and making the hooks and chain. The measurements required for a towel can vary, so there's some leeway in the fabrication—as long as the finished product is reasonably symmetrical.

The required skills include bending, tapering, flattening, and a new one, hole punching. The ability to punch a clean hole is important whenever you make something with a hole in it. The hole is usually created with an unusual tool resembling a hammer that has a beak instead of the usual flat striking surface. Blacksmiths often make these punches by drawing the face of a standard ball peen hammer to a taper.

You can give the towel bars you make a personal touch. Twist the center portion before bending it (see p. 267). Use square or hexagonal stock. Forge a more pronounced flare into the ends.

Towel bars can be made in various sizes, from large ones suitable for several towels to small hangers for hand towels or washcloths. The one shown here holds two standard bath towels. Two or three bars this size and a couple of smaller ones are plenty to add a rustic flavor to your bathroom, especially when mounted on wood.

The oil-finish process used on the towel bar is suitable for any forged object that doesn't come into contact with food. In this process, nondetergent motor oil is applied to metal heated less than cherry red. For hand-forged spatulas, choppers, or other kitchen items, coat the heated metal with vegetable oil instead of motor oil. The finish in either case makes the surface shinier (though not as much so as varnish would), and it protects against rust. This protection is important in humid environments—bathrooms, kitchens, damp basement workshops, or semiexposed areas such as screened-in porches.

Step-by-step instructions

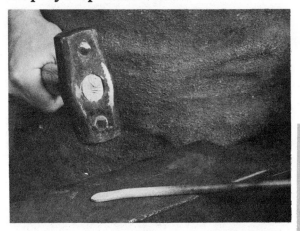

1. Flatten one end of the towel bar stock—a 28-in. length of ⅜-in. rod—by placing the orange-heated steel on the anvil face and striking with a medium-weight hammer held at a slight angle to the anvil. The procedure is similar to, though less pronounced than, flaring (see p. 282). The object is to thin the end evenly, with a slight taper to the tip.

Don't overwork the end. If the metal is hammered too thin, or worked too long, it begins to fissure and usually can't be repaired. To avoid the problem, hammer just enough to produce a smooth taper.

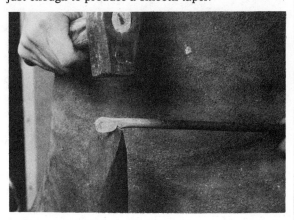

2. Reheat the flattened end and cut a notch in it by setting the edge of the flattened part on a cut-off hardie, 1 in. from the end of the stock. Strike directly over the hardie, driving it halfway through the bar.

What you will need

1 pc. ⅜-in.-dia. mild steel rod, 28″
medium-weight forging hammer
cut-off hardie
punch
file
nondetergent motor oil
basic blacksmithing equipment

Punching a Clean Hole

If you punch straight through a piece of orange-heated metal, the punch will form an indentation around the hole on one side of the workpiece and a bulge on the other. Even though you can hammer the bulge flat, you'll probably deform the hole in doing so.

To get a clean hole, punch only partway through from the first side. Then quickly flip the workpiece, and drive the punch through the center of the slight bulge on that side (created by the punch). Hammer

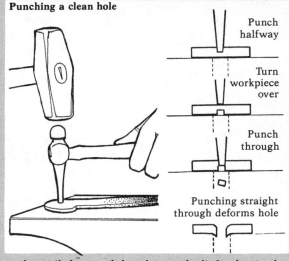

Punching a clean hole

Punch halfway

Turn workpiece over

Punch through

Punching straight through deforms hole

only until the punch knocks out the little plug in the hole; if you pound the tip too far through, you'll distort the shape of the hole.

Because the end of the punch is tapered thin, it quickly absorbs heat from the workpiece. In the time it takes to strike three blows, the punch will begin to soften. Keep it cool and hard by dipping it in the water bucket every couple of blows.

3. Draw out the stock behind the flattened end, placing the notch on the outer edge of the anvil with the body of the stock on the anvil face and the flattened end hanging over the edge. Hammer the stock behind the notch, tapering 2 in. of it.

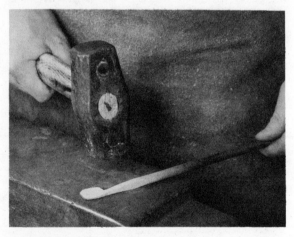

4. Work the end into a symmetrical shape, and flatten the part of the bar that joins it. The previous steps leave the end with partially rounded corners; take the time now to smooth out the curves. Then, to flatten, place the flat end of the stock on the anvil face, and hammer it out, as far along the stock as the drawn part from step 3. The result is a squared shank below the notch. Round these edges so the bar is roughly round again, but tapering from the stock size to the flattened end.

5. After reheating, set the flattened end on the pritchel hole and punch a hole (p. 265). Hammer the punch only partway through on one side. Flip the workpiece and punch completely through from the second side.

6. Make two 90° bends behind the flattened end. First, heat again, then set the stock on the outer edge of the anvil, with the notch 2 in. past the edge and the flattened end parallel to the anvil face. Hammer down, then in, bending the end against the anvil side. Then turn the workpiece 90°, so the end of the bar is now parallel to the outer edge of the anvil, and push the bar end 2 in. beyond the anvil edge. Hammer down and in, as before, to complete the second 90° bend.

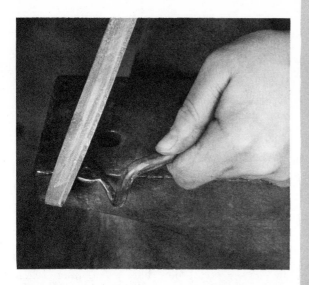

7. Repeat the preceding sequence of 6 steps on the opposite end of the stock to complete the shaping of the towel bar.

8. File away any burrs or sharp edges, exerting pressure only on the push stroke. (You'll dull the file if you press hard on the back stroke.)

9. Finish the surface with oil, both to improve the luster and to protect against rust. Heat the towel bar in the forge to less than cherry red, and dip it in a bucket of nondetergent motor oil. You may heat and dip the bar half at a time if you have trouble heating it all at once. For this step, use clean oil right out of the can to protect your towels. If you don't want to pour out the several quarts required to immerse the bar, simply wipe on the oil liberally with a brush or rag.

10. Mount the towel bar with either wood screws or hand-forged nails. If you use screws, use black ones, or paint the heads black after installation, to keep them from standing out against the bar itself. Forged nails are easy to make (p. 268) and would be an attractive addition to this project.

Mount the bar so that the mounting holes are above the bar. When towels are placed on the bar, the load will be exerted down on the nails, but not out from the wall, as it would be if the holes were below the bar. This will keep the nails from pulling out.

Twisting

Twisting is primarily a decorative procedure—a metal object with a twist is more interesting than a plain one—but it does stabilize a long piece, making it moderately hard to deflect in any direction, rather than easy across the narrow dimension and hard across the wide dimension.

It's important to complete the twist in one heat and one motion. Otherwise, the spiral will be uneven. It is a good idea, therefore, to have all in readiness, with your vise set and the tools close at hand, before you begin. As you heat the piece, move it back and forth in the fire to heat it evenly to light cherry.

Then quickly clamp one end of the piece in the vise. Hold the free end with pliers. Slip-joint pliers are okay, but locking grips are better. Twist in one smooth, continuous motion, pulling slightly to keep the metal from sagging. If the work does warp, you can reheat it and *try* to straighten it on the anvil with a hammer.

A variation is the reverse twist, which consists of opposite spirals on the same stem. Clamp one end of the heated piece in a vise, and have a helper hold the other end firmly with pliers. Then grasp the center of the stem with another pair of pliers and turn in a smooth, continuous motion.

Twisting

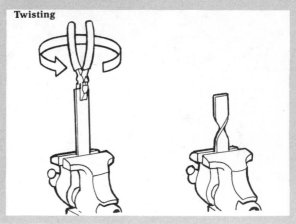

Nails and Rivets

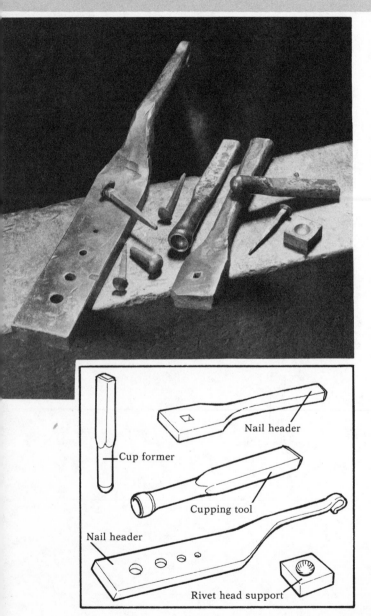

Nail header

Cup former

Cupping tool

Nail header

Rivet head support

Upsetting
Heading rivets

Forging quantities of nails was an important part of blacksmithing, a task for the apprentice, until mass production relegated it to craft shows and demonstrations in restored villages. But making nails and rivets remains a useful task for those who prefer the distinctive look of hand-forged fasteners and those who simply want to improve their skills at the forge.

To forge nails, you first must use a nail header—a metal bar that has a tapered hole through it. A red-hot nail with an unfinished head is inserted in the hole; a few hammer blows flatten the head for use.

Rivets can be worked from mild steel rod, and set using only a forging hammer and an anvil. You can even make simple rivets from cut-off nails, hammering the cut end until it clinches. But a more finished rivet is made using rivet-setting tools.

Making the nail header and one of the setting tools involves a procedure called upsetting, in which a metal bar, heated at one end, is stood on end on the anvil. Vigorous blows compress the heated end, causing it to bulge. It can then be worked into the required form.

Forged nails can be worked easily, since so little metal is involved. In fact, you have to be careful not to overwork them—if you do destroy a few, it's just part of the learning process. The dimensions for nails aren't terribly critical. As long as the head is attached firmly to a shank of reasonable length, it will do the job.

Rivets are a bit more exacting. The ones for movable-arm tools such as tongs must fit snugly without binding. Getting the right fit is mostly a matter of patience, though. Once you have the basic shape, just keep tapping away at the places that bind when you try to insert the rivet. Making nails and rivets is good practice.

Step-by-step instructions
Nail header

1. Upset one end of a 12–14-in. piece of ½ × 1-in. bar stock, widening about 1¼ in. of it to a width of 1¼ in. This will require strong blows with the forging hammer. Work at an orange heat.

2. Shape the head formed by upsetting and draw out the handle of the tool. Leave the thickness at ½ in., but taper the handle from ⅝ in. at the head to ¾ in. at the end. Bring the upset end to an orange heat. To establish the shape of the head, notch both edges on a hardie, about 1¼ in. from the end. Hold the piece on the anvil; then, with the notch just over the edge, work the hot iron, drawing the handle. Round all the edges and corners.

What you will need
1 pc. mild steel bar, ½″ × 1″ (12″–14″, for nail header)
¼-in.-dia. mild steel rod (for nails and rivets)
½-in.-dia. mild steel rod (for cup former and cupping tool)
1 pc. mild steel bar scrap, about ½″ × ½″ × ¾″ (for rivet-head support)
medium-weight forging hammer
cut-off hardie
punch
vise
file
grinder
knife
square drift
basic blacksmithing equipment

Upsetting

Upsetting to a blacksmith is a technique for making a piece of metal shorter and thicker. The end to be upset is forge-heated and stood on the anvil face. The opposite end, left unheated so it won't deform, is pounded forcefully with a medium-weight forging hammer.

The stronger the blows, the greater the length that will be thickened. For a single-hole nail header, medium blows will do, because you only need to upset a couple of inches, but for a header with several different holes in a line, you'll need very powerful blows. In fact, it's hard to appreciate just how hard you have to hit until you've tried it on some pieces of scrap.

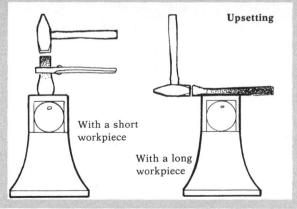

Upsetting

With a short workpiece

With a long workpiece

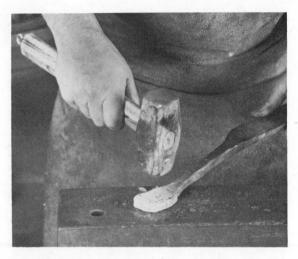

3. Bring the head to an orange heat again and place it on the hardie hole. Strike the center (directly over the hole) with the edge of the hammer, forming a depression, which on the opposite side is a shallow dome. When the nailheads are set, this dome will shape them, allowing them to grip wood better.

4. Cut the nail header to length, heating it orange and striking notching blows over the hardie. Strike a shearing blow to one side of the hardie when the pieces are nearly severed.

6. Enlarge the hole by reheating the head and driving a tapered square drift into the hole—from the same side as before. This makes the narrower part of the hole on the convex side. When the nails are inserted for heading, they won't get stuck.

7. Smooth the surface of the dome with a file, and the header is ready to start producing nails.

Forged nails

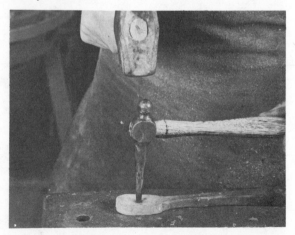

5. Bring the header to an orange heat and place it, dome side down, over the hardie hole, and hammer a round punch through the middle of the upset end. If the punch draws enough heat from the header to glow, quench it before continuing, or it may deform.

1. Lay a ¼-in.-dia. piece of rod, heated orange, on the anvil face, and draw the tip of it, rotating it as you do. As the part on the anvil face is drawn out, a shoulder will form at the anvil edge.

2. Continue until the shank at the shoulder is ³⁄₁₆ in. square and tapers to a point. With practice, you'll be able to draw the shank to just the length you need.

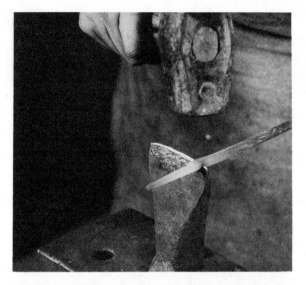

3. Lay the rod on a cut-off hardie, ³⁄₁₆ in. shy of the shoulder. Tap the rod with a medium-weight forging hammer, nicking the thicker portion of the rod, rotating the rod as you tap. Don't sever the nail free.

4. Place the nail header over the pritchel hole, and slip the shank of the still-hot nail into the header's hole. Break the rod free of the nail, then quickly strike the nail with several sharp blows to form the head.
5. Quench the nail and header in a slack bucket, and tap the nail out on the side of the bucket.

Cup former for rivets

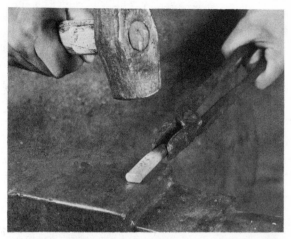

1. Shoulder and draw out to a length of 1½ in. one end of a ½-in.-dia. rod. Work at an orange heat. Make the drawn part ⅜ in. square. Turn the piece as you hammer to keep all four sides the same.
2. After reheating, set the thicker portion of the rod on a cut-off hardie, 1 in. from the shoulder. Hammer the rod as you turn it, cutting most of the way through. Use a shearing blow beyond the hardie to sever the pieces.

3. Round off the end you've just cut on a grinder, creating a rivet-head shape. This tool will stamp the shape into both the cupping tool and the rivet-head support. Grind with care, since the shape you create now will be the shape the heads of the rivets you make will have.

Cupping tool

1. Cut a 5-in. piece from the ½-in. rod, using a hammer and the cut-off hardie, as before.

2. Grip the cup former in a vise, leaving the dome exposed, and heat one end of the 5-in. piece. Hold the heated end of the rod on the cup former, and drive it onto the dome, forming a ¼-in.-deep depression.

3. The lip around the cup will be angled. Grind or file it flat, and remove burrs from the inner edge of the cup with a knife, scraping the blade completely around the edge.

Heading Rivets

Using the cupping tool and rivet-head support, you can head professional-looking rivets for such home-forged tools as tongs or pliers. Make the rivets for these tools as described in Nails and Rivets (see p. 268), but instead of squaring and tapering them, try to keep the shank at an even ¼-in.-dia. Place the completed rivet in a header—made like that for the nails, but with a hole large enough for the rivet-shank—and roughly form the rivet head by spreading the end with a ball peen hammer. Quickly place the cupping tool over the hot rivet and rap it, shaping the head. Quench the rivet and header.

Place the rivet-head support on the anvil face. Heat the unformed end of the rivet, and set the formed end in the rivet support. Quickly place the pieces to be riveted over the shank so that the heated end passes through the holes and protrudes ⅜ in. Spread the protrusion with a ball peen hammer, then head it by driving the cupping tool onto the spread end. Work quickly so you don't have to reheat for the heading operation. The rivet-head support will keep the bottom head true while you form the top rivet head.

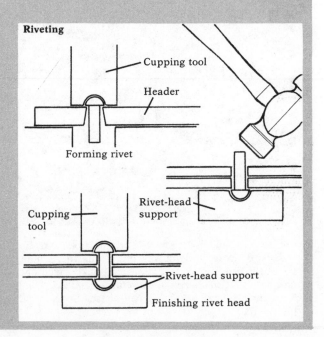

Riveting

Cupping tool

Header

Forming rivet

Rivet-head support

Cupping tool

Rivet-head support

Finishing rivet head

Rivet-head support

1. Cut a piece of bar scrap, ½ in. thick and at least ¾ in. square.

2. Heat this piece red-hot, and set it on the anvil face. Quickly place the shaped end of the unheated cup former on the piece (holding it with tongs) and drive the cup former into it, making a ¼-in.-deep depression. After the support has cooled, clean up burrs and rough edges with a file or knife blade.

Slide-Bolt Latch

Keepers

Slide bolt

Forming a shoulder

An effective way to add a rustic look to your home is to forge a set of hinges and a slide-bolt latch for each of the interior doors. The plainest door will become a worthy addition to your decor with forged fittings.

The slide-bolt latch can be used as a simple latch for the interior doors or as an additional security bolt for exterior doors. The latch consists of three U-shaped keepers that guide the sliding bolt. These keepers can be fastened to the door and jamb with screws or hand-forged nails.

The only part of the project that presents any difficulty is the finger loop. You'll need to form a shoulder in one end of the stock and hammer that end thin before forming the loop. Once you develop some blacksmithing expertise, you'll be able to forge the end of the bolt into a large ring, a touch that's both practical and decorative.

Stick to the measurements given in the step-by-step instructions so the latch won't wobble in use. When you install the slide-bolt latch, make sure the keepers are placed so that the screws or nails you use will be anchored in solid wood.

First, hold up the slide bolt as it would be with the door latched shut. Install the first keeper over the bolt next to the finger loop. Next, mount a keeper on the door casing. This keeper should cover the end of the slide latch and touch the latch stop. Now open the slide latch until it clears the keeper mounted on the door casing.

Mount the final keeper on the door, next to the latch stop (but on the opposite side of the stop from the previous keeper). The stops block the slide bolt both when it is fully opened and when it is shut. The two keepers on the door guide the slide bolt to the other keeper.

If you do use screws or lag bolts to mount your latch, and you can't find blued fasteners, drop cadmium-plated fasteners into the forge and burn the plating off.

What you will need

3 pcs. mild steel bar, ⅛″ × ¾″ × 3¾″ (for latch keepers)
1 pc. mild steel bar, ⅜″ × ¾″ × 5½″ (for slide bolt)
medium-weight forging hammer
light cross peen hammer
cut-off hardie
punch
header die
vise
file
basic blacksmithing equipment

Step-by-step instructions
Latch keepers

1. You'll need three keepers for each latch, each one shaped from a ⅛ × ¾ × 3¾-in. piece of steel. Heat one piece to a light cherry, and center it on the jaws of a vise opened to 1 in. Lay a piece of the ⅜ × ¾-in. stock to be used for the bolt on the keeper, parallel to the gap between the jaws. Strike with a medium-weight forging hammer, driving the bolt stock between the vise jaws, and forming a U-shaped bend in the keeper. Finish the bend by striking directly above the jaws, forcing the ends of the keeper against the top of the vise jaws and eliminating any bowing.

Forming a Shoulder

A shoulder, to a blacksmith, is the abutment that occurs where metal abruptly changes thickness. It's a natural consequence of forging part of a workpiece thinner without tapering it—the shoulder is the step between thicknesses. In the slide-bolt latch project, you must create a shoulder where the loop rises away from the slide bolt.

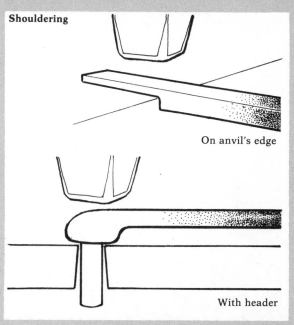

Shouldering

On anvil's edge

With header

Making this kind of shoulder is a simple matter of laying the workpiece across the inner edge of the anvil, with the area to be thinned on the anvil's face. Striking with a medium-weight forging hammer will thin the metal and at the same time form a step—the shoulder—on the underside of the piece.

Another kind of shoulder is formed using a header die. It is useful as a pintle for a forged door hinge. In this version, the shoulder surrounds the pintle—the hinge pin—providing a supporting surface on which the hinge strap will rotate. It helps to keep the pivoting action smooth.

To make a pintle shoulder, take a length of round stock and bend it at a right angle. With a header die placed over the hardie hole, insert the bent rod into the die and hammer directly above the die hole. As the metal flattens, it spreads around the hole, creating the shoulder at the base of the bent rod. Be sure the narrow side of the hole in the header die is up, or the pintle could get hopelessly jammed.

2. Using the latch stock to form the keeper jams the two pieces together. To separate them, lay the latch stock on the anvil face with the keeper on top. Tap the top of the keeper with a medium-weight hammer. The blow causes the sides of the keeper to spring apart, releasing the latch stock.

4. Smooth off the edges of the keeper with a file, applying pressure only on the push stroke. This is a finishing process that makes the completed piece look and feel hand-forged.

5. Since it takes three keepers to support one slide bolt, make two more in the same way.

Slide bolt

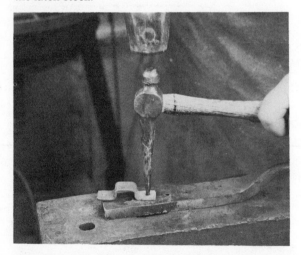

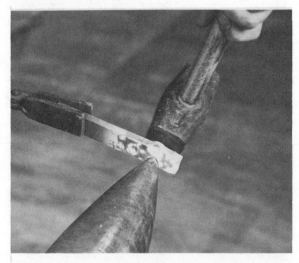

3. Punch a hole through each end of the keeper. Lay a header die over the hardie hole, and place one end of the orange-heated keeper over a die hole slightly wider than the base of the nail or screw you'll use for mounting. Hammer a punch through the keeper. The die will stop it and prevent a large bulge from forming on the underside. Flip the keeper over and flatten it out on the anvil face, with the U-bend extending past the anvil. Punch the hole on the other end of the keeper in the same way.

1. Make stops for the bolt by punch-flaring opposite sides of it, 1 in. from one end. Make each flare by holding the orange-heated bolt stock against the tip of the anvil horn and hitting it with a medium-weight hammer. This forms the main indentation. Lay the still-hot stock on the anvil face, and clean it up with a punch and hammer, flattening the bottom of the indentation and straightening its sides. Repeat the sequence to make the second flare.

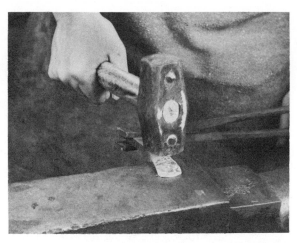

2. Form a shoulder ¾ in. from the end of the bolt stock farther from the two flares. Use tongs to grasp the orange-heated piece, and lay it on the anvil face so that ¾ in. of it rests on the anvil face next to the inner edge. Work the end until it is ⅛ in. thick and about 1½ in. long. If you hold the stock steady over the anvil edge as you work, a step or shoulder will form on the underside. As you forge, widen the piece slightly toward the end.

4. Flip the stock over, with the curled end extending past the anvil's outer edge. (The shoulder should be facing up, directly above the anvil edge.) Make a 90° bend by hammering down and then in.

3. Roll the end you've just forged. Heat the piece, then lay it on the anvil with ½ in. of it beyond the outer edge, the shoulder facing down. Drive the end in toward the anvil and up slightly, using a light hammer. Pull the piece back and close the curl with the cross peen end of the hammer.

5. Continue to form the end into a finger loop by heating only the upper half of the drawn part and placing the stock on the anvil face with the heated end facing up. Strike down on the end with a light hammer, aiming the first blows away from the body of the stock, then, as the end begins to bend over, aiming them toward the stock to form the loop. Heating only the end prevents the bend at the shoulder from being deformed while the loop is being shaped.

6. Smooth off all the edges with a file.

Hinges

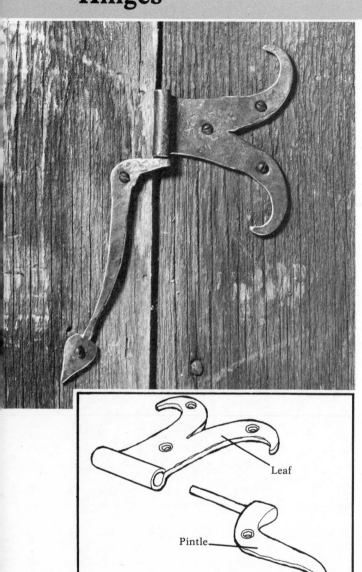

Leaf

Pintle

It's worth the trouble to forge your own hinges if you are trying for a handmade, country look. Forged door hinges, which are black when finished with oil, stand out handsomely when mounted on wood with a natural finish. Stamped metal fixtures may *look* similar at first glance, but seldom do they have the heft of forged ones— and they can't match the subtle texture of hand-forged pieces.

The plans that follow are for door hinges, but they can easily be scaled down to serve as a guide for making cabinet hinges, or even hinges for a small storage box. When hanging exterior doors, use three sets of hinges. Interior doors usually need only two sets, because they are lighter and thus easier to support.

Each hinge is in two parts: the hinge leaf, which fastens to the door, and the pintle, which is attached to the doorframe to support the hinge leaf and door. The pintle is forged of ⅜-inch-diameter stock. The hinge pin is drawn from this stock, and it must be perfectly straight and round so the hinge leaf will turn easily on it. The leaf must be flared at one end, and the flare rolled to fit snugly around the hinge pin without binding.

Before hanging the door, be sure that the hinge leaf turns easily on the pintle. If necessary, open or close the roll on the leaf slightly to get the proper fit. The surface where the pintle and the hinge leaf touch the door should be flat enough to allow both pieces to lay close to the door surface. To finish the surface of the metal, heat the pieces less than cherry red, and brush on 30-weight motor oil.

Mount the hinge leaves on the door, wedge the door in place, slide the pintles into the rolls of the hinge leaves, and screw the pintles to the doorframe. Remove the wedges, and see that the door swings fully.

The design of these hinges is very adaptable. If the door to be hung is very wide or very heavy, you may want to extend the length of the hinge leaf, making it almost as long as the door is wide. It would then be more of a strap hinge. The pintle, too, can be redesigned. If you are making hinges for a gate or a backyard shed, make a drive-in pintle. After drawing the hinge pin and bending the pintle, draw a taper on the pintle stem. You can then drive the pintle into fence or doorframe with a hammer.

What you will need

1 pc. ⅜-in.-dia. mild steel rod, 6'' (for pintle)
1 pc. mild steel bar, ¼'' × 1'' × 4'' (for hinge leaf)
medium-weight forging hammer
light ball peen hammer
cut-off hardie
punch
header die
file
basic blacksmithing equipment

Step-by-step instructions
Pintle

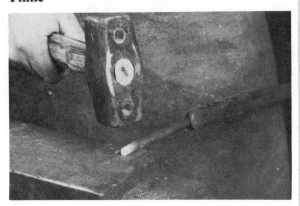

1. Start with a 6-in. piece of ⅜-in.-dia. round stock. Draw out ¾ in. of it, working at an orange heat with a medium-weight hammer. Turn the stock as you proceed, keeping the portion being worked round. Continue until the stock is reduced to ¼ in. dia. (which will nearly double the length of the drawn section).

Splitting

Your first impulse when splitting a metal strap might simply be to hold the orange-heated piece on the sharp edge of a cut-off hardie and hammer away. But, of course, you'd dull the hardie when you cut through. Instead, hammer most of the way through, with the bar held flat against the hardie. Then upend the workpiece, so that the end of the groove is resting on the hardie edge. Strike the opposite end of the bar, driving it onto the hardie. The sharp edge of the hardie will follow the line of least resistance, and split the bar neatly along the groove.

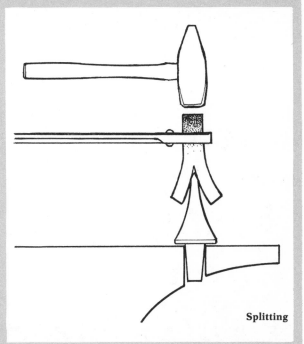

Splitting

If you need to make a split that's longer than the cutting edge of the hardie, start by hammering a groove in the strap, as described above. Then reposition the stock over the hardie edge, overlapping a short portion of the groove with the hardie edge, and continue your hammer blows. When the groove is the desired length, set the bar on end on the hardie and split it apart on the hardie edge.

Cutting a strap completely in two is similar, except that there will always be a small connection that can't be cut without dulling the hardie edge. Hold the bar so that the groove is along the anvil edge. Strike the part that extends beyond the anvil, separating the two halves, or simply twist them apart.

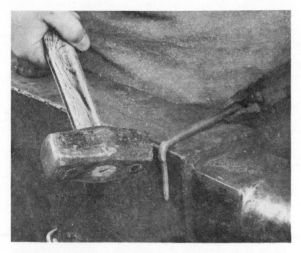

2. Drawing the stock creates a shoulder where the rod narrows. Measure ⅜ in. from this shoulder along the thicker portion, and make a 90° bend, by laying the orange-heated rod on the anvil with the drawn portion extending past the edge. Strike down, then in.

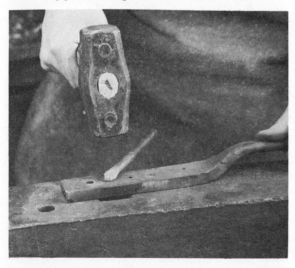

4. Hold the heated piece on the anvil with the bend extending over the outer edge, the drawn end up. Strike down, then in on the thickened shoulder, bending it in against the anvil side. Place the pintle on its side on the anvil face, so that the drawn hinge pin as well as the bent part and the unhammered body are all flat on the face. Still holding the end with tongs, flatten the body from the shoulder to the tongs. Don't flatten the part held by the tongs (about the last 1½ in.).

3. To support the hinge leaf properly, the shoulder must be wide and smooth. Place a header die on the anvil face, and center the hole that corresponds in diameter to the drawn part of the rod over the hardie hole. Heat the workpiece and insert the drawn portion in the die, then strike directly over the bent part of the stock, using a medium-weight hammer. Work the bent portion to refine its shape and thickness.

5. Heat the body of the piece to an orange heat. Then, holding the hinge-pin end with tongs, draw out the midsection. Taper this area from the bend to the short area at the end that has yet to be worked. As you draw out the midsection, you will form a shoulder just where the unworked section begins. As you work, turn the piece from side to side so it is thinned evenly and so the pintle remains flat.

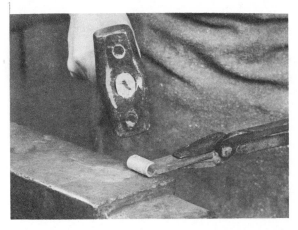

6. Forge the unworked end into a spadelike shape. To do this, bring the end to an orange heat, then flare it with a medium-weight hammer, making sure the flare is in the same plane as the bend. The shoulder created in the previous step contributes to the flare. Then hold the pintle so the flare is on edge, and use a light hammer to shape the flare to a point. Work until you have a uniform shape and thickness.

2. Roll the flared end into a socket for the hinge pin. To do this, reheat the piece and hold it on the anvil, shoulder up, with the flared end just extending over the outer edge. Bend the flare down with a couple of sharp hammer blows, then turn the piece over and, with moderate blows, begin curling the end. As you close the roll, insert the hinge pin and switch to a light hammer to tap the roll snug. The leaf should be able to turn easily on the pin.

7. Make two ⅛-in. mounting holes in the pintle, one through the flared end and the other below the hinge pin. Use a punch and header die to make the holes.
8. Remove burrs and round off sharp edges with a file, remembering to file only on the push stroke.
Hinge leaf
1. Flare and shoulder one end of a 4-in. piece of ¼ × 1-in. mild steel, placing ¾ in. over the inner edge of the anvil and working at an orange heat with a medium-weight hammer (see p. 247). Keep the piece in one position over the edge to form a shoulder.

3. Split the end of the stock opposite the roll (p. 279). To do this, lay the heated piece flat on the hardie and notch it almost through with several smart hammer blows. Stand the still-hot piece on edge, and drive it down over the hardie, splitting open the notch. Split about 2 in. of the leaf.

Flaring

Flaring is the process of spreading out the end of a piece of heated steel. The hammer blows usually thin the metal as it is spread. By modifying your blows or holding the flared end against different parts of the anvil as you work, you can produce any number of different shapes.

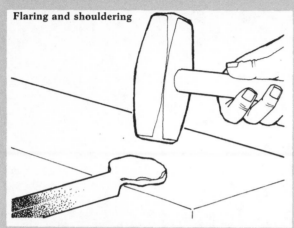

Flaring and shouldering

The flared end is essential for making tools from tongs to screwdrivers and for forming the ends of the towel bar (see p. 264). It can be used as a preliminary step, as in forming such parts as the roll for the hinge leaf (in the accompanying project) or the finger loop of the latch on p. 274.

For most projects, you can form a shoulder at the same time that you flare the workpiece by holding it over the anvil's edge. As the hammer blows spread the metal on the anvil face, they also create a step, the shoulder, at the anvil's edge. The shoulder can serve as a stop in a movable part, such as a door or window latch, or it can simplify the process of forming the flare into a loop.

To make a tapered flare for a chisel or a cut-off hardie, keep the workpiece toward the center of the anvil face, away from the edge.

When flaring, avoid forging any area too thin. It's nearly impossible to thicken the metal evenly once it has been tapered or flared—if you do get it too thin in one place, you may have to discard the piece and start again.

Flaring causes the workpiece to rise up at the edges. If you want a flat shape, work the edges back down by hammering them, but for decorative effect, or utensils such as spoons, you can exaggerate the curve by finishing the hammering in the middle, especially with a ball peen hammer.

4. Spread the split by driving the reheated end over an edge of the anvil. You'll have to strike the hinge-pin socket to do this, so be careful that you don't deform it. The completed angle between the two arms of the hinge leaf should be about 30°.

5. Draw each of the two split arms to a point. To do this, heat one arm and hold it over the inner edge of the anvil. Work the arm with a medium-weight hammer, turning the piece as you work, keeping the taper even and the thickness at ⅛ in. When the first arm is done, repeat the procedure on the second.

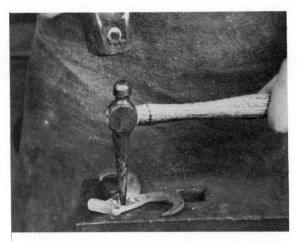

6. Bend the pointed arms over the anvil horn. While holding the rolled end with tongs, place one heated arm of the hinge leaf against the middle of the horn. Hammer-bend the arm against the horn, using a medium-weight hammer. Repeat the process to form the other arm.

7. Work the entire hinge leaf (except the rolled end) to make it as flat and as uniform in thickness as possible. After heating, grasp the rolled end with tongs and hold the hinge body on the anvil. Work carefully with the hammer to avoid denting the hinge surface.

8. Punch three holes in the hinge leaf, either by driving a punch through the leaf into a header die or by punching through the leaf into the anvil's pritchel hole. If you use the pritchel hole, first hammer nearly through one side of the leaf, then flip it over and punch all the way through (this will make a smooth hole). Place one hole in each tapered arm and the third next to the leaf roll.

9. Clean up the edges of the hinge leaf with a file, cutting only on the push stroke.

Brazing and Welding

Brazing and welding are, simply put, ways of joining metal. Knowing how to braze or weld doesn't make you a metalworker, but if you are a complete metalworker, you have welding equipment and know how to use it. There is a variety of relatively inexpensive welding rigs, both gas and electric, on the market. With some reading and more practice, you can master basic techniques to supplement other metalworking skills you may already have. The projects that follow can get you started.

Welding tends to be used as a catchall term. There are dozens of metal-joining techniques, including brazing, that are popularly lumped under this term. In the pages that follow, you'll learn to discern a braze from a weld. And you'll learn how to both braze and weld.

Setting Up Shop

The skills, equipment, and facilities you need for welding depend upon the kind of welding you want to do. There are more than 40 different welding processes in use today, some involving lasers and automated equipment. What's useful for home projects, like those in this book, is smaller scale and less sophisticated—the kind of brazing and welding rigs found in small auto body or machine shops.

There are two basic types of equipment— gas, typified by the oxyacetylene rig, and electric, typified by the arc welder. Either rig can be set up to braze or weld. The gas rig does better at welding lightweight materials, while the arc welder is better with medium-weight and heavyweight materials. Either rig can be used to cut metal, though the gas rig does a much cleaner job of it. The gas rig can be used to heat metal for bending or forging; the arc welder cannot.

You can get either a gas rig or an arc welder for an outlay of $200 to $300. In addition to the basic welding equipment itself, you'll need personal safety gear like goggles and gloves, miscellaneous hand tools, and supplies of welding consumables—gases or electricity, filler rods or electrodes.

In any case, the place to shop is a welding-supply company. These companies are listed in the Yellow Pages, and you shouldn't have difficulty finding one unless you live in a very rural area.

In some communities, welding and welding equipment are regulated, usually under the fire code. The welding process can *start* a fire, obviously, and pressurized gas and oxygen tanks are bombs in a fire. Clear your setup with anyone the law requires.

The work area

Whether you plan to use an arc welder, a gas rig, or both, setting up the work area isn't difficult. It's unlikely that you'll be setting up a shop *just* for welding, the way you *might* set up a place just for blacksmithing. Welding is something you get involved in as an adjunct to metalworking in general. It's likely, in other words, that you'll be making space in your metalworking shop for a welding rig.

The shop should already have a sturdy workbench; ample and accessible storage for your equipment; tools and metal stock; enough space for you to move around your work; and adequate access, so you can move your finished projects out of the shop when they're completed. These are all characteristics of a good welding shop.

To do welding in this shop, obviously, you should have a place to put the arc welder or the gas tanks (or both). An arc welder should have a 230-volt circuit dedicated to it alone.

A metal worktable is a must for fabricating things (as opposed to repair work). Suggestions for making a table are included on page 287.

A fireproof floor is essential. Flying sparks are a part of welding, and there's a chance that one could land on a wooden floor and smolder into a blaze hours later. It's also important to keep scrap wood, rags, and any other flammable material out of the area. To be on the safe side, keep a fire extinguisher handy.

Lighting—Although dim lighting is desirable for blacksmithing—allowing the smith to gauge the temperature of his work by observing the color of the glowing metal—welding is done in normal light. You can usually gauge the state of the work by the light of the torch flame or arc, but as soon as the joint is completed, the workpiece usually has to be repositioned, measured, or cut—all requiring good lighting.

An overhead, double-tube fluorescent fixture, perhaps supplemented by a window or two, provides good area lighting. Position another fixture, either incandescent or fluorescent, over the worktable. A single-bulb fixture equipped with a clamp is a good choice, because it can be positioned exactly where you need more light.

Ventilation—It's not necessary to have an elaborate ventilation system for welding—a window fan will do. Smoke is produced in fairly small quantities. As long as you avoid galvanized metal, which gives off toxic fumes, a fan will clear the air. Only in a closed area, such as a basement, will you have to set up a venting system.

Safety

A safe operation requires more than a clean work area. It's also important to dress the part, to maintain your equipment carefully, and to follow safe work routines.

Working with tools, metal stock, or hoses underfoot is asking for trouble. Working without a helmet or gloves, setting down the torch with the flame left on, leaving the rig unattended before it's completely shut down, even working when you are tired are all risky.

Gas rigs and arc welders have been refined over the years until they are as safe as possible. All that's required to keep your operation accident-free is a commitment to safety combined with common sense. It's worthwhile to establish a little formality in your routines, making safe procedures a habit.

Tools and Equipment

Getting into welding takes a substantial, once-and-done purchase of equipment. You have to buy a welding rig, some supplemental protective gear, and a few supplies. But so long as you've got basic metalworking tools, you've then got everything you will ever need for welding.

The big choice to make, once you've decided

to spend the $200 or $300, is between gas welding and arc welding. Despite the fact that both rigs will perform certain basic operations, they are different, and the choice you make should be based upon the type of work you want to do. If you figure the majority of your projects will involve welding lightweight rods (no thicker than ⅜-in. diameter) or sheets (no heavier than 20-gauge), go with gas. If the majority of your work will involve heavier metals, go with the arc welder.

Gas-welding equipment

Oxygen and a fuel gas are combined in the torch of a gas-welding rig to create a flame hot enough to melt steel. The basic gas rig, then, must include containers of the two gases, the torch, hoses to connect the gas containers to the torch, and some apparatus to regulate the gas flow. As

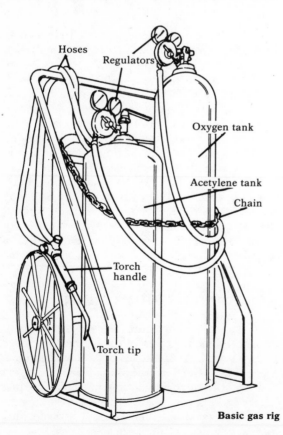

Hoses
Regulators
Oxygen tank
Acetylene tank
Chain
Torch handle
Torch tip

Basic gas rig

noted previously, such a rig, together with accessories and safety gear, can be purchased for a few hundred dollars.

The fuel gas you use can be acetylene (the most widely used fuel gas), Mapp gas (a proprietary acetylene product), or propane. Propane is too cool-burning to be satisfactory for welding. Mapp burns hotter than propane but less hot than acetylene. Its advantage is that it is economical, since more Mapp can be forced into a given container than acetylene.

You can purchase or rent tanks, which come in a variety of sizes.

The tanks of a gas brazing and welding rig must be secured in an upright position. If the rig isn't likely to be moved, you can chain the tanks to a sturdy post or to a wall. For more mobility, specially designed hand trucks are available to hold the tanks.

A basic rig—Every welding equipment manufacturer markets a basic gas-welding outfit, which includes tank regulators, hoses, a torch handle and an assortment of tips, perhaps a pair of goggles, a friction lighter, and a multipurpose wrench. Many outfits even include an assortment of filler rods.

The regulators control the release of gas from the tanks so there's a suitable working pressure at the torch tip. There is one regulator for each tank, and each regulator has two gauges, one showing the tank pressure and the other showing the working pressure. The correct working pressure varies with the type of fuel gas and the size of the tip opening. To adjust your regulators properly, check the specifications that come with your welding rig.

Hoses connect the regulators to the torch. The hoses are color coded and are threaded opposite to one another to prevent mix-ups. The fuel-gas line is red and screws counterclockwise into both the regulator and the torch handle. The oxygen line is green or black and screws clockwise into the oxygen regulator and the torch.

The torch handle has two small valves for fine adjustment of the gas pressure, allowing you to get exactly the kind of flame required for a particular job. The torch valves can also be used

A Steel Worktable

Whether you use an arc welder or a gas rig, you need a sturdy worktable. With a stable, metal-topped table, a half-dozen firebricks, and an assortment of clamps, you'll be able to set up all your projects for safe, easy welding. No awkward welding positions—no setups tumbling out of alignment at inopportune moments.

The table you need is a table you can make: a 2-ft. sq., 33-in.-high table with a ¼-in.-thick top. The project uses fairly thick steel, so you almost *have* to do the welding with an arc welder. You can try using a gas rig, but the welding can be troublesome, since the metals will act as heat sinks, making it difficult to concentrate the proper heat at the weld point.

Start by making two identical frames—one for the support of the top, one to support a shelf. To make each one, weld two 19½-in. lengths of ⅛-in.-thick ½ x 1½-in. steel channel to two 18½-in. lengths of the channel, forming a square. With an arc welder, use ⅛-in. E 6013 coated electrodes at 90-100 amps to make these and all other welds.

Cut four 33-in. lengths of ¼-in.-thick 2 x 2-in. angle iron for the legs.

Since the inside corner of the angle iron is rounded rather than square, you should grind a matching arc on the four corners of each support frame, so you will have a reasonably snug fit of leg against frame. After rounding off the corners, tack-weld one frame to the 2-ft.-sq. top plate. Use tack welds, since full-length welds could easily warp the assembly.

Clamp the legs to the outside corners of the top frame. Use C-clamps or locking-grip pliers for this. Now clamp the shelf to the legs, 12¾ in. from the leg ends. Use a framing square to make sure the assembly is square and true. Tack-weld the assembly together, clean the slag from the welds, remove the clamps, and run full beads at each joint of leg and frame.

Weld a scrap of ¼-in. steel plate to the end of each leg to support adjustable feet. Drill a ³⁄₁₆-in. hole through each of these supports. Using a ¼-20 NC tap in a standard tap wrench, thread each hole (see p. 310). Turn a hex nut onto each of four ¼-20 NC furniture

levelers, then turn the levelers into the holes in the supports.

Drill a ³⁄₁₆-in. hole through the top edge of each side of the shelf support frame. Cut a 19⅜-in. square of ½-in. plywood, lay it on the shelf support frame, and secure it with a ¾-in. #8 panhead wood screw driven through each hole.

Clean the assembly with solvent. Paint the legs, shelf, and support frames—but not the tabletop—with rust-resistant paint.

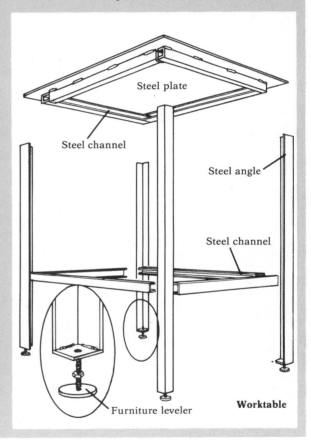

Steel plate

Steel channel

Steel angle

Steel channel

Furniture leveler

Worktable

to shut off the rig for short periods, such as when you are repositioning the workpiece.

The torch tips, which screw onto the handle, are easily interchanged and are normally hand-tightened. Having several tips makes the rig more versatile.

A hobby rig—An alternative to the equipment described above is the hobbyist's kind of rig sold in hardware stores and building-supply centers. These use oxygen and a fuel gas in tanks the same size as the propane tanks used for soldering. The limitation of these units is the oxygen. An oxygen cylinder lasts only about 20 minutes in continuous use. It doesn't take long for that to add up to a lot of cash. The hobbyists' rigs work well for brazing and are okay for occasional small repairs.

Filler rods—Filler rods used in gas brazing and welding provide the additional material needed to form a weld bead. For brazing mild steel, copper, or cast iron, the rod most often used is brass, a copper-zinc alloy. Rods made of bronze (a copper-tin alloy) are used less often, but in common usage, both brass and bronze rods are referred to as bronze rods.

The filler rod in brazing and braze welding melts before the parent metal and bonds to it, if the joint is clean, fluxed, and heated to the right temperature. The filler in this case provides all of the strength of the joint.

In fusion welding, the filler rod should be similar in composition to the parent metal—for the projects described later on, this would be mild steel.

Flux—The metal surfaces exposed to the air combine with oxygen to form oxides that interfere with brazing or welding. As metal is heated, oxidation occurs more rapidly, compounding the problem.

These oxides must be removed by flux. Use flux designed for the metal and filler rods you are working with. The correct flux will melt before either the filler rod or the oxides present, lifting the oxides as they melt and carrying them away just before the metals melt.

Mild steel does not require flux-coated filler rods, because the oxides on it happen to melt before the steel itself.

Arc-welding equipment

The alternative to gas welding is arc welding. Simplistically, the arc welder uses a controlled electrical short circuit to melt the metals being welded.

The basic arc welder—There is a wide variety of arc welders manufactured. The unit you buy should plug into a standard 230-volt outlet, just like a clothes dryer or a kitchen range. It should have a power range of 40 to roughly 225 amps, and it should be an AC (alternating current) device. Usually, such welders will have a knob or crank to adjust the amperage setting, an on-off switch, and two heavy cables. One, the work cable, terminates in a ground clamp that is attached to the work. The other, the electrode cable, terminates in the electrode holder. What the device does is convert your household's high voltage-low amperage power into low voltage-high amperage power.

To use it, you plug it in, adjust the amperage setting, connect the ground clamp to the work, insert an electrode in the holder, turn it on, strike an arc, and run the bead.

Just as with the gas equipment, manufacturers usually have a welding outfit available, which includes everything you need to get started, including a selection of electrodes. The outfit will include the basic unit, the necessary cables, an electrode holder and ground clamp, even a welder's helmet.

Carbon arc torch—An option you might consider buying is a carbon arc torch, which you can use

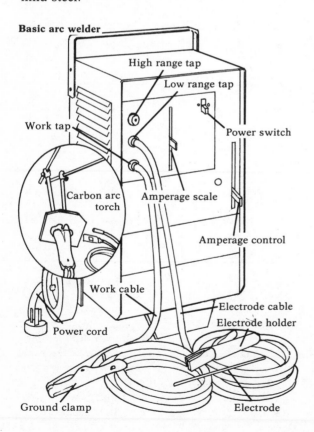

Basic arc welder

High range tap

Low range tap

Work tap

Power switch

Carbon arc torch

Amperage scale

Amperage control

Work cable

Electrode cable

Electrode holder

Power cord

Ground clamp

Electrode

to braze or braze weld. This device has two cables connected to it (one of which is the ground cable) and holds two carbon electrodes.

In use, the electricity arcs from one carbon electrode to the other, generating enough heat for brazing, but not enough for welding.

Electrodes—The filler rods used in arc welding are called electrodes. They vary in diameter from $\frac{1}{16}$ in. to $\frac{5}{16}$ in. The metal you are welding should dictate what diameter electrode you use; the diameter should roughly match the metal's thickness.

The electrodes are coated with flux, which floats impurities to the surface, depositing them in a layer atop the bead. This slag has to be chipped off.

Electrodes are coded to indicate the strength of their core metal, the weld position, and the type of current they are for. The salesman at the welding-supply company will help you select an appropriate electrode. The most common for general welding with mild steel is E6013, a good all-purpose rod for the beginner.

Protective outfits

When brazing and welding with gas, you're working with a very hot flame and extremely flammable gas. The process is often accompanied by showers of sparks, which are molten bits of metal splattering away from the weld.

When arc welding, there are the showers of sparks, and, though there's no gas or open flame, there is an intense glare, which produces enough ultraviolet light to give you a sunburn and damage your eyes.

With these kinds of hazards, safety gear is very important.

Begin with the clothes you wear, selecting fairly heavy garments of cotton or wool. Don't wear synthetic fabrics—they melt when exposed to high temperatures. Pockets, cuffs, and the like can catch sparks, so avoid clothes that have them if you can. Wear heavy, high-top boots.

If you will be doing a lot of cutting or fusion welding or any arc welding—these generate the most sparks—you may want to invest in a welder's cap and a leather apron. The sparks, you'll find, will riddle your clothes with pinholes; the

apron will protect them and help them last a bit longer. Professional welders wear special leather garments, but for the occasional welder, these may be a questionable investment.

On your hands wear gloves, preferably leather welder's gloves with wide gauntlets. *Always* wear these gloves for arc welding. While they aren't mandatory for gas welding, it won't hurt to wear them.

When using a gas rig, *always* wear welder's goggles or an appropriately tinted full-face shield, both to screen the ultraviolet glare of welding and to block spatters of hot flux or molten metal. The goggles have interchangeable lenses. Use #4 shades for brazing and light welding and #6 shades for heavy welding (pieces $\frac{1}{8}$ in. thick or more). The face shield will probably be more comfortable for you if you wear glasses.

For arc welding, get an arc-welder's helmet to protect your eyes and face. This heat-resistant mask shields your neck, face, and head. It has a

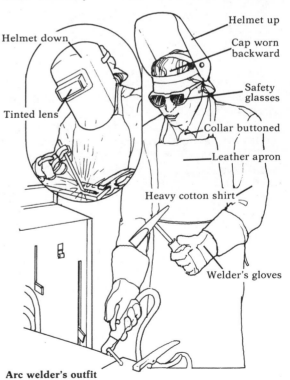

Arc welder's outfit

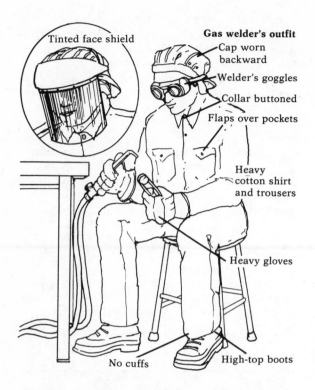

Tinted face shield

Gas welder's outfit
Cap worn backward
Welder's goggles
Collar buttoned
Flaps over pockets
Heavy cotton shirt and trousers
Heavy gloves
No cuffs
High-top boots

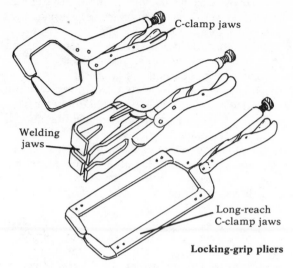

C-clamp jaws

Welding jaws

Long-reach C-clamp jaws

Locking-grip pliers

small, rectangular port that accepts interchangeable lenses. Use a #10 shade for welding with electrodes up to 5/32 in. and a #12 shade for thicker electrodes. Since the lenses are practically opaque under normal light—you can see the arc just fine through them—the helmet pivots on its headband so you can flip it up to see all work other than actual welding. It's a good idea to wear safety glasses under the helmet; cleaning the weld sends hot bits of slag flying.

Tools

Many of the other tools required for brazing and welding are found in typical home shops—pliers, hammers, cold chisels, and an electric drill with an assortment of bits and a wire-brush attachment.

Other common tools useful to the welder are locking-grip pliers, files, and C-clamps. Locking-grip pliers are invaluable for clamping pieces together until they can be brazed or welded. It's usually easier to get a good grip with these pliers than with C-clamps, although C-clamps can hold larger pieces, making them good for holding stock to the worktable. Files remove burrs and round off sharp edges of metal stock.

A hacksaw or a saber saw with a metal-cutting blade is essential for cutting lengths of stock to size. The saber saw can also be used to cut irregular shapes from heavy-gauge metal (for example, the figures of a youngster and a kite used in the weather vane project, p. 316). For cutting sheet metal, you'll need heavy-duty tin snips; for wire or thin rods, side-cutting pliers.

Either a bench grinder or a portable disk sander-grinder is an asset, though in a budget-minded operation, a file or two can do much the same work—primarily shaping, beveling, and smoothing metal.

For measuring and marking, several tools are useful. A soapstone pencil allows you to make layout markings that won't burn off in the heat of the torch or arc. A compass helps in making curves and circles. A try square and a framing square help keep layout markings straight and in proper alignment. A sliding T-bevel allows you to match and transfer angles. And, of course, you'll need a tape measure or folding rule.

Basic Procedures

Certain basics are intrinsic to all kinds of welding: definitions, the types of joints, the types of welds, and the weld positions.

The dictionary defines welding as being the uniting of metals by heating them to their melting points and allowing them to flow together. And this is, strictly speaking, what welding is. But an expert will distinguish between forge welding and fusion welding. Forge welding involves the application of pressure to cause or help the molten metals to coalesce. This is what a blacksmith does when he heats two pieces of metal white hot, then pounds them together into one with a hammer on an anvil. In fusion welding, there is no pressure. Rather, the pieces melt and form a molten puddle. A filler rod held in the puddle also melts, helping to fill the seam between the pieces.

Brazing, the other metal-joining process covered in this section, has a catchall quality. What many welders call brazing is technically braze welding.

Brazing is a soldering process, wherein metals are joined by a nonferrous filler that has a melting point above 800°F. but below that of the metals being joined and that fills the joint through capillary attraction. (In the process known as soldering, the filler has a melting point *below* 800°F.) In braze welding, the filler does not spread through the joint by capillary attraction. In neither brazing nor braze welding do the parent metals melt. But in both cases the filler metal does, bonding firmly to the pieces being joined.

Braze welding is used to join the same kind of joints that might be fusion welded. The joint gains its strength from the adhesion of the brazing rod to the surfaces of the joint, rather than from the coalescence of the parent metals.

Fusion and braze welding are sometimes used together when two nearby joints must be joined. The first is fusion welded and the second braze welded. Since the temperature required to braze weld the second joint is less than the melting temperature of the first, there is little chance of damaging the first joint. If both were braze welded or the second fusion welded, the first joint might be weakened by the heat generated in making the second.

Brazing or braze welding must be used when dissimilar metals are joined, because the parent metals, having different melting temperatures, are nearly impossible to join by welding—there won't be good penetration in both pieces. By brazing the pieces with a filler rod whose melting temperature is lower than either of them, however, a good union can be achieved.

Weld types—There are but five types of welds: bead, fillet, groove, plug, and tack.

The tack weld is used primarily in setup; the metal parts are welded together at intervals so they'll stay in alignment while you run the continuous weld. The bead weld is *the* basic weld, the one you should practice when you first take up welding. It is simply a single-pass deposit of weld metal—the bead. The fillet weld is a single or multiple pass of weld metal—one or more beads—in any sort of right-angle joint. The groove weld is one or more beads in any sort of groove, such as that formed in a beveled butt joint. The plug weld is essentially a bead that fills a hole or slot.

Weld positions—The weld position is determined by the orientation of the joint seam. It's either flat, horizontal, vertical, or overhead. In the flat position, the joint is horizontal (at least roughly it is; there will always be welds that don't fit the strict definitions), and the welding is done on the upper

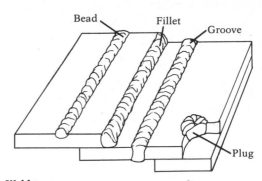

Weld types

Joint types

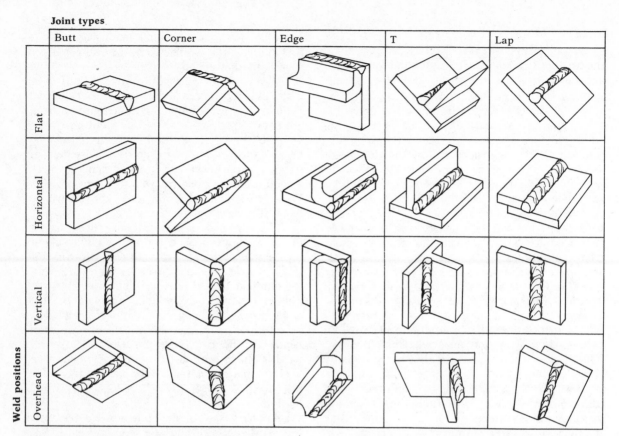

		Butt	Corner	Edge	T	Lap
Weld positions	Flat					
	Horizontal					
	Vertical					
	Overhead					

side. Conversely, the overhead position also has a horizontal joint, but it is welded from the underside. The horizontal position comes into play when a vertical piece is being joined to a horizontal or another vertical piece, and the vertical position when two vertical pieces are being joined.

Joint types—There are five basic types of joints in welding: the butt, the corner, the edge, the T, and the lap. All the joints you make will be variations of these.

Operating a gas rig

Setting up the equipment involves attaching the regulators to the fuel-gas and oxygen tanks, then adding in turn the hoses, the torch handle, and a torch tip. The gas pressure must be set for the tip being used, and the ratio of fuel gas to oxygen must be balanced. Each manufacturer provides specific instructions for setting up its equipment, so follow the directions provided with the equipment you have.

Setting up—Set the regulators to the working pressure recommended for the tip you are using. To do this, first be sure the regulator screws are closed (counterclockwise). Then open the tank valves—a one-quarter turn for the fuel gas, full open for the oxygen. Open the torch fuel valve (counterclockwise), then slowly open the fuel-gas regulator screw (clockwise) until the working-pressure gauge registers the required pressure. Close the fuel torch valve.

Open the oxygen torch valve; next, open the oxygen regulator screw until the correct working pressure is reached; then close the oxygen torch valve. You are now ready to light the torch. The regulator valves remain as they are set (unless you change tips), and the flame is adjusted by means of the torch valves.

Adjusting the flame—To light the torch, open the torch's fuel valve three-quarters of a turn, hold the tip about 1 inch from a friction lighter—*never a match*—and snap the lighter. If the flame smokes, increase the fuel-gas pressure until it burns clean. Slowly add oxygen by opening the torch's oxygen valve until you get a neutral flame.

The three basic flame types are: reducing (caused by excess fuel gas), oxidizing (too much oxygen), and the balanced, neutral flame, ideal for most welding. The reducing flame is also called the carburizing or the carbonizing flame.

As you begin adding oxygen to the flame, a brilliant white cone will form at the base of the flame, next to the torch-tip opening. The flame itself (or flame envelope) is green blue. This is a strongly reducing flame. Add more oxygen and a rounded cone will form inside the white one, indicating only a slight excess of fuel gas. Add a little more oxygen and you'll get the neutral flame, with a rounded blue inner cone. The sharp white cone, caused by excess fuel gas, has disappeared.

If you continue to increase the oxygen, the flame envelope shortens, and the inner cone takes on a purple tinge. A slightly oxidizing flame is hard to distinguish from a neutral one, but it does yield a weaker weld, and it does tend to burn the metal more readily. (A reducing flame introduces carbon into a weld, making it brittle, so it shouldn't be used for fusion welding. But because it is more forgiving of slight overheating, it may be the best brazing and braze welding flame for the novice to use.)

Backfire and flashback—There are two common failures in gas welding: backfire and flashback, which is actually prolonged backfire. In each situation, the flame is lost with a loud pop. What has happened is that the flame has backed up into the torch tip, disappearing from view. Though startling, backfire is harmless. If it hasn't resulted from a dirty tip or incorrect pressure, the most likely cause is touching the torch tip to the workpiece or table.

Flashback has the same causes as backfire, and it begins the same way, but the fire continues to burn inside the torch or hose with a shrill hissing. Immediately shut off the oxygen at the torch, then the fuel. If there's no apparent damage, check for leaks, then blow oxygen through the system for a few seconds to clear out soot before starting up again.

Shutting down—First turn off the fuel-gas valve in the torch handle, then the oxygen torch, turning both clockwise. Next, close both tank valves (clockwise). To exhaust the pressurized gas remaining in the regulator and hoses, open the torch valves. Finally, release pressure on the regulator diaphragms by turning the adjusting screws counterclockwise until you feel no resistance.

Brazing

A good process for the novice to start with is brazing. Brazing will help you get familiar with the equipment—gas or electric—but won't force

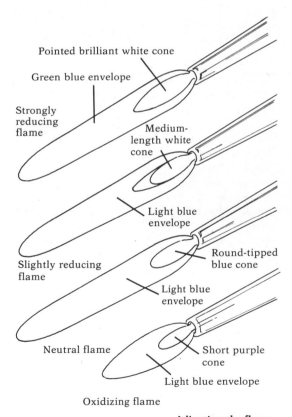

Pointed brilliant white cone

Green blue envelope

Strongly reducing flame

Medium-length white cone

Light blue envelope

Slightly reducing flame

Round-tipped blue cone

Light blue envelope

Neutral flame

Short purple cone

Light blue envelope

Oxidizing flame

Adjusting the flame

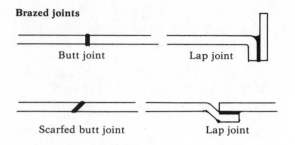

Brazed joints

Butt joint Lap joint

Scarfed butt joint Lap joint

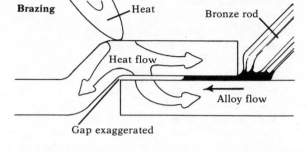

Brazing — Heat

Bronze rod

Heat flow

Alloy flow

Gap exaggerated

you to worry about synchronizing different hand motions. You merely have to heat the joint evenly—it does take some practice—and feed the filler rod into the seam.

Brazing depends upon capillary attraction to draw the molten filler rod into the joint. The surfaces must therefore be smooth, very close together, and perfectly clean.

Brazing is useful for joining pieces that require more strength than soldering can provide. For example, it is used to join pieces of sheet metal where it isn't possible to fold a seam (in which case solder would suffice to make the joint).

There are only two types of joints in brazing: lap and butt. The lap joint, largely because of its greater surface area, is the stronger of the two. Sometimes a butt joint is scarfed—that is, the mating surfaces are given matching bevels to increase their surface areas in an attempt to make the joint stronger.

The surfaces to be joined must be very clean and they must meet closely. The strength of the joint falls rapidly as the size of the gap increases, the optimum being only four-thousandths of an inch.

Clean the surfaces to be joined with a crocus cloth or fine steel wool. Avoid grinding wheels or files when preparing joints for brazing; they leave scratches that interfere with the capillary attraction of the fillers.

Using a brush, coat the surfaces with paste flux. Do this as soon as you've cleaned them. Clamp the pieces firmly together and heat them.

If you use a gas torch as the heat source, adjust the flame to neutral or very slightly reducing, and play it evenly over the work. If you are

using a carbon arc torch, adjust the gap between the carbons following the manufacturer's recommendations, turn on the welder, and ignite the arc by bringing the carbons together. Play the arc over the work, much as you would a gas flame.

When the work is a dull red, and the flux has a clear, watery look, remove the torch. Touch a preheated, fluxed filler rod to the parent metal. The rod should melt immediately and be drawn into the joint. If it does not melt readily, heat the joint a little longer.

Be sure to heat the pieces evenly, because otherwise the rod will be drawn toward the hotter piece, weakening the joint. Be sure, too, not to overheat the joint. Keep an eye on the flux and when it looks right, start testing the temperature of the metal with the filler rod.

Braze welding

Braze welding is a little quicker and a little easier to do than fusion welding. It requires you to grapple with the tiny torch movements that

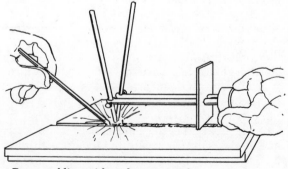

Braze welding with carbon arc torch

fusion welding involves, and it requires you to synchronize these movements with the manipulation of the filler rod that fusion welding also involves. But it doesn't require you to create a molten puddle and, using the torch flame, push it steadily across the joint, a process that's the heart of fusion welding.

Braze welding avoids problems such as warping or distortions of the metal that may be associated with the high temperatures required for fusion welding.

Successful braze welding depends upon careful joint preparation. Because the filler rod can't bond to the parent metal if there are oxides or other foreign material present, the surfaces must be clean and smooth and must match each other evenly. Clean the adjoining surfaces with a wire brush until the metal is shiny. If it is to be a flat weld, position the work with one end of the seam slightly elevated so the molten filler won't run ahead of the torch flame or arc.

The joint doesn't need to be fluxed, but the filler rod does. Either use coated rods or flux your own. Heat the rod in the torch flame—don't melt it, of course—and dip it into the flux. The flux will stick to the rod.

Use a neutral or slightly reducing flame with a gas torch, or the electrode tip gap recommended by the manufacturer with a carbon arc torch.

Hold either torch so the flame (or arc) plays over the metal, with the gas torch tip cocked at an angle of 45° to 60°. When using the forehand technique, it should point, roughly, in the direction you will weld. To heat the joint evenly, you must keep the flame moving in tiny circles—dime-size is too big. The cone is the hottest part of the flame; you want to play it close to the metal, but not touching it. Heat until the metal glows dull red.

The parent metals must now be tinned by rubbing the end of the filler rod over the joint. The filler should spread uniformly over the joint. If the metal is not hot enough, the filler will form drops that don't adhere to the surface; if the metal is too hot, the filler will boil and smoke as it melts.

After the joint is tinned, move the flame back to the beginning of the joint, continuing to play it in the tiny circles. Feed the fluxed filler into the seam, creating a little puddle. Move the torch along the seam, continuing the circular motion and continuing to feed fluxed filler rod into the puddle. The finished bead should be a slight ridge of bronze, of uniform height and width, marked with even ripples. A white residue on the weld is a sign of overheating.

If necessary, that is, if the metal is thick, build a second bead atop the first, being careful to clean the initial bead with a wire brush.

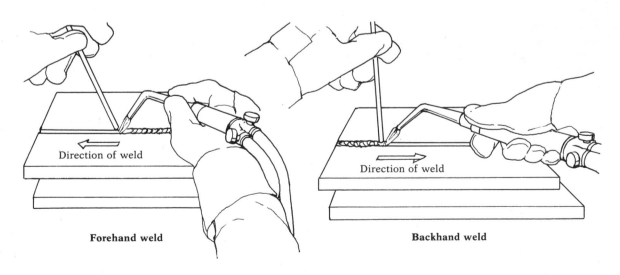

Forehand weld   Direction of weld

Backhand weld   Direction of weld

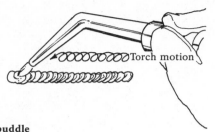

Carrying the puddle

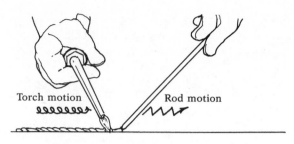

Don't expect too much of your first efforts. Lay in a supply of scrap metal and filler rods and practice braze welding until you are able to run consistently smooth beads.

Fusion welding

While a welder might tell you that the key to a good weld is proper penetration of the weld into the joint, as a novice you'll discover that the true key is a steady hand. When you fusion weld, you actually melt the parent metals, add a little reinforcement metal in the form of filler rod and, with the action of the torch flame, shape the weld into a rippled ridge called a bead.

The first skill you must learn is carrying the puddle. Just as you played the torch flame in tiny, tidy circles to heat the joint in braze welding, so must you do it to fusion weld. Play the flame at the head of the seam until you have a molten puddle, one no bigger than your little fingernail.

Once you've established the puddle, start inching it along the seam, still oscillating the torch. One end of the puddle will cool enough to harden and the other will take on new molten metal. With practice, you'll learn to carry the puddle, controlling its size and its movement. It takes a steady hand. If you tarry too long at one spot, the puddle will get too big and the flame will burn right through. If you progress too quickly, the puddle will shrink, perhaps even disappear. In the first situation, you have too much penetration; in the second, you have too little.

Start your fusion-welding training by practicing puddle control. Adjust the torch to a neutral flame. Hold the torch so the inner cone of the flame is just about ⅛ inch above the metal, the

Fusion welding choreography

torch tip held at a 45° to 60° angle to the metal. Play the flame in those little circles. As soon as the molten pool develops, start slowly across the metal, creating a bead. Your first beads will probably be somewhat blotchy and uneven. But once you've learned to carry the puddle, you must introduce the filler rod to the operation.

Adding filler to the pool requires you to introduce a new motion to the torch choreography, that being a very slight lifting and lowering of the flame coordinated with the dipping of the rod into the molten puddle.

To add unoxidized filler to the weld, the filler

Gas-welded beads

Poor—erratic movement, insufficient heat

Poor—erratic movement, too much heat

Good—fairly even movement, proper heat

Excellent—even movement, proper heat

rod must be dipped directly into the puddle. You can't just hold the rod in the puddle, for this will yield an excess of filler. You must develop a sense for how much filler to add, and you must add that amount by dipping the rod into the puddle. When you lift the rod out of the puddle, don't lift it out of the flame's envelope. You raise and lower the rod by a fraction of an inch, and you should bob the flame the same fraction.

This too takes practice to perfect, so set up a scrap plate and run beads, using filler rod. After a few beads, you'll be ready to weld two scraps together.

A good weld is smooth, with small ripples caused by the torch movement. It is slightly higher than the surface of the parent metal. This reinforcement gives extra support and because of it, the weld can be stronger than the parent metal.

Arc welding

The procedures for arc welding are similar to those of gas welding, but there's a considerable difference in the reaction time. The second you strike an arc, the steel is melting, and a puddle forms immediately amid a shower of sparks.

Successful arc welds require proper amperage settings, electrodes of the right size, and a rate of movement of the puddle that balances the amperage.

The electrode tip should be held within 1/8 to 1/4 inch of the work. As the arc lengthens, the arc voltage increases, dissipating heat and electrical energy at the expense of weld quality. An overlong arc whistles and hisses.

If you get it too close, the arc begins to make a sputtering sound. The resulting low-voltage arc creates a "cold" bead that swells above the work surface, with little penetration. The electrode is apt to freeze to the work.

A good arc produces a steady, sharp, crackling sound, yielding a smooth weld. If the arc is right, but the current (amperage) is set too high, the arc will make sharp, explosive, crackling noises. The result is a red-hot electrode end and splatter around the weld. If the current is too low, you'll hear a low-frequency, pulsating sound and get a shallow weld.

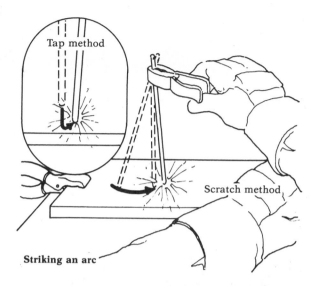

Tap method

Scratch method

Striking an arc

Learning to run a smooth bead requires some practice and experimentation with the various arc lengths and settings, but once you have heard the sound of a good arc and seen the results, it isn't too hard to duplicate.

Strike the arc by sharply tapping or scratching the work with the electrode tip. You must immediately lift the tip just enough to establish the arc—about 1/4 inch is plenty. If you pull up too much, the arc will break. If you touch the work and don't pull up, the tip will stick, and you'll have to twist it free.

Just as you have to play the flame in gas welding, so too must you play the electrode tip in

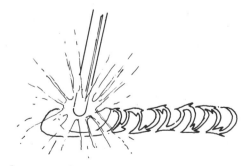

Electrode movement

Making a bead weld **Making a fillet weld**

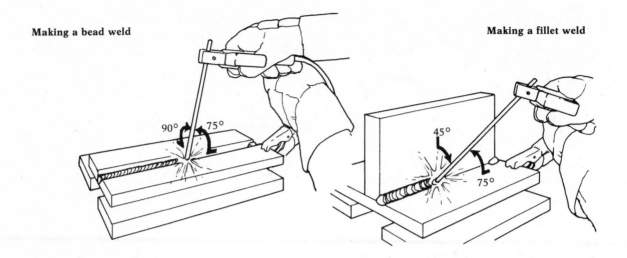

arc welding. Generally accepted motions include a waver of about ½ inch, either parallel to or arcing back and forth across the joint. Start at one end of the joint and oscillate the electrode in a tight, rhythmic motion. Carry the puddle along the joint by steadily moving the electrode tip.

To make the process a tad more challenging, the electrode gets shorter and shorter as the bead is run. You must continually compensate for its change of length to maintain the arc.

When the electrode has been reduced to a 2-inch stub, break the arc and clamp a new electrode in the holder. Before resuming the weld, you must chip the slag off the bead and scrub it with a wire brush. Strike an arc about ½ inch beyond the end of the bead. Carry the puddle back to the bead, then reverse directions and complete the weld.

Cutting

Cutting is a specialty of the gas rig. With a cutting tip, your home-shop rig will slice through plates and angle irons with ease.

The cutting attachment screws onto the standard torch handle. It has an adjustment knob for oxygen and a lever that, when depressed, releases a jet of pure oxygen through a center hole in the tip. The literature that comes with the attachment will list the recommended pressure settings.

Arc-welded beads

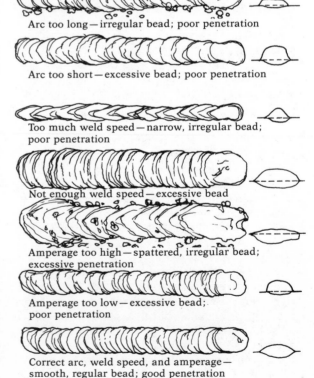

Arc too long—irregular bead; poor penetration

Arc too short—excessive bead; poor penetration

Too much weld speed—narrow, irregular bead; poor penetration

Not enough weld speed—excessive bead

Amperage too high—spattered, irregular bead; excessive penetration

Amperage too low—excessive bead; poor penetration

Correct arc, weld speed, and amperage— smooth, regular bead; good penetration

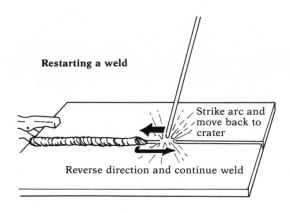

Restarting a weld

Strike arc and move back to crater

Reverse direction and continue weld

To use the device, first set the tank regulators to the desired working pressures. Open the oxygen valve on the torch handle a good full turn (though not necessarily fully open) and the fuel-gas valve a half turn. Light the torch. Using the valve on the cutting attachment, adjust the flame to neutral. Press the cutting lever, and, if necessary, readjust the valve to get a neutral cutting flame. It should have a consistent-size center streak. Release the lever.

Now hold the torch over the edge of the piece you want to cut. The tip should be about ½ inch above the metal, depending upon the tip. When the spot begins to melt, slowly press the cutting lever and raise the tip a fraction of an inch. The flame will blow right through the metal, and you can slowly move the torch, cutting the metal.

An arc welder *can* be used to cut sheet metal roughly, though the process isn't necessarily recommended. It is neither efficient nor pretty, but it will sever the metal. What you do is turn up the amperage as high as it will go and strike an arc, as though you were going to weld. The arc will simply burn through the metal. The edges will be rough, and the process won't work with metal that's too heavy, but in an occasional pinch, it can be done.

Safety

Before you move on to the projects, another word or two on safety is in order. There are specific hazards involved in the use of gas rigs and arc welders, but with proper care and caution, you should never run into trouble. The usual safety admonitions apply to welding as they do to all metalworking activities. If you follow the various caveats that have been presented here, if you follow the recommendations of the maker of your welding gear, if you use your common sense, you can make your welding experience an enjoyable, productive, and injury-free one.

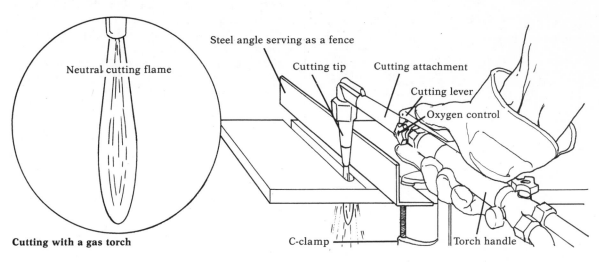

Neutral cutting flame

Steel angle serving as a fence

Cutting tip

Cutting attachment

Cutting lever

Oxygen control

Cutting with a gas torch

C-clamp

Torch handle

Brazed Stool

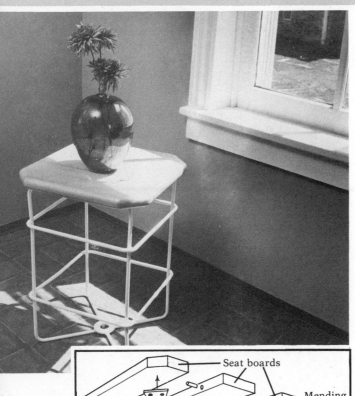

This utility stool has a quite contemporary design. It has a white pine seat mounted on a framework constructed of ⅜-inch-diameter steel rod. The framework is painted with enamel; the seat is given a natural finish.

It is an excellent project for the beginning welder, since it uses only brazed and braze welded joints. These are the easiest joints in the welder's repertoire. Moreover, the load on the stool is borne by the steel rods rather than the joints. Even if a joint should fail, the stool won't collapse.

Fabricating the framework introduces you to the ins and outs of bending heated stock. Every metalworker should master bending, and this project will give you a lot of practice. The bending here is done on a bending jig constructed from a length of 2 × 4 and several stubs of pipe. The jig will ensure that the bends are uniformly spaced, but it won't ensure that they are properly positioned in relation to the rod ends. *You* must ensure that by clamping them to the jig in the proper alignment.

Making the seat involves fairly basic woodworking skills, which are covered in the first section of this book, Furnishings to Make with Wood.

There are ways to personalize the project. You can boost the height of the stool from 18 inches to 30 inches or more to make a bar stool. To do this, modify the bending jig and use longer rods to make the legs. Add another leg support, too.

Another variation would be to cover the seat with foam padding and fabric.

Finally, you can make a set of stools. If you do try this, make one stool completely to get a feel for the entire process. Then make the others assembly-line fashion, first doing the bending, then doing the brazing and braze welding.

However you decide to approach this project, it's a perfect one for the welding beginner.

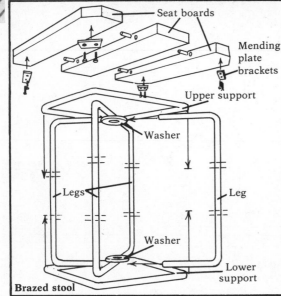

Brazed stool

What you will need

2 pcs. ⅜-in.-dia. mild steel rod, 48''
4 pcs. ⅜-in.-dia. mild steel rod, 30⅜''
2 pcs. 1½'' × 14-ga. round steel tubing, 4''
3 pcs. 2 × 6 clear white pine, 15''
1 pc. 2 × 4, 2'
1 pc. hardwood dowel, ½'' × 8'' (see step 8)
8 #10 sheet-metal screws, ¾''
2 machine bolts with washers and nuts, ¼'' × 4''
2 ³⁄₁₆-in.-thick ungalvanized flat washers,
   2½-in.-dia.
4 mending plates, ⅝'' × 2½''
white or yellow glue
paint thinner
metal primer
spray enamel
polyurethane
handsaw
hacksaw
router
drill
jointer or jointer plane
doweling jig
adjustable wrenches
file
C-clamps
bar clamps
hand screws
flux
¼-in. brazing rods
gas-welding rig and safety equipment

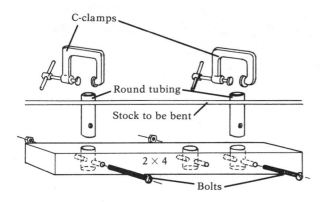

Bending jig

Step-by-step instructions
Making the bending jig

1. Drill three 1½-in.-dia. holes through the face of a 2-ft. length of 2 × 4, centering the holes between the edges. Position one hole near one end of the 2 × 4, then position the others 10⁷⁄₁₆ in. and 14½ in. from the first, measuring center to center. Use a spade bit and a ¼-in. electric drill to bore the holes.

2. Insert a 4-in. stub of 1½-in. × 14-ga. round steel tubing into two of the holes in the 2 × 4. Adjust the tubing so it is flush with one face of the board. Then drill a ¼-in. hole into the edge of the 2 × 4 at each tube, boring completely through the 2 × 4 and the tube. Move one of the tubes to the third hole and repeat the process.

3. Bolt the tubes in place with ¼ × 4-in. machine bolts with washers and nuts. Tighten the bolts with a pair of adjustable wrenches.

Bending Stock

Even the most elementary metalworking projects involve bending metal. For projects using lightweight stocks, the metal can be clamped in a vise and bent by hand. But if the stock is too heavy, it will have to be heated to make the metal plastic enough to bend.

The critical first step in any bending is layout. The location of the bend usually is important, and since the outer edge of the bend stretches while the inner edge compresses, the marking for the point of the bend must be exact. Always measure along the centerline of the stock. With square-edged stock—bars, squares, channels—use a try square to carry the mark across all dimensions of the stock. A felt tip marker is okay for cold-bending, but if the stock is to be heated, use a soapstone marker or a tool, like a cold chisel or a hacksaw, that will nick the metal visibly. For rods, you can use a pipe cutter to score the circumference.

For cold-bending, clamp the work to a sturdy workbench or in a vise with the mark just shy of the fulcrum point. Grasp the metal and bend. If you want to create a curve, rather than a right-angle bend, use a pipe as a form.

Heating metal for hot bending can be done with a propane torch, but if you've got a gas-welding rig, use it. It will bring the stock to the proper temperature much quicker. Just don't clamp the work to a wooden table; the table may catch fire.

To make the bend, heat the stock at the center of the mark. It's important to allow the heat to penetrate completely through for a smooth, accurate bend. If possible, play the flame on alternating sides of the stock. When the area glows cherry red, pause for 15-20 seconds to allow the heat to penetrate, then make the bend.

On freehand bends, complete only three-fourths of the bend before examining the curve to see whether it will match the desired shape. If the bend is on target, reheat at the same spot and complete. If it isn't right, compensate by reheating the bend closer to the desired location of the curve. Since the metal will weaken if you heat it more than three or four times, try to get a good fit the first time.

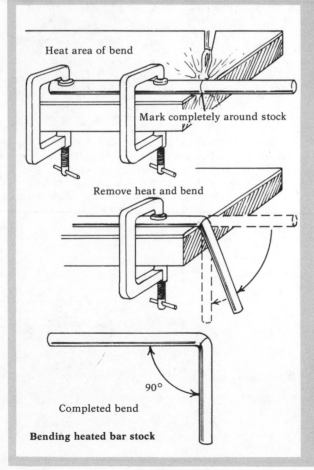

Heat area of bend

Mark completely around stock

Remove heat and bend

90°

Completed bend

Bending heated bar stock

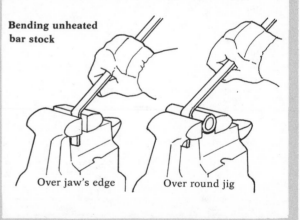

Bending unheated bar stock

Over jaw's edge   Over round jig

In some situations, especially where several pieces must be given matching bends, you should make a bending jig. A length of pipe can serve as a simple jig. A more sophisticated jig might consist of several pieces of pipe bolted to a stout board. Be sure the jig is sturdy enough to bear the pressure of bending and that it will yield parts of the proper size. If you are clever, you may be able to produce parts assembly-line fashion, without laying out each piece.

Making the stool

1. Set up the bending jig with the tubes in the more widely spaced positions, then clamp it, tubes up, to the worktable. Cut four 30¾-in. lengths of ⅜-in. steel rod, which will be bent into legs. Use C-clamps to secure one rod to the bending jig, positioning the rod well above the 2 × 4. When properly aligned, the rod should extend beyond the tubes of the jig an equal amount on each end. Torch-heat the rod on the rod-end side of the clamp until it is cherry red. Then withdraw the flame, let the heat penetrate the rod a few seconds, and bend the rod 90°. In like manner, bend the rod at the other clamp. Repeat the entire process to bend the other three legs.

2. Bend two rods to form leg supports. To do this, reposition one tube in the bending jig so the two are 10⁷⁄₁₆ in. apart, center to center. Cut two 48-in. lengths of ⅜-in. rod. Use the C-clamps to secure one rod to the jig, centering it on the tubes with an equal length of rod projecting beyond each tube. Heat and bend the rod at each tube. Shift the rod on the jig, so an unbent section of it is against one tube while a completed bend is against the other. Heat the rod and make the third bend. Shift the rod again, and make the fourth bend, closing the square now formed by the rod. Repeat the process to form the second leg support.

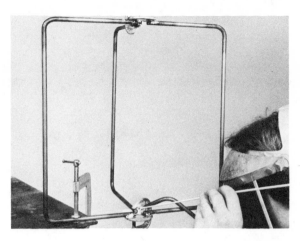

3. Assemble the legs into a single unit by braze welding them to two washers. Use ³⁄₁₆-in.-thick, 2½-in.-dia. ungalvanized flat washers. (Galvanizing would burn off during welding, emitting toxic fumes.) Clamp one leg upright to the worktable. Use a small C-clamp to secure a washer to each end of the leg; positioning the pieces so the butt ends of the rod align with the edges of the holes in the washers. The rods should be on the washers' diameters, not skewed. The bottom washer should be on top of the rod, the top washer beneath the rod. Run your beads on both sides of each rod end. Clamp a second leg to the washer on the same axis as the first, and braze weld it in place. Braze weld the third and fourth legs in place, forming a second axis at right angles to the first.

4. Fit one leg support over the legs, positioning it 5⅝ in. from one end of the leg assembly. Use a bar clamp to secure the support, positioning it so that it pulls the

Braze Welding Rods

Braze welding metal rods side to side can be difficult because their curved shape allows only a thin line of contact.

For rods ⅜ in. or less in diameter, you can get a strong joint without extra measures, but for heavier pieces, increase the contact area by flattening part of the rod, by either hammering, filing, or grinding it. Where two lengths of rod are joined, it's often enough to flatten just one, but for the best joint flatten both.

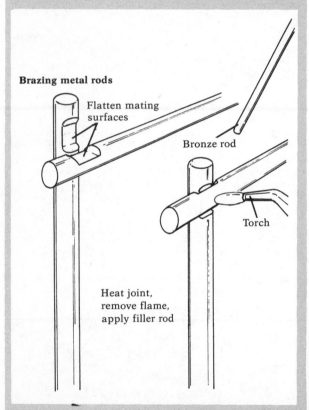

Brazing metal rods

Flatten mating surfaces

Bronze rod

Torch

Heat joint, remove flame, apply filler rod

Metal rod requires the same preparation as any other piece to be braze welded—smooth surfaces free of grease or oil and suitable flux to keep oxides from interfering with the bond. Rods are hard to clamp: C-clamps tend to slip off. When there's no alternative to C-clamps, persistence will eventually succeed, but often you can use locking-grip pliers instead, or even prop the work with bricks or other heavy material. The pieces don't have to be squeezed together for braze welding as long as they are in contact and the work is correctly positioned.

rod ends together and tightens the assembly by forcing the ends past each other. Cut off the overlapping section with a hacksaw, producing the perfect butt joint. Fit and cut the second leg support, positioning it 5½ in. from the first support.

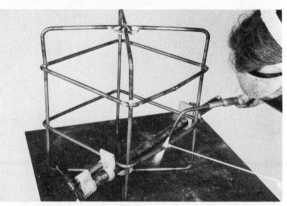

5. Braze and braze weld the unit together. Start by brazing the rod ends together. Back off slightly on the bar clamp to spread flux and align the butt ends, then retighten the clamp and braze the joint. Braze the second support together. Next, remove the clamps and braze weld the supports to the legs.

6. Braze weld the seat brackets in place. Each bracket is a ⅝ × 2½-in. mending plate, a standard hardware item. Set the leg assembly on the worktable, top end down. Slide a bracket under each leg near its bend, and braze weld.

7. File the joints smooth. Clean the assembly with a rag soaked with paint thinner. Prime the metal, then apply several coats of spray enamel.

8. The seat blank is made by edge-gluing three 15-in. lengths of 2 × 6 clear white pine. Each joint should be doweled with two 2-in. pieces of ½-in. dowel. Prepare the pieces by first dressing the mating edges of the boards on a jointer or with a long-soled jointer plane. Then mark the dowel positions on the pairs of boards making each joint; the center board will be dressed and doweled on both edges, the other boards on only one edge. Use a doweling jig to locate each hole and a ½-in. drill bit to bore each. The holes should be just over 1 in. deep.

9. Glue up the seat blank. Apply glue to the board edges and the dowels, insert the dowels in their holes, and fit the boards together. Use two bar clamps to draw the boards together until the glue sets. To prevent the blank from bowing under the bar clamps' pressure, clamp a scrap board across each face of the blank with hand screws.

10. Cut the seat blank to a 14 × 14-in. square. Measure and mark 2 in. along each edge of the seat from each corner. Scribe a diagonal from mark to mark at each corner, then saw off each corner.

11. Finish the seat by machining a radius on all the seat edges, using a ½-in. rounding-over bit in a router. Sand the seat carefully, then clean off all the sanding dust. Apply several coats of polyurethane. See Wood Finishing, p. 162, for complete finishing instructions.

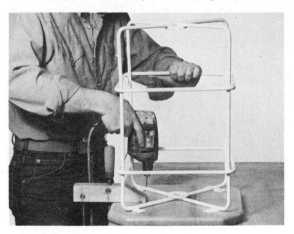

12. Install the seat on the leg assembly. Clamp the seat, top down, to the workbench. Set the leg assembly on the seat, positioning it squarely. Use a drill with a $5/32$-in. bit to bore pilot holes in the seat for mounting screws, through the holes in the brackets. Drive ¾-in. #10 screws through the bracket holes and into the seat to complete the installation.

Table Lamp and Shade

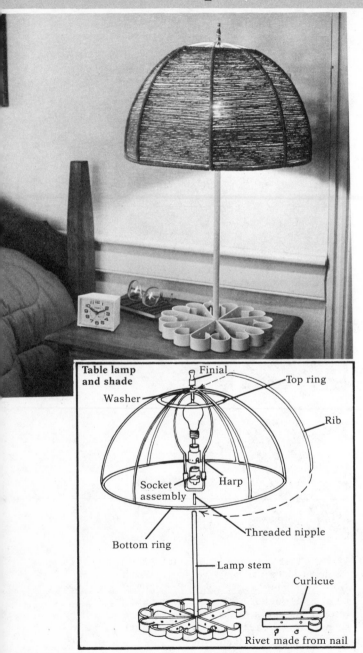

Table lamp and shade

- Finial
- Top ring
- Washer
- Rib
- Socket assembly
- Harp
- Threaded nipple
- Bottom ring
- Lamp stem
- Curlicue
- Rivet made from nail

Bending sheet metal and wire
Cutting threads
Making rivets

Here's an attractive table lamp and shade that will brighten any room. The lamp is made of strips of sheet metal formed and assembled into a sunburst pattern and braze welded to a slender stem supporting socket and shade. It is painted with enamel. The shade consists of a frame formed of bent rods and strung with ordinary jute cord.

The project doesn't involve a great deal of welding, though braze welding is an essential skill to have to complete it successfully. What it does do is expand your creative horizons by giving you experience with a variety of metalworking techniques, ranging from forming sheet metal and wire to riveting to cutting threads. The braze welding practice is a bonus.

Forming wire or sheet metal freehand can be fun, but if you must form more than one piece to exacting dimensions, the task can be maddening. The use of a form allows you to shape scores of pieces uniformly. In this project, two forms are used. A plywood disk is used to shape the shade's frame. A jig based on a stub of pipe is used to shape the lamp base pieces.

Riveting, which you may have tried in conjunction with a blacksmithing project, comes into play to assemble the base pieces. There's no heating involved here, however. The rivets are simply amputated nails, headed with a hammer.

The thread cutting that must be done is simple but unavoidable. To fasten the light socket and the harp that supports the shade to the lamp stem, you must screw an electrical fitting called a nipple into the upright. And to do that, you have to tap the inside of one end of the stem.

The braze welding required to make the lamp isn't difficult, though clamping the rods of the shade frame can be. If you can position the rods so they touch, you've got the problem licked.

What you will need

4 pcs. ⅛-in.-dia. mild steel rod, 29¼''
2 pcs. ⅛-in.-dia. mild steel rod, 24½''
1 pc. ⅛-in.-dia. mild steel rod, 19½''
1 pc. 1½'' × 12-ga. square steel tubing, 6''
1 pc. 1½'' × 12-ga. round steel tubing, 3''
1 pc. ½'' × 16-ga. round steel tubing, 15''
16 pcs. 14-ga. sheet steel, 1'' × 7⅞''
1 pc. plywood, ¾'' × 10'' × 18'' (see Making
  the Lampshade Bending Jig, below)
16 common nails, 16d
4 common nails, 2d
2 machine bolts with washers and nuts, ¼'' × 2''
1 ungalvanized washer with 5/16-in.-dia. hole
1 plastic lamp cord bushing, ⅜-in. dia.
1 threaded nipple, ⅛ IP × ¾''
1 lampshade harp with finial
1 electrical cord, 8', and plug
1 lamp socket
4-ply natural jute, 108 yd.
white or yellow glue
paint thinner
metal primer
spray enamel
hacksaw
saber saw with wood- and metal-cutting blades
drill
ball peen hammer
machinist's vise
bolt cutters
locking-grip pliers
box wrench
tap wrench and ⅛-27 NPT
file
C-clamps
flux
3/32-in. brazing rods
gas-welding rig and safety equipment

Step-by-step instructions

Making the lampshade bending jig

The jig for bending the rods that make up the lampshade is made from two disks cut from ¾-in. plywood. Lay out a 4½-in.-dia. disk on the plywood and saw it out with a saber saw. Then lay out a 10-in.-dia. disk with a 3 × 4-in. extension abutting the circumference. Cut this out with the saber saw. Then attach the smaller disk to the center of the larger one using glue and 2d common nails.

Making the lampshade

1. Form the bottom ring of the lampshade first. To form this ring, the top ring, and the ribs, use the bending jig. Clamp the jig to the worktable, using C-clamps. Press each of two 24½-in. lengths of ⅛-in.-dia. rod around the edge of the larger disk. Adjust the resulting curves freehand so that the two rods will make a smooth, even circle when placed end to end.

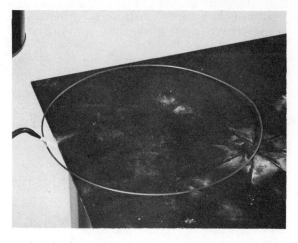

2. Place both curved rods on the table, forming a circle. Two of the rod ends should meet beyond the table edge, where they can be braze welded together without also being braze welded to the tabletop. Braze weld that joint. Turn the piece so that the other joint extends beyond the edge, then braze weld that joint, completing the circle.

Bending Sheet Metal and Wire

Sheet metal and heavy wire can be tricky to bend in smooth, even curves. The material bends easily enough that heating is unnecessary, but the results of bending it cold can be unpredictable. You have to bend it into a tighter radius than you really want because it *is* springy, but you dare not overcompensate and bend the metal into too tight a radius.

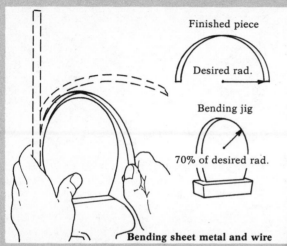

Bending sheet metal and wire

The solution is to use a form. A round form (or bending jig) cut from plywood works for heavy wire, strips of sheet metal, even lightweight squares and rods, while a length of pipe works for broader expanses of light-gauge metal. When sized properly, the form allows you to bend the metal just enough for it to spring back to the desired dimension. Just as important, a bending jig both helps to assure a smooth, even curve and allows you to repeat the same bend as many times as you need to.

As a rule of thumb, size the bending jig 25-35% smaller than the desired curve. That is, calculate the radius of the desired curve, and use a figure 25-35% smaller when laying out the jig. The results *are* somewhat variable, depending upon the material, its thickness, and the tightness of the curve, so a little experimentation is in order if you are designing your own project. But this rule of thumb will serve for the table lamp project.

Once the metal is bent to the approximate shape on the jig, it will retain an even curve when you make minor adjustments freehand. There's a good deal of leeway in the final adjustments you can make, so it is possible to use one form as a guide for bending different curves of roughly similar dimensions.

3. Form the ribs for the shade by bending four 29¼-in.-long rods on the larger disk of the jig. Even though the radius of the shade ribs isn't the same as that of the bottom ring, you can form both pieces on the same jig by making adjustments freehand.

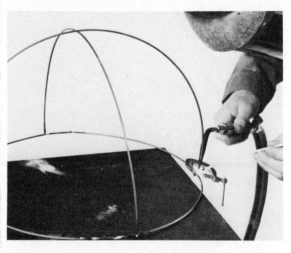

4. With the completed bottom ring still on the table, clamp and braze the four semicircular shade ribs to it, one at a time. Take care not to braze the clamp to the shade or the table: Keep the brazing rod out of direct contact with the clamp, and position the part being brazed beyond the table edge. Be sure the ribs are evenly spaced around the ring.

5. Bend a 19½-in. length of the ⅛-in.-dia. rod around the smaller-diameter disk of the bending jig, forming a 6½-in.-dia. ring. Since the diameter of the jig is only

4½ in., you'll have to overlap the rod a bit or bend only a section at a time. Braze weld the ends of this top ring together.

6. Secure the bottom ring of the shade assembly to the tabletop by laying two boards over the ring and clamping them to the table. Cut each shade rib in two where it intersects the others (at the highest part of its curve), using bolt cutters.

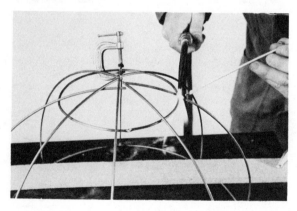

7. Clamp the top ring to a rib near the top of the assembly. The ring should be inside the assembly. The distance between the top ring and the bottom ring must be the same along each rib. Measure to be sure. Clamping the ring to one rib with a small C-clamp will bring it into contact with some of the others. Braze weld to the ring whichever ribs touch it. Then reposition the clamp at another rib, bringing more ribs into contact with the ring. Braze weld any new points of contact and continue until all are joined.

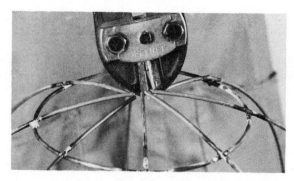

8. Trim back the ends of the ribs at the top of the shade assembly with the bolt cutters, providing at least ⁵⁄₁₆-in. clearance between each rib. The stud that supports the finished lampshade will protrude through this gap.

9. Turn the shade assembly upside down, with the gap you just cut resting on a firebrick. Support the sides of the assembly with two boards set on edge. Place an ungalvanized washer with a ⁵⁄₁₆-in.-dia. hole on the firebrick beneath the gap, and braze it to the shade ribs. (The brick won't drain away heat from the shade as the metal table would.) Make sure the hole in the washer isn't obstructed by any of the rib ends.

10. File off any sharp edges or burrs on the lampshade frame, and chip off any loose flux. Clean the wires with paint thinner to remove any grease or oil.

11. Apply a coat of metal primer to the exposed parts of the assembly. Let it dry, then turn it over and spray the remaining unpainted metal. For the finish coat, apply spray enamel in the color of your choice, using the same two-step method.

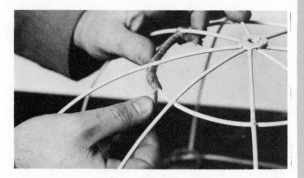

12. Wrap four-ply natural jute around the top and bottom rings of the shade. Wrap the small ring first. Tie one end of the jute to it, then wind the jute around the ring until the ring is covered completely. Tie the jute again when you reach the starting point. Trim the ends of the jute. Repeat the process on the bottom ring.

13. Tie the jute to one of the ribs, right below the small ring. Run it to the next rib, loop it around the rib and continue on, looping each rib, until you've circled the shade. Continue under the first row, looping around each rib and running one continuous length of jute to the bottom of the shade. When the last row is complete, tie off the jute and snip away the ends. The space above the small ring is not covered, to allow heat from the light bulb to escape.

Making the lamp base bending jig

1. The jig used to bend the sheet-metal curlicues that make up the base for the lamp is formed of a length of round tubing bolted to a length of square tubing.

Cutting Threads

Taps and dies cut threads: taps on the inner surfaces of holes, dies on the outer surfaces of rods and pipes. Basic tools of machinists, these items can be purchased by the hobbyist-metalworker in limited sets. A typical set will include a dozen or more of the most common taps, matching dies, a tap wrench used to turn the tap, a diestock used to turn the die, perhaps a reamer and a thread gauge. Because it is a collection of precision tools, a tap-and-die set won't be inexpensive.

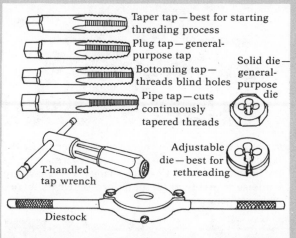

Taper tap—best for starting threading process

Plug tap—general-purpose tap

Bottoming tap—threads blind holes

Pipe tap—cuts continuously tapered threads

Solid die—general-purpose die

Adjustable die—best for rethreading

T-handled tap wrench

Diestock

Although taps and dies aren't difficult to use, you should understand the most basic of the several thread systems in use. The American National Standard thread system is the one most commonly used in the United States. In this system, there are three sizes of threads, coded NF for National Fine, NC for National Coarse, and NPT for National Pipe Thread.

Each tap or die is marked with a number-and-letter code that indicates the size of the hole or shaft, the number of threads per in., and the thread size. If the diameter is less than ¼ in., the size is given in terms of machine-screw gauges. Thus a tap marked 10–24 NF will cut threads to accept a 10-ga. machine screw with 24 threads per in. in the National Fine designation. A ⅜–24 NC tap will cut threads for a ⅜ in. bolt with 24 threads per in. in the National Coarse designation.

Before you tap a hole, you must think a bit. Select the tap you want to use first. Then consult the chart, which *should* come with your tap-and-die set, that tells what size drill bit to use for each tap. And use the correct bit to drill the hole.

The thread gauge comes into play when you want to cut threads to match a stock nut or bolt. Use the

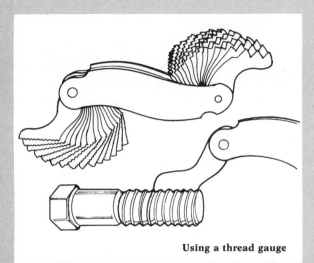

Using a thread gauge

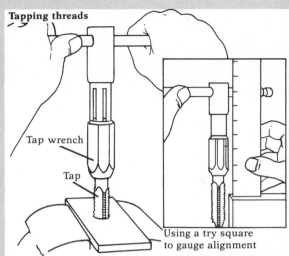

Tap wrench

Tap

Using a try square
to gauge alignment

blades in the gauge in a trial-and-error process to determine the number of threads per in. you must cut. A measurement with calipers and rule will tell you the diameter. This, in turn, will tell you the corresponding tap or die to use.

Electrical fittings, such as nipples, locknuts, and connectors, follow the NPT designations, although their threads are not tapered and although they are marked in IP (for Iron Pipe) designations. The IP designations are compatible with the NPT designations. If you have any doubt about what you are dealing with, use your thread gauge.

To tap threads, clamp the work to a workbench or in a vise at a comfortable working height. Unless you are cutting threads in cast iron or brass, you need to use a lubricant. Turpentine is a suitable lubricant for aluminum or copper, but steel requires an oil-base lube. Apply a few drops to the tap's threads before you start, then add more with each turn, dripping it on the tap shank just above the holes.

The first few threads you cut will determine the course the tap will follow, so align the tap carefully. Surely you don't want the threads to be cocked. If it will help, set a try square beside the tap and line up the tap with the vertical leg of the square.

When starting out, turn the wrench clockwise while exerting moderate downward pressure. Once the initial threads are cut, the pressure isn't necessary; the threads will pull the tap into the hole as you turn it. After each turn or two of the tap wrench, back off a quarter turn or so to cut off burrs and allow filings to clear.

To thread a rod with a die, you must clamp the rod in a vise. With a file, bevel the end of the rod, then mark where you want the threads to end. Fit the diestock over the rod and adjust the guide fingers to the diameter of the rod. Remove the diestock and fit the die into it. Put the diestock back over the rod, line up the guide fingers with the top of the rod and, grasping the center of the diestock in your fingers, carefully turn it onto the rod until the die gains a firm purchase. Then grip the handles and, exerting downward pressure, turn the unit clockwise. Every one or two turns, back off the unit about a quarter turn. Continue in this manner until you complete the threads.

Cutting threads on a rod

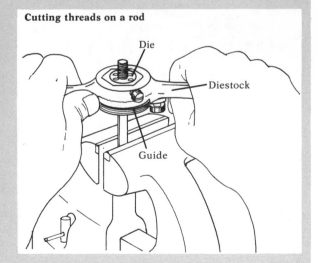

Die

Diestock

Guide

Fabricate the square tube first. Cut a 6-in. length of 1½-in. × 12-ga. square tubing. Drill two ¼-in.-dia. holes midway between the ends, one at each edge, 1 in. apart on center, penetrating both walls.

2. Cut a 3-in. length of 1½-in. × 12-ga. round steel tubing. Lay out the positions of two holes to be drilled along the length of the tube, 1 in. apart on center, toward one end, so that when the pieces are assembled, the bottom of the round tubing will be flush with the side of the square tubing. The round tubing should be at right angles to the square tubing. Drill the holes through one wall of the tubing with the ¼-in. bit.

3. Assemble the jig. Insert a 2-in.-long, ¼-in.-dia. machine bolt through one hole in the square tube, then put the round tube in place, fitting the hole farthest from the tube opening over the bolt end. Place a washer and nut on the bolt and tighten it with a box wrench. Install the second bolt in like manner.

Making the lamp

1. Cut 16 pieces of 14-ga. sheet steel, each measuring 1 × 7⅞ in. These will be bent into the curlicues forming the lamp base. Use a saber saw equipped with a metal-cutting blade. File off any burrs.

2. Stack the pieces in pairs, marking individual pieces, so members of the eight pairs can be readily identified at assembly time. In turn, set each pair on a scrap block of wood, clamp the works to the workbench, and drill two 3/16-in.-dia. holes through the metal. Position the holes along the centerline, ⅞ in. and 3⅛ in. from one end of the metal pieces.

3. Bend a curl in the end of each of the sheet-metal pieces by forming it around the bending jig made for the purpose. With the jig clamped securely to the workbench, clamp one end of a sheet-metal piece (the end farthest from the holes) to the jig's round tube. Bend the free end three-fourths of the way around the tube. Repeat for the remaining pieces. Keep the first piece you bend at hand to compare the remaining 15 to as you work. All should be as much alike as possible.

Making Rivets

One of the least complicated ways to join pieces of lightweight metal is to rivet them, using cutoff nails. By using nails of various sizes you can accommodate a fairly wide range of metal thicknesses.

For a good, sturdy connection, use nails whose diameter is equal to or greater than the combined thickness of the pieces being joined. That way you don't have to use too many of them. The length of the exposed shaft should also equal the diameter of the hole. This will have enough metal to spread into a sound rivet head.

In the lamp project, for example, the two 1/16-in.-thick sheets are joined with 3/16-in.-dia. 16d nails, cut off 5/16 in. from their heads.

To set the rivet, insert it through predrilled holes in the pieces to be joined, and place the assembly with nailhead down on an anvil or block of metal. Hammer down on the cutoff end, using the head of a 16-20 oz. ball peen hammer. Roughly form a rivet head, then switch to the hammer's peen to refine the shape, forming the head evenly around the hole and roughly as thick as the nailhead.

The table under a metal block must be very sturdy, or the rivet won't set properly. You'll get better results by positioning the metal block directly over one of the table legs, which will give extra support.

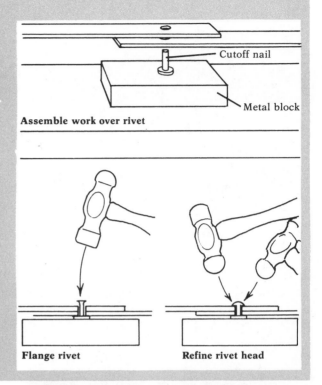

Assemble work over rivet

— Cutoff nail

— Metal block

4. Reassemble the pairs and rivet them together with rivets made from 16d common nails (see above). With a hacksaw, cut 16 of the nails 5/16 in. from the heads. Fit a pair of curlicues together and insert a rivet in each hole. Lay the assembly, nailheads down, on the anvil of a machinist's vise or a heavy metal block. Smite each rivet with a hammer to form the rivet head. The peen of a ball peen hammer can be used to refine the shape of the head. Repeat the process to assemble the remaining seven pairs.

Flange rivet   **Refine rivet head**

5. Clamp one of the riveted units in a vise, and drill a 3/8-in.-dia. hole through one of its curled ends. The lamp cord will be run through this hole into the lamp base.

6. Fabricate the lamp stem next. Clamp a 15-in. length of ½-in. × 16-ga. round steel tubing upright in a vise. Tap threads inside the top end, using a ⅛-27 NPT tap and tap wrench (p. 310). Continue turning the tap until the threads on it are no longer visible.

8. Cut out the metal between the hole and the end of the pipe with a hacksaw. The resulting notch will accommodate the lamp cord. File the notch edges to remove burrs that might cut the wire.

7. Clamp the pipe in the vise horizontally, resting it on a scrap of wood, if necessary, to hold it steady in the vise. Drill a ¼-in.-dia. hole through one wall of the pipe, ⅛ in. from the bottom end.

9. Braze weld the lamp base to the lamp stem. Position the eight pairs of curlicues in a circle, with the straight ends converging in the middle. Stand the lamp stem on end with the curlicues abutting its sidewall. The notch at the bottom of the stem must align with the hole for the lamp cord in the curlicue. Braze weld the ends of the curlicues to the stem.

10. Insert a ⅜-in.-dia. plastic lamp cord bushing into the hole in the lamp base, using a pencil or screwdriver to push it into place.

11. Chip off any loose flux, clean the base assembly with paint thinner, and spray on an even coat of primer, taking care to coat all metal surfaces without spraying any one part so much that the paint begins to run. When the primer is completely dry, spray on a coat of enamel in the color of your choice.

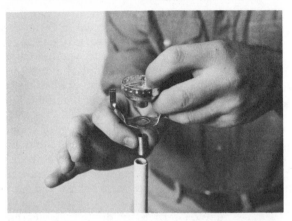

12. Screw a threaded nipple into the threads at the top of the lamp stem, then set the base of the lampshade harp assembly over the nipple, and screw the lamp socket base onto the nipple.

13. Insert the lamp cord through the lamp base, up through the stem and out the socket base. You should use about 8 ft. of cord. Separate the two conductors for about 3 in., then strip ½ in. of insulation from each. Tie the ends in an Underwriter's knot. Install a plug on the free end of the wire.

14. Form a loop in each end of the stripped wires, and place each loop over the socket terminals. Remember to position the loop so that the screw terminal will pull the loop closed as the screw is tightened. Place the cardboard insert in the metal socket shroud, and slide both over the socket and into the socket base.

15. Insert the ends of the harp into the harp base. In some cases there are small fittings to slide over the ends of the harp base (to hold everything securely). Hold these partway up the harp while inserting the harp in the base, then let them drop, and push them tightly in place.

16. Screw a 60-watt bulb into the socket, and attach the lampshade, setting the washer at the shade's top over the threaded stud on the harp. Secure the shade by screwing a matching finial onto the stud, and the lamp is complete.

Weather Vane

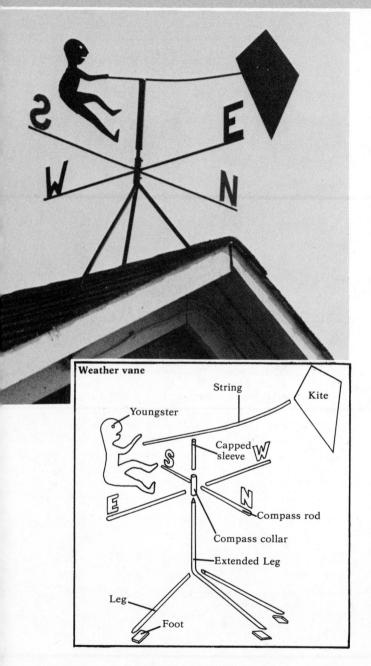

Weather vane

Youngster · String · Kite · Capped sleeve · Compass rod · Compass collar · Extended Leg · Leg · Foot

Using a bench grinder

In the old days, a weather vane decorated every barn. A horse or cow, the farmer's wife, even a fish or whale manned the weather vane, swinging in the wind and pointing the direction in which it blew. There are many distinctive designs, each created to give an individual touch to the farmstead.

And, because the weather vane told which way the wind was blowing, the farmer could use it to help him forecast the weather—he didn't have the advice of a television or radio weatherman. He mounted it on the barn so he could see it from the house.

You may construct this distinctive weather vane and mount it on your barn or other outbuilding to help *you* forecast the weather. Or you can simply mount it on your house for decoration.

The vane features an active youngster flying a kite. Since the kite has more surface area than the youngster, the wind pushes the kite with greater force, and the youngster will always point his kite in the direction the wind blows. He and his kite turn on a conical pivot point you grind on an extension of the tripod base.

A fixed crosspiece secured to the extension locates the four points of the compass.

You don't have to design your weather vane around a child and a kite, of course. Just as the old farmer chose a weather vane design that reflected his personality, so can you. Have a fisherman landing that BIG one. Or a horse pulling a cart. Or a child walking a dog.

As do all the projects in this section, the weather vane involves a variety of metalworking skills. The welding is, of course, an essential part of the work. But you also have to lay out and cut out relatively intricate sheet-metal figures—the letters, the kite, and the youngster. You will have to bend a rod, drill some holes, tap some threads, even do some fairly precision grinding.

This is the first and last of the projects to *require* the use of an arc welder, if only to weld together the tripod. If you try welding the tripod with a gas rig, you'll experience firsthand the difficulty of bringing big pieces of steel up to welding heat. On the other hand, the project should demonstrate that the arc welder is more versatile than you might think. While it does take a deft hand and a low amperage setting to weld the 20-gauge sheet-metal letters in place without mishap, it can be done.

What you will need

1 pc. ¾-in.-dia. mild steel rod, ¾''
1 pc. ½-in.-dia. mild steel rod, 30''
2 pcs. ½-in.-dia. mild steel rod, 18''
1 pc. ¼-in.-dia. mild steel rod, 24''
4 pcs. ¼-in.-dia. mild steel rod, 16''
1 pc. ¾'' × 18-ga. round steel tubing, 8''
1 pc. ¾'' × 18-ga. round steel tubing, 3''
1 pc. ⅛-in. sheet steel, 8'' × 11''
1 pc. 20-ga. sheet steel, 5'' × 18'' (see step 9)
3 pcs. 16-ga. sheet steel, 1'' × 2''
1 pc. 16-ga. sheet steel, 10½'' × 14½''
3 #14 flathead wood screws, 2''
2 10-24 allen setscrews, ½''
paint thinner
outdoor spray primer and enamel
small can asphalt roof cement
saber saw with metal-cutting blades
drill
bench grinder
ball peen hammer
machinist's vise
level
tin snips
layout tools
punch
sliding T-bevel
locking-grip pliers with C-clamp jaws
tap wrench and 10-24 NC tap
allen wrench
C-clamps
pocket compass
flux
3/32-in.-dia. E6013 coated electrodes
1/16-in.-dia. E6013 coated electrodes
arc-welding rig and safety equipment

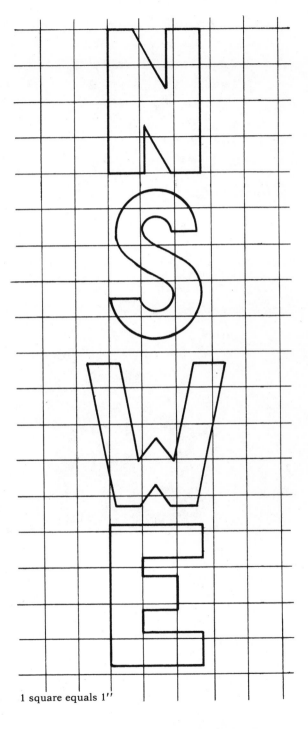

1 square equals 1''

Step-by-step instructions

1. Cut a 30-in. length of ½-in.-dia. rod for the extended leg of the tripod base. On one end, grind a conical pivot point for the vane. Hold the rod on the tool rest of a bench grinder (see p. 321), with the rod at a 60° angle to the abrasive wheel. Rotate the rod as you work to ensure an even shape. Be sure to wear goggles or a face mask.

2. Cold-bend this rod at a point 18 in. from the unpointed end. The 18-in. section will be one of the tripod legs. Clamp the rod vertically in a vise, with the point of the bend just clear of the jaws. Hammer-bend the rod, maintaining tension on the end of the rod with your hand. The rod must be bent to a 145° angle, so set a sliding T-bevel to this angle, and hold it against the rod periodically to gauge your progress.

3. Fabricate the other two legs of the tripod. Cut two 18-in. lengths of the ½-in.-dia. rod, and weld them together at a 60° angle. To complete the weld, clamp

the rods to the worktable so their ends meet at the desired angle beyond the edge of the bench (so you don't weld them to the bench). Use a ³/₃₂-in.-dia. electrode.

4. Set up the tripod and weld it together. Rest the leg with the vertical extension so its bend is in the notch formed where the other two legs are welded together. Adjust the pieces so the angles between the individual legs are equal and the extension is plumb. (Check it carefully with a level.) Then clamp them, and complete the weld.

5. Cut a foot for each tripod leg from 16-ga. sheet steel using tin snips. Cut each piece approximately 1 × 2 in. Drill a ¼-in.-dia. hole through each, ½ in. from one end.

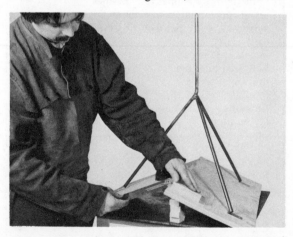

6. To weld the feet to the tripod at the correct angle for mounting, you must block up some scrap wood at the pitch of the roof on which the weather vane will be mounted, then set the tripod on it with the feet in place. Set a sliding T-bevel to the angle of the roof faces at the ridge, and set up the wood at that angle. Carefully set the tripod in place and adjust its position until the extension is plumb. Slip a foot under each leg with the mounting hole exposed. Attach the arc welder's ground clamp to one of the legs, and complete the welds, using a $\frac{1}{16}$-in.-dia. electrode.

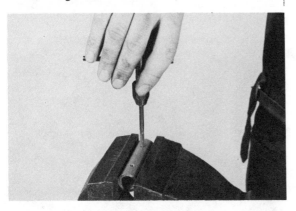

7. The next subassembly to be made is the compass. The compass collar is made from a 3-in. length of $\frac{3}{4}$-in. × 18-ga. round steel tubing. Clamp the tubing lengthwise in a vise, and drill two $\frac{5}{32}$-in. holes through one wall of the tubing. The holes should line up along the length of the tubing, with one about $\frac{1}{2}$ in. from each end. Thread the two holes with a 10–24 NC tap (see Cutting Threads, p. 310). Ultimately, a $\frac{1}{2}$-in.-long allen setscrew will be turned into each hole.

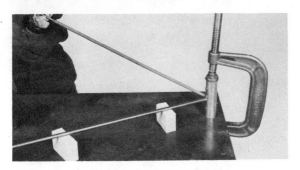

8. Cut four 16-in.-long compass rods from $\frac{1}{4}$-in.-dia. rod. Weld them to the collar so there is one rod extending from the collar every 90° around its circumference. To do this, stand the collar on end near the edge of the worktable, and clamp it with a C-clamp. Rest a rod on

two 1½-in.-high wood scraps set on the table. Adjust it so it abuts the collar squarely, then weld it in place with a $\frac{3}{32}$-in.-dia. electrode. Loosen the clamp, then rotate the collar 90°. Position a second compass rod, and weld it in place. Repeat the process to attach the remaining two rods.

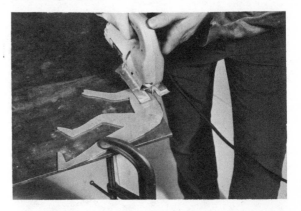

9. Cut out the sheet-metal letters to indicate the points of the compass. And while you are at it, cut out the youngster and his kite, too. Each 20-ga. steel letter is roughly 4 in. high and 3 in. wide. The 16-ga. steel kite is 14½ in. high and 10½ in. wide. The kid is cut from a 8 × 11-in. piece of $\frac{1}{8}$-in. steel. Lay out the pieces on the sheet metal, and cut them out, using a saber saw with a metal-cutting blade. Clamp the metal to the worktable with the area being cut extending just beyond the edge. Shift the work and reclamp as necessary to complete the cut.

10. Weld one letter to each of the compass rods. Be sure you position the E and the W on one axis and the N and the S on the other. Arrange the pairs so all four letters read correctly from one viewpoint. To complete the weld, clamp one rod on the table with the collar parallel to the edge. Lay the letter in place and run your bead, using a ¹⁄₁₆-in.-dia. electrode. (It may be advisable to experiment on some scrap sheet metal first to establish the proper amperage setting to use for this weld.)

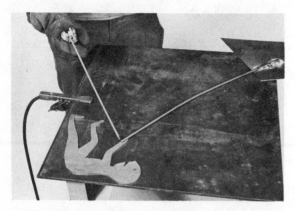

11. Assemble the vane, which consists of the kite and the youngster connected by a "string" of ¼-in.-dia. rod. Cut a 24-in. length of the rod, and form a slight curve in it. Lay the youngster on one corner of the table and the kite on the opposite corner, with the string extending diagonally across the table. The string should overlap the kid's hand by about 1 in., and it should extend about halfway across the kite. Weld the string securely to both the kite and the kid, using the ¹⁄₁₆-in.-dia. electrode. Watch the amperage!

12. In the finished weather vane, the vane is welded to a capped sleeve that fits over the tripod extension. The cap must be dimpled so it will bear on the conical pivot

point with as little friction as possible. To make the cap, first cut a ¾-in.-long stub of ¾-in.-dia. rod. Locate the center point by scribing several diameters across one end of the stub. (Since the diameter, the maximum distance between two points of the circumference, always intersects the center point, scribing two or more diameters will locate the center point.) Use a punch and hammer to mark the spot. Using a ³⁄₈-in. drill bit set on the center point, drill into the stub, just enough to create a conical dimple.

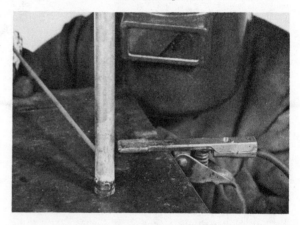

13. Cut the sleeve and weld it to the cap. The sleeve is an 8-in. length of ¾-in. × 18-ga. round steel tubing. Place the cap, dimple up, on the table, and align the sleeve atop it. Tack-weld them, using the ³⁄₃₂-in.-dia. electrode.

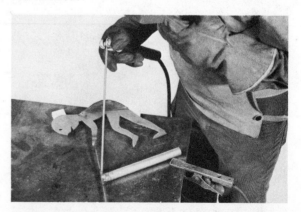

14. Weld the vane to the capped sleeve. Position the sleeve against the string, closer to the youngster than to the kite and angled slightly so the kite will be higher

Using a Bench Grinder

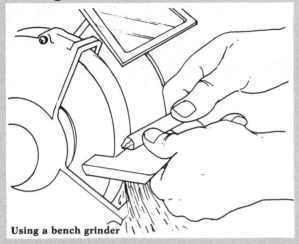

Using a bench grinder

A bench grinder is a handy tool for any shop, but it is especially so in the metalworking shop. It can be used to sharpen all sorts of cutting tools, from woodworking chisels to mower blades to scissors. In a metalworking shop, it removes burrs from newly cut edges, grinds bevels and chamfers, and can even be used for full-scale shaping.

The typical bench grinder looks like an electric motor with an abrasive grinding wheel on each end. The wheels are almost completely shielded on their sides and edges; only about a quarter of each is exposed. An adjustable tool rest is mounted in front of each wheel, along with a transparent shield. The grinder should be bolted to a workbench or stand.

To use the grinder, adjust the tool rest to within ⅛ in. of the wheel. Put on a pair of goggles or a face shield. Turn on the motor, and let the wheels work up to their full operating speed. Rest the object to be ground on the tool rest, and slowly and carefully feed it into the wheel. A great deal of pressure is seldom necessary. Examine the piece frequently to gauge your progress.

If the piece is broad, you will have to slide it back and forth on the tool rest to work the entire surface. If it is narrower than the wheel, you still work it back and forth, to avoid wearing the wheel unevenly. The tool rest should be long enough that you can grind pieces with the side of the wheel. And since the rest is adjustable, you can set it for the grinding of specific bevel angles.

The bench grinder can be a dangerous tool. The least of its hazards are the specks of abrasive and metal that fly about when it's in use. The worst that can happen is that a wheel can shatter. ALWAYS wear goggles or a face shield, even for the briefest of operations, all the tool-mounted guards and shields notwithstanding.

Take particular care of the abrasive wheels. Test each one for cracks before mounting it. Slip the wheel on the arbor, and tap it lightly with a scrap of wood. If it doesn't ring clear, toss it out. In use, be careful how you feed the work. It is all too easy to gouge and break the wheel.

than the youngster. The placement is not terribly critical. Complete the weld, using the 3/32-in.-dia. electrode. Fit the vane on the tripod and balance the vane by welding scraps of metal to the youngster. The vane should bear on the pivot point; contact between the sleeve itself and the tripod extension as the vane turns should be minimized.

15. Clean the entire unit for painting. Chip off any remaining slag, scrub all the welds with a wire brush, and wipe the metal with a rag doused with paint thinner. Paint all the parts with spray primer suitable for outdoor use. Apply several coats of an outdoor spray enamel.

16. Mount the tripod on the roof. Set it in position, and adjust it until the extension is plumb. If necessary, bend the feet so they bear solidly on the roof. Drill appropriate pilot holes, then drive a 2-in. #14 screw through each mounting hole and into the roof. Cover each foot with a blob of asphalt roof cement.

17. Fit the compass subassembly in place. Using a pocket compass, locate north. Rotate the weather vane's compass so the letter N aligns with north. Fit a ½-in. allen setscrew in each of the two holes in the compass collar and tighten each firmly. Fit the vane in place.

Fireplace Tools

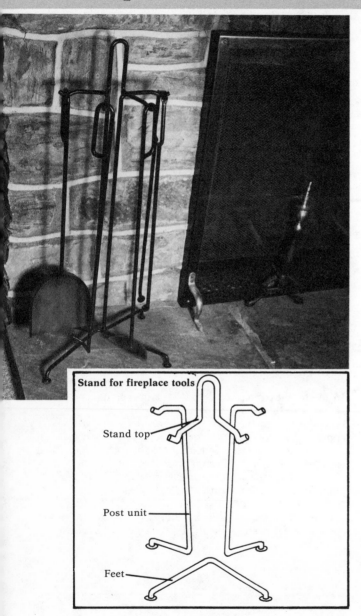

Stand for fireplace tools

Stand top

Post unit

Feet

Over the last few years, wood burning has grown faster than any other residential source of heat. If you have a wood stove or a fireplace, and you don't have the proper tools to move logs and rake ash, consider making your own set.

This design consists mainly of ⅜-inch-diameter mild steel rod, heated with an oxyacetylene torch and bent to shape. Some of the bending is done freehand, but the more intricate bends are made using a remarkably simple bending jig. You merely slip the heated rod between the jig's two prongs and pull the rod's free end, bending the rod around the prong closest to you.

Blacksmithing skills come into play in the course of this project. The poker's hook is forged, and parts of the tongs and the shovel must be forged to create an appropriate surface for brazing. While the instructions that follow specify the use of a torch for heating and the anvil of a large machinist's vise for the forging, you can more easily use a blacksmith's forge and anvil, if you have them. And using the blacksmith's forge would certainly ease the heating of the rods for bending.

All of the joints, except for the joints in the shovel's scoop, are brazed or braze welded. Unless you fusion weld the scoop together, brazing the handle to the scoop could weaken its joints.

Three of the tools—ash hoe, poker, and shovel—have handles that are identical but for their lengths. Make all three handles at once, then modify the end of each in turn to create the three distinctive tools. The tongs and the stand are entirely one-of-a-kind items.

These fireplace tools are simple in design and appearance, but if you feel like experimenting, try a variation following essentially the same steps, but use square stock rather than rods, introducing a few twists in the shafts for decoration (see Twisting, p. 267). However you choose to execute the project, these plans offer a simple, inexpensive way to acquire some useful tools for wood burners.

What you will need

3 pcs. ⅜-in.-dia. mild steel rod, 36″
1 pc. ⅜-in.-dia. mild steel rod, 32″
1 pc. ⅜-in.-dia. mild steel rod, 31″
1 pc. ⅜-in.-dia. mild steel rod, 25″
2 pcs. ⅜-in.-dia. mild steel rod, 18″
1 pc. ⅜-in.-dia. mild steel rod, 11″
1 pc. ⅜-in.-dia. mild steel rod, 5″
1 pc. 16-ga. sheet steel, 8″ × 8″
1 pc. 16-ga. sheet steel, 2″ × 5″
6 ungalvanized washers with ⁵⁄₁₆-in.-dia. holes
paint thinner
heat-resistant metal primer
heat-resistant spray enamel
hacksaw
saber saw with metal-cutting blade
lightweight forging hammer
machinist's vise
file
pliers
C-clamps
flux
¼-in. brazing rods
gas-welding rig and safety equipment

Before you begin

A key procedure in making the fireplace tools and stand is the torch-heating and bending of steel rods. It's a procedure you may want to practice a bit before actually tackling the project.

The bending jig used to bend the rods is a U-shaped device with just enough space between its prongs to allow you to drop in a ⅜-in.-dia. rod.

The routine is to heat the rod to a cherry red. Remove the rod from the flame and allow the heat to penetrate for about 15 seconds. Place the rod in the jig with the glowing section just outside the prongs. Rotate the free end in a horizontal plane until the desired bend is formed.

A soapstone pencil can be used to mark the locations of the bends, since its markings won't burn off.

The process of heating and bending the rods (as well as doing the forging this project requires) is most easily accomplished if you have three hands. The problem is, of course, that you need two hands to light and extinguish the torch. You also need a hand to hold the rod. If you are doing only one or two bends, it's no problem to light the torch, pick up the rod, heat it, carefully lay the rod down while you extinguish the torch, then quickly pick up the rod and complete the bend. But this routine gets old in a hurry.

The most obvious solution is to have a helper man the torch, allowing you to keep the torch burning while you complete a series of bends. A less obvious solution, though one not without its potential hazards, is to make and use a device called a torch stand. A simple one can be made by welding an 18-in. length of steel angle to a 1-ft.-sq. piece of steel plate so the angle rises at a 45° angle across the plate. The stand is clamped to a worktable, then the lighted torch is clamped to the stand. While the torch cannot be knocked over, you can burn yourself seriously if you let your attention wander.

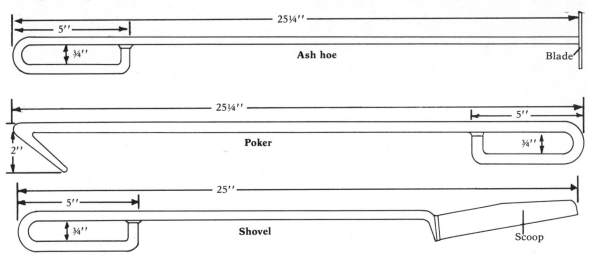

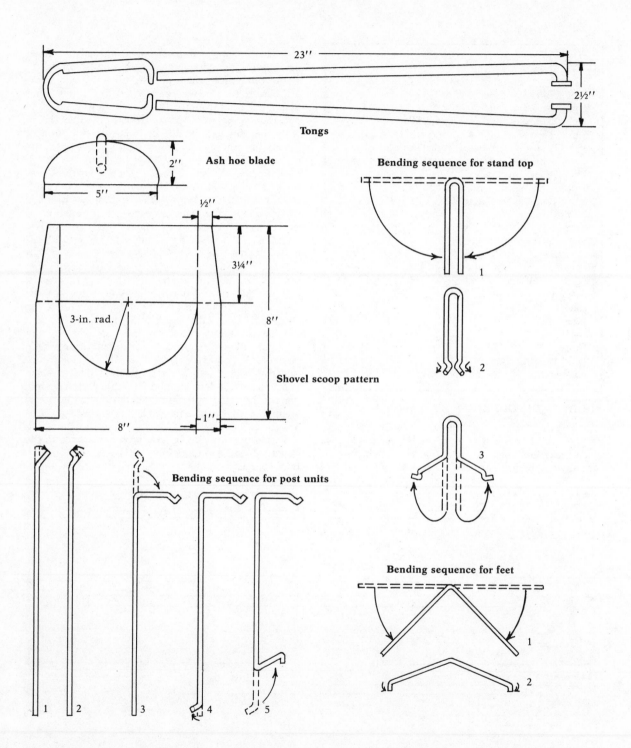

23''

2½''

Tongs

2''

Ash hoe blade

5''

Bending sequence for stand top

1

2

½''

3¼''

8''

3-in. rad.

Shovel scoop pattern

8''

1''

3

Bending sequence for post units

1   2   3   4   5

Bending sequence for feet

1

2

Step-by-step instructions
Making the bending jig

Clamp a 5-in. length of ⅜-in.-dia. steel rod in a machinist's vise. The rod should be positioned at one edge of the jaws. With a torch, heat the midsection of the rod, then grasp the free end with pliers and bend the bar into a U-shape. The ends of the piece should line up and be ⁷⁄₁₆ in. apart.

Making the handles

1. Cut three pieces of ⅜-in.-dia. steel rod: a 31-in. length for the ash hoe handle, a 32-in. length for the poker, and a 25-in. length for the shovel handle.

2. Clamp the bending jig in the vise with 1½–2 in. of the ends protruding above the jaws.

3. Begin forming the handle loop in one rod. Heat the area 1 in. from an end of the rod. Insert the heated end into the bending jig, and make a 90° bend. The distance from the rod end to the inside corner should be ¾ in.

4. Make a second bend, this a 180° one, at a spot 5 in. from the inside corner of the first bend. Heat the spot, then insert the rod in the bending jig and pull the rod, creating the bend. The rod should now loop around so the end abuts the shaft.

5. Repeat the process to form loops in the other two rods.

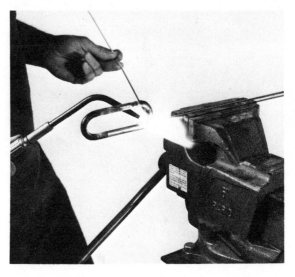

6. Braze weld the loop closed on each handle. Build up a fillet between the end of the rod and the curve of the shaft to smooth the joint.

Making the ash hoe

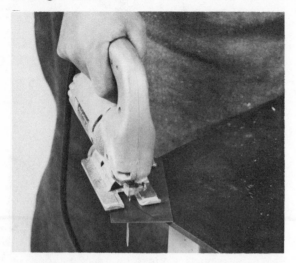

1. Cut the ash hoe blade from a 2 × 5-in. piece of 16-ga. sheet steel. Lay out the arc of the blade on the metal (see p. 324). Clamp the piece to the corner of the worktable, and cut along the line with a saber saw equipped with a metal-cutting blade. You may have to reposition the clamp during the cut to allow clearance for the saw.

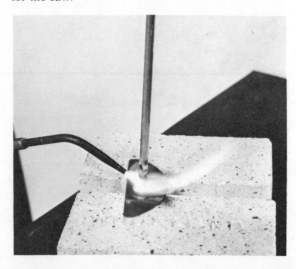

2. Braze the blade to the end of the handle. Butt the handle end against the blade at a spot midway between the blade sides and ½ in. above the blade's straight edge. To make sure you get a good joint, melt a bit of filler rod on the blade before you braze the joint. First, suspend the blade between two firebricks with the spot to be brazed over the gap. Flux the area to be brazed. Heat the blade until it's hot enough to melt the brazing rod. Let the bronze cool, then place the fluxed handle end on the now-hardened puddle. Reheat, directing the flame more toward the handle end than the blade. As the metal reaches the proper heat, feed a bit more filler rod into the joint.

3. Clean any rough spots on the hoe's two joints with a file, then scrub them with a wire brush. Finally, set the tool aside to be cleaned and painted with the other pieces of the set.

Making the poker

1. Draw a taper on the end of the poker handle (see Drawing a Taper, p. 260). First place the rod on the anvil of the machinist's vise with the end extending several inches beyond the anvil's edge. Heat the end with the torch, then pull the end onto the anvil and draw a taper on the end, using a forging hammer. The hammer should strike at a slight angle to the anvil's face. Strike several blows, flattening the rod, then turn it 90° and continue working, forging and turning until you have a four-sided taper. You may have to reheat once to draw the end out to the desired length of 2 in. Round the last ½ in. down to a tip of ⅛ in. diameter.

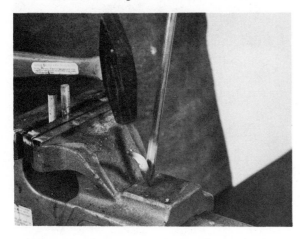

2. Reheat the poker where the taper begins, and position the rod with the heated part extending beyond the anvil's edge. Strike down, then in, bending the end 90°. Quickly turn the poker, rotating the bent end so it points up. Strike at the base of the bend, driving the tapered end further toward the handle shaft. Stop when it is at a 45° angle.

3. Reheat the poker end once again. Place the crook of the bend on the anvil face, holding the handle shaft nearly vertical. Strike first on the tip to blunt it slightly, then strike just behind it to put a slight curve in the hook, making it more useful for poking and pulling logs in the fireplace.

4. Smooth out any rough spots with a file, and scrub the poker with a wire brush. Then set it with the ash hoe.

Making the shovel

1. The end of the shovel handle must be shaped and bent to create a surface to which to braze the shovel scoop. Torch-heat the handle end, then flare it (see Flaring, p. 282). Work with a forging hammer on the vise's anvil. Spread the rod's end to a thickness of about ⅛ in. and a width, at its very end, of about ½ in.

2. Reheat the flare. Lay the handle with the flare extending about 1 in. beyond the anvil's edge. Strike on the flare, bending it down about 75°.

3. Cut out an 8-in. square of 16-ga. sheet steel. Mark the pattern for the scoop on it, using the illustration on p. 324 as a guide. Cut out the scoop, using a saber saw equipped with a metal-cutting blade. The two tabs at each side of the scoop will form its sides.

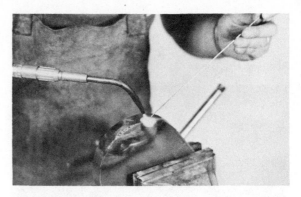

4. Place the cutout metal scoop in the vise, with the jaws gripping one of the tabs that will form the scoop sides. Bend the piece until it is at right angles to the tab, and hammer along the edge to complete the bend. Bend the other tab in the same way.

6. Fusion weld the tab ends together and then close the seam between the tabs and the scoop base. First, tack weld the joints every 1½ in., beginning with the corners of the tab ends, then continuing around the longer joint, repositioning the work to keep the spot being tack welded away from the vise itself. Finally, run the weld bead along the joints, again repositioning the work in the vise as necessary.

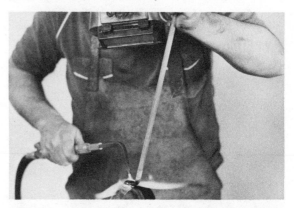

5. Bend the ends of the tabs together with pliers, then clamp the scoop in the vise with the joints to be welded up. The tab ends have a tendency to spring apart, but if you clamp them together, all the joints should remain correctly positioned.

7. Braze the handle to the scoop. First, carefully smooth the weld joining the two tab ends with a file or bench grinder. Clean the joint, flux it, and clamp the scoop in the vise with the back up. Heat the back of the scoop with the torch, and melt a small puddle of fluxed filler rod there. Then press the fluxed, flared end of the handle onto the spot. Since the filler will harden in the short time it takes you to do this, heat the flared end of the handle until the filler remelts, forming the bond. You'll probably feel the handle give slightly as the bronze melts, and a fillet will form around the joint. Feed more rod into the seam if necessary to create a fillet.

8. Clean the joints with a file, then scrub them with a wire brush. Set the shovel with the growing collection of tools, completed but unpainted.

Making the tongs

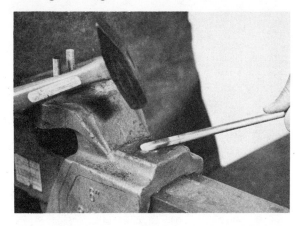

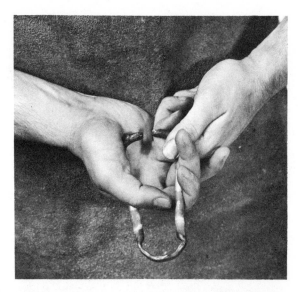

1. Cut an 11-in. length of ⅜-in.-dia. steel rod for the tong handle. Heat and forge each end of this piece flat. Work with a forging hammer on the vise's anvil. Work an area about ¾ in. long, and thin it to about ¼ in. Forge one end, then the other.

2. Reheat one end of the rod. Holding the flattened area over the anvil's edge, hammer-bend it down to an angle of 90°. Bend the other rod end the same way.

4. Heat the flattened section of the tong handle. Bend it in your hands until the tapered ends are about ¼ in. apart. Clearly, this operation can be done bare-handed, but you may want to don gloves to do it.

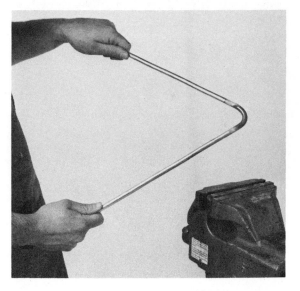

3. Heat and flatten 3 in. of the rod's midsection, reducing it to a thickness of ⅛ in. This flattened section will form the spring that holds the jaws of the tongs apart.

5. Cut a 36-in. length of ⅜-in.-dia. rod to form the tong shafts. Heat the rod's midsection, and bend it in half in your hands. The halves should be parallel, the ends even and about ½ in. apart.

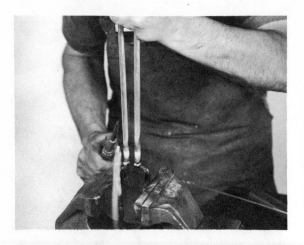

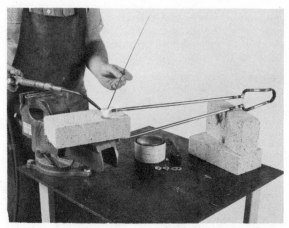

6. Clamp the handle in the vise with the flared ends up. Braze the shaft piece you just bent to the exposed ends of the handle. First, flux each handle end, then heat it and melt a puddle of filler rod on it. Press the fluxed shafts onto the cooled and solidified puddles. Heat the end of one shaft until you see a fillet of bronze form around the joint, indicating that the puddle has remelted and bonded to the shaft. Heat the other shaft for the same result. If necessary, feed more filler rod into either joint.

8. Prop the tongs on firebricks, as shown, with a firebrick inserted between the tong ends. Slip an ungalvanized washer with a $5/16$-in.-dia. hole between the top tong end and the firebrick, and braze tong end and washer together. Both pieces should be fluxed before brazing, of course. Turn the assembly over and braze another washer to the other tong end.

9. Smooth any rough spots with a file, and wire-brush the tongs. Then set it with the other tools. Only the stand is yet to be made.

Making the stand

7. Clamp the assembly in the vise with only the U-shaped bend of the tong shafts projecting from the vise jaws. Leave about 1½ in. exposed. Cut through the center of the bend with a hacksaw.

1. Cut a 36-in. length of ⅜-in.-dia. steel rod for the first of two post units. Make a 45° bend in one end. To do this, heat the rod end with the torch, and insert the rod in the bending jig, positioning it so that the distance from the rod end to the inside angle of the bend is ¾ in.

2. Make a second 45° bend behind the first, bending in the opposite direction to form an S-shaped section. To do this, heat the rod about ¾ in. behind the first bend, then fit the rod in the bending jig so the distance from bend to bend will be ¾ in. One of the fireplace tools will hang from the resulting hook.

3. Make a 90° bend 4 in. from the end of the hook. Again, you must heat the appropriate area of the rod with the torch. Position the heated rod in the bending jig so that the straight-line distance from the rod end to the inside corner of the bend will be 4 in. Make the bend.

4. With the hook formed at the top of the 36-in. rod, begin making a foot at the other end. First, make a 90° bend ¾ in. from the rod end. Torch-heat the end, and bend it in the jig so the inside of the bend is ¾ in. from the rod end.

5. Make a second 90° bend for the foot, 5½ in. from the first. Heat and bend the rod in the jig.

6. At this point, the 4-in. section for the hook and the 5½-in. section for the foot should be in the same plane. The foot must be bent 30° out of that plane. Place the long midsection of the post in the vise horizontally with the foot just free of the jaws to one side and projecting straight up. Torch-heat the shaft. Grasp the end of the foot with pliers and pull it *toward* you until the foot is 30° off vertical.

7. Cut a second 36-in. piece of ⅜-in.-dia. rod, and repeat steps 1 through 5 exactly, forming the second post unit. When you get to step 6, however, you must clamp the second post in the vise just as you did the first. But when bending the foot, you must push it *away* from you. If you repeat step 6 exactly, you'll get two identical posts, when what you want is a left one and a right one.

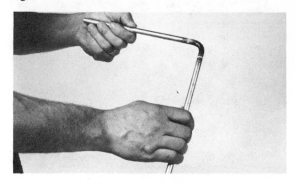

8. Cut an 18-in. length of ⅜-in.-dia. rod for the stand top. Bend this piece to form the last two stand hooks. First, torch-heat the middle of the rod. Hold one end in each hand and bend it in half. The ends should align and be 1 in. apart with the rod halves parallel.

9. Bend each rod end twice, creating a hook to match those atop each post unit (see steps 1 and 2).

11. Spread the tool hooks apart by placing the piece's U-shaped end in the vise, heating the 90° bends, and spreading the hooks 60° apart. Bend each hook 30°, so the bends will be even with respect to the U-shaped end.

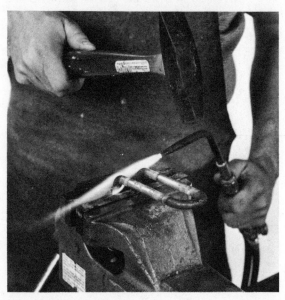

10. Bend the stand top 90°, 4 in. from its ends. Mark the location of the bend, then fit the piece in the vise, hooks down, with the bend location aligned with the jaw tops. Heat and hammer-bend the U-shaped end of the top until it's at a right angle to the hooks.

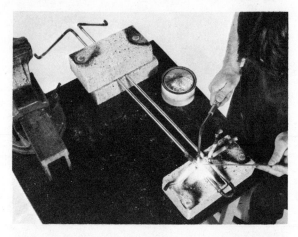

12. Position the posts and the stand top on firebricks, and braze weld them together. Lay the posts across two firebricks with their feet clear of obstruction and hanging below horizontal. The hooks should be flat on one firebrick, pointing in opposite directions. The shafts should be 1 in. apart and parallel. A third firebrick laid atop the posts near the feet will hold them in place. Butt the stand top in position and braze weld where the bend of each post meets a bend of the stand top.

13. Cut another 18-in. piece of ⅜-in. rod, heat its midsection, and bend it 90°. This piece will form the remaining two feet for the stand.

14. Heat one end of this piece, and make a 90° bend whose inner angle is ¾ in. from the rod end. Heat and bend the other end, making a matching 90° angle.

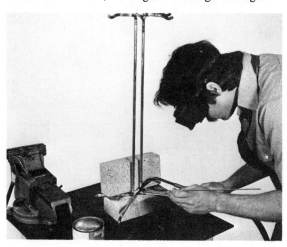

15. Stand the assembly on a firebrick, and hold it there by setting another firebrick on top of the two feet. Place the 18-in. foot piece against the stand assembly so its 90° bend rests in the space between the posts. Position the pieces so that all four feet are in a single plane, so that the finished stand will be stable. Braze weld the pieces together.

16. Stand the assembly on firebricks, and braze an ungalvanized washer with a ⁵⁄₁₆-in.-dia. hole to the bottom of each foot. When the feet have cooled, place the stand on the worktable, and adjust the position of the feet so the unit will stand without wobbling.

17. File any rough spots with a file, and wire-brush the joints.

Finishing the tools and stand

Carefully wipe each tool and the stand with a rag soaked in paint thinner to clean flux or oils from the metal. Coat each piece with a heat-resistant spray primer. Then apply several coats of a heat-resistant spray enamel. You can find such paints, used to paint auto engines, in auto parts stores.

Furnishings to Make with Fiber

For well over a hundred years, it has been standard practice to decorate our homes with machine-made rugs and fabrics. Store-bought textiles are now so much of a commonplace in our domestic lives that we tend to think of them only in their finished form.

Because we are so long removed from the work of cloth weaving and rug knotting, it is easy to ignore the elemental processes that bring these goods into being. Think of a rug as an orderly arrangement of hundreds and hundreds of knots. Imagine fabric as a multitude of horizontal threads passing in and out of an army of vertical threads. The painstaking, meticulous work of making knots and interlocking threads is the basis of the craft of textiles. These are simple activities which, despite their antiquity, still offer inexhaustible creative possibilities.

In the following section, you can learn basic fiber skills and apply them to projects to make for your home. There are seven detailed projects for making home furnishings on a loom and three for making off-loom rugs. The weaving projects progress in complexity from a tapestry hanging made on a small, hand-held frame loom to a set of three screen panels made on a multiharness loom.

In the section on nonwoven rugs, there are projects for making a latch hook rug, a punch needle rug, and a braided rug. All the basic information you will need to become a weaver or a rugmaker is included in special chapters and alongside the project directions. Because fiber crafts can be expensive, there are instructions for building two frame looms yourself and many suggestions for saving money on basic supplies and equipment.

Approach the challenge of creating your own textiles in the same way that you might undertake to produce a special meal. Start with tempting raw ingredients, cut them, measure quantities, experiment with promising combinations, and finally serve up the results as proof of your skill and care. The fun of creation may be all yours, but pleasure in the finished product can be shared with those around you and enjoyed for a very long time.

Handweaving

Why weave? The reasons are as varied as the thousands of weavers around the world, but at the heart of the matter is the desire to produce something aesthetically pleasing. We don't weave from necessity. That reason no longer applies. But the process still appeals to our elemental desire to produce a tangible product from dissimilar raw materials.

If the impetus to weave has changed, the process is remarkably like what it has always been: the passing of horizontal threads in and out of vertical threads. Within the severe limitations of warp and weft lies an extraordinary potential for artistic expression. To seize that opportunity, to take a crack at weaving, is to join the company of an unbroken thread of weavers down through the centuries.

For all weaving's complexity, it is surprisingly easy to learn. Intuitively, it makes sense to us. Watch children twist fibers together, intertwine grasses and plait flowers, weave pot holders and braid lariats. They grasp these possibilities as naturally as birds build nests or spiders spin webs.

The fascination with interlocking fibers has led to the development of knitting, crochet, tatting, and macrame. But weaving is the daddy of them all. The metamorphosis of material from strand to cloth, from yarn to clothing, and from string to lace, predates all other forms of handwork, which is in fact the old name for fiber arts.

Weavers are soothed by the rhythmic repetition of the work. They are stimulated by the scope for creativity and practical application. Handweaving is particularly adaptable to home furnishings. Displaying and using handwoven work captures good design and craftsmanship and releases it into daily life. (Imagine a house in which every room has a handmade article: that is a home indeed.)

Above all, weavers have fun. They amuse themselves through the exploration of fiber, and if they are skilled and lucky enough, they end up with a pleasing pile of decorative and practical articles to make them smile, keep them warm, and show off their skill. After all the trial and error, they can say, "I made it myself."

Learning to weave—Weaving requires a commitment of time and money, but it is possible to begin gradually, to test the waters a bit before plunging in. If the idea of weaving is appealing, start by simply watching a weaver at work, if at all possible. See what it is really like, and talk about it with someone already committed.

Then read a book on the subject, or take a course, or both. Best of all is to take individual lessons with a teacher who can concentrate on showing you how to use the particular equipment to which you have access.

Community colleges usually offer weaving courses and the accompanying opportunity to meet other student weavers. A course will impose some discipline on your efforts, and the personal contacts will be invaluable for encouragement and inspiration.

In the absence of a private teacher or a local course, learn from a book. To a degree, all weavers are self-taught anyway, because they learn by experimenting. The self-taught weaver proceeds at his or her own pace. Books provide the panorama of techniques without becoming sidetracked in any one area of expertise. Book glossaries provide good reference tools, for weaving jargon is often more difficult to master than the techniques themselves.

In the end, any method of learning to weave that is encouraging, challenging, and enjoyable will be effective. Books and magazines that include specific projects are useful for learning the basics and for review. Many weavers like project weaving, because the format frees them from a part of the process—complex decision-making—that they do not enjoy. Projects allow you to see the finished work before beginning and evaluate the

level of skill they require. You know at the outset that the design works and what equipment and material are necessary.

Modern craftspeople have an overwhelming number of choices of what to produce and what materials and colors to use. Freed from producing the necessities of life, and with exciting materials in spectacular colors readily available, it is easy to get swamped by this embarrassment of riches. Projects appearing in books and magazines allow the home weaver to benefit from the expertise of experienced weavers without the confusion of facing each minute decision involved in the planning process.

The weaving community—If you make an effort to meet weavers, you will find that they share generously and talk freely about textile work. By taking a course or finding weavers to observe, you will inevitably absorb some of their aesthetic vision and technical expertise. But take nothing for granted; the youngster may be a master weaver and the grandparent a beginner.

The more weavers you meet the better. Each one will bring to your acquaintance an individual weaving style that is complementary with that weaver's own personality. Each will expand the vocabulary of possibilities that you bring to your own work.

Weavers commonly establish guilds as a means of communicating with each other. These local guilds offer instruction, run workshops, loan books, and suggest projects to their members. Join a guild for practical help and for inspiration. The members befriend, encourage, and educate each other. Find information about a local guild through a local loom distributor, yarn store, or the national organization: The Handweavers Guild of America, Inc., 65 LaSalle Avenue, P.O. Box 7-374, West Hartford, CT 06107.

The HGA sponsors a biannual convention and publishes both a suppliers' directory and a quarterly magazine. The convention promotes weaving through workshops, exhibits, lectures, and displays of material from an international array of suppliers. The HGA magazine is one among several publications specifically addressed to home weavers.

Warp and weft

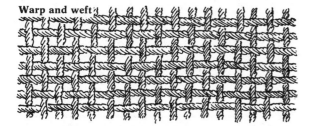

Buying Equipment

The best loom to buy is the one that you can afford, that fits in your house, and that can produce the kind of fabric that you're interested in. Whatever its size or style, it should definitely be constructed of hardwood. Nothing else will last as long, or retain its resale value as well.

Look at a lot of looms, watch them in operation, and talk about them with knowledgeable owners. If possible, borrow one and take it home. Your goal is ultimately to establish a special relationship with your equipment. The right loom will seem almost to develop a personality as it becomes your ally in the weaving process. If it is well designed, it will also make weaving physically easier.

Looms come in enough sizes and styles to make it possible for you to come very close to buying the ideal loom for your circumstances. They all have in common the basic mechanisms that hold warp threads taut while a horizontal weft thread is interwoven between them, but weight, size, and degree of automation vary tremendously.

Looms get more expensive as they get more automated and as the width of fabric they can produce expands. A frame loom you assemble yourself costs a small fraction of the price of a multiharness loom. A table loom with a 15-inch weaving capacity is cheaper than a floor loom with a 45-inch weaving capacity.

There are now looms available in inexpensive kits that are easy for an amateur to assemble. Assembling a loom yourself will save you a lot of money, but before you buy one, try to find a dealer who displays looms already constructed so you can examine their complexities.

Looms sometimes come up at auctions or estate sales. Before you bid, seek the advice of someone who knows looms. If there are parts missing, make sure they are ones that are easy to replace. Replacing heddles is no problem, but a cloth beam requires major work to replace, because it must be rebuilt by a woodworker. If an old loom costs almost as much as a new one, it is no bargain.

Types of looms

Looms fall into categories based on their degree of automation and the type of fabric they can produce. Within each category, there are several weaving widths. Once you choose the category that is right for you, choose a loom that is large enough and has enough features to allow you to grow as a weaver. You will be disappointed if you don't evaluate the limitations of a loom before you buy it.

The weaving projects in this book progress from items made on simple looms to those on looms that are more complex, starting with a project to be woven on a basic frame loom made with stretchers. Cheap and easy to build, a frame loom is very useful for learning the fundamental techniques.

Despite its simplicity, the frame loom is the vehicle for creating the breathtakingly intricate and beautiful works made by primitive peoples. Navajo, tapestry, and vertical or upright looms are all frame looms. At their simplest, they do nothing more then hold the warp threads, allowing the weaver to concentrate on experimenting with color, texture, and design, without being distracted by complex equipment. The weaver needle-weaves the weft threads into place. Adding a shedding device, which separates the warp threads so that the weft thread can be slipped into place, speeds the weaving process. The addition of a beater mechanism to push the weft thread quickly into its horizontal position also adds to the mechanization of the process. In

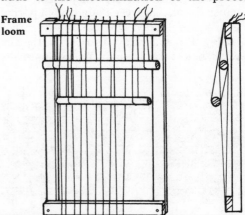

Frame loom

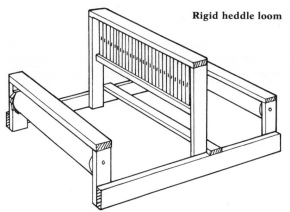

Rigid heddle loom

addition to a beater, some frame looms and all roller looms have shedding devices.

Rigid heddle looms are simple, two-shed roller looms that allow the weaver to produce plain weave, which is the basic weaving stitch. They are one step up in complexity from a frame loom. A reed-heddle bar separates the warp threads to create the shed, or opening, between them, which allows easy insertion of the weft thread. The reed-heddle bar also acts as a beater to position the weft thread. It is possible to work laces, knots, wrapping, and inlay techniques on a rigid heddle loom.

Adjustable rollers, located in the front and back of the loom, hold threads and finished fabric. As you weave, you can roll the finished work onto a roller, making it possible to produce cloth that is longer than the length of the frame of the loom.

Acquiring a small table loom would expand your weaving horizons one more step. A table loom is a small roller loom with harnesses. The harness structure creates the shed. The greater the number of harnesses on a harness loom, the more possibilities for intricate pattern weaving. The weaver can arrange the warp threads so that the loom is programmed to produce the desired pattern. A larger version of the table loom—a floor harness loom—adds a fourth level of complexity. Whereas the most common number of

Choosing a Loom

Type	Method of Producing Shed	Advantages	Limitations
Frame loom	Manual or needle-weaving	Inexpensive Uncomplicated Entire work visible Easy to store	Cloth can only be as long as the loom
Rigid heddle loom	Manual (raising reed-heddle)	Mechanical plain weave Relatively inexpensive Simpler than multiharness loom Can produce longer length of cloth than can frame loom	Cannot use bulky warp Limited to plain weave Can do open weaves with pick-up stick
Multiharness table loom	Manual (levers)	Unlimited pattern weaving Can produce longer cloth than can frame loom or rigid heddle loom	Complicated setting-up procedure Expensive
Multiharness table loom	Foot (treadles)	Unlimited pattern weaving Speed of production Can produce longer cloth than can frame loom or rigid heddle loom	Complicated setting-up procedure Expensive Large space required

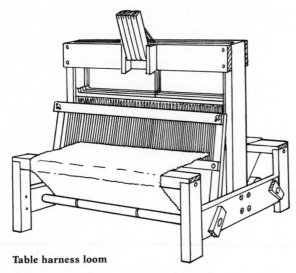
Table harness loom

harnesses found on a table loom (and even on many floor looms) is 4, large floor looms for home use may have as many as 16, and old-fashioned looms used commercially had even more. All the projects in this section can be worked on a four-harness loom.

The four-harness loom can create plain and twill weaves, and their hundreds of derivatives, all of which are formed by the weft's movement over and under a combination of 1, 2, or 3 warp threads. A satin weave such as damask requires a five-harness (or more) mechanism for production, because the weft material goes over and under 4 warp threads, thus demanding another harness to hold the weft in place.

There are three styles of harness looms, each differentiated by the way in which the shed is formed. The movement of the harnesses controls the movement of the warp threads. The warping process is the same on all three styles of harness looms.

On jack harness looms, the harnesses rise in order to raise their warp threads. This action forms the shed; hence, jack looms are also called rising shed looms. Jack looms are the most popular harness looms in the United States.

Early American looms, the second type, are counterbalance looms. The harnesses of the counterbalance loom work in tandem. They are attached to joints which rotate the pairs of harnesses so that as one is lowered, the other is lifted. An additional mechanism controls the pair of harnesses so that one pair can be worked against another pair. Counterbalance looms are returning to popularity, because they are particularly well suited to rug production. There are, however, some intricate patterns that are difficult to produce on the counterbalance loom. A jack loom is a better choice if you're interested in doing complex pattern weaving.

The third kind of harness loom is called contramarche. The shed on the contramarche loom is formed by the combined action of raising and lowering harnesses simultaneously. Each harness is independent of the action of the other harnesses. Contramarche looms are often used in Europe, particularly in Scandinavia, but less often in America. All of the harness loom projects presented in this book can be worked on any style of harness loom.

Harness looms are the most versatile looms available for home use. They are the only looms capable of reproducing the complicated overshot patterns developed in colonial times. These patterns are based on the star, cross, diamond, rose, and wheel. Overshot patterns are experiencing a renaissance, thanks to home computers that can alleviate the more strenuously labor-intensive aspects of this style of weaving.

Complex patterns engaged the imagination of colonial weavers while their hands attended to the production of items that were strictly utilitarian. Their weaving projects, while thoroughly practical in nature, and meant to last for several generations, were also one of their rare outlets for artistic expression.

Weaving of this complexity has long been superseded by styles that are more accessible to the hobbyist. The advent of graphic computers, however, may well signal a return to a generally more complicated level of weaving patterns. The graphics can be represented with great rapidity and experimented with visually. Using a pattern that has been translated into a program draft to be implemented when the loom is threaded is far less time-consuming for the weaver.

Other weaving equipment

Below is a list of weaving tools that you can buy, or, in some cases, make at home, to facilitate your work.

Bobbin—a spool which holds weft thread. There are two types: type A (see p. 342) is used in tapestry weaving and is pointed to act as a shuttle as well as a bobbin; type B fits into a boat shuttle. To make a type B bobbin, cut a piece of paper to the proper length, then wrap it around a pencil, and tape it in place.

Bobbin winder—a manual or electric machine which winds weft thread onto bobbins.

Cone or spool holder—a wooden base containing two or four vertical pegs. It holds cones of yarn while the weaver is winding a warp or bobbins. You can make a cone holder by sinking 3- to 4-inch-long dowels into a piece of wood.

Cross sticks—two slender sticks or dowels, each with a smooth finish and a hole drilled through each end so they can be tied together. Cross sticks are used to help hold the warp threads in the proper sequential order. They generally remain in place throughout the weaving process.

Pick-up stick—a pointed, flat stick used to enlarge the shed on a frame loom and to help pick up warp threads in some types of open weaves. Use to pick up warp threads on a frame loom or a rigid heddle loom to make pattern weaving possible.

Raddle—a wooden rod with nails protruding vertically at ½-inch intervals. The raddle is used in the warping process to spread the warp threads across the loom. Instructions for making a raddle are on page 385.

Shuttles—wooden tools that hold the weft thread and pass through the shed. Shuttles come in several shapes and sizes to accommodate the demands of the particular project, materials, and loom you are using. The three common shuttle types are explained below.

A boat shuttle is a boat-shaped wooden frame that holds a bobbin around which the weft thread is wound. The weft thread unrolls automatically as the shuttle is thrown across the shed.

A rag or rug shuttle is a wooden tool that can hold bulky materials. The rag shuttle is wider than the rug shuttle and is designed to hold rag strips.

A stick shuttle is a wooden or cardboard tool with notches at each end to hold the weft material in place. The yarn is wound around the shuttle and must be unwound before each row is woven. Stick shuttles are available in many lengths, or you can make one easily by cutting it out of cardboard.

Stretcher—made from metal or wood, stretchers are adjustable and keep fabric from drawing in during the weaving process. Sharp points at each end grip the cloth and hold it securely. Also known as a temple and template.

Tapestry beater—a wooden fork or comb used to beat the weft into place in tapestry weaving. A fork can be substituted.

Tapestry needle—a large, blunt-tipped needle used in tapestry weaving.

Threading hooks—the two common types are listed below.

A reed hook is a plastic or metal device used to sley the reed. Substitute a threading hook, an unbent paper clip, or a piece of cardboard cut in the shape of the reed hook.

A threading hook, also called a sleying hook, is a flat, metal hook used to thread the heddles and reed. A small to medium-size crochet hook can be substituted.

Umbrella swift—a foldable reel that holds a skein of yarn and twirls while the yarn is wound off onto bobbins, shuttles, or balls. The swift can also be used to wind skeins.

Warping board—a strong, rectangular wooden frame with pegs on which the warp is measured and wound before being placed on the loom.

Warping reel—a large, revolving, wooden frame around which the warp is measured and wound before being placed on the loom. A reel can hold more warp material than a warping board.

The efficient weaver will inevitably run into a need for scissors, a crochet hook, masking tape, measuring tape, and 3 × 5 cards. Keep a box or basket of these sundries close by as you work, to save yourself having to stop in mid-inspiration to hunt for them.

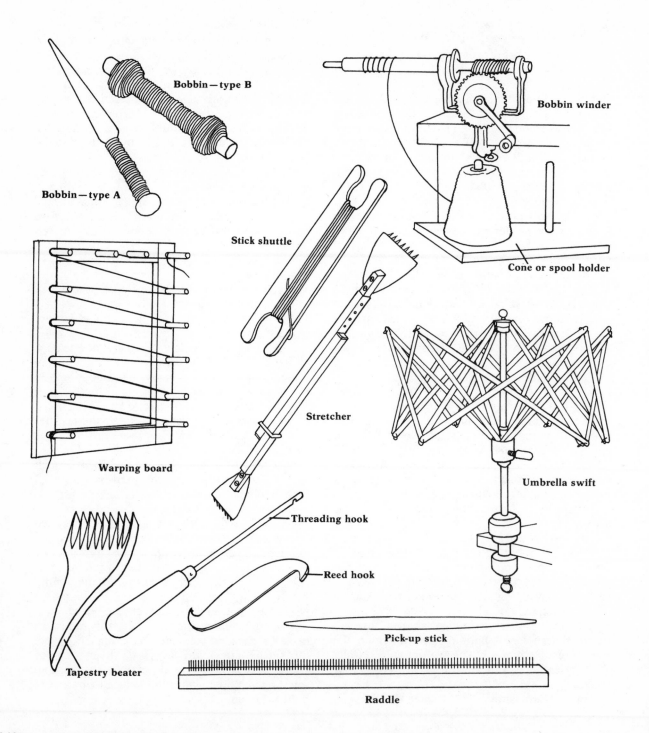

Bobbin—type B

Bobbin—type A

Bobbin winder

Cone or spool holder

Stick shuttle

Stretcher

Umbrella swift

Warping board

Threading hook

Reed hook

Pick-up stick

Tapestry beater

Raddle

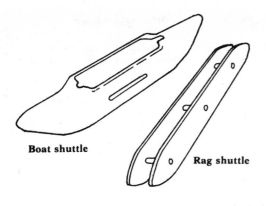

Boat shuttle

Rag shuttle

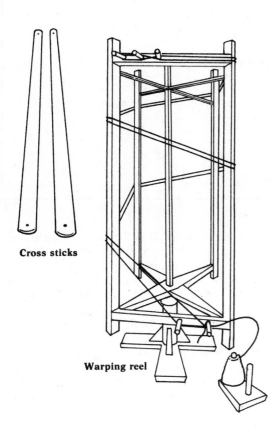

Cross sticks

Warping reel

Weaving tools

The illustration to the left shows the workaday tools of the weaver's craft. Many are made of hardwood and decorative enough in their own right to enhance your workspace.

Fiber

Strands of fiber are the weaver's raw materials, just as wood is the woodworker's and clay is the potter's. Acquiring a basic knowledge of fiber is just as important for the weaver as understanding wood and clay is for those who create objects from them. A fiber's qualities dictate the characteristics of the finished cloth, and no weaving project will be a success if the choice of fiber is inappropriate. A beautifully executed screen, for example, will be a disappointment if the fabric sags out of shape when it is fixed to a frame. The lesson: Know thy fiber.

Almost all fibers are chemically altered before they are sold commercially. They are often treated with mordants, which are chemicals that prevent dyes (yet another treatment) from fading, washing out, rubbing off, or changing color. Cotton is mercerized to improve its luster and strength.

The chart on page 344 lists the characteristics of fibers in their natural states, before any chemical altering takes place. Check the label on commercial fibers for a description of their characteristics. Ask a salesperson to explain the purpose of any process listed. Fabric characteristics are subject to constant change as new industrial processes are introduced.

Fibers fall into two categories: natural and synthetic. Natural fibers come from living organisms, either animals or plants. Wool, mohair, alpaca, and angora are animal fibers. Linen, jute, cotton, and hemp are plant fibers. Synthetic fibers are man-made. When first introduced, they were an attempt to copy natural fibers, but their strengths and unique characteristics made them attractive in their own right. Rayon, nylon, and polyester are among the most popular synthetics. Blending natural fibers and synthetics to get a specific mix of characteristics is now common practice.

Fibers for Home Furnishings

Fiber	Source	Advantages	Disadvantages	Other Information
Acrylic	Chemical (acetic acid)	Strong Resistant to sunlight	Nonelastic	Appears in many forms Blends well with cotton and wool
Cotton	Cotton plant	Easy to use Dyes well Strong Elastic	Wrinkles	Blends well with other fibers
Linen	Flax plant	Strong Long wearing Elegant	Nonelastic Difficult to use as warp Wrinkles Affected by humidity	Blends well with other fibers
Mohair	Angora goat	Warm Durable Elastic Dyes well	Expensive Fibers tend to cling to one another when used as warp	Hairy, textured yarn
Rayon	Wood pulp	Shiny Dyes well	Weak when wet	Blends well with other fibers
Wool	Sheep	Long wearing Resilient Absorbent Dyes well Elastic Warm	Static Attractive to moths	Can be spun thick or thin

Thread and yarn structure—Fibers can never be turned directly into woven fabric. There must first be an intermediate step of interworking the raw elements to give them strength. At the beginning of the process of yarn or thread production is the raw fiber. If a wool fiber is coarse, it will be spun into yarns that are appropriate for carpets. If the fiber is gossamer fine, it will be spun into yarns for clothing. The length and weight of the fiber determines its destiny.

To create a thread, minute, short, natural fibers are spun together. The twisting action forms a continuous strand, called a single. In making fabric, a single is the simplest structural unit possible. Man-made fibers are extruded in a continuous strand, sometimes miles long.

A plied thread is formed by spinning two single strands together. A plied thread is significantly stronger than a single strand. Technically, what we call a thread is always plied and is finer and more tightly twisted than yarn. While thread is almost always smooth and tight, yarn can be loose or tight, smooth or nubby. It can be single or plied. Often yarns are 3- or 4-ply, meaning that they are formed of three or four single strands twisted together.

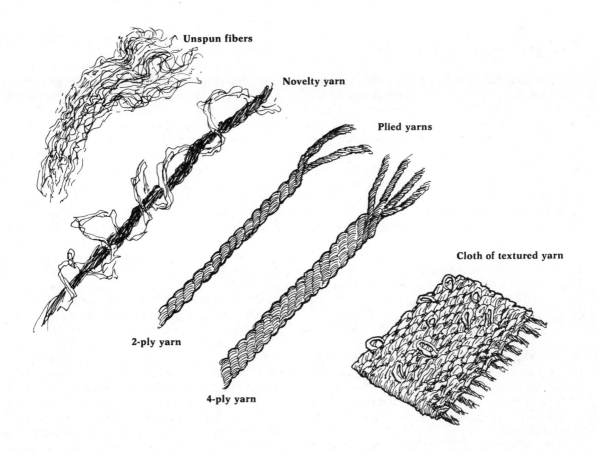

Unspun fibers

Novelty yarn

Plied yarns

Cloth of textured yarn

2-ply yarn

4-ply yarn

When you go shopping for yarn, you will be confronted with a useful code on the yarn labels. The smaller of the two descriptive numbers you will see refers to the number of strands plied together. For example, 22/2 is a 2-ply yarn. The higher number refers to the weight of a single strand of the fiber.

The way a plied yarn is twisted together helps determine its ultimate use. Roving, which is raw wool with no twist at all, is a good choice for rug weft, but it can never be used for warp, because it has no strength. A yarn that is tightly twisted will feel hard to the touch. Its strength will make it appropriate for home furnishing, but a poor choice for a sweater or other clothing that is worn next to the skin.

Yarns that add an interesting, nubby texture to the finished cloth are known as novelty yarns, and they are greatly favored by weavers. Chenille, slub, and bouclé yarns fall in this category. Each is constructed differently, but all appear nubby. Before mixing them with other yarns, check that their fiber content is compatible for washing purposes.

Found items like feathers, grasses, twigs, and leaves also make successful weft materials, particularly for wall hangings. Plastic bread bags used as weft make interesting place mats. Rag rugs, made with strips of fabric as weft, are also a thrifty and creative use of fiber. Any material that is slender enough to fit through the shed and suits your project is an appropriate fiber for weaving.

Planning and Design

Designing a weaving project requires both practical and creative decision-making. At the outset, you should be realistic about how challenging and time-consuming a project you are willing to undertake. If you're hoping for quick results with a minimum of frustration, make a table runner or some place mats. After all, weaving should be fun and it should suit your style. If you like to work slowly, planning as you go, try a tapestry that can remain on a frame loom for months, providing entertainment and accommodating revisions.

Always work with yarn that you are fond of. Often the yarn will suggest its own best use. If you like the yarn, and it seems to be particularly well suited to a project, the work will proceed enjoyably.

Closely related to choosing the fiber for a project is deciding on a form or structure. The stitches you choose become part of the structure of the piece. Should it be an open, lacy cloth or a dense, thick cloth? Should it have a pattern? These questions can only be answered in relation to the yarn you choose and the purpose of the finished product.

By its nature, all fabric has texture. Texture derives from the kind of thread you use and how you manipulate that thread on the loom. The best way to anticipate the texture that a particular yarn or stitch will yield is to keep a sample book of fabric and yarn snips from your projects as they accumulate. A sample book becomes the record of your weaving work, so the earlier on you start it, the better. Include disappointing results right along with the successful ones. The failures are equally educational.

To begin a sample book, get a notebook and set up a format for your notes. The notes should include the project, reed size, and sett per inch, technique, warp and weft sources, dates and personal notes. Use a consistent format for your notes, and they will remain coherent and useful years later. Personal notations in particular can be very helpful later. Did the fibers perform well in this project? Was the sett appropriate for the yarn?

Where does the initial inspiration for a weaving project start? Projects can develop from a number of possible starting points. One might begin with the selection of color, another from a motif or pleasing shape, and another from some experimentation with textures.

For weavers with training in art and design, sketching a design may be the most intriguing part of the weaving process. Some may find designing difficult and intimidating. Working with textiles demands an ability to visualize how a design sketched on paper will appear when translated into fiber. The transition from a two-dimensional sketch to a weaving subtly changes the overall effect of the design. A way to fuse the textile medium with the design ideas in one's imagination is to relate both to nature.

Nature is a never-ending source of ideas. Consider flower colors, tree shapes, and rock forms in relation to fabric color and texture. Art and architecture also suggest shapes, textures, and colors. Stained glass windows, architectural detailing, and symbolic forms are worth consideration when hunting for a weaving design.

To translate the design idea you have settled on into fiber, make a cartoon. A cartoon is a sketch drawn to scale with felt tip pens. Because it is almost impossible to touch up a design after it is woven, it is wise to perfect your ideas on the preliminary cartoon before you begin to weave.

Finalizing the design is not enough. Making a sample before you begin is also a good idea. Weaving a sample is the best way to test the warp sett, color combination, and shrinkage of the fabric. Time spent on a sample can save time, material, and disappointment later. Preserve the samples you make by adding them to your sample book.

Although good planning is vital, in weaving one also learns a great deal by experimenting. Don't get bogged down in the design stage. Many beautiful textiles are the result of lucky accidents in design. The goal is to weave and to enjoy it. The weaver's enjoyment of the process can itself be a subtle influence on the design.

The Ways of Color

Color is one of the most exciting components in weaving. Because colors are combined in stripes, plaids, and inlays, and with warp and weft of different colors, a sense of the interplay of colors upon one another is important to the weaver. The excitement of visualizing the woven result when choosing yarn colors makes working with color in weaving very stimulating. No amount of reading will teach as much as simply working with colored yarns. Weaving a color sampler and evaluating the interplay of colors as they affect the individual weaver is invaluable.

Though color theory is complex, there are some simple color tricks weavers use to help in color selection. A color circle simplifies the discussion. The color families listed on a wheel are either primary or secondary. These are shown in infinite gradations around the wheel. The primary colors—red, yellow, and blue—are the basic pigments from which the rest of the colors are formed. Colors resulting from combinations of primary colors are called secondary colors. Combining the primary colors blue and yellow, for example, makes green, a secondary color. Since each primary color is shown in its entire spectrum, the possible combinations that yield secondary colors are virtually limitless. Neutral colors—white, gray, and black—are not included on the wheel, since their addition determines the gradations of each primary color from dark to light.

There are several common types of color combinations (called harmonic colors) that generally appeal to our tastes. These fall into two broad categories: monochromatic and analogous combinations, which emphasize similar colors, and complementary and split complementary combinations, which emphasize differences in colors.

A monochromatic color alliance is made by combining one color family with neutral colors. Pale red (made by mixing red and white), pure red, and maroon (made by mixing red and black), for instance, form a monochromatic harmony. The weft-faced rug project (see p. 370) uses a monochromatic approach.

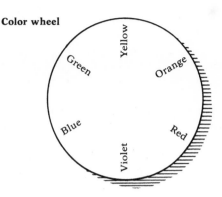

Color wheel

Analogous color combinations are those which use neighbors on the color wheel. For example, since violet is bordered by red and blue, the grouping together of red, violet, and blue constitutes an analogous color scheme. The screen panel project (p. 400) is an example of an analogous color harmony.

Complementary harmony is created by using colors that are opposite one another on the color wheel. Red and green, yellow and purple, and blue and orange are complementary color combinations.

Use of split complementary combinations is particularly effective in plaids. Split complementary agreement involves three colors—the dominant color and the two colors on each side of the complement. Orange, blue green, and blue violet form a split complementary harmony.

Dominance is important to consider when picking out harmonious color combinations. Choose the foremost color for the article first, then choose the minor colors. The dominant color should remain a stand-out; a blue striped fabric may have minor black and white stripes and still be called a blue fabric.

The single most important consideration in the use of color in weaving is the effect the colors surrounding a specific hue have on that hue. The same red stripe will appear as one hue when surrounded by black and quite another one when surrounded by yellow. If you are making a throw pillow to match drapes, first evaluate how the sofa color will interact with the pillow color. It may change the effect so that the pillow does not appear the same shade as the drapery color.

Working with color

1. Interweaving two yarns of different colors will give the impression of a third color. Similarly, checkered fabric will appear as a third tone when viewed from a distance.

2. Texture affects color. Fuzzy-textured chenille will appear dull compared to smooth rayon of exactly the same hue.

3. In analogous color combinations, the colors lean toward one another. Red appears orange when surrounded by yellow.

4. Using intense colors together will make the brighter color look more brilliant than it is and the less bright look dull.

5. Dark colors appear heavy compared with lighter ones. Use less of dark colors in stripes, and place them at the bottom of work when doing horizontal shading.

6. Complementary colors are intensified when used side by side, but they are dulled when interwoven.

7. Advancing colors—red, orange, yellow, white—jump out from a darker background.

8. Dark colors recede when surrounded by a lighter background. The dark circle on a wall hanging, for instance, will appear deeper than the surrounding fabric.

9. The type of weave affects the color's appearance. A weft-faced tapestry will hide the warp threads completely, so their color is unimportant.

The Language of Weaving

Apron bars—the rods which attach warp threads to the warp or cloth beams on a harness loom.

Balanced weave—work in which the number of warp threads per inch is equal to the number of weft threads per inch.

Basket weave—a variation of plain weave in which the weft goes over 2 warp threads and under 2 warp threads.

Batten—a beveled stick which makes a shed and acts as a beater on the upright frame loom.

Beater—a frame that holds the reed on a harness loom.

Beating—the process of positioning weft thread into its horizontal place in the woven work.

Bobbin—a spool which holds weft thread.

Bouclé—a looped novelty yarn.

Bubbling—the process of making waves in the weft thread as it is placed in the shed; it is used to avoid draw-in.

Buttonhole stitch—a decorative finishing stitch.

Carpet wool—a tightly spun, heavy yarn.

Cartoon—a sketch used as a guide in working a design into woven work.

Castle—the central structure on a harness loom, which holds the harnesses.

Chaining stitch—a technique in which the weft is wound around the warp threads to form a raised base for the work.

Chaining the warp—a process to prevent tangles in the warp while it is moved from the warping board to the loom; similar to crochet chain.

Cloth beam—the roller around which finished cloth is wound on a harness loom.

Contramarche—a harness loom on which the harnesses rise and sink simultaneously, creating a large shed.

Counterbalance—a harness loom on which the harnesses work in tendem; as one is raised, its partner is lowered.

Cross—crossing of threads as the warp is wound. It keeps the warp threads in order and simplifies the warping process.

Cross sticks—two slender rods that hold the cross in the warp threads while the loom is being warped and during the weaving process.

Danish medallion—an open, lacy weave in which oval medallions are formed by looping weft thread around itself.

Dent—a space in the reed.

Draw-in—the inclination of woven work to pull in during the weaving process.

Fiber—a material, either natural or man-made, that forms thread or yarn when it is spun.

Filler rows—the weft rows of cloth.

Fleece—a sheep's wool coat or fibers thereof.

Frame loom—a rectangular loom that usually lacks harnesses and a beater.

Guide thread—a short piece of string that is tied from the edge warp thread to the vertical structure on a frame loom to avoid draw-in.

Harness—a frame that holds the heddles on a harness loom.

H design—a design resembling a row of Hs worked with two colors in weft-face technique. Also called pick and pick.

Heddle—a wire or string with an eye in the center that holds and controls a warp thread on a harness loom.

Heddle rod—the stick around which string heddles are wrapped to make a shed for a frame loom.

Hole—the eye in a heddle on the reed-heddle bar of a rigid heddle loom.

Inlay—a free weave in which the weft is laid into the work to create a design.

Jack—a harness loom on which the harnesses rise from the rest position to form the shed.

Levers—the handles on table harness looms which control the harnesses.

Loom—any structure used for weaving that holds the warp threads taut and in place.

Maori edge—a finishing technique that makes a plaited edge to hold the weft in place.

Overhand knots—a finishing technique in which knots are formed with the warp threads to hold the weft in place.

Plain weave—the basic weave formed by the weft material going over and under alternate warp threads.

Ply—the number assigned to a yarn that designates the number of single strands that are spun together to form the yarn.

Pulled weft—a pile weave in which fleece or roving is laid loosely into the shed and pulled out between the warp threads to create a raised effect.

Raddle—a wooden rod with nails protruding at ½-inch intervals, used to spread the warp during the warping process.

Reed—a metal comb device that positions weft threads on harness looms. It is held by the beater.

Reed-heddle bar—the device used to create the shed and beat the weft into place on a rigid heddle loom.

Rigid heddle loom—a simple roller loom having a reed-heddle bar to form the shed.

Roving—a slightly twisted, thick strand of wool fibers which has been commercially carded.

Rya knot—a knot that creates a long pile that is particularly useful in rug-making. Also called ghiordes knot.

Selvage—the vertical edge of woven fabric.

Sett—the number of warp threads per inch.

Shed—the V-shaped opening formed as the warp threads are separated for the weft to pass into place.

Shed stick—a pointed, beveled stick used to form a shed on a frame loom.

Shuttle—a tool that holds weft material and passes through the shed.

Singles—yarn formed of one strand of spun fiber.

Skein—a length of yarn wound loosely in a coil.

Sley—to thread the warp threads through the dents in the reed on a harness loom.

Slot—the opening between heddles on the reed-heddle bar of a rigid heddle loom.

Soumak—a wrapping technique that gives a raised textural effect.

Spaced warps—the arrangement of skipping dents in the reed.

Splicing—a method of joining yarn lengths.

Stretcher—a tool which keeps fabric from drawing in during the weaving process.

Take-up—the decrease in length of the warp caused by interlocking weft and warp theads.

Tapestry—a type of decorative weaving in which only the weft shows. The warp is completely covered by weft yarn. Also called weft-face.

Tapestry beater—forklike tool used for beating the weft into place in tapestry weaving.

Tension—the tautness of warp threads when they are stretched the length of the loom.

Throw—a single movement of the shuttle through the shed to place weft thread in position.

Transparency—a technique in which the woven cloth has a translucent background and an inlay design, which becomes the decorative foreground.

Treadle—a pedal that controls the harness movement on a floor harness loom.

Warp—to string the warp threads on the loom.

Warp beam—the roller around which the warp threads are wound.

Warp threads—the vertical threads stretched taut along the length of the loom.

Weft-face—type of fabric in which only the weft material is visible on the surface of the work.

Tapestry/Pillow on a Small Frame Loom

Warping a frame loom
Plain weave
Bubbling
Chaining
Joining weft yarn
Soumak
Basket weave
Rya knots
Vertical stripes
Maori edge

This first project is a fitting introduction to the craft of handweaving. It combines practice in the fundamentals of tapestry weaving with the creation of a hanging that can also be folded, stitched together, and stuffed for use as a decorative pillow.

The work is done on an easily constructed frame loom, which, because of its small size and basic design, provides the simplest way to learn to weave. The very simplicity of the frame loom affords the weaver great control and flexibility. There is time to correct an error, change your mind, experiment, and explore.

Tapestry weaving is an ancient and useful art, well suited to frame loom methods. Tapestry technique is also called weft-face, because the weft completely covers a strong set of warp threads. The warp threads do not show on the surface of the work, but appear only as ridges in the fabric. The weft yarn creates the pattern, and special stitches provide the texture.

The densely woven nature of tapestry fabric once made it an excellent source of primitive insulation against the chill of cold stone walls. Probably more effective, however, was the psychological insulation evoked by its bright, warm colors.

While its R-value is of little consequence now, a tapestry is still a highly decorative source of vivid color. The one in this project serves as a primer of techniques that will provide the basis for creating the projects that follow.

What you will need

4 wooden canvas stretchers:
    2 in 20-in. size
    2 in 30-in. size
150 yd. 4-ply cotton rug warp
¾ lb. (800 yd./per lb.) 3-ply wool carpet yarn:
    ¼ lb. melon red (color A)
    ¼ lb. soft orange (color B)
    ¼ lb. light peach (color C)
2 blunt weaving or tapestry needles
1 fork or tapestry beater
1 pc. poster or mat board, 1½″ × 16″
1 pkg. hem tape to match color A
thread to match color A
12 oz. fiberfill (for pillow)
thin stick or 1 pc. dowel, ¼″ × 1′ long (for
    tapestry)

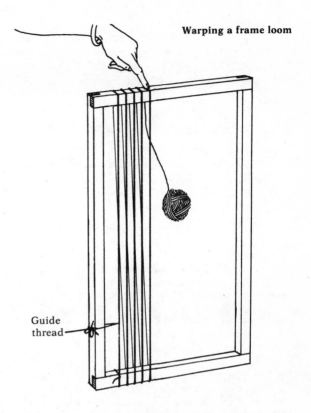

Warping a frame loom

Guide
thread

Making a frame loom

To make a simple frame loom, buy four canvas stretchers, two in the 20-in. size and two in the 30-in. size, at an art supply or hardware store. Assemble the frame by slipping the grooves of the longer and shorter stretchers together, then glue the corners in place to steady them. If you intend to take the loom apart again, use strapping tape instead of glue. When the loom is assembled, make pencil marks at 1-in. intervals across both the top and the bottom of the frame, starting 1½ in. in from the left. The marks will serve as guide lines when warping the loom.

Warping a frame loom

Hold the loom upright. Using the cotton carpet warp, tie a firm half bow on the lower left of the bottom frame at the 1½-in. mark. Draw the cotton over the top of the frame and around behind it. Place a finger on top of the thread to hold it firmly in place. Bring the cotton down the back of the loom, then around the bottom and up over the top again.

To maintain tension, always press the thread you are working on against the loom frame with your finger. Continue warping, spacing the threads ¼-in. apart, all the way across the loom. Stop when you have 113 warp threads extending over a 14-in. width, with a 1½-in. space remaining at the right side. In the upper right corner, tie the thread to the frame with a half bow.

Though the warp threads must be taut, they must still have enough elasticity to bounce if you strum

them with your fingers. If too tight they will not spring back, and if too loose they will shift position. If the tension is not uniform across the warp, undo whichever half bow is closer, press the thread against the frame where it is too loose or too tight, and rewarp the remaining thread back to the end. Retie the half bow. To help keep the warp threads in place, fix one piece of masking tape across the warp threads at the top of the frame, and another piece across the threads at the bottom.

To prevent the warp threads from pulling in as the work progresses, tie guide threads from the last warp thread on each side to the closest vertical frame member. Use pieces of thread about 8 in. long. The first ones should be about 6 in. from the bottom of the loom, and repeated at 1½-in. intervals as the work progresses. If you fail to add guide threads, the work may become distorted.

Finally, weave a narrow piece of cardboard through the bottom of the warp threads in order to eliminate the gap between the layers of threads caused by warping them over the frame.

Weaving Techniques

PLAIN WEAVE

Plain weave is the simplest, most frequently used weaving process. It is nothing more than interweaving yarn between alternate warp threads. Its simplest application is in making loop pot holders.

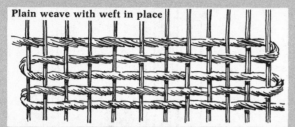
Plain weave with weft in place

To produce plain weave on a frame loom, first thread a tapestry needle with the weft yarn. Weave the yarn over the first warp thread, and under the second, then over the third and under the fourth. Repeat this interlacing process across all the warp threads. When the yarn is in place across the warp, push it firmly down against the cardboard with a fork, your fingers, or a tapestry beater. In the return row, lace the yarn over the threads you went under on the previous row and under the threads you went over.

At the top of the frame, every other warp thread is raised. The gap thus formed is called an open shed and is caused by the process of wrapping the warp on the frame. It can be used every other row when you are doing plain weave. Simply push the needle through the open shed and maneuver the yarn down into place. Weave the alternate rows by lifting alternate threads individually with the needle.

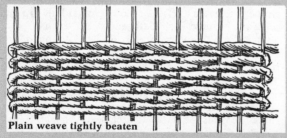
Plain weave tightly beaten

Plain weave will vary in appearance depending on the material used, how closely the warp is set, and how tightly the weft is packed. In tapestry, since the weft is very tightly packed against the previous row, the warp threads do not show on the surface of the work.

BUBBLING

Use the bubbling technique to prevent the sides of the work from drawing in. Because it takes slightly

Bubbling

more yarn to go over and under the warp threads than it does to lay the yarn flat across the width of the work, make waves in the weft yarn when you place it in the

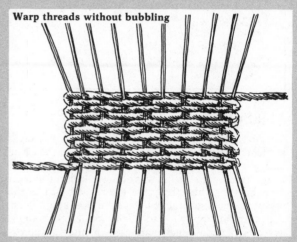
Warp threads without bubbling

shed. Bubbling eliminates the strain on the warp threads that might otherwise pull them out of their vertical alignment. After trailing the weft yarn across the shed, beat the yarn down against the previous row.

CHAINING

Chaining provides a firm starting edge for the first row of filling. Cut a length of yarn four times the width of the piece. Using a tapestry needle threaded with a single strand of yarn, start at the left edge and work toward the right. Moving counterclockwise in a wide

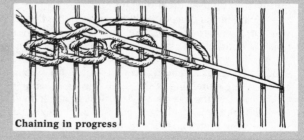
Chaining in progress

oval, trail the yarn over the space where the chaining row will fall. Insert the needle, pointing to the right, under 2 warp threads, then over the top of the oval made by the yarn, then pull the yarn up firmly, but not too tightly.

Leave a 2-in. tail at the left side; weave it invisibly into the work later. Now repeat the stitch by forming another oval with the yarn, inserting the needle again

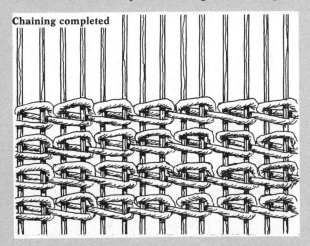

Chaining completed

from left to right under 2 warp threads, then over the top of the oval formed by the yarn, and finally pulling it firmly as before.

Continue the chaining stitch across all the warp threads. Whether loose or quite firm, the tension should be consistent across the row. The finished stitch is similar to a single crochet or to the chain stitch commonly found in embroidery.

JOINING A NEW WEFT YARN: SINGLE STRAND

To join a new length of weft yarn when you run out, splice the end of the current yarn with the new

Joining a single strand of yarn

Plies separated

length you wish to add. Simply unravel the plies of both ends of yarn, cut off two plies each from the old and the new lengths, then overlap them. This method prevents a lump from forming where the two layers are joined.

JOINING A NEW WEFT YARN: DOUBLE STRAND

First, double the strand of new yarn, and thread the loop through a needle. To join the new yarn with

the current length that has run out, put the loose ends from the current yarn through the loop of new yarn, then push the tails of both lengths into the back of the work. Weave them invisibly into the fabric later. The loop will disappear into the back of the work. This double-strand joining method creates a secure yarn splice which leaves ends to be reworked later.

Joining a double strand of yarn

SOUMAK

Soumak is a wrapping technique which creates a raised textural effect. It can be woven in several different ways, each method producing a slightly different appearance. Two rows of soumak wrapped in opposite directions resemble a chevron.

The stitch can be worked over any number of warp threads, right to left or left to right. Make the tension of the stitches and the number of warp ends wrapped consistent across the row. The soumak

Right-to-left soumak

stitches described here are the most basic among the many variations.

To produce right-to-left soumak, begin by carrying the weft yarn over the surface of the work, then insert the strand down between the warp threads toward the underside of the fabric. Turn the strand back under the one you are wrapping, and bring it up to the surface again. Draw the needle through so that the yarn is snug. Now carry the yarn over the top of the warp thread already wrapped and over the next 2 warp threads. Insert the yarn back under 1 warp thread and up to the top again as before. This completes 1 stitch. Continue across the row until all the warp threads have been covered.

(Continued on next page)

Weaving Techniques—*Continued*

SOUMAK—*Continued*

Left-to-right soumak

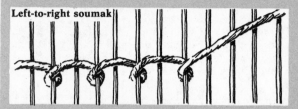

Making rya knots

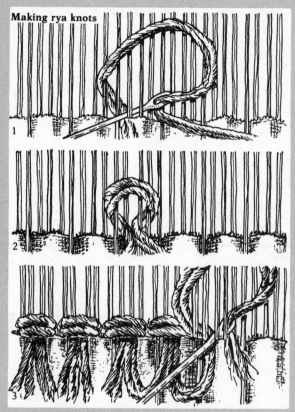

To produce left-to-right soumak, weave the weft yarn in precisely the opposite direction, carry the weft yarn over the surface of the work as in right-to-left soumak, insert it down between the warp threads, back under the one you are wrapping, then up between the warp threads, returning to the top of the work. Draw the yarn snug with a tug on the needle. Again as with right-to-left soumak, carry the yarn over the top of the warp thread already wrapped and over the next 2 warp threads, then turn the yarn back under 1 warp thread and up to the top again. Continue across the row until all the warp threads have been covered.

Soumak is similar to the back stitch in sewing. Since it does not have any structural strength, it must be used with plain weave or a variation of plain weave. For different effects with soumak, skip several warp threads, wrap 2 together, or wrap every warp thread.

BASKET WEAVE

Basket weave is a variation of plain weave. It is often used in tapestry work, because it covers the warp threads densely. The needle goes over 2 warp threads,

Basket weave

then under 2 warp threads, then over 2 and under 2 across the row. On the return row, the weft will be over the 2 warp threads it was under on the previous row and under the 2 threads over which it previously lay.

RYA KNOTS

Rya knots are usually associated with rugs, but they can provide an interesting texture for tapestry and pillows. Use at least 2 strands of multi-ply yarn to create the tufted effect. Starting at the left side of the work, weave over and under 2 warp threads in plain weave. Lift the weft over the next 2 warp threads, leaving a loop of weft yarn about 1 in. long. Insert the yarn back under the last 2 warp threads, carry it over the top of 4 warp threads, and wrap it back under 2 warps. Then pull it up firmly.

After leaving the loop, repeat the knot on the next set of 4 warp threads. Make knots with a continuous length of yarn, wrapping it around your fingers, thumb,

Uneven number of warp threads for rya knot

cardboard, or a ruler to help make the length of the loops consistent. Continue forming knots across the row of warp threads. Weave at least 2 rows of plain

Rya knots with plain weave between rows

weave between the rows of knots in order to hold them in place. After you complete each row, cut each loop open at the center to form a cut pile.

Make the next row of knots over the same warp threads as the previous row. If you discover that a row has an uneven number of warp threads, simply use 1 warp thread to maintain the space of 2.

VERTICAL STRIPES

In order to produce vertical stripes in weft-face weaving, use two colors of weft yarn on alternate rows. Basket weave is best for covering the warp threads and producing definite stripes. In order to create neat edges when using two colors, the yarns need to be interwoven beyond the end warp thread. By placing color B weft yarn under yarn of color A every time you reach the right side of the work, you will produce a tidy, looped effect.

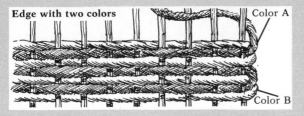

Edge with two colors — Color A — Color B

MAORI EDGE

The Maori edge is a useful finishing technique for producing a plaited edge that will not rip out. With the wrong side of the work facing you, start with the lower left warp thread. Weave the first warp thread, *A*, over the second warp thread, *B*, then under the third warp thread, *C*, and up on the back of the work. Pull snugly. Next weave the second warp thread, *B*, over the third

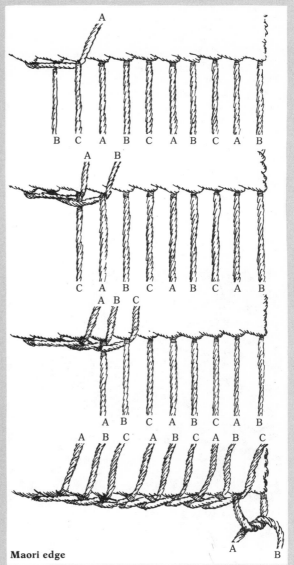

Maori edge

warp thread, *C*, under the fourth, *A*, and up in back as before. Finally, weave the third warp thread, *C*, over the fourth, *A*, under the fifth, *B*, and up.

Continue working across the fabric in groups of 3 warp threads, weaving them over, under, and up in back. At the right side, knot the last 2 warp threads together to hold them in place. All the warp threads will now be facing upward, and the plaited edging will hold the weft in place.

Step-by-step instructions

1. Cut a piece of wool weft yarn in color A, about 84 in. long. Thread a tapestry needle with a single strand of yarn, then, starting in the lower left corner, chain 1 row (see p. 352) with the loom flat on a table.

2. Prop the loom up. On the return row, begin a row of plain weave (p. 352). Bubble the yarn (p. 352) to keep the warp threads in place. Continue in plain weave with color A for 32 rows or 1½ in. Pack the weft rows tightly in order to hide the warp threads. As you progress, the first rows will become slightly more packed, but continue to beat each row as tightly as possible when it is in place. End the plain weave on a left-to-right row.

3. Slide the guide threads down to the top of the finished work. Make new guide threads now and every 1½ in. as the work progresses so there will be no distortion.

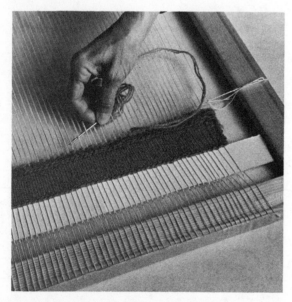

4. Weave 3 rows of soumak (p. 353) in color A. In row 1, use a single strand of weft yarn, and work from the right edge to the left. Go under the first warp thread at the edge, then over 2 warp threads and back under 1 warp thread. Next, weave right to left, going over 3 warp threads (counting the one wrapped) and back under 1 warp thread. Continue across the row. In row 2, thread the needle with a double strand of yarn. Begin at the right side again. Join the yarn at the edge.

Working soumak right to left, go over the first 2 warp threads and back under 1 warp thread for the first stitch. Then go over 3 warp threads and back under 1. You will be wrapping opposite warp threads from the previous row. In row 3, using a double strand again, work soumak left to right. Again wrap the warp threads which were skipped in the last row. They will be the same as in the first row. After completing the soumak, the piece should measure 1¾ in. long from the beginning of the work.

5. Starting at the right side, weave 3 rows of basket weave (p. 354) with a double strand of color A. There will be a single odd warp thread on the left side. Simply treat it as a double strand. At the end of the 3 rows, the piece should measure 2 in. long.

6. Add a double strand of color B at the left side. Continue the basket weave with both color A and color B on alternate rows. This will produce stripes of each color. Be careful to interlace the weft yarns at the edges (see Vertical Stripes, p. 355). Weave in basket weave for 1 in. End with a row of color A. You will have 8 rows of color B and 8 of color A (16 rows in all). The piece should now be 3 in. in length.

7. Drop color A. Add color C. Work in basket weave, alternating rows of color B and color C until there are 18 rows of each.

8. Drop color C. Work 5 rows of basket weave with a double strand of color B.

9. Working right to left, weave a row of soumak with a double strand of color B. Work on the top warp threads from the open shed. Then work a row of soumak left to right, wrapping the warp threads which were skipped on the last row. At the end of the soumak, the piece should measure 5½ in. long from the beginning of the work.

10. Weave another 5 rows of basket weave with color B, double strand.

11. Reattach color C and continue working basket weave with colors B and C in alternate rows for 2 in. End with a color C row. There will be 18 rows of color C and 17 rows of color B. The piece should now measure 7¾ in. long.

12. Drop color C. Reattach color A and continue colors A and B in alternate rows with basket weave for 1 in., completing 8 rows each of colors A and B.

13. Work an additional 3 rows of basket weave with color A. End with a left-to-right row.

14. Working right to left, work a row of soumak with color A, double strand. Work soumak on the return left-to-right row. The piece should now measure 9¼ in. from the beginning of the work.

15. Work 20 rows of plain weave, using a single strand of color A. End with a right-to-left row. The piece should now measure 10⅛ in. from the beginning of the work.

16. Thread the needle with 3 strands of color B to begin the rya knots (p. 354). Working from left to right, skip the first 2 warp threads. Make the first rya knot around 3 warp threads, starting with the third warp. To measure the length of the rya loop, wrap the yarn over your thumb and brace your thumb against the 2 rows of soumak. Make each knot around 4 warp threads except for the first (around 3) and the last (around 2). There will be 28 knots across the work.

17. Use a single strand of color A for the following 6 rows. Work the return right-to-left row in plain weave. Weave a second row in plain weave, and pack it tightly in order to hold the knots in place. After each of the next 2 rows, work extra plain weave at the sides over 6 warp threads on the left and 5 on the right. This extra filler will compensate for the large space taken up by the rya knots. Work 2 more rows of plain weave, to arrive at a total of 6 rows of plain weave.

18. Cut the rya strands at the middle of each loop.

19. Work the second row of rya knots left to right, with 3 strands of color B around the same warp threads as previous row of knots.

20. Repeat step 17, using color A. Packed tightly, the filler should measure ¼ in.

21. Work the third row of rya in the same way as the previous 2 rows, but vary the colors of the knots as follows: 4 B, 1 C, 3 B, 12 C, 3 B, 1 C, 4 B.

22. Turn the loom upside down. Leaving a space of ½ in., work 2 rows of plain weave with a single strand of color A.

23. With the loom upside down, work the fourth row of rya, *in the same holes as row 3.* The color sequence is 2 B, 24 C, 2 B.

24. Pack the 2 rows of filler against the knots. Turn the loom right side up, then work 4 rows of plain weave with a single strand of color A. Remember to work the extra at the edges to fill the warp evenly. Pack the plain weave tightly up against the knots.

25. Leaving a ½-in. space, weave 2 rows of plain weave with color A. Work the fifth row of rya in color B, using triple strands. Remember to skip the first 2 warp threads. Working left to right, form the first knot around 2 warp threads, then form 26 knots on 4 warp threads each, and the last knot around 3 warp threads. In this way your knots will be over the same warp threads as before. There will be 2 warp threads remaining at either side for plain weave.

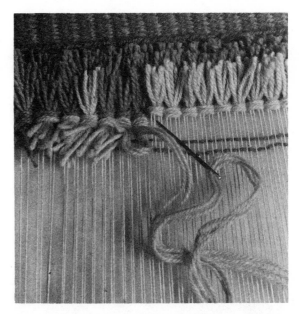

26. Pack the 2 rows of plain weave up against the knots. Work 4 more filler rows in color A with edge fillers as before.

27. Work the sixth row of knots with color B. Pack the 2 rows firmly up against the knots.

28. Turn the work right side up and, with color A, single strand, continue working in plain weave to ¾ in. beyond the rya knots.

29. Work right-to-left soumak with color A, double strand. Then work left-to-right soumak, also with color A, double strand.

30. Work 3 rows of basket weave with color A, double strand.

31. Reattach color B. Work basket weave in alternate rows of color A and color B for 1 in. The total should be 8 rows each of color A and color B.

32. Drop color A. Attach color C. Work basket weave with colors B and C on alternate rows for 2 in. There will be 18 rows of color C and 17 rows of color B. The piece should now measure 15½ in. in length from the beginning.

33. Drop color C. Weave 5 rows of basket weave with color B, double strand.

34. Working right to left, work a row of soumak with color B, double strand. Work on the top warp threads from the open shed. Then work a row of soumak left to right, wrapping the warp threads which were skipped on the last row. At the end of these soumak rows, the woven work should measure 15¾ in. long.

35. Work 5 rows of basket weave with color B, double strand.

36. Add color C. Work in basket weave with colors B and C on alternate rows until there are 18 rows of color B and 18 rows of color C for a total length of 2 in.

37. Drop color C. Add color A. Work basket weave with colors A and B on alternate rows. You will have 8 rows of color A and 8 rows of color B, totaling 1 in.

38. Drop color B. Weave 3 rows of basket weave with color A, double strand.

39. Work 3 rows of soumak. In row 1, work a row of soumak right to left with a double strand of color A. In row 2, work a row of soumak left to right with a double strand of color A. In row 3, using a single strand of color A, work a row of soumak left to right.

40. Weave 32 rows or plain weave with a single strand of color A.

41. Chain 1 row, working left to right.

42. Weave 2 additional rows of plain weave with color A, single strand.

43. Remove the tapestry from the loom by cutting the warp threads at the top and bottom of the frame.

44. Work a Maori edge (p. 355) at both ends of the piece.

45. Weave tail ends of the weft into the back of the work.

46. With the back of the work facing you, firmly hand-sew a piece of hem tape over the warp threads at each end. Catch the warp threads into the sewing for extra insurance against their pulling out. Sew both edges of the hem tape to the work. Cut off the excess warp ends.

For use as a tapestry wall hanging

1. Fold the top to the back at the top row of soumak, with the soumak showing on the front of the work.

2. Turn the work under again at the chaining so that a 1½-in. pocket is formed. Sew down at the chaining, using sewing thread which matches color A.

3. Insert a thin stick or ¼-in.-dia. dowel into the pocket. The dowel must be 1 in. shorter than the width of the tapestry so that you can sew the edges together to hide it. The dowel can be removed to dry-clean the piece.

4. Attach a small loop to the center and use it to hang the tapestry.

For use as a pillow

1. Fold along color B soumak (5½ in. from the ends), with soumak showing on the side which has the rya center. The chaining that began and ended the work should now meet in the center at the back of the pillow.

2. Match the color A soumak rows that are 1½ in. from the ends with the color A soumak that is on the front near the rya. Pin the pillow together at these points.

3. With color B, sew one side of the pillow together on the outside with a buttonhole stitch, starting at the corners and working toward the center. Place the stitches close together to keep the filling from showing.

4. Turn the pillow inside out.

5. With sewing thread matching color A, sew the edges of the hem tape together in a lacing fashion. Sew into the tapestry, but *not* into the Maori edge. Sewing into the edge would put undue stress on the warp ends. The edges should just meet in the center.

6. Turn the pillow right side out. Using color A yarn, join the 2 rows of chaining which began and ended your weaving. To join the chaining, catch one loop from the bottom chain and one from the top chain with a buttonhole stitch. Use color A (for clarity the photo shows the stitch worked in white). Push the needle between the outside loops and under both inside loops so that they are drawn together.

7. Pin the remaining open edges together at the color A soumak rows.

8. Starting from the corners, with color B yarn, sew the edges together with a buttonhole stitch. Stitch past the center.

9. Stuff the pillow.

10. Finish sewing the remaining edge. Overstitch the last stitch in order to secure it, then weave the end back down the side.

Alternate fastenings: Machine-stitch the pillow together from the inside, or fit a zipper closing at the center back.

Building an Upright Frame Loom

The construction of an upright frame loom is an elementary woodworking project. The finished loom, however, gives the weaver ample scope to use sophisticated rugmaking techniques. It is a variation on a Navajo frame loom, but it also belongs to a family of similar looms used throughout the world for centuries. In their simplest form, such looms were merely two trees growing close together. Branches lashed between them served as horizontals. Weaving was done from the top down, using needles; the warps were weighted to provide tension. Gradually, shedding devices replaced the needle technique.

Today, the bigger the loom the more expensive it is. But here is a big loom that is inexpensive to make, on which you can create works beyond the capabilities of even many expensive looms. It's also a good loom on which to hone your design skills, because the entire work is visible as you go.

Materials needed to build the loom are listed on the page opposite. Nominal lumber sizes are shown in parentheses.

The loom has two simply made shed mechanisms: a batten and a heddle rod (also called a pull rod). They automate the weaving process by creating the openings through which the weft passes. Beyond the loom's main task, which is to hold a warp securely in a vertical plane, it also has the virtues of taking up little floor space and of being easily dismantled.

The loom's frame is heavy and should be tipped against a doorframe, beam, or wall and tied to prevent it being pulled over. The weaver will be most comfortable kneeling on a cushion while working on the beginnings of a project, sitting and standing during the middle portions, and standing on a stool to complete the top of the work.

The loom is big enough, at 5½ × 8 feet, and weighty enough, to produce wide, heavy rugs. Weavers at any stage of competence will find it a useful investment, because it allows such wide scope for experimentation. At the end of this chapter are instructions for two projects well suited for production on an upright frame loom: a rya rug and a weft-faced rug. Each demonstrates one of the many variations the loom can accommodate.

What you will need

To build the loom:
2 pcs. lumberyard stock, 1½'' × 3½'' × 8'
   (2 × 4 × 8')
2 pcs. lumberyard stock, 1½'' × 3½'' × 66''
   (2 × 4 × 66'')
1 pc. lumberyard stock, ¾'' × 2½'' × 50''
   (1 × 3 × 50'')
1 pc. lumberyard stock, ¾'' × 1½'' × 5' (1 × 2 × 5')
   or 1 pc. dowel 1'' × 5'
8 bolts with nuts, ¼'' × 4''
16 washers, ¼''
2 lb. 4d finishing nails
hammer
yardstick
To warp the loom:
8/5 linen or heavy cotton carpet warp:
     250 yd. for rya rug
     500 yd. for weft-faced rug
25' twine

How to build the loom

1. Label the 66-in. frame pieces *top* and *bottom*. Label the 8-ft. frame pieces *left* and *right*.

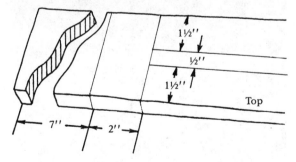

2. On both *top* and *bottom* pieces, measure 7 in. from the left end. Draw a vertical line on both faces of each board to indicate positioning for the two side pieces.

Draw a second vertical line, on the upper faces only, 2 in. to the right of the first line.

3. On both *top* and *bottom* pieces, draw horizontal lines 1½ in. from each side along the length of the boards. Draw these lines also only on the upper face.

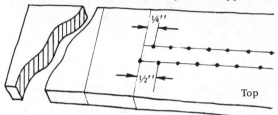

4. On the *top* piece, beginning on the lower line where it meets the second vertical line at the left end of the board, place dots at ½-in. intervals across the frame. Place the first dot on the vertical line. There should be 96 dots on each line. Now place dots on the top line in the same manner, starting ¼ in. *to the right* of the vertical line. The two rows of dots will be offset. Counting both rows, there should be 192 dots.

5. Count both rows of dots together from the left edge, and mark the lower row of dots at number 11. Then continue to mark every tenth dot (21, 31, 41, etc.). Writing these numbers at the appropriate dot will serve as a handy reference later.

6. Hammer nails with their heads slanting upward into each dot in the top frame. The slant keeps threads from falling off the nails when you weave.

7. On the *bottom* piece, also beginning at the second vertical line at the left end of the board, place dots on the top line at ½-in. intervals. As before, the first dot will be on the vertical line. Place dots on the lower line in the same manner, starting ¼ in. to the right of the vertical line. The rows of dots will be offset. Mark the upper row at 11, 21, 31, etc., as you did for the *top* piece.

8. Hammer nails slanting downward into the *bottom* piece at each dot.

9. Lay both *top* and *bottom* frame pieces over the pieces marked *left* and *right*. Position the *left* piece so that it lies to the outside of the first vertical line marked on the *top* and *bottom* pieces. Position the *right* piece beyond the rows of dots so that there is a 52-in. opening in the center of the loom.

10. Drill two holes for bolts at one corner. Insert a bolt in each hole with a washer on each side of the frame.

Tighten the nuts on the bolts. Repeat drilling holes and inserting bolts at each corner in the frame. Take care to keep the frame square. The loom is now completed and ready to be warped.

Warping a Frame Loom

Warping or stringing the loom is the preliminary step to weaving. The warp thread (linen or heavy cotton warp designed for rug projects) is strung up and down the loom on the nails you have placed in the top and bottom frame pieces. The nails are arranged so that each pair will share the warp tension, while at the same time the threads can hang straight from the top to the bottom of the frame. In order to benefit from the nails' unique positioning, warping must be done as directed.

1. Before starting, see the specific project you are doing for the width measurement. In the rya rug and the weft-faced rug projects, directions indicate the exact nail at which to begin and end the warping procedure.

Warping the loom

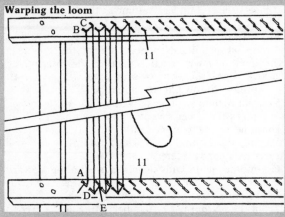

2. Begin by tying a half bow on nail A on the bottom frame. The half bow can easily be untied if adjustments are necessary.

3. Pull the warp thread to nail B on the top frame. Lay the thread to the left of nail B, then over the top and to the right of nail C and down the length of the loom. Now place the thread to the left and under nail D on the lower row of the bottom frame, then draw the thread to the right side of nail E and up the length of the loom. Pull the threads snug but not tight; you don't want them to break. Continue stringing warp threads in this manner across the width of the loom. When you are done, tie a half bow around the final nail on the lower row of the bottom frame.

Count the warp threads to make sure you have the right number for the project you are doing. Strum your fingers lightly across the warp threads to see if any threads are loose. If the warp thread tension is not equal across the warps, work the slack to the closer end and retie the half bow.

Making the shed mechanisms

The two shed mechanisms for the frame loom, a batten shed and a pull shed, will create openings between warp threads through which the weft shuttle will pass. The batten should be a 2½-in.-wide stick to create a shed when it is turned sideways in the warp threads. The pull shed, or heddle rod, is made by wrapping twine around a wooden stick or dowel and behind selected warp threads. With the heddle rod, selected warp threads can also be pulled from the rest of the warps to create an additional shed. As well as creating one shed, the batten does double duty to push, or beat, the weft yarns into their horizontal positions. This shedding design allows the weaver to manipulate the warp threads mechanically rather than having to lift them individually by hand.

1. To make a batten shed assembly, cut two pieces of twine, each about 6 ft. long, and loop and tie one around each end of the top frame, in the space between the warp threads and the vertical frames, so that each length of twine extends down 36 in. These lengths will hold the battens in place.

2. Weave the batten into the work by placing it over the first 2 warp threads, then under the next 2, and then over the following 2, continuing across the loom. Hang the batten in the twine holders made in step 1.

3. For a pull shed/heddle rod assembly, tie pieces of twine, each 54 in. long, to the top frame, as in step 1 of the batten shed directions. Hang a thin stick or a 1-in.-dia. dowel in place as the heddle rod.

4. Measure a length of twine 25 ft. long, and wind it into a ball. You will use the twine to make string heddles for the shed opposite that created by the batten.

5. Tie the twine in a half bow onto the left end of the heddle rod. As you work, hold the heddle rod out toward you so that there is a 1½-in. space between the warp threads and the heddle rod. Carry the ball of twine around behind warp threads 1 and 2, then between warp threads 2 and 3, to the front of the loom. Now carry the twine over the top, down the front, and under the heddle rod. Pass the twine in your hand up to the left of the twine in the space between the heddle rod and the warp threads, then carry the ball of twine to the right, over the top of the twine which started the loop around the heddle rod. Press the twine against the heddle rod with your index finger to keep the heddles from loosening. Skip warp threads 3 and 4 by passing the twine in front of them. Pass the twine between warp threads 4 and 5 to the back of the work, then carry the twine behind warp threads 5 and 6 and between warp threads 6 and 7 to the front of the rod. Wrap the twine around the heddle rod as before; over the top, down the front, under the heddle rod, through the space, and over the twine which started the loop. Skip warp threads 7 and 8. Continue across the work in this manner with each group of 4 warp threads. Since the string heddles are behind the warp threads which fall behind the batten, this setup allows you to produce basket weave in opposite sheds. When you reach the end of the warp threads, tie the twine onto the heddle rod.

6. To begin weaving with the batten, turn it sideways to create a shed.

7. Insert a shed stick (for wide work you will need two shed sticks to cover the width of the warp) in the shed just below the heddle rod and string heddles. Turn it sideways to hold the shed open.

8. Pass the shuttle through the shed on top of the shed stick across the width of the warp.

9. Remove the shed stick.

10. Bubble the weft yarn (see p. 352).

11. Beat the weft yarn down into its horizontal position with a tapestry beater.

12. Close the shed by returning the batten to its flat position.

13. Pull the heddle rod toward you to open the shed.

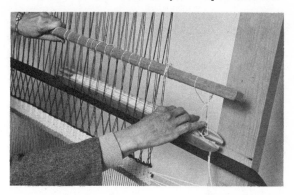

14. Insert the shed stick in the open shed just below the heddle rod and string heddles. Turn it sideways to hold the shed open.

15. Pass the shuttle through the shed across the top of the shed stick. Remove the shed stick.

16. Bubble the weft yarn. Beat the weft yarn down into its horizontal position with a tapestry beater.

17. After weaving 2 to 3 in., it is necessary to beat the fabric with the batten to compress the weft yarns. First, release the heddle rod from its holders. It will hang by the heddles across the top of the finished work. Release the batten from its holders and slide it down to the woven work. Beat the weft threads into place.

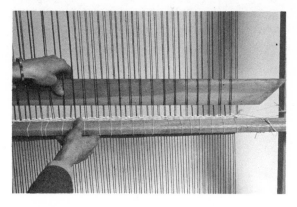

18. Replace the batten and the heddle rod in their holders. As the work progresses, move the batten and the heddle rod up by retying the twine holders in a higher position.

Rya Rug on an Upright Frame Loom

Rya knots
Plain weave
Basket weave using a batten and heddle rod
Overhand knots

Rya rugs with their thick, shaggy pile have a long history in Scandinavia. Originally used as blankets in fishing boats with the pile side wrapped around the body, ryas provided good protection from the elements. Later, the cheerful brilliance of their colors won them a place indoors, hanging on walls or resting on floors.

The rug in this project is made with the traditional materials: a linen warp and a pure wool weft. But making it on the upright frame loom is not the typical method. Weavers usually make ryas on a four-harness loom. Or they weave the backing, called ground fabric, to the right size first, then do the knotting. Nonweavers can buy a ground fabric made of a linen warp and wool weft and then make woolen rya knots.

The rya knot is simple and can be easily adapted to an unlimited number of designs and color combinations. It's the best-known rug knot in the world, known variously as the ghiordes knot, the Turkish knot, the Oriental knot, and by many other regional names as well. The number and length of strands, the closeness with which they are set together on the ground fabric, and the direction in which they are cut all affect the pattern. In Oriental rugs, the strands are very short and closely grouped; in rya rugs the strands are longer and more widely spaced.

The rug in this project measures 24 × 45 inches, plus fringe on each end. The two main colors are tan heather and soft rose, and the outline dividing the two sections is a deep, rich red. To produce a contrast in textures as well as color, two different kinds of wool yarn are used. If you substitute other materials, choose a tightly plied yarn for the rya knots, and use between 3 and 6 strands per knot.

What you will need

upright frame loom
2 shed sticks, each 2″ × 22″
rug, rag, or stick shuttle, any size
tapestry bobbin or tapestry needle
tapestry beater
12 oz. 8/5 linen
1½ lb. 4-ply wool rug yarn (640 yd. per lb.) for
   background (any color)
2-ply rug wool for rya knots:
   1¼ lb. tan (color A) (714 yd. per lb.)
   1¼ lb. rose (color B) (580 yd. per lb.)
   4 oz. deep red (color C) (580 yd. per lb.)
twine for guide threads

Step-by-step instructions

1. Begin warping on nail 49 of the bottom frame. End the warping procedure on nail 144, also on the bottom frame. For directions for warping, see p. 362. Count the warp threads to be sure that you have 96. The warp should be centered on the loom, and there should be a 14-in. space on each side between the vertical frame and the edge warp threads. Put masking tape over the heads of the nails so that the yarns won't get caught on them as you work. Now, measure up 7 in. from the inside of the bottom frame, and draw a line across the warp threads with a felt tip pen. This line indicates where to place the first row of weaving. Next, measure 22½ in. up from the first line, and draw a second line across the warp threads. This line is the midpoint of the rug.

2. Beginning on the bottom line, work ½ in. of plain weave (p. 352) with a double strand of linen. Though you can use a tapestry needle, a tapestry bobbin is better because it holds enough weft to work several rows without rethreading.

3. Weave basket weave (p. 354) for 1 in. with the background carpet wool. Use the shed mechanisms described on p. 362 for all basket weave work.

4. Tie guide threads from the vertical frames to the edge warp threads. The guide threads will help to keep the edges straight as you weave. Add guide threads at 1½-in. intervals as you progress. It is important to keep the rug centered on the loom at all times or it will be lopsided when you are finished. Keep a tape measure nearby, and check periodically that the rug remains 14 in. from the vertical frame on each side.

5. At this point you will begin the rya knots which will make the pile. The pile section of the rug is a repetition of four steps, enumerated below as A, B, C, and D. Each sequence of these four steps should add 1 in. of pile width.

A. Weave 2 rows of plain weave with a single strand of linen. Carry the linen up the side as you work.

B. Work rya knots (p. 354) across the row. Form each knot over 2 warp threads. See the instructions that follow for the colors to use for the rya knots. When knotting color A, use 6 strands of yarn. For knots of colors B and C, use 3 strands. The pile or rya loop is 2 in. long. At this length the pile will overlap and hide the preceding row of knots as well as the background between them. Make the knots over all the warp threads from one edge of the rug to the other. You will have 48 knots in each row, and there will be 43 rya rows worked as steps A—D.

C. Weave 2 rows plain weave with a single strand of linen.

D. Work ¾ in. basket weave with background color carpet wool.

The instructions below show you how to weave the rug, listing which colors to use in each rya knot row. To weave the rug, follow numbered steps 1—44 in the sequence below, using whichever color yarn is specified.

1. Perform steps A—D. Rya knots: all color A.
2. Perform steps A—D. Rya knots: all color A.

Rya and Weft-Faced Rug Techniques

H DESIGN

To create an H design, use two different color shuttles in opposite sheds. Color A, the background white color in the fleece project, always goes through the batten shed. Color B, the contrasting color black, is used in the pull shed. When the weft is compressed, it will completely cover the warp and create stripes that resemble teeth.

When the teeth are the required length, use color B in both sheds to create a block of color or crossbar for the H. To continue the teeth on the other side of the crossbar, reestablish the pattern of color A in the batten shed and color B in the pull shed.

OVERHAND KNOTS

The overhand knot is an easy finishing technique which keeps the weft from unraveling after the work is removed from the loom. To tie one, take a group of 2 to 6 warp threads, knot them together as shown to the right, and gently slide the knot up against the weft.

PULLED WEFT

The pulled weft technique is a form of pile weave in which the yarn rises above the background weaving.

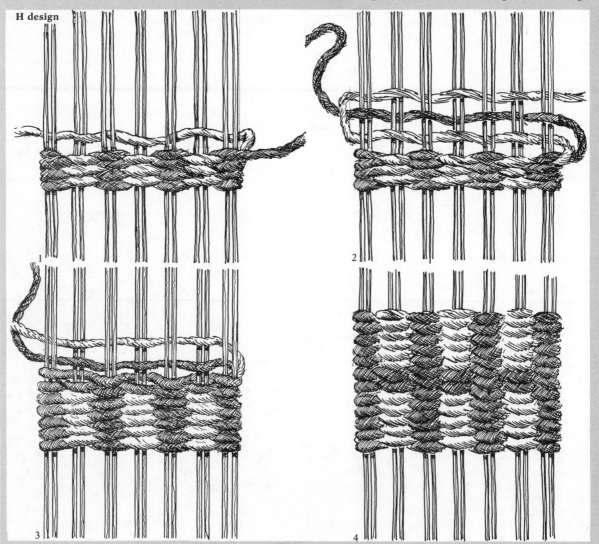

H design

1

2

3

4

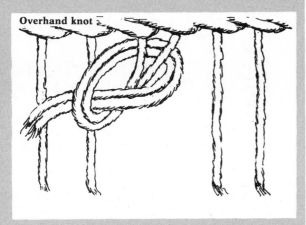

Overhand knot

The pile formed is not as high as rya pile. Usually a textured yarn is used to add some design interest to the work.

The weft-faced rug in the project that follows includes roving (see p. 370) used in pulled weft fashion, but raw fleece would create a similar effect.

Pulled weft

To produce pulled weft, first form an open shed, then wrap the roving around the edge warp thread and lay it loosely in the shed. Gently pull the roving out from the warp threads with your fingers to make small loops. Change the shed and repeat the process. Work the technique in multiple rows to create raised areas (rather than bumps) in the weaving.

3. Perform steps A—D. Rya knots: all color A.

4. Perform steps A—D. Rya knots: all color A.

5. Perform steps A—D. Rya knots: 18 color A; 27 color C; 3 color A.

6. Perform steps A—D. Rya knots: 14 color A; 4 color C; 24 color B; 4 color C; 2 color A.

7. Perform steps A—D. Rya knots: 12 color A; 2 color C; 30 color B; 4 color C.

8. Perform steps A—D. Rya knots: 10 color A; 2 color C; 35 color B; 1 color C.

9. Perform steps A—D. Rya knots: 10 color A; 2 color C; 14 color B; 6 color A; 16 color B.

10. Perform steps A—D. Rya knots: 11 color A; 2 color C; 12 color B; 8 color A; 15 color B. Remember to check that there is a 14-in. space between the rug and the vertical frames on each side. Add guide threads at 1½-in. intervals.

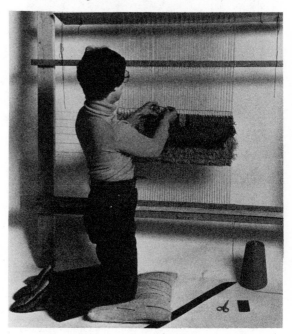

11. Perform steps A—D. Rya knots: 11 color A; 2 color C; 11 color B; 11 color A; 13 color B.

12. Perform steps A—D. Rya knots: 12 color A; 2 color C; 9 color B; 13 color A; 12 color B.

13. Perform steps A—D. Rya knots: 12 color A; 2 color C; 9 color B; 13 color A; 12 color B. (Row 13 is the same as row 12.)

14. Perform steps A—D. Rya knots: 13 color A; 2 color C; 10 color B; 11 color A; 12 color B.

15. Perform steps A—D. Rya knots: 13 color A; 2 color C; 11 color B; 8 color A; 14 color B.
16. Perform steps A—D. Rya knots: 14 color A; 2 color C; 32 color B.
17. Perform steps A—D. Rya knots: 14 color A; 2 color C; 32 color B. (Row 17 is the same as row 16.)

18. Perform steps A—D. Rya knots: 15 color A; 2 color C; 31 color B.
19. Perform steps A—D. Rya knots: 15 color A; 2 color C; 31 color B. (Row 19 is the same as row 18.)
20. Perform steps A—D. Rya knots: 16 color A; 2 color C; 30 color B. Check to be sure that there is a 14-in. space between the rug and the vertical frames on each side. Add guide threads at 1½-in. intervals.
21. Perform steps A—D. Rya knots: 16 color A; 2 color C; 30 color B. (Row 21 is the same as row 20.)
22. Perform steps A—D. Rya knots: 17 color A; 3 color C; 28 color B.
23. Perform steps A—D. Rya knots: 19 color A;

10 color C; 19 color B. This step is the center of the rug, which should now measure 22½ in. from bottom to top.
24. Perform steps A—D. Rya knots: 28 color A; 3 color C; 17 color B.
25. Perform steps A—D. Rya knots: 30 color A; 2 color C; 16 color B.
26. Perform steps A—D. Rya knots: 30 color A; 2 color C; 16 color B. (Row 26 is the same as row 25.)
27. Perform steps A—D. Rya knots: 31 color A; 2 color C; 15 color B.
28. Perform steps A—D. Rya knots: 31 color A; 2 color C; 15 color B. (Row 28 is the same as row 27.)
29. Perform steps A—D. Rya knots: 32 color A; 2 color C; 14 color B.
30. Perform steps A—D. Rya knots: 32 color A; 2 color C; 14 color B. (Row 30 is the same as row 29.)
31. Perform steps A—D. Rya knots: 14 color A; 8 color B; 11 color A; 2 color C; 13 color B.
32. Perform steps A—D. Rya knots: 12 color A; 11 color B; 10 color A; 2 color C; 13 color B.
33. Perform steps A—D. Rya knots: 12 color A; 13 color B; 9 color A; 2 color C; 12 color B.
34. Perform steps A—D. Rya knots: 12 color A, 13 color B; 9 color A; 2 color B. (Row 34 is the same as row 33.)
35. Perform steps A—D. Rya knots: 13 color A; 11 color B; 11 color A; 2 color C; 11 color B.
36. Perform steps A—D. Rya knots: 15 color A; 8 color B; 12 color A; 2 color C; 11 color B.
37. Perform steps A—D. Rya knots: 16 color A; 6 color B; 14 color A; 2 color C; 10 color B.
38. Perform steps A—D. Rya knots: 1 color C; 35 color A; 2 color C; 10 color B.
Toward the end of the rug it will be necessary to move the batten and heddle rod up to the top of the loom so that there is space to turn the shed stick sideways. The batten and heddle rod are held in place by the crossed warps. When the shed stick is removed, the batten and heddle rod fall to their string holders. Form the next shed.
39. Perform steps A—D. Rya knots: 4 color C; 30 color A; 2 color C; 12 color B.
40. Perform steps A—D. Rya knots: 2 color B; 4 color C; 24 color A; 4 color C; 14 color B.
41. Perform steps A—D. Rya knots: 3 color B; 27 color C; 18 color B.
42. Perform steps A—D. Rya knots: all color B.
43. Perform steps A—D. Rya knots: all color B. (Row 43 is the same as row 42.)

Work 1 in. of basket weave, using carpet wool background color. Do not beat tightly against rya knots. Work ½ in. of plain weave with a double strand of linen.

Remove the rug from the loom by cuting the warp threads near the nails. Cut the bottom warp threads first, then the top warp threads. Lay the rug on the floor.

44. Work row 44 of rya knots *in the same holes* as row 43, with the rug turned upside down. This row hides the base of the other knots and lies toward the fringe.

Now work overhand knots (p. 366) across both ends of the rug. Put 2 warp threads in each knot, then go back and tie 4 warp threads together with additional overhand knots. Push the second knots gently against the first. Cut the fringe to the same length at both ends of the rug.

Weft-Faced Rug on an Upright Frame Loom

Plain weave
Basket weave
Rya knots (optional)
Bubbling
H design
Overhand knots
Pulled weft

Weft-faced rugs are both a Navajo and a Scandinavian design form. The designs and colors differ from one culture to the other, but the technique is the same, and in both cultures the rugs are firm and long-wearing. The weft-faced rug in this project (shown here as a hanging) has the added feature of being worked partly with fleece. In Australia and New Zealand, where sheep are abundant, fleece rugs are popular.

The rug is 40 × 46½ inches. You can make it on a harness loom 42 inches wide, using a warp 68 inches long. With heavier yarn, use 4 warp threads per inch; with lighter yarn, use 6 warp threads per inch. Follow the step-by-step instructions for the weft work.

The instructions that follow are specifically for the upright frame loom. Even beginning weavers will have no difficulty, since there are no complicated techniques to master. This will be a particularly interesting project to those who do handspinning or raise sheep, or have other access to raw wool. The photographed example uses black handspun yarn and store-bought white carpet yarn. The pulled wefts are roving, which is commercially carded fleece. The optional rya knots are raw fleece, which is uncarded.

The rug is a series of design repetitions done in black and white. To simplify them, the directions are divided into sections. The cartoon on page 372 lists the correct width and the number of pattern repetitions for each section. Because handspun wool varies in thickness, inch measurements are given in the instructions when more than 2 rows are called for.

What you will need

upright frame loom or harness loom with 42-in.
  weaving width
rug or stick shuttle
tapestry bobbin or tapestry needle
tapestry beater
2 shed sticks, each 2″ × 22″
fleece or roving:
    1½ lb. white
    1 lb. black
carpet wool or handspun yarn (640 yd. per lb.):
    2 lb. white
    2 lb. black

Step-by-step instructions

1. Begin warping on nail 11 of the bottom frame. End the warping procedure on nail 180 of the bottom frame. For directions for warping, see p. 362. Count to check that there are 170 warp threads. Put masking tape over the heads of the nails to prevent the yarns from getting caught on them as you work. Measure up 7 in. from the inside bottom frame, and draw a line across the warp threads with a felt tip pen to indicate where the first row of weaving begins.

2. Using linen as weft, and starting at the bottom edge, begin working plain weave (p. 352) for ½ in. Use a tapestry bobbin or tapestry needle. Then, using white carpet wool as weft, work another ½ in. in plain weave.

3. Tie guide threads from the vertical frames to the edge warp threads to help keep the edges straight as you weave. Add guide threads at 1½-in. intervals as you progress. Work the following sections in basket weave (p. 354). Use the shed mechanisms described on p. 362, and use the rug or stick shuttle for the basket weave section of the rug. The last in. of the rug will be worked, as was the beginning, in plain weave.

Section I—pattern A

4. Work ½ in. with white carpet wool.
5. Weave 2 rows with black carpet wool.
6. Work 2 rows of pulled weft with black roving.
7. Weave 2 rows with black carpet wool.
8. Weave ½ in. with white carpet wool.
9. Weave 2 rows with black carpet wool, then repeat pattern A (steps 4—9) two more times.

Section II—pattern B

10. Work ½ in. with white carpet wool.
11. Weave 2 rows with black carpet wool.

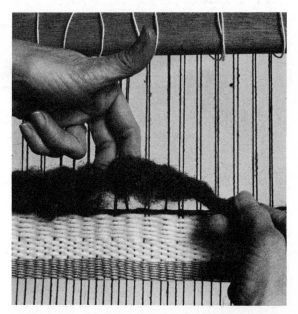

12. Work 2 rows of pulled weft. On the first pulled weft row, use black roving 6 in. in from each edge and white roving in the center of the row. Use white roving for the second pulled weft row.
13. Weave 2 rows with black carpet wool.
14. Weave ½ in. with white carpet wool.
15. Weave 2 rows with black carpet wool, then repeat pattern B (steps 10—15) three more times so that you have four complete repetitions of pattern B. Now repeat pattern B (steps 10—14 only) once more. Do not work step 15 on the last pattern B.

Section III—pattern C

Although pattern C is repeated three times in section III, the materials and measurements vary in each pattern. Therefore, complete step-by-step directions are given for section III.

16. Work the H design (see p. 366) with ⅜-in. teeth on each side and a ⅛-in.-wide crossbar. The design will be ⅞ in. wide when completed.
17. Weave ½ in. with white carpet wool.
18. Weave 2 rows with black carpet wool.
19. Work 2 rows of pulled weft. On the first pulled weft row, use black roving 9 in. in from each edge. Use white roving in the center of the row. Use white roving for the second pulled weft row.
20. Weave 2 rows with black carpet wool.
21. Weave ½ in. with white carpet wool. This completes the first pattern C design.

Weft-Faced Rug Cartoon

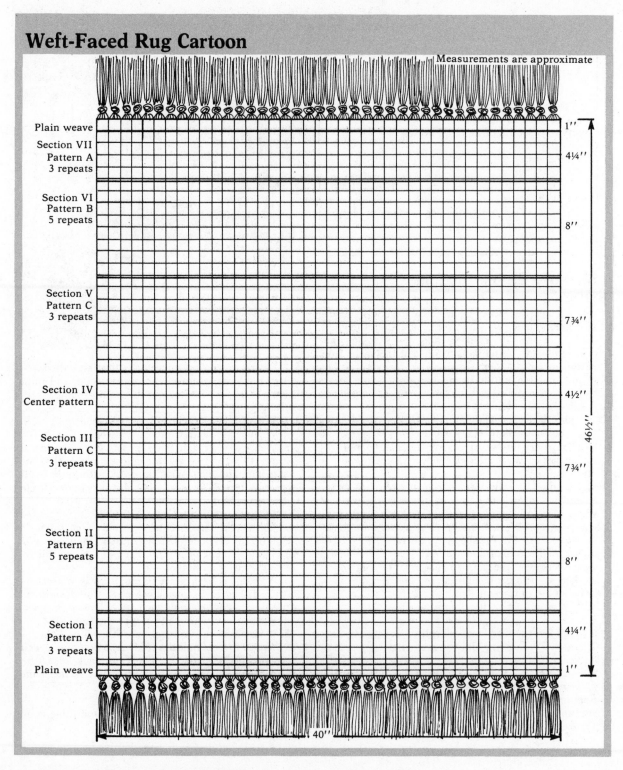

Measurements are approximate

Plain weave — 1″

Section VII
Pattern A
3 repeats — 4¼″

Section VI
Pattern B
5 repeats — 8″

Section V
Pattern C
3 repeats — 7¾″

Section IV
Center pattern — 4½″

Section III
Pattern C
3 repeats — 7¾″

Section II
Pattern B
5 repeats — 8″

Section I
Pattern A
3 repeats — 4¼″

Plain weave — 1″

46½″

40″

22. Work the H design with ⅜-in. teeth on each side of the crossbar. The crossbar is 1 row of black roving (laid in the shed, not pulled) followed by 2 rows of black carpet wool. The design will be 1 in. wide when completed.

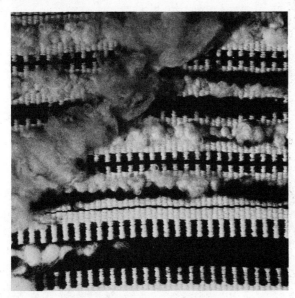

23. Weave ½ in. with white carpet wool.
24. Weave 2 rows with black carpet wool.
25. Work 2 rows of pulled weft. Use white roving for the first pulled weft row. On the second pulled weft row, use black roving 6 in. in on each side.
26. Weave 2 rows with black carpet wool.
27. Weave ½ in. with white carpet wool to complete the second pattern C design.
28. Work the H design with ½-in. teeth on each side of the crossbar. The crossbar is 5 rows of black carpet wool. The design will be 1¼ in. wide when completed.
29. Weave ½ in. with white carpet wool.
30. Weave 2 rows with black carpet wool.
31. Work 2 rows of pulled weft. Use white roving for the first pulled weft row. On the second pulled weft row, use black roving 25 in. across the row from the left edge. There will be 15 in. of white roving on the right side of the row.
32. Weave 2 rows with black carpet wool.
33. Weave ½ in. with white carpet wool to complete the third pattern C design and section III.

Section IV—center pattern
34. Weave 2 rows with black carpet wool.

35. Weave ½ in. with white carpet wool.
36. Work the H design with ⅞-in. teeth on each side of the crossbar. To make the H crossbar, first weave 20 rows of black carpet wool, and then 3 rows of pulled weft worked from left edge as follows:
    Row 1: 12 in. black roving; 16 in. white roving;
       12 in. black roving
    Row 2: entire row of black roving
    Row 3: 17 in. black roving; 11 in. white roving;
       12 in. black roving
Finish with 19 rows of black carpet wool. Remember to work ⅞-in. teeth after the crossbar.
37. Weave ½ in. with white carpet wool.
38. Weave 2 rows with black carpet wool to complete section IV, the center pattern of the rug.

Section V—pattern C
39. Weave ½ in. with white carpet wool.
40. Weave 2 rows with black carpet wool.
41. Work 2 rows pulled weft. On the first row, use black roving 18 in. in from the right edge. Work 22 in. of white roving on the left side. Use white roving for the second row of pulled weft.
42. Weave 2 rows with black carpet wool.
43. Weave ½ in. with white carpet wool.
44. Work the H design with ½-in. teeth on each side of the crossbar. The crossbar is 5 rows of black carpet wool. This design, 1¼ in. wide, completes the first pattern C design. The design has been worked backward from the third pattern C design in section III in order to make the rug symmetrical.
45. Weave ½ in. with white carpet wool.
46. Weave 2 rows with black carpet wool.
47. Work 2 rows of pulled weft. On the first row, use black roving 6 in. in from both edges. Use white roving for the center. Use white roving for the entire second pulled weft row.
48. Weave 2 rows with black carpet wool.
49. Weave ½ in. with white carpet wool.
50. Work the H design with ⅜-in. teeth on each side of the crosspiece. The crosspiece is one row of black roving (laid in the shed, not pulled), followed by 2 rows of black carpet wool. This design, 1 in. wide, completes the second pattern C design (steps 45—50).
51. Weave ½ in. with white carpet wool.
52. Weave 2 rows with black carpet wool.
53. Work 2 rows of pulled weft. On the first row, use black roving 6 in. in from both edges. Use white roving for the center. Use white roving for the entire second pulled weft row.
54. Weave 2 rows with black carpet wool.
55. Weave ½ in. with white carpet wool.

56. Work the H design with ⅜-in. teeth on each side and a ⅛-in.-wide crossbar. The design, ⅞ in. wide, completes section V, pattern C.

Section VI—pattern B

57. Weave ½ in. with white carpet wool.

58. Weave 2 rows with black carpet wool.

59. Work 2 rows of pulled weft. On the first pulled weft row, use white roving. On the second pulled weft row, use black roving 6 in. in from the edges. Use white roving in the center of the row.

60. Weave 2 rows with black carpet wool.

61. Weave ½ in. with white carpet wool.

62. Weave 2 rows with black carpet wool.

Repeat steps 57—62 three times more, so that you have four completed repetitions of pattern B. Now repeat pattern B (steps 57—60 only) once more. Do not work step 61 or 62 on the last pattern B. This completes section VI.

Section VII—pattern A

At the end of the rug it will be necessary to move the batten and heddle rod up to the top of the loom, leaving space to turn the shed stick sideways. The batten and heddle rod are held in place by the crossed warps. When the shed stick is removed, the batten and heddle rod fall to their string holders. Form the next shed.

63. Work ½ in. with white carpet wool.

64. Weave 2 rows with black carpet wool.

65. Work 2 rows of pulled weft with black roving.

66. Weave 2 rows with black carpet wool.

67. Weave ½ in. with white carpet wool.

68. Weave 2 rows with black carpet wool.

Repeat pattern A (steps 63—68) once. Then repeat pattern A (steps 63—67 only) also once. This completes section VII.

69. Weave ½ in. of plain weave with white carpet wool.

70. Weave ½ in. of plain weave with linen.

71. Remove the rug from the loom by cutting the warp threads near the nails. Cut the bottom warp threads first, then the top warp threads. Lay the rug on the floor.

72. Work overhand knots (p. 366) across both ends of the rug, with 2 warp thread ends in each knot.

73. Cut the top and bottom fringe to the same length.

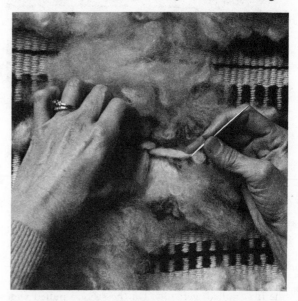

Rya knots (optional): When the rug is finished, you can add another design element with decorative rya knots. Work the knots with long-staple fleece 5 or 6 inches in length threaded through a needle, or use a long, fluffy fiber like mohair. Follow the design pattern in the project (see photo, p. 370), or add the knots where you like. Work a single knot over 2 warp threads at each point in the line.

Optional Rug Fringe Techniques

The easiest way to make rug fringes is to work one set of overhand knots with the warp threads. There are several other methods as well, all of which are attractive and keep the weft material from unraveling.

WRAPPING WARP THREADS

1. Cut a length of warp thread about 6 in. long. Count out 2 to 6 warp threads, so they form bundles ½ to ¾ in. thick. Form a loop with the 6-in. length of warp thread along the side of the bundle of warp threads close to the edge of the woven work.

2. Allow a short tail of thread to lie on top of the woven work. Wrap the other end of thread around the bundle of warps for the desired length. Push the tail of thread through the loop.

3. Pull on the end of thread that is sticking out of the top of the wrapping until the loop disappears. Either clip this tail or needle-weave it invisibly into the work.

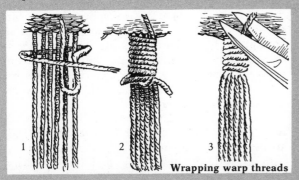

Wrapping warp threads

DOUBLE AND TRIPLE OVERHAND KNOTS

To give fringe a lacy look, form sets of overhand knots in series. After making an initial row of overhand knots, divide in half the number of warp threads in each bundle. Using half the warp threads from pairs of adjacent knots, form a second set of knots across the work. Repeat the dividing and knotting process for a third set of overhand knots.

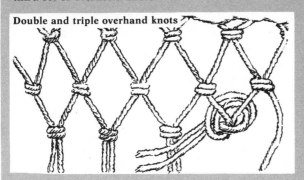

Double and triple overhand knots

BRAIDING

Grouping warp threads in braids adds weight to the fringe and makes it lie neatly in place. Each braid should use no more than a ¾-in. width of warp threads. Finish with an overhand knot or tightly wrapped length of warp thread to prevent the braid from unwrapping.

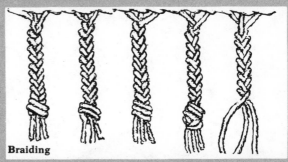

Braiding

TWISTING THE WARP THREADS

Like braiding, twisting makes the fringe lie flat. It's often used on afghans because it is so attractive. Count out an even number of warp threads to make a ½- to ¾-in.-thick bundle. Divide the bundle in half. Take one half in each hand, and hold it between the index finger and thumb about 1½ in. from the edge of the woven work. Roll both bundles clockwise, twisting both groups in the same direction. Pinch the bundles to hold the twist in place.

Still holding the bundles in each hand, wind them around and around one another in a counterclockwise direction. Repeat these two steps downward by 1½-in. intervals until the fringe is twisted to the desired length. For fibers that do not stay twisted in place, add an overhand knot. Repeat the two-step procedure with each set of warp threads across the work.

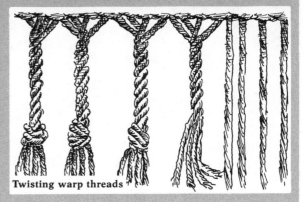

Twisting warp threads

Table Runner on a Rigid Heddle Loom

Warping a rigid heddle loom
Vertical warp stripes
Slip knots
Plain weave
Bubbling
Overhand knots

Despite their name, table runners are sedentary. Purely ornamental, they're one of life's little extras. Whether you are a beginning weaver or an expert, however, you will find that this project provides an opportunity to experiment a bit without regard to such considerations as the strength or warmth of the fabric. There's always the possibility, too, that you will produce an article that becomes a family heirloom—the special table runner that graces the table every Christmas day, perhaps.

The runner in the project measures 12½ × 60 inches plus fringe and is worked in vertical stripes of dark brown, natural, and cinnamon. To change the design, use stripes in different widths and combinations. Choose colors that complement the wood of your table, or the colors of your place settings.

To plan your own design, color a strip of paper with a diagram of your intended warp color. The warping method described for this project also allows you to design on the loom as you warp. If a stripe is too wide, remove a warp thread and change the color. If a stripe seems too narrow, change a warp thread and widen it.

Since table fabrics are subject to spills and stains, use fibers that wash well. Cotton, which is used in the project, is easy to wash and line-dry. Pure linen is elegant but requires ironing.

At the end of the step-by-step instructions for the runner project there are steps for making place mats and for making the table runner and place mats together. The latter projects (see p. 379) require that you warp the loom differently than for the table runner alone.

Before you begin

The rigid heddle loom is the simplest kind of roller loom. It is cheaper, more compact, and more portable than any other loom of its type. Like all roller looms, it has a back beam and a front beam on which to roll up either the warp threads or the fabric. The beams make it possible to weave fabric longer than the length of the loom.

The rigid heddle loom has a frame simple enough to build yourself. The reed-heddle bar can be purchased separately. It is considered a two-harness loom, producing two sheds which allow the weaver to create basic plain weave, the conventional structure for fabric.

Rigid heddle loom

Ratchet gear

Crank

Back beam

Back apron bar

Reed-heddle bar

Shed mechanism

Front apron bar

Front beam

Limitless variations of colors and stitches are possible on the rigid heddle loom. There are also limitations; complex patterns require the use of a pickup stick, and the size of the warp thread is limited to the size of the holes and slots in the reed-heddle bar.

The latter is the mechanism for raising and lowering the warp threads and for beating the weft yarn into its horizontal position in the fabric. It separates and raises or lowers alternate warp threads to provide a shed for the weft to run through. The reed-heddle bar is a wood or plastic frame which contains a series of vertical plastic strips called heddles, each with a hole drilled through it. The weaver laces warp threads through the holes in the heddles and through the spaces between them, which are called slots. The threads extend the length of the loom, passing alternately through the holes and slots, and are attached around the apron bar that is tied to the back beam.

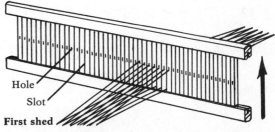

Hole

Slot

First shed

To produce plain weave, first raise the reed-heddle bar so that the warp threads passing through the holes will rise. The slot threads will remain in place, creating a shed for the weft to pass through. The reed-heddle

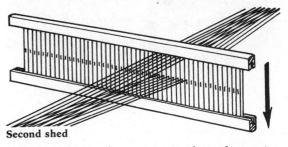

Second shed

bar now acts as a beater to tamp the weft yarn into place. Push the reed-heddle bar down. The hole threads will drop while the slot threads continue to stay in place. This creates the second shed. Passing the weft through this shed produces the second row of plain weave. Tamp the weft yarn into place again, using the reed-heddle bar as a beater. Repeat the process to produce as much plain weave as necessary.

Step-by-step instructions

1. Tie the reed-heddle bar in the holding position on the loom so that it will stay in place during the warping process. If your loom does not have a holding position, tie the reed-heddle bar to the loom frame.

2. Find the center of the reed-heddle bar. Measure 7⅞ in. from the center toward the left side. Mark the slot closest to the 7⅞-in. mark by tying a loop of thread or string over the top of the reed-heddle bar.

3. Cut a piece of color A warp thread 160 in. long. Use this piece as a measure to cut the other warp threads to the same length. Cut 13 additional pieces of color A warp thread for the first section.

4. Begin warping the loom. Starting at the left side, thread a length of color A through the slot you marked. Pull the thread to the back of the loom around the back apron bar, by first going over the apron bar, then under it. Sley (thread) the end through the hole next to the slot you just threaded. Pull the thread to the front of the loom.

5. As you warp, adjust the length of the threads so that they are the same length by pulling gently on the shorter end. Lay the threads out in front of the loom to keep them from tangling, though some tangling will be inevitable.

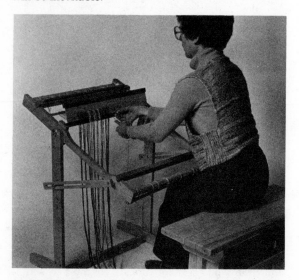

6. Warp with color A 12 more times to make a total of 26 warp threads (called warp ends) in color A at the front of the loom. Check carefully to be certain that you thread each slot and each hole. Repeating the phrase

slot — hole to yourself as you thread the reed-heddle bar is a helpful reminder.

7. Warp with color B two times to make 4 warp ends. (When you complete a color, always count the number of warp ends and check again that every slot and hole is threaded.)

8. Warp with color C four times to make 8 warp ends.

9. Warp with color B two times to make 4 warp ends.

10. Warp with color C three times to make 6 warp ends.

11. Warp with color B two times to make 4 warp ends.

12. Warp with color A ten times to make 20 warp ends.

13. Warp with color C seven times to make 14 warp ends. This is the center stripe on the table runner. When you finish warping with color C, you should be more than halfway across the table runner and there should be 86 warp ends.

14. Warp with color A ten times to make 20 warp ends.

15. Warp with color B two times to make 4 warp ends.

16. Warp with color C three times to make 6 warp ends.

17. Warp with color B two times to make 4 warp ends.

18. Warp with color C four times to make 8 warp ends.

19. Warp with color B two times to make 4 warp ends.

20. Warp with color A 13 times to make 26 warp ends. The warp ends should now total 158, and each slot and hole should be threaded.

21. Pull all the threads out at the front of the loom. The threads will appear tangled, but they won't be. The warp threads should all be even in length. If any are not, adjust with the adjoining partner thread to even them up.

22. Working from the left side of the loom, take a group of 8 warp threads, comb them with your fingers to work out any tangles, and make a loose slip knot close to the reed-heddle bar. Put another slip knot about 12

in. beyond the first, and add 4 more slip knots at equal intervals until you reach the end of the warp threads.

23. Repeat across the work the process of making slip knots with bundles of 8 warp threads each. The last bundle will have 6 warp threads.

24. Check to see that the apron bar and the back warp beam are parallel. If they are not, adjust the strings which hold them together until they become parallel. Make certain that the warp threads are straight and not overlapping.

25. Begin to wind the warp by rolling the back warp beam. The slip knots will serve to place a small amount of tension on the warp threads. The aim is to have the threads parallel and at equal tension.

26. Make one revolution of the back warp beam, stopping before the warp threads wind on top of each other, and slide a sheet of stiff paper between the warp threads to keep the warp threads from settling into one another and making the tension uneven. As the knots reach the reed-heddle bar, they should come undone.

27. When there are 20 in. of warp in front of the reed-heddle bar, stop winding the warp.

28. Starting at the left side, take 4 warp threads in your left hand and 4 in your right. The threads in your right hand go under the front apron bar; those in your left go over the bar. Make a half bow by wrapping the bundles of threads around one another twice. The technique is the same as the first step in tying a shoelace, only doubled. Tie a half bow by pulling one end through as you make a bow.

29. Repeat step 28, working at the right side of the loom with 8 warp threads.

30. Repeat step 28, working at either side, moving in toward the middle until all warp threads are used. There will be 6 warp threads in the central bundle.

31. Make sure that the front apron bar is parallel with the front beam. Roll the back beam until the threads are tight.

32. Retie any bundles as necessary to produce uniform tension across the warp, otherwise the work will later sag.

33. Tie one piece of rag or plastic bag to the front apron bar, and weave it over and under the bundles of threads. Go over the bundles which went over the bar and under the ones which went under the bar. Tie the rag to the apron bar on the opposite side of the loom.

34. Weave 2 rows of rags, 1 row in each shed.

35. Using color C, weave 2 rows in alternate sheds. Measure from the reed-heddle bar to the weft threads to be sure that the work is parallel. Be careful to beat straight across with the reed-heddle bar.

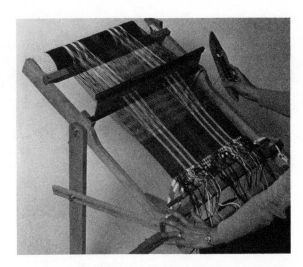

36. Using color C, weave 9 rows per in. in alternate sheds for the length of the table runner. Follow the directions for plain weave and bubbling (see p. 352). Until it is washed, the work will feel loose and stiff in texture. At the end of the weaving, there will be about 8 in. of warp left on the loom.

37. To finish, remove the table runner from the loom by cutting the warp at the back apron bar and undoing the half bows from the front apron bar. Tie overhand knots (p. 366) on the warp threads from the back apron bar. Remove the rows of rags from the opposite end of the table runner, and work overhand knots on the warp ends. Cut the fringe to about 6 in. on both ends. Wash the table runner by hand and machine-dry on a low setting. Turn under 2 warp threads along either side to make a firm hem edge, then stitch the threads in place.

To make place mats

To weave four place mats, each 18 × 15 in., follow the step-by-step directions for the table runner. Change the length of the warp threads to 216 in. Weave 18 in. for the first place mat, then weave in 6 in. of rags or plastic bags as a separator. Repeat for three more place mats. The finishing process is the same as for the table runner. Cut the mats apart in the center of the rags, and work overhand knots at the ends. If you prefer, zigzag the edges on a sewing machine at the end of the weft.

Making the table runner and place mats together

Wind the warp 5 yd. long. The longer length of the warp requires that you use a different winding technique (see p. 383).

Weaving on a Multiharness Loom

A multiharness loom is the Rolls Royce of home weaving—expensive, equipped for every contingency, beautiful, and made to last a lifetime—or longer. The oldest antique looms still work with all the efficiency of the newest manufactured ones. Both new looms and old are constructed of hardwood and are as pleasing to look at as they are to use.

The versatility of the multiharness loom is its major advantage. A weaver can create twills, plain weave, or intricate patterns merely by arranging the levers or treadles that operate the shed mechanisms. Rollers make it possible to produce fabric longer than the length of the loom itself.

Harness looms come in floor models and table models, as well as in different styles, weaving widths, and complexity. See page 340 for a description of the three loom styles: jack, counterbalance, and contramarche. The weaving width of the loom refers to the width of fabric the loom can produce. Table looms usually have a narrower weaving width than floor looms. There are also looms complex enough to produce lace and brocade, and the last word is patterns programmed on a home computer and then worked on a loom.

On a harness loom, the harnesses control the vertical motion of the warp threads. The raising and lowering of warp threads creates the shed (or opening) through which the weft is slipped into place. The weaver using a table loom uses levers to control the harness action. Foot treadles on a floor loom serve the same purpose and free the weaver's hands to work more rapidly.

This chapter explains the intricacies of warping the four-harness loom, the most popular home loom. Warping organizes and holds hundreds (sometimes thousands) of threads in parallel positions on the loom. Yet it is a surprisingly simple process. Three projects following this chapter—curtains, chair seat upholstery, and woven screen panels—explore the harness loom's potential for home weaving.

Aim to understand your loom and keep it operating. Though it has always had a significance that is more than the sum of its parts, the loom is primarily a tool. Above all, it is meant to be used.

Parts of a Multiharness Loom

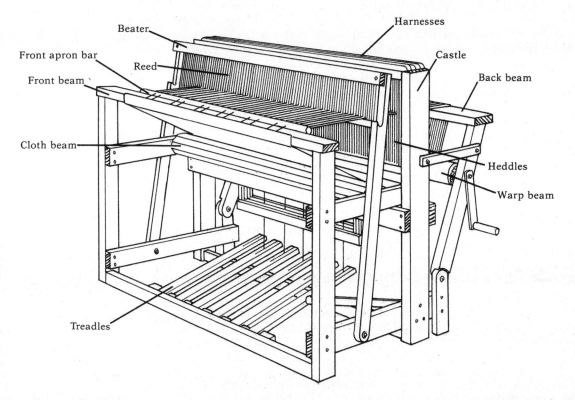

Four-harness floor loom

Back apron bar—rod attached to the warp beam. The warp threads are slipped over the back apron bar, which is then wound around the warp beam.

Back beam—structural frame at the back of the loom. Warp threads run over the back beam as they travel from the warp beam to the heddles.

Beater—frame that holds the reed, which in turn beats the weft threads into place.

Castle—central structural section of the loom. The castle holds the harnesses.

Cloth beam—roller around which the finished cloth is wound.

Cross sticks—two flat sticks used to keep the warp threads in order when warping the loom.

Front apron bar—rod attached to the cloth beam. The warp threads are tied to the front apron bar. As cloth is produced, the front apron bar and the cloth are wound around the cloth beam.

Front beam—structural frame at the front of the loom.

Cloth travels over the front beam as it moves to the cloth beam.

Harness—frame that holds heddles. Each harness in a loom slides up and down, controlling the movement of the warp threads that pass through the heddles it holds.

Heddle—a metal or string form that has a central eye. The heddle is held in place by the harness frame. Each heddle houses and controls 1 warp thread.

Reed—metal comb used for beating weft threads into place. Reeds come with different numbers of openings, called dents, per inch.

Treadles—foot pedals that control the up-and-down movement of the harnesses. They may be hinged at either the front or the back of the loom. There is normally one treadle for each harness, plus at least two or more to make combinations that allow for faster pattern changes.

Warp beam—roller on which warp threads are wound at the back of the loom.

Estimating Material

Before you can begin to work on the loom or warping board, you must first calculate how much material you will need. The width and length of your project will determine the quantity of warp material you need to use. These warp figures then determine the necessary amount of weft material.

First, decide how wide you want the finished article to be. Calculate extra threads at the edges if you need a firm seam. Second, decide how close together the warp threads should be; that is, the number of warp threads you will have per inch of cloth. This figure depends on the size of the reed you are using for the project. By multiplying the width you want by the number of threads per inch, you will arrive at the correct number of warp threads for your project. You must also allow for the fact that the warp threads naturally squeeze together as the weft is woven in. This is called draw-in. Add 1 inch worth of warp threads for every 10 inches of proposed finished width. Add this figure to the product obtained above to arrive at the total number of warp threads you will need for the project. For example, to calculate the number of warp threads for upholstery fabric 20 inches wide:

	22	inches (fabric width, including selvages)
×	10	warp threads per inch
=	220	warp threads
+	22	warp threads (draw-in of 10 percent)
=	242	warp threads needed for project

Therefore, wind 242 warp threads on the warping board for the project.

To figure the length of warp to wind, first decide how long you want the cloth to be. Some warp length cannot be woven, because it is used for knots or is slipped around the back apron bar where it cannot be used. Generally figure 18 inches for loom waste on a table loom and 1 yard for a floor loom. The warp length decreases slightly as the warp threads go over and under the weft. To allow for this reduction, called take-up, add 10 percent to the total length. Add these figures together to calculate how long a warp to put on the warping board to get the yardage you require. For example, to calculate the warp length for upholstery for four chairs:

	22	inches per chair
×	4	chairs
=	88	inches (desired length of cloth)
+	36	inches (loom waste)
=	124	inches (length of warp)
+	12.4	inches of take-up (10 percent of warp length)
=	136.4	inches (length to put on warping board)

To compute the total yardage needed for the warp, multiply the length of a warp thread by the number of threads needed for the project. Hence, for the upholstery:

	136	inches per warp thread
×	242	warp threads needed
=	32,912	inches or 914 yards needed for warp

Calculating the amount of weft is necessary whether or not it is a different fiber from the warp. Add the length of 1 weft thread (width of the warp) to 10 percent of the figure needed for weft take-up. Multiply the resulting figure by the number of picks (weft threads) per inch to find the amount of weft thread needed per inch of fabric. Multiply the amount of weft needed for an inch of fabric by the desired length of fabric to get the amount of weft required.

For example:

	22	inches (length of weft or width of fabric)
+	2.2	inches take-up (10 percent of weft length)
=	24.2	inches (weft needed per row or pick)
×	10	rows (picks) per inch
=	242	inches (weft needed per inch of fabric)
×	88	inches (length of fabric)
=	21,296	inches or 591½ yards of weft needed

Using a pocket calculator makes quick work of these computations.

The weft and warp requirements for all the projects in the textiles section are listed in each What You Will Need list, much like ingredient quantities in a recipe. Yardage is usually stated per pound (i.e., 2100 yards = 1 pound) in order to indicate a weight of thread or yarn. You can calculate the number of pounds of yarn you need for projects you devise yourself by dividing your yardage requirements by the number of yards in 1 pound of the yarn.

Winding the Warp

Having calculated the length of the warp you will need, the next step is to make a guide thread. Measure a thread the same length as the warp you will use, then add about 10 inches for tying around the pegs. Tie the guide thread on the warping board at peg A.

Guide thread on a warping board

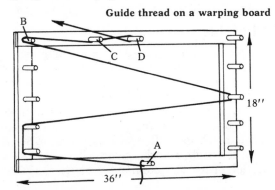

Then follow any wrapping pattern you find convenient, using as many pegs as you need to accommodate the guide thread. To tie off the guide thread, however, go over peg B, under peg C, and end at peg D. Tie the guide thread around peg D, and push it to the base of the peg. Position the ball or cone of warping thread so that it will unroll easily, in a small box or bowl perhaps. An umbrella swift (see p. 341) makes using a skein of thread easy, since the thread unwinds under slight pressure as you warp. Lacking an umbrella swift, put the skein over the back of a chair or on the arm of a patient friend, whatever will enable you to unwind the skein as you wind the warp.

It is easiest to work with the warping board hanging on the wall, but you can also lay it on the floor or on a table. Tie the warping thread around peg A, and begin to follow the guide thread. It is important to wrap the thread over peg B, under peg C, up around peg D, and back over peg C, thereby forming an × or cross with the threads. The cross must be repeated with every movement around the warping board in order to keep the threads in sequential order. The cross remains important throughout the warping process, so do not take shortcuts here. Place the threads side-by-side on the pegs; do not overlap them. Push the threads to the base of the pegs. Maintain an even taut tension on the warp thread throughout the warping procedure. If you must leave your work, wrap the warping thread tightly around a peg several times in order to maintain the tension until you return. Try to do all the warp winding at one time.

Keep count of the warp threads as you wind the warp; tie the warp threads loosely in bundles equal to the number of threads per inch for the project. For example, if you are weaving upholstery fabric with 10 threads per inch, tie bundles of 10 warp threads. By counting the number of bundles, you will know how many inches of warp-thread width you have wound.

In order to count easily the number of warp threads you have wound, count the warps at the top or bottom of peg C and double that number. The cross separates the warp threads on alternate revolutions; the threads on each side of peg C are half the total number of warp threads.

Tying the warp

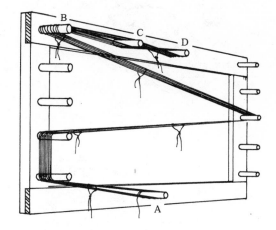

When you have completed winding the warp on the warping board, tie the end off at peg A. Using string of a contrasting color, loosely tie the

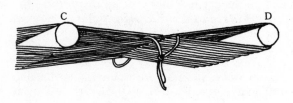

warp together at the beginning loop (peg A), the end loop (peg D), and every 2 to 3 feet in between. Tie the cross securely between pegs C and D, since it is important not to lose it.

If you do not have a warping board, you can easily use chairs arranged at opposite ends of a table to perform the function of pegs on a warping board. Form the cross between the chairs or by adding a third chair for the warp to wind

around (this will also lengthen the warp). Alternately, you can turn a table upside down and use the legs as pegs. To make a semipermanent warping board, sink dowels into small sections of 2×4. Attach the 2×4 to a table top with C-clamps in any desired configuration. Make certain that you form a cross with the warping threads. If you like, you can even drive stakes in the ground. Much of the world's best woven work comes from countries where that is the common warping practice.

Chaining

To take the warp from the warping board to the loom without tangling it, form a chain in the following manner. Starting close to peg A, loop the warp over on itself, then slide your hand through the loop and grasp all the warp threads in a bundle. Draw the bundle of warp threads through the loop. Repeat this action to form a giant chain, like a crochet chain. Allow the cross-end section of the warp to hang freely.

Chaining

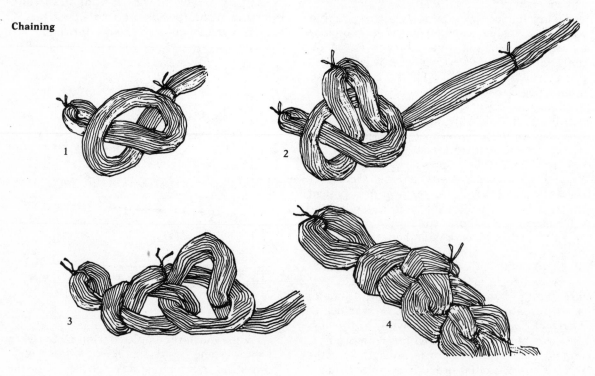

Warping the Loom

Many floor looms can be dismantled to make parts more accessible during the warping procedure. If you can, remove the front beam and beater (reed assembly), so you can sit inside the loom close to the heddles you will be threading. Unwind the back apron bar, and lay it across the back beam. Place the cross sticks near by. Push the heddles on each harness to the left side of the loom. If you are left-handed or find that you can work adroitly left to right, push the heddles to the right side of the loom. Center the raddle on top of the castle or back beam. If your raddle is designed to fit into the beater, remove the reed and place the raddle in its position. If your loom has a high castle and the raddle does not fit the beater, place the raddle on the back beam. Tie the raddle in place with string. The raddle spreads the warp threads evenly across the width of the loom while the warp is being wound around the warp beam. The warp threads must be centered on the back beam, and the raddle must be centered on the loom.

Making a raddle and cross sticks

The raddle, which resembles a rake, is easy to construct yourself. Use a length of wood as long as your loom is wide and approximately 1 × 1½ inches thick. Mark dots at ½-inch intervals along the length of the raddle. Hammer 2-inch

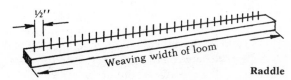

½''

Weaving width of loom

Raddle

finishing nails into the marked dots, leaving 1½ inch of each nail standing. Spread the warp threads across the loom between the protruding nails.

If your loom does not include cross sticks, use ¾-inch-diameter dowels as long as the loom's weaving width. Drill holes about ½ inch from the ends so that the cross sticks can be tied together.

Cross sticks

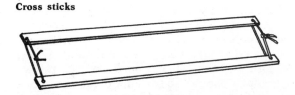

Placing the warp on the loom

Place the chained warp over the top of the loom on top of the raddle, which should be tied to the castle. Place the cross end toward the back beam. Slide the back apron bar or the stick attached to the back apron bar through the loop formed by the end of the warp. (The loop is formed where peg D was located on the warping board.) Slide the cross sticks onto either side of

Using cross sticks to warp the loom

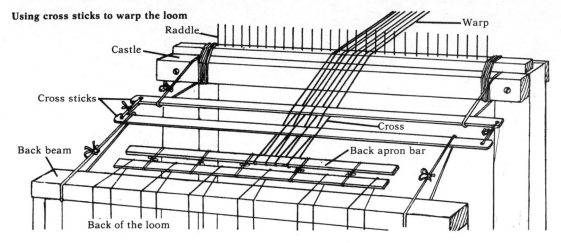

Raddle

Castle

Warp

Cross sticks

Cross

Back beam

Back apron bar

Back of the loom

the cross. One cross stick will be in the same loop opening as the back apron bar. The other cross stick will be in front of the crossing point in the threads. Tie the cross sticks together with a 2-inch space between them. The cross in the warp threads will be between the cross sticks. Tie a string through the front cross stick and around the castle on both sides of the loom. Tie the back cross stick to the back beam on both sides of the loom. Time spent now on the tying-up process will save time later.

Spreading the warp in the raddle

Clip the string that tied the cross in the warp; clip the counting string. Stand at the back of the loom, and note that the warp threads run alternately over and under the cross sticks. You can determine the warp threads' sequential order by lifting the first thread from over the cross stick and the second thread from under the same cross stick; lift the third thread from over the stick and the fourth from under the stick.

Starting at the right side of the work, count out the number of warp ends per ½ inch in the work plans. Place them between two nails at the

right side of the raddle. For example, if you are working on a piece which will have 12 warp threads per inch, place 6 warp threads in each raddle space. Continue arranging the warp threads by spreading them to the width of your item. Wind a string around the tops of the nails so that the warp threads cannot slip out of position. If your raddle has a top piece, or if you have placed it in the beater, close the top over the raddle. If your loom requires it, return to the back apron bar to redistribute the warp threads.

The warp threads should be in position on the back apron bar so that, when wound on the warp beam, they will stay parallel to one another. Count the warp threads to make certain that you have the correct number for your project. If you have far too many warp threads, tie the excess at the back of the loom until the warp beam is unwound. Plan to use them later in another project. If you do not have enough warp threads to match the desired width of the final article, wind the number of warp threads you are lacking on the warping board, tie the cross in place, place the threads on the loom through the cross sticks, and proceed.

Threads spread in raddle

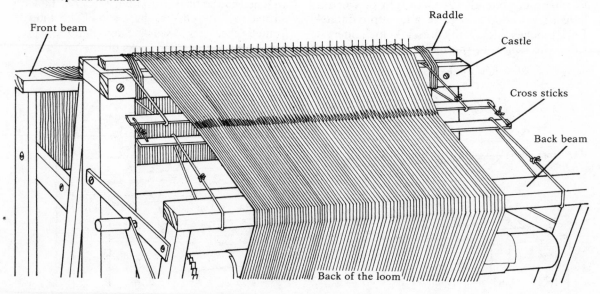

Front beam · Raddle · Castle · Cross sticks · Back beam · Back of the loom

Winding the warp on the warp beam

You will need an assistant to help in winding the warp. Wind the warp on the warp beam with all the threads parallel and under the same tension; none should sag. Stand at the front of the loom and hold the warp threads in both hands

Winding the warp on the warp beam

with fingers spread out like a comb. Maintain equal tension on all the warp threads while your assistant turns the crank to wind the warp on the warp beam. After one revolution of the warp beam, the assistant should lay paper (cut grocery bags or old wallpaper), trimmed to the width of the warp beam, between the layers of warp. The paper will keep the layers of warp threads from settling into one another and making tension unequal. In looms equipped with flat wooden sticks for this purpose, place them quite close together for the first revolution. Then use two sticks per layer, placed at uneven intervals.

Stop winding (cranking) the warp beam in order to comb tangles out of the warp threads with your fingers and to regain your grip on the

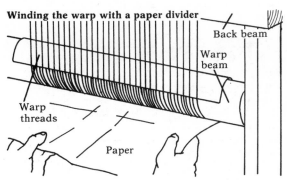

warp threads. Be careful when combing the warp with your fingers not to overhandle the warp. Stop your assistant from winding when you have about 12 inches of warp in front of the harnesses. Cut the warp threads as nearly equal as possible at the farthest point in the loop. Let the warp threads hang down in front of the harnesses.

Threading the heddles

The heddles are the wire or string pieces which are attached to the harnesses. The harnesses are frames which can be raised (or lowered on some looms) to separate the warp·threads. While the warp threads are separated, the weft is placed between the warp threads, thereby interlacing the threads and producing cloth. Looms are built with 2 to 16 harnesses. The following directions are for threading a four-harness loom, the most common size.

Stand in front of the loom and start by counting out four heddles from the left side of the harnesses. Take one heddle from each harness, working from the front to the back of the loom. The harness closest to you is number 1, and the harness closest to the back beam is number 4. Slide the heddles to the right side of the warp threads. Count the first four warp threads, starting from the right. Noting precisely which thread follows which through the cross, thread the heddles in order from front to back. Use a special sleying (threading) hook designed to thread heddles, a small crochet hook, or just your fingers.

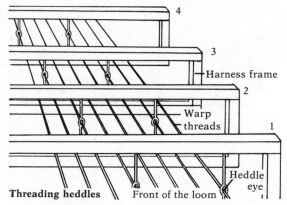

4

3

2 — Harness frame

Warp threads

1

Heddle eye

Threading heddles — Front of the loom

It is helpful to count the harnesses aloud as you thread up. When you have completed 1 inch worth of threading, check the order closely, then tie the warp threads in a slip knot. For example, if you are warping at 8 warp threads per inch, thread harnesses 1, 2, 3, 4, then 1, 2, 3, 4 again, and tie a slip knot in front of the harnesses with these warp threads. Continue threading across all the warp threads. It does not matter which harness you thread last. The method described here is called straight draw, the style used to produce plain weave and other patterns. It is the most widely used threading order and applies to all the weaving projects in this book.

Sleying the warp threads through the reed

If you have removed the beater from the loom, return it now. If you replaced the reed with the raddle, replace the reed. The reed is similar to a comb. Its purpose is to beat or push the horizontal weft threads firmly into place as part of the cloth. Reeds vary in size according to the number of dents per inch. Selecting the appropriate reed depends on the materials used. In the projects that follow, reed size is always specified.

When sleying, or threading, the reed, some weavers have the reed laying horizontally, supported by sticks which go over the front and back beams. Others place the reed in the beater. The warp must be centered in the reed and threaded through the dents. To do this, first mark the center of the reed. Measure half the width of the

warp to the right (or left) from the center of the reed. Mark the dent which matches the right edge of the warp. For example, start sleying the warp threads for a 20-inch-wide wall hanging 10 inches from the center of the reed. Draw the first warp thread from the right side of the warp through the

Sleying the reed

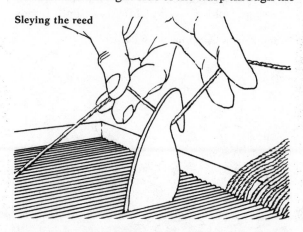

marked dent. Use a threading hook, sleying hook, or small crochet hook for this procedure. Sley the second warp thread through the next dent to the left. Continue across the series of warp threads. After sleying 1 inch worth of warp threads, recheck their order and tie a slip knot in front of the reed. An error in threading will necessitate resleying; check carefully. Continue across all the groups of warp threads until all the warp threads have been sleyed through the reed.

Tying the warp threads on the front apron bar

Untie the front cross stick from the castle, if you have not already done so. Return the front beam to the loom if you removed it previously. The final step in warping the loom is to tie warp threads to the front apron bar. Loosen the front apron bar to reach the warp threads as they hang down in front of the reed. Untie two slip knots of warp threads at the left edge of the work. Hold half the warp threads in each hand so that they are straight down the loom, through the heddles, and through the reed. The threads in the right hand go under the front apron bar; those in the

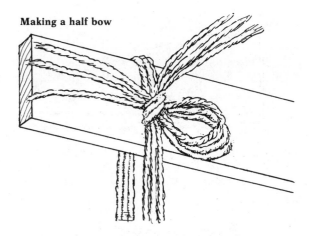
Making a half bow

left hand go over the bar.

Make a half bow by wrapping the bundles of threads around one another twice as in doubling the first step of tying a shoelace. Tie the half bow by pulling one end though as you make the bow. Repeat the procedure with the warp threads at the right edge. Continue alternating sides, tying the warp threads onto the apron bar. Strum your fingers over the warp threads to check the tension. Tighten or release warp threads or bundles which have uneven tension. Waves will appear in the finished fabric if the tension is not uniform. Time spent now will save disappointment later.

Tie a strip of rag on the front apron bar, and weave it over and under the bundles of threads. Go over the bundles which went over the bar and go under the ones which went under the bar. Tie the rag strip to the apron bar on the opposite side of the warp threads. This procedure brings all the warp threads to the same plane.

Warping a Multiharness Loom

1. Calculate amount of materials.
2. Wind warp.
3. Prepare loom to be warped.
4. Spread warp in raddle.
5. Wind warp on warp beam.
6. Thread heddles.
7. Sley reed.
8. Tie warp on front apron bar.

Plain Weave on a Multiharness Loom

Plain weave is the most frequently used process in cloth production. The multiharness loom projects that follow use plain weave or a variation of it. It is produced by raising or lowering alternate warp threads and placing weft threads between them. Observe that, if you number the warp threads, when you raise (or lower) harnesses 1 and 3, the odd-numbered warp threads are raised or lowered. Harnesses 2 and 4 control the even-numbered warp threads. To produce plain weave on the harness loom, simply manipulate the equipment to produce these two sheds alternately while throwing (passing) weft across the work with each harness change.

Weaving filler material in place

Open the shed so that harnesses 1 and 3 are raised or lowered. Weavers using table looms manipulate levers to raise the harnesses; weavers using floor looms step on a treadle (or two trea-

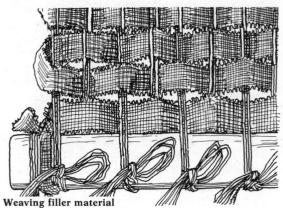
Weaving filler material

dles) that open the shed. Pass a row of ½-inch-wide rags, precut plastic trash bags, or newspaper inside and across the opening. Close the shed so that harnesses 1 and 3 return to their rest position. Draw the beater (reed assembly) toward the front of the loom, where you are sitting, in order to position the rags in a straight horizontal row. Raise or lower harnesses 2 and 4, so that the alternate shed is open. Throw a second row of filler material. The filler rows make the warp threads a uniform distance apart. (The knots that hold the warp on the front apron bar make clumps of them.) Weave enough filler so that the warp threads are equidistant and parallel running toward the back of the loom.

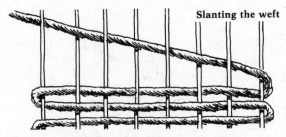

Slanting the weft

should be straight. Lay the weft in the shed at a 30-degree angle. Depending on the fibers used and the number of warps per inch, you may also

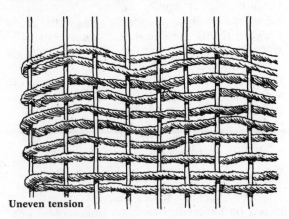

Uneven tension

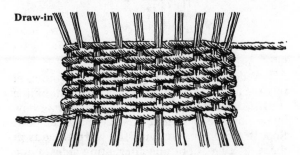

Draw-in

Check to see that the weft is forming straight rows. If the tension is not uniform, waves will form in the cloth. If a hill appears, the warp threads are loose at that point. The appearance of a valley indicates that the warp threads are tight in that area. Untie problem bundles and adjust the tension. When the tension is correct, you are ready to weave your project. Using the weft thread chosen for your project, continue weaving.

Beating

In order to position the weft thread in the cloth, draw the beater toward you until the weft is drawn into its horizontal position by the reed. Hold the beater in the center to avoid even the slightest slant; the horizontal threads must be straight. Neither draw the beater back with great force nor tap the weft thread so lightly that it won't become part of the cloth. A firm, definite beat is best. Try to beat at a steady rate to establish a uniform tension in the cloth.

Edges drawing in

Although there will be some natural draw-in by the weft (see p. 382), the edges of the work

need to bubble the weft thread as you lay it in the shed (p. 352). Bubbling provides enough weft thread to avoid extreme draw-in. Aim to keep the edge of the woven work parallel to the dent in the reed which holds the edge warp thread.

Winding cloth and warp forward

As you weave, the cloth will get closer to the beater. Eventually the shed will become too small to take the shuttle. Before that happens, release the warp slightly from the warp beam, and wind the cloth forward on the cloth beam. Secure the gears that hold the beams in place. To keep a large shed for ease of weaving, release and wind the warp forward often during the weaving process.

Removing cloth from the loom

When you finish weaving your project, decide whether you want to weave a few rows of filler to hold the weft in place until you do the finishing work. Next, remove the weaving from the loom. Cut the warp threads behind the heddles. Release the cloth beam, and untie the bundles of warp thread from the front apron bar.

Untangling Problems

Skipped heddle — If you discover a skipped heddle, fill it, otherwise an imperfection will appear in the cloth. If you simply failed to thread the heddle, but the warp thread is in place, thread the skipped heddle and the proper dent in the reed. If you totally skipped the heddle, cut a new length of warp thread the same length as the warp, then thread the warp thread through the skipped heddle and through the dent in the reed. Now, since you can't put the new warp length around the warp beam, wrap it around a nail or a fisherman's lead sinker to provide enough tension to keep it taut. Allow it to hang over the back beam.

Thread not in cross

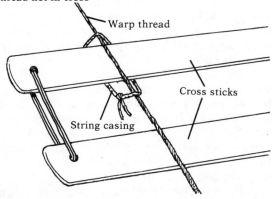

Warp thread

Cross sticks

String casing

Warp thread not in the cross — If you find a warp thread that is not included in the cross, try to figure out where it should fall in the warp. Attach it to its place with a string casing, which acts as a frame to hold the warp thread in place. The casing prevents the thread from getting lost.

Skipping a warp thread in threading heddles — If you skip a warp thread when threading the heddles, remove the thread as far back as possible. If you weave to the end of the warp length, tie a knot around the back apron bar to maintain tension on the removed thread's partner.

Warp threads twisted or reversed between heddles and reed — If you reverse or twist threads between threading the heddles and the reed, rethread and resley the warp threads. Otherwise an imperfection will show in the cloth and the warp threads will probably break.

Skipping a dent in the reed — Resley the reed if you skip a dent. Otherwise an open stripe will appear in the finished cloth.

Broken warp thread — If a warp thread has broken, measure a new warp thread about 30 inches long.

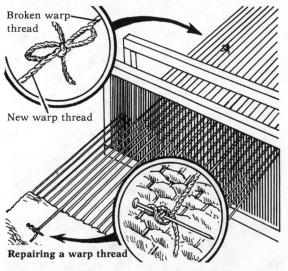

Broken warp thread

New warp thread

Repairing a warp thread

Locate the dent and the heddle from which the broken warp came. If it is still threaded, remove it. Carefully thread the new warp through its dent and heddle. Tie the new warp thread with a bow to the end of the broken warp just in front of the cross sticks. Return to the front of the loom, and place a straight pin 2 inches back from the woven edge in the cloth in line with the broken warp thread. Wind the front end of the new warp thread around the pin in a figure 8 to secure it.

Continue weaving. Watch the bow carefully to insure that it doesn't pull loose. Continue weaving until the end of the broken warp is long enough to reach about 2 inches into the woven cloth. Replace the new warp length with the broken warp through the heddles and reed. Place another pin on the cloth and wind the warp in a figure 8, maintaining the tension.

Threads in wrong heddle order — If you confuse the order in threading the heddles, you must rethread the heddles in the problem area.

Curtains on a Multiharness Loom

Warping a harness loom
Plain weave on a harness loom
Spaced warps
Danish medallions
Using two shuttles

Curtains are a satisfying undertaking, useful as well as a constant reminder of weaving pleasure. Since the fabric suffers no abrasion or pressure in use, the weaver can choose a design without being hampered by considerations of structural strength. Fabric that is too lacy or impractical for any other purpose can be attractively and easily displayed as curtains. The cloth need only be pliable enough to drape well and fall into soft folds.

The curtains in this project are woven of a sunny yellow mercerized cotton. The great advantage of weaving your own curtains is the chance to choose exactly the right colors and texture to complement the colors of your walls. Always work with good quality, colorfast, lightfast materials, since your work will be exposed to the deteriorating effects of sunlight.

The open, lacy effect that is the special delight of handwoven curtains is lost if you choose to line them, though lining them or hanging them in a northern window will prolong their life. In this project, the opportunity to have the sun streaming in through the texture wins out over concern for wear.

The open effect is the result of the spaced warp technique. This airiness in the pattern, however, can also cause the warp threads to drift across the open stripes. The Danish medallion pattern prevents this drift and provides a pleasing design that is relatively uncomplicated to produce. The technique is particularly easy to work in combination with spaced warps. Together, the spaced warps and Danish medallions produce a pleasing texture that drapes gracefully across the window. The only other new technique the curtain project requires is the use of two shuttles, one to help create the rows of plain weave and a second for the Danish medallions.

The project directions are for two curtain panels, each 25 × 43 inches, but the means of making curtain panels of other dimensions are also explained.

What you will need

multiharness loom, minimum width 25'' (proper loom width depends on desired curtain width)
12-dent reed
boat shuttle
short stick shuttle
1 lb. 5/2 mercerized cotton (2100 yd. per lb.)
seam binding
crochet hook (size 4 or 5)

Step-by-step instructions

1. Calculate the number of warp threads needed for curtain width. Because of the warp spacing, figure in multiples of 4 in. for the patterned area of the curtain. The pattern runs all the way across the curtain, with the patterned area averaging 9 warp threads per in. After deciding on the desired width, multiply the number (number must be divisible by 4) by 9 threads per in. For example, a 24-in. patterned curtain requires 216 warp threads (24 × 9).

Allow a 1½-in. seam allowance of solid fabric on both sides of the curtain. This allows a ½-in. hem at the edges to provide stability for the fabric. The seam allowances are threaded at 12 threads per in. Adding the seam allowance (12 threads per in. × 3 in. = 36 warp threads) to the requirements for the 24-in. patterned curtain brings the total number of warp threads to 252 (216 warp threads needed for the curtain + 36 threads for the seam allowance). Add 10% (25 warp threads) for draw-in, to yield a total of 277 warp threads. Thus:

$$
\begin{array}{rl}
 & 24 \text{ in. (curtain width} \\
\times & 9 \text{ warp threads per in.} \\
\hline
= & 216 \text{ warp threads (for curtain)} \\
+ & 36 \text{ warp threads (for seam allowance)} \\
\hline
= & 252 \text{ warp threads} \\
+ & 25 \text{ warp threads (draw-in of 10\%)} \\
\hline
= & 277 \text{ total number of warp threads to wind}
\end{array}
$$

2. Figure the proper length of warp for weaving your curtains. Measure the length from the top of the heading (the ruffle above the rod pocket plus the rod pocket) to the bottom of the apron (the wood molding under the window). Add 3 in. for the heading hem and 6 in. for the bottom hem. (The large bottom hem allows for shrinkage.) To weave two curtain lengths, double the final figure. If you work on a table loom, add 18 in. for loom waste. If you work on a floor loom, add 36 in. for loom waste. Add 10% of the final figure for take-up. Here is the computation:

$$
\begin{array}{rl}
 & 43 \text{ in. (length of curtain)} \\
+ & 3 \text{ in. (heading hem)} \\
+ & 6 \text{ in. (bottom hem)} \\
\hline
= & 52 \text{ in. (warp length per curtain)} \\
\times & 2 \\
\hline
= & 104 \text{ in. needed for two curtain lengths} \\
+ & 36 \text{ in. (loom waste for floor loom; 18 in. for table loom)} \\
\hline
= & 140 \text{ in.} \\
+ & 14 \text{ in. take-up (10\% of warp length)} \\
\hline
= & 154 \text{ in. (length to put on warping board)}
\end{array}
$$

3. Wind warp on the warping board. Mark the cross. Chain the warp and transfer it to the loom (see Winding the Warp, p. 383).

4. Spread threads across the raddle as follows: Spread 6 threads per ½ in. at the seam allowances; in other words, spread the warp threads in 3 groups of 6 in the raddle for the seam allowance. Then spread the spaced warp area of the curtain in groups of 4—5—4—5—4—5, continued across to the opposite seam allowance. Spread the warp threads 6—6—6 in the raddle for the seam allowance.

5. Wind the warp on the warp beam.

6. Thread the warp threads through the heddles.

7. Sley the warp threads through the reed, starting at the left edge. Sley 18 threads, one in each dent, for the seam allowance. Skip 4 dents; sley 12 warp threads, one in each dent. Continue the pattern of skipping 4 dents, sleying 4 dents, across the work (see Spaced Warps, p. 394). Finally, sley 18 threads, one in each dent, for the seam allowance at the right edge.

8. Tie the warp on the front apron bar.

9. Check the tension across the warp threads.

10. Weave 3 rows of rags to space the warp threads.

11. Recheck the tension. The filler rows of rags should be straight. If they are not, retie the bundles of warp threads to equalize the tension.

12. Using the boat shuttle, weave 9 in. in plain weave for the curtain hem and bottom of the curtain. The medallions should begin slightly below the level of your windowpane. The plain weave frames the medal-

Open-Weave Techniques

SPACED WARPS

Use this arrangement of skipping dents when sleying the reed to establish a pattern so that the open areas in the cloth occur at even intervals. Spacing warp threads is good technique for openwork fabrics. In the illustrations below and in the project, 4 dents are skipped and 12 are sleyed across the warp. With a 12-dent reed, this establishes stripes with a 1/3-in. space and a 1-in.-wide solid fabric with weft threads joining the fabric stripes over the open spaces.

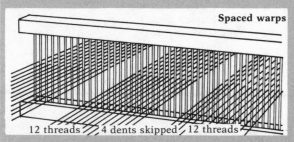

Spaced warps

12 threads 4 dents skipped 12 threads

DANISH MEDALLIONS

These are a series of oval, open patterns formed by manipulation of weft threads. When combining them with plain weave, end the plain weave at the left edge. Wind a short stick shuttle with a double strand of weft threads. Using a double strand of cotton, throw a left-to-right row. Weave plain weave for the desired size of the medallion center. With spaced warp threads, you must have an even number of rows in the center of the medallions, otherwise a warp thread will be excluded from the frame structure. Remember when deciding the number of weft rows to go in the center of the medallion, that this number determines the ultimate size of the medallion. The medallions in the project have 8 weft rows, with the eighth row ending at the right side of the work and the width of the medallion controlled by the spaced warp pattern.

Use the stick shuttle with the double strand of weft thread for the top medallion frame. Open the shed, and weave right to left across the seam allowance to the

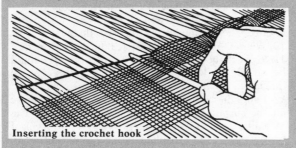

Inserting the crochet hook

first open area in the spaced warps. Bring the shuttle to the top of the work. Insert a crochet hook between the plain weave and the bottom frame row. When forming medallions with 8 weft rows in the center, insert the crochet hook back 9 rows. Catch a loop of the weft from the top frame row and pull it under the work and back to the surface. Pull on the loop so that it is big

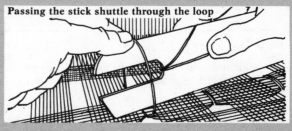

Passing the stick shuttle through the loop

enough for the shuttle. Pass the stick shuttle through the loop, thereby looping the weft through itself. Tighten the loop by pulling on the weft thread. An oval medallion shape will be formed as you tighten the weft thread. Experiment to find the dimensions you like.

Keeping the shed open, insert the shuttle through the shed to the next open space in the warp threads. Return the shuttle to the surface. Using the crochet hook under the bottom frame, draw the weft from under the work. Draw the loop to the surface and push the shuttle through it. Draw the medallion to the same tension as the first medallion. Continue across the row in this way.

USING TWO SHUTTLES

Two shuttles are necessary when using two colors, or using two different fibers, or using a double strand of weft for specific rows, including forming the frame structure for Danish medallions. Use one shuttle for the plain weave rows and a second for the medallion frame rows.

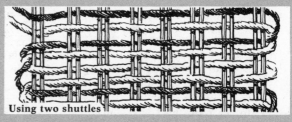

Using two shuttles

To use two shuttles, place the shuttle not in use on the table or loom frame out of the way. Intertwine the threads from the two shuttles at the edge of the work as you progress. Keep the threads loose at the edge of the work so that it will lie flat when completed.

lion area of the curtain. When measuring woven cloth, release the tension in order to get an accurate measurement (see Measuring Woven Work, p. 398).

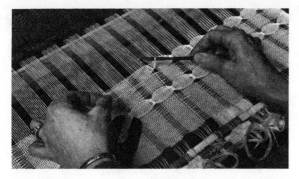

13. Work Danish medallions (opposite). The center of each medallion is 8 rows of plain weave.

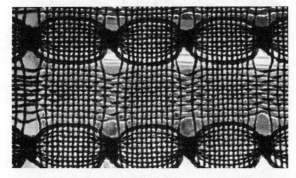

14. Measure the medallions when the final row is complete. If you are planning medallions to be a

uniform size throughout the curtains, write the size down so that you can check for uniformity as you weave, and tape the notation to the loom so it is readily available. To vary the medallion size from set to set, keep a log of sizes so that you can repeat the sequence on the second curtain length.

15. Weave 10 rows of plain weave between medallions, or the amount you choose for your curtains.

16. Alternate Danish medallions and plain weave for the desired length of the curtain. To frame the medallions with plain weave, end the medallions just beyond the top of the glass panes in the window.

17. Weave at least 3 in. of plain weave for the heading hem. In this project, 6 in. were woven because the medallions ended at the top of the windowpane.

18. If you are weaving only one curtain length, proceed to step 19. If you are weaving two curtain lengths, repeat steps 12—17.

19. Remove the curtains from the loom.

20. To finish, hand-sew or zigzag all the cut edges on a sewing machine. Cut the curtain lengths apart, and zigzag the cut edges. Hand-wash the curtains in warm water, and dry flat or steam press. Fold a ¼-to-½-in. hem back to the inside on each side of the curtain. Slip-stitch hems in place. You may cover the edge hem with seam binding.

At the top of the curtain, press ½ in. of fabric to the inside; them press an additional 2½-in. hem to the inside for the rod holder and heading ruffle. Before stitching, place seam binding inside the hem 1 in. from the top fold under the rod seam. Baste, then machine- or hand-sew both seams (the bottom edge and 1 in. from the top fold) for the rod pocket. Hang the curtains and mark the hem. Allow a 3-in. hem, press the excess under, and hem by hand.

Chair Seat Fabric on a Multiharness Loom

Designing striped fabric
**Winding a striped warp with an even number
of threads**
**Winding a striped warp with an odd number
of threads**
Sleying variations
Using stretchers
Measuring woven work

The fruits of your weaving projects can hang on the wall, lie underfoot, or cover your windows. Here is a project you can sit on—four chair-seat covers to fit the dining chairs that are described in a project in the woodworking section (see p. 120). The covers will also fit any dining chairs with seats 24 inches square or slightly larger.

The task of weaving chair-seat fabric is simplified, because full-width upholstery fabric is not required. These covers can be woven on either a four-harness loom or a rigid heddle loom. To use the latter, first make sure that the textured yarns will fit through your reed-heddle bar without undue abrasion. If they do not fit easily, constant wear will break the warp threads. To avoid this problem, you can replace the reed-heddle bar with a heddle rod you make yourself (p. 362).

Upholstery fabric should be strong and woven so tightly that it will not become fuzzy with wear. It must also have sufficient flexibility to fold easily around the chair inserts. To achieve this balance of characteristics, a combination of fibers are used in the fabric shown here: cotton, wool-viscose blend, rayon-linen blend, and cotton-linen blend. The raised area, which is most subject to friction, is a strong linen fiber. Cotton provides suppleness and depth. Rayon adds a shiny reflective color. The fabric can also be worked as drapes.

The seats are predominantly blue. The stripes are two shades of soft blue, off-white, and a bit of black. Before you begin, weave and wash a sample to insure that the fibers shrink evenly and do not pucker out of shape.

What you will need

multiharness loom or rigid heddle loom
4-dent reed
boat or stick shuttle
400 yd. blue linnay (750 yd. per lb.)
320 yd. off white Irish Lace (725 yd. per lb.)
240 yd. black linnay (750 yd. per lb.)
240 yd. blue Nubs n' Slubs (50 gr. = 72 yd.)
1 lb. blue perle cotton 3/2

Designing striped fabric

First, experiment with yarn combinations. There are five yarns in the seat upholstery shown. The stripes are narrow, to be in proportion with the dimensions of the chair, and asymmetrical, to add visual interest to the fabric. To add the illusion of depth to the cloth, two textured yarns are positioned alternately in the warp.

After the yarns were chosen, experimentation revealed that the black stripes must be narrow to keep them in balance with the blue color. The off-white textured stripes are almost as wide as the blue stripes, and the texture allows them to balance the richer blue. Because the textural warp threads take up more space than the smooth threads, there are fewer of them.

When designing stripes, it is helpful to wrap combinations of yarns next to each other around a ruler. When you've hit on a pleasing stripe sequence, make a sample to see how the weft thread affects the stripes, and how the fabric fits into your room's color scheme. Work the sample on a small frame loom or on stiff cardboard.

Before beginning to wind the warp, thread the textured yarns through the heddles to make sure that they will fit. Evaluate the reed size to insure that the thread will pass without abrasion.

Step-by-step instructions

1. Warp requirements are given for four chairs, each 24 in. square. Plan 27½ in. square to insure sufficient fabric to wrap around the chair cushion and to secure to the seat bottom.

Calculate the number of warp threads needed:

	27½	in. (fabric width)
×	12	warp threads per in.
=	330	warp threads
+	33	warp threads (draw-in of 10%)
=	363	total number of warp threads

Wind 363 warp threads for the chair seats.

Calculate the length of warp needed:

	27½	in. per chair
×	4	chairs
=	110	in. (desired length of cloth)
+	36	in. loom waste
=	146	in. (length of warp)
+	15	in. take-up (10% warp length, approx.)
=	161	in. (length of warp)
+	16	in. shrinkage allowance
=	177	in. (length to put on warping board)

Wind the warp 177 in. long (see p. 383).

2. Wind the warping threads in the following sequence (see Striped Upholstery Techniques, p. 398).

6 blue linnay threads
4 blue Nubs n' Slubs threads
2 black linnay threads
2 blue Nubs n' Slubs threads
4 blue linnay threads
2 black linnay threads
4 off-white Irish Lace threads
2 black linnay threads
3 blue perle cotton threads
4 off-white Irish Lace threads

Repeat this 33-thread sequence 10 more times to obtain a total of 363 warp threads.

3. Warp the loom (p. 385), following these steps:
A. Spread the warp in the raddle with 6 warp threads per ½ in.
B. Wind the warp on the warp beam.

Striped Upholstery Techniques

WINDING A STRIPED WARP WITH AN EVEN NUMBER OF THREADS

First tie a guide thread on the warping board, then tie the warp thread onto the starting peg. Now wind the designated number of warp threads. If the thread is to be used in later stripes, wrap it around an unused peg out of the way. This procedure maintains proper tension, while making the warp thread available when you need it. Tie the new warp thread onto the starting peg, and wind the number of warp threads needed.

When wrapping a series of stripes, it is often easiest to cut and knot the warp threads. Cut the old yarn at the starting peg. Knot the new yarn to the old and continue wrapping. Because of the number of warp changes, this method works best for the upholstery project shown in this chapter.

WINDING A STRIPED WARP WITH AN ODD NUMBER OF THREADS

Cut the thread at the final peg at the cross end after you've wound the number of warp threads you intend to use in that color. Leave a 9-in. tail on the warp thread. Tie the next warp thread to the cut end at the peg. The tails will allow for adjustments at the end of the weaving, if any are needed.

SLEYING VARIATIONS

The number of warp threads per in. (the sett) will often not be the same as the reed size. The warp yarn may have thick areas that will tear if you use a fine reed. If your reed size does not match the sett per in. you can calculate substitutions mathematically. For example, if an 8-dent reed is available, and a sett of 16 warp threads per in. is planned, sley the reed with 2 warp threads in each dent. With a 10-dent reed and a sett of 15 warp threads per in., the sleying order will be 1−2−1−2.

The reed with 3 threads through a dent

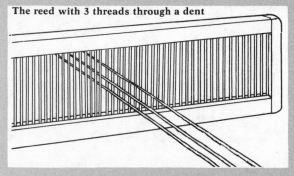

In the upholstery project shown, the textured rp yarns require a 4-dent reed (because they are too bby to pass through a 12-dent reed) and a sett of 12

warp threads to the in. Therefore, sley the reed with 3 threads in each dent.

USING STRETCHERS

Use stretchers when weaving fabric that should be held taut while you work. Using stretchers also gives an even width of fabric without the need to be constantly measuring.

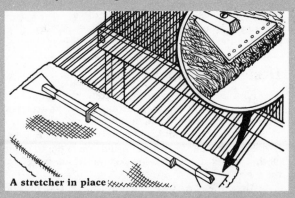

A stretcher in place

Set the stretcher for the desired width of the fabric. After weaving 2 or 3 in., attach the stretcher to each selvage. Press the stretcher in place so that the fabric is held taut. As the weaving progresses, move the stretcher along. Whenever you leave the loom, remove the stretcher first, then release the warp tension.

MEASURING WOVEN WORK

To measure the finished woven work, first release the loom tension. Measure the finished cloth with a tape measure. Tie a thread of a contrasting color around the edge warp thread at the closest in. measurement, then write the measurement on a card and tape it to the loom. Before the marker thread is wound on the cloth beam, measure again and record the measurement. Always measure with the tension released.

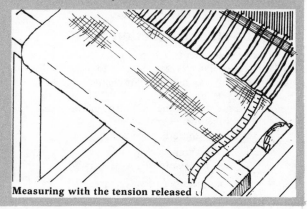

Measuring with the tension released

C. Thread the warp threads through the heddles.

D. Sley the warp threads through the reed. Sley 3 warp threads in each dent (see Sleying Variations, opposite).

E. Tie the warp on the front apron bar.

F. Check the tension and adjust as needed.

G. Weave 3 rows of rags to spread the warp.

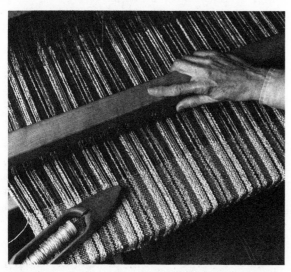

4. Wind the bobbins with blue perle cotton.

5. Work 2 to 3 in. of plain weave for the first chair seat (see Measuring Woven Work, opposite).

6. Place a stretcher across the width of the fabric (see Using Stretchers, opposite).

7. Continue to 28 in. in plain weave, moving the stretchers every 2 to 3 in.

8. Weave a row of contrasting color yarn, then throw 2 rows of cotton. Finally, throw a second row of contrasting color yarn. These rows of contrasting color yarn mark the cutting line for separating each seat.

9. Repeat steps 5—8 three more times to complete four chair seats.

To finish, cut the woven work from the loom. Either hand-stitch or machine-zigzag a line of stitching on the contrasting yarn rows and on the raw edges. Cut between the stitching rows. Hand-wash the chair seats in lukewarm water. Block and steam-press them. See p.125 for instructions on fitting the upholstery to the chair seats.

Woven Screen Panels on a Multiharness Loom

Weaving with a cartoon
Inlay
Horizontal color changes
Vertical joins in inlay
Color blending

This is a challenging project. Because it is worked in a linen fiber that has little elasticity, it is necessary to follow each step precisely. The end product will be impressive, however, even if worked on a small, 15-inch loom.

Screens are by definition intended to obscure the view but sustain an overall sense of space. To achieve this dual purpose, the screens are worked in a technique called transparency, which consists of two elements: transparent background and an inlay of additional weft threads which forms the design. The inlay design stands out, and the background fabric seems to disappear. The overall effect of this demanding, though uncomplicated, process is a translucent fiber.

The woven panels must be compatible in design with the wood frames supporting them. Since the panels in this project are tall and narrow, the emphasis of the design is in the upper section of the screens, where it will be most noticable. Though a substantial design mass is called for, each panel must also stand on its own as a design element. The panels each measure 15 × 64 inches. When installed in the wooden frame, the visible design area of each is 13 × 63 inches. There are three basic color combinations in each panel: dark blue purple, light lavender rose, and medium light blue.

The directions are for weaving the three panels one after another on either a table or a floor loom. If you have a loom with a 48-inch weaving width, work the panels side by side simultaneously. For complete instructions on making the mahogany frames to hold the panels, and the method of attaching the panels to the frames, see pages 78 and 85.

Before you begin

Choose colors for the background and inlay linen that will blend. Work the project with anywhere from three colors to a multitude. The screens shown use seven colors of inlay, starting with three basic colors, then blending them to obtain additional hues (see Color Blending, p. 404).

You may choose to use analogous shading of the colors in the screen. If you dye your own fibers, an unlimited number of hues is available to you. A monochromatic approach to color selection is also effective, as are natural fleece tones. Unplied wool will work as the inlay fiber if its weight is comparable to the tow linen #4.

Start by working a sample to practice inlay technique and experiment with color blending. The project directions include 18 in. additional warp on the loom for this purpose.

Step-by-step instructions

1. Draw a small cartoon of the panels on graph paper (scale: ⅛ in. = 1 in.). Color the cartoon to match as closely as possible your yarn choices. Our cartoon is 15 in. wide, as is the woven work. Thirteen in. will be visible when the screens are finished. The beading covers ½ in. on each side, and there is a ½-in. allowance for draw-in at the edges.

2. Using graph paper, draw a second small cartoon to the same scale as the first, but *reverse the image*. The cartoon must be reversed, because the weaving is done from the wrong side. Note that the cartoon shown for this project is the reverse of the screen design visible in the photo opposite. Keep the cartoon taped to the loom, and, to avoid confusion, mark your progress as you work.

3. To make the cartoons full-size, cut three wrapping paper panels, each 15 × 64 in., then measure the design onto the paper. Draw the cartoons *in reverse image* (see p. 402), marking the design with a heavy marker so that it will show through the warp threads as you work. Mark the measurements throughout the design on top of the cartoon lines. If you mark the cartoon in any other way, the finished work will obscure the numbers.

If you anticipate making any changes in the design as you work, make an extra set of full-size cartoons so you can judge how the change will look on the finished panels. Roll the cartoons up with the marked side out. Place paper clips on both sides of the rolls to keep them from unrolling.

(Continued on page 404)

What you will need

multiharness loom, minimum of 15″ weaving width
15-dent reed
boat shuttle
3 stick shuttles
blunt needle
5 skeins tow linen #8 singles (740 yd. per skein) for warp and background weft
1350 yd. tow linen #4 singles, divided according to color choices, for inlay
graph paper
6 yd. brown wrapping paper

Weaving with a Cartoon

To follow a design precisely, weave with a cartoon under the work. First, weave 1½ to 2 in. of plain weave in the background color, then align the cartoon under the warp threads and secure it under the finished work. Place one pin on each side, 1½ in. back from the edge, and place another pin on each side, 1½ in. below the first set, toward the front beam. The cartoon will hang by the pins under the work.

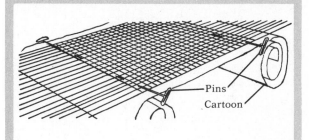

Pins
Cartoon

As you work, move the cartoon by placing the second set of pins in front of the first set, leapfrog fashion. Keep the cartoon pinned in place throughout the work. Removing both sets of pins simultaneously will make it difficult to get the cartoon back in position.

Coil the bottom of the cartoon into a roll as you work up its length, and attach paper clips to hold it in place. You will have two rolls under the work. To see your design through the warp threads, unroll the front cartoon and hold it under the warp. Continue unrolling and pinning the cartoon to the work until the design is completed.

Cartoons for Woven Screen Panels

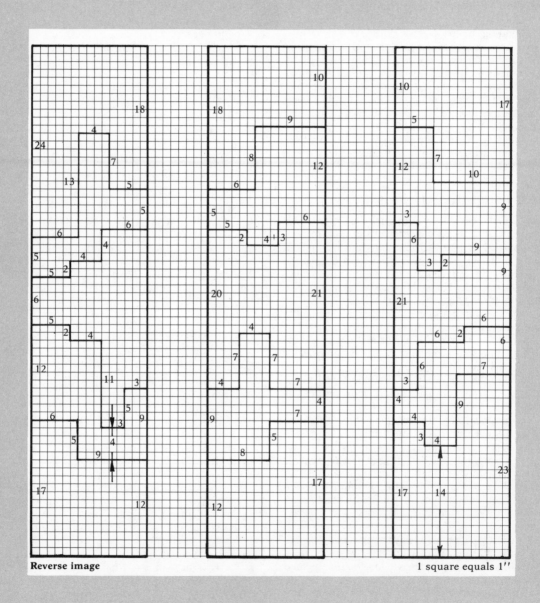

Reverse image

1 square equals 1''

Inlay

Inlay is a weave in which the weft is laid into the work to create a pattern. The inlay is usually basket weave woven into a background of plain weave. The inlay treadle or lever manipulation will raise harnesses in the following order:

1. Harnesses 1 and 3 (background—plain weave)
2. Harnesses 1 and 2 (design inlay)
3. Harnesses 2 and 4 (background—plain weave)
4. Harnesses 3 and 4 (design inlay)

This sequence is followed throughout the entire design area. Note that the background plain weave is worked throughout the design. The fabric will look like this:

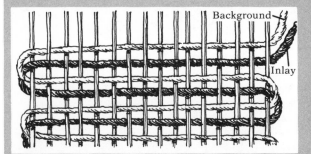

Here is the pictorial view of the weave structure. Try to maintain consistent tension when beating the plain weave background at 8 to 9 picks per inch. Take care to make the wrong side of the work neat.

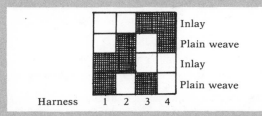

HORIZONTAL COLOR CHANGES

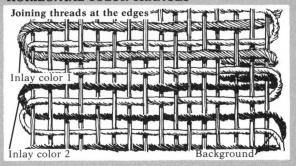

At the end of the color, leave a tail of weft thread at the edge of the work. Wrap the tail around the edge warp thread and lay it back into the same shed as the inlay row. Carry it over a few warp threads to secure it in the woven work. Begin a new thread at the same edge so that the joins remain at the same location. Weave the new inlay thread across the row, leaving a tail at the edge. Wrap the weft end around the edge warp thread and lay it back into the *same* shed as the inlay row. In this way the colors will form clear horizontal design patterns.

VERTICAL JOINS IN INLAY

There will be places in the design where two inlay colors meet in the middle of a row. When starting a row in which two colors meet, start the shuttles from opposite ends of the work. In this way the inlay threads will meet and be looped together to avoid a slit in the fabric. At the join, the thread that has been under the warp threads will lay on top of the weft thread that has been over the warp threads. The resulting loop will stick up slightly on the top of the work. Remember that the top of the work is the wrong side; and do not forget to weave the background row of plain weave into the work before weaving the second row of inlay.

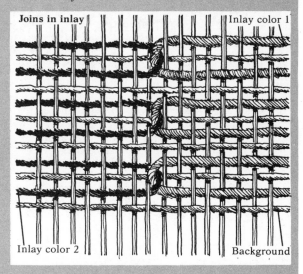

If a vertical line is being formed in the design, check every row to be certain that the loop is at the same place as in the previous row. Otherwise the vertical line will not be straight. From the front of the work, the loops will be invisible except as a shadow if light shines from behind.

Color Blending

There are three methods for producing varying hues from basic yarn colors. For clarity, the background rows of plain weave in the illustrations of methods 2 and 3 are omitted. Be sure to weave the background throughout the inlay area.

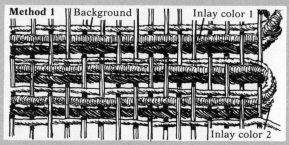

Method 1 | Background | Inlay color 1 | Inlay color 2

Method 1: In an inlay worked with 2 strands, simply use 1 strand of each color to be blended when winding the shuttle. This will create a melding of the two shades. The area between solid color areas can be woven with the combined threads.

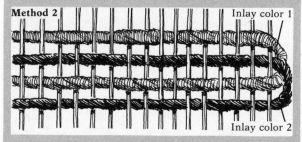

Method 2 | Inlay color 1 | Inlay color 2

Method 2: Weave alternate rows with different colors. This method requires two shuttles. Carefully intertwine the 2 weft threads at the sides to maintain a neat appearance and to let the work lie flat.

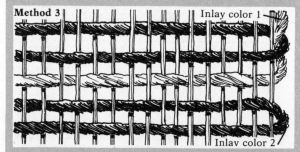

Method 3 | Inlay color 1 | Inlay color 2

Method 3: If you'd like less shading than method 2 produces, weave 2 rows with one color and the third row with the second color.

4. To calculate the number of warp threads needed:

$$
\begin{aligned}
& 15 \text{ in. (panel width)} \\
\times\ & 15 \text{ warp threads per in.} \\
\hline
=\ & 225 \text{ warp threads} \\
+\ & 7 \text{ warp threads (3 extra each side + 1 for even number)} \\
\hline
=\ & 232 \text{ total number of warp threads to wind}
\end{aligned}
$$

Wind the warp 110 in. long for each panel:

$$
\begin{aligned}
& 64 \text{ in. panel} \\
+\ & 36 \text{ in. (loom waste)} \\
\hline
& 100 \text{ in.} \\
+\ & 10 \text{ in. take-up (10\% of warp length)} \\
\hline
=\ & 110 \text{ in. (warp length per panel)} \\
\times\ & 3 \text{ panels} \\
\hline
& 330 \text{ in.} \\
+\ & 18 \text{ in. for sampler} \\
\hline
=\ & 348 \text{ in. (length to put on warping board)}
\end{aligned}
$$

This length allows removal of the panels as you finish each one. Adjust the tension as you retie the warp. The rigidity of a linen warp makes periodic readjustment necessary.

5. Wind the warp.

6. Warp the loom (p. 385). Spread the warp 15 threads per in. (8−7−8−7−8−7 etc.) in the raddle. Wind the warp on the warp beam, then thread the warp threads through the heddles.

Sley the warp threads through the reed. On each edge, sley 3 dents double (2 threads in each dent). Tie the warp on the front apron bar. Check the tension, and adjust as needed.

7. Wind the bobbins. Use the boat shuttle for the background weft thread, and the stick shuttles for the inlay thread. Wind the tow linen #4 double for the inlay.

8. Using tow linen #8, weave 1 in. to establish the warp width. Do not use rags to spread the warp threads; they're too bulky.

9. Work a sample piece to experiment with color and inlay technique (see Color Blending, to the left, and Inlay, p. 403).

10. Weave plain weave for 1 in., beating tightly (about 15 picks per in.). This in. of plain weave will attach to the frame. End with a row of contrasting color yarn to mark the beginning of the work. Weave a row of background weft thread (tow linen #8) in the *same shed* as the contrasting yarn. Take care to make the wrong side of the panels—the side you are working—neat. Whe the screens are in use, the back will often be visible.

11. Continue working plain weave, beating tightly

enough to give a firm substance to the fabric, but loosely enough to let light come through (about 10 – 12 picks per in.).

12. Pin the rolled cartoon under the finished work. Place the bottom of the cartoon on the row of contrasting color yarn (see Weaving with a Cartoon, p. 401).

13. Continue weaving plain weave to the beginning of the design. Move the cartoon as the work progresses.

14. Begin the design, working with 2 strands of tow linen #4 or material of comparable weight. Continue the plain weave with the tow linen #8 *throughout the inlay areas* from selvage to selvage, weaving 8 – 9 picks per in. on the inlay sections.

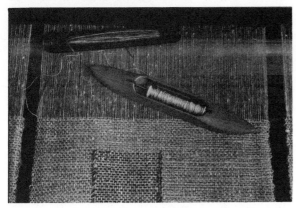

15. After the design is finished, continue the plain weave background at 10 – 12 picks per in.

16. Weave a row with a contrasting color yarn at 64 in.

(see Measuring Woven Work, p. 398). Throw a row of background weft thread (tow linen #8) in the same shed as the contrasting yarn, then change sheds and continue with 15 picks per in. for 2 in. more to provide tight fabric for joining to the wood frame.

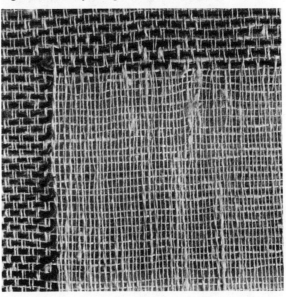

17. Remove the panel from the loom by cutting 8 in. *in front* of the reed (to avoid having to resley the reed). Put masking tape over the warp threads at both ends of the work to keep it from unraveling while you weave the next two panels.

18. On the horizontal lines between the design elements, use a needle to weave a double strand of the same color yarn into the work. When light is behind the panel, you will see the outline of the pattern changes. The vertical pattern changes show because of the loops used to join the inlay threads. Bury the ends from the needle weaving in the wrong side of the work.

19. Retie the warp threads. Weave the second and third panels, following the cartoons designed for them. Remove panel two from the loom before starting panel three. Remember to cut the warp threads in front of the reed so that you leave a length of warp threads to tie onto the front apron bar.

20. To finish, fold the sides under so that the design measures 13¾ in. across. Steam-press. At the top, fold the fabric under twice to make a ⅜-in. seam with the marker thread at the top edge. Stitch the seam in place by hand or machine. Install the screen panels in the frame according to the directions on p. 85.

Nonwoven Rugs

Nonwoven rugs first gained popularity in this country as a useful way to use up fabric scraps. Most of these rugs performed their humble task and disappeared, unmissed, forever. Those who first fashioned them out of scraps did not think of themselves as artists and would never have approached an easel, but in societies where goods must be handmade, everyone is an artist of sorts, and some of those early rugs turned out to be of lasting beauty. The ones that survived did so because they managed to combine ingenuity of design and lively color combinations with painstaking execution.

Nonwoven rugs are simple to create. They make use of inexpensive materials and easily mastered techniques, and the results are usually much greater than the sum of the parts. In the section that follows, there are directions for a latch hook rug in which small pieces of yarn are knotted through an open-mesh fabric backing; a punch needle rug, in which a continuous strand of yarn is pushed through a closely woven fabric backing to form loops; and a braided rug, made by interlacing strips of fabric. These rugs have no warp or weft and do not require a loom. (For rug projects woven on an upright frame loom, see Rya Rug, p. 364, and Weft-Faced Rug, p. 370.)

Nonwoven rugs offer the means for anyone — artistic or not — to make something beautiful. You do not need to know how to draw in order to sketch out a pleasing design for a nonwoven rug, nor do you need to possess skill with a needle or a loom. All you really need is careful pre-planning and the desire to see your imaginings become real.

Once your materials are assembled and the design chosen, you will find that the work itself moves along rapidly. In the time it takes to make a needlepoint cushion, for instance, you can hook, latch, or braid a small area rug. When you achieve a rhythm to your work, you will find it repetitive and relaxing. And when the finished product is resting underfoot, you may well be inclined to start all over again. Any household offers a multitude of areas where small rugs would be useful. Use them to define an activity area, provide some warmth under foot, or add color to a bare space.

Latch hook rugs

A latch hook rug has a thick pile formed by knotting cut pieces of yarn onto a base fabric with the help of a special tool called a latch hook. The result looks entirely different from a punch needle rug. Latch hooking works up very fast, making it possible to undertake a large rug or hanging you can be sure of having enough time to complete. (And, since latch hooking knots always come out the same, you can even pass the work among family members!)

Punch needle rugs

Punch needle rugs are a form of hooked rug, and have been called America's one indigenous folk art. Their invention, believe it or not, is credited to sailors and their wives—people skilled at repairing sails and nets—who lived along the Atlantic coast from Maine to Newfoundland in the first half of the nineteenth century.

To make use of discarded clothing and burlap, of which they had plenty, a hook was devised, based on a tool the sailors used for ropework, to push strips of cloth through the spaces in the burlap. Men worked at their rugs on long whaling voyages or in the winter when they could not fish or farm. Their themes, of course, were chiefly nautical. Anchors and ships were sketched on the burlap with the charred end of a stick or a piece of charcoal from the fireplace. Other traditional hooking themes made use of long strips of fabric looped into designs of flowers and trees, houses and barns, churches and people.

The hooked rug in this section is done with a punch needle and yarn, a combination that simplifies and accelerates the hooking process but has the same potential for highly detailed patterns. Like the earliest hooked rugs, punch needle rugs are made on a frame, using a base of tightly woven fabric and a continuous strand of fiber that is poked through the holes to form loops.

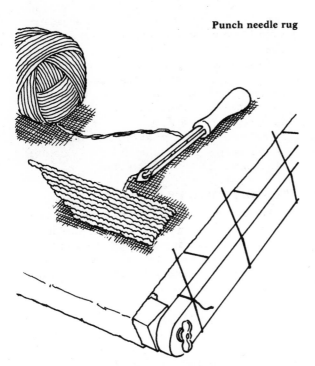

Punch needle rug

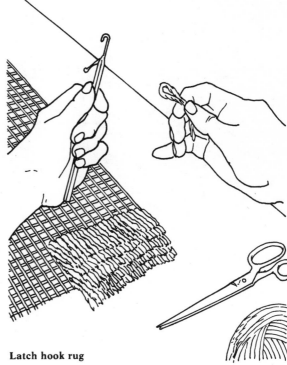

Latch hook rug

Braided rugs

Braided rugs are also a thrifty old device for using up scraps. The first braided rugs were probably grasses plaited together to cover a prehistoric mud floor, but it was in New England, during the nineteenth century, that the craft of braiding really hit its stride, and braided rugs, rich in color and varied in shape, had their golden age. Strips of wool from old clothing were braided to form long, thin bands that, when laced together, formed rugs that were both flexible and warm under foot. Since each strand of wool was folded several times before braiding, the finished rug provided a well-padded barrier between feet and floor.

Warm feet are no less a priority now than they were in rural New England 200 years ago, and braided rugs continue to be popular. Now as then, braiding is a skill quickly acquired. You can make the braided rug project from new wool torn into strips, or recycle old wools. There are directions here for both.

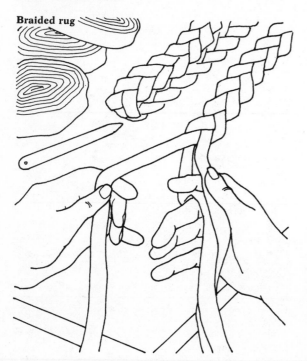

Braided rug

Choosing a rug design

Choosing a design idea can be made simpler by first looking at a lot of rugs, in stores, magazines, and books. Note that some rugs have a single motif that builds or radiates out from the center. Some rugs have border patterns (which tend to enclose and confine a design), and some have all-over patterns of such motifs as flowers, lines, or leaves. A design may also combine several elements—a border, a central image, and an overall background pattern.

Look at the relationship of one element of a design to another. Borders, for example, are generally wide in a rug with a bold pattern, and narrow in a rug with a more delicate pattern. Look at how shapes are arranged in relation to each other. Notice the size of each shape and how often it is repeated.

Study themes in rugs. Leaves, for instance, may be very straightforward in one rug, very stylized in another, arranged with rigid symmetry in one, and cast randomly over another. For inspiration, look at geometrical designs, seascapes, animals, crests and logos, abstracts, holiday images, sports, and children's themes.

A successful rug design will keep your eyes moving, in the same way that examining any object in nature will engage your interest and fascination. Examine a pebble, for instance, and note the presence of rings in it. Or look at tree bark as an example of pattern and movement. Any rug design that emulates one of nature's organic patterns is on safe ground.

Choosing the type of rug

Since all nonwoven rugs are easy to make, you need not start with any one type and graduate to others. To decide what kind of rug to make, first decide where you want the rug to go, then choose an appropriate size and shape for that location. Remember that a rug should neither be dwarfed by a large expanse of bare floor, nor should it overwhelm the space it is meant to fill.

Next, choose a suitable design. The design idea you come up with will lead you straight to the kind of rug you should make, because different

types of rugs favor different design possibilities.

Generally speaking, latch hook rugs, with their long, thick pile, lend themselves to large, bold designs which tend to be abstract. Their cut pile makes them more appropriate for the living room than for the kitchen, and they blend best with a modern selection of furniture.

Make a hooked rug if you're interested in detailed floral and geometric patterns or finely shaded representations of people, landscapes, buildings, letters, and numbers. These kinds of themes generally complement rooms whose styles are casual and traditional.

Make a braided rug for a room that is informal and furnished in colonial or Early American style. Since braided rugs are an exercise in color

and form, and usually have no pictorial content, they fit well into a wide array of other room designs as well.

A 3 × 5-foot rug is a reasonable size for a first project. Once you get into the rhythm of rugmaking, and the rugs you make take on a functional life in your rooms, you will probably try larger projects and other kinds of rugs.

Explore the many other varieties of nonwoven rugs you can knot, crochet, sew, or create with needlepoint or patchwork. Made with care, any nonwoven rug will be durable. Made with imagination, such a rug will also take its place among the centuries-old tradition of homemade floor coverings and become an heirloom to be handed down to future generations.

Latch Hook Rug

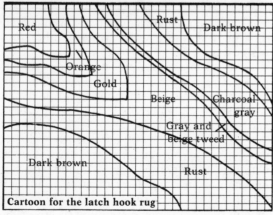

Cartoon for the latch hook rug

Red
Rust
Dark brown
Orange
Gold
Beige
Charcoal gray
Gray and Beige tweed
Dark brown
Rust

Preparing the rug canvas
Transferring a design
Latching
Creating your own design
Estimating yarn quantities
Making a cutting gauge
Sculpturing
Binding

The easiest way to make a knotted rug is to tie individual strands of yarn onto the crosswise threads of a rug canvas, using a latch hook. The amount of other equipment necessary is minimal; the work is portable and easily stored; and the result can be surprisingly luxurious.

The maker of latch hook rugs can produce many different kinds of cut pile simply by varying the type and length of yarn used. This project is made from rug yarn, purchased in skeins and cut into segments, but you can also use rya yarn, which is lighter and twisted like a rope. Each knot is made with two strands of yarn, each 5 inches long, and the result is a very dense, long pile.

The latching process is simple and repetitive. The value of the finished piece, therefore, relies heavily on the quality of the color combinations and the pattern. Pattern options for the rugmaker are, however, somewhat more restricted than are options for pile and color variations. Though realistic designs are possible, uncomplicated and abstract designs are usually more successful. Sharp definition of detail is only possible with a short pile worked on a large surface that can accommodate a larger number of knots.

The pattern in this project relies on subtle forms and interesting juxtapositions of color. It is worked in predominately dark colors with a contrasting element of red, orange, and gold that cuts across the middle. The finished rug measures 3 × 4 feet, an appropriate size for placing in front of a fireplace or a wood stove, on a landing, or beside a bed.

What you will need

rug canvas, 36″ × 52″, 5 holes per in.
latch hook, with either straight or bent shank
24 lb. rug yarn: 8 lb. dark brown; 6 lb. rust; 4 lb.
   beige; 2 lb. red; 1 lb. each orange, gold,
   charcoal gray, and gray and beige tweed
5 yd. 1½″ rug binding
felt tip markers
sharp scissors or rug scissors
masking tape, 1″ wide
heavy-duty needle
strong cotton thread
cutting gauge
tracing paper
shelf paper

Before you begin

The rug canvas should have the same dimensions as the finished rug, plus a 2-in. margin on all sides. If you purchase 36-in.-wide canvas for this project, however, the selvages can act as finished edges, eliminating the need for a 2-in. margin on the top and bottom of the design. Trim and tape the raw edges on the left and right sides of the canvas only.

If your canvas is cut from a larger width and, therefore, has four raw edges, allow a 2-in. margin at both top and bottom. In this case, buy canvas that measures 40 × 52 in., and trim and tape all four raw edges.

If, for purposes of economy, you intend to piece together odd bits of leftover canvas backing, first trim off any selvages that might overlap within the pieced area. Match all crosswise and lengthwise threads, overlapping the pieces 3 lengthwise rows. Whipstitch down the lengthwise rows to secure the pieces. Remember to hook through both layers when working the rug.

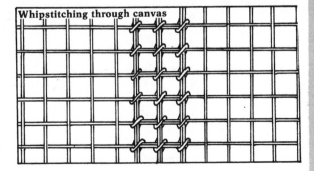

Whipstitching through canvas

Transferring the Design

It is necessary to transfer the outlines of your design to the rug canvas, where it will act as a guide for your work. To enlarge the design to the finished size of the rug, first trace it with a lead pencil. Then draw a small grid over the tracing paper, numbering each row of squares on the top and side of the grid.

Cut plain paper to the same dimensions as the finished rug, taping smaller pieces together on the back if necessary. Divide and number this paper into the same number of squares as the original small grid.

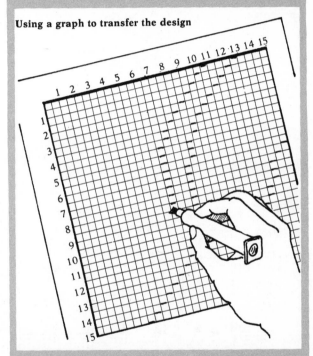

Using a graph to transfer the design

Using felt tip markers, copy the lines within the small squares onto the corresponding squares of the large grid by placing a mark where the design lines intersect the squares. Connect the marks and refine the lines as necessary. Fill in the colors if you want to see the finished effect. Mark the center of the design.

Position the canvas over the shelf paper grid, center it, and secure it with masking tape or pins. Trace the lines of the pattern onto the canvas, including the edge lines of the finished rug. This will ensure an even border. Use a yardstick to trace the border, to ensure that the lines stay within one row of mesh. Designate different areas of color by filling them in with markers or by tying a strand of the appropriate yarn in each section.

Latching

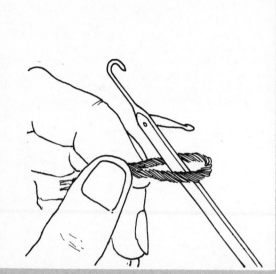

1. Loop the yarn (whether 1 strand or 2) around the shank of the hook. Hold the cut ends between your thumb and forefinger.

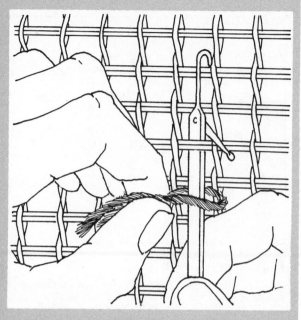

2. While holding the yarn, push the tip of the hook under a set of horizontal threads. As you push it up, the bar of the hook will fall open.

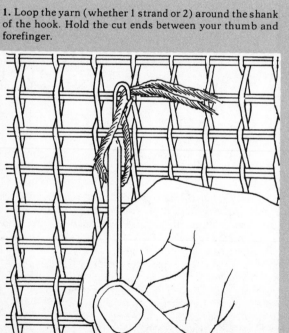

3. Draw the hook down, catching the yarn as the latch of the hook closes.

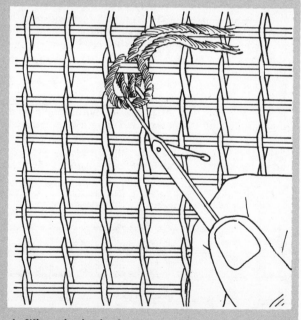

4. When the latch closes, release the yarn ends and continue pulling the hook until the knot is formed.

Step-by-step instructions

1. To prevent the canvas from unraveling, wrap all raw edges in 1-in.-wide masking tape.

2. Mark the exact center of the canvas and the center of each edge to help in transferring the design.

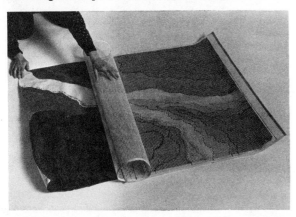

3. Transfer the design to brown paper, and pin the paper behind the canvas (see p. 411).

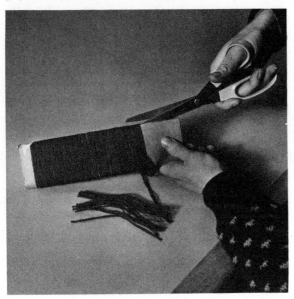

4. Make a cutting gauge to cut the cones of wool into 5-in. pieces: Cut a piece of cardboard 9 in. long and 2½ in. high. Wrap yarn around it, and cut along the top. Other cutting methods: Use an adjustable cutting gauge or a yarn cutter. The latter is a small, inexpensive reel that adjusts to cut various lengths of yarn. It is available at craft shops.

5. Begin latching. Use 2 strands per knot, treating them as a single unit. Unevenness in yarn length can be corrected later by trimming. Latch from left to right and from bottom to top, or by filling in one color section at a time. Working one color at a time is slightly more difficult, but using a bent-shank hook will make it easier to reach into tight places.

6. When the knotting is completed, lay the rug flat and brush against the direction of the pile. Snip all uneven yarn ends with a sharp scissors. If you wish, sculpture the pile by trimming certain colors so the pile is shorter and the rug takes on a three-dimensional effect. To trim areas of the pile, grasp several strands at a time and snip them straight across, then move on to another group of strands. The finished rug in the photo on p. 410 has not been sculptured.

7. Examine the back of the canvas to make sure all areas have been knotted. Fill in any areas where knots are missing.

8. Redo any knots that have only gone through 1 crosswise thread of the canvas instead of 2. With a little effort, these knots will come out for reworking, and no harm will be done to the rug or the canvas.

9. To sew the binding to the canvas, remove masking tape and trim excess canvas to 1 in. on each end.

10. Turn the rug canvas-side up. Cut a strip of binding tape equal to the length of a side, plus 3 in. The project calls for using 1-in. binding, because 2-in. binding is not readily available. If you can acquire it, use 2-in. binding to give the rug added strength.

Creating Your Own Design

Latch hook projects are readily available in kit form in craft shops and in chart form in craft magazines. For the beginner, they simplify the designing and enlargement processes considerably. Creating your own latch hook design, however, is not difficult and allows you the freedom to fit the size and colors of the piece to the space where you will use it and to choose among a wide variety of materials.

First, experiment on paper with forms and colors, bearing in mind the projected size of the finished piece. A small pillow, for example, will be overpowered by bright colors or pile that is too shaggy. The nature of the rug canvas itself will impose its own limitations on the design. It is necessary to step the lines of the design to conform to the places where knots are possible on the canvas.

Latch hook pile permits great flexibility. Make it long or short, or a combination of both, by sculpturing (trimming) sections of the finished piece. Choose the degree of density by making each strand with 1 knot or more. Produce a multicolored effect by alternating the colors of the knots in a row and then staggering the placement of colors in succeeding rows.

When you have settled on the design, transfer it to the canvas (see Transferring the Design, p. 411). Estimating yarn quantities is the next task. The amount of yarn you will need for the project depends on the number of knots your rug canvas allows (4 or 5 per in.) and the number and length of the strands per knot for each color you will use.

To calculate the total number of knots your design will entail, multiply the number of knots per square in. by the number of square in. in the design. Then multiply the number of knots by the number of strands per knot you plan to use. Roughly approximate what percentage of the total strand count each color uses up, then add 15% to each total to compensate for errors in estimating.

Yarn comes precut or in skeins. Precut yarn for rugs is 2½ in. long; for rya it is 4½ in. If you are buying it precut, you now have enough information to calculate the quantity you will need.

If you buy yarn in skeins, decide how long you want the pile to be, then double that figure and add ½ in. for the knot. For instance, to produce 2-in. pile, cut strands are 4½ in. long.

Multiply the length of each strand as determined above by the number of knots, and multiply that by the number of strands per knot. This calculation will provide you with the number of in. you need to buy. Divide by 36 to convert to yd. Remember to do the calculation color by color and to add 15% to the total to allow for errors.

As a beginning craftsperson, you should estimate wool in yd. Craftspeople, however, who use wool in quantity, usually buy yarns in bulk at minimal cost from textile mills and wholesale yarn outlets. Bulk yarns are usually sold by weight rather than yardage. Short pile of 1 strand per knot generally uses about ½ lb. of yarn per sq. ft. Double strands of long pile will use about 1 lb. of yarn per sq. ft. Experience will increase the accuracy of your yarn buying.

Latch hook yarns come in wool and synthetic blends. The latter are popular because they are less expensive and come in a wide variety of colors and textures. Wool is a better choice, however, because it is more durable and easier to work with. When choosing more than one kind of yarn for a single project, make sure the yarns all have compatible cleaning and care requirements.

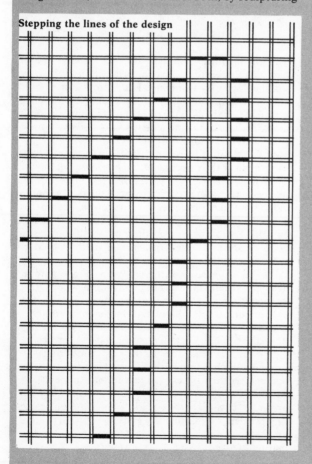

Stepping the lines of the design

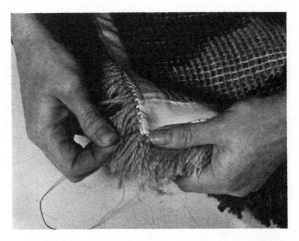

11. Turn over the 1-in. margin of canvas on that side of the rug. Leaving 1½ in. at either end for folding purposes, sew one edge of the binding as closely as possible to the last row of knots. Make 1 buttonhole stitch per canvas hole, using a heavy-duty needle and strong cotton thread 48 in. long and doubled.

12. Repeat the binding procedure on the other three sides of the canvas.

13. Tuck the 1½-in. binding ends under so they cover the jagged edges of canvas.

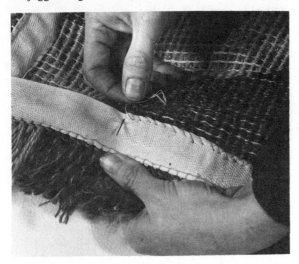

14. Fold the tapes toward the back of the canvas and whipstitch them down. Make 1 stitch per canvas hole, making sure to sew the tape through the canvas and not just through the knots.

15. Secure the corners. This method of binding is somewhat difficult, but very secure. By using the thread doubled, it has extra holding power in case 1 thread breaks against a rough floor. Making 1 stitch per canvas knot keeps the binding even and, therefore, better wearing.

Alternate finishing technique: Fold excess canvas back, leaving 1 row of unworked holes to border the rug. Whipstitch excess canvas to the back of the rug. Then, using overcast stitches, stitch the border in a color that complements the rug design. Take the needle from back to front, over the canvas, then back to front again. Work enough stitches in each hole to cover the canvas. This method of binding is both less arduous to sew and less sturdy than the tape method described above.

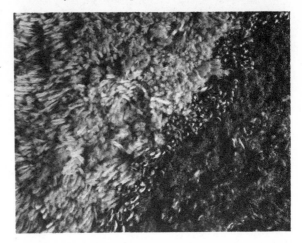

16. Give the rug a shake and it's finished.

Punch Needle Rug

Transferring the design
Using a punch needle
Working a punch needle design
Setting the fabric base into the frame
Creating your own design
Estimating yarn quantities

This punch needle project offers a fast and inexpensive way to learn hooked-rug rugmaking. The technique is in itself a simple one, but, once mastered, it can be applied to the creation of highly decorative floral and abstract patterns. Start slowly though, with this cheerful design, made in a workable size (20 × 36 inches) with readily accessible materials.

Hooking can be done with a hand hook or a punch needle, but the hand hook method, actually the ancestor of the punch needle method, requires much more effort. With a hand hook, the rug is worked from the right side of the fabric, with the hook serving to pull up loops of yarn or fiber strips from the underside of the backing. A punch needle rug, on the other hand, is worked entirely from the underside. The yarn is simply pushed or punched through the fabric to the right side, where the loops are formed that create the pile.

With either method the end result is basically the same—a short, uncut pile. Hand hooking, however, lends itself to great intricacy of design. While it is a useful outlet for leftover bits of fabric, it also requires greater skill and a larger expenditure of time to manipulate the length of each finished loop individually in order to create a uniform pile. The punch needle, on the other hand, scoots along the fabric backing, leaving a trail of loops behind it that are all exactly the same length. The pile forms quickly and has all the beauty of a hand hooked rug.

The semicircular rug you will be making will fit snugly up against a door opening or, as in the picture above, can rest underfoot next to a sink.

What you will need

easel frame
#6 punch needle
burlap fabric base, 32″ × 48″, 12- or 14-oz.
  weight
Aunt Lydia's rug yarn, 70-yd. skeins:
    1 skein tangerine
    2 skeins burnt orange
    3 skeins copper
    6 skeins antique gold
    6 skeins true blue
cotton muslin, 24″ × 40″
carpet thread
sewing needle
hot-iron transfer pencil
dressmakers' washable marker
brown kraft paper
5 dozen thumbtacks
6 sealing rings from canning jars

Before you begin

Hooked rugs must be worked on a fabric base that is firm enough to hold the loops of yarn securely. Burlap makes a good base because it is evenly woven, and its horizontal and vertical threads are easily visible for hooking. Burlap comes in several weights, but the 12- or 14-oz. weights are the only ones appropriate for rugmaking. Before you buy, hold the fabric up to the light to check for broken threads.

Monk's cloth is also an excellent rug base, but it is more expensive and harder to find than burlap, and it lacks the stiffness that makes burlap a favorite with beginners. Heavy linen and canvas are adequate substitutes, but they are woven too fine to make punching as easy as it is with burlap and monk's cloth.

The rug base must have the same dimensions as the finished rug, plus a 6-in. margin all around. The margin allows for setting the base into the easel frame without blocking any of the design area. It also provides material for turning under when the rug is finished. To piece together smaller, leftover pieces of burlap, overlap the raw edges 1 in. (cutting off any unnecessary selvages), and machine-stitch.

Woolen rug yarn is the best choice for hook work. The yarn used in this project is 100% polyester, because it is the most practical choice for a beginner. Polyester is very inexpensive, easy to find, and comes in dye lots that are always uniform. A cotton and rayon blend would have these characteristics as well. Whatever yarn you choose, buy all of it from one manufacturer to ensure consistency in weight and color.

Before you begin working, use an umbrella swift, the back of a chair, or the willing arms of a friend, to wind the skeins of yarn into balls. The yarn is easier to store in this form, it won't tangle, and it will feed more easily in the tube of the punch needle.

The punch needle itself is metal with a wooden handle. Use the #6 size to best accommodate the thickness of rug yarn. The punch needle will probably come with an adjustable pile gauge that makes it possible to form a very low, ¼-inch pile. The gauge is not necessary for this project. Without the gauge, the pile will measure ½ in., the proper size for the rug you will be making.

Yarn is threaded through an eye near the top of the punch needle. Then the yarn passes through a channel, and out through another eye near the handle. When you push the needle through the fabric base and then pull it back up, the yarn forms a loop on the opposite side. This push-pull technique is all there is to it.

Easel frame

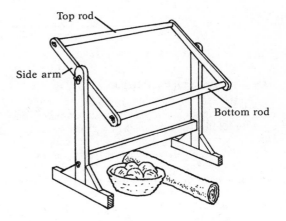

Rug hooking requires a strong frame to hold the fabric taut for even hooking. An easel frame exerts the necessary tension on the fabric base to make this possible. The easel tilts to provide a comfortable angle for working. Easel frames come in several sizes, based on the length of the top and bottom rods, which range in size from 20 to 60 in. Side arms are usually 17 in. long. Easel frames are available at craft or yarn shops.

Cartoon for the Punch Needle Rug

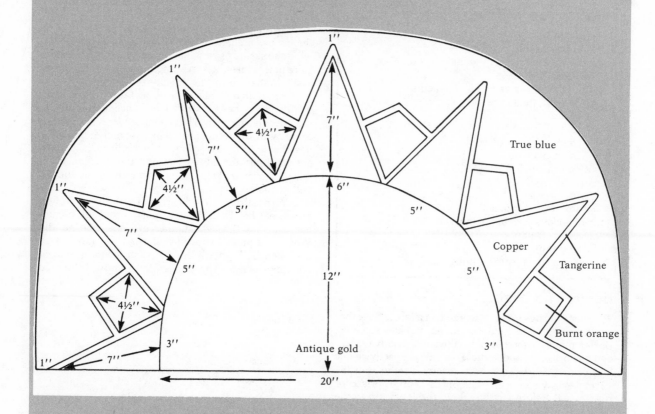

TRANSFERRING THE DESIGN

Use the grid method (see p. 411) to enlarge your design onto brown kraft paper. Tracing paper is too fragile for a full-scale cartoon. There are several methods for then transferring the cartoon to the fabric base.

You can simply trace the design, using dressmakers' carbon paper and a tracing wheel. Or you can prick along the lines of the design with a heavy needle, and then sprinkle a powder called pounce over the needle holes. While both these methods are useful, neither is appropriate for intricate designs.

The most popular and expedient way to transfer a design is to use a hot-iron transfer pencil, also called a hectographic pencil. Use it to redraw over all the lines of the design. Then turn the design over, and transfer the lines onto the fabric base by pressing with a hot iron. Make sure the fabric base is lying on a flat, hard surface. Smooth out any wrinkles or folds that might interfere with a good transfer. Place the right side of the drawing down on the fabric base, pin it in place, then press one area at a time. Use a wool or rayon setting to avoid scorching, and hold the iron in place only a few seconds.

Repeat if the transfer has not taken, but do not lift the entire drawing off the base to check. It will be impossible to reposition it exactly. Instead, just remove a few pins from the area you are working on, and lift a small section to look underneath. Repin when you are sure the lines have transferred. When the design is completely transferred, darken any faint lines with a dressmakers' washable marker.

Whatever method you use to transfer your design, the design side of the fabric base becomes the underside of the rug. In transferring the design, you are producing its mirror image on the base. When you have finished working the loops from the underside and you turn it pile side up, that side will be exactly the same as the original design.

Using a Punch Needle

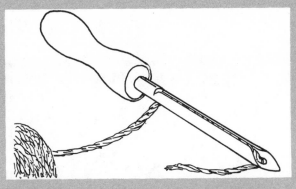

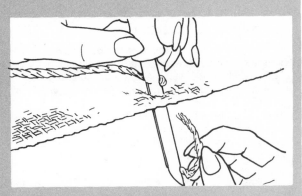

1. Thread the end of the yarn down through the eye nearest the handle. Pull the yarn through the shank of the needle and poke it out through the eye near the tip of the needle. The yarn should travel without friction through the shank and eyes of the needle.

2. Hold the punch needle like a pencil, with the gooved side facing the direction in which you are planning to punch. Push the needle into the fabric base as far as it will go. Pull yarn end down through the fabric base.

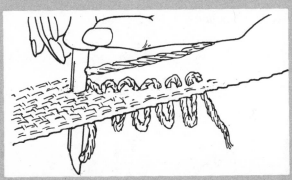

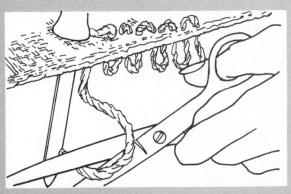

3. Pull the tip of the needle just to the surface of the fabric base. Skip over 2 threads (3 if yarn is heavy-weight), then reinsert tip. Push the needle down again, then pull up, keeping the groove of the needle facing in the direction you are working.

4. Always end a length of yarn on the pile side of the rug. Insert the needle into the fabric base, then snip off the yarn where it comes out of the eye at the tip of the needle. When the rug is finished, trim beginning and ending threads even with the pile.

HINTS FOR WORKING A PUNCH NEEDLE

Be sure that the yarn passes through the needle easily and that nothing interferes with its free movement. The least amount of resistance or tangling of yarn will stop loops from forming. Check the pile side of the rug from time to time to make sure the loops are forming. Never lift the needle too far off the fabric base, or you may pull out previously formed loops. To assure that the pile remains uniform, slide the point along the surface.

Always keep the grooved side of the needle moving in the direction you are punching. If the groove is facing the wrong way, loops will not form. Handle the needle like a drawing implement.

Work the details of the design first, outlining all the areas in the appropriate colors. Fill in the background last. For economical use of yarn, work from bottom to top within each color area, snaking back and forth from right to left and left to right. Or, fill the area concentrically by following the contours of each design.

Make the loops as close to each other as possible. Generally, leave 2 threads between loops with light yarn, 3 threads between loops with heavy yarns. If the rug begins to buckle, increase the space around the loops. If the fabric base shows through, decrease the space around the loops.

Step-by-step instructions

1. Turn under all raw edges of the burlap base ½ in., and machine-stitch to prevent unraveling.

2. Draw a full-scale version of the cartoon on p. 418 on brown kraft paper. Using a hot-iron transfer pencil, transfer the lines of the design onto the burlap (see Transferring the Design, p. 418). Center the design on the burlap so there is a 6-in. margin all around the design. Check to make sure the design has transferred clearly. Touch up faint lines with a dressmakers' washable marker.

You can transfer the design to either side of the burlap. The ½-in. hem you made in step 1 will be trimmed off when the rug is finished.

3. Secure the fabric base to the easel frame with the top of the design facing the side of the frame, to best accommodate the design (see Setting the Fabric Base into the Frame, below). Fasten top and bottom with thumbtacks; secure sides with whipstitches.

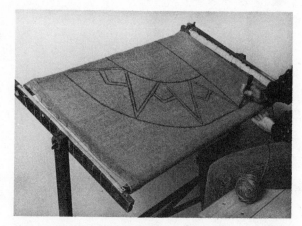

4. Begin punching by outlining each area of the design in the appropriate color. Start with tangerine. Form loops in every thread, 2 thread rows apart (see diagram, p. 422), beginning with the smaller areas.

Setting the Fabric Base into the Frame

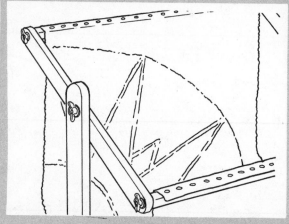

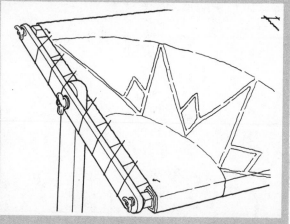

With the design side facing you, center the fabric base in the frame. Use thumbtacks spaced 1 in. apart to fasten the top end of the fabric to the top rod of the frame. Then tack the bottom end of the fabric to the bottom rod of the frame. To make the fabric taut, loosen the side screws which control the movement of the rods, turn the rods to take up the slack, then retighten the screws.

To secure the sides of the fabric base to the side arms of the frame, whipstitch the left and right sides to the closest arm. Use a heavy sewing needle and carpet thread. Begin the sewing with a knot and end it by taking a few stitches in the fabric base.

The fabric will have a tendency to slacken in the frame. To adjust the tautness, retighten the screws when necessary, and resew the whipstitched sides. As you finish working in an area, it will be necessary to move the fabric base by removing the thumbtacks and stitches, shifting the base to a fresh area, and refastening it to the frame.

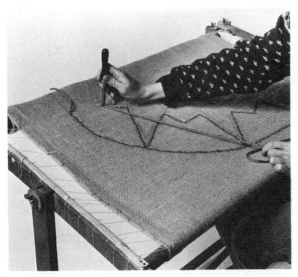

5. Go on to outline the other small areas. Start with burnt orange, then copper, antique gold, and true blue.

Check the pile side of the rug periodically to make sure that the loops are being formed. The yarn should feed freely into the punch needle tube; do not exert any tension on the yarn. Readjust the burlap in the frame as necessary.

7. When filling-in is complete, remove the rug from the frame. Trim off the excess burlap around the design, leaving a 2 in. margin. Clip the curved portion of the burlap margin so that it lies flat when folded back.
8. Cut cotton muslin for the lining to the same shape and size as the finished rug plus its 2-in. margin. Clip the curve on the muslin so it will lie flat. Fold back the edge so the lining is the same size as the finished rug. Pin, then iron to secure the margin hem.

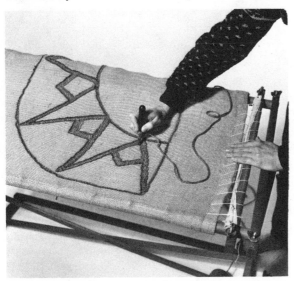

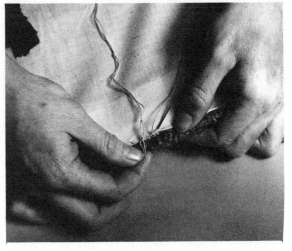

6. Beginning with the tangerine and continuing in the color sequence listed in step 5, fill in each color area (see Hints for Working a Punch Needle, p. 419).

9. Place the wrong sides of the rug and the muslin together. Whipstitch the two together as close to the edge of the design as possible.

Creating Your Own Design

Punch needle technique lends itself to chair seats and wall hangings, as well as to rugs. Use 10 oz. tapestry yarn and a #5 punch needle, and work on a needlepoint frame (round and 36 in. in diameter) when making chair seats. The result will be lighter weight and have a shorter pile than a punch needle rug but will still be very strong.

You can create a design that is highly detailed and realistic by using shading and minute variations of color. Use the lighter shades of a color in your design in order to create highlights. Use darker shades to give the illusion of receding areas. These effects will add dimension and impact to your project. To make a multicolored pile, thread strands of different colors through your punch needle. To vary the size of the loops, work part of your design with a pile gauge attached to the needle and part without.

Even if you doubt your drawing ability, it is quite possible to produce a design of great intricacy. There are tracing methods that make it possible for you to readily reproduce a design that you like. Start with a magazine photograph, for instance. Feel free to create your own design, or even to use parts of different photos that you blend together. Then start tracing.

Use tracing paper and a graphite pencil. For simple sketches, just hold the drawing and tracing paper up against a sunny window. For more detailed work, you can improvise a light table which will brighten the work space from underneath and make tracing surprisingly easy. Rest a piece of glass on two stacks of books. Keep the center area open and stand a flashlight under the glass. Place the image you wish to copy on top of the glass and tracing paper on top of that. Before you begin, make sure that the glass is well balanced, and tape the edges of the glass to avoid cuts and scratches. Trace your design, enlarge it by the grid method (see p. 411), and then transfer it to the fabric backing (p. 418).

ESTIMATING YARN QUANTITIES

As a general formula, 110 yd. of rug yarn are required to fill 1 sq. ft. of rug base. This formula is based on a normal pile length of ½ in., and a spacing of 3 threads between each formed loop. Dense pile, in which the loops are formed every 2 threads, will require twice that amount (or 220 yd. of yarn per sq. ft.). Extremely dense pile, such as in this project, and with loops formed every thread, will require three times as much; 330 yd. per sq. ft.

Since using a pile gauge on the punch needle shortens the pile length to ¼ in., only half as much yarn is required, and the standard formula becomes

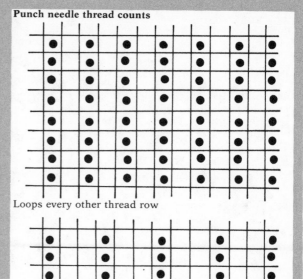

Punch needle thread counts

Loops every other thread row

Loops every third thread row

55 yd. of yarn per sq. ft., based on spacing of 3 threads per loop. For twice or three times this density, double or triple the yardage.

Tapestry yarn, which is thinner, is used with a #5 punch needle. It requires 220 yd. per sq. ft. since it is necessary to work twice as many rows to cover the same area using tapestry yarn instead of rug yarn. The formula is based on a ½-in. pile and should be halved when using a pile gauge. Double or triple the amount if you double or triple the loop density.

To decide on the loop density you like best, fit some spare burlap into a needlework frame. Try both tapestry yarn and rug yarn, varying the spacing between the loops, punching one area with an average pile thickness and another area with a dense pile. Once you have determined the area of your rug and the number of yards per sq. ft. you will require, apportion the yardage according to color areas. Add 10—15% to each area to allow for errors in estimating.

10. Steam-block the rug so it will lie flat on the floor. To do this, lay a big towel on the floor. Place the rug on the towel, lining-side up, then place a wet cotton cloth on top of the lining so it covers an edge. Heat iron on the rayon setting, and hold it on the cloth for ten seconds. Remove the iron and put some other very heavy, flat metal object (like a toolbox) on the area until the steam dissipates. Move on along the border, repeating the procedure.

If you choose not to steam the rug, it will take up to two weeks to lie flat. If you do steam it, it will only take a day or two at most. Rectangular rugs will lie flat readily, but rugs with a curved edge are much more likely to need steam blocking.

11. To prevent the rug from sliding on a wooden floor, take this precaution: Whipstitch six rubber rings from canning jars to the back of the rug. Sew one ring at each squared corner, three along the arch, and one at the midpoint of the straight edge.

Braided Rug

Gathering wool
Tearing strips
Joining strips
Folding strips
Storing strips
Starting a three-strip braid
Braiding a center strip
Making round turns
Lacing
Making color changes
Finishing a braided rug

New Englanders did not invent the braided rug (its history is much older), but more than the people of any other region, they came to excel at its production. The popularity of the craft in New England sprang from the necessity to use and use again the meagre resources of the colonial home. The women who carefully recycled the heavy clothes of a harsh climate into sturdy rugs, however, often managed to go beyond the practical nature of their task and produce work of museum-quality beauty and intricacy.

While rug braiding remains a useful and inexpensive craft, it is its potential for creative expression that keeps it a popular pastime. Like a wood stove or a fireplace, it is an enduring symbol of a cozy domestic environment. The best braided rugs are warm and springy underfoot, colorful and pretty to live with.

There are directions in this project for making a rug from either new or recycled materials. The rug shown in the photo was made with found materials, but you can duplicate it exactly by buying the wool fabric listed on the opposite page.

Even though precise instructions are given for making the rug, you will be undertaking what is essentially an inexact craft. Make your rug, if you like, with an entirely different assortment of colors. The rug shown measures 3½ × 4½ feet, but you can make yours smaller if your patience wears out or larger if you're having too much fun to quit. The near-random pattern of this rug, known as hit-or-miss, suggests just how flexible a craft you are embarking on.

Once you have completed a small oval rug, you may want to go on to try other shapes, patterns, and color combinations. There are patterns with enticing names like Jewel, Diamond, Arrowhead, and Butterfly. There are braiding techniques that allow for round, rectangular, and square rugs. And there are, of course, endless color combinations.

You will want to put the stamp of your own personality on every rug you braid. You might, for instance, include your favorite color somewhere in each of your rugs, or start every one with the same colors in the center. Resist the discreet anonymity of the women of early New England, and sign all your work with needle and embroidery thread.

What you will need

15¾ yd. 54-in.-wide, medium-weight wool:
- ¼ yd. dark purple
- ½ yd. lavender
- ¾ yd. bright light blue
- ¾ yd. dark red
- 1 yd. medium blue
- 1 yd. garnet
- 1½ yd. red
- 1¾ yd. charcoal gray
- 3½ yd. light blue
- 4¾ yd. navy blue

3 braiders (optional)
long sewing needle
lacing cord of linen, jute, or heavy cotton
blunt-tipped lacing needle or bodkin
spring-type clothespin
C-clamp

Gathering Wool

USING OLD WOOL

If you choose to make the rug from recycled materials, begin by gathering old wool clothes and blankets from friends, thrift shops, Goodwill Industries, or the Salvation Army. Collect wool, rather than other fabrics, because wool is the most durable and soil-resistant rug material. Cotton, linen, and silk are unsuitable because they will wear out quickly. Polyester is adequate only for small area rugs or chair seats. Gabardine is difficult to tear and braid because it is so stiff.

The ideal wool for braiding is heavy or medium weight, soft, strong, and tightly woven. Look for suits, bathrobes, and coats that still have a reasonable amount of wear left in them. When selecting clothes, try to find items of similar weight of wool so wear will be uniform. The tighter the weave, the longer the wear and the more durable the rug. Wools that are loosely woven or bulky are very difficult to rip by hand and therefore very time-consuming to prepare for braiding.

It takes between ¾ and 1 lb. of material to produce 1 sq. ft. of rug from recycled wool. For the rug in this project, which covers 15¾ sq. ft., assemble about 18 lb. of fabric to allow 10—20% extra for waste. After removing the unusable portions discussed below, you should have about 15 lb. of usable wool left over. Yardage estimates, however, are far from precise, because

of individual variations in braiding. Some rugmakers make tight braids, others make looser ones. Some like to work with wide braids, others prefer to work with narrow ones.

Having gathered a sufficient quantity of wool for your rug, remove all buttons, linings, facings, snaps, zippers, collars, cuffs, and worn areas. Machine-wash the material in warm water in order to preshrink it, remove any sizing, and make it colorfast. Washing will also draw the threads together, making them thicker and more durable.

While the material is still wet, do any necessary dying. If you are using found fabrics they will probably not be in the colors you can use. Old wool will accept dye easily. Light colors can be overdyed, and slight variations in color will not be noticeable in the rug. Use only commercial dyes that are permanent, and follow label instructions. After the dying process, rewash the fabric to remove excess dye.

USING NEW WOOL

If you buy fabric by the yd., expect 1 yd. of 54-in.-wide fabric to yield about 1 sq. ft. of braiding. Thus, for this project, the rug measures 15¾ sq. ft. and, so, requires 15¾ yd. of material. Machine-wash the fabric before you begin the work of tearing it into strips, separating out the colors so they do not bleed into one another.

Preparing Fabric Strips

TEARING STRIPS

Once all the material has been washed and dyed, cut or rip it into lengthwise or crosswise strips, whichever direction will yield the longest strip. The strips should be of different lengths so that when they are sewn together, their seams are staggered along the braid rather than all coming at the same point. Strips should be at least 12 in. long, but the longer the better. Using a lot of strips under 12 in. long will produce a lumpy braid.

The width of the strips is determined by the weight of the wool. Generally, tear medium-weight wool (from skirts, for instance) into 2½-in.-wide strips. Tear heavy-weight wool from coats or blankets into 2-in.-wide strips. The difference in width will compensate for the differences in thickness and assure an even braid. Wider braids are easier for beginners to work with. However, too wide a braid will produce too bulky a rug.

JOINING STRIPS

When all the fabric is ripped into strips, sew enough strips together to form lengths 8—10 ft. long. The strips you sew together do not have to be the same color, as long as they are close in value. Variations will give texture to the finished braid. To combine strips,

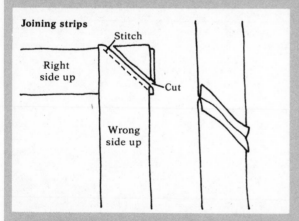

Joining strips

Stitch

Right side up

Cut

Wrong side up

place the ends of two strips together, right side to right side, so they form a right angle. Securely machine- or hand-stitch them together on the diagonal. Trim the seam allowance to ¼ in. and press the seam open.

FOLDING STRIPS

After the strips are joined into long lengths, it is necessary to fold in the raw edges of each strip. You can fold them by hand and press them with an iron, or you can use a set of metal cones, called braiders, which do the job for you.

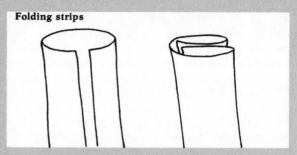

Folding strips

If you fold the strips by hand, fold the sides of the strip into the center. Fold the strips in half and press.

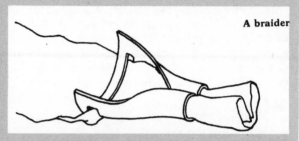

A braider

Braiders eliminate manual folding and pressing by automatically folding the raw edges in and under as you braid. They are available in different sizes, to accommodate light to heavy braiding strips. Or, you can buy the braiders first and then tear strips to accommodate the size of the cones. Feed the fabric strip into the larger opening of the braider. It will come out of the small end folded and ready for braiding. Tear up strips of different widths and experiment with folding and combining them.

SORTING STRIPS

Roll several of the strips into a roll. Stack rolls of the same or similar color together to get an idea of the quantity you have in each color. Secure each with a large safety pin, a blanket pin, or a rubber band.

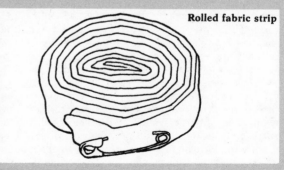

Rolled fabric strip

Braiding Techniques

STARTING A THREE-STRIP BRAID

It is important to start the rug off neatly and firmly. First, square off the ends of three fabric strips, each of a different length. Varying the length will allow you to join on new fabric strips later in a staggered pattern that will prevent noticeable lumps. Put on the braiders, sliding them down about 1 ft. from the squared-off ends. You will have to tuck the outer edges in and under by hand at the very start, but as you braid along the braiders will take over the job.

Join two of the strips with a bias seam (see Joining Strips, opposite). Trim the seam allowance and press the seam open. Fold the raw edges of the strip in

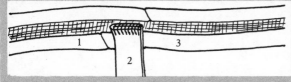

toward the middle. Place the end of the third strip, folded in and under, inside the fold at the bias seam to

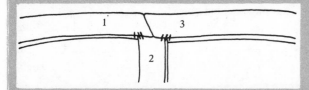

form a T, with the open edge facing right, and stitch. Fold the horizontal strip over the end of the vertical strip. Stitch in place at the corners.

Anchor the T-shape securely to a table, using a C-clamp. Fold the right strip over the center, pulling the strip sharply to the side (not down) for a tight braid. Always keep the open edges to the right as you braid.

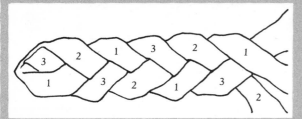

Bring the left strip over the new center strip. Twist before crossing so that the open edge stays to the right. Continue braiding, alternating right over center, left over center, right over center, left over center, and so on.

Maintain a firm tension by braiding close to the clamp, shifting the braid periodically so you stay near the clamp. Sew on new strips by hand as you need them. When you stop braiding, use a clothespin or safety pin to hold the braid in place.

BRAIDING THE CENTER STRIP

An oval rug begins with a straight center braid. To calculate the length of the center braid, you must first decide what size to make the rug. Subtract the width of the rug from the length. Use the remainder as the length of the center strip. For the rug in this project, the length is 4½ ft.; the width is 3½ ft.; the length of center strip will therefore be 1 ft.

MAKING ROUND TURNS

Oval rugs are the easiest to get to lie flat, but at the point where the rug first coils around the center strip a special braiding technique is required to avoid forming a bulge.

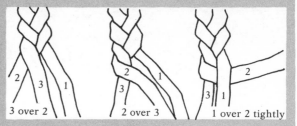

3 over 2   2 over 3   1 over 2 tightly

Braid the length of the center strip, then bring the left strip over the center strip. Instead of bringing the right strip over the center strip next, bring the new left strip over the new center strip. Then bring the right strip over the center strip, and tug it tightly to make the braid curve toward the right. Repeat three times. Braid to the next turn, and make three more round turns to coil the rug around the tip of the center strip. Make the regular three-strip braid for the rest of the rug.

Working with Form and Color

LACING

Lacing is a method of joining braids by interweaving them. It forms a stronger bond than sewing, and it is faster. When you have produced about 2½ to 3 times the length of the center braid, fasten a clothespin over the end of the braided strip, then mark the length of the center strip and fold it at that mark. Lay the folded strip on a flat surface, and curve the braid around it (see Braiding the Center Strip, p. 427).

It is a good idea to sew, rather than lace, the first few feet together, using a long, thin needle and strong thread. Beginning at the bend, sew back and forth through the folds of the two inside loops. Continue until you go around the second row.

Next, thread a bodkin or blunt-tipped lacing needle with some lacing cord, double it, and knot the ends together. Turn the rug over, and position the braids so that the loops of adjoining rows are at an angle to each other. Go back and forth from one braid to another, working the lace between the inside loops of each braid. Do not push the lacing needle through the material. Slip the needle under the loop and out the other side. Every few inches, pull the thread tightly enough to hide it, but not so tightly that it causes the rug to pucker or buckle.

Lacing

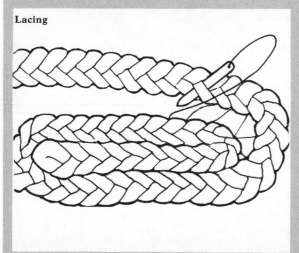

Continue this under-and-up rhythm along the straight part of the rug. When you come to a curve, you will have to skip some loops, or the rug will buckle. If you mark the loops you skip with a pin, you will be able to space the skips from one row to the next. Remember that the rug curves in four places, twice at each end. If the rug starts to buckle you have not skipped enough loops. As a general rule, if the next loop on the braid is ahead of the thread, lace it; if behind the thread, skip it.

When you need to add more lacing cord, attach a new double length of cord to the starter lacing cord with a square knot.

MAKING COLOR CHANGES

The random nature of the hit-or-miss pattern makes it a good choice for a first rug. The pattern has several variations. You can use color entirely at random, adding new shades when you run out of old, or you can use one color throughout for one strip, plus two strips of any other color.

The most controlled hit-or-miss variation is similar to the pattern of the rug in this project. It's based on using one or two of the major colors in the room where the rug will go, using them throughout the rug, and adding complimentary colors along the way. The rug shown on these pages is mainly in shades of blue, with shades of red, garnet, and lavender added for contrast. If you can, braid your rug in the room where it will ultimately be used, in order to simplify your color selection.

Using mostly dark colors will give the rug a flat appearance. It is generally a good idea, though, to use dark colors around the perimeter of the rug to give it a finished look. For an interesting textural effect, combine solids with tweeds.

Color changes should occur slowly in a rug. Change no more than one strip per row, and confine all color changes to the same curve to make the changes less obvious. It should take 3 rows of braiding for a complete color change in the braid to occur.

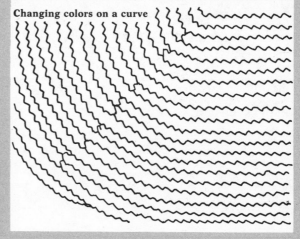

Changing colors on a curve

As you braid, use the joining technique on p. 426 to add on new strips. When you are ready to add a new length of a color or to make a color change, first hold the braid in place with a clothespin. With the strip in the center position, unfold it or remove the braider. Place the right sides of the old and new strips together, backstitch on the bias, and trim the seam allowance to ¼ in. Conceal the seam as you braid.

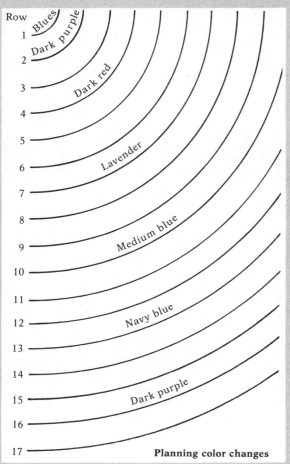

Planning color changes

To plan a pattern in advance, draw a wedge-shaped diagram equal to one-quarter of the rug, and indicate the color changes that occur on the curve. The hypothetical pattern above shows a design with two of the strips in shades of blue and a third strip that changes color throughout the rug. The first color change is in row 2. In row 4, dark red replaces dark purple and continues through rows 5 and 6.

Step-by-step instructions

1. Tear the wool into strips 2½ in. wide (see Tearing Strips, p. 426).

2. Join strips of the same color to form lengths 8–10 ft. long.

3. If you are intending to use braiders, roll each strip up and secure it with a safety pin. If you are folding the strips by hand, turn the raw edges under, fold the strips in half, and press (see Folding Strips, p. 426).

4. To begin braiding with braiders, square off the ends of a strip of light blue, a strip of dark blue, and a strip of dark purple. Slip each end through a braider.

5. Form a T-shape (see Starting a Three-Strip Braid, p. 427).

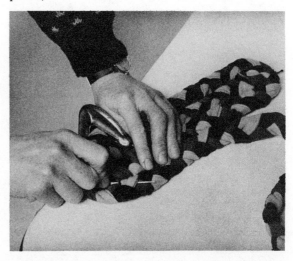

6. Anchor the center of the T-shape to a table with a C-clamp. Use the clamp to keep the rug steady while you are braiding and lacing in succeeding steps.

7. Begin braiding. Braid for 1 ft. to make the center strip. Make three round turns (see Making Round Turns, p. 427). Braid to the next curve and make three more round turns. As you braid, remember to pull each strip firmly to the side rather than down. To check the tension of your braiding, try to insert a pencil between the loops. If it slides through, the braids are too loose. If the braids pucker, they are too tight. Make sure the open edge of each strip faces right as you braid.

8. When you have braided 9½ ft., stop. Form the first ft. into the center strip. Then form 4 rows around it. (Note that each row in the rug increases in length approximately 11 in. over the one before. Row 1 is 1 ft., row 2 is 1 ft. 11 in., row 3 is 2 ft., 10 in., etc.

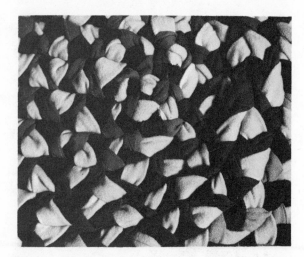

9. Lace the braids together, using lacing cord and a lacing needle (see Lacing, p. 428). Continue braiding a row and lacing it to the rug. You must lace as you braid, or the rug will become tangled and cause errors in color changes.

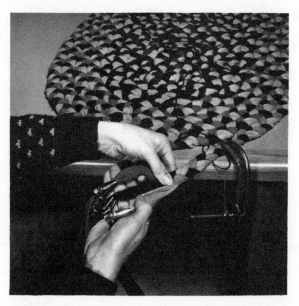

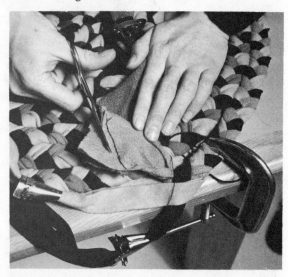

10. In row 5, change from dark purple to dark red (see Making Color Changes, p. 428). This is the first of ten color changes in the rug. Braid this combination in rows 5, 6, and 7. Try to make each color change on the same curve of the rug (see Sequence of Colors, to the right).

11. In row 8, change from dark red to medium blue.

12. In row 12, change from medium blue to lavender.
13. In row 13, change the light blue used in rows 1—12 to charcoal gray.
14. In row 14, change lavender to garnet. Braid this combination in rows 14 and 15.
15. In row 16, change charcoal gray back to light blue.
16. In row 17, change navy to light bright blue.

Sequence of Colors

Row	Colors of Braid
1-4	light blue, navy, dark purple
5-7	light blue, navy, dark red
8-11	light blue, navy, medium blue
12	light blue, navy, lavender
13	charcoal gray, navy, lavender
14-15	charcoal gray, navy, garnet
16	light blue, navy, garnet
17	light blue, light bright blue, garnet
18	light blue, light bright blue, red
19	light blue, navy, red
20-21	charcoal gray, navy, red

17. In row 18, change garnet to red.
18. In row 19, change light bright blue to navy.
19. In row 20, change light blue to charcoal gray.
20. Row 21 is the last row. Finish the rug with charcoal gray, navy, and red.

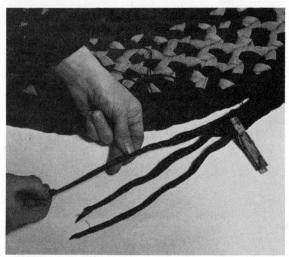

21. Taper the end of each strip (see Finishing the Rug, to the right).

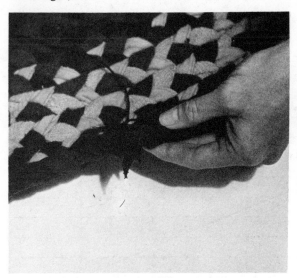

22. Slip the ends under the loops and stitch to secure. If you wish to enlarge the rug later, snip the stitches and join on more strips.

Finishing the Rug

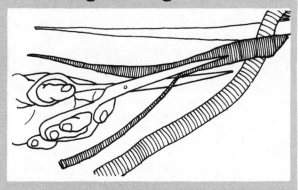

1. Begin finishing the rug at a curve. Clip each of the three fabric strips down to a point that tapers for about 1½'. Make each strip a slightly different length.

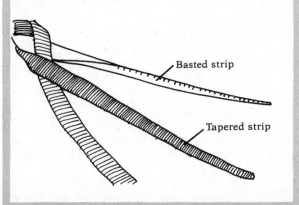

Basted strip

Tapered strip

2. Turn the raw tapered edges under, and baste them down to the point. Continue braiding and lacing as far as possible. Wrap the lacing cord around a braided strip and tuck it inside the braid.

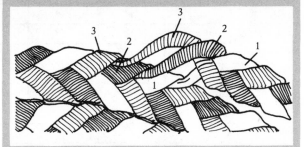

3. Using a lacing needle, tuck each of the three ends into an adjacent loop. Sew each point invisibly to its loop, using thread that matches each loop's color.

Caring for Textiles

Handcrafted textiles deserve careful cleaning on a regular basis. Don't wait until major cleaning is required. If you make it a point to vacuum up loose dust often, you'll save yourself the more strenuous effort that will be required to remove ground-in dirt later. Attend to stains immediately before they have time to set. Start with simple spot cleaning before you graduate to total surface care. Yarns and threads often have a protective coating that is washed away with the first major cleaning. The fibers are then prone to pick up dirt more readily than before. General cleaning instructions follow.

VACUUMING

To remove loose dirt, use the carpet or upholstery brush attachment with the vacuum cleaner. Make sure the brush is clean, and then gently, but thoroughly, run it over the article. Vacuuming is the best preventive approach to cleaning textiles. To prolong the life of the article even further, rotate it to a new position each time you vacuum it. For instance, turn pillow cushions 180° to even out the wear.

BEATING AND SHAKING

Good, old-fashioned elbow grease works wonders on a small or medium-size rug. Hang the rug on a clothesline, and beat it vigorously with a broom or a paddle-shaped instrument. Loose dirt and dust will fall out, and the pile will revive dramatically.

WET-WASHING

Do not machine-wash handwoven work, because the spin cycle may distort the fabric by twisting it too roughly. Instead, wash handwoven fabric by hand, using a gentle liquid detergent (such as Ivory Liquid with warm water or Woolite with cold water). Unless otherwise specified, use lukewarm water and squeeze suds through the article. Avoid putting your fingers through open fabric. Soak the article in sudsy water for 10–15 minutes. Squeeze suds through it a second time, then press the water out without wringing the material. Finally, rinse the article in lukewarm water, squeeze out the excess, and dry flat or on a line in the shade. Reshape the article with your fingers, then steam-iron when dry. Starch if necessary.

SNOW TREATMENT

Dry crunchy snow makes a great cleanser for articles with a pile. Choose a sub-freezing day so the snow you are using won't melt. First, shake the article to free it of loose dirt, then lay it pile side down on the snow, and rub vigorously. Shake the snow off, and leave the article outside to air.

GENERAL RESTORER AND FRESHENER

If a washable article has a low pile or is fixed in place, sponge it with a clean rag dipped into foam produced by whipping ½ cup Ivory liquid or Woolite with 2 cups of warm water, or use upholstery or carpet cleaner. Clean a small section at a time. Do not rub, or you may alter the texture. To rinse, wipe with a damp, clean rag, and dry in the shade.

DRY-CLEANING

For articles that must be dry-cleaned, use the procedure above, but substitute Carbona, a dry-cleaning fluid, as the cleaning agent. Follow label directions.

Cleaning the Fiber Projects

Project	Vacuuming	Beating and Shaking	Wet-Washing	Snow Treatment	General Restorer and Freshener	Dry-Cleaning
Tapestry/Pillow	✔				✔	✔
Rya rug	✔	✔		✔		✔
Weft-faced rug	✔	✔		✔		✔
Table runner			✔			
Curtains			✔			
Chair seat upholstery	✔		✔		✔	
Screen panels	✔					
Latch hook rug	✔	✔		✔		✔
Punch needle rug	✔	✔			✔	✔
Braided rug	✔	✔			✔	✔

Stain Removal

Stain	Washable Fabrics	Dry-Cleanable Fabrics
Alcoholic beverages	Blot up excess liquid immediately. Soak stain in cold water. Treat with prewash laundry product. Launder article. If wine has fruit base, treat as fruit stain.	Place fabric face down with a clean rag under stain. Sponge stain with cool water. Turn the rag as it becomes stained.
Blood	Soak stain in cold water until stain turns brown. Rub with liquid detergent. Rinse in clear water. Launder article.	Sponge with cool water. If necessary, apply ammonia to stain. Rinse. Sponge with hydrogen peroxide to remove traces.
Chocolate	Soak stain in lukewarm water. Treat with prewash laundry product and launder article.	Sponge with cool water. If stain remains, sponge with dry-cleaning agent.
Coffee and tea	Blot up excess liquid immediately. Stretch fabric over a pan, and carefully pour boiling water through spot. If liquid contains milk, sponge with dry-cleaning agent.	Place fabric face down with a clean rag under stain. Sponge stain with cool water. Turn the rag as it becomes stained. If necessary, apply a small amount of liquid detergent and cool water.
Fruit and berries	Wash immediately. Rub with white vinegar if stain remains. Rinse. Alternately, treat like a coffee stain.	Rub with liquid detergent or white vinegar. Rinse.
Grease	Put a clean rag under stain. Scrape off surface grease. Rub grease solvent on stain. Repeat as necessary. Launder article.	Scrape off surface grease. Rub grease solvent on stain. Dry-clean article.
Ink		
Ball-point pen	Spray with hair spray or sponge with dry-cleaning agent. Soak in warm water. Launder article.	Rub with dry-cleaning agent.
Fountain pen	Blot up excess ink immediately. Place fabric face down with clean rag under stain. Sponge stain with cool water. Turn the rag as it becomes stained.	Blot up excess ink immediately. Cover with absorbent powder (i.e., cornstarch). Vacuum or brush powder out. Repeat until no more ink is absorbed. Then mix powder with water to make a paste. Apply to stain, allow to dry, vacuum or brush off. Repeat as many times as needed.
Lipstick	Apply liquid detergent and rub. Repeat until the stain is gone. Launder article.	Sponge with dry-cleaning agent. Repeat if necessary.
Milk	Blot up excess liquid immediately. Soak stain in cool water and liquid detergent. Launder article.	Sponge with dry-cleaning agent. If stain persists, sponge with water.
Mud	Allow mud to dry. Brush off. Launder article.	Allow mud to dry. Brush off. Sponge with dry-cleaning agent.
Pencil	Erase. If necessary, rub detergent into mark. Rinse. If necessary, sponge ammonia on mark. Launder article.	Erase. If necessary, pretest fabric and follow directions for washable fabric.

Index

Page numbers in boldface indicate table entries.

chisels (continued)
  metal cutting with, 192, 196-97, 202
  for piercing sheet metal, 221
  for *repoussé*, 236
  sharpening of, 33
  storing of, 247
chocolate stains, removal from fabric, **433**
cigarette burns, repairing on furniture, 182
circular saw, 21
  cutting compound angles with, 28
  making crosscuts with, 23
circular-saw joinery, 50-51
  dado cut with, 51
  rabbet cut with, 50
clamping, 41, 44-45
clamps, 44-45. *See also under kinds of clamps*
  types of, 44
classic drawer, 99, 101
  construction of, 101
clear finish
  characteristics of, 171
  nonpenetrating, 171
  penetrating, 170-71
clinker, on coke, 242
closed-coat abrasive paper, for sanding, 164
cloth, removing from loom, 390
cloth beam, on loom, 348, 381, 390
clothes-drying rack. *See* drying rack, clothes
clothing, for felling trees, 10
coal, types of, 242-43
coated sheet steel, types of, 187
coffee stains, removal from fabric, **433**
cold-bending stock, instructions for, 302
cold chisel, 290, 302
  for metalworking, 192
Color, Temperature, and Forging Operation, **256**
color changes, in braided rugs, 428-29

colors
  blending of, 404
  forging, 254
  in weaving, 347-48
combination set, for metalworking, 201
combination square, as measuring tool, 17-18
Common Glues, **64-65**
common lumber, appearance of, 5
common nails, 74
common snips, for metal cutting, 201
compass, as measuring tool, 17-18, 290
composition board, as wood by-product, 9
  types of, 9
compound-action bolt cutters, for metalworking, 192
compound angles, circular saw for, 28
concave curve, smoothing with sandpaper, 165
concealed hinges, mounting of, 76
conductor stake, for metal shaping, 202-3
cone holder, for weaving, 341
conical shape, creating with sheet metal, 233
contact cement, for gluing, **64**
contemporary drawer, 99-100
  construction of, 100
contramarche, in weaving, 348
contramarche loom, for handweaving, 340
coping saw, 20
  to make pins, 151
  sawing curves with, 25
copper, 187-88
  annealing of, 189, 235
  drawbacks of, 187
  patina on, 187, 189
  tinning of, 187
  verdigris on, 187
corner guide, for drawer hanging, 102
cotton fibers, properties of, **344**

counterbalance, in weaving, 348
counterbalance loom, for handweaving, 340
cracks, repairing on furniture, 182
crayon marks, repairing on furniture, 183
crevices, sanding of, 165
crimpers, for metal shaping, 203
crimping sheet metal, 216
crochet hook, for sleying warp thread, 388
crocus cloth, for cleaning brazing joints, 294
cross, in weaving, 348
crosscuts
  circular saw method for, 23
  handsaw method for, 22
crosscut saw, uses for, 20
crosscut teeth, filing of, 29
cross-filing, of metal, 197
cross peen hammer, for forging, 248
cross sticks
  on loom, 381, 385
  in weaving, 341, 348
cup former, for rivets, 271
cupping tool, for rivets, 272
curtains, on multiharness loom, 392-95
  cleaning of, **432**
  instructions for, 393, 395
  materials for, 393
  open-weave techniques for, 394
curved-tooth files, for metalworking, 192
curves, instructions for making, 258
cutoff nails, to join metal, 313
cutters, for metalworking, 192
cutting
  attachment, 298
  with gas rig, 298-99
  tip for, 298
cutting gauge, as measuring tool, 17, 19
cutting oil, for metal drilling, 198
cutting steel, process for, 254
cutting tip, for gas rig, 298